P9-BJC-395

THE OSLO SYNDROME

"Ken Levin explains why so many Jews and Israelis delude themselves about the malevolent intentions of their enemies. His analysis is persuasive, insightful, illuminating. Readers of *The Oslo Syndrome* will better know how to prevent the recurrence of a perilous political process that endangered Israel and the world."

—Ruth Wisse, Martin Peretz Professor of Yiddish Literature and Professor of Comparative Literature, Harvard University.

The Oslo Syndrome

Delusions of
a People
Under Siege

Kenneth Levin

SMITH AND KRAUS GLOBAL

Smith and Kraus, Inc.
177 Lyme Road, Hanover, NH 03755
www.smithkraus.com

First edition: March 2005
Printed in the United States of America
9 8 7 6 5 4 3 2 1

Jacket and text design by Julia Gignoux, Freedom Hill Design, Reading, Vermont
Author photo by Denise Passaretti, Passaretti Photography

Library of Congress Cataloging-in-Publication Data
Levin, Kenneth, 1944–
The Oslo syndrome: delusions of a people under siege / Kenneth Levin. 1st ed.
p.cm.
Includes bibliographical references.
ISBN 1-57525-417-4
1. Arab-Israeli conflict—1993—Psychological aspects. 2. Jews—Israel—Psychology. 3. Israel—Foreign Relations—Arab Countries—Psychological aspects. 4. Israel—Politics and government—20th century—Psychological aspects. 5. Arab-Israel conflict—1993—Peace.
I. Title
DS119.76.L4752004
909'.04924—dc22   2004057795

Contents

SECTION ONE
THE DIASPORA

SECTION TWO
ISRAEL

FOR JONATHAN
AND IN MEMORY OF IDA

PREFACE

What follows is primarily a study of the delusional thinking that underlay Israel's attempt to achieve peace with its neighbors through the so-called Oslo process. The book will demonstrate that Israel's Oslo-era diplomacy was inspired mainly by the nation's predicament of being a state under chronic siege, with the delusions that spawned and sustained the Oslo approach reflecting a desperation on the part of many Israelis in their desire to extricate themselves from the siege. In exploring the evolution of the particular delusions represented by Oslo, the book also considers similar thinking embraced by Diaspora Jewish communities under the conditions of marginalization, disparagement, and abuse that were typically their lot.

While the subject is thus one of Jewish history and psychology, the psychological and historical phenomena described are applicable to many other communities. In particular, as noted in the book, other besieged minorities — groups likewise subjected to chronic denigration, defamation, and assault — have exhibited psychological stigmata similar to those found in Diaspora Jewish communities, an observation supported by the literary records and the histories of such groups.

It is hardly surprising that other abused or besieged populations, whether minorities within nations or citizens of small states under attack by their neighbors, would develop psychological responses of the sort discussed in the book — both the wishful thinking divorced from reality and some defenses against such psychological stigmata of the besieged. But the book's themes have a still broader relevance. Even ostensibly powerful and secure populations, under conditions that entail ongoing threat and vulnerability, can manifest similar responses.

This observation has been greatly reinforced for me by trends in the United States in the wake of the terrorist attacks of September 11, 2001. Those who perpetrated the carnage, as well as their supporters, have conveyed in word and deed their grievances against America and their objectives. They have declared their deadly hostility not only to America's military and diplomatic presence in the Moslem world but to its cultural presence as well. They have informed us of their determination to pursue a militant path to a recreated Islamic caliphate cleansed of all Western "pollution" and to fight for imposition of their Islamic rule worldwide. They have asserted that to do so is their religious duty. They have made clear that their war against America is predicated on their perception of America as the chief obstacle to their aspirations; and they have demonstrated that there are no constraints in the methods and weapons they are prepared to use. While much of the American public recognizes the gravity of the challenge, there are also many in the country who have sought to recast the threat, to rationalize it, and to urge policies aimed at appeasing the terrorists and their supporters in the delusional hope of thereby extricating the nation from the dangers it faces.

Interestingly, although the subject of America's response to the terrorist assault is never discussed in the book, those who have been kind enough to read the work in manuscript form and to offer their comment have repeatedly noted this relevance of the book's themes to what they see in their newspapers and hear in broadcast coverage about the range of American reactions to the war launched against the United States.

Noting this relevance is hardly, of course, to confound the predicament of Diaspora Jews living amid hostile surrounding societies, or of Israel facing enemies whose declared objective is the state's annihilation, with America's challenge. But the Jewish experience, and its psychological impact, is germane in a way that can be construed as adding a new dimension to an old observation about the place of the Jews in Western society.

It has been said that the Jews are the miners' canary of Western civilization. That is, like canaries taken into the pits by miners for the purpose of signaling — should they suddenly expire — the presence of poisonous fumes, attacks on Jews are an early sign of some social and political toxin that inevitably threatens a broader population than just the Jews. The point of the metaphor is to alert people to this truth and disabuse them of dismissing attacks on the Jews as merely a Jewish problem.

One broader application of the metaphor has been recognized, and acted on, by American officials who have not only, like much of the American population, sympathized with Israel's plight but have also seen the terror war against Israel as relevant to the threats facing the United States. In the wake of the 9/11 attacks, officials charged with protecting the country against future terror have looked at Israel's horrendous experience of terror assaults and the means it has devised to defend its population, and they have worked with Israel to apply that nation's expertise to the defense of America.

But the metaphor of Jews as the West's miners' canary is no less applicable to the themes of the present study. Significant numbers of Jews have repeatedly responded to the noxious fumes of chronic assault in the Diaspora and in Israel by deluding themselves into believing they could win peace through embracing the indictments of their enemies and seeking to appease them. These psychological responses, their translation into communal and national policy, and the disasters that have followed offer lessons for those whose predicaments are in many ways so very different and yet similar, including an America under attack.

Oslo — A Delusional "Peace" Process

Arafat promised that he would make his appeal against violence as soon as the Declaration of Principles was officially signed. Not unreasonably, the Norwegians, Americans, and Israelis all expected him to do this in his speech at the signing ceremony on the White House lawn [on September 13, 1993]. Waiting for the magic words to be uttered any moment, Ehud Ya'ari, the Israel Television commentator who covered the proceedings, used every break in Arafat's speech to announce, "Now he will denounce terrorism . . . now he will say it . . . now he simply has to say it. . . ." Only after the last paragraph did Ya'ari give up: "He is not saying it," he reported, crushed.[1]

A PECULIAR PATH

For any Oslo enthusiasts paying attention, there was within hours even more reason to feel crushed. Shortly after the signing of the Declaration of Principles and the famous handshake between Arafat and Yitzhak Rabin on the White House lawn, Arafat was declaring to his Palestinian constituency over Jordanian television that Oslo was to be understood in terms of the Palestine National Council's 1974 decision. This was a reference to the so-called Plan of Phases, according to which the Palestine Liberation Organization would acquire whatever territory it could by negotiations, then use that land as a base for pursuing its ultimate goal of Israel's annihilation.[2]

But not many people were paying attention. Both Israeli government leaders and the Israeli media ignored Arafat's words and most Israelis celebrated what they chose to see as the arrival of the deeply longed-for era of peace. There were also supporters of Israel, both Jewish and non-Jewish, who saw the events of the day as Israel's embarking on a dangerously deluded course that would end not in peace but disaster. But such views were drowned out by Oslo enthusiasts in Israel and abroad as well as by the many Israelis and Israel-backers who had misgivings but hoped for the best and trusted in Yitzhak Rabin not to do anything that would compromise Israel's security and survival.

Events in the ensuing months quickly reinforced the doubters in their grim expectations. Allusions to the Plan of Phases became a staple in Arafat's addresses in Arabic, with more than a dozen such references within a few weeks of the White House ceremony.[3] So also were Arafat's comparisons of Oslo to Mohammed's dealings with the Quraysh, a tribe on the Arabian Peninsula. Mohammed negotiated a treaty with the Quraysh in 628, but two years later, when his forces had grown stronger, he attacked and defeated them. Likewise featured in Arafat's speeches during this time were calls to Jihad, or holy war, against Israel.

Arafat's arrival in the territories, in July, 1994, and his assumption of control over Palestinian schools and an expanded Palestinian media system were marked by the promoting of these and related themes in Palestinian school curricula and media. Palestinian children were to be taught that all of "Palestine" from the Jordan to the Mediterranean — that is, the West Bank, Gaza, and all of Israel — belongs to them and is holy Islamic land. Jews have no historic connections to the land and no legal claim to any of it but are merely evil usurpers. Palestinian children were also to learn that it is not only their right but their obligation to dedicate themselves to Israel's destruction. Arafat-controlled Palestinian television, including children's television, and other Palestinian media outlets promoted the same claims and the same agenda.

Nor were the Oslo skeptics reassured by the Israeli government's response to such systematic defamation and incitement. It did not insist upon Arafat's adherence to clauses in the Oslo agreements in which the Palestinians explicitly foreswore incitement, asserted their recognition of Israel and of the state's legitimacy, and agreed that all disputes would be settled by peaceful means. Rather, the Labor-Meretz coalition government was typically silent on the anti-Israel indoctrination. At the same time, the Israeli media, generally Left-leaning and enthusiastically supportive of the Oslo accords, supported this silence by suppressing coverage of Arafat's incitement-laden speeches and of the prominence of the same themes in Palestinian schools and media. Indeed, a kind of underground system evolved to monitor hate-mongering in Palestinian school texts and media in the absence of coverage by the Israeli government and mainstream Israeli news outlets.[4]

Some Israeli government leaders, when confronted with the issue, even insisted that incitement was less important than advancing the "peace process." How they could imagine that educating another Palestinian generation to believe in Israel's illegitimacy and to dedicate itself to the state's destruction could be congruent with peace, or less significant than signed agreements, was, of course, difficult for many to fathom.

A similar pattern prevailed regarding Palestinian terror. The Israeli government, in embracing the Oslo accords, assured the public that the agreements' anti-violence clauses would bring an end to anti-Israel terror. Yet over the two years from Arafat's arrival in the territories until the fall of the Labor-Meretz coalition government in May, 1996, Israel suffered a spate of terror that, while paling beside the onslaught of suicide bombings and other terror attacks the country has endured since the collapse of Oslo, was far beyond what it had experienced in any comparable period since its birth. One hundred and fifty-two people were killed and hundreds more wounded. Indeed, the terror of those years introduced suicide bombing to Israel and foreshadowed later events.

The government, in response to public outrage, would occasionally insist that Arafat's regime comply with its Oslo obligations regarding terror and do more to combat the Hamas and Islamic Jihad terror groups. It would call for the dismantling of their organizational, recruiting, bomb-making, and terrorist-training infrastructures. But the government never made such steps a condition for additional Israeli concessions. Nor did it reveal to the public what it knew to be Arafat's indirect collusion with, and often direct support of, the terror organizations, and his frequent praise of the terrorists and their operations.

The government's policy of hiding incriminating information about Arafat from the public was dramatically if indirectly illustrated by an episode in 1994 when Shimon Peres, conversing with Arafat at the Erez checkpoint and apparently unaware that his comments were being recorded by a French filmmaker, threatened to reveal to the media Arafat's flouting of his Oslo obligations. Peres did not go into detail about Arafat's violations but did regard them as serious enough that their revelation would be a "catastrophe" for Arafat and would, among its consequences, "kill the Palestinian story in the American Congress."[5]

But rather than expose Arafat's malfeasance, including his role in the terrorism, the government at almost every turn sought to promote a perception of distance and conflict between Arafat and the terrorist organizations and to characterize Arafat as Israel's "peace partner," in contrast to the terrorist "enemies of peace."[6] It worked also to cast the latter as primarily dedicated not to killing Jews but to killing the Arafat-Israel "peace process." Government ministers even insisted at times that the proper response to the terror would be to speed up the concessions to Arafat so as to thwart the supposed aim of the terrorists.[7]

The Rabin government demonstrated in other ways as well its determination to pursue the Oslo process and to comprehend Oslo as the path to genuine peace despite all the evidence that the other side was aiming for something very different from peace. The Labor-Meretz coalition's commitment to ignoring any such evidence and remaining fully invested in Oslo as an article of faith, impervious to question or debate, was further illustrated, for example, by the fact that among those generally supportive of Oslo there was none of the public debating of details and elements that one might expect within a democratic parliament and government making momentous decisions.

Those opposed to Oslo, those who saw it as leading the nation to inevitable disaster, articulated their opposition, but such voices were smeared by the government and the Israeli media as more "enemies of peace." Indeed, for their daring to challenge the Oslo accords, they were characterized as little different from the Islamic fundamentalist "enemies of peace" who were perpetrating anti-Israel terror. Representative of such rhetoric was the following exchange between Rabin and a BBC interviewer:

Rabin: "I believe that we should address the problem that is really bothering the Israeli citizens: personal security in the face of the extremist Islamic terror of Hamas and the Islamic Jihad. Today, it is those groups, as well as the rejectionist fronts, that are the enemies of peace and which carry out the attacks . . . They want to influence the Israeli public on the one hand and the Palestinian public on the other to stop the peace process."

BBC interviewer Yisrael Singer: "They are quite successful, are they not?"

Rabin: "Excuse me. They are successful because the Likud has turned into a collaborator with Hamas and Islamic Jihad."[8]

Meanwhile, within the ranks of the Labor-Meretz coalition, there were many individuals with military backgrounds and others who earlier in their careers had demonstrated sensitivity to pragmatic details of strategic challenges presented by policies of state and an appreciation for the vital need to address those details. Yet among these people, or others in the Labor-Meretz camp, no public discussion or debate over the strategic challenges of Oslo ever emerged.

How much land could Israel safely surrender to Arafat? Clearly, even if Arafat, despite all countervailing evidence, proved a trustworthy peace partner, a responsible government must factor into its calculations the situation that would prevail if a peace-loving Arafat were overthrown by parties less committed to peace or if his reign were followed by the accession of such parties. How much territory could Israel cede and still defend the country were the ceded areas controlled by a hostile regime? What would be Israel's military needs, and their cost, in guarding what would in any case be greatly extended borders without the benefit of natural barriers? How would Israel defend its major population centers, virtually all of which — whatever the dimensions of Israeli withdrawals — would be within artillery range of ceded areas? How would Israel respond to military provocations?

Such questions are elementary. They should have been questions that even those supportive of Oslo would have been eager to address and debate. Yet no such public debate ever occurred. On the contrary, when questions of this sort were placed to members of the governing coalition, even to former high-ranking

IDF (Israel Defense Forces) officers, a common response was one to the effect that in the coming era of genuine peace such narrow strategic concerns would be passé. Peace would be so mutually beneficial that there would be no military threat and so no need to worry about the details of managing such threats.

The determination to hold fast to a particular comprehension of reality no matter what the strength of countervailing evidence, to be impatient with all invoking of such evidence and brook no debate, is virtually a textbook definition of "delusional." (An actual textbook definition of delusion is "[a] false belief, based on incorrect inference about external reality, not consistent with [the] patient's intelligence and cultural background, that cannot be corrected by reasoning."9) It is not surprising then that many observers responded with a sense of something being psychologically amiss in the avid and unshakable embrace of Oslo by its Israeli and Jewish-American enthusiasts (the latter typically no more open to countervailing evidence or tolerant of challenge than their Israeli counterparts). Thus, I found myself in September, 1993, and increasingly in the months and years that followed, being asked again and again by acquaintances, both Jewish and non-Jewish, variations on questions of the sort: Why are the Israelis doing these insane things? Why are Jews so self-destructive? So suicidal?

Such questions, and the events that prompted them, brought to mind the extensive literature dating back to the first decades of the twentieth century, some of it by psychologists and psychoanalysts, attempting to address what was perceived as a distinctively Jewish self-denying and self-destructive pathology. The literature related this pathology to the particular travails of Diaspora Jewish life in the nineteenth and twentieth centuries. But those difficulties were, at least superficially, very different from the circumstances confronted by a free people in a sovereign Jewish state.

Yet the reactions of Diaspora Jews to the corrosive indictments and assaults they suffered in that earlier period are relevant to the delusions many Israelis have embraced in the face of chronic besiegement. Diaspora Jews' efforts to respond to the attacks upon them took specific forms and included particular delusions about measures that would win them acceptance. These responses were played out both on the individual plane of accommodations made in people's personal lives and on the plane of communal accommodations made to placate European besiegers. Immigrants to the pre-state Jewish community in Eretz Israel and then to the state brought with them predilections learned in the Diaspora. While they may have foreseen in the prospect of being citizens of a Jewish state a release from the persecutions of life in exile, a solution that would free them from old patterns of attack and old responses, some also promoted in their new society self-deluding concepts of proper, accommodating Jewish behavior born of the Jewish predicament in Europe. They did so not only as parents but as teachers, journalists, and writers. And many Israelis, confronted with the chronic Arab assault, have reacted in ways reflecting those responses introduced into Israeli culture by Diaspora immigrants.

Consequently, a look at the stresses of Jewish life in the Diaspora and the corrosive effects those stresses have had on the people subjected to them is crucial to understanding the particular forms taken by Israeli self-delusion in the face of the Arab siege. At the same time, Jewish life in an independent Jewish state is indeed very different from the daily travails to which Diaspora Jews were often subjected. The questions raised by Oslo therefore require at least some rethinking of the explanations for Jewish "pathology" offered in those earlier writings on the subject.

Delusions of the Abused

Clues to the psychology of those who embraced Oslo can be found in the rationales with which they sought to defend their position. Those arguments were very often either delusionally self-deprecating or delusionally grandiose.

Illustrative of the former was the burgeoning of a largely bogus revisionist history of Israel, the so-called New History, beginning particularly in the late nineteen eighties, and its embrace by a substantial following in Israel. This rewriting of the history of the state implicitly or explicitly placed the onus on Israel for perpetuation of the Arab-Israeli conflict over the previous half-century: It was Israeli militancy and Israeli occupation of the territories in the face of Arab openness to compromise that initiated and sustained the conflict. Therefore, Israel's ceding of the territories would end the conflict and bring about a new era of genuine peace.

Many Israelis were drawn in by the new historians' claims that, despite the Palestinian Arabs' rejection of the UN partition plan in 1947 and despite the subsequent invasion of Israel by five Arab armies, Israel was actually the villain in the story. They took to heart assertions that the Arab terror of the 1950s really was not so onerous and Israeli counteractions were too heavy-handed. But even someone unable to analyze the new historians' specific claims and discern the lies in them should have been able to see the overarching lie in their authors' assessments of the nature of the Arab-Israeli conflict. There was abundant evidence of Arab intent available to any Israeli, evidence in the form of anti-Jewish rhetoric and policy aimed at undermining the legitimacy of the state and reflecting an Arab perception that the only just outcome would be Israel's dissolution. It still, therefore, required a major exercise in self-deception to perceive Arab intentions as "moderate," as having always been "moderate," and as consistent with genuine peace were only Israel to change its ways and be forthcoming enough in its concessions.

At the same time, delusional grandiosity was also apparent, as in arguments that Arab quiescence could be won by Israel's proffering benefits to Arab partners in economic, environmental, medical, and other endeavors. According to this thinking, the lure of economic gains would drive the Arabs to enter into peace agreements and would assure Arab adherence to those agreements — if only Israel were sufficiently forthcoming. Such arguments ignore, of course, the relative inconsequentiality of the economic strength of Israel, however impressive for a country of six million, and the relative insignificance of opportunities potentially provided by cooperation with Israel, in the context of the vast Arab world of over a quarter billion souls. They ignore the obvious consideration that hostility to Israel may have a utility in the domestic and inter-Arab politics of Arab governments that far outweighs in those governments' calculations the benefits any rapprochement with Israel might provide. They ignore the fact that the fundamentalist threat to so-called moderate regimes is another reason for those regimes to keep Israel at arm's length. They ignore the reality that for the Arab world in general peace with Israel is of too insignificant benefit to warrant much risk taking and that there are various considerations that weigh in the other direction and weigh more heavily. They ignore the example of Egypt, which has reneged on virtually all of the numerous accords touching on economic cooperation that were part of the 1978 Camp David treaty.[10] The accords would no doubt have brought economic benefits to Egypt, more so than to Israel. But those benefits are obviously something which the Egyptian regime has been willing to forego, perceiving them as outweighed by the negative impact for the regime, in both domestic and inter-Arab politics, of such cooperation with Israel.

Both the self-deprecating and the grandiose distortions of reality have a common source: A wish to believe Israel to be in control of profoundly stressful circumstances over which it, unfortunately, has no real control. Genuine peace will come to the Middle East when the Arab world, by far the dominant party in the region, perceives such a peace as in its interest. Israeli policies have, in fact, very little impact on Arab perceptions in this regard, much less than the dynamics of domestic politics in the Arab states and of inter-Arab rivalries. Israeli strength may deter Arab assaults and fend them off when deterrence fails and assaults occur, but it cannot force peace. This is a painful reality that does cast its shadow over life in Israel. Some Israelis are so pained by it that they prefer to take refuge in delusions of Israeli culpability, the subtext of which is that the proper self-reforms and concessions by Israel can and would suffice to win peace, despite all evidence to the contrary. Indeed, some continue to embrace such delusions even in the face of developments after September, 2000, the Palestinians' overt rejection of the peace-seeking premises of Oslo and their pur-

suit of a war of terror against Israel; events that altered the views of many previous Oslo enthusiasts in Israel, but hardly all.

The inclination to retreat to delusions of transgression, and of salvation
through self-reform and concessions, is common, even endemic, within communities under chronic siege. This is true whether the situation is that of a state
besieged by foreign forces or of a vulnerable community that, within its polity, is
under chronic attack — physical assault, bias, defamation, marginalization — by
other groups in the surrounding society. The syndrome has been so prominent
within Jewish Diaspora communities subjected to chronic manifestations of anti-
Semitism that, as noted, an extensive literature examining the phenomenon was
produced over the last century. This literature, much of it the work of psychiatrists and psychologists, often applied to the syndrome the rubric "Jewish self-
hatred."

Some observers have seen a particular propensity toward this mode of thinking among Jews, and they have often attributed Jews' predilection to assume
responsibility and guilt for their victimization by surrounding societies to the
traditional historicism of the Jewish faith: the Biblical, and subsequent rabbinical, comprehension of Jewish history as a playing out of the relationship
between God and the people, with disaster and exile perceived as consequences
of the people's transgressions, and adherence to the Covenant envisioned as the
path to prosperity and a flourishing in the Land. But there are problems with this
thesis. First, such interpretations of communal disasters have been far from an
exclusive characteristic of the Jews. While other faiths and cultures may be less
history-oriented in comprehending the relationship between the communal and
the divine, societies have commonly interpreted disasters as the product of religious transgression and divine retribution.

More significantly, the recurring propensity among segments of the Jewish
population to take to heart the indictments of besiegers and persecutors, and
to ascribe to themselves the power to change dramatically the attitudes of their
enemies by self-reform, is in important respects a contravention of the religious tradition. For it shifts the focus of redemption from the rapport with
God to the rapport with the Jews' tormentors, from self-reform in conformity with religious-moral codes of behavior to self-reform in conformity with
the indictments of the besiegers. If this propensity has been particularly marked
among Jews, its being so is a product of the Jews' particular, long history of oppression, slaughter, and dislocation.

Biographical, autobiographical, sociological, and historical writings touching on different communities living under conditions of chronic besiegement
of one form or another offer evidence that other peoples subjected to such duress
manifest similar psychological responses. Additional evidence is provided by the
sociological and psychological literature addressing prejudice and its ravages
more generally. As one astute observer who has considered particular examples

of the phenomenon has written, "When the history of Western attitudes toward those perceived as different, whether black or Jew or homosexual, is studied, the very idea of black, Jewish, or homosexual self-hatred seems a mordant oxymoron. Why hate yourself when there are so many willing to do it for you! But the ubiquitousness of self-hatred cannot be denied. And it has shaped the self-awareness of those treated as different perhaps more than they themselves have been aware."[11]

The professional literature seeking to explain in psychological terms this tendency among at least some members of besieged or abused groups to embrace the indictments and calumnies of their abusers has often invoked the psychoanalytic concept of "identification with the aggressor." The concept, and the term, were introduced by Anna Freud in the 1930s.[12] They have been used to refer to a defense mechanism in which the individual blunts the pain of negative interactions with others, such as criticism or rejection, by embracing the indictment, making it one's own self-criticism. The individual thereby at least attains a sense of being in control of the indictment rather than simply feeling the passive victim of assault by others, and he or she attains also a sense of shared comprehension and rapport with the attacking other rather than feeling simply the targeted outsider.

Psychoanalysts and others who have written on "identification with the aggressor" have also typically emphasized what they perceive as an additional essential aspect of the defense: the subject's projecting the painful indictment onto others, directing at others the same criticism and becoming the victimizer, thereby further "mastering" the indictment and further reinforcing the sense of rapport with the subject's own attackers.[13] In the context of the psychodynamics of besieged communities, one might comprehend as an expression of this phenomenon those members of such communities who accept the indictments of the attackers but see others in the community rather than themselves as embodying the derogatory ascriptions. An example would be Jews who are inclined to perceive other Jews as fitting anti-Semitic caricatures.

"Stockholm Syndrome" is another term that has become prominent in recent decades in both professional and popular discussions of people's embrace of the perspectives of their abusers. It largely parallels in its meaning "identification with the aggressor." The term had its origin in an attempted bank robbery in the Swedish capital in 1973 that went awry, with several people being held captive by the would-be robbers for six days in the bank's vault. The captives emerged displaying notable empathy for and emotional bonding with their captors.

The concept of identification with the aggressor and related terms and concepts clearly have their applicability and utility in explicating the psychodynamics of populations under chronic besiegement. But they also have the weakness of painting with too broad and unnuanced a brush what are, in fact, a range of responses within such populations that reflect the phenomenon those terms and concepts seek to explain. Consider a Jewish community subjected to chronic anti-Semitic assault and those within it who are inclined to embrace the indictments of the surrounding society. Some such individuals will seek to escape their Jewish identity, to distance themselves entirely from a community that they see as indeed bearing the ugly taints that the haters ascribe to it. They will perhaps convert to the dominant religion and strive to take on fully the identity of a member of the society's dominant group. Others will continue to feel a bond to the Jewish community, perhaps even assume leadership positions in it, and dedicate themselves to reforming their fellow Jews in conformity to the indictments of the surrounding society. Both groups are identifying with the aggressors, but in markedly different ways and also with radically different objectives and what is likely to be dramatically different impact on their community of origin.

Anna Freud construed identification with the aggressor to be to some degree a universally employed defense. She saw its paradigmatic expression in a universal childhood response to parental criticism. In fact, she saw the child's inclination to embrace at least in part any parental criticism — in order to lessen the pain of the parental attack and to feel more connected to parents — as the foundation of development of the child's conscience, or super-ego. The more particular phenomenon being examined here, the embrace by at least some members of abused groups of the indictments of their abusers, can perhaps be most usefully illuminated by considering a more particular developmental paradigm: the predicament, and psychological responses, of children subjected to chronic abuse.

A response widely noted and studied in children victimized by early abuse and related traumas is a self-indictment more intense and pervasive than Anna Freud's universal childhood identification with parental criticisms. A recurrent theme in such children's comprehension of their trauma is that bad things have happened to them because they have been "bad." Some psychiatrists and others, looking at possible additional factors — beyond the wish to "master" parental abuse and to feel a sense of rapport with the abusing parents — in accounting for this more extreme self-indictment, have suggested that the predilection also reflects children's naïveté. They note that abusive or neglectful parents typically convey to their children the message that actions against them are a response to offending behavior, and they suggest that the children, in their innocence, absorb such messages at face value. Other observers have emphasized the role of childhood narcissism: Children are inclined to see themselves as the center of their world and to ascribe to themselves grandiose powers, and this predisposes them to assume responsibility for whatever befalls them, good or ill.

But for a more basic psychological explanation, consider the existential predicament of abused children. Having typically no avenue of escape from their harrowing environment, such children are left with essentially two choices. They can perceive themselves as the victims of circumstances entirely beyond their control and endure the hopelessness that would flow from that insight. Or they can ascribe the abuse to their own misbehavior, assume responsibility, and endure the "guilt" of that comprehension but thereby also create and sustain an illusion of control, a hope that by reforming, by becoming "good," they can elicit an end to the abuse and set their lives right. While the former perspective is the truer one, the latter offers the irresistible attraction of enabling the child to stave off despair.

It can be argued that it is, in general, children's intense investment in fantasies of winning desired responses from parents that underlies their predisposition to take to heart parental criticism and that sustains children's grandiosity, their wish-driven faith in their own powers to transform their situation.[14] It is this factor amplified by circumstances of abuse that underlies the more extreme and more pervasive self-indictments and concomitant grandiosity of abused children.

In the context of chronically abused populations, it is similarly investment in fantasies of thereby transforming their situations, ending the abuse, that underlies predilections within such populations to take to heart the abusers' indictments and to advocate and pursue self-reforms congruent with those indictments. The pain of the abuse and the fantasies of relief — however divorced from realistic expectations those fantasies may be — generate both self-denigration, the inclination of some in such circumstances to blame themselves for their predicament, and grandiosity, the inclination to believe that they have the power by their own actions, by their self-reform, to alter the behavior of their abusers.

These dynamics can be seen at work repeatedly in the attitudes and behavior of significant segments of Diaspora Jewish communities subjected to anti-Semitic pressures from surrounding societies. The same dynamics also underlie the investment of significant segments of the Israeli population in delusions that ascribe to Israel responsibility for the persistence of the Arab siege and that anticipate Israeli self-reform and concessions inexorably bringing about an end to the siege and establishment of a genuine and enduring peace.

The embrace by members of an abused community of the indictments of their abusers is obviously both debilitating and potentially dangerous. It is debilitating insofar as it entails perceiving oneself and one's community as tainted and reprehensible, and dangerous in those instances where it diverts the individual's, and the community's, gaze from external peril, and from substantive defensive measures in the face of external threats, as they focus instead on self-reform.

But clearly there are tremendous variations within besieged communities, and between such communities, regarding people's actual response to pressures that might promote an embrace of besiegers' indictments and an investment in delusions of salvation through self-reform. There are differences in how much those pressures do in fact elicit such responses in people's comprehension of themselves and the world and in their behavior. Factors that play a role in these variations include individuals' temperaments and personalities, family dynamics, the nature and intensity of the duress to which a community is subjected, and the character and strength of a community's institutions and leadership.

On the communal level, leaders and members of besieged groups are confronted with the task of constructing and sustaining institutions that will provide psychological defenses for a sense of self-worth and wholeness even as members' valuing of themselves and of their group identity are assaulted by the indictments, and very often as well the allures, of the besieging culture. Consider again the paradigm of the psychological predicament of abused children. Some such children are fortunate enough to be exposed to counter-experiences that help arm them against assuming responsibility for their predicament and devoting themselves to pursuing self-reform to appease their abusers, a course that too often leads to lives of self-abasement, frustration, and unending misery.

The most common such counter-experience is a relationship with a more consistently nurturing adult, a grandparent perhaps, who conveys to the child a sense of being valued and worthy of better treatment despite the parental persecution. On the level of a besieged community and its institutions, it is the comparable task of those institutions to be sufficiently strong and nurturing to serve as an effective counterweight to psychologically debilitating assaults.

The embrace by substantial segments of the Israeli population of the false accusations and bogus claims directed against Israel by its enemies, and the militant advocacy by these Israelis of delusions of transforming the Middle East through Israeli self-reform and concessions, represent a failure of communal institutions. So also do the comparable responses within Diaspora communities to what have been typically conditions entailing at best significant degrees of chronic duress. But to understand these phenomena also requires that attention be given to those both in Diaspora communities and in Israel who did not surrender to the corrosive effects of besiegement. And it requires some consideration of the institutions that worked successfully within their communities as counterweights to the corrosive impact of chronic assault, the institutions that helped members of those communities sustain a sense of wholeness, of their and their community's essential validity, despite the drumbeat of deprecation and accusation directed against them by their neighbors.

I had written, in the months immediately preceding the first Oslo accords, about what I saw as largely self-deluding Israeli assumptions concerning the capacity of Israel, through concessions, to transform Arab attitudes toward the Jewish state and elicit genuine acceptance and peace, assumptions that were increasingly shaping Israel's political dialogue and policies.[15] I continued to write on this subject in the wake of revelation of the initial Oslo agreements.[16] An article in which I took up what I saw as the psychodynamics underlying such self-delusions appeared in Hebrew in the Israeli quarterly *Nativ* in the fall of 1996.[17] This last piece led to suggestions by a number of friends and readers that I expand the thesis into a book and became the starting point of the present work.

The book is divided into two sections, one on the Diaspora and the other on Israel. The former traces the evolution of those Jewish self-delusions that served in various ways as prototypes for the rationales that engendered Oslo. The second section considers manifestations of the same self-delusions in the history of Israel, culminating in Oslo and all that has followed upon the initial Oslo accords.

Section I
THE DIASPORA

Since the Six Day War, and at an increasing pace, we have witnessed a phenomenon which probably has no parallel in history: an emotional and moral identification by the majority of Israel's intelligentsia, and its print and electronic media, with people committed to our annihilation; people who openly declare their intention to expel us from this land . . . Whoever researches the dimensions of this phenomenon, possibly rooted in the Diaspora proclivity for self-abasement and sycophancy toward Jew-haters, *would have to go through enormous quantities of material.* [emphasis added]

Israeli novelist and essayist
Aharon Megged, June, 1994[1]

ONE

The Modern Era: New Anti-Jewish Indictments and Their Toll

Stunned by the hailstorm of anti-Semitic accusations, the Jews forget who they are and often imagine that they are really the physical and spiritual horrors which their deadly enemies represent them to be. The Jew is often heard to murmur that he must learn from the enemy and try to remedy the faults ascribed to him. He forgets, however, that the anti-Semitic accusations are meaningless . . .

Max Nordau, Austro-Hungarian Jewish
writer and early Zionist, 1897[2]

In the late eighteenth and nineteenth centuries, Jews in central Europe were told by much of the surrounding society that Yiddish was a crude, bastardized, unwholesome language that reflected the degenerate nature of the Jews and illustrated their unfitness for citizenship rights. Many Jewish leaders and members of the cultural elite in the Jewish community embraced this attack and urged the abandonment of Yiddish as, in the words of one such figure, "a language of stammerers, corrupt and deformed, repulsive to those who are able to speak in a correct and orderly manner."[3]

Jews were also told at that time that their being primarily engaged in commerce and trade was another mark of their degeneracy and inappropriateness for citizenship, as vocations in trade were intrinsically unproductive and exploitative.[4] And again many leading voices in the Jewish community took to heart the assault and urged Jews to cast off their reprehensible endeavors and devote themselves to more wholesome occupations like farming and the crafts in order to render themselves more worthy of acceptance by their neighbors.

Some gentile observers, even early in this period, offered much more positive assessments of Jewish involvement in commerce. The English playwright and essayist Joseph Addison, writing in *The Spectator* early in the eighteenth century, opined that, "[The Jews] are, indeed, so disseminated through all the trading parts of the world, that they are become the instruments by which the most distant nations converse with one another, and by which mankind are knit together in a general correspondence: They are like the pegs and nails in a great building, which, though they are but little valued in themselves, are absolutely necessary to keep the whole frame together."[5] The American statesman George Mason, who was a prominent delegate to the Constitutional Convention and played an important role in framing the Bill of Rights, likewise viewed Jewish engagement in trade in more positive terms. The Jews, he wrote, are "not only noted for their knowledge of mercantile and commercial affairs, but also for their industry, enterprise and probity."[6] But such perspectives were rare in central Europe. What the Jews heard there were predominantly derogatory, disparaging assessments of their endeavors, and all too often they chose to embrace those attacks as reflecting some transcendent truth and as answerable only by Jewish reform.

In the course of the nineteenth century, Jews in substantial numbers abandoned Yiddish as their primary language to speak, for example, "good" German, and significant segments of the community succeeded in leaving behind the commercial occupations of their fathers to become poets, composers, philosophers, and intellectuals of various other stripes. Many leading voices in the surrounding society then argued that Jews may gain command of the German language or master German poetic or musical forms or the subtleties of German philosophy but they were still doing so with alien Jewish minds and Jewish sensibilities. Such voices maintained that Jews were still unable to employ their learning to true aesthetic or intellectual creativity but were rather subverting what they learned to some lesser, alien end. Even this indictment was embraced by some in the Jewish community, people who insisted that Jews were indeed being too pushy in their cultural endeavors and that most who took part in those endeavors were, in fact, introducing alien and lesser "Jewish" elements that were coarsening German culture.

In the last decades of the nineteenth century, the racist strain in central European anti-Semitism became more sharply defined and more popular, with declarations that the Jews are biologically inferior and therefore incapable of assimilating into European society no matter what their efforts at acculturation. And there were Jews who embraced even these assertions of intrinsic and immutable Jewish inferiority.

All of these instances of Jewish absorption of anti-Jewish indictments were propelled by Jews' desires to propitiate their attackers, and they all reflected delusions of propitiation. Of course, minorities can and do take pragmatic steps that they believe will increase their chances of entering more fully into the wider society, and, for example, Jewish exertions to give up their dialect and master normative German could be perceived as such a pragmatic measure. But that is very different from endorsing the derogation of Yiddish as intrinsically primitive, inferior, corrupting. Such endorsements were founded on the desire to believe that Jews are regarded with distaste and loathing and treated as inferior because they speak an inferior language and have been coarsened by their language and that becoming linguistically equal to their neighbors will assure their being treated as equal — a wish-driven delusion.

Given the level of anti-Jewish sentiment in surrounding societies, conversion too could be perceived as a pragmatic step necessary if one wanted to enter more fully into the life of the wider world. But a recurrent theme in the writings of those who formally abandoned their Jewish ties during this period, and wrote about their doing so, was their perceiving their conversion not simply as a pragmatic measure but as the abandonment of an intrinsically inferior identity, a connection with an unwholesome and inferior people, for a superior self-definition. Underlying this comprehension was a wish to believe that anti-Jewish sentiment was grounded in a fair and truthful assessment of the Jews and therefore full abandonment of the Jewish community would indeed pave the way to full acceptance. Even those who embraced the concept of Jewish biological inferiority did so with the implicit hope that "honest" acknowledgment of their own inferiority would set them apart from other Jews and win them some greater status in the eyes of the surrounding society.

The delusional nature of these endorsements of Jewish taint and Jewish inferiority is not simply a matter of their failing to elicit the desired effect. At times, embracing the indictments of one's tormentors and reforming oneself accordingly do yield the desired results. Even in Germany, where Jews' efforts to propitiate their neighbors by taking to heart their neighbors' denigrating attacks failed so spectacularly to avert disaster, there were, for example, many Jews who in the previous century had abandoned what they saw as a tainted Jewish identity, who converted and intermarried, and whose descendants escaped the Nazi slaughter. But irrespective of such occasional "positive" outcomes, embracing hostile and bigoted indictments as truth and acting accordingly is delusional because doing so entails confounding hateful distortions with reality. It is delusional also because it is premised on the wishful belief that taking to heart the attacks and reforming accordingly will lead inexorably to acceptance, whereas the outcome, like the Israeli quest for peace, will typically be determined by forces outside the control of the embattled minority and its members.

Examples of Jews during the late eighteenth and nineteenth centuries endorsing the anti-Jewish indictments cited above are myriad. Moses Mendelssohn, born in 1729 in Dessau, was virtually the founding father of the Jewish Enlightenment (Haskalah). At age fourteen, he followed his teacher Rabbi David Frankel to Berlin, gaining admission to the city, where Jewish residency was strictly controlled, as a supported student. He subsequently expanded his studies beyond Jewish subjects, learned English, French, and Latin, took courses in classical philosophy, and began writing on philosophical subjects. Within liberal-minded circles in the surrounding society he was soon hailed as proof that with proper reform and education Jews could be worthy of civil equality.

Mendelssohn adhered to the practice of traditional Judaism throughout his life, was concerned about the welfare of his fellow Jews, and extended what help he could to Jewish communities across Europe in distress from the actions of local authorities. His aspiration was for Jews to win acceptance in surrounding societies without abandoning their faith, as he himself had won some modicum of acceptance. It is hardly surprising that Mendelssohn would advocate to other Jews a better command of German as a pragmatic step that might ease their way — as an education beyond Yiddish had eased his — to greater acceptance within the wider society. But it is Mendelssohn from whom the quote was taken about Yiddish being "a language of stammerers, corrupt and deformed." In another instance, when asked by a jurist in Breslau in 1782 for his opinion on revisions of the oath Jews were obliged to swear in court proceedings, Mendelssohn focused on the language of the oath. He voiced his opposition to the legal authorization of Yiddish and asserted, "I am afraid that this jargon has contributed more than a little to the immorality of the common man; and I expect a very good effect from the increasing use of the pure German idiom."[7]

These comments regarding Yiddish are obviously not simply in the vein of pragmatic advice but reflect some absorption by Mendelssohn, for all his sensitivity to things Jewish, of the crude biases and caricatures incessantly aimed at the Jews and their language by the surrounding society.[8] And the underlying motivation to his endorsement of the denigrating of the Jews' language and of the Jews who spoke it can best be explained by the dynamic that has been suggested: If one accepted the arguments of the Jews' critics who characterized elements of the Jews' culture as tainted and corrupt, accepted the attacks of the wider society as fair, then one could thereby bolster a hope that Jewish reform congruent with those attacks would inexorably win admission to the wider society.

Mendelssohn's absorption of the anti-Jewish indictments of the larger society can also be seen in his attitude toward Jewish occupations, although here his views were more nuanced. In published statements on the issue of civil rights for Jews, Mendelssohn argued against claims that Jewish concentration in occupations related to commerce ought to count against them. He pointed out that those who ply such vocations provide as valuable and indispensable a service to society as the practitioners of other endeavors. Elsewhere, however, he does write of Jewish engagement in trade coarsening "the common rabble."[9]

Vehement attacks on Yiddish in the vein of the ugly diatribes of anti-Jewish writers became a staple in the works of the maskilim, the German Jewish promoters of Haskalah, or Enlightenment, many of whom regarded Mendelssohn as their inspiration and mentor. And while Mendelssohn was hardly blind to the lie in claims that Jewish involvement in commerce was intrinsically reprehensible and justified anti-Jewish attitudes, the maskilim often echoed such anti-Jewish canards. They routinely advocated Jewish vocational reform as leaving behind a debased existence, and as a panacea for reshaping the Jews and making them fit to be assimilated into European civil society.

More particularly, maskilim urged that Jews give up trade for occupations like crafts and artisanry or farming, and they even conspired with governmental authorities to push Jews out of commerce. For example, maskilim promoted the formulations of an edict issued in 1782 by Emperor Joseph II of Austria, a ruler in the "enlightened despot" mold. The edict, among other provisions, placed restrictions on Jews' participation in some of their traditional occupations while easing Jewish admission into a number of alternative endeavors. The targeted Jewish community largely opposed the reforms, not least because their current vocations filled economic niches not taken by others. There was much historic precedent indicating that occupational shifts in which Jews would pursue endeavors popular in the surrounding societies, bringing them into direct competition with their non-Jewish neighbors, would likely not only put them at a competitive disadvantage but also exacerbate anti-Jewish feeling rather than ameliorate it. But such arguments had generally little impact on the maskilim's enthusiastic embrace of the indictments of the Jews as corrupted by trade and despised for their corruption or on the maskilim's visions of winning acceptance and an end to hatred and bias through vocational self-reform.

The claim that Jewish involvement in trade is intrinsically degenerate was taken up and expanded upon by the Jewish convert to Christianity Karl Marx. Marx argued, along with various Jew-baiters at the time, that it is not simply that Jews are coarsened by their involvement in commerce but, rather, that the Jews and their religion are immutably materialistic and degenerate and this drives them to engage in trade.

Marx underwent conversion in his native Trier at age six, in 1824. His father had converted seven years earlier, at least in part for career purposes, and had thereafter cultivated a German cultural identity. The elder Marx appears to have regarded his path as having abandoned a lesser identity for a superior one and to have encouraged the same perspective in his son.

From his earliest entry into the public arena, Marx was clearly interested in distancing himself from "the Jews." In the words of Isaiah Berlin: "[Marx] was determined that the sarcasms and insults, to which some of the notable Jews of his generation, Heine, Lassalle, Disraeli, were all their lives a target, should, so far as he could effect it, never be used to plague him."[10] The persistent heat of his anti-Jewish diatribes suggests that, when he continued to be the target of anti-Jewish barbs, he chose to blame not his tormenters but rather "the Jews" for casting the shadow of their tainted existence over his life, and he responded by striving even harder to separate himself from them.

In his essay "On the Jewish Question" (1844), Marx argues that the Jewish mind is too limited and Jewish thinking too concrete to have fashioned a true religion. Instead, it produced a pseudo-religion whose practical expression is materialism and occupation in trade. Also as a consequence of their limited nature, the Jews are incapable of creativity and lack aesthetic sensibility. (As noted earlier, this last indictment, while of long pedigree, had recently gained greater prominence in the German-speaking world. It had done so in the context of greater Jewish entry into the cultural mainstream and exertions in poetry and other artistic endeavors. This elicited attacks to the effect that Jews might superficially master German and faithfully emulate poetic forms but that the limits of the Jewish mind still meant their exertions would inevitably be devoid of true aesthetic value.)

Marx writes in the essay, "What is the worldly cult of the Jew? Huckstering. What is his worldly god? Money[11] . . . That which is contained in an abstract form in the Jewish religion — contempt for theory, for art, for history, and for man as an end in himself — is the real, conscious standpoint of the man of money."[12]

Moreover, according to Marx, to the degree that money has become the basis of the social order in the West, the West has been Judaized. "The god of the Jews has been secularized and has become the god of this world."[13]

From this perspective, the radical agenda becomes for Marx not just a transformation of modern society to bring about the liberation of everyone, including the Jews, but rather a transformation of modern society whose essence will be a liberation of the world from the ethos of the Jews!

Variations on the same anti-Jewish themes are a feature in Marx's writings throughout his life. One can see in Marx's published anti-Jewish arguments not only an attempt to distance himself in the public eye from the Jews but a more direct retort of sorts to those critics who, in their attacks on his writings, characterized them as ill-conceived products of the alien, primitive, and malevolent Jewish mind. (By 1850, there were already published attacks on Marx in an anti-Semitic vein, casting him as a revolutionary determined to impose a Jewish dictatorship on Germany. Such attacks continued throughout his life.[14]) Marx insists that the defenders of the status quo, of bourgeois society, are themselves "Judaized" and are making common cause with the Jews as obstacles to human development.

This tack of Jews or Jewish converts responding to anti-Semitic invective against them by insisting that their critics are themselves behaving like "Jews" is a recurrent one during this period. For example, Heinrich Heine, another convert, was subjected to arguments from critics that his poetry was inexorably marred by the aesthetic limitations and lack of artistry of the Jewish mind. Heine retorted that his critics, by engaging in excited, fantastical arguments against him, were themselves emulating the primitive Jewish ways of Talmudic disputation instead of more measured and reasoned critical discourse. But however much Marx's gentile critics were a target of his arguments, those arguments remain, of course, crude assaults on the Jews, assaults that regurgitate and amplify the popular canards of contemporary Jew-baiters. And Marx's ultimate aim in employing them was to gain credibility by demonstrating his separateness from "the Jews."

Attacks on Jewish entry into the cultural mainstream by elements in the surrounding society were not limited to critiques of Jewish literary and other artistic efforts and claims that Jews lacked aesthetic sensibility or that they invariably introduced alien elements into German culture. Such attacks also targeted Jewish entry into journalism, politics, and other endeavors and entailed declarations that these efforts too were illegitimate and tainted. Perhaps the best known Jewish voice mimicking this genre of bigoted assaults was that of the Austrian Jewish satirist Karl Kraus.

Vienna at the end of the nineteenth century had a large Jewish population, segments of which played a central role in the intellectual and cultural life of the city and of Austria. At the same time, the new political anti-Semitism in the German-speaking world attained its first important electoral victory in Vienna with the election of the Christian Socialist Party's Karl Lueger as mayor in 1897, and the Jews of the city were chronically subjected to social, cultural, and political pressures. Kraus's life and attitudes were largely shaped by the predicament of Viennese Jewry in those years.

Born in 1874, Kraus spent his adult life in Vienna pursuing a writing career that brought him unique prominence as a satirist and as a social and political critic. The major vehicle for his writing was the widely read journal *Die Fackel*, which Kraus founded in 1899 and edited until his death in 1936. Until 1911 he published some pieces from contributors; thereafter the material in *Die Fackel* was entirely his own.

Kraus declared his estrangement from the Jewish community in 1898 and converted to Catholicism in 1911. Nevertheless throughout his career he was attacked as a Jewish writer, indeed often as the quintessential Jewish writer, supposedly using an alien and corrupt Jewish literary language and stylistic mode to disseminate equally alien and corrupt Jewish ideas. Kraus in turn focused his critical and satirical assaults on other Jews, indicting them for being the true purveyors both of an alien, Jewish literary language and style and of alien, Jewish ideas.

Among Kraus's targets were Herzl, the writers Hermann Bahr and Arthur Schnitzler, and the children's writer Felix Salten (author of *Bambi*), as well as various Jewish newspaper editors and reporters. In generic terms, his targets were wealthy Jews, the Jewish bourgeoisie, and the Jewish cultural elite.

Kraus's animus toward Jews permeated his politics. He initially embraced Lueger, then cooled to him because he decided that once in the mayor's office Lueger was not adequately following through on his earlier populist anti-Semitic rhetoric and was too accommodating of the city's Jews, particularly the middle class and its business interests. In the Dreyfus affair, Kraus was convinced of the Jewish captain's guilt and argued that the theory of a conspiracy against Dreyfus was concocted by liberal Jewish journalists. He published numerous attacks on Dreyfus and his supporters, including suggestions that they were examples of the sort of Jewish malefactors whose behavior accounted for anti-Semitism. When a Jew in Bohemia was accused of the ritual murder of a Christian girl and wrongfully convicted, Kraus did not take issue with the anti-Jewish outrage but rather attacked the Jewish press in Vienna for defending the accused. During the years when he was still publishing articles by others in *Die Fackel*, Kraus accepted pieces from the anti-Semitic race theorists Lanz von Liebenfels and Houston Chamberlain.[15]

Kraus acknowledged that by racial definition he was a Jew. But he consistently chose to believe that the anti-Jewish animus directed against him and so prominent in the larger society was actually inflamed by faults that were alien to him, the faults of the people he was targeting. He also chose to embrace much of that animus as deserved and even wrote that his Jewish targets were precipitating the "destruction of Austria by Jerusalem." Other statements by Kraus that in tone and content mimicked the anti-Semitic press include: "Jew boys are the poets of a nation to which they do not belong"; "the inevitable pogrom of the Jews against ideals"; the depiction of Austria as "a state which has the most corrupt Jewish influences circulating in its veins"; and the declaration that "*Gemutlichkeit* and Jewishness" were "the driving forces of Austrian decay."[16] Kraus also insisted that the gentile anti-Semites did not really mean much of what they said, and he seems to have believed that they posed no real threat to the Jews.

Kraus's writings convey his obvious if futile desire to separate himself in the public eye from what was popularly comprehended as Jewish. They also convey his belief that sufficient Jewish self-reform, Jews divesting themselves of what he argued were their negative cultural, linguistic, and intellectual attributes, would indeed overcome the surrounding society's anti-Jewish hostility. It was only with the rise of Nazism in Germany and the burgeoning of Nazi influence in Austria (Kraus died in 1936) that he began to rethink his anti-Jewish assumptions.

Even the most virulent racist attacks on the Jews, arguments that the Jews' alien, inferior, and dangerous nature is essentially immutable and that neither conversion nor any other attempts by Jews to better themselves can have much salutary effect, had their Jewish defenders.

Such indictments of the Jews were a major element in the arguments of the Jew-baiters even at the beginning of the period being considered. In the latter part of the nineteenth century, with emergence of a new pseudoscience of race and racial studies, this notion of the inherently alien and inferior nature of the Jew became an even more prominent and established concept both in German political discourse and in German popular belief. And some Jews incorporated the concept of the racially inferior Jew into their image of Jews and of themselves as Jews. The figure most often cited as an example of this phenomenon is another Austrian, Otto Weininger.

Weininger[17] was born in Vienna in 1880, into a liberal, assimilated family. His father was a renowned goldsmith who produced museum-quality art objects. Otto's sister later wrote of their father: "[He] was highly anti-semitic, but he thought as a Jew and was angry when Otto wrote against Judaism."[18] The father apparently approved when Weininger converted to Christianity in 1902, and the rest of the family subsequently converted as well. Also in 1902 Weininger earned his doctorate from the University of Vienna.

A year later he published *Sex and Character*,[19] a work based on his university studies and devoted largely to arguing and documenting the supposed inherent inferiority of women, also a pseudoscientifically buttressed and widely popular concept at the time. For example, women, according to Weininger, are constitutionally devoid of genius, of dignity, of morality. But Weininger also devotes a chapter of his book to the Jews and argues that Jews are intrinsically even more limited than women. Here he repeats many of the old, if at times mutually contradictory, canards against the Jews: They are incapable of the highest forms of thought; they lack aesthetic sensibility; they are materialistic; they are communists who lack an appreciation of property; they are excessively emotional. But, in regurgitating these old attacks, Weininger invokes elements of the new racial science and the language of genetically transmitted racial character.

How did Weininger see himself? In other writers of Jewish origin who endorse the concept of supposedly inherent negative Jewish traits, writers such as Marx, there appears to be a cognitive disjuncture through which they somehow exempt themselves from what they declare to be universal and inescapable. But this was not true of Weininger. On the contrary, he seems to pride himself on consciously recognizing the same racial traits in himself and hating them in himself as he does in others. Weininger writes:

"The bitterest Antisemites are to be found amongst the Jews themselves . . . [But] only the commoner natures are actively Antisemitic and pass sentence on others without having once sat in judgement on themselves in these matters; and very few exercise their Antisemitism first on themselves. This one thing, however, remains none the less certain: whoever detests the Jewish disposition detests it first of all in himself; that he should persecute it in others is merely his endeavor to separate himself in this way from Jewishness; he strives to shake it off and to localize it in his fellow-creatures, and so for a moment to dream himself free of it."[20] But, Weininger suggests, he himself is too self-aware and too honest to entertain such a dream; he sets himself apart from other inexorably racially inferior Jews at least in this brutal honesty.

Weininger committed suicide a year after appearance of the book, at age twenty-three, and his death has been widely linked to his inability to come to terms with what he hated in himself but could not exorcize, what he perceived to be the immutable Jew within him.[21]

The Jewish experience in central Europe during the late eighteenth, nineteenth, and early twentieth centuries was marked by high levels of defection from the Jewish community motivated by the desire to escape the depredations to which Jews were subjected. This entailed both formal defection through conversion and simply emotional distancing and practical disengagement. But in the preceding eighteen centuries, Diaspora Jews had been exposed typically to much more severe pressures from the societies in which they lived. An obvious question, taken up in the next chapter, is how did Jewish communities during those centuries manage to survive at all — to the degree that they did survive — the corrosive impact of their besiegement.

TWO

Decimation and Survival:
The Ancient and Medieval Diaspora

When one of Friedrich II's courtiers was asked by his monarch how he knew that there was divine providence in the world, he cited as overwhelming proof the survival of the Jews.[1]

In considering what enabled Jews in premodern centuries to resist the corrosive effects of the chronic denigrating assaults to which they were subjected, one must recognize that resistance was, of course, far from universal. The pressures on Jews were onerous indeed. Even when not physically at risk, they typically lived amid societies in which they were widely viewed with antipathy and hostility. Leading institutions in those societies stigmatized them as lesser, often as intrinsically evil, beings practicing an alien, flawed, and benighted faith and routinely imposed on them legal and extra-legal handicaps and humiliations.

Many Jews over the centuries sought to escape their plight by voluntarily converting, if any defection under such conditions could properly be characterized as entirely "voluntary." Jews who did so and wrote about it typically cast their conversion not just as taking a pragmatic move but as divesting themselves of an inherently inferior and unwholesome identity. While it was no doubt politic for those who described their conversion in writing to present it in such terms, there is little reason to believe that they had not actually embraced the surrounding society's indictments of the Jews and believed much of what they were writing.[2]

One can also see among some who remained Jews a predilection, as in modern centuries, to endorse aspects of the anti-Jewish animus of the surrounding society, to choose to believe that its hostility was based on the lamentable behavior of some subset of the Jewish community, and to harbor wishful expectations that Jewish self-reform would end the hostility. The twelfth-century Jewish traveler Benjamin of Tudela wrote of his visit to the Jews of Constantinople:

"Among [them] there are craftsmen in silk and many merchants and many wealthy men . . . They dwell in a burdensome exile. And most of the enmity comes about because of the [Jewish] tanners who make leather and fling their filthy water into the streets at the entrance to their homes, polluting the street of the Jews. And therefore the Greeks [Constantinople was at the time, of course, still in Byzantine hands] hate the Jews, whether good or bad, and make their yoke heavy upon them and beat them in the streets."[3]

The historian H. H. Ben Sasson observes of the passage:

"This information certainly did not reach [Benjamin of Tudela] from the tanners; it was how wealthy Jews explained to themselves and to others the animosity of the Greeks towards the Jews. It resulted from the filthy habits of those who followed such a despicable craft, and because of them all Jews, good and bad, suffered. In this context 'good' meant the silk-maker or physician, and 'bad' meant the miserable tanner, blamed as the source of this animosity."[4] The besieged Jews chose to ignore the actual roots of the hostility directed against them, hostility about which they could do little, and instead to focus their resentment on elements within the Jewish community on the other side of the social-occupational divide. They did so in the service of fantasies that "reform" of those others would radically ameliorate the community's predicament.

Still, as has been pointed out again and again by both Jewish and non-Jewish historians, whatever the dimensions of "voluntary" conversion during these premodern centuries, or of Jewish embrace of anti-Jewish indictments, the ability of the Jews to survive at all as a faith and a people in the face of the tremendous pressures to which they were subjected during these two thousand years is a remarkable phenomenon that calls out for explanation. (Indeed, some, both Jews and non-Jews, have seen Jewish survival as so remarkable as to defy, or transcend, worldly explanation. Friedrich II's courtier referred to in the opening of this chapter is but one example of such an assessment.)

Discussions of the increased defections from the Jewish community in the modern era have often focused on the new opportunities for assimilation that started to open to Jews, beginning around two hundred years ago, in some of the societies in which they lived. The implicit suggestion has been that the absence of greater defection in earlier eras was due to absence of opportunity. But this explanation — developed in large part by writers of Jewish origin whose own attachments to the Jewish community were weak at best and who were predisposed to view Jewish identity as of little intrinsic value and something people would be readily inclined to shed if only given the chance — is largely a misrepresentation.[5]

On the one hand, of course, those new opportunities for assimilation were, more often than not, limited by *de jure*, and more pervasively *de facto*, restrictions on Jews. More importantly, all through the centuries of the Diaspora, assimilation was, in fact, readily available in return for apostasy, or at least as available as assimilation through most of the modern era.

Some observers have attributed the increased defections from the Jewish community in the modern era to the rise of secularism and the supposed diminished significance of religion in people's lives. Certainly, many defecting Jews embraced the widespread modern alienation from traditional religious belief and chose to see Jewish affiliation as exclusively religious and Judaism as irrelevant to their lives and their values. But modern secularism represented mainly an opportunity for defection and a rationale for it; it was not the "cause" of defection. Or, it was a "cause" only in the sense of working in tandem with pressures on Jews and offering a justification for defection to escape those pressures.

In earlier periods, in the face of chronic besiegement from surrounding societies, including often intense persecution, the check on large-scale demoralization, devaluation of Jewish identity and defection, when they were checked, was not absence of opportunity for defection or absence of rationales for it. Rather, it was the nature and strength of Jewish communal institutions in those earlier eras, institutions that underwent dramatic weakening and dissolution with the political and social upheavals that marked the emergence of modern Europe.

Those Jewish institutions that provided a significant bulwark against the corrosive psychological impact of the denigration and abuse to which Jews were subjected, and were consequently a defense against defection, were not, of course, a defense against physical assault. Largely as a result of losses to recurrent massacres, to talk of Jewish survival from the beginning of the Common Era to the beginning of modernity is to talk of the survival of a much decimated and depleted Jewry.

Scholarly estimates of the world Jewish population two thousand years ago tend to converge on the view that Jews living around the Mediterranean likely numbered six to seven million and represented about 10 percent of the estimated population of sixty million within the Roman Empire, while another million Jews lived in Mesopotamia and surrounding regions. The Mesopotamian Diaspora was largely a continuation of the exile communities of the Babylonian Captivity. Of the approximately six to seven million Jews in areas of Roman hegemony, perhaps half to two-thirds lived outside Eretz Israel, with Syria (particularly Antioch and Damascus), Asia Minor, and Egypt (mainly Alexandria) each possibly having Jewish populations in excess of a million people.[6] In 1800, the world Jewish population was a little over two million, approximately 800,000 of whom lived in what had been, until its recent dissolution, Poland.

There was large-scale destruction of Jewish populations even before the establishment of Christianity as the state religion of the Roman Empire. Roman suppression of the two Jewish rebellions in Eretz Israel, in 66–70 CE and 132–135 CE, entailed massive loss of life. An intervening Jewish uprising (115–117 CE) that engulfed Egypt, Libya, nearby Cyrenaica (corresponding roughly to the northeastern area of modern Libya up to Benghazi) and Cyprus depopulated huge areas and resulted in the virtual annihilation of their Jewish communities, including the perhaps million-strong community in Egypt.

In contrast to the Romans' brutal retaliation against the Jews when they were in revolt, Roman policy did not typically target Jews for denigration and abuse. This was not entirely true of populations in the empire among whom the Jews lived. In Egypt, writings of cultic priests attacking the Jews date at least from the early third century BCE, and mob assaults on the Jews of Alexandria, the first in 38 CE, entailed extensive slaughter. (The atrocities of that first episode are vividly described by the Alexandrian Jewish philosopher Philo, who was a survivor of the rampage.) Recurrent Egyptian depredations were likely the trigger for the Jewish rebellion of 115, which encompassed those lands that were within the Egyptian sphere of influence.

Anti-Jewish literature emanating from Egypt ultimately gained wide dissemination in the Greek-speaking world of the eastern Mediterranean and broadened anti-Jewish sentiment. This sentiment may have contributed to the rebellion of 67 CE since many of the Roman administrators in Eretz Israel prior to the uprising were Greek and were notably hostile to Jewish religious sensibilities.

But Egyptian and Greek hostility was distinct from Roman imperial policy. If Diaspora Jews were under any state-related pressure in the empire, it was mainly the pressure that a dominant culture invariably exerts on minorities and did not entail particular denigration. Nor is there any indication of significant Jewish defection to the dominant cults of the era. On the contrary, the flow of affiliation seems to have gone largely in the other direction, with numerous citizens of the empire, including members of Rome's aristocratic families, adopting elements of Jewish belief and practice.

With Constantine's establishment of Christianity as the imperial religion, in 313 CE, the situation of the Jews changed dramatically. They were now subject to official defamation, indeed demonization, and discriminatory legal constraints. Although official church policy permitted the Jews to practice their religion and did not support forced conversion, the subsequent centuries saw recurrent episodes of large-scale forced conversions and mass murder. Similar conditions prevailed in the Moslem world in the wake of Arab conquests in the Middle East, North Africa, and Spain in the seventh century. Most of the conquered areas had majority Christian populations with often substantial Jewish minorities. Islam prescribed protected *"dhimmi"* status for Christians and Jews, as "peoples of the Book"; but both groups were subjected to chronic discrimination and denigration and episodic campaigns of forced conversion and slaughter.[7]

Beyond what limited capacity they might have had to intervene effectively with Christian or Moslem authorities, Jewish institutions could not protect their communities against such depredations. Their efficacy in terms of defending their communities lay rather in helping arm Jews to resist the psychological corrosiveness of the abuses to which they were subjected and to preclude their being overwhelmed and beaten down to the point of abandoning the faith and the community. The ability to resist such pressures meant in large part the capacity of the Jews to maintain their faith in the Jewish mission and in the Jewish comprehension of history, according to which adherence to their Covenant with God, their fealty to the Covenant, would culminate ultimately in an end to their travails, national Redemption, and a world transformed by the light of God's Law. This was the common denominator among those who remained loyal to Judaism, however varied among them might be their understanding of Redemption and worldly transformation.

One institutional factor important in supporting this faith was the success of Jewish sages in proffering an understanding of Jewish exile and suffering that reconciled those travails with Jewish hope. Such comprehensions went beyond simply interpreting the torments of exile as punishment for transgressions, a punishment that would end when consistent and unwavering rededication to God's Law opened the way to Redemption, or as a testing and tempering of the faithful as prelude to Redemption. It is likely that many of those who were enduring the tribulations of the Jewish predicament viewed neither of these explanations as entirely satisfactory. They had seen too many good people suffer and die, too many of the just and the righteous in the world laid low and the unjust raised up high, to accept with equanimity such interpretations.

What appears to have been more compelling among the proffered explanations had less to do with casting the Jewish predicament in terms of inferences of God's purpose than with reconciling that predicament with scriptural prophecy, prophecy of the dark night of Jewish suffering that would precede the dawn of Redemption. The sages readily acknowledged that God's reasons were far beyond human understanding. On the other hand, they promoted scriptural prophecy, with its prediction of the rise and fall of empires under whose yoke Israel would suffer before being redeemed, as a faithful guide to history's course prior to Redemption. They also championed an understanding of the vagaries of current exile as aspects of that prophesied course.

The historian Yosef Hayim Yerushalmi has written about the virtual absence of Jewish history writing from the time of Josephus and the failed rebellions against Rome until the nineteenth century. He argues that throughout this long period there is nothing in the legacy of Jewish writing comparable, for example, to the chronicle of events in Jewish life that form so much a part of Hebrew scripture.[8] There are certainly records of some occurrences in Jewish life, particularly of Jewish catastrophes and also of Jewish escape from catastrophe. But these are less works of historical chronicle than martyrologies written for the purpose of mourning and remembrance or tales of escape written for celebration. The dearth of *bona fide* history, ironic given the popular association of the Jews with supposed historical awareness and mindfulness, is even more remarkable in view of the extensive development of historiography in both the Moslem and Christian cultures in which the Jews lived. Moreover, in virtually every other area of intellectual inquiry and endeavor pursued by the surrounding cultures, the Jews were eager participants and contributors to an extent that very often surpassed in relative terms that of the surrounding populations.

Yerushalmi's thesis has been challenged by other historians, who have suggested in particular that his definition of what constitutes *bona fide* history writing is too narrow. But aspects of his argument seem unassailable, and his explanation for this dearth of Jewish interest in chronicling Jewish history after the failure of the rebellions against Rome is likewise compelling. He proposes, in effect, that eschewing the chronicling of Diaspora history was a rhetorical choice that began to take shape at the point where it became clear that the liberation of Eretz Israel was not going to be achieved in short order and that Judaism had to adjust to survival in exile. It was a rhetorical declaration that the details, the novelty, and uniqueness, of Jewish experiences in the Diaspora were less important than their comprehension in ways that would sustain hope. To this end, new Jewish experiences were to be understood first as a reprise of experiences familiar to Jews — the cycle of exile and return, from slavery in Egypt to liberation and the reclaiming of Eretz Israel to exile in Babylon and again return. Secondly, they were to be understood as a fulfillment of scriptural prophecy of further exile and subjugation to oppressive empires prior to ultimate Redemption.

From this perspective, the ubiquitous practice in Jewish writing during the Middle Ages of applying to the Christian world, or the Moslem world, or to particular Christian or Moslem regimes, appellations that are drawn from Biblical adversaries of the Jews did not simply represent an effort to identify the Jews' persecutors with enemies who were overcome by Israel or enemies whose practices were offensive to God and whom God chose to punish. Rather, it was part of a broader, ongoing determination to understand current circumstances as reprises of earlier travails ultimately surmounted. It was part of the overarching effort to comprehend Jewish experience during the Middle Ages not as history spinning off in novel and appalling directions further and further from scriptural antecedents but as a recurring living out of experiences grounded in both Biblical precedent and Biblical prophecy and consonant with the expectation of ultimate Redemption.

Moreover, beyond the promotion of such affirmative and reassuring comprehensions by their sages, the Jews of the period, implicitly if ironically, drew further affirmation even from their tormentors. They lived in a world, particularly in Christendom, in which virtually everyone embraced a vision of history as moving toward ultimate transformation and redemption, a reign of justice and righteousness, derivative variations on the Jewish vision, so that those concepts in Jews' own belief and hope were, if anything, reinforced by the surrounding culture. Of course, there were many other aspects of Jewish belief beyond Jewish eschatology, including major elements of Jewish ethics, that the Jews could see embraced and affirmed as well by the dominant culture. Where Christian and Moslem formulations differed, where the other faith, particularly Christianity, took some Jewish principle or aspect of Jewish scripture and Jewish prophecy and transformed its meaning, Jews were inclined, and supported by the teachings of their sages, to comprehend these reinterpretations as bowdlerizations of the Jewish original rather than as more enlightened interpretations, as those around them insisted.

But it was not only through competitive comprehensions, in which Jews perceived flaws in the other faiths and saw them as defective imitations of Judaism, that Jews derived from Christianity and Islam affirmations of their own beliefs. There was also a perception of Christianity and Islam as, however flawed, and however terrible and shameful in their treatment of Jews, still representing an historical advance over the paganism that had earlier prevailed in the world. They were seen as reflecting at least a progressive acknowledgment of and lip service to the ethical precepts that are at the core of the Jewish belief system. Christianity and Islam had adopted much of Jewish ethics as their own, and had done so in the context of embracing at least an assertion of adherence to Judaic monotheism. This progressivist perspective was endorsed by various Jewish sages and seen as indicative of an historic dynamic that was further testimony to the truth of Judaism.

Nor was this a concept limited to rationalist thinkers such as Maimonides and his followers, thinkers who perceived in history a naturalistic progression toward Redemption. In a variation on the same theme, the twelfth-century Spanish Rabbi Judah Halevi, someone whose religious philosophy was very different from that of Maimonides, could write of being moved by the demonstrations of faith and piety exhibited by Christians and Moslems at their prayers. Halevi observed that, seeing the dissonance between these people's piety and their deeds, their supposed intentions and their manifest actions, he felt reinforced in his belief that only by their ultimately drawing closer to the precepts put forward in Hebrew scripture, in Hebrew scripture as the Hebrews understood it, and to the integration of faith and deeds prescribed there, would that dissonance be resolved.

(Moreover, this inclination to perceive in widespread adoption of elements of Jewish theology and moral prescriptions progress consonant with Jewish aspirations has deep roots in Jewish understanding. Judaism, since the Second Temple period and even in its epochs of active proselytizing, has conceived its universal role in ways consonant with such a perception. It has most typically formulated that role as an obligation to promote not general conversion to Judaism but rather general adherence to what is known as the Noachide Laws or characterized as the Noachide Covenant; that is, laws inferred from divine injunctions directed to Adam and Noah in the Bible and presumed to be incumbent upon all their progeny and therefore all humanity. They are traditionally rendered as entailing the eschewing of idolatry, blasphemy, bloodshed, sexual transgressions, theft, and eating from a living animal, as well as requiring establishment of a legal system, presumably to promote adherence to the laws. In Jewish tradition the Noachide Laws have significance in defining both the Jews' universal mission and the obligations of non-Jews living under Jewish sovereignty.)

But to note the arguments of sages in support of the Jewish vocation as an explanation for Jewish resistance to the surrounding society's indictments is at once valid and yet begs the question: One still must explain what enabled the sages to maintain their communal influence when the corrosive denigrations cast at the Jews included arguments that they were being misled by their benighted leaders.

The success of the sages was predicated in large part on Jewish communal and intercommunal organization, on structures for educating leaders, for conferring religious authority, and for disseminating the work of the sages between and within communities. But the importance of communal organization and intercommunal contacts in combating the psychologically corrosive effects of the Jews' predicament went beyond their role in fostering Jewish education and making transmission of the messages of the sages possible. On the most basic level, a community of believers, in addition to being necessary for Jewish ritual and religious practice, provided mutual support and affirmation and an emotional refuge in the face of the depredations of the surrounding society.

It can be argued that the unit of Jewish faith is the family. The symbolism and power of, for example, the Sabbath meal and Sabbath ritual in transporting the family beyond worldly travails, in palpably reinforcing the substantiality of the Jewish covenant, is indicative of the centrality of the family in propagating and sustaining Jewish faith. Jewish education was also a commitment of families. A twelfth-century monk, a student of Abelard in Paris, wrote, "The Jews, out of their zeal for God and their love of the law, put as many sons as they have to letters, that each may understand God's Law . . . A Jew, however poor, if he had ten sons, would put them all to letters, not for gain, as the Christians do, but for the understanding of God's Law; and not only his sons but his daughters."[9]

But it is likely that Jews living in virtual isolation from co-religionists or in very small communities of a few families, particularly if those communities did not have close ties with some nearby larger center, if they were not, in effect, satellites of some larger center, were much more vulnerable to being lost to apostasy. Indeed, a recurrent tactic of aggressive Christian proselytizers, such as those from the mendicant orders, was to advocate policies that would break up Jewish communities and isolate Jews from each other as an effective step toward converting them.

But the additional affirmation, beyond affirmative education, provided by

Jewish communal life and intercommunal contacts entailed, in fact, much more than simply mutual support and emotional refuge. In various ways, Jewish communal life and intercommunal relations provided Jews evidence of the ongoing, pragmatic viability, indeed vitality, of Jewish peoplehood and faith, the ongoing meaningfulness — in the sense of worldly measures of meaningfulness — of the Jewish vocation.

Intercommunal contacts meant, for example, that communities in distress were aware of Jewish communities elsewhere in the world that were prospering, even flourishing. Jews in Christian Europe, for instance, shared, at least into the thirteenth century and the sacking of Baghdad by the Mongols, and for many even beyond then, the image of a flourishing "Babylonian" Jewry. Such images, if at times in various respects exaggerated, helped bolster a sense of Jewish vitality and stave off despair qua the Jewish vocation in the face of local distress. In a letter to an apostate written in 1391, a Spanish Jew lists as one of his conjectured four possible reasons for the man's apostasy a comprehension of the disasters recently visited upon Spanish Jews as evidence that God had abandoned Israel. However, he then discounts this as a possible explanation, noting that "this day the majority of our people is in Babylon and Yemen," in addition to independent Jewish tribes elsewhere, as reported in travelers' tales. Consequently, he goes on, "even if it be divinely decreed that all the Jews living among the Christians should perish, the Jewish people as such remain whole, and this will not cause trust in God to fail."[10]

Similarly, the awareness of Jewish communities in Eretz Israel, communities continually being reinforced by immigrants — often renowned figures — from both East and West, gave a sense of the spark, the kindling of national Return, being kept alive.

Another important element of this pragmatic bolstering was that Jews, even in the face of the social and economic restrictions, vilifications, and other depredations that they endured, could often look around them in the societies in which they lived and not find very much in their neighbors' lives to envy or wish to emulate. While they would no doubt have preferred to share various prerogatives, and the general freedom from abuse, enjoyed by others in the society, they did not particularly see segments of that society, its social groups, as presenting attractive alternatives to their own group.

This sentiment went beyond convictions of holding to the truer religious faith or of being generally much more literate and better educated than the surrounding society. The Jewish presence in any realm was invariably predicated on its rulers perceiving some gain in their presence. When the rulers' perception was of that gain being exhausted or outweighed by other considerations, the Jews were most often expelled, or given a choice of conversion or expulsion. Consequently, the typical situation was that as long as Jews were within a country, however exploited by their rulers, they also enjoyed a position that was in various pragmatic ways — in terms of rulers' protection and in comparison to what was generally people's difficult lot in medieval societies — superior to that of most of those around them. The eminent Jewish historian Salo Baron observed in this regard that "medieval Jews at their worst were better off, both politically and economically, than the masses of villeins who usually constituted the majority of each European nation."[11] And Jews' sense of their community being more attractive even in pragmatic terms than alternative identities in the wider society was another boost to the forces sustaining their Jewish identity.

To be sure, there were various instances in which rulers' hostility and exploitation led to the impoverishment of Jews, often their reduction to desperate straits, certainly to a condition worse than that of most of those around them; hardly a situation of pragmatic reinforcement of their faithfulness. But in such circumstances either there existed as well a still relatively unmolested segment of the community that could and did extend support to their impoverished brothers and sisters and sustain them, or, in the absence of such relief, it would be very likely that the impoverished would be lost. They would either die or convert to gain relief. While some of the latter might later find an opportunity to leave their realm and return to their Judaism elsewhere, it is likely that this was not the destiny of most. Indeed, impoverishment where no Jewish relief was available often led to involuntary servitude — enslavement in one form or another — with a breaking up of families, individual isolation, and additional pressures to conversion from which there would be little chance of escape or return. In fact, just as the aggressive proselytizers in the church urged steps to break up Jewish communities as an aid to conversion, they likewise often advocated policies leading to Jewish impoverishment, family dissolution, and forced servitude as another way to promote apostasy.

The phenomenon of Jews living in chronically impoverished conditions, their circumstances essentially unchanged by what aid they obtained from other Jews, and yet maintaining their Judaism, is in all likelihood largely a phenomenon of more recent centuries. Then, particularly in the territories of what was or had been Poland-Lithuania, Jews lived predominantly in towns and villages that were almost exclusively Jewish, or in cities where they made up a very large percentage of the population. In such situations, impoverishment did not mean isolation from Jewish communal life. Nor did it entail overwhelming exposure to a surrounding hostile population and subjection to abuses and the threat of enslavement or death for faithfulness and, at the same time, blandishments of relief from poverty and perhaps from servitude for apostasy.

An indication that Jews in medieval Europe were not, in general, particularly attracted in pragmatic terms to the alternative communities and communal affiliations to which they were exposed in the societies around them was their typical behavior when faced with expulsion or conversion. Conversion would have meant entry into one of the alternative social echelons in the country that was their home. Yet Jews appear overwhelmingly — in expulsions from England, from France, from German cities and states, from Italian cities and states, even from Spain — to have chosen leaving.

But the most important element in the additional affirmation, beyond affirmative education, provided by Jewish communal life, the element perhaps also most difficult to appreciate today because it is so remote from Diaspora life in the modern era, was that of Jewish autonomy. This autonomy, often based on rights and privileges explicitly granted by charter to Jewish communities, entailed not just rights and privileges concerning religious practices but extended to authority over most areas of civil and even criminal jurisprudence. It provided effective control over the civil as well as religious life of the members of the community. Even members' employment fell within the aegis of Jewish autonomy, and not just in terms of community leaders setting and enforcing standards for vocational practice. Leaders also determined to a large extent who was allowed to practice particular vocations and with whom among other Jews or among the surrounding gentile population they could do business. (The Jewish leadership often established and enforced measures that prevented competition among community members. This was not simply a Jewish practice; the concept of the normality and appropriateness of vocational competition is a modern one. Medieval guilds, which excluded Jews and worked to eradicate Jewish competition, also had as a central function overseeing the practices of their members so as to preclude competition among them.)

This wide authority meant that Jews every day experienced in practical terms the reality of Jewish peoplehood. Moreover, this autonomy was conferred by rulers who comprehended the Jews as a distinct community; it was an expression of that understanding. So Jews saw their peoplehood not only as continuing to have practical meaning but as having its meaningfulness acknowledged by the highest authorities in the surrounding societies.

In addition, Jews experienced Jewish autonomy as essentially positive, and not just in the sense of protecting Jews from the depredations they were likely to endure had they been, in civil and criminal matters over which they had autonomy, subject instead to the jurisdiction of the surrounding societies. Again, Jews perceived their situation as, despite the social constraints, disabilities, and abuses to which they were subjected, in various practical respects preferable to that of most of those around them, indeed in some respects privileged by virtue of their relationship with their realm's secular elites. They likely did not regard these positive practical circumstances as due simply to individual talents, or simply to the fact that they belonged to a community of particularly talented people. They associated it rather with being part of an autonomous community whose leadership had established, and now sustained for its members, the practical advantages they enjoyed. That is, they perceived what was positive in their situations as emanating from their membership in the Jewish community.

Jewish autonomy gave the very tangible lie to the assertions of those around the Jews who insisted that Jewish nationhood had ceased to exist, or to exist in any positive sense, with the loss of Jewish national independence and the rise of Christianity as the successor faith. Administered by a leadership that included those sages and teachers who assured Jews not only of their ongoing place in history but of their ultimate redemption, autonomy gave additional weight to those spiritual assurances.

Again, Jewish autonomy did not provide assurance against physical depredations. Rulers invited Jews into their realms, extended protection to them and granted them autonomy in return for services they derived from the Jews, but there was an obvious tenuousness to this arrangement. A ruler could decide that the Jews were no longer useful to him or, more commonly, that their use was outweighed by other considerations. But, looking particularly at medieval Europe, rulers' usual action then was not physical assault but revocation of charters and exile.

Physical assault most often occurred at times when a ruler's authority was compromised to a point where other elements in the society hostile to the Jews — often clergy and their followers — could attack them with impunity. Indeed, it was characteristic of this period, in contradistinction to later centuries, that assaults on the Jews — including the extensive slaughter associated with the First Crusade, lesser assaults connected with later Crusades, and the widespread murderous attacks related to the Black Death — were almost invariably instigated from below, by lower clergy, marauding armed bands, town burghers, in defiance of, rather than in accord with, the policies of heads of state. On a number of occasions rulers executed leaders of the Jews' attackers. The phenomenon seen not only in Germany during the Nazi era but throughout eastern Europe between the world wars, and in Czarist Russia and Rumania in the late nineteenth and early twentieth centuries, and in Communist Russia and, later, Communist eastern Europe, where governments initiated and choreographed assaults on the Jews, was the exception rather than the rule in this earlier era.

Moreover, when rulers decided that it was politic to rid themselves of "their" Jews, there were almost invariably during the Middle Ages other sovereigns in other realms who saw gain to be had by inviting the Jews to immigrate. And these other rulers would typically extend to the immigrants wide-ranging rights and privileges, including broad autonomy, as enticements to their immigration and as protection both of the Jews and of their own interest in them. There was no medieval precedent for the situation that prevailed during the rise of Nazism or during the Nazi slaughter of the Jews, when anti-Jewish sentiment was so widespread and so rabid that no one offered the Jews refuge.

A Brief History of Jewish Autonomy

The granting of extensive autonomy to Jews in return for services rendered to rulers developed most formally in western Europe beginning in the eighth century.

In the pre-Christian Roman Empire, imperial authorities had allowed Jews extensive autonomy in Eretz Israel even after suppression of the two rebellions there. Within decades of the second rebellion the Jewish leadership had reestablished in Galilee, which had been less devastated by the war, the Sanhedrin, or Council of Elders, under the Patriarchate of Rabbi Judah the Prince. The revived Patriarchate and Sanhedrin assumed wide civil jurisdiction over the Jewish community of Eretz Israel, virtually autonomous government, and was able to extend some of that authority even to the Diaspora. The Diaspora communities acceded to the religious and extra-religious authority of the leadership in Eretz Israel and to payment of taxes to support the Sanhedrin and Patriarchate. The imperial government, which, under Caracalla, broadly conferred Roman citizenship on the Jews in 212, generally recognized the powers of the new Jewish leadership and even enforced its taxing rights in both Eretz Israel and the Diaspora.

The exercising by the Patriarchate and Sanhedrin of civil as well as religious authority and the levying of taxes continued even at times when official recognition was withdrawn. Indeed, Jewish autonomy in Eretz Israel under the Patriarchate endured for more than a century after establishment of Christianity as the imperial religion, ending only at the initiative of Theodosius II around 425.

The "Babylonian" Jewish community, in Roman times under the sway of the Parthian Empire and constituting the largest Jewish community outside of Roman dominion, likewise enjoyed a high degree of autonomy in civil as well as religious matters. It did so under the leadership of the "exilarchs," who were regarded as descendants of the House of David, and the exilarchs were accorded the rank of high royal officials by Parthian kings.

The Moslem conquerors of the seventh century destroyed the Parthian Empire and seized control of much of the Byzantine Empire. Jews living in the conquered territories were spared the severer depredations meted out by Moslem authorities largely to the extent that they provided what were perceived as useful services, and in such circumstances they were also accorded elements of autonomy.

In western Europe, in the wake of the Germanic invasions and with consolidation of Frankish rule in Gaul and Visigoth control in Spain, Jews were the targets of increasingly aggressive anti-Jewish measures. In Spain, which had the larger Jewish population, the assault included campaigns of forced conversion and ended only with the Moslem conquest of the peninsula in the late seventh century. But Moslem successes had a dramatic impact on trade relations around the Mediterranean and on the situation of Jews in the Christian realms of western Europe, precipitating an era in which Jewish communities were granted more formal, chartered rights of autonomy.

Arab control of North Africa and Spain led to the remaining Christian realms of western Europe losing traditional Mediterranean trade routes, and this loss was exacerbated by the frequent hostility of Byzantine rulers toward western Christian states. In the eighth century, Christian rulers in France succeeded in retaking areas in the south of the country from Arab forces that had crossed the Pyrenees and had established a presence of some decades. Jewish communities in the region then rapidly grew in importance as contacts between them and Jewish centers in Moslem territories served to reestablish trade routes. These Jewish communities in the West became the major trade bridge between the Christian West and the East.

From the latter half of the eighth century, under Charlemagne and his successors and in response to the new importance of the Jews in international trade, and increasingly in local trade as well, the earlier intensifying pressure on the Jews in the territories of the Germanic dynasties was reversed and Jews were given charters entailing rights of settlement, trading concessions, imperial protection, and self-government. In the ninth century there are complaints by Frankish church officials over privileges being granted the Jews and over rulers' failures to enforce old anti-Jewish measures.

In the tenth and eleventh centuries, with the early expansion of urban life in the Germanic territories, Jews were actively recruited to foster the growth of trade in urban centers. Jewish families, largely from southern Italy, migrated to northern Italy and to towns along the Rhine — both ancient Roman cities that had long had small Jewish communities and new towns — drawn by charters which, again, accorded them significant rights and privileges, including rights of self-defense. The Bishop of Speyer, in his grant of privileges to immigrant Jews in 1084, wrote, "Desiring to make a town out of the village of Speyer, I thought to raise its dignity many times by getting the Jews to settle there."[12]

Over the ensuing centuries, two broad factors figured in exacerbating anti-Jewish sentiment, spurring attacks on the Jews from below and compromising the utility of the Jews to western European rulers. The increased religious fervor that accompanied the Crusades had negative ramifications for Jews beyond the assaults of marauding Crusader bands. Among its consequences was the emergence of religion-based libels against the Jews in the twelfth and thirteenth centuries. The blood libel, the claim that Jews killed Christians, particularly children, to collect the blood of Christian innocents for use in Jewish ritual, first appeared in Norwich, England, in 1144, when Jews were accused of murdering a Christian child. (Similar libels had actually been directed against Christians by their pagan foes in the early centuries of the common era.) Such claims were frequent over the subsequent centuries and were often accompanied not only by the murder of the accused but by massacres of entire communities.

Both secular rulers, like Holy Roman Emperor Frederick II in 1236, and various popes — Innocent IV and Gregory X in the thirteenth century, Martin V and Nicholas V in the fifteenth century — issued emphatic statements condemning the blood libel and declaring that Jews did not prey on Christian children and did not use blood in their rituals. But such libels and their devastating consequences continued.

A variation on the blood libel, likewise dating from the thirteenth century, was the accusation that Jews were desecrating the communion host. This claim, particularly popular within the German Empire, was also often accompanied not only by murder of the supposed perpetrators but by the annihilation of entire communities. A claim of host desecration in Roettigen in Bavaria in 1298 triggered the massacre of Jewish communities throughout Bavaria and surrounding territories.

The second factor deleteriously affecting the position of the Jews, in addition to increased religion-based hostility, was social and economic changes during the period. In the earlier Middle Ages, from the late eighth through the eleventh centuries, Jews in France, England, and the German Empire were primarily tradespeople and artisans, with some engaged in finance, or medicine, or plying other professions. The growth of urban centers in the eleventh to the thirteenth centuries drew people from the countryside into the towns and to employment in trade and the crafts. This new urban entrepreneurial class organized itself by trade or craft into guilds that, moved in part by popular religious fervor but motivated also by economic considerations, explicitly excluded Jews and gained official sanction for doing so. Their aim was to diminish competition in the crafts and to counter the Jewish advantage of a network of trade ties. The successes of the Crusades and the opening of old trade routes to Christian merchants were effectively pushing Jews out of international trade, and developments in the towns were pushing them out of local trade and the crafts as well.

The one economic niche left to the Jews was moneylending, which was disapproved of by the church and largely forbidden to Christians, and Jews were increasingly forced into this niche with relatively few exceptions. Moneylending became the occupation of Jews at all financial levels. Wealthier Jews were the financiers of royalty, nobility, and even churches and monasteries; poorer Jews forced out of trade and crafts turned to extending small loans to the traders and craftspeople who had supplanted them and now required such loans to buy stock or raw materials for their endeavors.

Neither religion-based nor economy-based attacks on the Jews necessarily of themselves swayed rulers against the Jews. Indeed, clergy-led anti-Jewish campaigns or burgher-led attacks were at times seen by rulers as challenges to their own authority, as part of broader struggles between the Crown and the church or between the Crown and urban centers, and rulers would construe defense of the Jews as defense of their own interests against these other parties. But over time rulers did perceive the economic utility of the Jews diminishing, largely in the context of other parties filling some of the Jews' former roles, and saw the residual usefulness of the Jews as outweighed by other considerations of state. In addition, rulers' own religious feelings might at times have played a role in such calculations, although the significance of this factor should not be overstated. Mainly due to rulers' financial and political calculations, the Jews were expelled from England in 1290 and were subjected to a series of expulsions from French territories throughout the fourteenth century.

That the expulsion of the Jews from France required a number of decrees over the course of the fourteenth century was due to various factors. Some of the decrees were partial and left elements of the community temporarily intact. In other instances, the loss of Jewish loans had a deleterious effect on the economy, both because there was no adequate alternative source of loans and because what non-Jewish moneylenders there were, now freed of competition, charged sharply higher interest rates, and the expulsion decrees were therefore reversed and the Jews invited back until some later expulsion. But expulsions did follow on each other over the century. By 1400, except for some small communities in the south, mainly in French papal states, virtually no Jews remained on French soil.

Religious demonization of the Jews, together with economic antagonism toward them, particularly in the increasingly powerful towns, figured in the massacres that occurred in 1348 in the context of the Black Death, when a new libel, that of the Jews poisoning the wells and thereby causing the plague, triggered new assaults. The worst assaults, starting in Switzerland, were those in the towns and cities of the Rhine valley and then elsewhere in German-speaking realms. Some Jews who succeeded in fleeing subsequently returned to the German towns and cities, but typically under terms much more onerous than before.

The municipalities of the Rhine valley and elsewhere insisted that any reconstituted community now be chartered by them, that the Jews be legally defined as "belonging" to the town or city, with the municipality having rights of taxation over them. This was, of course, used to place the Jews at an economic disadvantage. In addition, earlier charters had admitted Jews with the intent of having them foster economic activity and so had given the Jews areas of residence close to the towns' commercial centers as well as areas that provided the Jews the ability to defend themselves. The burghers who formulated the new charters preferred to place the Jews away from the centers of commercial activity and also to restrict them to vulnerable locations.

Many of the survivors did not return to the previous areas of Jewish settlement. Some of those who had fled to the domains of friendly nobles settled instead in small towns under the nobles' control, where they did not face the hostile populations around their former communities. Others, following a pattern that had begun in the wake of the Crusader massacres of 1096, moved farther East, to eastern German and western Slavic dominions and into Poland.

Spain had by far the largest Jewish population in western Europe, and its Christian rulers, from the beginning of the Reconquesta, made the most extensive use of "their" Jews and granted to them in return far-reaching communal autonomy and privileges.

The origins of these policies can be traced in part to the influence of Charlemagne and his positive stance regarding the Jews. Certainly, Spanish Christian leaders during his reign looked to Charlemagne as their model and sought his help. They were aware of the rights and privileges he extended the Jews, and of the benefits he derived from them, and they could see much of this firsthand after Charles' forces captured Barcelona from the Moslems and extended similar rights and privileges to the Jewish community there.

But if Frankish policies provided a model, the embrace of similar policies in Spain was spurred as well by the particular conditions of the Reconquesta. The areas gradually regained by the Christian kings had been largely depopulated by the ravages of events since the Moslem invasion; and, in their eagerness for settlers, the kings encouraged Jewish immigration. More particularly, eager to man border outposts to counter Moslem raids on Christian frontiers, the kings recruited Jews to garrison frontier citadels, in some instances putting fortresses exclusively in Jewish hands, and would grant the Jews surrounding lands for cultivation as well as other concessions. Jews were especially sought after as many — both those who had been living in recaptured territory and those who responded to Spanish recruitment and benign Spanish policies by immigrating from elsewhere around the Mediterranean — were artisans and craftsmen. Such skills were in short supply under conditions of sparse population and of dedication of much of the available manpower to the military effort. Jews were recruited as well to participate directly in military campaigns. Commerce had also suffered under the prevailing conditions and Jewish merchants and traders were likewise welcomed. As in Frankish territory, trade ties that the Jews had with Jewish communities in the Moslem world made their presence particularly valued.

Many of the Jews in Christian Spain were people who had been living in areas from which the Moslems were pushed back, as well as people who immigrated from other Moslem-controlled territories, and these Jews spoke Arabic, which was itself useful for the Christian monarchs. They also brought other skills relating to professions they had practiced under the Moslems, professions which were in short supply in Spain and, indeed, in Christendom generally. In addition to plying farming, soldiering, trade, and crafts, the Jews served the Spanish kings also as, in one historian's synopsis, "physicians, land surveyors, engineers, mathematicians, salt miners, tax collectors, tax farmers, administrators, translators, diplomatic emissaries, and functionaries in a variety of other professions."[13]

A major influx of Jews from Moslem areas into Christian Spain occurred in the twelfth century when Moslem Spain, partly as a consequence of losses to the Christians in preceding decades, was invaded and overrun by the Almohades, fundamentalist Moslems from North Africa, who proceeded to attack Jewish communities as part of their "purification" of Moslem territories. While some Jews fleeing the Almohades left the Iberian peninsula — Maimonides' family, for example, fled to Egypt — most sought refuge in Christian Spain.

The elevation of talented Jews to high administrative posts by Spanish kings occurred to an extent not found in any other royal courts in the Moslem or the Christian world. While occasionally an individual Jew might attain high standing in a Moslem court in Spain or elsewhere in Moslem realms, in Christian Spain, "We can note [for example] that for three hundred years (from approximately 1075), there was not a reign in Castile in which Jews did not occupy high offices in the royal administration — above all, in diplomacy and finance."[14]

That the Spanish kings came to depend for so many services on the Jewish community, to support Jewish immigration, and to value and defend their Jewish subjects was due not only to the particular talents and skills the Jews provided. It also reflected the fact that they did so essentially without any conflicting agendas. The Jews owed their civil status to the kings, were almost invariably allied to no other group in internal political struggles in Spain, and could be counted on for their loyalty as well as their skills.

The status accorded the Jews by Spanish kings hardly meant that Spanish Jewry escaped the depredations that dogged Jews elsewhere in western Europe. There were anti-Jewish riots and massacres of Jewish communities in the eleventh, twelfth, and early thirteenth centuries. But such events occurred virtually always at times of royal weakness — after the death of a king, for example — when royal protection was compromised. Situations of competing contenders to a Spanish throne also presented particular dangers to the Jews, as did conflicts between kings and powerful nobles. In such circumstances enemies of the Crown could, and at times did, appeal to anti-Jewish sentiment by attacking kings for their pro-Jewish policies. They would fan animosity toward the Jews as a way of rallying support to themselves. Such conflicts also, of course, would often at least temporarily weaken the Crown and for this reason, too, would render the Jews more vulnerable. But the greatest threat to the Jews in Spain came, as elsewhere in Europe, from elements of the clergy and from the growing and increasingly powerful urban populations and their leaders.

Again as elsewhere in Europe, anti-Jewish sentiment in the urban centers, in addition to its church-inspired content, was fed by two further factors: professional competition with the Jews, and resentment of the Jews as agents of the Crown. Jewish artisans and merchants constituted a larger population and were more firmly established in Spain than in other areas of Christian Europe, and pushing Jews out of these professions proceeded more slowly in Spanish towns and cities. Concomitantly, Jewish involvement in moneylending, with Jewish merchants and artisans yielding to growing pressures and shifting at least part of their resources and employment to making loans to the growing gentile mercantile and artisan class, also evolved more slowly. But by the fourteenth century resentment of indebtedness to Jewish moneylenders was well established as another grievance of the urban population.

Urban resentment of the Jews as agents of the Crown was part of a larger competition of the cities and their leadership with kings, nobility, and even the church. The rights and privileges of the cities were defined by royal charter, and the cities were continually seeking to expand their own control over their domains and to diminish privileges and prerogatives still held within their boundaries by other parties — the Crown, nobility, and the church. By royal charter, Jewish communities within the cities were not subject to the city's courts; internal Jewish legal matters were settled by Jewish authorities and those between Jews and Christians were adjudicated by special royal courts. Jews also by charter had their own notaries for business documents and other legal transactions and were not subject to the scrutiny or discretion of city-appointed notaries.

By charter the Jews typically lived in separate neighborhoods within cities, given them by the kings with a view both to their convenience for commercial activities and their defensibility. Defensible locations held by the Jews in some instances dated back to the time when the kings enlisted the Jews as local garrisons, and there is evidence that the kings often regarded the Jewish sectors of cities as their own strongholds within the cities. In addition, Jews paid their taxes mainly not to the municipalities but to the king. Perhaps most importantly, Jews were often the kings' tax collectors, or tax farmers (an arrangement by which someone would be granted the right to collect taxes in an area in return for a fixed pledge to the royal treasury). Royal tax farming and tax collecting were also conducted by non-Jews, given over to nobles or to non-Jewish royal officials; the cities vigorously pursued an end to all tax farming and a restriction of royal tax collecting in urban centers to individuals approved by the municipalities. But Jews played a particularly prominent role in tax farming and tax collecting, and successive kings vigorously resisted the efforts of the cities to curtail the Jewish role.

The series of devastating catastrophes that befell the Jews of Spain from the mid-fourteenth century until the expulsion in 1492 were primarily fueled by the intense anti-Jewish sentiment in the Spanish cities together with situations of compromised royal authority. After the accession of Pedro I as king of Castile in 1350, his claim to the throne was challenged by his half-brother Count Enrique. In the civil war that followed and lasted almost two decades, Enrique consistently tried to muster support, particularly in the cities, by attacking Pedro's pro-Jewish policies. Jews living in the cities Enrique captured not only fell defending urban strongholds against his forces but suffered much larger loss of life in popular anti-Jewish riots that Enrique encouraged. (His support of these pogroms both reinforced the allegiance to him of anti-Jewish forces and also gave the cities involved another reason to stand steadfast against Pedro as they then had to fear retaliation for their attacks on the Jews should Pedro regain control over them. In cities he did recapture, Pedro did, in fact, severely punish the pogromists.)

It is testament to the value the Spanish kings placed on the services to their administrations provided by Spain's Jews that when Enrique finally killed Pedro and gained the throne of Castile he reversed his anti-Jewish policies — apparently always more cynically opportunist than ideological — and adopted the benign policies of his predecessors. But the civil war had weakened the Crown and also provided precedents for anti-Jewish forces of devastatingly successful assaults on Jewish communities.

Further weakening of the Crown ensued through the rest of the fourteenth and into the fifteenth century, and concomitant Jewish vulnerability led to repeated catastrophe. A clergy-inspired campaign of forced conversion swept Spain in 1391, at a time when the Castilian throne had passed to a minor and the court was in the hands of a divided and weak regency. A second wave of attacks on Jewish communities and forced conversion was unleashed in 1412, when Castile was again under the titular control of a weak and divided regency.

In subsequent decades, the Crown revived somewhat and began to turn to the Jewish converts, or conversos, and to Spain's remaining Jews to play the role the Jews had formerly played, and this effort encountered the same "anti-Jewish" resentment as previously, particularly in the cities. A rebellion in Toledo in 1449 targeted the city's conversos. The rebel leaders, in subsequently negotiating for clemency from the Crown, justified their assault on the conversos by insisting that the latter were heretics secretly practicing Judaism and urged an inquisition to investigate converso practices. The conversos and leading church officials vigorously denied the accusation and no inquisition was authorized.[15] But the King, feeling insecure in the face of widespread urban resentment, did grant far-reaching clemency to the rebels.

This only emboldened the cities and led to more anti-converso and anti-Jewish challenges to the Crown. In 1480, King Ferdinand decided it was politic to accommodate the pressures of the cities and their clerical supporters and allowed implementation of an inquisition. In 1492, again apparently more out of political calculation than as a step that he otherwise desired, Ferdinand approved the expulsion of the Jews, an action demanded by the Jews' enemies to end their supposed role as the heretical conversos' co-conspirators.

The end of Spanish Jewry was followed five years later by the forced conversion of Portuguese Jews, many of whom were refugees from Spain, and the demise of the Portuguese Jewish community. In addition, the expulsion from Spain also involved the estimated 50,000-strong Jewish community of Sicily and Jewish enclaves in parts of southern Italy that were under Spanish control. The Jewish presence in Italy was reduced to generally small communities, mostly in the Papal States but also in the mercantile towns of the North.

The influx into the towns of central and northern Italy of refugees from Spain, and of earlier refugees from expulsions in France and the depredations in Germany, was offset by various expulsions over the next century. While the Jews of the Papal states were generally, with a few episodic exceptions, free of the threat of expulsion, under conditions of the Counter-Reformation they experienced increased pressure to convert and were confined to the ghetto in Rome for the purpose of facilitating the promotion of conversion. Confinement to ghettoes occurred elsewhere in Italy as well.

By the end of the sixteenth century, except for these limited enclaves in Italy, the remnant surviving Jews in the German states, and the small community in the Netherlands, the Jewish presence in western Europe had virtually disappeared, the communities that had been the cradles of Ashkenazi and much of Sephardi civilization destroyed.

But refugees from the western European expulsions and the German massacres had been continually making their way eastward and had been welcomed by regimes that saw value in the skills and services the Jews offered and were prepared, as western European jurisdictions had been in earlier centuries, to offer extensive rights of autonomy in return for Jewish immigration. For example, in 1244, well after the onset of greater pressures on the Jews in most of western Europe, the Duke of Austria granted a particularly liberal charter to the Jews coming into his realms; that is, liberal in terms of rights and protections in disputes with non-Jews and also rights of land ownership. In fact, Jewish authority over civil and most criminal matters, as well as religious affairs, is not even spelled out in the charter but is simply taken for granted, as they were assumed elements of Jewish autonomy at the time. This Austrian charter was subsequently a model for charters elsewhere in eastern Europe, as in Silesia, Bohemia, and Hungary, and also influenced those granted in Poland and Lithuania.

Ultimately the most important of the Jewish communities that evolved in eastern Europe was Polish Jewry, and from its earliest establishment until the demise of independent Poland in the late eighteenth century, Polish Jewry was largely self-governing.

A Jewish presence in Poland is well documented from the twelfth century onward, and from its first foundations consisted primarily of people emigrating from the west and southwest, including families fleeing German lands in the wake of the Crusader massacres of 1096. The early immigrants were mainly traders and artisans, and evidence of their presence includes twelfth-century royal Polish coins with Hebrew inscriptions, produced by Jewish minters. The devastation and depopulation of much of Poland by the Mongols in the thirteenth century led Polish rulers to encourage immigration and settlement from the West and to be particularly receptive to Jewish immigrants as providing the skills and occupations needed to revive and develop the country. The first royal charters granting rights to Jewish communities date from the mid-thirteenth century.

To some degree, the difficulties experienced in the West followed the Jews into Poland. The Polish receptivity to immigration in the thirteenth century drew many Germans into Polish towns, so much so that Polish town life became dominated by these German arrivals and their descendants, and the immigrants brought with them the anti-Jewish attitudes and practices that prevailed in Germany. For example, commerce and crafts became dominated by the guild policies of the West and efforts were made to push Jews out of trade and crafts and restrict them to moneylending. Some towns sought to expel Jews entirely and succeeded in winning royal acquiescence to this, as least for a time.

But there were also factors that weighed in the Jews' favor in Poland and abetted their winning particularly extensive and effective self-governance. These factors included the converging ones of: liberal Lithuanian policies toward the Jews and the gradual merging of Poland and Lithuania; the growing power of the Polish nobility and the relationship between the nobles and the Jews; and Polish territorial expansion and the role accorded the Jews in colonial policy.

The first Lithuanian charters granted to Jews, dating from the late fourteenth century and referring to Jewish communities in Brest-Litovsk and Grodno, were modeled after Polish charters but in fact offered Jews exceptionally wide rights not only in economic terms, relating to the practice of trade and crafts and land ownership and cultivation, but also in terms of civil privileges. The extensive territories that had come under Lithuanian dominion were even more depopulated and in need of settlement and development than Poland, and Lithuania's generally liberal policies toward the Jews largely followed from this.

Beginning particularly in the fifteenth century, the power of the Polish nobility and its control over greatly expanding territories worked in the Jews' favor. The Polish nobles were interested in commercial development and exploitation of their estates but were averse to submitting to the commercial terms of the German burgher class in the old royal cities, a class whom they tended to view as competitors for power in Poland. They preferred to deal with the Jews. The nobility employed the Jews widely in the management of their estates and in the introduction onto estate lands of urban crafts and trades, and supported the Jews' settlement in estate towns.

The Polish conquest in the sixteenth century of large tracts of what is now the Ukraine added to the power and wealth of the nobility, which greatly expanded its land holdings. The nobility brought in Jews to settle and manage its newly acquired estates, with new Jewish communities serving not only as managers and as traders and craftsmen but as garrisons, playing a role similar to that Jews had played in Spain on the frontiers of the Reconquesta. The gradual merging of Poland and Lithuania, culminating in their full union in 1569, opened up areas of Lithuania and White Russia to the Polish nobility and additional opportunities for nobility-sponsored Jewish settlement and economic activity. The status of the Jews in these eastern realms was further enhanced by what had been liberal Lithuanian practice regarding Jewish rights and privileges.

Economic factors also figured to the favor of the Polish nobility and Polish Jews. For example, by the sixteenth century western Europe had become a net importer of timber, and its major source was the forests of the Polish nobility managed by Jewish foresters. Produce and cattle were also exported from Polish estates to western Europe. In addition to exports from Poland, Jews were prominently involved in new and extensive overland trade between Turkey and the East and western Europe.

The movement of Jews to towns and villages on the huge estates of the nobility, many of them new settlements and often entirely Jewish, led to considerable expansion of the Jewish population, which reached an estimated 300,000 by the mid-seventeenth century. The growth of the community in Poland and its absolute size were unprecedented in the history of Ashkenazi Jewry and was comparable in Europe only to the earlier Jewish experience in Spain.

For much of this period, Jewish autonomy in both Poland and Lithuania functioned under the overarching guidance of a strong national Jewish leadership, the Councils of the Lands, elected by local leaderships. Among the issues of particular concern to the Councils were security, complicated by the wide dispersion of the Jews in Poland, and standards of proper behavior in relations with the surrounding gentile world. The latter, like security, was always an issue for Jewish leadership but made more so in Poland by various factors. For example, the nobles often established Jews as virtual proxies on their estates, transferring to Jews the nobility's own prerogatives including legal and judicial authority that extended even to capital issues, and the Councils would consider standards for moral execution of such vast authority. Also, by 1600 the Jews in Poland had become net borrowers rather than lenders, and the Councils sought to establish oversight mechanisms to prevent Jews taking out loans, particularly from Christians, which they were unlikely to be capable of repaying.

The dramatic Polish-Lithuanian military and political reversals of the mid-seventeenth century, in the form of multifront struggles with Sweden and

Moscow in the north and Tatars and Cossacks in the south, were disastrous for many Jewish communities. In particular, the successful Cossack rebels in the Ukraine routinely annihilated Jewish communities falling into their hands, both those that offered armed resistance and those that did not, killing perhaps 200,000. In addition, the stresses on Polish society at all levels led to increased intolerance toward the Jews and a recurrence of blood libels and similar attacks as well as increased punitive taxation of surviving Jewish communities.

Various factors worked, in the context of these disasters and stresses, to weaken central Jewish leadership in Poland and Lithuania. Financial demands on the central leadership, both the funds required to satisfy the Polish government's increased taxation of the Jews and money needed to address the worsening threats to the Jews within what remained of Poland-Lithuania, led the central leadership to increase its assessments on communities. But the financially strapped communities, which suffered from the general economic downturn and from the influx of destitute survivors fleeing the lost territories of the East, were less able to pay. In addition, the Polish Court was itself weakened by the defeats Poland-Lithuania had suffered, was less in control of events throughout the country, and many Jewish communities saw their interests better served through a local leadership dealing with local authorities than through the central leadership.

Nevertheless, while the Polish government, in the face of weakening of the Jewish central authority, ultimately withdrew its support from the authority (1764), it never interfered with essential Jewish autonomy; and Jewish self-governance persisted and suffered very little compromise despite external pressures.

The communal autonomy that had been the norm for Jews in Europe throughout the Middle Ages came to an end in Poland only with the dissolution of the state in the late eighteenth century; and the end of Polish independence is, despite its late date, as appropriate a divide as any between the Middle Ages and the modern era in a Jewish context. At the time, the Jewish community in Poland, which, despite the events of the mid-seventeenth century and their after-effects, had generally been able to exercise its previous practices not only in terms of communal autonomy but also in terms of professional endeavors and demographic distribution in what remained of Poland, had grown to what is estimated as approximately 800,000 souls. It constituted by far the largest Jewish community in the world and at least a third of all surviving world Jewry.

THREE

Outside Looking In: Europe's Jews in the Late 1700s to 1880

I do not forget this shame [of being a Jew] for a single second. I drink it in water, I drink it in wine, I drink it with the air; in every breath . . . The Jew must be extirpated from us.

Rachel Levy, Berlin salon mistress
and patron of Goethe (1771–1833)[1]

THE NEW ISRAELITE HOSPITAL IN HAMBURG

A hospital for sick and needy Jews,
For the poor sons of sorrow thrice accursed,
Who groan beneath the heavy, threefold evil
Of pain, and poverty, and Judaism.
The most malignant of the three the last is:
That family disease a thousand years old,
The plague they brought with them from the Nile Valley . . .
Will Time, the eternal goddess, in compassion
Root out this dark calamity transmitted
From sire to son? — Will one day a descendant
Recover, and grow well and wise and happy?

Heinrich Heine[2]

TWO JEWRIES: POLAND VERSUS GERMANY

In Europe during the Middle Ages, the granting of charters to segments of a ruler's population, with the establishment of a corporate relationship between the ruler and those subjects through a formal spelling out of each party's rights and obligations, was a standard element of governance. Consistent with this practice, there was no concept of one universal legal code equally applicable to all in a realm. Charters to, for example, barons or municipalities typically entailed the concession of rights to the chartered entities to have their own courts and jurisprudence within the territories under their control or with regard to their subjects or constituents. In this sense, the granting of rights and privileges to Jewish communities through charters, with those rights and privileges including autonomy in civil and even many criminal matters, was reflective of broader practice.

So, too, the end of Jewish autonomy was part of a broader historical shift. In the latter decades of the eighteenth century and through the nineteenth, the evolving political frameworks in the nations of Europe varied widely. They ranged from the republican structures that followed on the 1789 Revolution in France to the despotic regimes — some headed for a time by so-called enlightened despots, others under the control of more conservative absolutists — that especially prevailed in central and eastern Europe. But a common characteristic among state regimes across Europe, however republican or absolutist, was the drive toward centralization of national authority and the dismantling of alternative power structures within their states such as the prerogatives still retained by particular groups as legacies of the medieval period. Regimes, with varying rapidity, dissolved, for example, the special rights and privileges accorded their nations' urban centers and burgher leaderships and moved against the special civil prerogatives of the nobility. Regimes also targeted whatever remained of the communal autonomy of the Jews.

Most significant for Jewish life were the policies toward the Jews and Jewish autonomy pursued by the states that joined in the division of Poland-Lithuania over a course of three partitions between 1772 and 1795, the last of which completed the dissolution of independent Poland. The three successor states were Prussia, Russia, and Austria. Russia, prior to this acquisition of Polish territories, had officially allowed no Jews at all to live within its borders. Austria and Prussia had been home to small Jewish populations that, as in other German states, were comprised primarily of the remnants of old Jewish communities together with some immigrants from Poland and, particularly in commercial centers, Sephardic groups whose members had immigrated as converso Christians and then returned to Judaism.

Under the centralized, absolutist administrations that were evolving in many German states, Jewish communities were tightly controlled. Only those Jews were tolerated who were perceived by the state as filling some open and useful niche in the state economy. Those whose utility was expended, or children of tolerated Jews who could not themselves find appropriate niches, were expelled. While these state policies may seem in some ways to resemble medieval conditions, they were different in the centralization and rigidity of controls over the Jews and in their severe circumscription of Jewish autonomy. Again, the era of chartered corporate rights and privileges on the medieval model was now gone.

For example, decrees issued by Friedrich the Great of Prussia in 1750 governing conditions Jews would need to meet in order to be allowed to live in Prussia placed tight restrictions on numbers, permitted places of residence, and permitted activities. The decrees also explicitly stated that the authority of rabbis and community elders would be strictly confined to religious matters and that "[the rabbis and community leaders] shall not presumptuously undertake to make any real decision and settlement of a case in matters of secular law, for the rabbi and the elders have no right to real jurisdiction. On the contrary, matters must be referred to the proper court of justice."[3]

Living under such conditions, the small Jewish communities in the German states even in the earliest part of the period being considered, in the late seventeenth and early eighteenth centuries, had experienced some attrition. Rigid controls over what Jews were tolerated in these states meant that Jewish communities typically remained small and relatively affluent and their leading figures tended to be well connected with centers of power and other elite elements in the surrounding society. Factors contributing to attrition included these extensive contacts with higher echelons of the larger society and the allure of those echelons, unhappiness with the disabilities that followed on being Jews, and the absence of a sizable and strong Jewish community with communal institutions that could have served as a counterweight to external allures and to the self-doubt attendant on exposure to chronic bias. Together, these factors led a number of Jews to abandon their Judaism and either themselves convert or baptize their children. That many of these people had converso roots, had grown up in families that had in their background some Christian education and extensive familiarity with Christian milieus, likely further eased the way to apostasy for a portion of the community.

Once again those who took such steps tended not to construe them simply as pragmatic measures to improve their lot in life, but rather to view them in a manner congruent with the anti-Jewish biases of the surrounding society, as casting off an intrinsically atavistic and inferior affiliation for an inherently superior one.

The spread of Enlightenment ideas in these small and weak Jewish communities in the latter part of the eighteenth century further eased the path to conversion for some. The Enlightenment devaluation of traditional religion, the vision of a new society liberated from the supposed shackles of traditional belief, had its particular allure for some Jews, who shared with other Jews the awareness of having been victimized for nearly two millennia by Christianity and who additionally seized upon this Enlightenment perspective as intellectual justification for disavowing Jewish belief and divesting themselves of a burdensome identity.

Enlightenment thinking in the German-speaking world had additional impact on the small Jewish communities there. Enlightenment ideals in part promoted the notion of the value of the individual irrespective of religious affiliation. But while various Enlightenment figures endorsed the breaking down of old barriers against the Jews and their fuller inclusion in European society, attitudes of Enlightenment enthusiasts toward the Jews in fact varied widely and were often hardly less hostile than those of their conservative opponents in the church, state governments, and the universities.

Traditionalist adversaries of the Jews, and of Enlightenment liberalism, maintained that the Jews were a separate nation and so could not be absorbed as citizens into European nations. They often argued as well that the Jews were irredeemably morally corrupt and this too disqualified them from integration into European society. Among Enlightenment figures, virtually all insisted that the Jews would need to give up their concepts of Jewish nationhood, that they would have to comprehend their Judaism in purely religious terms, as a condition for admission to fuller citizenship in European states. Some went further and attacked Judaism at its foundations as immoral, inhumane, and inconsistent with civilized society.

Whereas Christianity, of course, embraced Hebrew scripture as Holy Writ, Enlightenment philosophers such as Voltaire and some of his followers attacked the Hebrew Bible as testament to the barbaric and contemptible nature of Judaism. Voltaire's writings, and those of others who shared his views, have often been regarded as primarily indirect indictments of Christianity. According to this interpretation, Voltaire and his allies, unwilling to risk criticizing Christianity directly, chose to attack its roots in Hebrew scripture. But the anti-Jewish cant of these authors reflects more than a subtle swipe at Christianity. It is first and foremost a regurgitation of old anti-Jewish canards and slanders by people who embraced those defamations as truth and chose not only to endorse them but to promote and set their imprimatur on them.[4]

A common theme among other writers associated with the Enlightenment was, again, that the Jews were indeed morally corrupt and would have to be reformed to facilitate their wider acceptance as equals. Jewish corruption, as noted in Chapter One, was connected in part with the occupations Jews pursued, and the more liberal among Enlightenment authors suggested that it was medieval Christian restrictions and persecution that had forced Jews to focus their energies on trade and moneylending and led to their corruption. But a generally held view was, in any case, that reform in Jewish occupations would be required to render Jews more suitable for fuller citizenship.

Other reforms often suggested as necessary for Jewish absorption into the wider society were the giving up of Yiddish and Hebrew for European vernaculars, reform of Jewish education under government supervision, and some government oversight of other Jewish communal activities to make certain those activities were purely religious and free of political import. Finally, a widely held view among advocates of Jewish integration was that the Jews would be absorbed, even after their reform, on the lower rungs of European society. They would be extended universal prerogatives of citizenship but no more than that. Some writers insisted that Jews would still need to be barred from particular niches in the society, such as areas of state service.

There were also advocates of Jewish integration who were more open and benevolent in their attitudes toward the Jews. But, particularly in the German states, these were a small minority among Enlightenment thinkers. For the most part, the arguments swirling around the Jews in the German states and elsewhere in the West were between opponents to accommodation of the Jews who argued that the Jews were unfit for integration and supporters who advocated integration but typically with limits to the citizen rights to be extended the Jews and with those rights coming only upon the Jews' renunciation of much of their heritage.

It was in the context of these pressures that Jews in the German-speaking world endorsed the view that Yiddish was intrinsically unwholesome and corrupting and that Jewish employment in commerce was degenerate. The inclination of many Jews in the German-speaking world to embrace the indictments of the surrounding society manifested itself in additional ways, including the recurrent pattern of pitting one segment of the Jewish population against another. For example, in Prussia and Austria, the two German-speaking states that had annexed parts of Poland, those Jews who lived elsewhere in the two nations and who took to heart the indictments of the surrounding society tended to view the Jews in the former Polish territories negatively. They were inclined to regard "Polish" Jews, among whom Yiddish was most ensconced as the lingua franca and who were largely engaged in petty trade, as the obstacles whose reform was necessary to win over the surrounding society to a more benign attitude toward Jews. (Much as the rich Jews of thirteenth-century Constantinople discussed by Benjamin of Tudela chose to construe the foul-smelling work of Jewish tanners as the source of anti-Jewish sentiment in the surrounding society, and reform of the tanners as the path to acceptance.)

The support given by Prussian and Austrian maskilim to Joseph II's efforts to push Jews out of their established occupations was aimed essentially against the Jews of Galicia, or Austrian-controlled Poland. And these pro-reform Jews did not perceive reform of Polish Jewry as simply a pragmatic step but chose to construe it rather as the exchange of an intrinsically primitive, corrupt, degenerate life for a better, more wholesome one.

Both Prussia and Austria, on acquiring their Polish territories, severely restricted the movement of Jews from the newly annexed regions to other parts of their realms. In addition, the catastrophes that had befallen Poland-Lithuania over the previous century had impoverished much of its Jewish community, and the successor powers adopted policies that worsened still further the economic straits of Polish Jewry. For example, Prussian policy promoted controls over Polish exports to German areas and created obstacles to exports that might compete with German goods. This particularly hurt Jews, who played a predominant role in Polish exports of timber, farm goods, and other commodities.

Prussian and Austrian policy more generally was to keep the Polish territories segregated from their other domains. Consequently, they tended to retain to a considerable degree elements of the governmental structures already in place in the territories. While introducing some instruments of their own authority, they were less aggressive in replacing established institutions than they would have been had their intention been to pursue expeditious integration of the new territories. As a consequence, while Jewish autonomy was diminished, significant elements of autonomy also persisted for a time, at least *de facto*. Prussian Poland and Galicia, or Austrian Poland, were thus home to an increasingly impoverished Jewish community but one still largely managing its own affairs.

This self-governance, however diminished from earlier eras, provided vital services and cohesion to Jews in those areas. But among many Jews elsewhere in Prussia and Austria, and in the German-speaking states more generally, including many maskilim and their supporters, these vestiges of Jewish autonomy were viewed with abhorrence and hostility.

Elements of the surrounding society were telling them that Jewish communal organization must be stripped of all non-religious roles, all secular or civic jurisdiction, that Jews' comprehension and definition of themselves as a community must be freed of all "national" meaning, all significance other than the purely religious, as a condition for winning civic rights in the wider society. Once again many Jews not only endorsed such Jewish self-reform as a pragmatic step that might gain Jews greater acceptance but cast Jewish autonomy as intrinsically primitive and unwholesome. They chose to regard it as the vestige of an externally imposed separation and ghettoization that supposedly became a wall sustained by Jews to keep themselves separate from the wider world and stuck in their atavistic ways, a Jewish perpetuation of the ghetto that must be expunged. Those who embraced this view wished to believe that self-reform vis-à-vis Jewish autonomy, together with sufficient other self-reforms and self-improvement by "Polish" Jews, would inexorably win for Jews a place in the wider society. And they were predisposed to blame "Polish" Jews for the persistence of anti-Jewish prejudice and Jewish disabilities should they reject proffered programs of self-reform.

Of course, the historical narrative that underlies this critique of Jewish autonomy is largely wrong. For example, if Jews lived separately in the East, it was not because of ghettoization but, rather, because they sought privileges of separate residence for protection, economic well-being and communal cohesion, and they were granted those privileges in exchange for services to rulers. The ghetto was for the most part a late development — one of fifteenth and sixteenth century Italy and some German states — and not a phenomenon of earlier ages or of eastern Europe.[5]

But Jews such as many maskilim and their supporters, caught up in their delusions concerning self-reform, were blind to the positive side of autonomy in earlier centuries as well as in their own age. And various maskilim worked to advance Prussian, Austrian, and even Russian steps to dismantle the vestiges of autonomy that persisted in formerly Polish territories, impervious to the damage they were doing to the Jewish communities in those regions.

It is noteworthy that despite the difficulties encountered by Jews in recent centuries, culminating in the unprecedented horrors of the Holocaust, much of Jewish historiography concerning the dawn of modernity has largely followed the biases of the maskilim. It has cast Jewish life as emerging from medieval conditions that were uniformly bad into a modernity that was essentially good as it opened the way to Jewish integration into surrounding societies. The first major voice to challenge this grossly oversimplified slant was the Russian Jewish historian Simon Dubnow. Dubnow particularly emphasized the vital role of Jewish autonomy in providing a bulwark against the corrosive impact of anti-Jewish depredations in the Middle Ages and helping sustain a positive national consciousness.[6]

But the bias outlived Dubnow. Another major figure of Jewish historiography, Salo W. Baron, reiterated the same message in the middle of the twentieth century. Baron noted that not only the early maskilim but many subsequent Jewish champions of Jewish assimilation have been inclined to portray the changes of early modernity, the so-called era of Jewish emancipation, as an absolute good for Jews and the earlier, medieval period as absolutely bleak. Baron, like Dubnow, countered that this is a gross distortion, that there was much of value to the Jews in their situation during the Middle Ages and much lost with "emancipation." He pointed particularly to the benefits of Jewish self-government in the earlier era.[7]

Among the additional self-reforms promoted by maskilim and their supporters were reforms in the education of Jewish children. Maskilim militated particularly for the enrollment and secular education of Jews in state-sponsored schools. There were obviously good pragmatic reasons for Jews to learn what their non-Jewish neighbors were learning in schools, as a step toward entering more fully into the life of the surrounding society. But once again the advocates of Jewish self-reform were not simply promoting the pragmatic. In Austria, maskilim endorsed Joseph II's promulgation of mandatory public school attendance for the Jews of Galicia and excoriated those Jews who spoke out against such mandatory state schooling, even though it was clear that the Austrian regime viewed the schools as a vehicle for promoting the conversion of the Jews. The government appointed a Berlin maskil, Naphtali Herz Homburg, as chief inspector for the state schools for Jews. Homburg urged government censorship of Jewish books to enforce conformity with Haskalah principles of Jewish self-reform and threatened with prosecution rabbis who resisted his educational program.

Maskilim subsequently abetted Czarist Russia's institution of a system of state schools for Jews, and some advocated the use of coercive measures to enforce Jewish participation, despite the Russian system being even more blatantly geared to promoting conversion than was the case in Austria. Like Austria, the Czar's government hired a German maskil, in this case Max Lilienthal, to run the system of special schools for Jews. The Jewish community in Russian Poland, like the community in Galicia, overwhelmingly resisted participation and even some of the maskilim ultimately acknowledged that the government's aim was advancement of conversion rather than integration of Jews as Jews. (Lilienthal emigrated to the United States in 1845 and became a prominent Reform rabbi there.)

The maskilim's advocacy of state education for Jews was congruent with their characterization of the traditional Jewish leadership's stance toward education, particularly in the former Polish territories, as stuck in a primitive, "medieval" commitment to exclusively religious learning incapable of preparing the young for the modern world. This was an echo of non-Jewish indictments of Jewish education and advocacy of Jewish educational reform. It was also to a significant degree a caricature of Jewish education in the East and of its medieval antecedents.

In the early medieval period, Jews in the Moslem world shared in the rediscovery of Greek philosophy and science. Jews subsequently became the chief transmitters of Moslem-Greek culture, particularly philosophy and science, to western Europe. They served as translators of Arabic and Greek into Latin, as mathematicians, and as physicians to the courts of Christian Spain and also to courts and church circles in Italy and the Christian kingdoms of the north.

In the Diaspora of the Moslem world and Christian Spain, philosophical and scientific learning were highly valued and thought a fit complement to religious education by the religious sages, the educated elites, and broader Jewish society. While this has generally been thought of as less characteristic of Ashkenazi Jewry, there is much evidence to the contrary, including statements by rabbis in the north on, for example, the virtue of scientific knowledge and the value of books on the sciences.

Nor did this tradition die in subsequent centuries. A visitor to Moses Mendelssohn's circle in Berlin in 1777 was a Russian-born rabbi, Baruch of Shklov, who had studied various sciences while pursuing rabbinic duties in Russia, had then gone to England to study medicine, and spent time in Berlin on his way back to the East. Baruch published works on anatomy, mathematics, and astronomy. A year after his stay in Berlin, Baruch met with the Vilna Gaon, Rabbi Elijah ben Solomon Zalman, the chief figure at the time in traditional eastern European Judaism. Baruch later reported that Rabbi Elijah had encouraged him to translate into Hebrew as many scientific texts as possible because, he quoted the rabbi as asserting, Torah and science are "bound together" and ignorance of the sciences makes one "a hundredfold more ignorant of the Torah."[8] The Vilna Gaon himself published, in addition to religious texts and writings on Hebrew grammar, works on mathematics and astronomy.

To be sure, his attitude toward secular studies was not ubiquitous among eastern European Jews and was notably less popular among the Hasidim. Rabbi Elijah was the chief figure in the traditionalist campaign against the Hasidim in the late eighteenth century, and one of his major criticisms was what he perceived as Hasidim's anti-intellectualism. This, he argued, was antithetical to the essential rationalism of Jewish belief and would inevitably lead to a falling away from basic Jewish tenets.

But the maskilim's blanket condemnation of traditional Judaism for its supposed negative attitudes toward secular education was more a parroting of biased, non-Jewish indictments of Jewish education than a reflection of reality.

Likewise an echo of the surrounding society's anti-Jewish biases was the maskilim's call not only for state-sponsored "expansion" of Jewish schooling but also for a curtailing of Jewish religious education. More particularly, the maskilim embraced the attacks on Talmudic studies that had for centuries figured prominently in anti-Jewish indictments of Jewish religious learning and practice. Mimicking those attacks, maskilim characterized Talmudic studies as primitive, arcane, even corrupting, and certainly inconsistent with Jewish entry into the modern world and participation in the surrounding civil society.

Beyond simply being an embrace of indictments by the Jews' attackers, the campaign against Talmudic studies was also driven by the maskilim's desire to bring Jewish religious practice more into conformity with Christian practice and by a perception that a more exclusive focus in Jewish religious education on the Hebrew Bible, holy to both faiths, would serve this end. In addition, the Talmud was, of course, the major source of the body of law that guided Jewish self-governance. The effort to curtail Talmudic studies served the push for an end to all vestiges of Jewish autonomy and accommodation of those in the surrounding society who insisted upon Jews stripping their identity of all "national" content as a condition for gaining greater civil rights. But the Jewish critics of Talmudic studies did not cast their critiques in terms of accommodating anti-Jewish opinion but rather in terms of doing away with something inherently "bad" in the march to something intrinsically better. The emphasis on state schools as the proper place for Jewish secular education was geared in large part to diminishing Jewish self-governance by stripping the community of control of education, but that emphasis was justified rather in terms of the traditional Jewish community supposedly being incapable of instituting adequate secular education.

Those Jews who promoted Jewish self-reform to win over the Jews' attackers urged not only changes in Jewish religious education but also modifications in Jewish religious practice. Very few, if any, of the maskilim shared Mendelssohn's commitment to traditional Jewish observance. Rather, there was almost unanimous support for doing away with it. There were as well efforts to reform the book of prayer and to replace Hebrew with German. Maskilim also criticized the informality of traditional worship as indecorous and advocated more formal services. In general, many of the maskilim sought to impose on Jewish religious practice at least a superficial resemblance to Protestant practice, with the expectation that this would make the Jews' religion seem less alien to their neighbors and thereby win the Jews greater acceptance. But, once more, the maskilim's arguments were not cast in these terms but rather in terms of shedding the primitive and tainted for the progressive and modern and good.

Maskilim also advocated removing from the liturgy all references to Zion and Jerusalem and anything else that might suggest Jewish nationhood and devotion to a national home other than the state jurisdictions in which the Jews were then living. This was, of course, intended to counter the arguments both by conservative circles and by many Enlightenment voices that the Jews were a "separate nation" and therefore were not suitable candidates for citizen rights. Another general principle widely endorsed by the maskilim, and likewise a response to such arguments, was that Jewish religious obligations must be secondary to state obligations. But the maskilim cast their suggested modifying of liturgy and relegating of religious duties to a secondary status vis-à-vis state duties not as self-reforms to mollify the Jews' indicters but rather, again, as a principled divesting of the outmoded in favor of the modern and progressive.

Along with their advocacy of jettisoning all references to longing for Jerusalem and to the goal of Jewish Return, many of the maskilim promoted the reformulation of Jewish messianic hopes into an entirely universalist and assimilationist mission: The Jews were to be a light unto the nations in the sense of becoming citizens of the world's nations and promoting by example Enlightenment principles of individual worth, reason, and liberty. Movement toward worldwide dissemination and embrace of these principles would be the mark of progress toward realization of Jewish messianic aspirations. Indeed, the loss of Eretz Israel was to be comprehended not as a national catastrophe but as a divinely ordained historical development intended to disperse Jews among the nations and thereby advance their universal mission.

This reformulation was another facet of the effort to mollify the Jews' detractors, in this case by further altering Jewish self-definition, reinforcing the deletion of "national" elements, and redefining Jewish aspirations in terms of a humanitarianism that would presumably be offensive to no one. But again such redefinition was not cast by its advocates as intended to appease the Jews' indicters but rather as an enlightened and progressive advance beyond traditional Jewish aspirations.

As noted, the maskilim and their allies grossly distorted historical reality when they cast traditional Judaism and its practitioners as having typically walled themselves off from their non-Jewish neighbors and from cultural and intellectual developments in surrounding non-Jewish societies. Yet there were, indeed, significant differences between Jewish openness to surrounding cultures in the premodern era and the sort of responses cultivated and promoted by many of the maskilim. These differences have at times been written of as a distinction between "synthesis" and "assimilation." For example, medieval Jewish scholars of secular subjects routinely interacted with non-Jewish scholars throughout the Middle Ages. They drew upon discoveries and innovations in the wider culture and had their own work studied in turn by others beyond the Jewish fold. But an elemental aspect of how Jewish scholars comprehended the significance and thrust of their exertions was their perception of those efforts as enriching Jewish civilization by a synthesis of traditional Jewish wisdom and understanding with new discoveries and new insights.

In artistic realms, the Jews of, for example, southern Italy adopted contemporary Italian verse forms, but the poetry they produced using these forms had largely Jewish content and various poems written in Italy between the ninth and thirteenth centuries entered the Ashkenazi liturgy. Similarly, in medieval Spain Jews wrote sophisticated poetry, both secular and religious, reflecting the contemporary poetic modes of their non-Jewish neighbors. But their work was largely geared to Jewish audiences and elements of this poetry became part of Sephardic liturgy. In both cases, the poetry was construed as representing an enriching synthesis of the new with traditional elements of Jewish culture. The evolution of Jewish religious philosophy and religious practice in response to Jews' interaction with the evolving cultures around them was likewise comprehended primarily in terms of the enrichment of the Jewish experience and Jewish civilization.

In contrast, the maskilim's promotion of their own image of secular education and their advocacy of reforms in Jewish religious philosophy and practice were primarily driven not by a wish to enrich Jewish culture but by a desire to woo non-Jewish opinion and win assimilation into surrounding cultures and societies.

Consider similarities and differences between the religious philosophy of Maimonides and Moses Mendelssohn. Maimonides, writing in twelfth-century Spain and Egypt, was profoundly influenced by the contemporary ascendancy of rationalist philosophy, a vogue emanating from the rediscovery of Greek philosophy. His *Guide for the Perplexed* is an exercise in reconciling faith and reason. His *Mishnah Torah* is an effort to offer a rational, systematic codification of the Oral Law that would cut through all the complicated dialectics of Talmudic literature. In all of his work, Maimonides was directing his exertions essentially to fellow Jews and was striving to strengthen their understanding and their faith.

Mendelssohn, six centuries later, became an enthusiastic student of Maimonides' work early in his life. It is likely that his later receptiveness to the writings of philosophers such as Leibniz and Christian Wolff was due at least in part to the resonance of their perspectives on the relation of faith and reason with Maimonides' rationalist exegeses of Jewish texts and Jewish belief. Mendelssohn subsequently wrote at length on the rational foundations of Jewish belief and Jewish practice. But Mendelssohn's efforts in this vein, as with much of his other writings on Jewish themes, was largely outwardly oriented, aimed at rendering Judaism and its followers more acceptable at least to the more educated and enlightened strata of the surrounding society.

This was even more the case for the efforts of Mendelssohn's maskil protégés, for their recasting of Jewish belief and their promotion of other Jewish reforms, however much they chose to characterize their proposals as aimed at Jewish self-improvement.

The shift from earlier eras is further illustrated by the maskilim's comprehension of the role of the Jews as a light unto the nations, destined to provide the world by teaching and example a model of a more ethical and humane society. It is reflected also in their comprehension of the messianic age as a time when the Jews will have succeeded in winning the world to their message, when that more ethical and humane society will be universally established.

This understanding of the Jewish mission had, of course, an ancient pedigree in Jewish belief. But formerly these concepts were essentially of internal significance and were articulated for internal consumption. They were intended to help define for Jews their role and obligations in the wider world as a particular nation in a unique Covenant with the One and Universal God. Later, they served to reemphasize for Jews their shared, national destiny, the ongoing meaningfulness of their Covenant with God, even under conditions of exile and even when the surrounding societies had taken on elements of Jewish belief as their own and were attacking the Jews as a people whom history had passed by and whose role in the world had been superseded.

But these same comprehensions of the Jewish place in history were now being invoked for a new purpose, now being emphasized to render the Jews and Judaism more acceptable to the Jews' neighbors. To the same end, these comprehensions were now linked to advocacy of a casting off of Jewish peoplehood and Jewish longing for Jerusalem and aspirations for Return, however much those renunciations were defended as Jews leaving behind the primitive for the modern.

But to pursue religious reforms, or other reforms, for the purpose of winning a benign response from the surrounding society inevitably renders the surrounding society arbiter of those reforms, indeed arbiter of the faith and of the people who are its adherents. There is then a high likelihood that ongoing rejection by the surrounding society will elicit, from those who pushed reform for the sake of acceptance, a spiritual capitulation and abandonment of the faith and the people. In fact, in the face of obstacles to acceptance in those circles of the surrounding society most attractive to acculturated maskilim — academia, literary and artistic elites, government service — a number of maskilim converted. So too did four of the six of Mendelssohn's children who survived into adulthood.

Apostasy in such situations is not, however, inevitable. People can reinterpret or modify practice and belief for the sake of acceptance and assimilation and, if acceptance is not forthcoming as they had hoped, can then balk at further accommodation. But to do so likely requires that one feel part of a larger community of faithful, a community whose consensus is against further accommodation, and that one value one's affiliation with the community to a degree that serves as an effective counterweight to the lure of greater acceptance by the wider society. But even for Mendelssohn, with all his dedication to fellow Jews and indeed to traditional Judaism, the counterweight of identification with the larger Jewish world was compromised. The larger Jewish world meant for him primarily the Yiddish-speaking world of Polish Jewry. And the members of the small German Jewish communities around him were either Yiddish-speaking, Talmud-oriented, like their Polish cousins, or as attracted to the allures of the Enlightenment as he. As indicated in his echoing of the wider society's prejudices against Jewish language and some other elements of Jewish life, Mendelssohn clearly felt more attracted to the intellectual and cultural world of Enlightenment circles in Berlin than to the wider Jewish community as defined particularly by Polish Jewry.

The early maskilim, Mendelssohn's protégés and successors, while often differing among themselves in the details of their vision of Jewish reform and of a reconciliation between Jewish life and an "enlightened" world, shared many basic perspectives. Not least was their alienation, both intellectual and emotional, from much of what characterized the wider Jewish community, meaning, again, more particularly, Polish Jewry. The maskilim exhibited this estrangement in their various expressions of distaste, or ridicule, or censure, vis-à-vis aspects of Polish Jewish life. They demonstrated it also in their willingness to endorse, and even to initiate, measures by central and eastern European despots to force reforms upon the Jews even when the relevant Jewish communities opposed such reforms and even when the communities had well-founded reasons to anticipate often severe negative consequences as a result of those reforms.

RELIGIOUS REFORM, DEFECTION, AND COMMUNITY IN GERMANY

The religious reforms suggested by the early maskilim were initially almost universally rejected, even in the small and weak German Jewish communities of the late eighteenth and early nineteenth centuries. This was not only because they were such a radical break with tradition but also because they were being proposed by people who often had no standing and no moral suasion in the communities. Reform took root when community leaders became advocates of reform.

There were ultimately numerous movements of religious revision within German Jewry through the nineteenth century, all of which embraced at least some elements of the programs proposed by the early maskilim and all of which were motivated in large part by the desire to facilitate Jewish integration into the wider society. These movements led to the establishment of an array of reformist congregations, which varied widely in the extent to which they were able to retain their congregants or suffered erosion and dissolution through members abandoning the Jewish community because of indifference or for the sake of self-advancement. Some such congregations disappeared entirely, while others stabilized and served as the foundations of the major nontraditionalist branches of Judaism extant today, from Reform Judaism to "modern Orthodoxy."

But none of the reformist movements developed a definitive answer to erosion. Advocates of reform often argued against critics that reform was necessary to retain Jews who found traditional Orthodoxy incompatible with the demands of modernity and would otherwise be lost to the community. Traditionalists countered that reform was itself a step toward conversion. Both were right. German Jewry, by virtue both of small family size and continual erosion that affected all communities to some degree, was, in its internal dynamics, a constantly shrinking community. Only ongoing immigration from formerly Polish areas — to the extent that migration was liberalized and people fled the straitened conditions in "Poland" — accounted for the stabilization and expansion of many community populations.

A number of people have written about the extensive defections from Judaism and the Jewish community in the German-speaking world and elsewhere in central and western Europe in the nineteenth century, a pattern that of course continued through the twentieth century and was replicated in the Western hemisphere. Observers have tended, by way of explanation, to emphasize particularly the gradual lifting of legal disabilities directed against Jews and the growing extension to them of citizen rights and fuller inclusion in the wider societies in which they lived. As noted earlier, this emphasis in fact explains little and itself represents a kind of anti-Jewish bias in its suggestion that what had earlier held Jews to their faith and their community were primarily legal and quasi-legal barriers that separated them from the broader society around them.

A more substantive accounting for this phenomenon of increased defection would relate it to such factors as the alienation of significant segments of German Jewry from the larger Jewish community, in particular from the Jews of former Poland. This in turn stemmed from the acculturation of these segments of German Jewry to German society and their embrace of German anti-Jewish biases. It derived also from the weakening of Jewish communal institutions in Germany. All of this rendered some Jews more prepared to abandon Judaism and the Jewish community; it inclined them to see relatively little lost in their doing so when confronted with defection as the price of shedding disabilities and entering more fully into the surrounding society.

Those who would emphasize the supposed role of new opportunities in increasing apostasy might argue that the lowering of barriers against the Jews contributed to their acculturation to German society and whetted their appetite for fuller entry. Or, that greater accessibility was at least a factor that worked in combination with persisting obstacles to win Jews away from their community, the former increasing acculturation and interest, the latter pushing Jews to defect to gain still more access. An example would be Jews enjoying greater educational opportunities but encountering obstacles to applying their education to academic careers or government service; or, at a later date, enjoying greater access to government service but confronting impediments to advancement and a *numerus clausus* that would limit the educational and employment opportunities of their children.

Someone often cited as an early example of a Jew in the modern era responding to the anti-Jewish animus of the surrounding society by blaming not the haters but the Jews is Rachel Levy, and Levy's history would seem to fit such a pattern of partial admission to the wider society whetting her appetite for more and persistent barriers to fuller access prompting her defection. Levy was mistress of a celebrated salon in Berlin and a patron of Goethe. She chafed at the slights she experienced because she was a Jew and her reaction is captured in such statements as, "How loathsome it is always having to establish one's identity first [as a person of talent and worth despite being Jewish] . . . That alone is enough to make it repulsive to be a Jew."[9] Elsewhere she wrote: "I do not forget this shame for a single second. I drink it in water, I drink it in wine, I drink it with the air, in every breath . . . The Jew must be extirpated from us."[10] Levy ultimately converted and married a Prussian diplomat.

Heinrich Heine's career in the early nineteenth century could similarly be construed as his exposure to German culture having spurred his desire for a life of poetry and the limits of his access as a Jew having then prompted his conversion. Heine famously said of his defection, "A baptismal certificate is a ticket of admission to European culture."[11] A variation on the same theme of the impact of partial access combined with persistent obstacles is reflected in a story concerning Jewish academics at the end of the nineteenth century: "The *Allgemeine Israelitische Wochenschrift* reported in 1898 . . . that of the ten or so Jewish professors at the University of Strasbourg — none of whom was himself baptized [Strasbourg, a lesser institution at the time, was apparently more open to Jews obtaining professorships than were the major German universities] — not one failed to baptize his children. They, like other German Jewish parents, sought to protect their children — boys and girls alike — from humiliation and insult as they grew up and ease their way later when, as adults, they made their way in the world."[12]

But the combination of accessibility and obstacles existed in former ages as well. Strata of Spanish Jewry obtained extensive secular educations and entered into many levels of government service, including very high levels, but were also prohibited from major positions because of their Jewishness. Yet this combination of access and prohibition — in many ways more liberal than that found in the German states in the early nineteenth century — existed for centuries without leading to wide-scale defections. The strength of Jewish communal institutions and Jewish autonomy, even when riven by class differences, and the value Jews placed on membership in the community largely by virtue of those institutions, held them to the community despite the allures of the wider society. It was only when confronted in 1391 and 1412 with the choice of defection or death, or at least of defection or a dramatic deterioration in the conditions of their lives, and in 1492 when the remnant community faced the choice of apostasy or expulsion, that the acculturation of segments of the community to Spanish society, and rifts in the community, eased the way to large-scale defection.

In the German states in the early nineteenth century, Jews obviously defected in the face of lesser pressures to do so than the threat of death or impoverishment or exile, but they had weaker communal institutions than had Spanish Jews and many had a weaker sense of connection with the bulk of Jewry, and so they had less in their lives to counter what pressures there were to defect.

It has been estimated that about 200,000 Jews converted through the nineteenth century.[13] However reliable this figure, it represents at most, of course, only a portion of the defections. In the early part of the century, when there were still extensive legal barriers to Jewish integration, baptism to address these obstacles was the primary path for those who left the community. As legal barriers fell and obstacles to Jews became more *de facto* than *de jure*, falling away from the community increasingly took the form simply of disassociation, nonidentification, and a high rate of intermarriage, with children being raised as non-Jews.

That all communities in "non-Polish" German areas suffered significant erosion was in large part a consequence of the fact that communities in these areas retained hardly a shadow of their former legally recognized authority and centrality in the lives of their members. The communities had, in this regard, lost much of their earlier meaningfulness for their members. They were no longer potent daily confirmations of the continued vitality and meaningfulness of Jewish peoplehood. They were no longer in the same position to address with authority and their earlier effectiveness the needs, material, social, and spiritual, of their members.

Yet, for all the defections, something did hold many German Jews to their faith and their community despite the weakening of community and despite the assaults and allures of the surrounding society. Was that something an intellectual commitment to Jewish theology and Jewish belief? Or an emotional, nostalgic sense of connection with and obligation to one's Jewish heritage, the immediate, familial legacy and the longer, historical bond? Or a positive response to the particular reformist compromises and adaptations of ritual and practice adopted by one's congregation? Each could play a significant role for some. But to hold large numbers to their Jewish identity in a meaningful way, it would seem that such ties would have to be supported by something more, by a sense of connection with and attachment to a community, a connection whose loss could not, to one's perception, be adequately compensated for by prospective alternative attachments. (Indeed, the pioneering sociologist Emile Durkheim, himself Jewish, famously observed that all religion is a celebration and ritualization of communal ties.[14])

There are, it is true, people who have been drawn to Judaism and moved to embrace it while never having met a Jew, simply by reading of the Jewish past, belief system, and ethics in the Bible and elsewhere. Certainly many Jews by birth have retained a loyalty to the faith on the same grounds, even under conditions of attenuated or absent connections with other Jews. But such people are exceptions. Similarly, there are isolated Jews, or Jews with very limited contacts with others, who will continue to value their Jewish identity out of loyalty to heritage and history; a higher likelihood if parents valued it as well, but possible even when parents did not. But these too are exceptions. More typically, attachment, if it is to be sustained, must be anchored in connection with a valued community. Even those able to maintain attachment on intellectual grounds, or on the foundation of loyalty to their heritage, even non-Jews drawn to the faith by their reading, typically seek out a community to deepen their sense of attachment and connectedness.

To the degree that German Jewry sustained itself, it did so through its forging of relatively stable communities whose members valued their ties to their community sufficiently to want to preserve and nurture them and pass them on to their children. At the heart of these communities were generally reformist congregations of one stripe or other, ranging from Reform to modern Orthodox. Such congregations and their members forged syntheses, in their beliefs, in their rituals, in their lives, of the traditionally Jewish and the German; and members' shared sense of communality entailed a shared valuing of their particular synthesis above alternatives — but the anchor was primarily the community itself.

Yet the stability of these communities, however sufficient to retain the loyalty of large proportions of their members, was also intrinsically precarious. Recognition of this is not based simply on the history of ongoing and significant defections that marked these communities, or the fact that many required the continual arrival and acculturation of Jews from the East to sustain themselves. Nor does it reflect merely observation that they did not have the institutional strength that was typical of Jewish communities in earlier eras and could still to some degree be found in many areas of eastern Europe.

The precariousness can be seen also in the nature of the Jewish-German syntheses that characterized these communities. Their reformist Jewish elements represented more than divergence from traditional, Orthodox Judaism. They reflected alienation from traditional Judaism, and from the large majority of Jews, the Jews of the East, whose lives remained centered around traditional observance. Moreover, that alienation was conditioned not merely on an assessment of the requirements of modernity, an assessment that comprehended the ways of the East as passé. It was in no small measure the product of German Jews adopting the biases of the surrounding German society. It was inspired by the seemingly particular hostility of the Germans toward Eastern Jewry, the fact that the caricatures of Jews that pervaded German anti-Semitic writings and art were most often of Eastern Jews. It reflected the eagerness of many German Jews to separate themselves from the objects of those caricatures and from that venom and to embrace the hope that by distancing themselves from those despised other Jews they could assuage the anti-Jewish hostility directed at themselves and their communities.

In addition, the German elements incorporated into these communities' Jewish-German syntheses were also determined not simply by impulses of adaptation, of adopting what seemed positive and valuable in the surrounding culture, but again by impulses of ingratiation, of aspiring to win over hostile, anti-Jewish opinion in the surrounding society. Both these communities' alienation from the majority of other Jews and the fashioning of their Jewish-German syntheses largely with the objective of assuaging anti-Jewish opinion rendered their communities' stability intrinsically precarious, vulnerable to increasing defection and potentially even dissolution when hostility toward them as Jews did not dissipate. It is unclear what would have been the fate of these communities had they not been overwhelmed by the Nazi actions of 1933 to 1945.[15]

Besiegement and German Jewish Political Sentiment

The efforts by Jews in the German-speaking world to respond to the bigotry of the surrounding society and win acceptance by their neighbors were not limited to promotion of Jewish religious and social self-reforms congruent with anti-Jewish indictments. They also entailed political steps. But here, too, Jewish exertions were very often characterized not by pragmatic weighing of the Jewish predicament and how it might be improved but by wishful, delusional comprehensions that the right Jewish behavior, often in the vein of self-reform or self-renunciation, would inexorably elicit the desired results.

A somewhat poignant example of this involved the actions of Prussian Jews in the context of the Prussian struggle against Napoleon. It was not unreasonable that Prussian Jews might look to demonstrations of patriotism as positive, pragmatic steps toward winning the acceptance of the surrounding society. But note the more wishfully definitive expectations contained in a call to arms issued then by two leaders of the Berlin Jewish community, Eduard Kley and Carl Siegfried Gunsburg: "There upon the battlefield of honor . . . where all work for a single goal: for their fatherland; . . . there also will the barriers of prejudice come tumbling down . . . Hand in hand with your fellow soldiers you will complete the great work; they will not deny you the name of brother, for you will have earned it."[16]

In fact, from 1813 to 1815, seventy-two soldiers from the small Prussian Jewish population won the iron cross; fifty-five Prussian Jewish officers died at Waterloo.[17] But, as has so frequently happened, the Jews in post-Napoleonic Germany faced political and social forces that transcended anything they as a community did or did not do.

What actually ensued was virtually a preview of events that would follow a hundred years later, when the exemplary record of German Jewish soldiers in World War I did nothing to dampen the postwar explosion of German Jew-hatred that culminated in the rise of Nazism. In this earlier instance, the defeat of the French triggered a reactionary, anti-Enlightenment and anti-modern, backlash in much of the German world. On an intellectual level, this reaction entailed a dismissal of Enlightenment values of legal equality and justice as illusory abstractions, and French abstractions at that, unrelated to the life of nations in the real world. The new German perspective regarded nations, and Germany in particular, as properly built on organic, "Volk," connections of shared history, culture, and faith. It promoted an idealization of the Middle Ages with its supposedly more stable, more ordered, more "organic" and "civilized," institutions; that is, its system of social corporations supported by church and Empire.

In this context the Jews were regarded as inexorably alien, and the movement engendered by the post-Napoleonic reaction was militantly opposed to the extension of citizen rights to Jews. It was in fact vehemently anti-Jewish, and its followers engaged in extensive anti-Jewish rioting. The movement, accompanied also by an outpouring of new anti-Jewish literature, was particularly strong in intellectual circles, among university faculty and students, circles that had formerly been the bastions of enlightened thinking. The rallying cry of the anti-Jewish rioters at the time was "Hep! Hep!," a resurrection of the rallying cry of medieval anti-Jewish gangs during the first Crusade and derived, it is believed, from the initial letters of *Hierosolyma est perdita,* "Jerusalem is lost."

The major political issue for German Jews in subsequent decades continued to be the pursuit of legal equality despite the reverses of the post-Napoleonic years, and many Jews sought to advance this agenda in pragmatic ways. The widespread support among Jews for liberal parties and ultimately for the liberal drive for German unification was due in large part to the vocal and intense antagonism of conservative forces in Germany to Jewish integration and the hope that liberal victories would bring about an end to Jewish legal disabilities. But in the face of attacks from many quarters to the effect that the Jews were inexorably a separate and unintegratable people, or, within more liberal quarters, that Jews must demonstrate their willingness to give up their particularism before they can be integrated, many in the Jewish community, including in the leadership, responded by seeking to de-emphasize particularly Jewish political issues. They sought to demonstrate Jewish dedication to issues of supposedly more general and more widely shared concern. This was a political response to the same pressures that led to reformist attempts to revise what it meant to be a Jew from a concept of peoplehood to a more exclusively religious concept, and that inspired reformist revisions of Jewish litany to delete all references to peoplehood and aspirations for Return.

There was, of course, no intrinsic inconsistency between, on the one hand, Jewish peoplehood and Jewish concern about issues affecting the Jewish community and, on the other, Jews' loyalty to the states in which they lived. Nor was there typically a perception of such an inconsistency in previous ages. Moreover, Jewish "particularism" does not intrinsically warrant being conceived differently from other particularisms; those of class and occupation, for example, or regionalism, or affiliation with a particular Christian denomination, all of which can have political ramifications that distinguish groups from other segments of a state population. Yet under the weight of widespread anti-Jewish animus in the German states in the nineteenth century, Jewish particularism was elevated to the status of a unique problem and made the target of anti-Jewish attacks, and much of the Jewish community accepted the indictment at face value and sought to demonstrate conspicuously its disavowal of particularism.

Those Jews who did so would often cast their arguments in high-minded terms, as reflecting a concern with all mankind above any parochial agenda, and they might convince themselves that this was indeed their primary motivation.

But the perspective was in large part a defensive one in the face of attacks on the Jews and, in its censure of Jewish particularism, reflected an absorption and endorsement of the canards of the Jew-baiters. There was, indeed, an intrinsic anti-Jewish bias not only in the attacks but in the Jewish community's response, to the degree that the response implicitly attributed merit to the indictment. For, in fact, Jews did face disabilities that were unique, and the ignoring or downplaying of those disabilities was itself prejudicial. Yet there was wide sentiment in the community in support of this stance of accommodation to the indictment.

Some legal disabilities were gradually removed in the course of the century, and Jews whose priorities were assimilation and career advancement in previously proscribed areas were less obliged to convert. One consequence was that many individuals remained nominally within the community — that is, eschewed conversion — whose connection with the community was attenuated at best and whose attitudes toward things Jewish were indifferent or even hostile. Among German Jews who became political activists, demonstration of a particular concern with the Jewish predicament and persisting Jewish disabilities was rare and such activists were often among the very marginally affiliated.

But the eschewing of particularly Jewish issues was to a large degree the political stance even among those activists more committed to the community and concerned about its fate. Gabriel Riesser, a leading liberal who was almost unique among Jewish political activists in his vocal and energetic pursuit of the cause of Jewish legal equality, nevertheless repeatedly reiterated views subsuming the problem of Jewish disabilities to broader political and nationalist matters. Riesser declared at one point: "Give me Jewish equality in one hand and the realization of the beautiful dream of Germany's political unification in the other . . . and I will unhesitantly choose the latter, for I am convinced that unification also encompasses equality."[18]

Perhaps not surprisingly, Riesser was critical of anything suggestive of transnational Jewish interests or of Jews constituting a distinct nation. He asserted that German Jews desire no "national existence of their own, such as had formerly been imposed upon them by their enemies, but . . . [to] think and feel as Germans."[19]

Indeed, even leaders of the Jewish community who sought to promote Jewish equality in Germany often went to pains to make clear both that they subsumed their efforts under wider German goals and that their brief for German Jews did not at all reflect concerns for Jewry more broadly. The response of German Jewish leaders to the Damascus blood libel in 1840 was illustrative. (In a revival of the medieval blood libel, Jews in Damascus were accused of having killed a Capuchin monk and his Moslem servant to use their blood for ritual purposes.[20]) A number of prominent European Jews spoke out forcefully against the libel and several joined a delegation to Egypt to bring their concerns to the authorities there, as Damascus was then under the control of the Egyptian ruler Mohammed Ali. Among the delegates were Moses Montefiore, a leading figure in British Jewry, and the French Jewish statesman Adolph Cremieux. But Abraham Geiger, a key founder of Reform Judaism, was critical of the delegation. Geiger declared, "For me it is more important that Jews be able to work in Prussia as pharmacists or lawyers than that the entire Jewish population of Asia and Africa be saved, although as a human being I sympathize with them."[21]

The proclivity of Jewish political activists to eschew particularly Jewish issues was vividly exhibited in the context of the liberal revolutions of 1848, especially in Berlin and Vienna. Jews were among the leading figures in the briefly successful revolutions. Riesser was elected deputy-speaker of the all-German parliament that met in Frankfurt; Adolf Fischhof and Joseph Goldmark played major roles in the uprising in Vienna, where Fischhof was appointed head of the General Security Committee that controlled the city. Fischhof, discussing the multi-ethnic composition of the Austrian Empire, advocated communal rights for the national groups in the empire but excluded the Jews. Representatives of other ethnic groups argued their groups' cause; but Jews, cowed by indictments of Jewish self-concern, were reluctant to do the same. Yet they often cast their reluctance as a matter of principle. A rabbi in Austria's parliament stated, "What should be done for us now? Nothing! Everything for the people and the Fatherland . . . No word about Jewish emancipation unless others speak for us . . . First the right to live as men, to breathe, think, speak, first the right of a citizen . . . afterwards comes the Jew. They should not reproach us that we always think first about ourselves."[22]

Many Jews chose to construe Jewish self-effacement in response to anti-Jewish indictments not only as proper and principled but as also a strategy that would lead inexorably to desired goals. Consistent with this, many German Jews chose to see their alignment with liberal parties in Germany, certainly a pragmatic tack, as more than a pragmatic political alliance. They chose to construe it as a submersion of Jewish particularist interests and a fusion with a broader constituency that would inevitably win the Jews in return the full equality and acceptance they desired. But once more, Jewish fantasies of positively controlling the Jewish community's fate and ending biases through self-reform and self-renunciation proved overly sanguine.

While the Jews gained some support for Jewish emancipation from their non-Jewish liberal "allies," the extent and depth of that support was often disappointing. The agenda of the wider liberal forces was focused in large part on breaking the power of old elites in the German states and had a strong economic component to it. The drive for German unification by the broader liberal constituency was concerned with ending the taxing prerogatives and other economic controls still exercised by the landed gentry, local sovereigns, and related elites. But non-Jewish liberals often saw Jews as also economic threats, as competitors; a situation familiar from the urban politics of the Middle Ages. Many were consequently less than sympathetic to the Jewish quest for equality.

As rights were extended to Jews and *de jure* obstacles fell, many so-called liberals were eager to limit Jewish competition in the professions and the universities and supported *numeri clausi* that increasingly restricted Jewish access to academia and the professions in the wake of the lifting of *de jure* restrictions. Many viewed the Jews' desire for full equality and full access as overreaching. They thought — not unlike members of more conservative strata who acceded grudgingly to some concessions to the Jews — that the mere extension of basic citizenship rights ought to be appreciated as sufficient by the Jews. Events around the revolutions of 1848, while ultimately resulting, with setbacks, in some Jewish gains in legal rights, gains attained through liberal support, also demonstrated the limits and ambiguities of the Jewish-liberal "alliance."

This pattern was even more marked in the context of Germany's unification, achieved in 1871 primarily through liberal efforts. Unification yielded Jews virtually full *de jure* equality, but *de facto* restrictions on them subsequently intensified and did so with the support of many middle-class "liberals." The rise of anti-Semitic political parties in the last decades of the century was in large part a reaction against the Jews' achievement of *de jure* equality, and sympathy with the sentiments of the anti-Semitic parties existed among some "liberal" elements.

The extent to which many Jews had chosen to idealize the agenda of German liberals and the fruits of Jewish self-effacement is captured in an exchange between Gabriel Riesser and the conservative German academic and theologian H.E.G. Paulus. Paulus argued that as long as Jews adhered to their religion they constituted a separate nation and were entitled to be protected subjects in Germany but not full citizens. Paulus also suggested that the Jewish push for full integration as Germans would end in their expulsion or even extermination. Riesser responded that German unification would inexorably be built on Enlightenment principles of justice and equality and so would inevitably entail the providing of full equality to Jews.[23]

The issue is not that Riesser proved so dramatically and catastrophically wrong. It was not impossible that events could have unfolded very differently and more in keeping with his hopes. The point is his willful, self-deluding certainty, despite much countervailing evidence, that the right Jewish alliances and self-effacements would inexorably yield the results he desired.

While most German Jews aligned themselves with liberal parties, some, from the early decades of the century, were attracted to radical ideologies of the left, socialism and communism. Their numbers included some Jews who valued their Jewish identity but, faced with the anti-Jewish animus abroad in the wider society and the slow pace of positive changes in the Jewish predicament, believed that only a radical revision of social and political institutions would improve the Jews' situation. Or, a variation on the same theme, they believed that only by Jews immersing themselves in some imagined broader brotherhood of the aggrieved could they improve their lot and so they chose to see some transcendent congruence between the needs of the Jews and the aspirations of the working class. But more commonly it was Jews interested in distancing themselves from the Jewish community and taking on a different identity that were attracted to the politics of the far Left.

Some Jews who chose to shed their Jewish identity immersed themselves in right-wing politics. The convert Friedrick Julius Stahl, a professor of law at the University of Berlin, became head of the anti-Jewish Christian Conservative Party early in the nineteenth century and fought against the extension of political rights to Jews. But politically active converts and disaffiliated Jews more typically drifted leftward. The total numbers who embraced such ideologies, and the percentages they represented of all disaffiliated Jews and Jewish converts, were small. Many more in both groups, like those Jews who remained within the community, became enthusiastic middle-class Germans than radicals. But those who did join the ranks of the radicals played a disproportionately large role in the politics of the ideological Left.

Various observers have attributed this overrepresentation to a displaced Jewish messianism. Having implicitly or explicitly abandoned Judaism, such people, the argument goes, transformed Jewish messianic images and hopes into a secular utopianism. Perhaps the theme of the Jews' universal mission, of the Jews as a light unto the nations, that was then being increasingly emphasized to the exclusion of particularist concerns in German Jewish religious thought, did figure, in displaced, deracinated form, in the utopian radicalism of some disaffiliated Jews and converts. But there was a more direct, more personal source of this radicalism for many. What led disaffiliated Jews and converts to be disproportionately involved in such movements was their eagerness to separate themselves emphatically from the Jewish and immerse themselves in a broader identity, together, often, with their sense of being dogged by their Jewish roots under prevailing social conditions and being refused the acceptance they desired despite their disaffiliation or conversion from Judaism. In their frustration with this exclusion, and their wish for acceptance and achievement, they chose to ally themselves with larger groups in a perspective of shared victimhood and to comprehend resolution in terms of radical social reform that would bring relief to all of established society's "victims."

Radical attitudes were also in themselves, in their rejection of all that was "traditional," in their secular utopianism, a dramatic break with these people's Jewish background, a social and political repudiation of the "Jewish."

Not surprisingly, given that these people were typically eager to distance themselves from any connection with matters Jewish and immerse themselves in an alternative identity, issues of Jewish emancipation rarely figure in their programs of radical social reform. If they are mentioned at all they are invariably comprehended as an equality that can be attained only by the undoing of more universal inequities. More usually, these writers join in critiques and caricatures of the Jews and even in the anti-Semitic diatribes popular within many radical leftist circles at the time and, of course, in the society more broadly. They too, in the common parlance of far Left cant, often castigate "the Jews" for their middle-class liberal values and supposed betrayal of society's truly disadvantaged, the working class.[24]

Nor are such attacks on the Jews limited to the most radical among these people, as represented by Marx and his anti-Semitic rants. Ferdinand Lassalle's course is illustrative. Lassalle was a founder of the German labor movement, first president of the General German Workers Association, and a major spokesman for socialism in the German arena.

Lassalle's break with the Jewish community seems to have been driven in large part by temperament and ambition but also entailed some absorbing of the broader society's anti-Jewish animus. In his diary at sixteen he writes — in the context of the contemporary news story of the Damascus blood libel — of imagining himself a Jewish military hero, and he expresses distaste for what he sees as the Jews' passivity in the face of their tormentors.[25] He returns to this theme in later years in articulating his alienation from the community and the faith, but his later comments also clearly include attempts to assure others of his distance from the Jews and reflect as well his embrace of popular anti-Jewish canards. He writes at one point:

"I do not like the Jews at all, I even detest them in general. I see in them nothing but the very much degenerated sons of a great but vanished past. As a result of centuries of slavery, these people have acquired servile characteristics, and that is why I am so unfavorably disposed to them. Besides, I have no contact with them. There is scarcely a single Jew among my friends and in the society which surrounds me [in Berlin]."[26]

Lassalle had ambitions that could not be fulfilled within the Jewish community, ambitions that — given the biases of his time and place — could only be satisfied in his lights by turning away from the Jews. This apparently made him all the more open to embracing the anti-Jewish bigotry of the surrounding society. He never converted or denied his Jewish origins, and he could even joke at himself in his anti-Jewish remarks, as when he wrote: "There are two classes of men I cannot bear; journalists and Jews — and unfortunately I belong to both."[27] But indeed after his late teens he showed little sympathy for the Jews and was mainly their critic, indicting them in contemporary anti-Jewish veins, even as he himself was the object of anti-Semitic attacks by his critics and political enemies.

The broader palette Lassalle chose was the German labor movement and socialism. Lassalle complained at times of the passivity of German workers, in statements resembling his comments about Jewish passivity. But that did not compromise his sensitivity to workers' plight as a disadvantaged and abused population in German society or his energetic and often courageous championing of their predicament, not just as a writer and theoretician but as activist organizer. In contrast the adult Lassalle was more inclined to embrace the canards cast at the Jews than to take offense at the abuses and disabilities heaped on them.

Moreover, in his championing of German labor and socialism, Lassalle himself introduced anti-Jewish themes as he attacked middle-class liberalism. For example, he wrote of the Jewish editor of the liberal newspaper, *Berliner Volkszeitung*, "A man who cannot even write German but is slowly but surely corrupting our nation's language and its character with the peculiar gibberish with which he feeds his readers — that so-called Jewish-German."[28]

No doubt some of those who sought to shed their Jewish identity and immerse themselves in an alternative identity as socialist or communist brother-in-arms with the downtrodden working class succeeded in being accepted as they wished with their alternate persona. But what drove them was still largely a delusion, a wish to believe that embracing the anti-Jewish indictments of the surrounding society and associating themselves with one faction of the indicters would inexorably end their being seen as Jews and spare them the arrows shot at "the Jews." Reality, of course, is not subject to such inexorable control.

It was not simply that the radicals' opponents commonly labeled these people Jewish agents of a nefarious Jewish agenda. Even within the ranks of the radical Left, and certainly among much of its working-class constituency, Jewish radicals were often still identified with the Jewish community more broadly as unreformable capitalist enemies. Even among those fellow radicals who were relatively free of anti-Jewish biases, the radical universalism so common among the former Jews — their dismissal of all ethnic, cultural and national distinctions as insignificant, atavistic, and to be discarded in the future radical utopia — was commonly viewed as a particularly Jewish vision of the socialist future. Indeed so it was, born of those Jews' eagerness to discard and render insignificant their own ethnic connections.

The Jewish attraction to universalist perspectives has not been limited to the radical universalism of those who sought to shed their Jewish identity by remaking themselves into deracinated champions of the revolutionary Left. As noted, even many Jews who valued their Jewish identity have, in the face of anti-Jewish pressures, sought to placate their neighbors by eschewing particularist Jewish concerns and emphasizing the universal in Jewish aspirations. Of course, those who did so would typically cast their universalism not as a tack to mollify anti-Jewish sentiment but as a principled embrace of the modern and progressive. In any case, so common has been this predilection, and so transparent its motivation, that the writer Cynthia Ozick trenchantly observed, "Universalism is the ultimate Jewish parochialism."[29]

But, again, those who embraced left-wing radicalism were a small percentage of disaffiliated Jews and an even much smaller percentage of Jews who were interested in preserving their Jewish identity. The great majority of the latter, as of the former, were most concerned with being good middle-class Germans. This shaped their political tastes and their cultural tastes as well, and in both spheres their choices reflected the persistent wish to believe — even in the face of much counterevidence — that behaving as good Germans would inevitably lead to their being accepted as good Germans. The self-delusions that this entailed were at times startling.

For example, Richard Wagner, ultimately the premier artist of German nationalism, attracted many admirers from among committed Jews despite his vicious anti-Jewish ravings. Indeed, the fawning of Wagner's Jewish admirers, at least one of whom committed suicide in despair at Wagner's death, was the subject of widespread comment and ridicule at the time. (As was also Wagner's hypocrisy in seeking out and availing himself of, and depending on, the help of Jews even as he proclaimed his hatred of them and called for their extermination.) The German nationalist tenor of much of Wagner's work, particularly his later work, and his celebration as the embodiment of German high culture, were part of the attraction to his work for many German Jews, a facet of their self-conscious pursuit of cultural integration.

The self-delusion is made more clear by the contrast of these Jewish sentiments with the stance of someone like the philosopher Friedrich Nietzsche. Nietzsche is widely construed to have been an anti-Semite, in large part because of the use made of his work by anti-Semitic parties, including the Nazis. In fact, Nietzsche in his writings vigorously attacked anti-Semitism and opposed militant German nationalism on various grounds including what he perceived to be its intrinsic anti-Semitic strains. An early friend and devotee of Wagner, Nietzsche broke with him when Wagner returned to Germany and embraced militant nationalism. He later wrote bitterly: "I suffer no ambiguity; and since Wagner had moved to Germany, he had condescended step by step to everything I despise — even to anti-Semitism."[30] Yet many German Jews refused to let Wagner's ugly anti-Semitism interfere with their adoration of him.

There were numerous additional instances as well in which affiliated and committed Jews in the German-speaking world during the nineteenth and early twentieth centuries, in their eagerness for acceptance, lent their support to political and cultural figures and causes whose agendas were viciously hostile to their own interests and well-being but whose inimical aspects self-deluding Jewish enthusiasts chose to ignore.

FOUR

Besiegement East and West, 1880 to 1914

. . . Go any Sunday through the Thiergartenstrasse midday at twelve or evenings glance into the foyer of a Berlin theater. Unique Vision! In the midst of a German life, a separate, strange race, lustrous and impressively costumed and with hot-blooded, active gestures. On the sands of the Mark Brandenburg, an Asiatic horde. The forced humor of these people does not betray how much old, unsatiated hatred rests on their shoulders. They do not imagine that it is only living in an age that has controlled all natural violence that has rescued them from that which their fathers suffered. In close relationship among themselves, in strict rejection of all that comes from outside — thus they live in a half-willed, invisible ghetto, not a living part of the people [Volk] but a strange organism in its body.

German Jewish industrialist and statesman
Walther Rathenau, 1897[1]

In the youth of every German Jew there is a moment that he remembers his whole life: when he becomes fully conscious for the first time that he has entered the world as a second-class citizen, and that no degree of ability, or merit can ever free him from this position.

Rathenau, 1912[2]

We have honestly endeavored everywhere to merge ourselves in the social life of surrounding communities and to preserve the faith of our fathers. In vain are we loyal patriots, our loyalty in some places running to extremes; in vain do we make the same sacrifices of life and property as our fellow-citizens; in vain do we strive to increase the fame of our native land in science and art, or her wealth by trade and commerce. In countries where we have lived for centuries we are still cried down as strangers, and often by those whose ancestors were not yet domiciled in the land where Jews had already had experience of suffering . . . If we could only be left in peace . . . But I think we shall not be left in peace.

Theodor Herzl, *The Jewish State*, 1896[3]

The 1880s ushered in a period of increased pressures on Jews throughout Europe, and a significant element of the Jewish response to this worsening besiegement continued to be an embrace of anti-Jewish indictments and a pursuit of self-reform to appease the indicters. Particularly significant were developments in the states that had participated in the division of Poland, as Austria, Germany, and Russia were still home to the world's largest Jewish populations.

The decades from 1800 to 1880 had seen a dramatic expansion of the world Jewish population generally, and more particularly in the number of Jews in formerly Polish territories. The total increased from somewhat more than two million worldwide to about seven and a half million. This growth was due not to increased fertility but to decreased infant and adult mortality. Improved conditions affected Jews during this period more than non-Jews, and this was so even outside the former Poland. For example, in Frankfurt in 1855, the average life span of Jews was about 49, of non-Jews not quite 37.[4] By way of explanation, one historian notes, "There can be no doubt that the greater stability of the family, the smaller number of illegitimate children, the infrequency of venereal diseases, the higher status of the woman within the family, the care lavished on babies and small children, abstinence from alcohol, the readiness of the individual and the community to undergo considerable economic sacrifice in order to help others and the lengthy tradition of charitable deeds combined, among the Jews, to serve as the basis for their demographic development."[5]

During these same eighty years, there was some Jewish emigration out of Russia, Austria, and Prussia/Germany, with a number of Russian Jews moving to German states, for example, and German Jews going to France and England or to the United States. But by far, most Jewish movement out of formerly Polish territories was to elsewhere within the successor nations: gradually increasing emigration out of Galicia to other parts of the Austrian Empire, out of Prussia's Polish territories to elsewhere in areas under Prussian control, out of Russian Poland to territories added to the Pale of Settlement. (The Pale refers to those limited areas of Russia beyond which Jews, by statute, were not allowed to reside. It initially consisted of only those provinces that Russia had seized from Poland.) Consequently, of the seven and a half million Jews in 1880, four million lived in Russia, another one and a half million in the Austrian Empire, and half a million in Germany.

THE RISE OF POLITICAL ANTI-SEMITISM IN GERMANY[6]

In Germany, the last two decades of the nineteenth century saw a burgeoning of anti-Semitic themes in the public arena, including the emergence of political parties whose platforms were built almost entirely of anti-Jewish planks. Various factors contributed to this phenomenon.

While the liberal camp had provided the main political support for German unification, unification had unleashed distinctly anti-liberal sentiments. The Prussian wars that accompanied the drive to unification (against Denmark, Austria, and France), and the impetus that unification gave toward further defining a national culture, led to the emergence of a popular militant Germanism that built on the reactionary cultural Germanism of the post-Napoleonic era and viewed Jews as alien, unabsorbable, and inimical to its spirit. These sentiments, as conveyed in nationalist and anti-Semitic literature, were reinforced by the incorporation of elements from the new pseudo-discipline of racial science and from the new social Darwinism. Both were invoked to propound theories of inexorable racial competition, especially between Germans and Jews.

Social factors that fed the burgeoning anti-Jewish sentiment and the emergence of anti-Jewish politics included the legal gains toward equality of the Jews in the previous two decades, the success of some Jews in the professional, business, and cultural mainstream, and the negative response of the urban middle class to Jewish competition. This was, as noted earlier, a reprise of the urban hostility to the Jews during the Middle Ages. That earlier hostility had only been exacerbated by Jewish conversion and consequent liberation from legal disabilities, and anti-Jewish rancor now was similarly exacerbated by Jewish legal equality and Jewish pursuit of integration and assimilation.

Additional key reservoirs of anti-Semitic sentiment were groups that had been protected by pre-unification structures and were hurt by the new situation — artisans and small farmers, for example, who had benefited from old tariff arrangements and from the patronage of formerly privileged nobility. Many of these people perceived the urban factories, with which small craftsmen and artisans could not compete, and the liberal rolling back of old tariffs and old privileges, as a consequence of Jewish machinations, a view promoted by socialist attacks on "Jewish capitalism" and socialist claims that modern capitalism was a Jewish phenomenon. Yet another social factor feeding the new wave of anti-Jewish feeling and anti-Jewish politics was what there was of Jewish immigration from the East, portrayed in the anti-Semitic literature as a hostile invasion threatening to overwhelm Germany.

The Jewish response to the rise of anti-Semitic parties and to the broad embrace of anti-Semitic perspectives and anti-Jewish sentiment by the German public varied widely. Many Jews, likely most of the Jewish community, had nurtured a whiggish or progressivist view of history, and of Jewish history in particular, as a process of consistent improvement. In this view, the modern age was a dramatic advance in the Jewish situation over all preceding, benighted eras, and the recent achievement of *de jure* equality marked an historical high point. For those who entertained this perspective, the subsequent persistence and amplification of *de facto* discrimination and the intensification of popular anti-Jewish sentiment came as an essentially unanticipated and rudely disconcerting turn of events.

Some Jews, in response to the increasingly pervasive and shrill anti-Jewish content of German social-political discourse, concluded that there was something shamefully demeaning in the Jews' efforts to take on a German identity and win an acceptance that clearly was not to be had. It was this perspective that gave rise to the early literature on "Jewish self-hatred" alluded to previously. Its authors saw in the wider society's hostility evidence that efforts by many to attenuate their Jewish identity and subsume it to a German one were intrinsically pathological, a sick self-abnegation that could only end in disappointment, disorientation, and self-loathing.[7]

To the extent that these authors regarded efforts to shed one's Jewish identity as inexorably doing violence to one's essential self and as inevitably ending in psychological disorientation and angst, their argument was clearly an overstatement. Insofar as those German Jews who perceived their Jewish identity as primarily a burden and who sought to shed that identity subsequently experienced distress and some modicum of self-loathing, they did so in large part because their efforts were widely met with rebuff. They were in turmoil because much of the larger culture told them that they remained Jews no matter what their desires and efforts to become German were, and not simply because the quest to cast off their Jewishness was intrinsically anxiety-producing and disorienting.

Some people, perhaps because they so successfully hid their origins, found their way to a new identity more open to them. They encountered in their personal experience a greater willingness among those around them to regard them as they wished to be regarded. Among such people were many who — particularly if they had been reared with an already attenuated Jewish identity — likely experienced very little angst or psychological disequilibrium or fractured sense of self, who shed their Jewishness without ever looking back.

Still, the term *self-hatred* and the concept capture in a dramatic manner something of the psychological turmoil and diminished sense of self commonly experienced by members of a minority aspiring to acceptance by the broader society in which they live but stigmatized by that society as in various ways alien and unfit.

The early authors of this literature were themselves to varying degrees assimilated Jews, and some of them, in response to the hostility of the surrounding society, turned back to the Jewish world for meaning and identity.

Other German Jews, coming up against a hostility and exclusion that seemed impervious to all efforts of accommodation and commitment, felt hurt, dejected, but stuck. They could find for themselves no satisfactory escape from their predicament of being rejected suitors for German acceptance and could only lament the unfairness of their situation. Still others fled even more determinedly from all things Jewish and sought even more intensely to immerse themselves in the wider society, a tack marked, among other indications, by an upsurge of conversion and intermarriage during these decades.

Much of the affiliated community felt obliged to demonstrate still more explicitly its loyalty to things German and its aloofness from any Jewish particularism. Not a few, among both the affiliated and the alienated, blamed German Jew-hatred primarily on Jewish immigrants from the East and focused their own hostility on "Polish" Jewry. Some affiliated Jews, and many more among the alienated, interpreted the epidemic anti-Semitism as further evidence of the need for a radical transformation of society and threw themselves into the politics of the radical Left. They either ignored the anti-Semitic sentiments of the socialist parties and the workers, or regarded them, particularly the latter, as due to ignorance and the propagandizing of reactionary forces and as curable by proper education. Some, especially among the alienated Jews who remade themselves into ideologues of the Left, chose to construe the Jew-hatred of the working class as an inevitable reaction to "Jewish capitalism" and "exploitation."

Among the many within the Jewish community who responded to the surrounding society's increased expression of anti-Jewish sentiments by further embracing elements of anti-Jewish litany and blaming the Jews themselves for the hostility directed against them, there were a number of recurrent themes. These included arguments that Jews, usually other Jews, were still being too particularist in their concerns and not demonstrating enough devotion to German priorities, or were not shedding quickly enough the dross of religion, or were still being too distinctive by virtue of manners and habits brought from the East, or were still too immersed in the mentality of commerce. The writings of the industrialist and statesman Walther Rathenau — who at times considered conversion but never formally broke with the Jewish community — convey his embrace of several of these indictments. In an essay published in 1897 and filled with echoes of anti-Semitic cant and caricature, Rathenau declared,

" . . . Go any Sunday through the Thiergartenstrasse midday at twelve or evenings glance into the foyer of a Berlin theater. Unique Vision! In the midst of a German life, a separate, strange race, lustrous and impressively costumed and with hot-blooded, active gestures. On the sands of the Mark Brandenburg, an Asiatic horde. The forced humor of these people does not betray how much old, unsatiated hatred rests on their shoulders. They do not imagine that it is only living in an age that has controlled all natural violence that has rescued them from that which their fathers suffered. In close relationship among themselves, in strict rejection of all that comes from outside — thus they live in a half-willed, invisible ghetto, not a living part of the people [Volk] but a strange organism in its body."[8]

Some years later Rathenau declared: "I have . . . no other blood than German, no other stem, no other people . . . I share nothing with the Jews [except] what every German shares with them . . . I am hurt more if a Bavarian declaims against the Prussians than if he does so against the Jews."[9] In 1915, Rathenau stated that he considered the vehemently anti-Semitic race theorist Wilhelm Schwaner to be the last person in his life for whom he had any genuine feelings.[10]

Rathenau's endorsement of anti-Jewish themes reflects a response so widespread in the community during this period that it prompted the Jewish writer Max Nordau to observe, "It is the greatest triumph for antisemitism that it has brought the Jews to view themselves with antisemitic eyes."[11] Rathenau's arguments, and the course of his life, also reflect the self-delusion inherent in the Jewish embrace of anti-Jewish themes. Rathenau wished to believe that the Jews' dedicating themselves more determinedly to Germany and working aggressively to make themselves more German would resolve the anti-Jewish biases of the wider society. He wished to construe the Jewish predicament as soluble by Jewish self-reform.

Interestingly, Rathenau did not blind himself entirely to the truth that the anti-Jewish animus of the surrounding society was more than a response to particular irritations and was impervious to Jewish efforts to please. He wrote in 1912, "In the youth of every German Jew there is a moment that he remembers his whole life: when he becomes fully conscious for the first time that he has entered the world as a second-class citizen, and that no degree of ability, or merit can ever free him from this position."[12] But Rathenau's desire for acceptance was so powerful that this insight did not stop him from still advocating self-reform as the answer to German Jew-hatred, still resenting those he saw as unreformed Jews, and still seeking to ingratiate himself with the wider society.

In reality, not only was much of the anti-Jewish animus in the wider society impervious to the types of self-reform Rathenau advocated, but many Germans even looked upon such self-reforms with suspicion and comprehended them in a way that reinforced anti-Jewish feeling. They viewed the efforts of Jews to make themselves more German as Jewish intrusion and pretension, Jewish arrogance, Jewish overreaching, Jewish invasion, Jewish subversion.

Later, the exceptional record of valor forged by German Jewish soldiers in World War I did not protect the community at all against anti-Semitic claims of Jewish betrayal in the war. Rathenau's own substantial contributions to mobilizing German industry for the war effort and his exertions on Germany's behalf as statesman after the war did not spare him from being regarded by many in Germany as an alien Jew. Despite his patriotic achievements, his appointment as foreign minister infuriated many Germans because of his Jewishness and impelled some to seek, and successfully execute, his assassination.

The element of wishful thinking in Jewish endorsement of the wider society's bigoted indictments, and in Jewish advocacy of self-reform consistent with those indictments as the path to acceptance, has been alluded to by others. These observers, too, recognized the self-delusion in Jews believing that the other side saw things as they did and would respond as they wished them to respond to Jewish self-reform; in Jews believing that the dialectic between them and the wider society would inevitably play itself out as they hoped. Gershom Scholem, looking back on these years and the period that followed, wrote of the delusional aspect of Jewish comprehensions of a German-Jewish rapprochement, "To whom, then, did the Jews speak in that . . . German-Jewish dialogue? They spoke to themselves."[13]

FIN-DE-SIECLE AUSTRIA

In Austria, the migration of Jews to Vienna and the other cities of Austria proper from elsewhere in the empire — particularly, of course, from Galicia — together with some immigration from Russia, exacerbated hostility toward the Jews much as immigration did in Germany. At the same time, a number of the other social stresses that contributed to the intensification of anti-Jewish sentiment and the emergence of anti-Semitic political parties in Germany in the last decades of the nineteenth century actually figured even more prominently in Austria.

For example, the efforts by many Jews to eschew Jewish "particularism" and immerse themselves in a national identity encountered in Austria the problem of competing national identities within the fractious empire. Was a Jew in Prague to associate himself with German culture and Austrian nationality or with Czech culture and Czech national aspirations? Similar questions arose in Hungarian territories, in Galicia in the context of Polish-German competition, and elsewhere. Partisans of each national group were typically predisposed to perceive the Jews as in the camp of the other side and to view them with suspicion and hostility, whatever the actual sentiments of the local Jewish community or actual division of its sympathies. This had long been a difficulty for Austria's Jews, as reflected in attacks on them during the 1848 revolution. It once more became a prominent issue in the context of heightened nationalist feeling among the empire's ethnic groups during the last decades of the century.

Also, in Austria, as in Germany, the extension of fuller rights to the Jews led to greater Jewish entry into the professions, civil service, and commerce and increased competition with the German middle class, particularly in urban areas. But, unlike the situation in Germany, Jews and ethnic Germans in Austria were competing for slices of a shrinking pie. Through the latter part of the century the imperial government made a series of concessions to the empire's minorities in the form of substituting local languages for German in the schools, courts, and government offices in various ethnic regions. Such concessions entailed the loss of jobs in teaching, law, and the civil bureaucracy for the German-speaking middle class, exacerbating its hostility toward the German-speaking Jews competing for those jobs. This middle-class resentment toward the Jews figured prominently in the emergence of a German nationalist anti-Semitic party in Austria. Its platform emphasized anti-Jewish planks, sympathy with anti-Semitic politics in Germany, and a looking to Berlin with the aspiration that Austria proper would be absorbed into the new Germany and that a militant Germany would reassert German cultural hegemony in the East.

In addition, Austria, like the unified Germany, undertook a dismantling of the system of local tariffs that existed throughout the empire and of the economic privileges of local nobilities. These liberalization steps were intended to promote Austria's economic development. Groups hurt by the reforms, such as, again, artisans and small farmers who had been protected by the old tariff and patronage arrangements, here too blamed the urban manufacturers and what socialist activists identified as "Jewish capitalism" for their predicament. There evolved in Austria a politics of what might be called "reactionary socialism"; that is, a socialism whose constituency was not urban factory laborers looking to state control of manufacture to improve their lot but rather artisans and farmers and others who saw both the urban factories and their workers as enemies and looked back to medieval models of church and castle patronage and protection for salvation. This form of "socialism" existed in Germany as well as in Austria. But in Austria it had the support of important elements of the Catholic clergy, representatives of the church that had in fact been a key patron of this constituency in earlier centuries.

The clergy's backing spurred the emergence in Austria of an anti-Semitic populist "socialist" party built on this constituency, and the party enjoyed a success unmatched by any comparable forces in Germany during these years. Its leader, Karl Lueger, was elected mayor of Vienna in 1895 and, when Emperor Franz Joseph refused to ratify the election of someone perceived as a potentially destabilizing demagogue, Lueger won reaffirmation at the polls. The Emperor finally capitulated in 1897 and Lueger remained mayor until his death in 1910. Meanwhile, his party became the largest in the Austrian parliament and continued to enjoy its plurality until Austria's Anschluss with Nazi Germany.

The range of Jewish responses to the emergence of political anti-Semitism in Austria and to the general intensification of anti-Jewish sentiments mirrored the Jewish reaction in Germany. It included an increased hostility on the part of acculturated Jews both within the community and alienated from the community toward unassimilated "Eastern" Jews as the source of anti-Jewish sentiment. It entailed as well the absorption of other anti-Semitic biases by both affiliated and disaffiliated Jews. (This is the era in Austria of Otto Weininger and Karl Kraus, discussed in Chapter One.) Many Austrian Jews, particularly among the intellectual, cultural, commercial, and professional elites, sought to distance themselves from the community either through conversion or simply through disaffiliation, intermarriage, and immersion in the wider society. Among those who remained within the community, major elements strove with even greater determination to eschew issues that could appear too "particularist" and immerse themselves rather in wider political agendas. A small but growing minority of Jews, especially among the disaffiliated, chose to see salvation in the casting aside of all established political and religious institutions, to seek a radically reformed society, and to throw themselves into the politics of the socialist Left, and such people often embraced the anti-Semitic formulas particular to the Left.

There were also, as in Germany, those who responded to the broader society's rebuff of efforts at integration and assimilation by perceiving the attempts to exchange one's Jewish identity for another as intrinsically pathological, a sick self-abnegation that could lead only to frustration and despair, and who turned back to the Jewish world for meaning and identity. Most notable among these was, of course, Theodor Herzl, an assimilated Viennese journalist. In 1896, Herzl published *The Jewish State*, in which he argued that the painful predicament of the Jews — their abuse and degradation as victims of anti-Semitic prejudice in the societies amid which they lived — could only be resolved by creation of a Jewish national home: a national solution to the problems of the Jewish nation.

Herzl wrote of the Jewish situation: "We have honestly endeavored everywhere to merge ourselves in the social life of surrounding communities and to preserve the faith of our fathers. In vain are we loyal patriots, our loyalty in some places running to extremes; in vain do we make the same sacrifices of life and property as our fellow-citizens; in vain do we strive to increase the fame of our native land in science and art, or her wealth by trade and commerce. In countries where we have lived for centuries we are still cried down as strangers, and often by those whose ancestors were not yet domiciled in the land where Jews had already had experience of suffering . . . If we could only be left in peace . . . But I think we shall not be left in peace."[14]

Despite the heightened level of anti-Semitic sentiment to which Jews were routinely exposed in Vienna, the key experience in precipitating Herzl's shift from assimilationist predilections to immersion in advocacy of a Jewish national renaissance was the Dreyfus affair in France. Herzl, working for a Viennese newspaper, covered Captain Dreyfus's court-martial in Paris on trumped-up charges of treason and witnessed the explosion of public displays of Jew-hatred triggered by the trial. In the face of anti-Jewish depredations at home, Herzl, like many other Jews in Austria and Germany, had cultivated an idealized image of France. He had tended to view France, home of well-established anti-conservative and anticlerical institutions and of the Declaration of the Rights of Man, as more liberal, more progressive, less militant, chauvinistic, and bigoted, than other nations: in many ways a model for other nations. Herzl responded to the anti-Jewish convulsions around the Dreyfus affair as a rude awakening.

In fact, political anti-Semitism — on the socialist Left as well as on the Right — had been growing in France in recent years as it had been in Germany and Austria, in part under the influence of events in the latter nations. Increased Jewish immigration from eastern Europe, and a backlash against it, were factors also operative in France. In addition, various economic crises in the country were exploited by conservative and clerical forces to whip up anti-liberal and more specifically chauvinistic and anti-Jewish feeling and by socialist forces to rail against "Jewish capital." As in Germany and Austria, France experienced a proliferation of anti-Jewish propaganda, the emergence of anti-Jewish political platforms, and a widespread and popular perception of the Jews as a hostile and alien element in the French body politic.

Also as in Germany, and elsewhere in Europe, many Jews in France responded to the hatred around them by seeking the more eagerly to prove their patriotism and to eschew any demonstration of "particularist" sentiments. Very few French Jews, for example, actively supported Dreyfus. One who did, the journalist and political writer Bernard Lazare, complained that most of his fellow French Jews were too concerned with proving themselves "good" Frenchmen free of any other loyalties.[15]

Herzl's publication of *The Jewish State* and his efforts to disseminate its ideas elicited an enthusiastic response from a number of Jews in the West who were disenchanted with the difficulties faced by Jews despite their *de jure* emancipation. But further to the East, in Russian domains, a literature arguing the need for a national solution to the Jewish predicament and for a Jewish national home had been evolving for several decades before Herzl's book. Such sentiments had even established a foothold in Vienna among recent immigrants from the East, although Herzl appears to have been largely unaware of these stirrings.

Herzl was also apparently unaware of the earlier writings in a Zionist vein of the German Jew Moses Hess. Hess, born in 1812, had by the 1840s fled his Jewish background and immersed himself in the ideology of the radical Left, writing for Marx's newspaper the *Rheinische Zeitung* and collaborating with Marx and Engels on other publications. But, in a rare development for Jews who had abandoned the Jewish community for the religion of the radical Left, Hess was put off by the utopian universalism of the socialists, thought it misguided to dismiss what was positive in people's national and ethnic ties, and was particularly offended by the anti-Jewish sentiments among German socialists and in Germany more generally. He returned to the Jewish fold and advocated a Jewish national reawakening, establishment of a Jewish national home in Eretz Israel and Jewish participation on an equal footing with other nations in what he construed to be the great social tasks confronting humanity. Hess elaborated these views in his 1862 book *Rome and Jerusalem*, the reference to Rome being to the recent reunification of Italy under the leadership of Garibaldi and Cavour and its value as a model for Jewish national rebirth.[16]

It was somewhat more common in the 1890s than in Hess's time to see Western Jews who had attempted to discard their Jewish identity respond to the hostility of surrounding European societies by returning to the Jewish fold. But those who returned were still a small minority and those prepared to embrace Zionism smaller still. Even Western Jews who consistently cultivated and valued their bonds to the community more typically endorsed the view, first articulated by Enlightenment thinkers and other gentile reformers, that Jewish identity should be comprehended as exclusively a religious affiliation and stripped of notions of peoplehood. They maintained that one's sense of national identity ought to be invested entirely in the state of one's citizenship and, accepting and echoing a popular anti-Jewish indictment, that concepts of Jewish peoplehood were somehow inconsistent with loyal national citizenship, and so they were not particularly receptive to Herzl.

Of course, Jews in central and western European nations were confronting a rise in anti-Jewish sentiment despite consistent demonstrations of Jewish good citizenship and Jewish loyalty. Indeed, there was much evidence that Jewish success at assimilating actually exacerbated anti-Jewish feeling. Nevertheless, many Jewish voices insisted that only more emphatic Jewish immersion in European national identities would ameliorate European Jew-hatred. Many Jews in the West consequently responded to Herzl's arguments with hostility, as regressive in their promotion of Jewish national consciousness, in their driving Jews back toward a supposedly premodern communal identity and away from an identity as individual state citizens of the Jewish faith. They argued that Herzl's program was likely to feed the claims of the anti-Semites about Jews being a foreign element and so was a threat to Jewish integration and the acquisition and maintenance of citizen rights.

Much of the hostility Herzl encountered in the West stemmed also from his implicitly tying Western Jews to "Polish" Jewry, that impoverished and, to many Western Jews, primitive and exotic Jewry from which they were eager to distance themselves and with which they felt they had little if anything in common.

There were segments of the community in Russian domains as well that were averse to Zionism. Some took issue with what they saw as its impracticality. Still others were opposed on religious grounds, perceiving it as sacrilegious to contemplate a return to Zion in political terms rather than in the context of religious messianism, as an event to follow only on the appearance of the Messiah. But in the Pale of Settlement there still survived vestiges of Jewish autonomy, a greater social and political dimension to Jewish communality, and a living and positive sense of distinctive Jewish peoplehood;

Enlightenment concepts of citizenship and the weakening of old communal forces were less at play. Consequently, the nationalist idea encountered less of the particular sorts of resistance noted in the West.

THE PLIGHT OF RUSSIAN JEWRY

Despite the greater sense of Jewish peoplehood prevailing among Russian Jews as compared to the Jews of central and western Europe, the exigencies of Jewish life in Russia in the nineteenth century had created substantial fissures in the community. Here too, in the face of intense anti-Jewish pressures from the surrounding society, Jews on one side of communal divides would not infrequently blame those depredations on the ways of the Jews on the other side and would see reform of those other Jews as a panacea that would assuage anti-Jewish sentiment.

The major factor creating and exacerbating divisions in the Jewish community was the czarist policy of choreographing Jewish impoverishment, a policy consistently pursued by czarist regimes throughout the nineteenth century if varying at times in intensity of execution. Jews were banned from some occupations that had long been key fields of employment for them; they were expelled at times from villages and townlets that were at once their homes and the base of their livelihoods; they were often forbidden from moving to other areas of the state to seek employment even as increasing population density meant more and more people competing for fewer and fewer opportunities to earn a living. While the source of the problem was government policy, the inability of the traditional communal leadership to intervene effectively with the government led to extensive alienation from that leadership.

Other anti-Jewish policies by czarist regimes exacerbated this alienation. For example, the primary overarching aim of the government was to push Jews to conversion, and, in addition to using special Jewish schools to this end, the Russian government also formulated in the early part of the century the "cantonal" decrees. These mandated conscription of Jewish males starting at age twelve — some younger children were also inducted — for twenty-five years of service in the Russian military. The children were sent to special preparatory schools and were subjected to starvation, physical abuse, and incessant pressure to convert. Many died from abuse, entire units were forcibly baptized, and suicide was widespread, including instances of mass suicide to avoid forced baptism. Some Jews converted to end the abuse while secretly practicing Judaism; others converted and ultimately merged into the surrounding Christian society. The Jewish community leadership was assigned responsibility for enforcing conscription regulations, and for dispensing the limited exemptions allowed, and the system engendered widespread corruption and exacerbated class tensions within the community.

To some degree, Hasidic institutions and the yeshivot, or religious schools, of the traditionalist rabbis filled the void created by loss of faith in the traditional leadership and became major forces in maintaining community cohesion and exercising what remained of community autonomy. The Hasidic movement split into often competing camps but its leading figures enjoyed wide respect and exercised broad authority, civil as well as religious, in their respective strongholds. The yeshivot became the central force in the daily life of Lithuanian Jewry.

The musar (ethics) movement that evolved in Lithuanian yeshivot placed a major emphasis on the study of ethical and moral behavior and became very popular. It helped counter the corrosive impact of disenchantment with established communal institutions and further reinforced community cohesion.[17]

But the worsening impoverishment of Russian Jewry ultimately ate away at the authority even of these alternative institutions, which could provide no answer to deteriorating conditions. They were impotent in the face of government policies that promoted Jewish impoverishment and had no leverage that might allow them to intercede effectively with hostile czarist regimes.

In addition, some of the religious-civil bodies responded to the maskilim's push for government-sponsored secular education, and to the Russian authority's co-option of that push as a tool in efforts to convert the Jews, by seeking to insulate the community from secular influences and secular learning with a rigidity virtually unprecedented in former ages. This further undermined those institutions' authority, particularly among an increasingly urbanized Jewish population.

That growing urbanization involved primarily cities within the Pale but also, to the small degree permitted by czarist regimes, locations outside the Pale. It evolved in response both to Jews being pushed out of the villages and townlets of the Pale and to the cities containing what limited opportunities there were for employment. Elements of the urbanized Jewish population developed their own ad hoc accommodations of religious orthodoxy to secular life in the city and to secular learning. But other Jews who drifted into the cities responded to the intense pressures on Jews and to the failure of religious institutions to ameliorate the Jews' predicament by adopting a militantly anti-religious perspective. They embraced the view that Jews abandoning their religious beliefs and practices would be the path to their shedding their pariah status and winning acceptance by the wider society.

But while some Jews jettisoned Jewish religious practice and adopted a militant secularism, they, along with most other Russian Jews, still retained a sense of Jewish peoplehood. This reflected primarily their experiences of vestiges of Jewish autonomy and of meaningful social and political dimensions to Jewish communality. This strong sense of peoplehood among Russian Jews was demonstrated in their responses to the ever more aggressive assault on the Jews pursued by the Russian government in the last decades of the nineteenth century.

The assassination of Czar Alexander II in 1881 and ascension of Alexander III ushered in the new anti-Jewish measures, largely under the direction of Alexander III's mentor, Pobedonostsev, head of the ministry responsible for church affairs. Pobedonostsev is widely believed to be the source of the remark to the effect that the core of Russian policy was to have one-third of Russian Jews emigrate, one-third die out, and the remaining third convert to Christianity.[18] The new czar's coronation was followed by widespread pogroms in the Ukraine. These had extensive popular support in a society whose anti-Jewish bigotry had been exacerbated in recent decades by increased economic competition and growing Ukrainian nationalist feeling, but there are also indications that the riots were instigated by Moscow.

The new regime also soon subjected Jews to additional occupational restrictions in commerce, crafts, and the professions, further residential limitations, even within the Pale, and new constraints on education. The last of these likely marks the most dramatic departure from earlier governments, which were hardly benevolent in their policies toward the Jews. In the preceding decades, those regimes had promoted Jewish entry into state secondary schools and institutions of higher learning as a means of integrating the Jews into the society, eroding Jewish cohesiveness and distinctiveness, and, again, facilitating conversion. From the mid-1870s there was some movement away from this policy and expression of concerns that the presence of Jewish students in these institutions was depriving Christians of opportunities. Alexander III introduced for the first time strict *numeri clausi* severely limiting Jewish access to both secondary schools and higher institutions.

Also, military service was once more used as a weapon against the Jews, and, in fact, succeeded in promoting all three government aims of increased conversions and deaths (one or the other being the fate of many conscripts under the particularly harsh conditions reserved for Jews) and increased emigration (to avoid conscription). Very few in Russia raised their voices against the anti-Jewish measures. On the contrary, they had wide popular support, enjoyed the endorsement of the radical Left as well as right-wing groups, and received at least tacit backing from the press and intelligentsia.

Anti-Jewish measures were intensified still further after the ascension to the throne in 1894 of Nicholas II. The government financed anti-Semitic publications, organized local anti-Jewish committees, and, beginning in 1903, choreographed widespread pogroms much more brutal and deadly than those of the 1880s. These continued for four years until, faced with Western condemnation and eager for Western investment, the regime halted the attacks. But the anti-Jewish campaign continued, taking the form in the next decade of, for example, dissemination of blood libels and even a high-profile indictment and trial for ritual murder.

From the early 1880s onward, Jews responded to their worsening predicament in part with a proliferation of Zionist groups, some entirely new and others building on associations established in preceding decades. Even many Russian maskilim, those Jews who had advocated assimilation and immersed themselves in Russian culture only to be confronted with the wider society's hostility and rejection, its virtually universal support of or at least acquiescence in the government's assaults on the Jews, now expressed their disappointment by becoming Zionists. Russian maskilim seem to have been much more likely to answer the wider society's persistent Jew-hatred with a return to their community, including involvement in Zionist organizations, than was the case among their counterparts in the West.

The various Zionist groups had different agendas and often worked at cross-purposes. Some focused on a political program aimed at securing a national homeland. Others emphasized vocational projects reminiscent of those encouraged earlier by the maskilim as a means of facilitating Jewish integration, in particular agricultural endeavors. These were now perceived as necessary for preparing Jews to become a "normal people" in their future national home. Still others stressed cultural preparation, especially the promotion of Hebrew and its dissemination in place of Yiddish as the national language and as the foundation of a revitalized national culture. (The push for Jewish farming and for replacement of Yiddish by Hebrew were both driven in no small part by surrounding societies' denigration of Jewish involvement in trade and of Jewish use of Yiddish, the latter cast as "degenerate" even outside of German-speaking areas where it was seen as a bastardized, corrupt form of proper German.) There were also tensions between religiously Orthodox Zionist groups, most notably Mizrachi, and more secularly oriented organizations. During the last decades of the nineteenth and the beginning of the twentieth century, the different Zionist bodies had only very limited success in establishing and maintaining communities in Eretz Israel, but they did succeed in winning the Zionist concept growing and substantial support among Russian Jews.

In addition to the proliferation of Zionist groups in Russia, the increased pressures on the Jews during the last decades of the nineteenth and early years of the twentieth centuries fostered also the emergence of Jewish socialist organizations.

In Russia, as in the West, there were Jews within the community, especially among the most assimilated, and, even more, Jews alienated from the community, who had embraced socialist ideology. These were people who chose to comprehend Jewish aspirations for equality and an end to bias as related to and dependent on a broader rectification of social injustices through socialist revolution. Or, among the alienated, they were often individuals who chose to regard the Jews as part of the capitalist problem, even echoed socialist anti-Semitism, and immersed themselves in the utopian universalism of socialist ideology. As in the West, the increasing pressure on the Jews drove some of these people to distance themselves even more aggressively from any Jewish identity and embrace with still greater fervor an alternative identity of socialist activists.

For example, some Jews associated themselves with the anti-czarist and anti-Semitic revolutionary group Narodnaya Volya. In 1881, the group called for a popular uprising against the czar, the nobility, and the Jews. Three members of the executive committee that issued the call, and many of the organization's members, were themselves Jews.[19]

But, to a degree unparalleled in Germany or Austria, Jews in Russia who had been attracted to socialism as a cure for social ills became involved in political activism within the Jewish community and helped develop Jewish socialist organizations that had as a major aspect of their agenda the pursuit of Jewish national autonomy or independence. This development, too, reflected the greater cohesion of the Jewish community in Russia, more particularly in the areas formerly Poland and Lithuania and now under Russian control, and the influence of what vestiges of Jewish communal autonomy remained.

In 1897 representatives of such organizations throughout Russia formed the General Union of Jewish Workers in Lithuania, Poland, and Russia, popularly known, from its Yiddish abbreviation, as the Bund. The Bund pursued its political activities in the context of the All-Russia Social Democratic Party, which focused its agenda on the general relief of the working class in Russia through social change. But within this broad coalition the Bund preserved its independence in advocating for the Jewish working class.

Initially this advocacy emphasized gaining civil equality for the Jews, but over time increased attention was given to the national question. At its 1901 conference, the Bund resolved to advocate that Russia become a "federation of nations, each of them with complete national autonomy, independent of the territory on which it resides. The conference recognizes that the term 'nation' also applies to the Jewish people."[20]

The Bund was anti-Zionist, but other groups emerged that combined socialist and Zionist goals in their agendas. These groups varied widely in their relative emphasis of Zionism or socialism, their involvement in domestic politics, and whether they focused their national aspirations on Eretz Israel or were willing to pursue an alternative national home.

Suppression of the 1905 Revolution in 1907 entailed suppression of all the Jewish socialist parties. But all the Jewish parties — the Bund, the Socialist-Zionists, and the Zionist parties — reemerged in dramatic fashion with the February, 1917, revolution, and all demanded Jewish national autonomy. The Zionist parties insisted on both internal autonomy in Russia and Jewish national independence in Eretz Israel. In the months following the revolution, several hundred Hebrew educational institutions were established, as were many publications advocating national autonomy.

In the latter part of 1917, democratic elections were held in Jewish communities across the country for community councils, representatives to a Jewish conference embracing all of Russian Jewry, and representatives to the proposed All-Russian Constituent Assembly. The Zionists gained about two-thirds of the overall votes. During this period the centrist and leftist non-Jewish parties — in particular, the Social Revolutionary Party, the Mensheviks, and the Constitutional Democrats — generally supported the concept of Jewish national and cultural autonomy. Only the Bolsheviks were opposed.

Although the Bolshevik Party had many activists of Jewish origin, its following within the Jewish community was minute and those activists were typically people who were estranged from the community and had essentially abandoned their Jewish identity for an alternative identity as socialist revolutionary. Chaim Weizmann wrote of the contempt with which, for example, Trotsky (born Lev Bronstein) "treated any Jew who was moved by the fate of his people and animated by a love of its history and its tradition. [He] could not understand why a Russian Jew should want to be anything but a Russian. [He] stamped as unworthy, as intellectually backward, as chauvinistic and immoral, the desire of any Jew to occupy himself with the sufferings and destiny of Jewry."[21]

The Bolshevik Revolution in October, 1917, soon quashed the hopes of the Jewish parties. The Jewish Conference never convened and the Russian Constituent Assembly, which met in January, 1918, was quickly dissolved by the Bolsheviks. In the same month, the Communists established a Jewish commissariat with the aim of increasing Communist influence among the Jews and fighting the Jewish parties.

The Red Army's campaign in ensuing months against White Army forces and Ukrainian nationalists, who had murdered tens of thousands of Jews in territories that fell under their control, won the Communists some Jewish support. So too did Communist Party statements condemning anti-Semitism. This garnering of support occurred particularly among Left-leaning members of the Jewish socialist parties, and the shift in allegiance of some of these people, together with Bolshevik pressures on the parties, led to the Jewish socialist groups' rapid dissolution. Steps toward liquidating the Zionist parties intensified in 1919, and when an all-Russian Zionist conference met in Moscow in 1920 all the attendees were arrested. Underground Zionist organizations persisted for about a decade despite ongoing persecution and large-scale arrests.

One of the Jewish commissariat's first acts was to seize control of Jewish schools. Subsequently, all Jewish religious institutions were closed and the teaching of Hebrew to children was prohibited. Other Jewish communal structures were also suppressed and even charitable institutions such as orphanages and hospitals were seized. The democratically elected community councils were, of course, dissolved. Within a few years virtually all vestiges of Jewish communal autonomy had been eradicated. (Some Jewish religious activity persisted despite all the Soviet measures against its practitioners, most notably among the Habad Hasidim.)

Opponents of the Bolsheviks both within and outside the Soviet Union, certainly the anti-Semites among them, commonly labeled Bolshevism a Jewish phenomenon during these and subsequent years, even as the Communists were aggressively suppressing Jewish identity and persecuting Jews who sought to preserve that identity. Anti-Communists would point to the presence of numerous individuals of Jewish origin in the cadres of the party, very likely in numbers exceeding those of their presence in the general population, and to the achievement by some of very elevated positions in the party, obviously achievement of an order far beyond anything accessible to Jews in czarist regimes. But those of Jewish origin who immersed themselves in party activity were almost invariably Jews alienated from the Jewish community and aggressively seeking to dissociate themselves from it and to cultivate an alternative identity. Many were individuals not only indifferent to but actively hostile to all things Jewish, even harboring Jew-hatred of the dimensions one finds in Marx.

The Jewish Immigrant Community in the United States

The large numbers of Jews who emigrated to the United States during this period encountered stresses and difficulties common virtually to all immigrant groups as well as additional problems peculiar to them, including what there was in the United States of anti-Jewish animus at the time. The responses of the immigrants, and of the established Jewish community, to pressures from the surrounding society mimicked in various ways Jewish reactions to such stresses in Europe.

Whereas Jewish migration out of the former Poland-Lithuania prior to 1880 mainly entailed movement within the three partitioning powers, the period 1880–1914 saw large-scale migration westward, most notably to the United States. Over 2.5 million Jews left eastern Europe during these years, about two million going to the United States. The great majority fled Russia, eager to escape both the increased persecution to which the Jews were subjected during these years and the ever deepening and increasingly inescapable poverty to which the Jews had been reduced by czarist policies.[22]

During these years other groups also emigrated in large numbers to the United States, particularly from eastern Europe and Italy. But the Jewish migration was distinctive in a number of ways. It comprised a higher percentage of the source population than did other immigrant groups. It was, much more so than other groups, a migration of entire families; the percentage of children among Jewish immigrants was more than twice that in other groups. It was also much more a permanent migration. In the years immediately preceding World War I immigrants from other groups returned to their countries of origin at a rate about six times greater than did Jews. (About one-third of other immigrants returned.)[23]

The Jews were also the most impoverished immigrants, ranking last among all groups in the amount of money per capita with which they arrived in the United States. About one-half of the Jewish arrivals of working age had no defined occupation, as compared to one-quarter of other immigrants. (In contrast, about a third of the Jews were skilled craftsmen, compared to 20 percent of other immigrants.)[24]

The Jewish immigrants were also distinguished by the manner in which elements of their experience in America, and their responses to their new situation, recapitulated in significant ways both the tribulations to which the Jews had been subjected in Europe and Jewish reactions there. Aspects of these distinctive experiences and responses can be seen in tensions between the new Jewish immigrants and Jews who had arrived earlier and in stresses within the communities of new Jewish arrivals.

To be sure, one would expect to see dynamics characteristic of marginalized, unacculturated, and at least to some degree denigrated minorities at work within the communities of other immigrant groups as well. Indeed, evidence of such dynamics within other groups abounds in the historical record.

Some modicum of hostility was encountered by a number of immigrant groups. Whatever U.S. government policy at the time in opening America's gates to these new waves of immigrants, there was also much populist anti-immigrant sentiment in the country. Even more pronounced within the general populist feeling was anti-Catholic sentiment. This was directed particularly at the time against the large numbers of Polish and Italian Catholics entering the United States.

Moreover, many earlier immigrants from both countries, and from other nations of immigrant origin, responded to the new arrivals from their own mother country with some degree of ambivalence, distaste, and even resentment. These reactions were born of such factors as fear that the new arrivals would exacerbate antagonism toward the particular groups who figured prominently in recent immigration and would thereby make life more difficult for members of those groups who had arrived earlier. Another, related, factor was discomfort, perhaps embarrassment, that new arrivals were imposing on earlier-arrived former compatriots, or at least represented to them, a past that those earlier immigrants were energetically trying to leave behind them in their own efforts at acculturation. Distaste or hostility also derived at times from earlier immigrants having embraced the biases abroad in the wider society, adopting them as part of their own acculturation and now directing them against the newer arrivals.

Obviously, there were many possible permutations and combinations of these dynamics. Even among earlier immigrants who worked to help new arrivals from their own country of origin adapt to their new homes, the motivation to do so was often not simply, or even primarily, philanthropic. Rather the aid was driven at least in part by a desire to speed the new immigrants' acculturation, help them shed as quickly as possible their foreignness, their alienness — so as to render the new arrivals, and themselves as linked to the new arrivals, less obvious targets of hostile sentiment within the surrounding society.

In addition, within all the communities of new immigrants, pressures to acculturate often had a corrosive effect on social cohesion. Families, for example, were exposed to generational stresses brought about by children more easily learning English and more readily picking up the manners and ways of their new society. Children often looked upon their elders with declining respect and even embarrassment, as representing a devalued past of which the young were eagerly and successfully seeking to divest themselves. These people's elders, in turn, would suffer having their former authority and pride of place in family and community slip away with no effective remedy available to them. Whatever hostility the immigrants encountered in the wider society only exacerbated these corrosive dynamics and the resultant familial and communal fissures.

But if the corrosive effects of pressures to acculturate, and also of some degree of hostility from the surrounding society, took their toll within all the communities of new immigrants, and in relations between all the new communities and their compatriots who had arrived earlier, those effects were at work with particular intensity among the Jews.

Several factors rendered relations between the new Jewish arrivals and their co-religionists who had immigrated earlier distinctively troubled. The American Jewish community before the upsurge of immigration in the 1880s consisted predominantly of German Jews. (The earliest Jewish immigration to what became the United States, starting in the seventeenth century and continuing through the eighteenth, was mainly of Sephardic Jews. But descendants of these early Sephardic communities were greatly outnumbered by the nineteenth-century arrivals from Germany and their offspring.) That these people had encountered some anti-Jewish bias in the United States is hardly surprising given that the American population had its origins overwhelmingly in former Europeans, many of whom had brought their biases with them. There was only very limited European-style *de jure* discrimination or government-supported bias, but anti-Jewish prejudice was real. Moreover, as these earlier Jewish immigrants achieved some financial success, they sought but were often blocked from entry into what were the professional and other institutional preserves of America's older elites.

There were parts of the country, especially in the Midwest and the South, where Catholics were more the focus of local hostility. But anti-Jewish feeling was a fact of life. The upsurge in Jewish immigration in the 1880s unleashed an intensification of popular anti-Jewish sentiment, which itself rendered many in the established Jewish community less enthusiastic about the new arrivals.[25] Indeed, a short time earlier, in 1879, the Jewish World Conference in Paris had considered the predicament of eastern European Jews, particularly in newly created states in southeastern Europe, and representatives of the American Jewish community had sought to discourage unrestrained Jewish immigration to the United States.[26]

Given that the new wave of Jewish immigrants did fan anti-Jewish sentiment in the United States, or at least provided grist for the mill of Jew-baiters, fears in the established Jewish community about this consequence of the immigration were hardly delusional. But the categorical perspectives reflected in the response of the established community to the new immigrants, particularly the categorical conviction that the new immigrants' taking on the accoutrements of American ways and divesting themselves of all distinguishing characteristics beyond elements of their faith would assure acceptance, while all foreignness and all particularism would lead to rejection, entailed wishful thinking not borne out by reality. For example, the late nineteen twenties and the nineteen thirties were not a time of new immigration and were rather a period when most American Jews were well along the path of acculturation, and yet those years were marked by an intense upsurge of anti-Jewish feeling triggered by events in Europe and domestic developments beyond the influence of what the Jewish community in America was or was not doing. In a similar vein, the established Jewish community's conviction, in those earlier decades, that its own path was the modern, progressive, enlightened route and any retention of foreign ways or particularist affinities was primitive and passé, was not as anchored in transcendent truth as that community's members chose to believe.

This predilection on the part of the established Jewish community to see Jews on the other side of the immigrant divide as the source of anti-Semitic venom, with salvation lying in their reform, was amplified by differences between the earlier arrivals and the new ones beyond the dates of their immigration. That alienation from and prejudice toward "Polish" Jewry that had been a significant element of the German Jewish community's reaction to German anti-Semitism was in large part carried to America by German Jewish immigrants and shared by them with their descendants. The distinctive tensions separating the older community from the new arrivals in part reflected this divide between German and "Polish" Jewry and entailed ramifications of this divide.

The two groups were separated to a considerable degree by differences in language and culture; not just by the English acquired by earlier arrivals and the native-born but by language of origin and related culture, German versus Yiddish. (Some of the German immigrants had spoken Yiddish, others not.) There were differences in religious belief and practice as well, with the established community largely embracing reformist models of Judaism first developed in Germany and the new immigrants bringing with them a more traditional Judaism. (In 1880, only twelve of two hundred synagogues in America did not identify themselves as Reform. These reformist congregations, while deriving from German antecedents, had evolved to reflect American influences. Reform Rabbi Isaac Wise observed, in the latter part of the nineteenth century, that the quest of Reform congregations to emulate their Protestant neighbors could be seen in their frequently resembling in their practices the locally dominant Protestant denomination: "There were Episcopalian Jews in New York, Quaker Jews in Philadelphia, Huguenot Jews in Charleston . . . everywhere according to the prevailing sect."[27])

There were also dramatic differences in class, with the established community having largely replicated and even surpassed in America the impressive economic success of German Jewry. In contrast, the new immigrant community suffered from what had been the ever worsening, state contrived, impoverishment of "Polish," now Russian, Jewry — an impoverishment, again, exceeding that of other immigrant groups during this period.

Of course, many among the German Jewish immigrants and their descendants had either converted or simply drifted out of the community and abandoned their Jewish identity, immersing themselves in the wider society, perhaps marrying non-Jews and having their children reared in another faith. They had done so under the pressure of anti-Jewish biases, or because they had lost any meaningful connection with the Jewish community and saw little value in retaining their Jewishness even if pressure to give it up was limited. Or they had aspired to positions in the wider society to which anti-Jewish biases represented an insurmountable obstacle and they had valued those aspirations over affiliation with the faith and the community. The reactions being discussed of earlier Jewish immigrants to new Jewish arrivals were essentially the reactions of those who did value their Jewishness and stayed within the community. But, again, the community of which they were a part and which they valued was very different — in religious belief and practice, in cultural tastes and affinities, in social and economic status — from the new arrivals. The attitude of many in the older, German Jewish, community toward the new arrivals is captured in the statement in the *Hebrew Standard* that, "The thoroughly acclimated American Jew . . . has no religious, social, or intellectual sympathies with them. He is closer to the Christian sentiment around him than to the Judaism of these miserable, darkened Hebrews."[28]

With regard to religious differences between the two Jewish communities, just as German Jewry had adopted religious reforms of various stripes to render themselves more acceptable to the surrounding population, so too the established American Jewish community tended to perceive its reformist beliefs and practices as "American" in ways adherence to traditional Judaism could not be. The Reform Rabbi Isaac Mayer Wise, comparing reformist Jews to those who cling to traditional practice and belief, stated this explicitly: "We are American and they are not."[29]

As in Germany, a major element of religious reform within the established Jewish community in America, again inspired by the desire to make itself more acceptable to the wider society, was renunciation of the concept of Jewish peoplehood and of liturgical focus on national Return. For example, Reform Rabbi Kaufman Kohler wrote that, "To pray for a return to Jerusalem" was unacceptable.[30] Many in the established community therefore viewed as an intolerable threat both the new immigrants' traditional messianic hopes and their general assumption of Jewish peoplehood, an assumption born not only of traditional Jewish comprehensions but also of political sensibilities related to the recent immigrants' experiences in eastern Europe of communal cohesion and relative self-sufficiency. No less intolerable to much of the established community, of course, were the Zionist sympathies that many of the new immigrants brought with them from eastern Europe.

Along with its renunciation of Jewish peoplehood and of aspirations to national Return, the reformist credo embraced by much of the established American Jewish community echoed reformist themes in Germany also in what it embraced as alternative aspirations. It too sought to redefine the Jewish vocation in terms of a worldwide mission to promote moral and ethical improvement in the human condition. It too strove to vest Jewish messianic hopes in establishment of such a better world and to strip Judaism of all that is particularist in it. A 1909 resolution by leaders of the Reform movement declared Israel's mission to be to advance "among the whole human race . . . the broad and universalist religion first proclaimed by the Jewish prophets."[31]

As noted earlier, such a comprehension of the Jewish vocation, as a light unto the nations, obviously has an ancient pedigree, but in earlier eras it was essentially inward-focused and was understood as complementing rather than replacing aspirations to national Return. In this modern context, however, it was understood as a substitute for national aspirations and was largely outward-focused, another aspect of accommodation to the wider society, even if its promoters, as in Europe, typically cast it as representing a more modern, more ethical and humanitarian, comprehension of the Jewish mission. From the perspective of this reformist tenet as well, the inward-focused traditionalist beliefs of the immigrants, together with the Zionist sympathies of many, were viewed with dismay.

Efforts to eschew Jewish "particularism" in an attempt to demonstrate to the larger society Jewish devotion to wider social and political agendas were as much a concern of the German Jewish community in America as they were of Jews in Germany and went beyond reforming some elements of religious belief. Leaders of the preeminent German Jewish congregation in New York, Temple Emanuel-El, articulated a policy that it is "a mistake for Jews to act together for social and political purposes."[32]

Against this perspective predisposing much of the established community to avoid political and social exertions that were "particularist," and against the eagerness of much of the community to distance itself from the new immigrants, stood the impoverishment and more generally difficult straits of the new arrivals. In fact, many in the established community did extend substantial help to the new immigrants. Some did so out of purely philanthropic impulses and a desire to aid their co-religionists. Others were eager to see the new arrivals acculturate and assimilate into the wider society as quickly as possible in the hope that their doing so would diminish the increase in shrill anti-Jewish sentiment and rhetoric that was triggered by the upsurge in Jewish immigration. In the view of much of the established community, that increased Jew-bashing was exacerbated by the immigrants' poverty and alien appearance and ways. Many of those who extended help were no doubt moved both by philanthropic impulses and by their own anxieties and an eagerness to address what they saw as the new arrivals' undermining of their own position in the wider society. An article in the *American Hebrew* stated: "All of us should be sensible of what we owe not only to these . . . co-religionists, but to ourselves who will be looked upon by our Gentile neighbors as the natural sponsors for these, our brethren."[33]

The established community's concerns about the negative impact the new immigrants were having on the wider society's attitudes toward Jews inspired steps beyond simply seeking to hasten the acculturation and assimilation of the new arrivals. The established community also sought to assure that its voice, rather than any emanating from among the new immigrants, would be the voice of American Jewry heard by the broader society. In 1906, some leading members of the established community founded the American Jewish Committee as a vehicle for articulating American Jewish views. One of the founders, Louis Marshall, gave as a rationale for this self-appointed assumption of overarching communal leadership the argument that, if it were not done, "indiscreet, hotheaded, and ill-considered oratory might find its way into the headlines of the daily newspapers inflicting untold injury upon the Jewish cause."[34] By "indiscreet, hot-headed, and ill-considered oratory," Marshall was clearly referring to the concerns he and his colleagues had regarding voices from among the new immigrants, voices that did not reflect his and his colleagues' Americanized sensibilities.

Efforts by the established Jewish community in America to reform the faith so as to strip it of references to Jewish peoplehood, and its broader exertions to eschew anything suggestive of Jewish particularism in order to render American Jewry more acceptable to the wider society, were consonant to a large degree with what the community, along with other immigrant groups, was hearing from the wider society. Theodore Roosevelt declared: "We can have no fifty-fifty allegiance in this country. Either a man is American and nothing else, or he is not an American at all."[35] Woodrow Wilson, speaking to a group of immigrants in the following decade, stated, "You cannot become thorough Americans if you think of yourself in groups. America does not consist of groups. A man who thinks of himself as belonging to a particular national group in America has not yet become an American."[36]

Yet it is very likely that Jews, both within the established community and among the new arrivals, took to heart the warning against divided loyalty to a degree other groups — although hardly impervious to pressures to divest themselves of their former identities — did not and sought self-consciously to redefine themselves in an effort to win acceptance to an extent other groups did not. They did so both because of the recent legacy of their experiences in Europe and because of the particular, anti-Jewish bias and particular challenges they encountered in the United States. They did so in response to pressures, even as they cast their actions as high-minded and progressive and as the abandonment of an intrinsically inferior self-comprehension for an intrinsically superior one. It is perhaps significant in this regard that it was a Jew, Israel Zangwill, who coined the phrase "melting pot," with its comprehension of becoming an American as a process entailing the laudable cooking out of all ethnic and national differences related to people's origins.

Efforts within the established community to eschew "parochialism," whether in religious belief or in social and political action, were not universally endorsed. The most notable and prominent exception at the time to this predilection was Louis Brandeis, who in 1916 became the first Jew to be appointed to the U. S. Supreme Court. Brandeis dissented from those who viewed Zionist sentiment as reflecting a divided loyalty, or at least an appearance of divided loyalty, which Jews needed at all cost to avoid. On July 4, 1915, he delivered a commemorative speech whose context was clearly the upheaval of the war then being waged in Europe and the demands for self-determination by Europe's minorities that had preceded the war and would need to be addressed in its aftermath. Brandeis declared, "The new nationalism adopted by America proclaims that each race or people, like each individual, has the right and duty to develop, and that only through such differentiated development will high civilization be attained"[37]; and he construed Zionism as consistent with this American perspective.

It is in this context that, in another address the same year, Brandeis posed the question, "While every other people is striving for development by asserting its nationality, and a great war is making clear the value of small nations, shall we [Jews] voluntarily yield to anti-Semitism, and instead of solving our 'problem' end it by noble suicide?"[38] He also argued, "Let no American imagine that Zionism is inconsistent with Patriotism . . . Every Irish American who contributed towards advancing home rule [in Ireland] was a better man and a better American for the sacrifice he made. Every American Jew who aids in advancing the Jewish settlement in Palestine . . . will likewise be a better man and a better American for doing so . . . Indeed, loyalty to America demands rather that each American Jew become a Zionist."[39] This was especially so, Brandeis elaborated, as "The Jewish spirit, the product of our religion and experiences, is essentially modern and essentially American. Not since the destruction of the Temple have the Jews in spirit and in ideals been so fully in harmony with the noblest aspirations of the country in which they lived."[40] From this perspective, as he succinctly put it in another speech around the same time, "To be good Americans, we must be better Jews, and to be better Jews, we must become Zionists."[41] Brandeis persistently reiterated the same themes in subsequent years.

But, among prominent Jewish Americans at the time, Brandeis was virtually alone in articulating such views, and he was criticized by other members of the German Jewish elite for his stance. Much more common within the Jewish leadership were fears that Brandeis's declarations of Jewish peoplehood and his encouragement of Jewish group loyalty would trigger an increase in anti-Semitic sentiment. *New York Times* publisher Adolph Ochs, hewing to the line adopted by Jews in the face of anti-Semitic assertions in Germany and elsewhere in Europe that Jews represented an alien nation, insisted Jews must eschew all ethnic or "national" group identity. Ochs wrote, "I'm interested in the Jewish religion — I want to see that preserved — but that's as far as I want to go," and he attacked Brandeis for having become "a professional Jew."[42]

Just as tensions between the new Jewish immigrants and the established Jewish community were in various respects more intense and corrosive than those between other recent immigrants at the time and their compatriots already established in America, so too do stresses within the immigrant Jewish community appear to have been distinctively more intense than those within other groups.

Again, other immigrants too found themselves in the position of being marginalized, unacculturated, and to some degree denigrated minorities and endured the corrosive effects of such a predicament. Among the difficulties shared by many immigrant communities was, once more, the undercutting of family and community cohesion that followed from the circumstance of children more rapidly learning English and in general — through experiences in the schools and the streets — more quickly adapting to their new culture. The children's elders lost that command of their environment that had been theirs in their former homes, typically had greater problems in adjusting, and indeed often became dependent to some degree on their children for navigating the new environment. Consequently, they lost much of their former authority in the eyes of their children and not infrequently lost self-respect as well, and many families and communities were rent by forces that defied repair. But among Jewish immigrants these common familial and communal dynamics were exacerbated by several factors.

The particular poverty of the Jewish immigrants and their difficulties extricating themselves from their poverty further sapped the authority of elders in the eyes of their children. In eastern Europe, too, in the Pale of Settlement, Jewish communal institutions had lost authority in part because of their inability to intervene effectively to address the severely straitened circumstances to which much of the community had been reduced by Russian government policies, and this translation of impoverishment into diminished authority recurred in America.

But Jews in the Pale lived in predominantly, often almost exclusively, Jewish villages, towns, and cities, even after their expulsion from many of the villages and townlets, and saw most of those around them sharing their predicament. In addition, they generally found little alluring in the non-Jewish communities with which they interacted. These circumstances mitigated to some degree the divisive impact on community and family of corrosive forces and encouraged the development of alternative Jewish institutions that might more effectively address communal problems. In contrast, in the environment of their new lives in America, the young had many opportunities to be exposed to conditions of life much more attractive and alluring than those of their impoverished homes, a situation that reinforced the divisive impact of negative forces at work in family and community.

The anti-Jewish sentiment that they routinely encountered outside their home or immediate neighborhood was experienced by many as yet another downside to an identity that they in any case associated with the foreign and unacculturated and with poverty, a downside that further distinguished the corrosive forces within the Jewish immigrant community. Many of the young responded by turning away, in varying degrees, from both faith and community, in pursuit of assimilation and acceptance into American society. Those who did so typically perceived their path as leaving behind inferior, tainted affiliations for the accoutrements of a superior and more wholesome identity.

FIVE

The War Between the Wars

Every prejudice one thinks disposed of breeds a thousand others, as carrion breeds maggots. Vain to present the right cheek after the left has been struck. It does not move them to the slightest thoughtfulness; it neither touches nor disarms them; they strike the right cheek too. Vain to interject words of reason into their crazy shrieking. They say: He dares to open his mouth? Gag him! Vain to act in exemplary fashion. They say: We know nothing, we have seen nothing, we have heard nothing. Vain to seek obscurity. They say: The coward! He is creeping into hiding, driven by his evil conscience. Vain to go among them and offer them one's hand. They say: Why does he take such liberties, with his Jewish obtrusiveness? Vain to keep faith with them, as a comrade-in-arms or fellow citizen. They say: He is Proteus, he can assume any shape or form. Vain to help them strip off the chains of slavery. They say: No doubt he found it profitable. Vain to counteract the poison. They brew fresh venom. Vain to live for them and die for them. They say: He is a Jew.
  Jakob Wassermann, *My Life as a German and a Jew* (1921)[1]

Almost no Jew could make a free, personal decision about his education and career. At every turn, the fact of his Jewishness meant that many, if not most, options were simply not available to him.
  Arthur Hertzberg, on the situation of Jews in the
  United States in the period before World War II[2]

HOPES DASHED IN EASTERN EUROPE

The years between the world wars saw a broad intensification in Europe and elsewhere of anti-Jewish bigotry. This increased hatred was expressed both in popular Jew-baiting and in governmental imposition of *de jure* and *de facto* measures against Jews. Once again a major aspect of the Jewish response to such pressures was embrace of anti-Jewish indictments and acting out of fantasies of winning over the indicters by ingratiating self-reforms, whether that entailed reform as Jews or reform by abandonment of the Jewish community.

A number of events in 1917 had initially raised the prospect of better times for Jews in eastern and central Europe. The autocratic czarist regime was over-thrown in the February revolution. America's entry into the conflict and President Wilson's proclamation of his "Fourteen Points" also served to ignite widespread hopes. Wilson's program offered self-determination and independence for the peoples living in the empires of central and eastern Europe. But it also promised international guarantees of the rights of minorities within the nations to be carved out of those empires and a League of Nations to assure the coming peace and its arrangements. The Jews took heart as well from Britain's issuance of the Balfour Declaration giving support to the creation of a Jewish homeland in Eretz Israel and from the broad international backing extended to the British proposal.

But by the time the victorious allies convened the Paris Peace Conference, in early 1919, Jewish hopes were already clouded by recent events. Following the Bolshevik Revolution in October, 1917, the new rulers of Russia had quickly undertaken their assault on Jewish political and other institutions. Elsewhere in the East, most notably in the Ukraine, widespread pogroms that grew in some areas to a virtual campaign of annihilation had already killed thousands of Jews. (Between 1917 and 1920, some 75,000 Jews were murdered in the Ukraine.) Yet Jewish delegations from throughout Europe and from the United States attended the Peace Conference still hopeful of being able to lobby effectively for international protection of Jewish rights and interests, particularly in central and eastern Europe.

The efforts to establish and guarantee Jewish and other minority rights in the new nations of eastern Europe ultimately failed. Wilson and others were aware of the history of dominant powers in the region having earlier enforced restrictive and discriminatory policies against members of minority groups, including the Jews, and having pursued the eradication of minority cultures and languages. They saw the need to extend protections and guarantees to the minorities. But the Peace Conference's attempts to do so proved grossly inadequate. The Supreme Council of the Peace Conference established, in May, 1919, a Committee on New States and for the Protection of Minorities, which was charged with drawing up treaties with the new states that would include guarantees of minority rights, with the Jews recognized as a distinct minority community. But the resulting treaties included no provision for monitoring compliance or for implementing sanctions in response to violations. Rather, minority issues were designated to be within the purview of the League of Nations and complaints were to be addressed to the Permanent Court of International Justice in The Hague.

Moreover, the League of Nations subsequently established rules whereby complaints on behalf of minorities could only be brought by member nations or by recognized organizations. While several Jewish bodies were among the organizations recognized by the League, the Jews of eastern Europe were at a distinct disadvantage compared to other minorities in not having a sovereign state, a League member, controlled by their kin and able to advocate for them. The weakness of the Jewish situation was demonstrated by the fact that most of the new states refused to recognize the Jews as a distinct minority to which minority protections applied. The only new state readily to acknowledge the Jews as a national minority was Czechoslovakia, and even this was due essentially to anti-minority sentiment. (The Jews in Czech areas were mainly German-speaking, those in Slovakia Hungarian-speaking. Certain regional autonomous rights were dependent on the percentage of a minority in the regional population, and the Czechoslovak government therefore preferred to have the Jews counted separately rather than included, on the basis of language, in the count of ethnic Germans and Hungarians.)

All of the new nations contained significant minority populations and in all areas there was a history of hostility and competition over the past century or more between the majority group and both local minorities and the former imperial authorities. The newly empowered groups that dominated the new nations typically harbored long-standing grievances against other groups and extreme nationalism and chauvinism quickly became the rule. The common attitude among the new nations toward the minority protections enacted by the Peace Conference and made part of the mandate of the League of Nations was that they represented an intolerable assault on the new nations' sovereignty. In the two decades between the wars, abuse of minorities was virtually the rule from the Baltic to the Adriatic, with the Jews being particularly vulnerable and particularly victimized. Pogroms ravaged communities in Poland, Hungary, and Rumania as well as the Ukraine and occurred with government support and media incitement.

The most important state for Jews among the new nations was reconstituted Poland, which inherited the largest Jewish population in Europe. Developments in Poland during these decades, the minority situation in Poland, and the continually worsening predicament of the Jews there, were in many respects representative of conditions throughout central and eastern Europe between the Wars.

Reconstituted Poland, whose borders were not established until 1921, contained about three million Jews (of a worldwide postwar Jewish population of around fourteen million), approximately a tenth of the national population. Another roughly 25 percent of the people living in Poland belonged to other minorities; they were ethnic Germans, Ukrainians, Byelorussians, Lithuanians. Elements of all four of these other minorities had engaged in armed conflict with the Poles, abetted by forces in Germany, the Ukraine, Russia, and Lithuania, and Poland's borders were ultimately determined by the outcome of those clashes.

The Polish government pursued policies that discriminated against all minorities but did so with particular intensity against the Jews. Jews were largely barred from government service. While, in contrast to a number of other states, there was no explicit *numerus clausus* in higher education, Jews were widely excluded from the universities and those admitted were often attacked and driven from campuses. Discriminatory taxation policies were applied to Jewish businesses. Discriminatory examinations were required to practice skilled crafts and were used to bar Jews. Government credit was denied Jews. The government progressively nationalized various industries and dismissed Jews who worked in them.

Poland instituted other anti-Jewish measures as well. One of the reasons Jews suffered more than other minorities in Poland was that the others consisted mainly of small farmers in rural areas and so governmental efforts to "Polonize" government, higher education, commerce, crafts, and the professions were targeted mainly against the Jews.

There had also been a history over the previous century and a half of an upsurge in anti-Jewish actions by Polish populations and leadership whenever imperial powers had allowed some autonomy in Polish territories. For example, measures against the Jews became chronic in Galicia from the time that Austria granted the Poles administrative autonomy there in 1866. (This may have accounted for the uniquely high level of Jewish emigration from Galicia in the last decades of the century.) In areas of Russian dominance, the semi-autonomous Duchy of Warsaw, created in 1815, had likewise instituted aggressive anti-Jewish policies, imposing disabilities that in various ways exceeded those in areas directly administered by Russia. This persisted until autonomy ended in the wake of the failed 1863 Polish rebellion, when the territories were fully absorbed administratively into Russia.

Anti-Jewish policies similar to those pursued in reconstituted Poland were introduced throughout eastern and central Europe; in the Baltic States, Czechoslovakia, which was the most "liberal" state in the region, Austria, Hungary, Rumania, and even Greece. What checks there were on measures against the Jews came from the influence of Western governments which protested abuses and could exert some economic, political, and cultural clout. But with the rise of Nazism, the influence of the Western democracies declined and the Eastern nations now had the model of Nazi policy to follow in their own anti-Jewish measures. From 1935 onward, state after state adopted Nuremberg-type laws, and pogroms again swept Poland and other lands of eastern Europe.[3]

Jewish Responses in the East

In these years between the wars, there were again Jews in the East who responded to the stresses of anti-Jewish bias and depredations by taking to heart elements of the anti-Jewish litany of the surrounding societies. If they nevertheless remained attached to the community, they often sought internal reform to address the dominant society's indictments. Alternatively, they strove to excise from themselves what they saw as the faults that drew the ire of the larger society and to separate themselves from the community that embodied those faults. They chose to exchange their Jewish identity for another by self-reform, detachment from the community, and immersion in the surrounding society. But as in the past, particularly in reconstituted Poland and Lithuania, several factors made these responses less common and widespread in the East than they were elsewhere.

The strength of communal institutions was, again, particularly important. Where Jewish institutions had weakened in the East, whether due to internal dynamics or those institutions' inability to serve the community effectively in the face of deteriorating political, social, and occupational conditions, those structures were typically superseded by new ones that took on the strength of earlier institutions and continued to foster communal cohesion. New structures such as Jewish labor unions, artisans' cooperatives, and political parties served as successor bulwarks against the corrosive effects of the anti-Jewish messages broadcast so incessantly and insistently by the surrounding society.

Related to this impact of strong communal institutions and concomitant cohesiveness, both a consequence of them and at the same time reinforcing them, was the circumstance that most Jews did not find the surrounding societies, their people and those people's lives, so alluring as to abandon their own community to become part of them. Such allure is always predicated not simply on the assets of the surrounding society but also on the perceived weaknesses and inadequacies of one's own group, and perceptions of the latter are based not only on exposure to the larger society's indictments but on the failure of the minority group to offer its young an attractive enough alternative. This was much less the case in the Jewish communities in eastern Europe than elsewhere.

The size of the community, again particularly in Poland, and its living in large part separate from the surrounding society also contributed to this cohesiveness of the Jewish community. Much of the Jewish population still lived in towns and villages that were largely Jewish. Even in the big cities the Jews constituted a very substantial proportion of the population, often a third or more, and lived in their own neighborhoods.

Jewish political activity in eastern Europe between the wars, particularly in the old Jewish heartland of what had earlier been Poland-Lithuania, was organized overwhelmingly around Jewish political parties, parties that were affiliates or successors of the earlier strong and influential Jewish communal institutions in these areas. Jewish political parties ranged from Agudah — ultra-Orthodox and non-Zionist — to the Orthodox Zionist party Mizrachi, the Zionists, the socialist-Zionist groups, and the anti-Zionist labor movement, the Bund.

The various Zionist groups were the political parties that enjoyed the most support within the Jewish population of eastern Europe. In Poland, the Bund garnered extensive support as well by virtue of its energetic trade-union activity. Its strong anti-Communist stance also won favor among those — the vast majority of Polish and other eastern European Jews — committed to Judaism and the Jewish community.

All parties engaged in communal work, including education and support of charitable and other institutions, in the face of the social and economic depredations of the Eastern regimes. Much of the communal activity of the Zionist parties revolved around preparing people for emigration to Eretz Israel, despite severe British restrictions on immigration. This preparation included training in agricultural work and other vocational endeavors and the mastering of Hebrew.

Jews did play a disproportionate role in Communist parties in the East, which operated essentially underground. But those who joined the Communists represented a very small proportion of the community and were typically, again, Jews who were unaffiliated and estranged from the Jewish community and so were undeterred by the Soviet Union's anti-Jewish policies. While no doubt the persecution endured by Jews living under the reactionary regimes of the East contributed in leading some among them to believe that only a radical restructuring of society could right prevailing social and political wrongs, those who valued the community and the faith looked elsewhere for solutions. It was particularly individuals who sought to divest themselves of their Jewish identity and to take on another, as champion of the proletariat or as utopian internationalist, that gravitated to Communism.

The appeal of the Communists increased somewhat within the Jewish community during the late nineteen thirties, when the Western democracies did nothing to rein in the Nazis and it seemed that only the Soviet Union and the Communists were prepared to oppose Hitler's regime. But the Hitler-Stalin pact of 1939 put an abrupt end to this attraction for most people outside the circle of those who were so detached from the Jewish community and Jewish concerns that their Communist sympathies were little affected by this Soviet accommodation with Nazism.

No Refuge

The ultra-nationalist regimes of eastern Europe would have been glad to be rid of their Jews through emigration, but the Jews had no place to go. For all that seems familiar in the Jewish predicament between the wars, a reprise of earlier, long-recurring torments, in fact there was much that was distinctive and unusual. For example, large-scale assaults on the Jews in earlier eras were typically not promoted by national rulers. They were, rather, popular mob assaults, often organized by leaders drawn from the lower ranks of the clergy, or were instigated by the urban entrepreneurial class, or at times by nobility at odds with the Crown. (The instigation of pogroms by czarist governments in Russia were likewise a modern break with earlier patterns in Europe.) Rulers typically saw the Jews as assets and, whenever the Jews' usefulness seemed to have been exhausted, rulers would simply expel them.

In addition, there was most often someplace else for the Jews to go, some other jurisdiction that saw potential gain in allowing in the Jews. This was in large part the case even in the decades before World War I. But the situation changed dramatically in the war's wake.

Britain had already sharply curtailed Jewish immigration well before World War I, in response to anti-immigrant, and often distinctly anti-Semitic, sentiment in both the Conservative and Labor parties. Only the liberals in Britain had favored continued immigration. France began to impose severe limitations on Jewish entry shortly after the war. The major force in France militating for restrictions was the socialist labor unions, which claimed to be concerned that an influx of low-paid Jewish workers would compromise union gains. But the most important policy changes in the West were those of the United States, which had been the primary haven for Jews fleeing the East in the decades before the war. Laws limiting immigration and particularly affecting the Jews were enacted in 1921 and, in even more restrictive form, in 1924.

The impact on Jewish immigration was dramatic. From the turn of the century until the start of World War I, about 1.3 million Jews had immigrated to America. In the twenty years between the wars, despite the horrendous circumstances under which the Jews lived in the East, their eagerness to leave, and the eagerness of the eastern European nations to be rid of them, only 400,000 arrived in the United States. Even more dramatic was the drop in immigration after passage of the more restrictive 1924 limits. From 1926 to 1938, which encompasses, of course, the rise of Nazism, the accompanying heightened persecution of Jews throughout central and eastern Europe, and ever-mounting Jewish desperation to flee Europe, only 115,000 Jews were allowed into the United States.

What should have been an obvious refuge for eastern and central European Jews, the Jewish national home in Eretz Israel mandated in 1922 by the League of Nations, likewise admitted only limited numbers of Jews during the two decades between the wars. The many new nations created from Russian, Austro-Hungarian, and German imperial lands in eastern and central Europe had immediately been independent; but the new national entities carved out of the Turkish Empire in the Levant had all been placed under the control of mandatory authorities, which were charged by the League of Nations with fostering national development prior to the granting of independence. These entities included a French mandate to create an Arab nation in Syria (covering territory that subsequently became Syria and Lebanon), a British mandate for creation of an Arab state in Iraq, and the British mandate for creation of a Jewish national home in what became known as Mandate Palestine. But from the time of the allied nations' endorsement of the mandate for the Jewish national home, in 1920, the British had been backtracking on their mandatory obligations.

In 1921, even before League of Nations ratification of the Mandate, Britain detached about 75 percent of Mandate Palestine to create a new Arab nation of Transjordan. Although Transjordan formally remained part of Mandate Palestine until the end of the mandate in 1947, its territories were closed to Jews. In 1923, Britain also detached the Golan Heights from the Mandate and ceded it to the French Mandate in Syria in exchange primarily for French concessions regarding Iraq. Extensive Jewish landholdings on the Golan, much of them purchased by the Rothschilds to establish Jewish agricultural communities, were subsequently nationalized by Syria after that country won its independence from France in 1946.

Even more significant for Jewish immigration than the shrinking of the territories presumably open to the Jews was the hostility of the British administration in Mandate Palestine to the Jewish community generally and Jewish immigration in particular. The League of Nations mandate called for Britain to promote "close settlement" of the land by Jewish immigrants; the British administration was determined to do no such thing.

Both the military and civilian elements of the initial British administration were drawn largely from the British colonial apparatus in Cairo and were generally sympathetic to the Arabs and hostile to the Jews. Churchill, colonial secretary at the time and the person who choreographed the creation of Transjordan, estimated that 90 percent of the British military in Palestine were opposed to Britain fulfilling its Mandate obligations to the Jews.[4] The civilian echelons were so recalcitrant that Churchill circulated a memorandum to the Cabinet in 1921 suggesting "the removal of all anti-Zionist civil officials, however highly placed."[5]

This anti-Zionist animus had various sources. In part it was an expression of anti-Semitic sentiment in the colonial ranks. It also reflected a favorable and largely patronizing view of the Arab population of the Middle East, particularly a self-deluding belief that the Arabs welcomed the British presence throughout the Middle East, including in Mandate Palestine, and would be more pliable than the Jews in acquiescing to the perpetuation of British control.

The authorities in the Mandate immediately began clashing with the government in London, which was generally more committed to fulfilling Britain's undertakings to the Jews. But the local authorities, being the force on the ground, wielded tremendous power to undermine the Mandate. One device used by the administration from as early as 1919 was that of the *agent provocateur*, with British agents encouraging Arab assaults on Jews. The administration would typically have British forces refrain from intervening to end the attacks, and at times even prevent available Jewish forces from doing so. The authorities would then communicate to London that the attacks demonstrated Arab hostility to the Zionist enterprise, that the administration was incapable of controlling such outbursts, which might ultimately get entirely out of control, and that the only solution was for London to retreat from its commitments to the Zionists.

One British officer in Palestine, exceptional in his sympathy for the Jews, wrote of Arab attacks on the Jews and of the administration's machinations: "The anti-Jewish outbreak . . . was carefully fostered, and the hooligan element amongst the Arabs openly encouraged to acts of violence by certain individuals who, for their own ends, hoped to shatter the age-long aspirations of the Jewish people . . . There can be no doubt that it was assumed in some quarters that when trouble, which had been deliberately encouraged, arose, the Home Government, embarrassed by a thousand difficulties at its doors, would agree with the wire-pullers in Palestine, and say to the Jewish people that the carrying out of the Balfour Declaration, owing to the hostility displayed by the Arabs, was outside the range of practical politics."[6]

Sabotaging tactics by various echelons of the administration continued throughout much of the Mandate period and did often weaken resolve in London. Some British governments, those in any case less sympathetic to the Zionist cause, were particularly receptive to anti-Zionist arguments from Mandate authorities. In contrast, when there was a High Commissioner appointed by London who was committed to fulfilling Britain's Mandate obligations and took a clear stand with both the local Arabs and his own administration, the former, seeing less to be gained, diminished their attacks on the Jews, while the latter curtailed its sabotage.[7]

Largely as a consequence of Mandate administration sentiments and machinations, Jewish immigration was closely controlled and limited. In contrast, the administration allowed large-scale and essentially unfettered Arab immigration from surrounding lands. The attraction for Arabs living in neighboring states was mainly the employment opportunities created both by the British authorities and by what Jewish economic development in the Mandate Britain permitted. In the decades between the wars, the total number of Jews admitted to the League of Nations-mandated Jewish refuge from among the oppressed millions trapped in central and eastern Europe was about 330,000.

With the rise of Nazism and the even greater desperation of Jews to flee Europe, and with the dangers to the Jews increasingly obvious, the British responded by ultimately imposing still more severe restrictions on Jewish immigration to the Mandate. Promises by Berlin to the Arabs of Iraq, the Mandate, and Egypt to help them throw off the yoke of British colonial control, and the responsive chord these blandishments elicited among the Arabs, worried London and bolstered the impact of messages from the Mandate authorities that Jewish immigration had to be curtailed to placate Arab opinion. An Arab revolt within the Mandate from 1936 to 1939, instigated by the Grand Mufti of Jerusalem, Amin Muhammad al-Husseini, encouraged by the Nazis, and directed against both the British and the Jews, further reinforced British resolve to impose draconian restrictions on Jewish immigration.

In addition, the stature of the League of Nations had been undermined by its failure to prevent Japanese aggression in Manchuria and China, the Italian occupation of Ethiopia, or German repudiation of the Treaty of Versailles. This weakened the impact of demands from the League that Britain fulfill the terms of the Mandate and made it easier for Britain to renege on its obligations to the Jews. In 1939 Britain issued a White Paper limiting Jewish immigration over the subsequent five years to 75,000, after which all Jewish immigration would be halted. In fact, over the course of the next five years, although there were many Jews who could have made their way to Mandate Palestine despite the war and were desperate to do so, and although for most of that time the British government was fully aware of the Nazis' campaign of genocide against the Jews, Britain did not even allow into Mandate Palestine the White Paper's 75,000.

THE GERMAN-SPEAKING WORLD BETWEEN THE WARS

The increase in anti-Jewish sentiment between the wars was, of course, not limited to eastern Europe. In Germany, well before the rise of Nazism, the already endemic anti-Semitism reached new intensity. Right-wing circles, eager to obscure their own responsibility for the war and its calamities, and those large swathes of the general public that imbibed right-wing claims and were likewise eager for a scapegoat, blamed the Jews for Germany's defeat in the war. They scapegoated the Jews also for the straitened economic circumstances and hyperinflation that wracked postwar Germany, and for the severely punitive sanctions of the Versailles Treaty. The Bolshevik Revolution, and the anti-Semitic propaganda brought to the West by fleeing Russian nobility and white army cadres, many of whom were in fact ethnic Germans, fed the growing equation of Bolshevik with Jew and further inflamed Jew-hatred in Germany.

This welling of anti-Jewish sentiment was not limited in the West to Germany, as demonstrated, for example, by the dissemination and popularity of *The Protocols of the Elders of Zion* throughout western Europe and beyond in the years after World War I. *The Protocols,* cast as a Jewish plan for world domination, was apparently written by the czar's secret police shortly before the turn of the century and plagiarizes almost verbatim an attack on Napoleon III published several decades earlier. It simply substitutes the Jews for Napoleon III as the target of the forgery. It had been in circulation in Russia for about two decades with little impact. But in the wake of the Bolshevik Revolution and World War I, and with the push to its dissemination given by White Russian exiles, it won wide popularity throughout Europe. In Britain and France as well as Germany, right-wing and Catholic Church groups used it to inflame anti-Jewish sentiment in the years of postwar economic difficulties and social unrest.

In France and Britain, as elsewhere in Europe, this increase in hostility toward Jews continued beyond the immediate postwar period. Throughout the decades between the wars, anti-Semitism was, in today's terminology, "politically correct," a staple of opinion not only within right-wing circles or the hardcore Left but virtually across the political spectrum and among all classes. It was embraced in universities and in literary and other artistic circles no less than by the uneducated.

But anti-Jewish sentiment reached a particularly intense pitch in Germany, at a time when the largest community of Jews in central and western Europe, west of old Poland-Lithuania, was still the Jews in the German-speaking world.

Jewish responses there to the worsening anti-Semitism that followed World War I were consistent with earlier Jewish reactions to anti-Jewish sentiment in these areas over the previous century. Many Jews chose to avert their eyes as much as possible to the anti-Semitism around them or sought to comprehend it in ways that diminished its significance. Some, including Jews who remained connected to the community and valued their Jewish identity, continued to blame other Jews, particularly "Eastern" Jews, for the anti-Jewish attitudes in the German world, although this was perhaps somewhat harder to do when a major theme of the postwar anti-Jewish rhetoric was that German Jews had somehow betrayed the war effort.

Another recurrent theme in postwar attacks on Jews was, again, the equation of Jews with Bolsheviks. This reflected not only widespread adoption of White Russian anti-Jewish propaganda but also a concomitant focus on the prominent participation of people of Jewish extraction in postwar leftist uprisings in Bavaria, Hungary and elsewhere. Some Jews in the German-speaking world chose to see the embrace of radical politics by a segment of the Jewish population as the key to the hostility directed against Jews. They chose to ignore the reality that, while "Jews" were overrepresented in the echelons of some

radical groups, the attention given to this, and the Jew-baiting significance attached to it, was more a symptom than a cause of anti-Jewish sentiment. They
chose to ignore that those who dedicated themselves to radical politics represented a very small percentage of the "Jewish" population, were often themselves
"anti-Jewish" in their attitudes, were also far outnumbered by their gentile fellow radicals, and that the misrepresentation of these facts in anti-Jewish propaganda itself demonstrated how much "Jewish" radicalism was less a source of
anti-Semitism than a convenient tool of it.

Many in the Jewish community could no doubt see the distortion in blaming German anti-Semitism on "Polish" Jews or Jewish radicals, and virtually
everyone in the community could see the lie in claims of Jewish betrayal in the
war — a particularly painful lie given the extraordinary war record of so many
German Jews and the large number of Jews who had lost their lives on the battlefield for Germany. (Of a German Jewish population of about 500,000,
92,000 had served in the army during the war, 78 percent at the front. Twelve
thousand were killed in action; 35,000 were decorated for heroism.[8])
Nevertheless, a persistent popular response among members of the Jewish community to the hatred directed against them was to strive to demonstrate even
more clearly their embrace of things German and to avoid even more resolutely
all "particularism."[9] Among its self-deceptions, this tack ignored the reality that
Jewish efforts toward ever more thorough self-effacement as Jews and ever more
comprehensive assimilation often of themselves elicited a negative response from
many in the surrounding society and were themselves fodder for anti-Semites.

Another response by some Jews to the hatred directed against the community in the wake of the war was, of course, as in earlier years, to separate
themselves from the community and often to embrace — even more thoroughly
than those who retained some attachment to Jewish identity — elements of the
broader society's anti-Jewish litany. Once again, many sought to cleanse themselves of what they had come to despise as "Jewish," to assume another identity and to immerse themselves in the wider society, perhaps using intermarriage
to this end and for some using conversion as well. A small percentage of those
who fled the community continued to drift to radical politics, seeking to attach themselves to an imagined brotherhood of the downtrodden and dedicate
themselves to utopian radicalism and choosing to ignore, or to be indifferent
to, the vehemently anti-Jewish rhetoric that was, as before, a fixture of the radical Left.

Certainly, there were also many who continued to see themselves as Jews
and to value their Jewish identity who likewise during these years were attracted
to the Left. They drifted leftward in the face of the anti-Jewish drumbeat and
the failure of centrist and liberal political forces to respond forcefully against
it. But such shifts in sentiment were generally more a reaction against rightist
involvement in fanning the anti-Semitic fires than a reflection of any deeper

attraction to the ideological Left; and the great majority of Jews, even among those disenchanted with politics as usual, did not see succor there. This, however, was likely due as much to the Jews' general disposition to cling to the mainstream as to their attunement to the lack of sympathetic allies on the radical Left.

Again, the most common response among Jews in the German-speaking world to the ongoing indictment and vilification of the Jews was to seek even more eagerly to make themselves German, to assimilate, to separate themselves from what they chose to construe as offensive to the German in the Jew. But both among Jews who retained some attachment to the community and to Jewish identity and among those more alienated from them, not a few ultimately came to the realization, in the face of the hatred around them, that such efforts were in vain. They acknowledged that the tack of embracing anti-Jewish indictments and seeking by self-reform to win acceptance was a doomed course. A number of these people described articulately their chasing after German acceptance, their efforts to remake themselves in answer to anti-Jewish indictments, and the continued rebuffs and rejection and hatred they encountered despite all their exertions and accommodations.

Some of these individuals ultimately responded by finding their way back to a greater connection with the Jewish world and Jewish identity. Others, too removed and alienated from Judaism and the Jewish community — comprehending "Jewish" more in terms of the hostile perspectives that they had absorbed from the surrounding society than of any positive meaningfulness, were left more adrift. They felt in many respects homeless, rejecting the identity of their progenitors and rejected by those with whom they wanted to identify.

In numerous instances those in this latter group ultimately killed themselves. This dynamic figured significantly in the high rate of Jewish suicides in Germany, particularly after the Nazis seized power. It is noteworthy that such suicides also occurred among Jews who had escaped the German-speaking world, the lands under Nazi control, but who carried with them a rootlessness, frustration, and despair over their rejection by those they had wooed. The writer Stefan Zweig and his wife killed themselves in Brazil in 1942. In a final note Zweig wrote, "Now I do not belong anywhere, everywhere a stranger and at best a guest."[10] One historian notes Zweig's attempt to reconnect with his Jewishness five years earlier, in his novella *The Buried Candelabrum*, but observes: "Zweig's affirmation of Judaism is unconvincing. It seems as though the Viennese aesthete who remained indifferent to Jewish facts throughout the first third of the twentieth century . . . wished to record his faith in its continued survival at a time when this survival was being questioned by many. But once this literary document was completed, Zweig resumed his attitude of aloofness from the contemporary currents."[11]

Such suicides were generally different from those of Weininger and people like him, who had literally come to hate the Jew in themselves, found it unexpungeable, and so found life intolerable. These others were typically people who felt they had made themselves Germans, or Europeans, or cosmopolitans, or some other identity not Jewish, but were rejected by those with whom they would identify, those from whom they had sought to win acceptance by their cultivation of an alternative identity. Their despair stemmed from this rejection despite their efforts. But there was, no doubt, some overlap in the two groups. Some among these others no doubt did comprehend the wider world's rejection of them as evidence of something shameful of the Jew still in them that they had not succeeded in expunging.

An example of someone who found his way back to a Jewish identity was the writer Theodor Lessing.[12] This period saw a burgeoning of the literature on Jewish self-hatred and Lessing himself published a book entitled *Jewish Self-Hatred* in 1930. The perception, conveyed by Lessing and common to this literature, is that there is an intrinsically pathological element, a sick self-abnegation, in Jews embracing the anti-Jewish animus of a surrounding society and seeking to divest themselves of their Jewish identity and assume the identity of the dominant group. Such a course, it is argued, can only end in psychological disequilibrium, frustration, and misery. This perception was not infrequently based at least to some degree on the authors' own experiences, and it was so for Lessing. (The writers of this literature were predominantly German-speaking and by and large assimilated Jews.) Lessing's writings offer a vivid picture of someone who had followed the course of, by his own subsequent lights, "self-hatred," had encountered rebuff, rejection, and frustration, and had finally "healed" himself.

Early in his life, Lessing had enthusiastically embraced German nationalism, distanced himself from the Jewish world, even converted to Lutheranism while a university student, and had written disparagingly of Jews, regurgitating popular anti-Jewish themes. For example, writing of a trip to Poland in 1906, he offered an account that echoed anti-Semitic caricatures of Polish Jews: They are filthy, corrupt, degenerate, and hypocritical in their piety. His newspaper articles in which he discussed the trip were ostensibly about the effects of political repression on Eastern Jews, but his focus was on the allegedly ugly nature of Polish Jewry. Elsewhere, he denigrated, in popular anti-Semitic fashion, the cultural contributions of Jews. Lessing's writing in this vein elicited a reproach for his bigotry from Thomas Mann, a non-Jew.[13]

Lessing had earned doctorates in medicine and philosophy, wrote extensively on philosophy and the history of ideas, and pursued a successful teaching career in Hanover, where his family had resided for more than three centuries. In the postwar period, however, he recognized that efforts by Jews such as himself to divest themselves of their Jewish identity and make themselves into Germans did nothing to ameliorate the anti-Jewish animosity of those around them or its rationalizations and pseudo-justifications. He observed in

1930, in *Jewish Self-Hatred*, in the context of the recent Arab massacres of Jews in Palestine and the growing strength of the anti-Semitic right in Germany: "We were told: you are parasites on the land of others — and so we tore ourselves loose. We were told: you are middlemen among the peoples — and so we raised our children to be farmers and peasants. We were told: you are decaying and becoming cowardly weaklings — and so we went into battle and produced the best soldiers. We were told: everywhere you are only tolerated — and we answered: our greatest longing is to be an object of tolerance no more. But when we insisted on maintaining ourselves as a distinct people, we were told: have you not yet learned that your preserving your distinctiveness is treason against all international pan-human values? And so we replied by quietly disbanding the Jewish Legion, by giving up our self-defense, and by placing our just cause under the protection of the European conscience. And what is the result?"[14]

By the time he published his book on Jewish self-hatred, Lessing had reconnected with his Jewish past and become an ardent Zionist and articulate writer on Zionism. He also wrote attacks on the Nazis and, with the Nazi seizure of power, was forced to flee Germany. He and his wife moved to Marienbad in Czechoslovakia. But the Germans posted a bounty on them and, in August, 1933, Lessing was murdered by Nazi assassins.

One of those who was left more adrift by his attempts, in the face of German anti-Semitism, to divest himself of a Jewish identity and take on a more German one, and by the wider society's rebuffs of his efforts, was Ernst Toller. Toller also wrote an enlightening record of his experiences. In his autobiography, *I Was a German*, he describes a painful childhood in which he was derisively taunted by other children for being a "Jew" and relates his "overwhelming joy" on those occasions when he was mistakenly assumed to be an "Aryan."[15] As a young man he sought to free himself of any remnants of a Jewish identity and cultivate an alternative persona. This initially manifested itself in an enthusiastic embrace of German nationalism and an eagerness to participate in the fighting in World War I. Disillusioned by his experiences in the war, he next threw himself into the radical politics of the Left and joined in the leftist Bavarian uprising of 1919. After spending five years in jail for his involvement in the rebellion, he then embraced internationalism and pacifism.

Toller comprehended both his former leftist radicalism and his new politics in the context of a German identity, immersing himself in causes he associated with German colleagues. When, with the rise of Nazism, those around him rejected him for being a Jew even more emphatically than earlier in his life, he felt bereft of any identity, having been scorned by those he sought to cultivate and having no connection with the Jewish world. He had come to this impasse largely by virtue of his absorption of the hatred directed against him as a Jew throughout his life and by his lack of any countervailing attachment to anything Jewish. Toller committed suicide in 1939.[16]

FATHERS AND SONS IN THE GERMAN-SPEAKING WORLD

That path, taken by many Jews in the face of anti-Jewish sentiment in the surrounding society, of separating themselves entirely from the Jewish community and seeking to cultivate an alternative identity, has often been characterized as a rebellion against parents. Abandonment of the community has been comprehended as a repudiation of the faith and values of the preceding generation. Various steps pursued by people disassociating themselves from Jewry, such as converting, or changing one's surname from one's father's to another less Jewish-sounding, are particularly suggestive of a sharp break from, or even repudiation of, parents. (Some name changes seemed to be declaring such a break from Jewish parents with exceptional explicitness, as when the psychoanalyst Eric Homberger, on escaping Nazi Germany and coming to the United States, became Erik Erikson, in effect recasting himself as his own, non-Jewish, creation, the son of his own fathering.[17])

But autobiographies such as Lessing's and Toller's, and the biographies of many others who chose to separate themselves from an embattled Jewish community and assume an alternative identity, suggest also a different, and perhaps more common, dynamic. They point to a dynamic in which the repudiation of one's Jewish identity is less a rebellion against parents than a further step along a path already embarked upon by parents, often indeed a step that was at least implicitly encouraged by parents.

Lessing wrote of knowing virtually nothing of his own Jewishness growing up. This was so much the case that when, as a child — picking up the prejudice of those around him — he had called another child a "Jew" and the other had responded that he himself was one, he did not understand what the other boy meant and responded emphatically that he was not. When he asked his mother about it, she ducked the question. Lessing states, "The word took on a sinister meaning for me. Since I had childishly absorbed all the patriotic and religious prejudices of the school, and there was nothing to counterbalance them at home, I became convinced that being Jewish was something evil."[18]

Toller writes of how his own casting off of his Jewish identity and throwing himself into German patriotism was consistent with his father's enthusiasm for everything German and discomfort with his Jewishness. Toller's mother retained a greater attachment to her Jewish background and Toller saw his course as a repudiation of his mother, but it was still a course to which his father had pointed the way. In the face of the pressures brought to bear on him as a Jew in a hostile society, Toller chose his father's model as the easier and seemingly more promising one.

Parental drift from connection with the Jewish community in response to anti-Jewish animus in the wider society not only predisposed children to a more thorough break from the community and the faith but likely contributed to the attraction of some to the politics of the radical Left. This was likely so even where there was no particular inclination in that direction at home. The parental disconnection from the community and the faith often left a spiritual vacuum at home. Some children who chose to make a more thorough break did so toward another faith, or German nationalism, or both, seeking spiritual, emotional engagement in those directions. But the hostility of the surrounding society toward those of Jewish origin made such choices seem less viable to others, who found the faith of the radical Left, with its promise of a transformed society, more attractive as a source of meaningfulness that filled the spiritual void in their lives. Still others chose to find meaning in an apolitical direction, becoming devotees of science, or culture, or career.

One of the first to write about how estrangement from Judaism and the Jewish community, while perhaps seeming a break from or rebellion against Jewish parents, was often a living out of an at least implicit parental message, was Franz Kafka.[19] Kafka grew up in the German-speaking Jewish community in Prague, a community subject to depredations and bigotry by both its ethnic German neighbors and the surrounding Czech majority. Kafka recognized the spiritual corrosiveness of this Jewish predicament in Prague and was drawn to Martin Buber's message — he heard Buber lecture in Prague — on the greater spiritual integrity, the greater centeredness and sense of self-worth, of Polish Jewry. He was also attracted to Yiddish and responded with particular enthusiasm to the Yiddish theater when he was first exposed to it in 1911.[20]

But when he traveled to Belz in 1915 with his friends Max Brod and Jiri Langer (Langer, who wrote in Czech, had immersed himself in the Orthodox religious community around the rabbi of Belz), Kafka was at once drawn to and repelled by what he saw. He was too acculturated to German Jewish perspectives, including an alienation from Eastern Jewry, to share the enthusiasm of Langer or Buber, or even Brod. He returned to Prague and dedicated his energy to writing in German and in a German mode.

Yet Kafka did not delude himself about his situation as a Jew in Prague, or as a Jew in the German-speaking world. Indeed, the impossibility, the spiritual corrosiveness and intellectual and moral absurdity, of the Jewish predicament, of his predicament, is the theme dealt with metaphorically in, the theme that animates, virtually all of his writing. The Jewish meaning of the stories is never explicit but is not far from the surface. Three of his stories appeared in 1916 and 1917 in Buber's journal, *The Jew,* and one of these, "A Report to the Academy," is a tale of an ape taken out of his natural habitat and transported in a cage to the land of his captors. He decides to leave behind him all connection with his earlier life as a free ape, to no longer aspire to that freedom and no longer cling to his identity as an ape, but rather to adopt the ways of humanity. He learns the manners of his captors in order to escape the confines of his cage and is even able to emulate his captors' discourse. But he is still seen as an ape, an alien creature now liberated from his cage but on display on "the variety stage."[21]

Kafka's other fablelike stories offer variations on the same theme of the absurd but inescapable Jewish predicament. "Investigations of a Dog" is about dogs who are impelled by a communal impulse, drawn to each other, but who are too dispersed and take on alien and even self-destructive ways.[22] Another, "Josephine the Singer, or the Mouse Folk,"[23] tells of hunted mice and is in some respects the most straightforward of his fables in its allusions to Jewish tribulations and Jewish responses. Kafka at times, in his nonfictional writings, uses creature similes to describe the condition of the Jews, similes reminiscent of his fables. A comparison of Jews to caterpillars incapable of effective movement, because "with their posterior legs they were still glued to their fathers' Jewishness and with their waving anterior legs they found no new ground,"[24] reminds the reader of Gregor Samsa in "The Metamorphosis."

Elsewhere in his fiction, Kafka addresses the Jewish predicament in still implicit but nevertheless more straightforward ways, through protagonists done in by an arbitrary, unfathomable and unstoppable hostility. In "The Hunter Gracchus,"[25] the protagonist is dead but doomed to wander the world in a kind of limbo. His plight is not his own fault, but he has no escape from it and no one will help him. In *The Castle*, the protagonist is cut off from all access to a sanctuary.

Joseph K. in *The Trial* has been called "a caricature of [Jewish] deracination."[26] K. has no substantial attachments, personal or professional; he has no full name, no cultural connections, no identity. He seems to trust that his anonymity and intelligence will save him but he is actually defenseless and ultimately accepts his execution without even learning the charges against him. K. is not entirely passive in the face of his ordeal but has stripped himself of all capacity for effective response.[27]

The tremendous popularity of Kafka's work has been due, of course, to readers' perceiving his tales of absurd, soul-corroding, inescapable, and often ultimately dooming situations as metaphors for the human predicament, revelations of existential truth. But they were more immediate tales of Jewish life in central Europe in the early twentieth century as Kafka perceived and experienced it.

Kafka could conjure up images of escape into a Jewish identity, images of immersion in Orthodox or Zionist communality. But these were largely abstractions for him and emotionally he was cut off from such an identity. Again, he was too thoroughly acculturated to his German Jewish milieu. But in discussing being irreversibly blocked from finding his way back to a tenable, meaningful Jewish identity, Kafka notes that this situation is less a drifting away from his father's course, an Oedipal rebellion, than a following of tacitly conveyed paternal direction. In a letter to Brod, Kafka observes, "Most who begin to write in German [that is, seek to pursue a literary career in German] want to flee from Judaism, often with the unclear agreement of the father (and it is this unclarity which is aggravating)."[28] In *Letter to His Father*, Kafka writes of how his father's failure to convey to him very much of his Jewish heritage led to his predicament: "[Your Judaism] was too little to be handed on to the child; it all dribbled away while you were passing it on."[29] What religious observance his father clung to, and introduced his son to, largely entailed going through the motions of rituals in which his father obviously invested little meaning and so taught his son little of their meaning. Deprived of necessary knowledge, Kafka would sit through services bored and fearful of being called to the Torah. His bar mitzvah was "ridiculous learning by heart."[30]

"What sort of Judaism was it I got from you? . . . It was . . . impossible to make a child . . . understand that the few flimsy gestures you performed in the name of Judaism, and with an indifference in keeping with their flimsiness, could have any higher meaning. For you they had their meaning as little souvenirs of earlier times, and that was why you wanted to pass them on to me, but this, since after all even for you they no longer had any value in themselves, was something you could do only by means of persuasion or threats."[31]

Kafka adds that "the whole thing is, of course, not an isolated phenomenon. It was much the same with a large section of this transitional generation of Jews, which had migrated from the still comparatively devout countryside to the towns."[32]

This was the ultimate source, to Kafka's perceiving, of his inability to find his way to a meaningful and enduring Jewish connectedness, for all his sense of painful solitary drifting, for all the allure that such a connectedness had for him and for all his grasping for an anchor in the Jewish world.

Many Jews who sought to immerse themselves in an alternative identity that reflected their having grown up, and been educated, in a German social and cultural milieu, and who subsequently ran up against the wider society's refusal to endorse that alternative identity, came to fathom the apparent impossibility of fulfilling their quest. Many arrived at this point in response to the broader society's Jew-hatred well before the rise of Nazism. Lessing had recognized the at once protean and adamantine nature of German Jew-hatred in the early 1920s, Wassermann's *My Life as a German and a Jew* was published in 1921, and Kafka died in 1924. But even after Hitler's rise to power there were still Jews, even among those who remained connected to the community and placed some value on that connection and not simply among the disaffected and alienated, who chose to ignore the storm clouds. There were still Jews who chose to believe that the unpleasantness would soon fade and who still sought to cultivate their connection to Germany, their German identity. Some among them even chose to see the fault for the unpleasantness in the Jews, typically in other Jews, and to believe that further Jewish self-reform — or, among the alienated, their own distancing themselves further from any Jewish identity — would ultimately set their world right.

THE JEWS IN AMERICA BETWEEN THE WARS

The sharp curtailment of Jewish immigration to the United States after World War I reflected not only general anti-immigrant sentiment and popular support for broad immigration restrictions but more specifically anti-Jewish sentiment and a policy of limiting Jewish arrivals. There had been some militating for such restrictions before the war, but it was particularly in the context of the postwar dissemination in the States of the new European anti-Semitic literature and anti-Jewish canards, most notably those purveyed by White Russian emigrés, with the *The Protocols of the Elders of Zion* being the foremost anti-Jewish tool, that anti-Semitic sentiment became sufficiently mobilized and organized to affect policy.

Most active and effective in circulating anti-Jewish literature in the United States was Henry Ford. In 1920, Ford serialized the *Protocols*, with commentaries, in his newspaper, the *Dearborn Independent*. Later that year, he published an anthology of the *Independent*'s anti-Semitic articles under the title *The International Jew*.[33] White Russian immigrants to the United States also played a role in inciting anti-Jewish feeling. The Ku Klux Klan, which had earlier focused its attacks primarily on blacks and Catholics, now increased its targeting of Jews.

Anti-Semitism in the United States during the postwar period did not reach the intensity of anti-Jewish feeling throughout most of Europe. But it was widely embraced at all levels of society, by educated and cultural elites as well as the general public, becoming a "politically correct" bias in the States as it was in Europe.

The Depression further exacerbated anti-Jewish sentiment as straitened circumstances made many people all the more receptive to anti-Semitic demagogues who blamed the Jews, or Jewish capital, for the nation's problems. The rise of the Nazis, and Germany's pouring of large amounts of money and organizational effort into the United States to establish and support groups dedicated to purveying anti-Jewish propaganda, added another dimension to the assault on the Jews.

In the years immediately before World War II, and in the period from September, 1939, to December, 1941, anti-Semitic and right-wing groups, which were overwhelmingly isolationist, began to attack the Jews, and Jewish support for steps against the Nazis, as warmongering. They argued that the Jews were trying, for their own narrow interests, to drag the United States into another conflagration in Europe. This too hit a responsive chord in segments of the population. The late 1930s was also the era of Father Coughlin, whose anti-Semitic sermons were broadcast on Sunday radio and reproduced in print media and who orchestrated a nationwide anti-Jewish campaign.

Day-to-day consequences for American Jews of this epidemic anti-Semitism went beyond the painful exposure to denigration and vilification. Jews were excluded from many areas of employment, among them some entire industries, such as banking, which accepted virtually no Jews. Jews faced restricted access to universities and professional schools and blackballing from myriad clubs, hotels, and residential areas. Jews in America had been subject to many such prohibitions in previous decades as well, but the institutionalized bias became much more widely established and entrenched in the decades between the wars. Rabbi Stephen Wise observed, "The only profession I know that does not bar Jews is the rabbinical profession."[34] Historian Arthur Hertzberg states that in the pre-World War II period, "Almost no Jew could make a free, personal decision about his education and career. At every turn, the fact of his Jewishness meant that many, if not most, options were simply not available to him."[35]

The response of American Jews to the increase in anti-Semitism and the new exclusionary measures followed the pattern of Jewish reactions in the German-speaking world and elsewhere during the modern era, particularly in situations of weakened communal institutions. Flight from the community increased. Among children of immigrants, the intensification of anti-Jewish sentiment pushed many to separate themselves even more eagerly and definitively from parents who were struggling with all the immigrants' problems of acculturation. Among grandchildren of immigrants, the anti-Semitism now permeating the surrounding society hastened many along a course already embarked upon by their parents, a path associated with weakened communal affiliation and cohesion, with faith and community having become often mere form emptied of meaningful content. It pushed them in a direction that reflected at least in part the ambivalence of their parents, in the face of American realities, American pressures, American opportunities, between adherence to traditional ties and traditional communality and a degrading of those affiliations in pursuit of assimilation. The grandchildren, in their flight from a Jewish identity, perhaps comprehended their path as a rebellion against parents — and perhaps their parents comprehended it similarly — but in fact, as Kafka saw, they were often simply completing the march already started by their parents.

Some Jews converted, often in the context of marriage to non-Jews. Most who sought to detach themselves from their Jewish identity simply drifted away, taking an alternative identity without converting to Christianity, also often marrying non-Jews and having their children reared in another faith. Many of those who fled their Jewish background imbibed elements of the anti-Jewish bias of the surrounding society. Some were exquisitely hostile to other Jews, not least because they were embarrassed by them and feared those Jews would call attention to, and reinforce the bias against, their own Jewish background, dredging up what they were seeking to expunge from their identity.

This hostility and embarrassment could be found also in many Jews who did not entirely cast aside their Jewish identity but wanted to separate themselves from their co-religionists in the eyes of the wider society. Barry Rubin cites a 1943 quote that captures much of this mind-set, from "Laurence Steinhardt, the first American Jewish career ambassador, [who] complained, 'A single individual can frequently draw attention . . . by his conduct just as the diners in a restaurant are made conscious of the presence of a Jew by his loud or rowdy conduct or bad manners, whereas prior to his entry there may have been a dozen well-behaved Jews . . . of whose identity . . . the other diners were not conscious.'"[36]

Those who aspired to careers in areas largely blocked to Jews, such as academia, or to high-profile public careers as in the arts and entertainment, were often particularly eager to jettison their Jewish identity. The examples of Jews during this period who pursued careers in entertainment and who, in doing so, changed their names to less "Jewish-sounding" ones are, of course, myriad, and examples of the negative attitudes toward things Jewish harbored by many of these people are also legion. Irving Berlin (born Israel Baline), the quintessential American songwriter, mentions Jews in his songs only in negative terms, complained, while staging "They're in the Army," that there were "too many Jews in the show," married a non-Jew, and reared his children as Protestants.[37] Other Jewish entertainers followed a similar course.

The Jewish founders of the Hollywood movie industry assiduously sought to omit Jewish names and Jewish themes from their movies and in large part from their lives. They were eager to accommodate both art and life to the surrounding bias and to render both more "American." Far from using the power of their media to address the biases directed against Jews, the movie moguls in general aggressively rejected such a course. The producer David Selznick remarked, "I am not interested in Jewish political problems. I'm an American and not a Jew."[38] Such attitudes continued even after World War II. It was a non-Jewish producer, Darryl Zanuck, who made the first film addressing anti-Semitism in America, *Gentleman's Agreement* (1947), and Zanuck reported that Jewish producers urged him to drop the project. They feared it would only draw more negative attention to Jews.

The flight of Jewish intellectuals and academics from Jewish identity during this period and their frequent embrace of anti-Jewish biases were also widespread and have been illustrated in numerous biographies. The political theorist and commentator Walter Lippmann, scion of a wealthy German Jewish family and for many decades one of the most influential political writers in the country, sought to distance himself from his origins and from other Jews and repeatedly in his writing embraced popular anti-Jewish indictments and blamed Jews for the hatred directed against them. "The guilt is not one-sided, as most Jews would like to believe," he asserted in a letter to a friend defending anti-Jewish statements that he had published.[39]

Ronald Steel, in his acclaimed biography of Lippmann, notes, "The faults Lippmann saw — 'bad economic habits,' ostentatious dress, gaudy manners — were those of any *nouveaux riches*, just as the celebrated Jewish "clannishness" was that of any oppressed group. Instead of demonstrating the irrational basis of anti-Semitism — how the Jews, like other minority groups, were used as scapegoats — Lippmann accepted its premises by blaming the Jews."[40] Of a later assault on the Jews in a similar vein published by Lippmann in 1922, Steel observes, "The crudeness, even the cruelty, of Lippmann's attack on his fellow Jews was in dramatic contrast to the sensitivity he had shown to other minority groups and to individuals suffering discrimination or poverty. It was inconceivable that he would have written anything comparable about, for example, the Irish, the Italians or the blacks, all of whom had their parvenus."[41]

Lippmann supported immigration quotas in the 1920s, quotas that fell particularly heavily on eastern European Jews, and also supported limitations on the admission of Jews to his alma mater, Harvard. In a letter to Harvard regarding the latter, he wrote: "[Jews] hand on unconsciously and uncritically from one generation to another many distressing personal and social habits, which were selected by bitter history and intensified by a pharisaic theology."[42] Of course, Lippmann knew little of the Jewish community or of either Jewish history or theology, and as an intellectual embracing contemporary anti-Jewish biases he had no great interest in the people, their history or their theology. His interest was in cultivating an identity as a cosmopolitan internationalist aloof from anything that might be construed and censured — in the vein of the popular anti-Semitic indictment — as Jewish parochialism.

The casting of one's flight from a Jewish identity in lofty terms, as abandonment of the supposedly backward-looking, atavistic, parochial, and benighted for an identity more progressive, future-oriented, cosmopolitan, and universal, was, of course, a common ploy for many of those eager to shed the stigma of "Jew" in Europe; and it was no less popular in America. This cant, as in Europe, was particularly common among those with intellectual, political, or artistic ambitions. The novelist Henry Roth, whose *Call It Sleep* (1934) is perhaps the most evocative rendering of Jewish immigrant life by a member of the immigrant generation (he came to America as a young child), is another example. Roth immersed himself in the politics of the radical Left, joined the Communist Party, rebelled against all things Jewish as too particularist and backward-looking, and even urged Jews to disappear as a boon to humanity. Roth later acknowledged that this "alienation from my own faith" had "a strong anti-Semitic element." It was an imbibing of the anti-Semitism of the surrounding society in the context of seeking to separate himself from the objects of the anti-Semites' attacks.[43]

The tack of choosing to comprehend one's flight from Jewish identity as divesting oneself of narrow and atavistic allegiances in favor of broader and more progressive commitments again drew many of those wishing to shed their Jewishness to embrace, like Roth, the utopianism of the radical Left. To be sure, even among those Jews who continued to value their ties to Judaism and the Jewish community and who remained committed to both, there were factors — indeed factors related to those very sentiments — that led many to leftist sympathies. As in Europe, the anti-Jewish bias and institutionalized anti-Semitism of the surrounding society inclined many to perceive relief as achievable only in the context of a radical restructuring of society; and the rhetoric of the socialist Left — the promise of a more egalitarian social order that would transcend old biases and divisions — reinforced such perceptions. The popular comprehension among Jews that modern anti-Semitism is a continuation of old biases related to the persistence of old, traditional institutions further buttressed this view. The legacy of Jewish socialist parties in Czarist Russia and the example of such parties in the new nations of eastern Europe, the Bund and the Zionist-Socialist parties, as chief champions of the Jewish community against czarist and nationalist depredations, further predisposed Jewish immigrants to socialist sympathies. The crushing poverty of the immigrant Jewish community and the terrible working conditions of Jewish laborers also, of course, contributed to Jewish receptiveness to the cause of the socialist Left.

Even Communism and sympathy for the Soviet Union struck a receptive chord among some committed Jews, who looked positively at the Bolsheviks for having brought an end to viciously anti-Semitic czarist policies. In the nineteen thirties, after the rise of Nazism, many also viewed the Soviet Union as standing up to Hitler while the Western democracies retreated into appeasement and capitulation. But among those committed to their Jewish identity and the Jewish community there were also countervailing forces, particularly vis-à-vis Communism and the Soviet Union. Many Jews who had come from Russia were fully aware of how the Soviet Union had crushed Jewish religious and charitable institutions, Jewish labor organizations, and the Jewish political parties, and they had little sympathy for the Bolsheviks. Indeed, Jewish labor leaders in the United States, people like David Dubinsky, born in Byelorussia and reared in Lodz, and Sidney Hillman, born and reared in Lithuania, played key roles in stifling and reversing Communist penetration of the American labor union movement in the years between the wars. What persisted of sympathy among committed Jews for the Bolshevik regime was dramatically curtailed by the Hitler-Stalin pact of 1939.

But among many of those eager to divest themselves of a Jewish identity, the broader and supposedly more progressive identity offered by the radical Left retained a special attractiveness. Immersion in socialist and Communist universalism, in the international brotherhood of the working class, and in socialist images of a utopian future, seemed a liberating alternative to the narrow and embattled world of the Jews. Bolshevik depredations against the Jews, and the betrayal of the Hitler-Stalin pact, were widely dismissed by Communism's ex-Jewish acolytes as parochial issues insignificant against the greater drama of fighting for a universal egalitarian utopia that would transcend all narrow allegiances and divisions.

There were also Jews who did not seek to sever entirely their connection with their Jewish background but who, under pressure of the anti-Jewish sentiment of the surrounding society, chose to comprehend their Jewishness in universalist terms, to see its legacy as primarily a sympathetic humanism, and to shed much of the rest of that legacy as dross. No doubt this perspective often reflected such people's having been exposed to little Jewish education and having in many instances been given the message by parents, however indirect, that what parents retained of Jewish observance, Jewish commitment, Jewish identity, was less to be valued than "Americanization." In any case, the perspective was at once an embrace of the indictments of Jewish "particularism" and Jewish identity more broadly, and an answer to those indictments. It was an accommodating reinterpretation of the Jewish, of what was "valuable" in the Jewish legacy, and an appeal to the surrounding society to acknowledge one's virtuous reform.

Playwright Arthur Miller's autobiography, *Timebends*, evocatively illuminates this pattern of Jewish response as it manifested itself in many young Jews growing up in the decades between the wars. Miller recalls an incident at age six in which he was ashamed to tell a librarian his father's Jewish-sounding name and fled rather than do so. He observes, "I had already been programmed to choose something other than pride in my origins."[44] Yet he could not fathom the elements of that programming. Both his parents were self-confident and assertive, seemingly not people who perceived themselves as victimized or living under siege. Their family's milieu was largely Jewish and there was no awareness in the child of confrontation with a hostile surrounding society. He could recall no exposure to anti-Semitism. But somehow, he assumes, comprehensions of besiegement and denigration must have so permeated the culture that it was transmitted to the children even in this relatively confident and protected environment.

In addition, in Miller's growing up, aside from the warmth of experience with family, there was no countervailing education to give positive meaning to Jewish identity. Both his parents were uninformed and uninterested in religion. He had a bar mitzvah but his formal Jewish learning was very meager.

Miller's later course can be seen as his response to the dynamics of his growing up, to his awareness of a broader society that looked upon "Jewish" as a tainted, suspect, lesser identity — indeed, to his direct exposure to anti-Semitism as a teenager — and to his possession of no strong countervailing comprehension of what it meant to be Jewish. Miller did not repudiate his Jewish identity but chose to distance himself from it and to cast his doing so in high-minded terms. Religion, he decided, is based on fear; "the transaction called believing comes down to the confrontation with overwhelming power and then the relief of knowing that one has been spared its worst."[45] Leaving behind Judaism meant growing beyond that primitive fear. Speaking of himself and his Catholic bride whom he had met at the University of Michigan and married two years after their graduation, Miller declares: "Judaism for me and Catholicism for Mary were dead history, cultural mystifications that had been devised mainly to empower their priesthoods by setting people against one another."[46] In marrying, they were "leaving behind the parochial."[47]

Not surprisingly, given the time and place, the supposedly more evolved, more humane and tolerant creed to which he had advanced and which he was now embracing was socialism and its visions of a utopian egalitarian and pacific future.

Miller's refusal to see that what he chooses to cast as moral evolution was in large part simply flight from a demeaned and disadvantaged identity leads at times to statements that are unintentionally self-revealing and laughable. For example, he relates looking for a job in his late teens and routinely coming across ads that specified "White" or "Gentile" or sometimes "Chr." "There were even ads specifying 'Protestant' and, very rarely, 'Cath. firm.'" Miller concludes: "My disdain for such clannishness probably helped move me later to marry a gentile girl."[48]

Miller retains some feeling for his Jewish roots and there seem at various points in the book to be moments of self-recognition, but they are quickly replaced by his chosen verities. Miller writes that, when he was embarking on his career as playwright, he imagined himself in the "role of mediator between the Jews and America"; but it is clear that he conceived of that mediation as via the dramatic rendering of universalism, identifying the Jew with the socialists' everyman, free of any particularism; and he immediately adds that his imaginings in this vein included mediating "among Americans themselves as well."[49] Miller describes his visit after the war to a compound in southern Italy housing Jewish refugees hiding from the British and awaiting passage to the Mandate, and he remarks, "In coming years I would wonder why it never occurred to me to throw in my lot with them when they were the product of precisely the catastrophe I had in various ways given my writing life to try to prevent. To this day, thinking of them there on their dark porches silently scanning the sea for their ship, unwanted by any of the civilized powers, their very presence here illegal and menaced by British diplomatic intervention, I feel myself disembodied, detached, ashamed of my stupidity, my failure to recognize myself in them." But he quickly universalizes the sentiment. "It reminds me of a similar hole in my heart regarding my response to the first report of Hiroshima. How could I have felt such wonder? Such relief, too . . ."[50]

Elsewhere, Miller relates an encounter with an Orthodox Jew on a subway platform during the war. He recalls: "That people like him were being hunted down like beasts was once again incredible."[51] The distancing is noteworthy, given that, of course, Jews like Miller were also being hunted down like beasts.

Miller speaks at other points of wishing to identify with humanity as a whole rather than some small segment of it. He suggests that insofar as he values his Jewish heritage, he does so most for its pushing him toward broader sensibilities, toward seeking universal justice. Similarly, he chooses to comprehend the ordeals of the Jews as simply a variation of universal tribulations, the Jewish predicament as emblematic of the universal predicament.

Even among American Jews who remained fully committed to the faith and the community, even among those who immersed themselves in community causes and community leadership, there was, as in Europe, a predilection to eschew Jewish "particularism." Under the pressure of the anti-Jewish bias of the surrounding society, there was an impulse to emphasize communal commitment to broader, less parochial agendas, as a way of assuaging anti-Jewish hostility. Many chose in this context to emphasize the universalist elements of the Jewish mission and Jewish message. While these predilections were often cast in lofty terms, they in large part, as in Europe, reflected fears that Jewish advocacy of Jewish issues would exacerbate anti-Jewish sentiments. They were also driven by a wishful belief that sufficient Jewish self-effacement would assuage anti-Jewish feeling and win the Jews acceptance by the wider society.

SIX

American Jews and the Holocaust: Catastrophe and Failure

There is a possibility that the Germans or their satellites may change over from the policy of extermination to one of extrusion, and aim as they did before the war at embarrassing other countries by flooding them with alien immigrants.

British Foreign Office memorandum to the State Department opposing efforts to rescue Europe's Jews, spring of 1943[1]

Report to the Secretary on the Acquiescence of This Government in the Murder of the Jews

Title of memorandum presented by U.S. Treasury Department officials to the Secretary of the Treasury, January, 1944

Now let's be frank about this, our dear Leaders. Isn't it a fact that for ten years you have been trooping up to the State Department with bated breath and hat in hand — and getting the run-around? Politely, of course.

Then why didn't you report back to us, the Jewish people of America, so that we could try to do something about it before it was too late? What could we have done? We could have done what other Americans do when their kinsmen are threatened with danger and death. We could have brought pressure to bear on Congress, on the President, on the State Department — mass pressure, not just the backstairs 'diplomacy' of your hush policy. It is too easy for a government official to say No when he knows it isn't going any further.

When you found that you were getting nowhere with your back-stage wire-pulling you should have stood up and said so, loud and clear, so that every Jew in America could hear it, and every Gentile too. That would have been the democratic thing to do. Then we, the people, could have done the next democratic thing. We could have organized a mass movement to back you up. Instead of doing that you hushed up your failure.

Editorial in Bulletin of the *Independent Jewish Press Service*, March, 1943.[2]

The deep-seated and widespread anti-Jewish animus in the United States in the decades after World War I, particularly as this prejudice permeated the corridors of power, had a profound impact on America's response to the Nazi campaign of extermination against Europe's Jews. In addition, the corrosive effects on American Jews of the surrounding society's anti-Semitism colored significantly American Jewry's response to the European catastrophe.

Some historians and others have been reluctant to address weaknesses and failures in American Jewry's reaction to the Nazi campaign. They have been concerned in large part that to do so might distort the limits of American Jews' capacity to influence events, obscure the tremendous obstacles the American Jewish community faced in efforts to promote rescue, and, in a perversion of historical truth, shift the onus of responsibility for the failure of rescue away from those who must bear the overwhelming burden of that responsibility and to the Jews for the limits of their effectiveness.

Certainly, American Jewry did confront determined and very powerful obstructionist opponents of rescue within the American government, opponents well placed to stymie rescue efforts,[3] and American Jews had very few allies. At the same time, the belated rescue efforts the U.S. government did finally authorize, through the War Refugee Board, managed — despite limited administration support and still frequent obstructionism — to help save about 200,000 European Jews; and the War Refugee Board would never have been created were it not for the action of elements of the American Jewish community. Also, as the Roosevelt administration withheld funds from the Board — even though discretionary funds were available and were used to rescue non-Jews — Jewish charities provided 90 percent of the Board's budget. Establishment and funding of the War Refugee Board through the efforts of concerned Jews was a victory, however belated and limited, over obstacles to rescue. In an ideal situation that victory would have been won much earlier and been much more effective. Its occurring when it did was less a consequence of external conditions than of a more effectively mounted effort by some American Jews. It is reasonable — and important for the light it casts on the Jewish predicament during this period — to consider what within American Jewry figured in compromising and undermining its earlier efforts to promote rescue.[4]

News of Genocide, Calls for Rescue, and Administration Obstruction

From the summer of 1941, reports were reaching the West regularly, through diplomatic and other channels, of large-scale massacres of Jews in areas of eastern Europe under Nazi control. In May, 1942, a message transmitted to the West through the Polish Government-in-Exile in London contained a compilation, by the Jewish Bund in Poland, of confirmed massacres. The Bund estimated that 700,000 Polish Jews had already been killed and surmised that the Nazis had embarked on a campaign to annihilate all the Jews of Europe.[5] On July 21, 1942, several Jewish organizations sponsored the first large-scale demonstration protesting the Nazi slaughter and calling for Allied action. It was held at Madison Square Garden and drew a crowd well in excess of the Garden's 20,000-person capacity.[6] Other rallies followed.

The summer of 1942 also brought confirmation, from a well-placed German source, that the Nazis did indeed have a plan for the murder of all the Jews in Europe and were in the process of executing it. Rabbi Stephen Wise, the most prominent American Jewish leader, president of both the American Jewish Congress and the World Jewish Congress and a key figure, often chief officer, in perhaps a dozen other organizations and institutes, received this information in late August. At the urging of the State Department, Wise agreed to defer any public announcement until the Department had received additional corroboration. Undersecretary of State Sumner Welles withheld news of such corroboration until November 24. Over the subsequent twenty-four hours, Wise convened two press conferences — one in Washington, another in New York — informing the media that the State Department had confirmed that two million Jews had been killed by the Nazis in an "extermination campaign."[7]

In the preceding months, the Jewish leadership had formulated no comprehensive program of steps it wanted to promote in response to the catastrophe in Europe. The most concrete proposal was one which Wise, in October, had urged Secretary of the Interior Harold Ickes to present to President Roosevelt: The opening of the Virgin Islands — administered by the Interior Department — as temporary refuge for a few thousand Jews. (A sympathetic Ickes brought the plan to Roosevelt, but the President rejected it.)[8] However, in the months following public announcement of the extermination campaign, various proposals to, in Wise's words, "save those still alive," were formulated.

Key elements of these plans were: strong public announcements by Allied leaders of postwar prosecution of those involved in the murder of the Jews (November, 1942, had seen a crucial reversal in the Nazis' military fortunes, with defeats at El Alamein and virtual encirclement at Stalingrad, and threats of prosecution had some promise of having an impact); opening up of refuges in Allied-controlled territories for Jews escaping the Nazis; encouragement of neutral states, such as Turkey, Spain, Switzerland, and Sweden, to accept Jewish refugees by promising to subsidize costs and to evacuate the refugees after the war; and broadcast of Allied appeals to the populations of occupied countries to hide Jews and help them escape the Nazis.[9] (Such broadcasts would also be warnings to Jews of the Nazi plan and would likely have led many of those now going unwittingly to their deaths to flee into hiding or to put up greater resistance to "relocation.")

But the American Jewish community and its leadership faced substantial obstacles in their effort to promote implementation of such steps. Foremost among these was State Department obstructionism. State Department operatives at the European desk and visa and immigration posts in Washington, and in European embassies and consulates, had already exhibited their attitudes and associated policy decisions regarding the plight of Europe's Jews in the years after the Nazi ascension to power, when Jews were desperate to leave Europe.[10] These same attitudes and policies persisted despite awareness of the Nazi genocide program.

State Department officials throughout this period typically held strong anti-immigration sentiments and seem to have been especially determined to block the immigration of Jews into the United States. Policies adopted by State regarding issuance of visas were in fact much more restrictive than even the strict immigration laws of the period. Thus, the number of visas issued to Jews during the war, including during the years when the Nazis' genocide program was fully known, was barely 10 percent of those potentially available to European Jews under the immigration quota legislation then in effect. From Pearl Harbor to the end of the war, approximately 21,000 immigrants, mostly Jews, were allowed into the United States, out of about 210,000 visa slots available during the same period to citizens of countries controlled by the Nazis and their allies.[11]

But State Department opposition to extending help to Europe's Jews went beyond simply wishing to prevent emigration of Jews to the United States. The State Department, both before and during the war, fully supported the broader anti-rescue policies of the British Foreign Office. The Foreign Office perspective, in addition to being animated by as much distaste for the prospect of Jewish immigration to Britain as the State Department was of Jewish immigration to the United States, was shaped primarily by determination to prevent enlargement of the Jewish population of Palestine. The consequences of this agenda entailed more than simply implementation of Britain's 1939 White Paper restrictions on Jewish immigration into Palestine.

The Foreign Office believed that even if sanctuary were found outside of Palestine for European Jews, many Jewish refugees — particularly if the sanctuaries were obtained on the basis of assurances to the sovereign powers that the Jews' presence would be "temporary" — would ultimately seek to come to Palestine. The Foreign Office also anticipated that sympathetic governments would bring increasing pressure on Britain to live up to its unilaterally abrogated League of Nations obligations in Palestine. At times the Foreign Office seemed to support searches for refuges other than Palestine. But this was in large part to counter pressures from the British public for efforts at rescue and to do so in a manner that would shift the focus away from Palestine. Its more typical stance was one of seeking to block, and certainly to not abet, any flight of Jews from Europe and lobbying the State Department to do likewise.

The lengths to which the British Foreign Office went to prevent the rescue of Jews is indicated by an episode involving Japan. In 1940, the Japanese vice consul in Kovno, Lithuania, Chiune Sugihara, issued several thousand visas to Jews desperate to escape Europe. Hillel Levine, a professor of sociology and religion at Boston University who was working on a book about Sugihara, did research in the archives of the Japanese Foreign Ministry in Tokyo to investigate to what extent the Japanese government was aware of Sugihara's efforts to save Jews. He not only discovered documents there charting Sugihara's activities but also complaints from the British Foreign Office (this is, of course, before Britain and Japan were at war) protesting Sugihara's visas and warning that the rescued Jews would become a burden on Japan.[12]

This policy of discouraging and obstructing rescue by other parties, and, of course, the Foreign Office's own eschewing of any rescue effort, persisted even after the Allies learned of the Nazis' extermination program. Indeed, the attitude at the Foreign Office seems to have been that if no Jews were rescued from Europe and no European Jews survived the war there would then be no basis for advocacy of a Jewish homeland and the British grip on Palestine would be all the more secure. In any case, Foreign Office communications to the State Department opposing rescue proposals, even after the genocide program was known, refer repeatedly to, in the words of one memo, "the difficulties of disposing of any considerable number of Jews should they be rescued."[13]

In this context, Jewish proposals for promoting rescue by promising neutral countries and other potential refuges that the Jews they sheltered would be evacuated after the war ran up against the key Foreign Office concern vis-à-vis Palestine and elicited only hardened objections from Britain. The State Department may have resisted such promises of postwar relocation of rescued Jews out of concern that there would be pressure for some of that relocation to be to the United States. But State also fully endorsed British Palestine policy and readily followed British objections to rescue of any sort in the service of ultimate British concerns about political pressure to open Palestine to those saved.

Even small-scale rescue was opposed by the Foreign Office and by State out of fear that successful rescue might lead to pressure to save more Jews, and that the Nazis, or at least their allies, might "exploit" rescue programs to "unload" additional Jews. Thus, public statements regarding rescue made by the Foreign Office and by State in the wake of learning of the genocide program typically speak of the practical difficulties of extracting Jews from Europe, but confidential communications between the Foreign Office and State speak instead of concern that "too many" Jews might be rescued, that a small stream of saved Jews could become a flood. For example, a Foreign Office memorandum to the State Department in the spring of 1943, opposing even modest rescue steps, expresses the concern that: "There is a possibility that the Germans or their satellites may change over from the policy of extermination to one of extrusion, and aim as they did before the war of embarrassing other countries by flooding them with alien immigrants."[14]

That State Department opposition to the rescue of Jews throughout the Nazi period went beyond anti-immigration attitudes and involved also endorsement of British policy toward Palestine and Jewish refugees is illustrated by an event that occurred in the fall of 1941, before America's entry into the war. Since September, 1940, when the fascist government of Ioan Antonescu had seized power in Rumania, several thousand Jews had fled the country via Rumania's Black Sea ports and many had died when their dilapidated ships — "coffin ships," as they were popularly called — sank either in transit through the Black Sea or in attempts to evade the British blockade of Palestine. One ship sank when, having reached Palestine, it was forced back to sea by the British. This traffic, opposed, of course, by the British, was also of concern to Turkey, which was under pressure — from the Germans, Arabs, and British — not to aid the Jews arriving in Istanbul harbor in transit to Palestine and also not to admit them to Turkey. By the fall of 1941, agents of the Rumanian regime, together with German death squads, had already slaughtered 200,000 of the approximately 800,000 Jews within Rumania's borders. But it was widely known that Rumanian strongman Ioan Antonescu was not entirely committed to the slaughter and was willing to go on allowing Jews to ransom their way out of the country. The Turkish ambassador in Budapest then proposed to the American ambassador a plan for the orderly transport of 300,000 Rumanian Jews through Turkey to Palestine and urged the Americans to push the plan with the British.

But the State Department objected to the plan and refused to present it to the British. Its stated objections, listed in a memorandum by Cavendish W. Cannon of the European Division, were: concern about upsetting the Arabs; fears that a rescue of Rumanian Jews would lead to calls to save Jews being persecuted in other countries; anticipation that such a rescue would trigger pressure to offer asylum in the Western hemisphere; and the problem of transportation. The first three of these arguments against rescue would sway State Department policy in the years after exposure of the genocide program as well. The last argument — not enough shipping — would be trotted out repeatedly in response to pressures for rescue. It was bogus, as much neutral shipping was readily available and was, indeed, employed by the Allies throughout the war to rescue many thousand non-Jews — from Greece and Yugoslavia, for example — and transport them to safe havens. In addition, over 400,000 German prisoners of war were transported to the United States between 1942 and 1945.[15]

When strong evidence of the Nazi extermination program first reached the West, the State Department initially tried to block the information from

Jewish leaders and from the public more generally. State subsequently, as noted, delayed until November, 1942, informing Rabbi Wise of its confirmation of the genocide plan. Afterwards the Department denied that it in fact had confirmed the plan to Wise or indeed possessed concrete evidence of it. Beyond sowing doubt in some minds, this tack also had other negative consequences. In the months immediately following disclosure of the extermination program, the Jewish leadership tried to enlist the Office of War Information to publicize what was happening to European Jewry. But the OWI would disseminate only information coming from the State Department, and State would not officially release information on the genocide. Similarly, the Advertising Council — an industry association promoting advertising in support of the war effort — indicated that it would mobilize a publicity campaign about the killings but only if the Office of War Information supported the plan, and so this too was indirectly stymied by State Department obstruction.[16]

In response to what information about the mass killings and the genocide plan did get out to the public, there evolved some pressure, beyond the Jewish leadership, for government action. This broader public reaction emerged, in fact, primarily in England, not in the United States. From the fall of 1942, with leak of the earliest reports of the Nazi extermination policy, William Temple, Archbishop of Canterbury, spoke out forcefully to urge rescue efforts and sharply criticized allied inaction. He was joined in his efforts by Arthur Cardinal Hinsley, leader of Britain's Catholics, and the exertions of both men far exceeded any steps taken by church leaders in the United States. There was similarly greater attention to the issue and calls for rescue efforts in Parliament than in the U. S. Congress. (It should also be noted that Britain admitted over 8,000 unaccompanied Jewish children in the so-called *Kindertransport* of 1938–1939, with the children being placed in the care of Jewish and non-Jewish families. A parallel attempt to admit 20,000 children to the United States over a two-year period aroused intense opposition and was stymied.)[17]

The Foreign Office and the State Department quickly colluded to defuse what public pressure there was for rescue by organizing a conference to discuss the Jewish problem. They deferred the conference — a strictly British and American affair — until April, 1943. They set it in Bermuda, which was then a closed military zone, so as to limit media access and prevent the presence of representatives of the Jewish leadership and of other parties potentially sympathetic to the Jews. They then proceeded to accomplish nothing by way of aid to Europe's Jews. Minutes of the conference show that the Foreign Office and State Department continued to be preoccupied with fears that rescue steps might result in a large-scale release of Jews from Axis-controlled Europe.[18]

Also, in the first months of 1943 information reached the West from Rumania that, of 130,000 Jews earlier deported to the Transnistria region, 70,000 remained alive, although destitute and starving, and that Rumania, presumably for a price, was prepared to release these 70,000 to the Allies and even provide ships to transport them to Palestine or some other Allied territory. The State Department dismissed the offer out of hand, refusing to explore the proposal. It also refused to consider undertaking negotiations that may have led the Rumanians to extend protection for a time to the Transnistrian Jews even if State had no intention of supporting a rescue.[19]

These patterns of obstruction to intervention continued to characterize the State Department's answer to the Nazi genocide throughout the war. It routinely deferred responses to plans for rescue, dismissed plans out of hand as impractical, and invoked bogus impediments to rescue, such as the supposed shipping problem. Among its false arguments against action were claims that rescue projects would somehow impede the war effort. Another tack was State's persistent withholding of visas from Jews who had reached neutral countries and whose evacuation would have made those countries more amenable to admitting additional refugees. The State Department even sought to block broadcast of threats to bring to justice the perpetrators of the genocide, as well as broadcast of appeals for the people in occupied Europe to aid the Jews.

Of course, the president could have forced State Department officials to abandon their obstructionism and abet rescue efforts, and the Jewish leadership appealed to the president to support rescue measures. But Roosevelt was himself an obstacle to rescue. He rarely spoke out on the predicament of the Jews, even though aware that his doing so would have given the issue a higher public profile and led to greater public support for rescue activities, and he refused to intervene with the State Department. His one significant measure aimed at aiding the Jews, the executive order establishing the War Refugee Board, came only when faced with looming pressure from Capitol Hill demanding administration action and with a potential rebellion from inside the executive branch that would have exposed State Department obstructionism and the administration's callousness. Moreover, Roosevelt again would do nothing when the State Department, War Department and other arms of the executive failed to cooperate with the War Refugee Board as they were mandated to do under the executive order.[20]

Some have argued that Roosevelt was too busy conducting the war to pay much attention to the Nazi genocide. But he could have had a major impact on government policy with little effort, and he seems in fact to have expended as much energy in ducking the issue as would have been required of him to effect some positive steps. Another argument often made has been that Roosevelt's actions were determined by political expediency; that, given the level of anti-Semitism in the country, he viewed sympathetic discussion of the plight of the Jews and support for rescue as likely to alienate many voters whereas, in contrast, he had the Jewish vote locked up even if he did nothing to aid the Jews of

Europe. In addition to the obvious point of the cold cruelty of such a calculation, of the preparedness to sacrifice so many lives for electoral gain, there are other problems with this explanation. The president could have chosen to use exposure of the Nazi genocide program to win over public sympathy for the Nazis' victims; there is good evidence that most anti-Jewish sentiment in America was not so fixed as to be entirely impervious to counter-argument. But beyond this, and more clearly, there is much the president could have done outside of public scrutiny and without courting an anti-Semitic backlash. Again, throughout the war the State Department issued only 10 percent of the visas available for Jews from Axis-controlled Europe. Roosevelt could have ended this restrictiveness and saved at least tens of thousands of lives without going beyond prevailing immigration quotas and so without having to take any steps, such as requesting Congressional action, that would have invited public scrutiny.

When, finally, under pressure, Roosevelt created the War Refugee Board, he failed to support it. He could have financed the WRB from discretionary funds — funds that he in fact drew upon to support other humanitarian efforts aimed at mainly non-Jewish groups, but he did not. Roosevelt could have moved against failure of the War and State Departments to extend to the WRB the cooperation mandated in the executive order that created the board, but he did not.

A comprehensive explanation of Roosevelt's behavior must go beyond suggestions of his distraction with other, war-related issues, or his sensitivity to political considerations and to the popularity of anti-Jewish attitudes, and must factor in Roosevelt's own infection with what was at the time epidemic anti-Jewish sentiment.

It is certainly true that Roosevelt appointed many talented Jews to high positions in his administration. Moreover, employment in the new federal agencies created by the "New Deal" was typically much more accessible to Jews than employment in the society at large, where restrictions against the hiring of Jews was commonplace. At the same time, Roosevelt was not averse to invoking people's being Jewish as a slur and making denigrating comments about Jews.[21] Elsewhere, Roosevelt even parroted Nazi anti-Jewish assertions. For example, at the Casablanca conference in January, 1943, while discussing possible projects for resettling rescued Jews in North Africa (projects subsequently torpedoed, mainly by the United States), Roosevelt suggested restricting the number of relocated Jews allowed to practice the professions, as this "would further eliminate the specific and understandable complaints which the Germans bore towards the Jews in Germany, namely that while they represented a small part of the population, over 50 percent of the lawyers, doctors, school teachers, college professors, etc. in Germany were Jews."[22] The figure for Jewish involvement in these occupations is, of course, wildly exaggerated.

There is much to support the view that Jewish suffering, even suffering on this unprecedented scale, simply did not elicit the same level of concern or sympathy from Roosevelt as did the lesser tribulations of others.

Faced, in its efforts to promote rescue, with what was at best the general indifference of the president, and with the hostility of the State Department, the Jewish community also confronted the reality that, of other political and social institutions and segments of the society that one might enlist as allies in attempts to advance a cause against administration intransigence, none was particularly sympathetic or prepared to be helpful. Congress was staunchly anti-immigration, even more so after the congressional elections of November, 1942; and openly anti-Semitic sentiments were not uncommonly heard in speeches on the floor of the House and Senate. While some individual Christian religious figures could be enlisted for support, church leaderships were in general unresponsive to the plight of Europe's Jews. The Nazi extermination program never elicited much attention or sustained moral outrage within American religious bodies.

The media, of course, could have helped sway public opinion and also exert pressure on both Congress and the administration. But the American media chose typically either not to cover at all stories regarding the genocide or to relegate coverage to a few lines or paragraphs in some corner of an inside page. A brief spate of higher profile reporting in some segments of the press followed Rabbi Wise's announcement in November, 1942, of the Nazis' extermination plan and of two million Jews already dead. But in subsequent months, news of the genocide became largely invisible.[23]

The Response of American Jews

With that flurry of more extensive media coverage that had followed Wise's two press conferences, the Jewish leadership did succeed in getting news of the extermination program in a convincing manner to a substantial portion of the American population. A January, 1943, Gallup poll posed the following: "It is said that two million Jews have been killed in Europe since the war began. Do you think this is true or just a rumor?" Forty-seven percent of respondents believed it to be true; 29 percent thought it a rumor; 24 percent had no opinion.[24]

But the Jewish leadership's — mainly the American Jewish Congress's — plans, formulated in December, 1942, for steps to arouse public opinion in support of rescue efforts floundered in the face of the nation's general indifference. Attempts to win Christian churches to hold a Day of Mourning and inform their parishioners of the genocide gained very little church cooperation. Hopes of enlisting the media to disseminate information on the slaughter and to advocate for rescue likewise fizzled. Some rallies were held, but plans for marches in major cities accompanied by store closings and work stoppages never materialized.[25]

A separate campaign to increase awareness of the genocide and win support for rescue efforts was undertaken in early 1943 under the leadership of Peter H. Bergson. Bergson was one of a group of Palestinian Jews who had come to the United States several years earlier with the aim of gaining support for the Zionist struggle against Britain's anti-Jewish policies in Palestine, particularly the struggle against Britain's closure of Palestine to Jews trying to flee Europe. With news of the Nazis' extermination program, the Bergson group shifted its focus more entirely to responding to the catastrophe in Europe.

In early 1943 the group ran several large advertisements in major American newspapers dramatically conveying the predicament of Europe's Jews and urging rescue efforts. The ads, composed by such writers as the Dutch-Canadian journalist and author, and dedicated Christian Zionist, Pierre van Paassen, and the playwright Ben Hecht, were explicit and hard-hitting. One, for example, that appeared in February, bore the headline — referring to the offer by Rumania to release 70,000 Jews then in Transnistria, an offer dismissed by the State Department and Foreign Office — "FOR SALE to Humanity, 70,000 Jews." It went on: "Seventy Thousand Jews Are Waiting in Rumanian Concentration Camps . . . Rumania Offers to Deliver These 70,000 Alive to Palestine . . . The Doors of Rumania are Open! Act Now!" It urged pressing the government to take action.[26]

The ad campaign of the Bergson group came under withering attack from the Jewish leadership, which criticized the campaign's "sensationalism" but was clearly also responding to what was, in effect, a challenge to its own activities in addressing the European catastrophe. In fact, the work of the Bergson group helped galvanize the leadership to greater action. For example, having deferred its plans for mass rallies, it now responded to the Bergson group's organizing of a Madison Square Garden rally in March, 1943, by organizing one of its own. The leadership also started to run its own ads calling for rescue measures.[27]

The leadership also formulated an eleven-point rescue proposal. It emphasized actions to gain the release of Jews from occupied Europe, to promote fuller use of U.S. immigration quotas, to pressure Britain on accepting some refugees and opening Palestine, and to loosen rigid immigration restrictions in Latin America. It also proposed steps to work with neutral countries to evacuate refugees already there and to encourage their admission of additional refugees, to provide financial support for rescue efforts, to form an agency dedicated to rescue, and to appoint a war crimes commission and begin assembling evidence and formulating procedures for prosecutions. Additionally, Wise now revived the earlier Temporary Committee, as the Joint Emergency Committee on European Jewish Affairs, to coordinate the leadership's efforts.[28]

The leadership's Madison Square Garden rally, under the banner "Stop Hitler Now," won the co-sponsorship of the AFL and the CIO, was addressed by New York mayor Fiorello LaGuardia and AFL president William Green, and received messages of support from Wendell Willkie, New York governor Thomas Dewey, the Archbishop of Canterbury, and the leader of British Catholics, Arthur Cardinal Hinsley. (No major American church leaders involved themselves in the rally.) It drew some 75,000 participants. The Joint Emergency Committee subsequently helped organize forty more such meetings across the country during the spring of 1943, many of which received the cooperation of local Christian groups as well as organized labor.[29]

The Bergson group's Madison Square Garden event, a week after the leadership's, featured a pageant entitled "We Will Never Die," the creation of Ben Hecht, Billy Rose, Moss Hart, and Kurt Weill. Its large cast included Paul Muni and Edward G. Robinson. The organizers, particularly Billy Rose, tried to obtain a statement of support from the president — Rose had contributed his talents to various Roosevelt charitable projects — but none was forthcoming. The Bergson group performed its pageant in a number of other cities in the ensuing months, but plans for a broader tour were frustrated by the opposition of the Jewish leadership, which effectively lobbied sponsors in many localities to withdraw their support.[30]

Both the leadership's rallies and the Bergson group's pageants spurred a new flurry of media coverage and, again, won significant support beyond the Jewish community. But they did not lead to any change in administration policy. The leadership tried to generate movement in Congress in favor of rescue, but to no avail. But the bulk of the efforts, and the hopes, of Wise and those around him was still directed to the administration and the State Department and there they encountered only obstacles and resistance. A meeting in late March with British foreign minister Anthony Eden, then visiting Washington, exposed Wise to the Foreign Office's indifference to the Jews' plight and unwillingness to take any steps to help the Jews.[31] (At about the same time, Eden was conveying to the White House and State Department that the Foreign Office's main objective was to block any large-scale escape of Jews from Europe.)[32]

The subsequent failure of the Bermuda Conference came as a crushing blow to the leadership. In the following months it seems to have sunk into despair. The Joint Emergency Committee became essentially moribund.[33] There were some additional approaches to the administration, which again got nowhere. Plans for a march on Washington, for mass demonstrations, and for threats to the administration of extensive Jewish defections in the 1944 elections if no efforts at rescue were made, were never pursued.

The Bergson group, in the wake of Bermuda, resumed its ad campaign, in which, among other points, it denounced the Bermuda Conference as "a mockery and a cruel jest."[34] Bergson and his circle also organized an Emergency

Conference in late July and were able to involve in the conference a prominent array of noted non-Jewish figures despite attempts once more by the Jewish leadership to sabotage their efforts. The Conference resolved that effective rescue efforts could be made without compromising the war effort (claims to the contrary were a staple of the administration's obstructionist armamentarium) and advocated the establishment of a federal agency dedicated to rescuing Europe's Jews. The Conference ended with creation of an Emergency Committee to Save the Jewish People of Europe.[35]

The Conference's deliberations garnered yet another flurry of media coverage and some notable supportive editorials, including one by Max Lerner entitled, "What About the Jews, FDR," challenging the president, the State Department, and the Foreign Office to cease their inactivity and take up the Conference's recommendations. Subsequent actions by the Bergson group included an open letter to Roosevelt and Churchill by Pierre van Paassen likewise urging rescue and another ad by Ben Hecht dramatizing Roosevelt and Churchill's silence and apparent indifference while the Jews of Europe were being slaughtered.[36] The group also organized, in the fall, a rabbis' march in Washington, involving 400 Orthodox rabbis in a pilgrimage for rescue. The group stopped at the White House but the president refused to meet with them.[37]

The Emergency Conference's appeals to the administration, and efforts to move the administration by exposing its callous inactivity thus far, as well as its attempts to enlist broad-based church support, got nowhere. But it made a concerted effort to cultivate support for rescue in Congress. By late fall of 1943, it had succeeded in winning some substantial backing in Congress for a Rescue Resolution that would establish a rescue commission and support its operation in North Africa and neutral European nations.[38]

The administration sought to scuttle the Rescue Resolution and almost succeeded as the State Department, testifying before the House Foreign Affairs Committee, grossly misrepresented its own record on rescue. It suggested, for example, that 580,000 refugees had entered the country in the course of the war, whereas barely 21,000 had, and it insisted that nothing more could be done.

The *New York Times* carried State's testimony as true. (State's claims of rescue were the only Holocaust story during the war to be covered by the *New York Times* on page one above the fold.) But other publications quickly revealed that the testimony was fraudulent, and momentum in support of the Rescue Resolution again grew.[39] The Jewish leadership around Wise never lent its backing to the Bergson-sponsored legislation, but the Bergson group was able to win endorsements from some prominent church figures and increasing sympathy in both houses of Congress.

It was in the face of looming passage of the Rescue Resolution, and the prospect of political credit going to major rivals in Congress, that Roosevelt finally moved to take action and establish the War Refugee Board.

At the same time pressure for action was also coming from within the administration, from the Treasury Department, apparently accompanied by threats to expose the administration's abysmal record of obstruction of efforts to help Europe's Jews. This pressure also seems to have played a role in changing the president's stance.[40] (There is also evidence that the Bergson group's ad campaign, with its explicit indictment of the administration, was having a direct effect on the president.[41])

The Treasury Department's involvement in the rescue issue began in mid-1943. Earlier, in February, Treasury Secretary Hans Morgenthau had brought to Roosevelt the just revealed story of Rumania's offer to allow the 70,000 surviving Jews in Transnistria to leave the country and even to provide transport for them to Palestine, but Roosevelt had simply referred him to the State Department. State, of course, dismissed the proposal. But in April the Rumanians revived the offer, and Gerhart Rieger, the World Jewish Congress representative in Geneva and a major conduit for information on the genocide, requested a transfer of funds from Jewish groups in the United States to help support the Transnistrian Jews and convey American interest to the Rumanians. He also hoped to support Jews being hidden in France and help finance underground escape routes into Spain. The request was not for a transfer of money to Axis-occupied areas — which in any case would not be allowed — but rather placement of funds in accounts in Switzerland that would be frozen until after the war but could serve as collateral for obtaining local money to finance the plans. (Sources of local funds that agreed to these terms had already been obtained.)[42]

But even such a transfer of money to Switzerland required government approval. The State Department tried to block dissemination of the Rieger proposal and, when it did become public, raised objections. In July Rabbi Wise, frustrated at State, was able to see Roosevelt and presented the plan to him. In a rare act of cooperation Roosevelt agreed to the fund transfer and informed Morgenthau, as all such transactions fell under Treasury's purview.[43] Treasury officials quickly approved, but what they assumed would then be rapid State Department action — the Jewish funds still had to go through the U.S. embassy in Bern — did not follow. Instead, the transfer encountered, despite the president's approval, the now routine State Department obstruction. State also enlisted the Foreign Office, which weighed in with its own objections.

In the ensuing months, the key figures at Treasury involved with money transfer licensing were exposed to State Department and Foreign Office tactics and their obvious intent to sabotage any rescue efforts. (Despite presidential approval, State and the Foreign Office only acquiesced to a partial transfer of the approved funds, and that only in December.) In addition, much of the information on the genocide reaching American Jewish organizations involved in the campaign for rescue was being transmitted through the American embassy in Bern, and Treasury officials discovered State's efforts to stop these transmissions. They also learned of State's subsequent attempts to cover up what it had done to prevent news of the exterminations from getting to the public.

The Treasury Department officials exposed to State Department tactics urged Morgenthau to intervene with the president, but Morgenthau held back. Meanwhile, Oscar Cox, executive at the Lend-Lease Administration, had been advocating a separate rescue agency since the spring of 1943 and, in the wake of his own ongoing frustrations with State, likewise urged Morgenthau to intervene with Roosevelt. Still Morgenthau held back. Finally, in January, 1944, members of Treasury's Foreign Funds Control Staff presented Morgenthau with a memorandum entitled, "Report to the Secretary on the Acquiescence of This Government in the Murder of the Jews," documenting State Department obstruction of rescue efforts.[44] With this in hand, Morgenthau finally agreed to go to Roosevelt, confront him with State's actions, and urge the establishment of a new agency dedicated to rescue efforts.

THE WAR REFUGEE BOARD[45]

From its inception, the War Refugee Board functioned under many handicaps. The administration never provided meaningful funding. (The WRB obtained over 90 percent of the money it actually used for rescue efforts from Jewish charities, but Jewish agencies did not have the capacity to finance the Board at a level that would have maximized its effectiveness.) The State Department not only failed to cooperate with the Board as mandated in the executive order that created the WRB but, in fact, continued to pursue its obstructive policies. Other executive branches, most significantly the War Department, likewise withheld cooperation. The Board was also confronted repeatedly with British sabotage of its efforts, and received no cooperation from the administration to counter British anti-rescue policies. Yet, while its achievements were far less than they would undoubtedly have been had it had the support mandated in executive order 9417, the WRB did succeed in saving many thousands of Jews.

WRB's office in Turkey managed to get about 7,000 Jews out of the Balkans and ultimately into Palestine. In addition, the Turkish office successfully negotiated the transfer of the 48,000 Jews still alive in Transnistria into the interior of Rumania and the provision of effective measures for their security there.

WRB efforts in neutral Spain and Sweden, and in allied-controlled southern Italy, made little headway. In Sweden, efforts to extract Jews from the Baltic states were too late, as very few Jews remained alive there. In Spain and Italy, State Department and Foreign Office obstruction in the former and War Office and British military impediments in the latter effectively confounded steps toward rescue. In Switzerland, however, WRB provision of financial support for refugees admitted to the country and assurances of postwar evacuation of refugees helped ease Switzerland's restrictive policies toward letting in Jews. (While about 27,000 Jewish refugees were taken into Switzerland during the war, at least 30,000 others were either turned back at Switzerland's borders or, having crossed the border, expelled from Switzerland into Nazi-controlled territory.)

In all, the WRB succeeded in extracting about 15,000 Jews (as well as 20,000 non-Jews) from axis-controlled areas. In addition, the office in Switzerland was effective, despite being hamstrung by limited funds, in getting money across the border to underground forces in Nazi-occupied areas for the rescue, hiding, and care of Jews, and it is estimated that at least 10,000 Jews survived largely because of these efforts.

Both the impact of the WRB's work and the undermining of its efforts by American and British obstructionism are illustrated by events in Hungary in 1944. Hungary, an ally of the Nazis, had enacted Nazi-style anti-Jewish legislation but had left the nearly 800,000 Jews in the country for the most part physically unscathed — by far the largest still intact Jewish community in Europe. However, in March, 1944, the Germans, concerned that Hungary might negotiate a separate peace with the allies, occupied the country. In mid-May, the Nazis, under Adolf Eichmann, began the deportation of Hungarian Jews to Auschwitz. Steps in the concentration of Hungarian Jews into collection centers and in their deportation to the death camp were known in the West virtually as they were happening.

In April, details of the Auschwitz death camp and its "processing" of Jews had reached the West. The fate awaiting Hungary's Jews was clear. Also at this time, American Air Corps facilities in southern Italy had evolved to the point where they were mounting an intensive schedule of missions over eastern and central Europe. The WRB joined other voices urging the bombing of Auschwitz and of key railheads on the route from Hungary to the death camp, but to no avail. (Were the gas chambers destroyed, the Nazis would no doubt have tried to kill as many Jews as possible by other means. But to do so would have required much more manpower than the death camp. It was obvious that, with Nazi forces in retreat, the killings could not have proceeded nearly as thoroughly whatever the effort.) Despite the fact that bombing flights were passing over Auschwitz and attacking industrial sites near the gas chambers and crematoria, and also operated near the railheads, the Americans and British rejected plans to target either.[46]

On May 19, 1944, four days after the start of the mass deportations from Hungary, Eichmann sent Joel Brand, a Hungarian Jew, to Istanbul with an offer to exchange one million Jews for 100,000 trucks, ostensibly to be used only on the Eastern front. The significance of the offer is not fully known, although some scholarship suggests it may have been a feeler to the West by Himmler in the context of pursuing a separate peace. Brand sought to transmit the offer to the Jewish leadership in Palestine but was arrested by the British, taken to Cairo, and incarcerated.

Brand was interviewed by the WRB there, and the WRB, with some additional American Administration backing, urged that, even if the plan was thought unacceptable, Brand ought to be allowed to return to Budapest with at least hints of Allied interest. It was argued that such a tack, rather than the current message of rejection, might well buy time and some interim protection for those Jews still alive. But Britain refused to release him, fearing, again, according to British documents, that negotiations might, "lead to an offer to unload an even greater number of Jews onto our hands."[47]

In the face of the British stance, the WRB lent its support to two efforts by European Jewish leaders to convey to the Germans that the Allies were secretly considering the offer and thereby to play along the negotiations and perhaps even elicit some release of Jews from the Germans as signs of the sincerity of their offer. Although these contacts proceeded with no substance behind them on the Jewish side, with WRB support some 15,000 lives seem to have been spared through the ruse. (The Nazis transported nearly 1,700 Hungarian Jews to Switzerland. Another 18,000 were sent to a labor project in Austria rather than to Auschwitz, with three-quarters of them surviving the war.)[48]

In addition, in June, 1944, the WRB arranged through the head of its Swedish office to have Raoul Wallenberg go to Hungary. Wallenberg, working as, in effect, the WRB's representative in Hungary but with the authority and the cover of a Swedish diplomatic appointment, aggressively issued protective Swedish papers and provided safe houses to more than 20,000 Jews.[49]

Between mid-May and early July, about 440,000 Hungarian Jews were deported to Auschwitz and murdered. Throughout this time Western pressure on Hungary, much of it generated by the WRB, intensified. In early July, in the face as well of mounting German setbacks, the head of Hungary's fascist government, Admiral Horthy, demanded an end to the deportations. At that point about 350,000 Jews remained alive in Hungary, 230,000 of them in Budapest.

Horthy offered to let all Jewish children with visas, and any Jew with an entry permit to Palestine, leave the country. The WRB urged rapid action on the offer; the British balked and managed to delay even provisional British-American acceptance for a month.[50] By then, however, the Germans had taken steps to block any large-scale exit of Jews. Two months later they deposed Horthy and installed a radically pro-Nazi regime that soon embarked on wholesale massacre of Jews in Budapest.

The killing ended only in February, 1945, when the Russians took the city. At that point only 120,000 Jews were still alive. But the survival of these was due in large part to the WRB, which had figured in bringing the pressure to bear that led to Horthy's stopping deportations and which had sponsored Wallenberg's work. In addition to the more than 20,000 people he directly protected, Wallenberg had also been instrumental in mobilizing other neutral legations to extend protection to Budapest Jews and played what appears to have been a crucial role as well in preventing the final liquidation of the Budapest ghetto and its 70,000 inhabitants.

LESSONS

From its inception, in January, 1944, until the end of the war, the WRB, despite the very limited support given it by the Roosevelt Administration, made the difference in the survival of what appears to have been between 150,000 and 200,000 Jews. Available evidence strongly suggests that several times that number among the dead, perhaps many more, could have been rescued had the United States taken steps that had been urged upon it from the earliest reports of the massacres and that were readily within its power to take. That the American Jewish community was unable to sway the administration to give up its obstructionism and pursue a determined and committed policy of rescue represented a catastrophic failure of political power.

In large part this was due, of course, to the Jewish community's inexorably compromised political leverage in the face of the powerful anti-Jewish sentiment that pervaded American society at the time.

But what effective rescue measures were ultimately taken, through the WRB, came about largely through Jewish efforts. They were the result, in particular, of a campaign to shift congressional sentiment toward supporting rescue and challenging administration inaction, thereby putting pressure on the administration finally to change its policies. The WRB was created in significant part through the work of a small group of Jewish activists unconnected with the mainstream Jewish leadership and often undermined by the mainstream leadership. This suggests that the failure to move the administration to act sooner and with more determination despite its obvious antipathy to doing so represented not only a failure due to the dearth of Jewish political power but also, at least in part, a failure in the wielding of that political power the Jewish community did have available to it.

This latter failure, in turn, can be traced largely to the corrosive impact upon American Jewry of the bias and hostility to which it was so widely subjected.[51] Again, many Jews fled their Jewish identity entirely, while even those who continued to attach some value to that identity and did not seek to jettison it were still commonly cowed enough by the surrounding bias that they sought to maintain a low profile regarding their Jewishness. Both patterns were even more characteristic of the more successful strata of American Jewry, those subpopulations who, despite the obstacles confronting them, had managed to establish niches for themselves in the wider world of the professions, or academia, or business, or public life, or entertainment. Many, in pursuing their aspirations, had eased their path to achievement by detaching themselves from their Jewish past. Others, perhaps feeling more vulnerable than those Jews on lower rungs, either because they were living in a wider world or because they felt they had more to lose, latterly sought to break or at least to attenuate their connection with matters Jewish, certainly not to emphasize those connections.

As noted before, those who chose to eschew Jewish concerns and Jewish causes often cast their doing so in a noble-sounding rhetoric of rejecting the particularist for the more universal. But they were typically motivated in large part by fear, by a cowing anticipation of being seen as separate and different, by intimidation in response to the anti-Semitic claim that, as Jews, they were unassimilable, were indeed separate and different, and by an eagerness to demonstrate otherwise. Intimately bound up with such feelings was a wish to believe that sufficient self-effacement vis-à-vis their Jewish identity would ultimately win them the full acceptance that had so far eluded them.

This defensive predilection to shun the "particularist" even infected Jews comfortable enough with their Jewish identity to assume positions in the Jewish leadership, and it did so, as it infected and inhibited others in the community, even in the face of the Nazi genocide. Judge Joseph Proskauer, president of the American Jewish Committee, remarked, "For Jews in America, [as] Jews, to demand any kind of political action is a negation of the fundamentals of American liberty and equality."[52] Proskauer opposed the Jewish leadership's "Stop Hitler Now!" rally in March, 1943. The American Jewish Committee agreed to lend fuller backing to Wise's initiatives only after Proskauer and his associates had seen that the rally had engaged the support of organized labor and of some Christian groups, and had been "decently conducted; it was addressed by prominent speakers; it was not flamboyant or vulgar." The Committee gave its endorsement only after being convinced that efforts to promote rescue would proceed "in a decent and decorous way."[53]

Others in the Jewish leadership shared at least to some degree Proskauer's views and concerns. Indeed, throughout the previous decade, from the time of Hitler's rise to power, major Jewish organizations, including the American Jewish Congress under Wise's leadership, repeatedly either voiced opposition, or responded with silence, or at best gave lukewarm support, to efforts introduced in Congress to liberalize immigration statutes. They took this stance essentially out of fear of an anti-Semitic backlash should Jews be perceived as pushing for relaxation of immigration restrictions in order to gain admission for their fellow Jews. Moreover, this pattern of response to initiatives touching on immigration continued throughout the war as well.[54]

Concerning other avenues of rescue, many of the plans formulated by Wise and his committee in December, 1942, including marches in major cities and a mass convergence on Washington to increase public awareness and pressure Congress and the administration to act, were never carried out. A crucial reason was that the leadership was unable to rally more than very limited non-Jewish support for these efforts and was reluctant to proceed with any tack that at once was not "decorous" and did not have sufficient compensatory sanction from non-Jews, any tack that was both somewhat confrontative and too exclusively Jewish.[55]

Would more aggressive steps by the Jewish leadership to promote rescue have resulted in an anti-Jewish backlash? No doubt in some quarters such steps would have been attacked as Jews pressing their own narrow interests, even acting in an unpatriotic manner, supposedly compromising shared goals for parochial ends and comfirming suspicions of their insularity, differentness, and disloyalty. There were certainly precedents for such responses and both Jewish and non-Jewish voices of warning. Prior to the 1936 Olympics in Berlin, for example, numerous public statements, most notably from American Olympic Committee president Avery Brundage and American representative to the International Olympic Committee Charles Sherrill, cast efforts to organize an American boycott of the games as a nefarious Jewish plot and warned American Jews that a boycott campaign would trigger an anti-Semitic backlash.[56] Joseph Kennedy, the isolationist patriarch of the Kennedy family, advised American Jews more generally to refrain from protesting events in Germany or risk facing increased anti-Jewish sentiment in America.[57] During the same period American Jewish entrepreneur and diplomat Jesse Strauss complained that Jewish efforts to promote measures against Nazi Germany would confirm to other Americans that Jews are indeed "a race apart, with a group solidarity that prevents them from becoming a sincere and patriotic part of the country in which they live."[58]

The Jewish leadership's unhappiness with the Bergson group's efforts was, in fact, not simply a matter of political competition but entailed discomfort with the hard-hitting rhetoric of the Bergson group's newspaper campaign, particularly its ads, with their "undecorous" demands for action to rescue European Jews and attacks on government foot-dragging. Indeed, according to a State Department memorandum, Wise and several other Jewish leaders, in a meeting with Breckinridge Long in October, 1943, expressed concern that the Bergson group's tactics would "lead to increased anti-Semitism" in the United States.[59]

Yet, if the leadership's mass meetings and news conferences increased public awareness and rallied some support, the more dramatic efforts of the Bergson group appear to have been notably more successful in heightening awareness and winning support. In particular, it was the hard-hitting efforts of the Bergson group that won backing for rescue in key quarters in Congress despite the prevalence in Congress of sentiments that did not predispose it to concern with European Jews and efforts for their rescue.

While anti-Semitism was epidemic in American society, the rabid, hardcore anti-Semites incapable of recognizing Jews as fellow human beings were distinctly in the minority. For much of the country, anti-Jewish sentiment was not so impervious to issues of human suffering and human decency. Events during the war demonstrate both the real impediments to rescue that flowed from American anti-Semitism and the reality that the intimidating impact of that anti-Jewish animus on American Jews led them to compromise appeals for rescue to a degree that underestimated the surrounding society's capacity to respond positively.

Illustrative of this was the attempt, after creation of the War Refugee Board, to establish "free ports" in the United States. The WRB executive order had called for setting up temporary havens for rescued Jews. Various groups, including Bergson and his allies and Morgenthau and his associates at Treasury, urged arrangement for such refuges in the United States. But Roosevelt dragged his feet on the temporary haven, or "free port," proposals and major American Jewish organizations did not aggressively lobby for their establishment, largely, still, out of fears of an anti-Semitic backlash. Yet important non-Jewish voices endorsed the plan and a Gallup poll revealed that 70 percent of Americans supported temporary havens on American territory. (Ultimately, in June, 1944, Roosevelt granted temporary asylum to 1,000 refugees, 918 of whom were Jews, and would allow no more.)[60]

It is noteworthy also that many Jews, including individuals within the leadership, had, under the weight of the surrounding anti-Semitism, internalized the "parochialism" canard and genuinely struggled with the propriety of aggressively demanding special steps to rescue Jews threatened with extermination. In contrast, it was largely non-Jewish voices, starting with some key church figures in Britain but ultimately joined by prominent individuals in the United States, who cast the martyrdom of the Jews as a crime against humanity. In their calls for rescue efforts, they pointed out that, if Jews were the victims, this was nonetheless not simply a Jewish issue, that the genocide was an assault upon and a test of Western civilization.

Aside from the successes of the Bergson group, there are other indications that more aggressive steps by the leadership might have advanced rescue efforts significantly. As David Wyman notes in discussing the aborted plans for mass demonstrations in large cities and a mass convening in Washington: "The mere threat of a march on Washington by 50,000 to 100,000 blacks in 1941 had extracted an executive order from President Roosevelt that helped increase employment opportunities for black Americans"; a step for which there was hardly much congressional or administration or popular predisposition. "A massive demonstration of concern in late 1942 or early 1943 might have influenced [Roosevelt] to take action many months sooner than he did."[61]

If internalization of the "parochialism" canard and an associated hesitancy to act affected even members of the Jewish leadership, this phenomenon, and more generally a defensive shying away from specifically Jewish issues, was, again, characteristic of large segments of the Jewish community, particularly within more successful echelons of American Jewry. Among the Jews closest to Roosevelt and wielding influence on the administration, none other than Morgenthau appears to have taken up the rescue issue with the President. Bernard Baruch and Herbert Lehman seem to have avoided the subject entirely. Felix Frankfurter and David Nolan, a presidential assistant, did very little.[62]

Samuel Rosenman, special counsel to the president and an advisor on Jewish matters, worked consistently against the president's taking steps that would have abetted rescue. When the Bergson group organized a delegation of Orthodox rabbis to visit Washington and lobby Congress and the administration for intervention, Rosenman tried to block the visit and then encouraged Roosevelt in his decision not to meet with the rabbis.[63] When the WRB pressed the White House for a more explicit statement threatening war-crimes prosecutions against those involved in the slaughter of the Jews, Rosenman worked to quash the effort and subsequently to water down the statement, placing less emphasis on crimes against the Jews. (The statement he diluted had been approved by three Cabinet departments and had even gained State Department support.)[64] Rosenman also fought Morgenthau on creation of the WRB. Rosenman's explanation for his actions was concern that government help to Europe's Jews would increase anti-Semitism in America and also hurt the administration.

Among Jews with strong and prominent ties to the administration, Morgenthau was the one figure distinguished by efforts to advocate for rescue. But it is noteworthy that even Morgenthau, although aware for much of the previous year of State Department obstructionism and although obviously concerned about the fate of Europe's Jews, hesitated to confront the president. He acted only after months of urging by key figures on his staff (Josiah DuBois, Randolph Paul, John Pehle, Ansel Luxford) and by Oscar Cox of the Lend-Lease Administration, all of them non-Jews, and only after being presented by his staff with their "Report to the Secretary on the Acquiescence of This Government in the Murder of the Jews."

Of Jews in Congress at the time, David Wyman writes, "Only Emanuel Celler persistently urged government rescue actions. Samuel Dickstein joined the struggle from time to time. Four others [out of the total of seven] seldom raised the issue. Sol Bloom [as Wyman documents] sided with the State Department throughout."[65] Bloom was chairman of the House Foreign Affairs Committee and in a particularly good position to exert some pressure to promote rescue. But he appears to have been most concerned with overcoming whatever prejudice there might be toward him as a Jew, especially in the State Department, by demonstrating his capacity to rise above "particularist" issues like the fate of European Jewry.

The failure of most media outlets to give prominent coverage to news related to the Nazis' campaign of extermination compromised efforts to increase public awareness and rally support for rescue, and prominent Jewish-owned news outlets shared in this failure. The *New York Times*, in the years before the war, had already established a pattern of limiting discussion of the Nazis' depredations of the Jews. When, shortly after Hitler's ascension to power, the paper was challenged to open its letter columns to the plight of Germany's Jews, publisher Adolph Ochs refused. He explained that to do so would generate too much mail and would require, under *Times* rules, that he give equal space to the other side.[66] (Almost two decades earlier, in 1915, Ochs had warned an editor against giving too prominent coverage to an American Jewish Committee campaign for aid to Jewish civilian populations that were enduring particular hardship in eastern European war zones. The publisher suggested that the campaign was too parochial.[67]) When news of the mass killing began to emerge, the *Times* consistently buried the story. The revelation by Rabbi Wise in November, 1942, of two million Jews murdered was reported on page 10, next to an article about a truck hijacking in New Jersey.

People who have worked for and written about the *Times* have spoken of management's not wanting the *Times* to appear to be concerned with Jewish issues or to be thought of as a Jewish paper.[68] But this explanation for the paper's subdued coverage of the plight of Europe's Jews is not simply a retrospective one; the nature of the *Times'* coverage, and the explanation for it, were perceived similarly by many people then. For example, Deborah Lipstadt writes that publisher and newsman Oswald Garrison Villard complained in 1944 that a resolution by 500 Christian ministers and laymen denouncing the "systematic Nazi destruction of the Jewish people" was given only a few lines by the *Times* and buried on page 7, and a similar event was reported on page 17. Villard blamed the paper's "unfortunate trait" of not wanting to appear "a vigorous defender" of the Jews.[69]

As Lipstadt points out, the *Times'* dereliction in refusing to give the plight of Europe's Jews the prominence it warranted had consequences far beyond the *Times'* readership. As America's newspaper of record, the *Times* was looked to by other papers and exerted considerable influence over what stories were deemed important and given prominence, and what stories were not, in newspapers across the country. In addition, many papers subscribed to the *Times* wire service and reprinted important *Times* stories.[70]

The *Washington Post*, also a Jewish-owned paper in a position to influence the level of public awareness and attention, likewise gave little prominence to coverage of the genocide. Moreover, publisher Eugene Meyer strongly objected to calls for rescue. The paper ran a four-part front page series — much higher profile than it gave any Holocaust story — attacking the Bergson group; a series that it subsequently had to retract because of inaccuracies.[71] In addition, Meyer wrote a letter to the U.S. solicitor general accusing those promoting rescue of harassing the president, and concluded that he felt it is not "necessary for any pressure group, however well meaning, to devote its time and money to the business of 'molding American opinion' on this subject."[72]

Walter Lippmann, perhaps the most influential news columnist of the day, wrote nothing about the genocide. Lippmann's discomfort with his Jewish identity and hostility toward other Jews were noted in Chapter Five. In 1933, he defended Hitler and the Germans and insinuated that the Jews were responsible for their ill treatment.[73] In November, 1938, after a five-year silence on the issue of Germany and the Jews, he wrote two columns touching on refugees. Without explicitly mentioning Jews or anti-Semitism, he characterized the problem as simply Europe's "overpopulation" and its having "too many shop keepers, professional men, artists and intellectuals." He opposed liberalizing America's quota system and suggested the excess population could perhaps be relocated to Africa.

Lippmann's influence translated into his views being invariably espoused by others, including others in the media. *Time* magazine, in December, 1938, describing Lippmann as the nation's "most statesmanly Jewish pundit," approvingly cited his stance on immigration.[74] Through the course of the war, Lippmann was silent on the plight of Europe's Jews.

The attitudes and actions of the Jewish leadership and of many others in the Jewish community in their responding to the European catastrophe reflect an additional impact of anti-Semitism. This was an impact somewhat distinct from the shrinking from an aggressive public stance, or very often from any public stance, out of fear of fanning anti-Semitic flames, fear of being identified as too Jewish or being labeled with the canard of acting too narrowly or parochially or unpatriotically. It was distinct also from the internalization and embrace of that canard and the championing as a "virtue" eschewing "Jewish" concerns for supposedly broader and less "particularist" interests.

Again, in America as in Europe, many Jews, in the face of anti-Jewish sentiment in the surrounding society, abandoned their Jewish identity for some alternative one, often political, and more typically an identity on the political Left than on the Right. Similarly, once more as in Europe, those who continued to value their Jewish identity very often sought, in the face of anti-Jewish animus, to connect themselves in self-deluding ways with broader causes, to see a self-deluding complementarity between the latter and their Jewish identity. That is, they perceived such connections in a manner that went beyond simply taking on, for example, an additional identity, as state citizen, or beyond simply seeking political alliances with other minorities or other workers or others striving for a more liberal and open and accepting society. They were inclined rather to see such connections in a manner that entailed assumptions of transcendent shared interest and shared perspective that was a distortion of realities.

In Europe, from the early nineteenth century and even earlier, many Jews reasonably saw liberal political forces as potential allies in their effort to break down barriers of *de jure* discrimination, and indeed such alliances at times bore fruit. But Jews often chose to comprehend Jew-hatred as simply emanating from ruling elites, from a conservative nobility and conservative churches, or, if infecting other segments of the population, doing so because of the manipulations of the elites and the ignorance of the lower classes. They chose to believe that by making common cause with the middle class and the working class they would diminish the power of the elites, improve the conditions and the awareness of the lower classes, and bring about a radical resolution of anti-Jewish sentiment. This comprehension was, of course, a gross distortion of reality. It ignored the strength of anti-Jewish bias, amplified by commercial and professional competition, that characterized much of the European middle class, as well as the force of populist anti-Semitism. It ignored the anti-Jewish rhetoric that figured in much of liberal and socialist polemic. Such willful blindness rendered Jewish communities unprepared for the political betrayals they recurrently suffered from the Left.

The same phenomenon figured prominently in the United States. American Jews, overwhelmingly part of the urban working class and even more overwhelmingly having working-class roots, commonly chose to perceive anti-Semitism as emanating from and sustained by the nation's conservative elites, or, when encountered in the street, as due to Old World ignorance and the manipulations of the nation's elites. They chose to invest in liberal politics, and particularly in Roosevelt's grand alliance of the common man and programs for the common man, expectations of a new social force that would transcend old biases and, by educating, lifting up, and demonstrating shared interests, would bring about a radical end to those biases, including anti-Semitism. In the context of such comprehensions, of such self-deluding simplifications of liberal and conservative, working-class and privileged, biased and unbiased (or, irredeemably biased and biased but educable and reformable), it was very difficult indeed for many Jews to look objectively at Roosevelt. American Jews were largely unprepared to recognize that the leader who had forged the alliance of the underprivileged, who had shown such feeling for the downtrodden common man and worked so hard to bring him succor, whose Administration employed Jews at all levels in a manner that contrasted dramatically to the obstacles to employment Jews routinely encountered in the wider society, could be at best indifferent to, could be unwilling to offer any succor to, the Jews of Europe being murdered by the thousands daily in a program of total annihilation.

What Jews commonly construed to be inexorably linked sensibilities and sympathies were largely linkages of their own imagining, a form of wishful thinking, and did not conform to reality. Their resistance to recognizing this mitigated against their responding more effectively to the Roosevelt Administration's foot-dragging and obstructionism regarding rescue.

Rabbi Wise, over the entire four decades of his career, had been active in the social justice movement, working alongside Christian reform leaders to advance workers' rights, black rights, and honest government. He was an early supporter of Roosevelt and helped him win the New York governorship in 1928. He withheld his support in the 1932 presidential campaign because of Roosevelt's refusal to confront Tammany Hall corruption in New York City, but thereafter became once again an enthusiastic backer. An early advocate, with the development of the Depression, of indigent relief and unemployment insurance, Wise was obviously sympathetic to Roosevelt's New Deal programs and remained consistently loyal to Roosevelt throughout his presidency. He appears to have been convinced, despite all the evidence to the contrary, despite Roosevelt's actions, that Roosevelt did want to help Europe's Jews in the 1930s and during the war. He was unable to grasp the president's indifference and callousness toward Hitler's Jewish victims.[75]

Even in the face of Roosevelt's refusal to intervene when intervention would have cost him nothing politically and would have required virtually no effort, Wise continued to defend the president. In the midst of the Bermuda debacle, in a note to a colleague, Wise wrote, "[Roosevelt] is still our friend, even though he does not move as expeditiously as we would wish."[76] In August, 1943, speaking before an audience of mainstream Jewish leaders, Wise responded to criticism of Roosevelt's inaction on rescue coming from some Jewish quarters. He declared, "I choose to register my unchanged faith in the deep humanity of the foremost leader of free men in the world today, Franklin Delano Roosevelt. This body of delegated and widely representative American Jews, dedicated to the triumph of our Nation's cause, declares its deep and unchangeable confidence in the integrity and goodwill of its Commander-in-Chief."[77] When the Republican National Convention, in June, 1944, put a strong pro-Zionist plank into its platform for the upcoming election and criticized Roosevelt for not pressing Britain to open Mandate Palestine to Jewish refugees, Wise wrote to Roosevelt, "As an American Jew and Zionist, I am deeply ashamed of the reference to you in the Palestine Resolution adopted by the Republican National Convention. It is utterly unjust, and you may be sure that American Jews will come to understand how unjust it is."[78]

Wise's trust in Roosevelt, and the distorted assumptions that underlay it, were shared by many American Jews, including many in the Jewish leadership, and compromised the American Jewish effort to help the Jews of Europe. It reinforced the inhibitions born of intimidation. It figured, for example, in the leadership's refusal to take more aggressive and confrontational steps such as mass demonstrations, work stoppages, and a march on Washington, or a hard-hitting advertising campaign. It was also a factor in the leadership's reluctance to bring pressure to bear on the administration by working more effectively with Roosevelt's political foes in Congress.

The Jewish leadership's protectiveness of Roosevelt was an additional and significant element as well in its antagonism toward the Bergson group, in its criticism of the group's confrontational and very effective advertising campaign and in its attempts to undermine the group's mobilizing of support for rescue in Congress by working with a broad array of congressional allies, including leading Republicans. The leadership did at times solicit and receive support for its public rallies and other rescue-related events from prominent Republicans such as Wendell Willkie, Roosevelt's 1940 election opponent, and New York governor Thomas Dewey. But the Bergson group, eager to forge as wide a coalition as possible to bring pressure to bear for rescue, made much more use of Republicans and other political figures seen by the White House as opponents and rivals. Willkie and former President Herbert Hoover were particularly forthcoming throughout the war in their efforts to promote and support rescue.

Not only members of the Jewish leadership were uncomfortable with this use by the Bergson group of the president's political foes. Many other Jews took issue with the Bergson group's work with Republican leaders either because of loyalty to Roosevelt or more broadly because of their uncritical loyalty to the political Left. In a similar vein, some Jews attacked the Bergson group for enlisting the support of conservative publisher and Roosevelt critic William Randolph Hearst, even though Hearst was unique among the nation's newspaper publishers in repeatedly using editorials in his syndicate's papers to expose what was happening to Europe's Jews and to demand rescue efforts.[79]

The determination to mount an aggressive challenge to Administration obstructionism and to forge as broad a coalition as possible in support of rescue figured prominently in the effectiveness of the Bergson group, and the self-deluding political orthodoxies embraced by a substantial portion of American Jewry, including key figures in the Jewish leadership, played a significant role in compromising Jewish efforts to promote rescue.

SEVEN

Responding to Acceptance:
American Jewry After the War

Jews are as rich as Episcopalians but . . . they vote like Puerto Ricans.
Irving Kristol[1]

DECLINING ANTI-SEMITISM, PERSISTING PSYCHOLOGICAL STIGMATA

In the aftermath of World War II the pervasiveness and intensity of anti-Semitism in the United States diminished. Fuller revelations of the horrors of the Nazi campaign against the Jews, of that fruit of anti-Jewish bigotry and hatred, were one factor in this change. But even those revelations did not automatically alter attitudes. The change evolved and progressed over a number of years and was reinforced by such other factors as expansion of government-protected civil rights in the decades after the war and legislation outlawing bias in employment, housing, and other spheres. Economic prosperity, and reform in immigration law and immigration patterns that rendered the United States a more multicultural society, also figured in the lessening of anti-Jewish sentiment. While more tolerant attitudes evolved gradually, and while reservoirs of anti-Jewish sentiment, and outright Jew-hatred, still persist, it can very reasonably be argued that the United States in the last decades of the twentieth century offered the most benign environment for a Diaspora Jewish community in the 2,600-year history of the Diaspora.

Yet many within the American Jewish community have continued to exhibit psychological stigmata that are characteristic of the corrosive impact of a bias, prejudice and marginalization much more intense than anything most of these people have experienced. These include, among some people, an eagerness to separate themselves from any Jewish identity, not to be seen by others as Jews. One finds also in segments of the community, whether together with such an impulse to flee Jewish identity or distinct from it, a diminished sense of self, a sense of being flawed, connected with their being Jews, or a more specific incorporating of traditional negative comprehensions of Jews. There is still to be found among some Jews a feeling of having to prove oneself, or one's community, to be different from anti-Jewish stereotypes and canards, or of having to reform oneself or one's community in conformity with anti-Semitic indictments.

The explanation for this phenomenon appears to lie in a number of forces at work in American Jewish life since World War II. Anti-Semitism, although much diminished, has not disappeared. Particularly in the years immediately after the war but even subsequently for some, it has figured in a significant way in many individuals' personal experience, including their early, most reverberative experience, that which is likely to have the greatest impact on one's understanding of the world. Perhaps more significant for others has been the impact of parental attitudes, the perspective of parents who grew up in the years before and during World War II and bore the psychological scars of the pervasive anti-Jewish sentiment of that time. Even if they in most cases did not overtly convey to their children fear and distrust of the surrounding society, or openly display a sense of victimhood, they may commonly have exhibited a defensiveness, a sense of some ambivalence toward and discomfort with their Jewish identity, a diminished sense of self related to that identity, inspired by their exposure to a more intense and incessant anti-Jewish sentiment. These sensibilities may have been learned by their children despite the children's not having been themselves directly exposed to anti-Semitism; and such attitudes, once learned, could likewise be conveyed by some of these children to the subsequent generation even in the absence of significant direct experience of anti-Semitism.

Polls of American Jewish opinion regarding anti-Semitism are suggestive of such a dynamic. In a 1990 survey of affiliated Jews, half "strongly agreed" and another quarter "agreed" less emphatically that anti-Semitism is a serious problem in the United States,[2] results likely reflecting at least in part the transmission of family experience and associated wariness. They probably also reflect a sense that what anti-Semitic attitudes persist in the society, even if seemingly much diminished from earlier periods and no immediate threat, retain a potential to flare up dramatically and become threatening — a sense founded on popular understanding of events in Europe in the last century and popular comprehensions as well of other historical precedents.

The ongoing perception among Jews of substantial anti-Jewish bias in the surrounding society continued to manifest itself, through the decades after World War II, in embrace of that bias by many Jews, in their comprehension of Jewish identity as indeed defective, and, for some, in flight from the community. Most Jews, however, continued to retain a sense of connection with the Jewish community and to value that bond, and the diminishing level of anti-Jewish bias and of its overt expression in the surrounding society no doubt made it easier for many people to feel good about their ties to the community. But even developments in Jewish communal life that would seem to reflect a more intense and confident identification often represented a much more complex reality.

For example, in the 1950s and 1960s, as American Jews were largely freed of earlier impediments vis-à-vis educational and vocational opportunities, shared in the nation's growing prosperity, and joined the widespread urban exodus to the suburbs, there was an unprecedented boom in the forming of new congregations and construction of synagogues. Synagogue affiliation rose during those years from an estimated 20 percent of American Jews in the prewar decade to about 60 percent.[3] But various observers have argued that this development should be understood less as a confident assertion of what distinguished Jews from those around them, their particular faith, than as an exercise in conforming.

Community life in the surrounding society was largely organized around church affiliations, which were an element of normality. The organizing of Jewish life in new communities around synagogue affiliation was consistent with this pattern and therefore with the Jews' quest to make themselves like everyone else. It converged with the comprehension that emulating non-Jewish models was the key to acceptance, to tamping down anti-Jewish attitudes and fending off such attitudes' flaring up again. Moreover, as also has been noted by many observers, the element in the synagogue culture that most distinguished it from church culture, the Jewish religious content, was largely attenuated. Synagogue-sponsored religious education and literacy were typically superficial.[4]

Some have argued that conformity was indeed a condition for the acceptance of Jews in postwar America. But even if there has been a pragmatically sound element to the Jews' pursuit of conformity, there have also been notably delusional aspects to that pursuit's actual unfolding. Casting adaptations undertaken for the sake of winning acceptance as intrinsically superior to older Jewish ways, as "progressive" vis-à-vis older practices, is one such aspect; and the impulse to comprehend conformity's utility in moralistic and categorical terms — to claim that the preservation of differences was rightly perceived with distaste by the surrounding society, that pressures to conform were reasonable, and that embracing conformity would inexorably win acceptance — were more a reflection of wishful thinking in the face of trepidation than of ethical sensitivity or realistic assessment.

Moreover, elements of Jewish self-effacement and eschewing of "parochialism" have persisted even through later decades, even as the United States has grown to be much more a "multicultural" society and as ethnic and religious particularisms have become more accepted. Insofar as stigmata of corrosive external pressures have continued to mark Jewish life in America, they do not seem explicable simply in terms of what remains of anti-Jewish feeling, or actual pressures to conform, or even in terms of transmitted memories of earlier abuse and belief in its potential recrudescence. The phenomenon requires additional explanation.

At least part of the answer lies in the diminished meaningfulness of Jewish identity for many in the community. One of the consequences of American anti-Semitism earlier in the century was its inculcation in many Jews of a sense of the faith and the community as more stultifying and encumbering than supportive and vital. This was so even for large numbers of those Jews who held to their Jewish identity and to a connectedness with the community. Again, the tribulations of acculturation confronted by the immigrant generation, and worsened by the exceptional poverty of the Jewish immigrants, and the associated loss of authority of that generation, contributed as well to this sentiment by sapping the capacity of communal institutions to provide more effective countervailing weight against corrosive pressures from the surrounding society.

As a result, for large numbers even of those second- and third-generation Jews who remained connected to the community and continued to attach value to the faith, that connection and attachment became more *pro forma* and nostalgic than alive. It was characterized by perhaps an attenuated religious observance, certainly a lessened perception of observance providing an essential rhythm and meaning to their lives, by the investment of essential meaning elsewhere, and by an ambivalence toward what of their Jewish legacy they wished to convey to their children. On the one hand, they wanted to pass on what they continued to value in their Jewish identity; on the other, they harbored aspirations for their children that were focused elsewhere and they did little to transmit to them a meaningful Jewish legacy. This was the ambivalence and the empty legacy, the legacy that had largely poured away like sand between one's fingers, that Kafka had written of receiving from his father.

Surveys of those American Jewish children whose parents cared enough about their Jewish identity to send them to supplemental school for religious studies and have them prepared for bar and bat mitzvah have routinely reported the overwhelming sentiment among such children that their religious education was a negative experience, one that even pulled them away from rather than pushed them toward a closer affiliation with faith and community. It was a largely empty chore that took them from more attractive and meaningful after-school activities. This common sentiment is not due simply to the pedagogical shortcomings of Hebrew school programs. It reflects more profoundly the experience of that schooling as not essentially related to the rest of their lives, certainly not to their home life. It reflects parental ambivalence of wanting to convey a Jewish legacy but not being interested in living that legacy at home. It is symptomatic of the negative complementarity between a home in which there is a vague and ambiguous Jewish spiritual connectedness devoid of much content and a religious-school experience in which there is content devoid — largely because of the disconnect from home — of spiritual meaningfulness.

In many of those who grew up before and during World War II, the mix of anti-Jewish sentiment in the surrounding society and a dearth of countervailing forces in the Jewish community led to, at best, ambivalence toward Jewish identity. One result was the transmission over several generations of a Jewish legacy progressively emptied of content, which rendered still more dramatic erosion almost inevitable. Under such conditions, within a few generations little remains to hold children to any connectedness even in the absence of anti-Jewish pressures in the wider society. They will simply drift away — and what there is of anti-Jewish sentiment in the broader society, however diminished from earlier periods, will accelerate the process.

For those who do retain a sense of connectedness, the diminution of meaningful content engenders more vulnerability to self-doubt and defensiveness even in the face of attenuated anti-Jewish pressures. They are more subject to having their perception of Jewish identity defined by the wider society, to embracing negative images from the wider society and feeling obliged to reform oneself or one's community in conformity with anti-Jewish indictments. In this way, parentally programmed ignorance supplements parentally transmitted self-doubt, ambivalence, and defensiveness learned in an age of greater pressures from the surrounding society.

An obvious question is to what degree might the diminished meaningfulness of Jewish learning and literacy to large swathes of American Jewry simply be part of the broad secularization of American society. How much is it a product primarily of the social and cultural forces that have figured in this broader phenomenon rather than a consequence of the Jews' predicament as a minority that had earlier in the century been the object of intense vilification and discrimination and is even today the target of some anti-Jewish sentiment? But there is much that weighs against this alternative explanation.

The drift among American Jews from religious practice and literacy has been much greater than that of other religious groups in the United States, even adjusting for idiosyncratic demographic characteristics of American Jewry such as high education level and concentration in major urban centers. For example, surveys have indicated that Jews practice their religion least among college students, both at elite colleges and at schools more generally.[5] This difference reflects the corrosive impact of anti-Jewish pressures from the surrounding society, particularly earlier in the century. It reflects the consequent generational transmission, in large segments of American Jewry, of religious connections that were progressively drained of their former meaningfulness as American Jews defined aspirations for their children among which Jewish religious connectedness had less and less of a place. This is in contrast to the central role that such connectedness has retained for much of non-Jewish America.

Also noteworthy is that in the second half of the twentieth century American Jews were dramatically overrepresented among those drawn to exotic religions and cults in the United States. This is another indication that the widespread abandonment of Jewish religious and spiritual connectedness reflected more than simply secularizing trends in the surrounding society. Judaism has been so drained of its spiritual and religious meaning in Jewish homes that those seeking bonds of faith and spirituality have frequently been unaware of the reservoirs of both in their own backgrounds and were left to look elsewhere — and their doing so has exceeded any similar phenomenon in other groups.

Another salient pattern is that of secular Jews often reserving a particular hostility toward those Jews who continue to find meaning and comfort in their faith, a hostility in contrast to their much more benign, positive regard for adherents of other faiths. Clearly such responses represent something other than simply secularist distaste for religious commitment. They reflect the embrace of negative attitudes toward the Jewish religion that were once, and are presumed to be still, abroad in the wider society. They are largely motivated by some mix of ignorance — a background in which Jewish identity had been drained of all substantive content and meaning — and the determination to distance oneself from the "parochially" Jewish and to aver different, broader and more mainstream sympathies and allegiances.

The particular hostility of some secularized Jews toward religious Jews is, most typically, one manifestation of a broader phenomenon, an embarrassment and discomfort and often hostility of some Jews — religiously affiliated as well as secularized — in the presence of the more overtly identifiably Jewish, whether identifiable in a religious context, hasidim, for example, or even modern Orthodox wearing kippot, or Jews identifiable in terms of manifesting ethnic stereotypes. Again, this is typically a response not felt in the presence of those overtly manifesting some other religious affiliation or other ethnic stereotype and is related to a particular discomfort with Jews calling attention to themselves. It is a reflection of people's own self-consciousness and defensiveness and ultimately of their sense of a vulnerability as Jews despite the broad tolerance of American society and even despite some acculturated expectation of that tolerance. Fearfulness, and a wish to believe that Jewish self-effacement will be the path to acceptance, lies at the heart of such Jewish intolerance of the Jewish, even if those who practice that intolerance choose to construe their doing so as the cultivation of an ethically or intellectually superior stance.

THE HOLOCAUST AND ISRAEL IN AMERICAN JEWISH LIFE

Seymour Martin Lipset and Earl Raab note three types of needs that a group identity must meet in order to sustain group cohesion: "(1) the need to mount group defense against disadvantage; (2) the need to belong to a familiar and accepting community, marked by 'a developed set of customs and traditions'; and (3) the need to draw on such customs and traditions to give unique form, meaning, and direction to personal life."[6] For Jews, the unique form, meaning and direction to life derived from membership in the community has emanated, of course, from the religious-historical tradition of faith and people. This has been so even more emphatically in the wake of the dissolution of Jewish autonomy and the end of what shape and direction to life was given by Jewish autonomous institutions. The decline of religious literacy and meaningfulness has consequently eroded the significance of Jewish identity for many.

The need for defense in response to external pressures is in itself a very weak basis for group cohesion in the long term. Such pressures are intrinsically corrosive and many will flee the group to escape them, while even for those who remain true, the external assaults will often undermine people's sense of themselves and of their group. As the cogent meaningfulness derived from their religious-historical legacy is lost among Jews, defensiveness becomes a still weaker reed and defection inexorably becomes more widespread. Even under conditions of much diminished external pressure, many will see little reason to hold to their Jewish identity.

Nor is a connection to Jewish identity founded on nostalgia or on a more purely ethnic sense of affiliation stripped of religious literacy and spiritual immediacy likely to suffice to counter corrosive forces. In the American environment, as Lipset and Raab point out, other ethnic groups such as Italian Americans have surrendered their group cohesion, through, for example, intermarriage, at even a greater pace than have American Jews.[7]

One factor that, in the view of Lipset and Raab, has very likely slowed erosion of the American Jewish community has been the emergence of Israel, which has not only reinforced group cohesion on ethnic terms and evoked concomitant impulses to group defense but has served to reinject some religious and historical content into Jewish self-comprehension.[8] The other major transforming event in Jewish life in the twentieth century, the Holocaust, has also loomed large in American Jewish self-comprehension and self-definition. But it has done so mainly in terms of connectedness on an ethnic level and defensiveness, with little substantive impact on the void left by the decline in religious literacy and connectedness and by the particular loss of meaning derived from that decline.

Remembrance of the Holocaust has touched in various ways on American Jewish self-consciousness over the last half-century. American Jewish focus on the Holocaust increased dramatically in the 1960s. This occurred in significant part in response to events not directly involving the American Jewish community, events such as the Eichmann trial in 1961 and the prelude to the Six Day War, when much of Jewry seemed again faced with potential annihilation and analogies were widely drawn to the Holocaust. But since the 1960s Jewish organizations, and many individual Jews acting independently, have obviously played major roles in bringing about the current high level of Jewish, as well as non-Jewish, indeed worldwide, awareness of the Holocaust.

People engaged in Holocaust remembrance efforts have been motivated largely by convictions that they have a moral obligation — to the memory of the slaughtered and to the integrity of Western civilization — not to allow the history of those in many respects unique and uniquely horrific events to slip from the world's consciousness. Many have also believed that keeping the memory of those events alive could contribute to the prevention of a recurrence of such a catastrophe, whether again with Jews as victims or with some other vulnerable population as target. These motivations are obviously laudatory and their objectives indeed valuable.

But some voices within American Jewry have questioned the extent of the community's focus on the Holocaust. They have expressed misgivings regarding the place given it as perhaps the central defining element of contemporary Jewish experience, as demonstrated by the proliferation across America of community-sponsored Holocaust memorials. They have questioned the significance and impact of that focus both within the Jewish community and in relations between Jews and non-Jews. In terms of intercommunal relations, some have articulated doubts about the value of emphasizing to the surrounding society images of Jews as victims rather than the positive, soul-enhancing, confident, and life-affirming aspects of the faith.

But more corrosive, in the view of many, has been the significance and impact of this focus within the community. Various voices, perhaps particularly from among the more religiously observant within American Jewry, have suggested that the prominent place given the Holocaust reflects the fact of so much of the community having lost touch with other potential defining elements of Jewish identity, elements embodying those positive, life-affirming, and soul-enhancing aspects of the faith. They argue, in essence, that the Holocaust has taken on additional meaning — even beyond that central meaning it would have in any case — because it has come to fill the vacuum left in Jewish self-definition by the diminution of religious and spiritual literacy and connectedness.

Observers have also been troubled by the potential effects of this emphasis within the community. They have acknowledged that some people may respond to the events of the Holocaust by rededicating themselves to faith and community, to the spiritual and cultural legacy of those who died, to honor their memory and defy the murderers. But they have suggested that many more, educated in the comprehension of victimhood as a central defining element in Jewish identity, will be moved, particularly in the context of a dearth of more positive education in and connectedness with faith and community, to disassociate themselves from Jewish identity and to seek what is life-affirming, soul-enhancing, and confident elsewhere. Many critics who comment on what they see as troubling aspects of the American Jewish focus on the Holocaust question whether some of the resources dedicated to Holocaust memorials would not be better spent on promoting more meaningful Jewish education or in other programs building for a future rather than commemorating the past.

Another aspect of American Jewry's focus on the Holocaust that has been the subject of some discussion and debate concerns the organized community's explications of the Holocaust and of its significance in history. It entails disagreements on the relative weight to be given to comprehension of the Holocaust as an exclusively Jewish catastrophe versus understanding of it as a catastrophe for all humanity, an event of significance for everyone.

Obviously the victims were Jews targeted specifically because they were Jews, and obviously the Holocaust was the product of particular historical circumstances that converged with almost two millennia of marginalization and demonization of Jews in Christian Europe. Generalizations about the victimization of abused minorities that blur the unique savagery and brutality of the Holocaust and the particulars of its victims and of the history and circumstances that led to the crimes against them do violence to the history and a disservice to the victims. On the other hand, other vulnerable populations have, of course, also been subjected to horrendous victimization, including mass murder, and discussions of the Holocaust that seek to draw general lessons about bias and bigotry and the crimes they are capable of generating have their clear legitimacy and value.

The debate is one of balance, with some arguing that various attempts to generalize the significance of the Holocaust have at times virtually airbrushed out the Jewish identity of the victims. A subtext of such concerns has been the perception that predilections in that direction reflect the modern Jewish unease, shared by much of the community, with Jewish particularism. There is a sense that what is at work here is an eagerness for the sake of promoting acceptance to demonstrate that Jews are like everyone else, that even their tragedies are like everyone else's, and a pushing of this agenda even at the expense of bowdlerizing the history of the Holocaust and doing a disservice to its victims.

Those who discern these proclivities in some American Jewish work on the Holocaust have mustered data in support of their concerns. For example, "Facing History and Ourselves," a program for Holocaust education founded with funding mainly from Jewish philanthropists, has been extremely successful in introducing the Holocaust and Holocaust-related studies as a self-contained curriculum in American schools. The basic curriculum workbook, *Facing History and Ourselves: Holocaust and Human Behavior*,[9] consists of didactic material along with suggested class exercises and relates the Holocaust and its origins to all manner of bias and prejudice. To the argument that many of the analogies suggested in the text reflect a bowdlerization of the Holocaust and its history, the framers of the program have pointed to the didactic and social utility of their methodology.

But it is noteworthy that while the workbook addresses in some detail the general refusal of asylum to Jews by the world's nations, including the United

States and the other major democracies, during the prewar years, the first edition was silent on the closure to the Jews of the land explicitly created by the world's powers, and ratified by the League of Nations, as a refuge for Jews in danger, Mandate Palestine, and the second edition offers very little on the subject. (It does note British statements at the July, 1938, Evian Conference to the effect that while many European Jews wanted to go to Palestine, letting them do so was not practical. It also quotes Golda Meir on the British policy during World War II of keeping Palestine closed to Jewish refugees. But there is no mention of, for example, Britain's Mandate obligations to admit Jews to Palestine and foster their settlement, or League of Nations protests against Britain's violation of its Mandate responsibilities toward the Jews.) This is difficult to explain other than in terms of the authors' eagerness to avoid the "particularist" issue of the Arab-Israeli conflict.

Even more startling is that, while the workbook is replete with examples of more recent manifestations of bigotry and hate-mongering and their often deadly consequences, and, in the first edition, refers briefly to some recent incarnations of anti-Semitism including anti-Semitism in the guise of anti-Zionism, it is silent on the major contemporary manifestations of anti-Semitism and contemporary calls for completion of the annihilation of the Jews undertaken in the Holocaust. The government-sanctioned anti-Semitism continually purveyed by many Arab nations is entirely ignored, even where the anti-Jewish propaganda is reminiscent of, or indeed entails reproduction of, Nazi material attacking the Jews, and even though it has included calls for extermination of the Jews.[10]

(Facing History and Ourselves did introduce in 2003 — "with anti-Semitism in the news once again" — a collection of readings under the title *Anti-Semitism: The Power of Myth,* available on its Web site "facinghistory.org." Topics addressed in the readings include the manifestations of anti-Semitism at the United Nations' World Conference on Racism, Racial Discrimination, Xenophobia and Related Intolerance in Durban, South Africa, in August, 2002; the distribution at San Francisco State University in the spring of 2002 of pro-Palestinian materials invoking the blood libel against Jews; a 2002 French law suit concerning anti-Semitism, including blood libels, in editions of the Egyptian government newspaper *Al-Ahram* distributed in France; and Harvard President Lawrence Summers' speech of September, 2002, on widespread anti-Semitic actions triggered by recent events in the Arab-Israeli conflict and particularly on the burgeoning expressions of anti-Jewish bias in academia.)

In a related vein, there are institutions in American society and abroad — media outlets, political entities, charitable organizations, religious groups — that express sympathy for the dead Jews of the Holocaust but are silent or even hostile in situations where living Jews are threatened, silent or hostile particularly with regard to the dangers faced by Israel. Nevertheless, one finds Jewish organizations embracing these institutions for their positions vis-à-vis the Holocaust and letting the rest pass, seemingly unwilling to challenge them with a "particularist" defense of Israel.

The significance of Israel in enhancing the meaningfulness of Jewish identity for a very large proportion of American Jews is indicated by the breadth and intensity of American Jewish support for the state. That meaningfulness has religious and spiritual content, even if not translated into any dramatic increase in religious observance and even if most Israeli Jews are "secular." It has therefore served, in a way that nothing else has, toward countering the spiritual anomie that has been for so many one result of the decline of religious literacy and connectedness.

Support among American Jews for a Jewish state in Eretz Israel was overwhelming in the years leading up to Israel's founding and has remained as strong since then. In the wake of World War II, some anti-Zionist voices were still to be heard, the most powerful being from among the old German Jewish elite. But the horrors of the genocide, and the obvious truth that earlier fulfillment of Britain's League of Nations Mandate obligations and creation of an independent Jewish homeland would have saved hundreds of thousands, perhaps millions, of lives, convinced many who had earlier been hostile or indifferent to Zionism of the moral and pragmatic necessity of a Jewish state. Perhaps more importantly, these factors pushed many who had earlier been passive to a more active advocacy of the Zionist cause. The plight of the several hundred thousand displaced Jewish survivors in Europe, the remnant of European Jewry, and their need for a safe refuge, reinforced these sentiments. In addition, many were haunted by the failure of American Jewry — through political weakness, political ineptness, and hesitation — to intervene more effectively in the face of the enormous catastrophe in Europe, and support for Israel provided an opportunity for redemptive action. The effort to establish a Jewish homeland also offered a prospect of new hope and vitality in Jewish life as against the despair and gloom and aura of doom that followed on the catastrophe in Europe.

Also significant was that in this instance the advocacy of a "particularist" Jewish issue was made easier by the fact that the Zionist cause enjoyed substantial support within key circles of the wider society. During the war both the Bergson group and the Jewish leadership around Rabbi Wise had argued the necessity of the Jewish state as the answer to Jewish vulnerability and a refuge for those saved from Europe, and this view won wide political support, including congressional support, even in the face of Administration hostility articulated mainly by the State Department. In the 1944 election campaign, both the Democratic and Republican national committees included pro-Zionist planks in their platforms. While some mainstream church establishments were cool to Zionist aspirations, and various religious leaders were actively hostile to them, there were also important voices in the religious community who spoke out in support of the Zionist cause and worked to advance it.

As the horrors of the genocide became more fully revealed with the end of the war, and as the harsh and heavy-handed British measures against survivors seeking to enter Eretz Israel garnered wider publicity, significant sympathy for the Zionists also evolved among the American public. Invasion of the newly declared state of Israel by surrounding Arab armies, Arab expression of determination to annihilate the Jews, and the Jewish struggle to defend the country elicited additional public sympathy for the Jewish state.

In the first two decades after World War II, there remained groups within American Jewry unsympathetic to Zionism, and in some circles this sentiment actually increased. But such groups continued to represent a very small, if at times disproportionately vocal, minority. Still active were elements of the old anti-Zionist elite, originally inspired in large part by fears that creation of a Jewish state would raise charges of dual loyalty and thereby fuel anti-Semitism and undercut the Jewish quest for fuller acceptance as equal citizens. A leading figure in this group and outspoken opponent of the Zionists in the immediate postwar years was Arthur Hays Sulzberger, who had succeeded Adolph Ochs as publisher of the *New York Times* in 1935.

The role played by fears of an anti-Semitic backlash in shaping the *Times* dynasty's antagonism to the Zionists is suggested by the long-standing policy at the *Times* of eschewing sympathetic stances on "Jewish" issues in order to avoid being labeled a "Jewish" paper and eliciting anti-Jewish hostility. The *Times'* failure to give prominent coverage during the war to the genocide in Europe, or to address the rescue issue, has been noted. When, in the wake of the war, President Truman pressed the British to admit 100,000 Jewish survivors to Mandate Palestine, the *Times'* national correspondent, James Reston, whose columns generally reflected the newspaper's editorial opinion, attacked the proposal as unprincipled, politically motivated, and contrary to America's foreign interests.

Echoing the rhetoric of the British foreign office, Reston argued that, "the plight of the Jews in Europe is only one aspect of the melancholy story of the displaced persons of Europe, of whom the Jews are a minority," and therefore hardly merited special consideration. The *Times'* headline writers introduced the column with "Truman's Palestine Plea Flouted Foreign Advisers: Swayed by Political Aides, President is Held to Act Counter to U.S. Policy." So exercised by the issue were the *Times'* editors that they apparently forgot it is the president who sets U.S. policy.[11]

A group, also a small minority, whose hostility to Zionism actually increased in this period was the hard Left, those Jews sympathetic to Soviet Communism. This was a constituency made up almost entirely of people who had abandoned any meaningful connection with Jewish faith and community and exchanged a Jewish identity for one centered on their embrace of the far Left. The Soviet Union had in 1947 supported the creation of Israel, essentially out of considerations of realpolitik and a desire to weaken Britain's strategic position in the Middle East. But in subsequent years, Stalin and his successors, hostile to the growing expression of Zionist sympathies and identification with Israel among Soviet Jews, and discerning strategic advantage in supporting the Arab states against Israel, shifted Soviet policy to a stridently anti-Israel course. Soviet sympathizers in the United States, including those of Jewish origin, widely followed in their sentiments the Kremlin's lead, even as the Kremlin propagandized against Israel with a rhetoric that was often blatantly anti-Semitic.

There was also a larger body of Jews, some who had essentially abandoned their Jewish identity, others who continued to value it and to feel some connection with faith and community, who were intellectual heirs of those in the preceding generations in Europe and America that had responded to the anti-Semitism of surrounding societies by seeking to detach themselves from Jewish particularism and to embrace universalist sentiments. They saw themselves as citizens of the world, identified with all peoples, especially all those perceived as downtrodden and victimized, and often found value in the particulars of all the world's cultures except Jewish culture. They were not especially enamored of Soviet Communism but were sympathetic to leftist-internationalist political ideology and to socialist dogma, not simply out of pragmatic pro-labor sentiments but more out of an ideological connection with the working class as a disadvantaged, abused part of their imagined international brotherhood. They embraced these sympathies either as an alternative to Jewish identity or as what they chose to construe to be the universalist essence of the Jewish mission. Such people tended to be wary of all nationalisms, but were often especially critical of Jewish nationalism as it posed a particular challenge to their chosen self-comprehension and their understanding of proper Jewish aspirations.

(A related wariness toward Jewish nationalism — related, that is, in the sense of being often, but not exclusively, articulated by people predisposed to universalist sentiments — entailed a focus on the vastly disproportionate intellectual and artistic contributions of individuals of Jewish origin to modern Western society. Perception of this creativity as deriving at least in part from the situation of the Jews as a distinctive and to varying degrees embattled minority in Western societies led some to fear that as the Jews acquired national independence and indeed became, as Herzl had hoped, a more "normal" people, their exceptional contributions would diminish. Even if one regards this Jewish creativity as the most valuable gift of Judaism and the Jewish people to the world, a weighing of that contribution as more significant than all the suffering that also followed on the status of Jews as a distinctive and all too often victimized minority is a dubious moral stance indeed. Nevertheless, anti-Zionism based on this perspective — a perspective entailing what is likely in any case an overstated linkage between creativity and vulnerability, with some valid kernel — continued to have its adherents even after the Holocaust had demonstrated the horrendous price of Jewish vulnerability.[12])

A small nexus of anti-Zionist sentiment also existed within the Orthodox community in American Jewry, among a distinct minority circle of Orthodox Jews who regarded the creation of Israel as sacrilege in that, they believed, Jewish national redemption must properly await the coming of the Messiah. Most Orthodox Jews were, particularly in the wake of the Holocaust, supportive of the Zionist endeavor. They were more inclined to see the creation of Israel as indeed a fulfillment, at least in part, of millennia-old Jewish longing.

This was so even if many Orthodox leaders were critical of the demise of religious literacy and religious practice and connectedness among both Israelis and American Jews. Similarly, they were supportive of the state even while some were troubled by what they saw as Israel, like the Holocaust, being enlarged in the consciousness and the "Jewishness" of many beyond its "proper" bounds to fill the void left by the falling away from religious literacy and practice.

Of course, an obvious and critical difference between the focus on the Holocaust and the focus on Israel was that the former reinforced in the Jewish consciousness images of Jewish helplessness, suffering, and vulnerable marginality. It emphasized images likely to bolster the impulse of many to flee their Jewish identity, or at least to question the value of preserving it, in the absence of religious and communal literacy and connectedness. In contrast, the creation of Israel lent to Jewish identity images of vitality, capacity for positive action, and the promise of a brighter Jewish future even in the wake of the Holocaust, and so was more likely to enhance people's valuing of their Jewishness. But there remained some uneasiness among Orthodox leaders even with this positive bolstering of Jewish connectedness in the sense that they saw it as serving for many not simply as an additional bond to their Jewishness but as a substitution for the bonds of meaningful religious practice and connection.

But despite pockets of ambivalence or even hostility toward Israel within American Jewry, sentiment regarding Israel among American Jews in the first decades after her creation was overwhelmingly positive.

The 1967 Middle East war elicited even greater, more vocal and activist, support for Israel from American Jews. The buildup to the war, with Egyptian President Gamel Abdul Nasser mobilizing his forces, deploying them in the Sinai, forging a united Arab command with Jordan and Syria, and openly declaring that the moment had come in which the Arabs would annihilate Israel, raised fears among American Jews of another slaughter of their brothers and sisters. The United Nations' withdrawal, at Nasser's demand, of peacekeeping forces deployed by international agreement on the Israeli-Egyptian border, presented to Jews images of the world once again abandoning them and further heightened

American Jews' concerns and spurred their rallying to Israel's cause. So too did the failure of the United States, France, and Britain, in the face of an Egyptian blockade, to live up to their decade-old commitment to keep open to Israel the Straits of Tiran, Israel's lifeline to Asia.

What had been a largely passive sympathy without much actual involvement for most American Jews rose for many, in the context of the fears that preceded the war, to a much more intense and more active engagement. This response persisted and was even amplified across American Jewry with the relief and joy of Israel's subsequently emerging victorious from the ensuing conflagration, and the widespread heightened involvement continued for many beyond the war.

This rallying to Israel was again made easier by the broad support for Israel among American leaders and the American public, who reacted to Arab threats to annihilate the state and to Israel's subsequent victory by identifying and sympathizing overwhelmingly with the Jewish state. In addition, the years after the 1967 war saw the gradual development of a strategic alliance between the United States and Israel, rendering American Jewish support for Israel more than ever consistent with American national policy and so still easier to embrace.

The evolution of this strategic alliance was not primarily a result of any newfound support for Israel among the American public or American leaders, or more effective Jewish pro-Israel lobbying. Rather, it reflected a change in the strategic assessment of Israel within American administrations. As noted, there had been broad support for Israel among the American public and American leaders, including American administrations — except for persistent State Department pro-Arab sympathies — from 1948 onward. Even President Eisenhower, who in the 1950s advocated Israel's ceding the Negev to Egypt to assuage Egyptian hostility — Israel, under Ben-Gurion, refused, of course, to do so — and who in 1956 insisted on Israel's full withdrawal from the Sinai in the wake of the Sinai war, was generally sympathetic to Israel. Indeed, he is reported to have stated in the mid-1960s that he had erred in forcing Israel's withdrawal from Sinai.[13] (It was in the context of that withdrawal that the United States, along with Britain and France, pledged to guarantee freedom of shipping for Israel through the Straits of Tiran, the pledge which all three failed to honor when the Egyptians blockaded the Straits in 1967.)

But prior to 1967, all American administrations had kept Israel somewhat at arm's length, at least in military terms. They generally refused arms sales, for example, or only allowed limited arms transfers through third parties or limited sales that balanced some particular American arms package to an Arab regime. The overriding reason for this stance even in the face of widespread sympathy for Israel seems to have been less concern for inciting Arab hostility, which was a consideration beyond 1967 as well, than American perception of Israel as militarily vulnerable. Administrations were reluctant to be too closely identified with a vulnerable country, perhaps being put in a position of having to come to Israel's direct military aid in a war and having to fight a coalition of Arab nations that would include generally pro-Western states. They were also wary of an even worse prospect, of likely being unable to save an Israel under attack because of the logistical difficulties of intervening effectively in a fast-moving war, and so suffering the diplomatic defeat before the world of having an ally annihilated.

However, in the wake of the 1967 war, a war won by Israel with Western arms, mainly French aircraft, over Soviet arms, and which therefore redounded to the West's, including America's, diplomatic advantage, the American strategic view of Israel changed. It was now seen as indeed capable of defending itself given only the military equipment necessary to counterbalance arms sales, whether Soviet or Western, to the Arab states, and so the United States felt free to avail itself of the gains of a strategic alliance with Israel. Those gains included fuller access to Israeli military and political intelligence, to Soviet arms captured by Israel and to the battlefield capabilities of Soviet equipment as encountered by Israel. They also entailed other military lessons learned from Israel's battlefield encounters, including the performance of American equipment under battlefield conditions and modifications of military doctrine in response to battlefield experiences. An additional gain was the diplomatic advantage of being allied to a nation now perceived by the world as the regional power, in contrast to the Soviet Union's vanquished allies.

To be sure, circles in the American Jewish community previously cool to Israel remained so in the wake of the war. *New York Times* editorials, while generally acknowledging the extreme danger Israel had faced from the Arab mobilization, and even characterizing prewar Arab rhetoric as incitement to genocide, tended to focus on the difficulties that the editorial writers believed would flow from Israel's victory. Jews who embraced the radical Left, either abandoning their Jewish identity for a socialist one or choosing to comprehend their Jewishness in radical "universalist" terms, and who were critical of Zionism from this perspective, typically persisted in their critical stance. Indeed, development of the strategic alliance between Israel and the United States increased negative attitudes toward Israel among those Jews or former Jews whose primary spiritual allegiance was to the radical Left. The burgeoning unhappiness, in subsequent years, with the American involvement in Vietnam, and the consequent increased hostility toward American strategic policy generally, both expanded the ranks of those sympathizing with the ideological Left and intensified the ideological Left's negative take on Israel for its alliance with America.

This period saw the emergence of the New Left, largely from the ferment of opposition to the Vietnam War. The New Left's focus on pacifism, its anti-Westernism and perception of Western economies as inexorably abusive and Western democracy as a cruel, exploitative hoax, its sympathy for the Second World and even more for the Third World, and its universalism, created another nexus of anti-Israel sentiment. Particularly in its penetration of American university campuses, the New Left purveyed pro-Arab attitudes, often outright anti-Semitic rhetoric — the old socialist rhetoric of Jews as capitalist exploiters — and even more intense anti-Zionist rhetoric. Some Jews, again especially on campuses, eager to join the rising tide of this new popular movement, uncomfortable with their being identified with a targeted group and ill-equipped, knowing little or nothing, to rebut the assaults, embraced the anti-Zionist line. Some even endorsed New Left anti-Semitism.

Others responded in the opposite way. Some who previously sympathized with the socialist Left were put off by the strident anti-Americanism and anti-Zionism, and at times anti-Semitism, of elements of the New Left and turned away from their former political predilections to a new connectedness with the United States, with Israel, and with Judaism. But in any case, the ranks of the New Left and old Left Jewish critics of Israel remained very small, if vocal, and Israel enjoyed continued, even increased, support from the vast majority of American Jews.

This support was further reinforced by events in the decade and a half after the war, as Israel continued under siege. In August, 1967, Israel had its postwar offer of trading land for peace rejected by the Arab League. The organization, meeting in Khartoum, adopted instead the "three no's" — no negotiations, no recognition, no peace. Israel subsequently faced the war of attrition, the 1973 Yom Kippur War, and incessant terrorist assaults.

But there have also been developments in Israel over recent decades that have elicited more complex responses from American Jews and eroded aspects of support for Israel among some segments of the community.

In the years immediately after the Six Day War, Israel awaited a change in the Arabs' Khartoum policies and the appearance of Arab interlocutors with whom it could conduct the negotiations prescribed by Security Council Resolution 242. The most difficult situation confronting the nation in holding the territories captured in the war lay in the West Bank and Gaza. These areas, unlike the Sinai taken from Egypt and the Golan Heights captured from Syria, had a large Arab population now living in political limbo. (International law established standards for administration of populations in disputed territories, and supported Israel's maintaining control of the territories until its Arab neighbors agreed to recognition and negotiations and until peace agreements were forged that defined permanent borders. But, of course, this still left the Palestinian Arabs politically and legally adrift.)

Government policy, formulated initially by Moshe Dayan and generally continued by all later Israeli governments, was to allow the Palestinian Arab population to run its own affairs as much as possible. But tension and clashes between the local population and Israeli authorities, including security forces, were inevitable.

In the wake of Israel's 1978 peace accord with Egypt, which at least formally took the most powerful of Arab nations out of the ongoing military confrontation with Israel, increased attention was focused on the predicament of the Palestinian Arabs. Their situation, rather than Arab hostility to Israel's existence, was now perceived more and more widely as the crux of the Middle East conflict, even as Arab states around Israel and beyond continued to militate for the nation's destruction.

The most important Palestinian Arab military group and perpetrator of terrorist attacks against Israel was Fatah. Fatah had been established in 1958, before the Six Day War, when the West Bank and Gaza were still, of course, in Arab hands. It was founded with an operational agenda of launching raids into Israel. In 1964, still three years before the war, the Palestine Liberation Organization, ultimately an umbrella federation of militant Palestinian groups, was formed and adopted a covenant focused on pursuing Israel's annihilation, and by 1969 Fatah had become the dominant force in the PLO. In 1974, when much of the world was promoting Arab-Israeli negotiations in the wake of the Yom Kippur War, Yasser Arafat, leader of Fatah and of the PLO, formulated what he called the "Plan of Phases." The plan declared that the Palestinian Arabs would seek to acquire territory by negotiations and would then use that territory as a launching pad for military pursuit of Israel's annihilation. With this agenda as backdrop, Arafat offered to enter into negotiations with Israel.

As increased attention was placed on the Palestinian Arab situation after Israel's accord with Egypt, voices outside the Middle East began pressing Israel more forcefully to agree to such negotiations. This push gained further momentum in the wake of the Lebanon War of 1982, which expelled the PLO from the mini-state it had established in southern Lebanon, rendered it less able to pursue terrorist operations against Israel, and so led it to begin emphasizing its preparedness to negotiate.

But it was particularly after the outbreak of the Intifada, in December, 1987, that Israel came under intense international pressure to enter negotiations with Arafat and the PLO. In the context of the Intifada, Jordan withdrew, in favor of the PLO, its claim to the West Bank territories that it had lost in the 1967 war. This further heightened pressure on Israel to deal directly with the PLO. In addition, even as Arafat continued to emphasize to the Palestinian Arabs and to the Arab nations that negotiations would be only phase one and that the goal was still Israel's destruction, before Western media and diplomats the PLO leadership would stress its willingness to negotiate "peace."

Still Israel refused to enter into talks with the PLO, given its history of bloody terrorist assaults on Israeli civilians and its still articulated dedication to Israel's ultimate annihilation. But outside demands to do so continued to mount.

These developments were accompanied by some shift in perspective on the

Arab-Israeli conflict by relatively small but influential segments of American society, such as the liberal media.

The fringe Left media, media reflecting Soviet views or the perspectives of the New Left, had typically cast Israel as the villain, particularly in the wake of its post-1967 closer ties with the United States. Israel, through this lens, was a colonialist extension of Western imperialism encroaching on, exploiting, and dispossessing native populations. After the Camp David agreement with Egypt, as the predicament of the Palestinian Arabs gained greater attention and the wider Arab conflict against Israel settled into a *de facto* cease-fire, variations on these distortions gained wider popularity in American media. Particularly with the outbreak of the Intifada and its daily newsreel footage of Palestinian Arab stone throwers versus Israeli soldiers and police, the conflict was more and more cast as a reprise of the American civil rights movement. The ongoing Arab push to delegitimize, isolate, weaken, and ultimately destroy Israel was largely airbrushed out of the confrontation, which was now recast as dominant Israel refusing to address the legitimate aspirations and demands of a subject people.

This to some degree reflected the success of Palestinian Arab leaders, who sought to separate their conflict from the broader Arab war against Israel and to cast it in the guise of a struggle for national rights. In the 1948–1967 period, when the West Bank was controlled by Jordan and Gaza by Egypt, the inhabitants of the former at least were regarded as Jordanians. When the PLO was formed in 1964 it did not press Jordan and Egypt to cede the territories for creation of a Palestinian national entity but rather pressed for the destruction of Israel. Earlier, in the Mandate period, a common refrain among Arab political leaders and intellectuals was that, rather than Palestine being a distinct political entity, the home of a distinct Arab nation, the entire concept of "Palestine" was an illegitimate Jewish invention intended to break off from Arab control part of the territorial patrimony of all Arabs. The Arab historian Philip Hitti testified to this effect in 1946 before the Anglo-American Committee of Inquiry (created at Britain's instigation in its attempt to counter pressure from Truman for admission of Jewish refugees to the Mandate). Hitti declared, "There is no such thing as 'Palestine' in history, absolutely not."[14]

Indeed this same comprehension was offered by Yasser Arafat as late as 1991 in the context of his supporting Saddam Hussein's conquest and annexation of Kuwait. Arafat insisted that all borders between Arab states are artificial constructs imposed on the region by Western colonial powers and that there are properly no Iraqis or Kuwaitis or Syrians or Jordanians or Palestinians but all are part of one nation sharing a common territorial patrimony.

But the new rhetoric regarding the Palestinian Arabs, the rhetoric of a subjugated nation seeking its national rights, played well in the West. In addition, the tack was bolstered by the obvious circumstance of the Palestinian Arabs being in a position different from that of the surrounding Arab nations. It was also reinforced by conflicts between Arafat and other Arab leaders, particularly King Hussein. And it was an easy gloss to put on the visuals of the Intifada and fit a liberal American — as defined in this period — frame of reference.

On American campuses, the penetration of New Left ideology had already established a receptive environment for anti-Israel rhetoric and even for assaults on the very legitimacy of the Jewish state. The increased focus on the Palestinian-Israeli clash and the events of the Intifada led to a popularization of the casting of the conflict in terms of abusive, imperialist Israelis and victimized Palestinians. Like the media's gloss on the conflict, the campus version essentially ignored ongoing calls by Arab regimes and in the Arab media, and by the Palestinian leadership and Palestinian media, for Israel's ultimate annihilation. Similarly ignored were the strategic threats that confronted Israel and were a vital part of the equation in Israeli calculations of possible concessions, especially territorial concessions, to the Palestinians.

The liberal churches in America, many of them deeply engaged in recent decades in embracing Third World causes, likewise commonly chose to cast the conflict in terms of a civil rights struggle, or of colonizers versus the colonized. Many of them fervently championed the Palestinian cause and were silent on the existential threats to Israel and ongoing Arab, including Palestinian, demands for Israel's destruction.

This assault on Israel, particularly in the media, and the media images that cast Israel in a negative light, discomfited and embarrassed many American Jews. It put them on the defensive, roused old concerns about how negative publicity would play in the wider society's attitudes toward Jews and what hostility it might ignite, and spurred an eagerness to placate that potential hostility.

But for the great majority of American Jews there appears to have prevailed against such fears an awareness of Israel's essential rightness, a recognition of the distortions and biases in the critical media coverage and in the campus and church attacks on Israel, and an alertness to the unacknowledged existential threats that confronted the state. The continued high level of American Jewish connection with Israel is indicated by, for example, a 1993 survey by the American Jewish Committee that found that 68 percent of those questioned agreed with the statement: "If Israel were destroyed, I would feel as if I had suffered one of the greatest personal tragedies of my life."[15]

This sense of vital connectedness has existed in the context of, and very likely has been easier to maintain because of, a broader American society that has remained strongly sympathetic to the Jewish state.

AMERICAN JEWS AND THE POLITICAL LEFT

Despite American Jews' strong identification with Israel and the fact that support for Israel in the broader society has become greatest on the American political Right, American Jews overwhelmingly vote Left. Similarly incongruous is that they do so despite their economic place in American society, an incongruity that is virtually unique. As Irving Kristol famously observed, "Jews are as rich as Episcopalians but . . . they vote like Puerto Ricans."[16]

Various factors have contributed to this trend. In western and central Europe, it was typically, although not exclusively, liberal parties that supported the granting of civil equality to Jews and conservative parties that opposed it, and Jews brought with them to America the political predilections formed in this context. Polls of American Jews in recent decades have continued to reveal that a vast majority believe anti-Semitism is more rife among American conservatives than liberals, even though actual surveys of American opinion regarding Jews do not support this assumption.[17] In addition, in eastern Europe the opposition to czarist autocracy was led by socialists. Also, as Jews migrated to cities in the Russian Empire and became employed increasingly as urban laborers they became more and more involved in socialist politics. Again, Jewish immigrants brought their political attitudes with them to America, with Jews of eastern European origin, particularly secularized Jews, initially supporting socialist candidates here and then shifting to mainstream liberalism.

But the liberal predilections of American Jews have additional roots as well, roots reflected in the redefinition of the Jewish vocation, formalized by the nineteenth century reform movement, as an exclusively universalist one of promoting transcendent humanitarian values. This reformulation of what it meant to be a Jew was motivated by Jews' hopes of making themselves more acceptable to their neighbors, countering antagonism and winning equality, by eschewing particularism and embracing an unthreatening and unimpeachable agenda. For many, it was fed as well by the hope that they could also advance their quest for acceptance and counter anti-Jewish hatred by identifying the aspirations of the community with the interests of a much larger, and likewise in some respect disadvantaged, part of the body politic, such as the working class. The clinging to liberal politics by American Jews still reflects in part this quest for acceptance through emphasis on humanitarianism and through identification with broader, disadvantaged groups, even though American Jews are not confronted by the lack of acceptance that helped shape these predilections.

In this regard, American Jewish liberalism is a defensive response to anti-Semitism, an embrace of and reaction to the anti-Semitic indictment that Jews are different and alien. In fact, this defensively self-effacing element of American Jewish self-definition has grown more marked as the religious content of being Jewish, that aspect of Jewish "parochialism," has further eroded. The self-definition of what it means to be Jewish and share in the Jewish vocation has become more narrowly focused on a universalist humanitarian agenda.

Yet another facet of Jewish social liberalism as an exercise in conformity and ingratiation has been noted by Lipset and Raab: "[This emphasis] within the Jewish community [has] become most explicit when some of the main streams of American Christianity, usually the higher status denominations, have established a moralistic rather than a theological cast and espoused the 'social gospel.'"[18]

That social liberalism became, in the post-World War II era, the common denominator of the greater part of the Jewish community is indicated, for example, by the results of a meeting in 1964 of rabbis from the three major branches of Judaism intended to try and reconcile differences. The only common ground they could agree upon was support for the civil rights movement and the War on Poverty.[19] A 1988 survey conducted by the *Los Angeles Times* found that when Jews were asked which among three facets of Jewish identity they most valued, many more chose the pursuit of social justice and equality (50 percent) than either Israel (20 percent) or the "religion" (20 percent).[20]

There is much to support the observation that alliances formed by the Jewish community around the promotion of social justice were motivated by more than simply the community's pragmatic self-interest in advancing social justice and equality. Nor was it merely a matter of the community's religious-ethical dedication to social justice as an abstract good. Rather, it reflected also the community's desire to demonstrate its benevolence, its transcending of parochialisms, and its identification with larger groups, as a response to traditional anti-Jewish indictments. In particular, there is the evidence of the eagerness of major elements of the Jewish community to embrace and cultivate and cling to such alliances with larger groups, and perceive an identity of interests in them, even when the interests of the parties clearly were different and even when aspects of the alliance were inimical to Jewish well-being. That eagerness has entailed an essentially delusional pursuit of an abstract concept of "proper Jewish behavior," born long ago in an atmosphere of Jews under siege, largely maladaptive even then, and clung to despite changing circumstances and different realities.

For example, American Jews had always overwhelmingly supported first the movement for black emancipation and later for black civil rights, and their doing so was obviously both morally correct and pragmatic. The National Jewish Community Relations Advisory Council (NJCRAC) — renamed in recent years the Jewish Council for Public Affairs (JCPA) — is an umbrella group of local Jewish Community Relations Councils across America. It has convened yearly to formulate objectives, and Jewish-black cooperation on social justice issues has perennially been a centerpiece of the NJCRAC/JCPA program. However, citing the organization's 1953 statement on the issue, Rabbi Arthur Hertzberg, himself a man of impeccable liberal credentials, notes that the statement, while touching on what were indeed shared concerns and aims, suggests an identity of black and Jewish interests that was not true.

Hertzberg also points out that when, in the 1960s, elements of the black civil rights movement, and other groups that gained prominence within the American black community, became radicalized, adopted a rhetoric that was often anti-Semitic, and pursued militant confrontations with segments of the Jewish community, "The richer and better established [segments of the Jewish community continued] to talk the older language of social conscience . . . The National Jewish Community Relations Advisory Council persisted in believing that the riots in the cities, in which Jewish stores in the black ghettos were main victims, were of little importance. In 'program plan' after 'program plan' the doctrine was reiterated that Jews should remain committed to every form of help for blacks. In late May, 1967, the Anti-Defamation League published a study in five volumes on black anti-Semitism, to assert that there was less such prejudice among blacks than among whites. The Anti-Defamation League would soon change its estimate of black anti-Semitism, but in May 1967, this was the dominant 'orthodoxy' of the American Jewish establishment."[21]

Jews have again and again embraced an uncritical, wishful, self-deluding comprehension of their interests being identical to all minorities' interests or all interests couched in the rhetoric of supporting the underdog or the disadvantaged — a comprehension born largely of the anxieties and self-doubt engendered by chronic marginalization and bias. Their doing so has often left them unprepared for and unresponsive to the recurring phenomenon of anti-Jewish rhetoric and action emanating from their imagined soul mates.

In a similar vein, American Jewish groups have often closely allied themselves with liberal churches, those churches Lipset and Raab are referring to when they speak of "higher status denominations [espousing a] 'social gospel.'" They have joined with them in shared social action endeavors on a wide range of issues related to aiding the disadvantaged and promoting government programs to do the same. But when some of those church groups have been openly hostile to Israel and indifferent to threats against her and attacks on her, indifferent also to the anti-Semitism purveyed by Arab countries and by the Palestinian Authority (PA) since its establishment in 1994, those same Jewish groups have again and again been virtually silent. They have put the preservation of their alliance around social action issues above addressing clashing views on "parochial" matters, even when those matters have life and death import for many Jews.

This predilection among various Jewish groups and individuals to give precedence to preserving alliances around socially liberal agendas even at the cost of failing to address divergent interests and perspectives on issues of vital significance to Jews has been prominent also in international contexts.

The United Nations, in its formal mandate, obviously offers much that makes it an attractive institution to Jews simply from a pragmatic perspective, and even more to recommend it from the perspective of the Jewish embrace of internationalist humanitarian causes. That mandate includes working against racism and bigotry and against the abuse of populations due to prejudice, and, more broadly, working against violence and for the peaceful resolution of conflicts. The United Nations' special agencies are charged with promoting world health, advancing education worldwide, and fighting the ravages of poverty and natural disasters as well as of war. It is hardly surprising that American Jews and their communal organizations have been broadly supportive of the United Nations since its inception. What is noteworthy in the present context is how slow much of the Jewish community has been to change its position and challenge the United Nations and various of its constituent bodies even as those bodies have for decades been in the forefront of hostility to Israel and indeed to Jews generally.

Virtually every fall, no matter what acts of war, enslavement, and even genocide are unfolding elsewhere in the world, more General Assembly resolutions are devoted to attacks on Israel than to any other subject.[22] In 1975, the Assembly, at the instigation of the Soviet Union, its satellites, and the Arab states, passed a scurrilous resolution equating Zionism with racism — its chief proponents being states that routinely practiced the most horrendous abuses of their ethnic and religious minorities. The General Assembly only repealed the resolution, under intense American pressure, in 1991.

The UN's special agencies like UNESCO and WHO have been subverted to anti-Israel agendas; conferences on women's rights or vital medical issues have routinely become forums dedicated to Arab attacks on Israel. The UN Commission for Human Rights has been particularly ugly in its acquiescence to what is an almost exclusive devotion to indicting and defaming Israel, a path that culminated in the commission's choreographing an orgy of Jew-hatred at the August, 2001, Durban conference intended to address racism and other forms of bigotry. An April, 2002, vote by the commission's member states endorsed terrorist attacks against Israeli civilians.[23]

The United Nations early and eagerly embraced the PLO even though the PLO charter calls for the annihilation of a UN member state. The UN Relief and Works Agency for Palestinian Refugees, whose responsibilities over the last half century have included educating young Palestinians in schools in UN-administered refugee camps, routinely taught the anti-Semitism that was a staple of the Arab school texts used in the West Bank and Gaza before 1967. After the 1967 war, Israel expunged anti-Israel and anti-Jewish material from textbooks in the territories but did not do so with books used in UNRWA schools, and those schools continued to purvey the same hate-filled "education."

Since the establishment of the Palestinian Authority in 1994 and the subsequent introduction of PA texts, UNRWA has been providing its students with the PA version of that education, teaching that Jews are evil, that they have no legitimate presence in the land of Israel and are merely usurpers, and that it is not only the right but the duty of Palestinian children to pursue Israel's annihilation.[24] The stipulations of the Oslo accords calling for an end to incitement had no more impact on the policies of this UN organ than it did on the Palestinian Authority. When questioned about the hate-mongering and incitement to anti-Israeli and anti-Jewish violence in UNRWA school texts, UNRWA commissioner-general Peter Hansen responded, "We cannot expect a people under occupation fighting every day to have textbooks which idealize, praise and express love for their occupiers."[25]

UNRWA has also allowed its facilities to be used as recruiting and training grounds and armories for terrorists, and those facilities have been an important strategic resource for terrorist groups targeting Israeli civilians.[26]

Yet through all this, while some American Jewish organizations have challenged the nefarious role of the United Nations, others have been loathe to do so, because of the UN's formally liberal, internationalist agenda. They close their eyes to the UN's role in promoting Jew-hatred and supporting the Arab war against Israel because the UN's official objectives render it the kind of organization that Jews whose self-identity is centered on social liberalism and universalism are supposed to support.

The organized Jewish community has shied away to a remarkable degree even from challenging Arab states. Arab education systems, state-controlled media, and religious institutions have made anti-Jewish hate-mongering standard fare, including promotion of a frankly genocidal agenda. *Mein Kampf* and *The Protocols of the Elders of Zion* are widely published and distributed, often with Arab government subsidy. Holocaust denial is commonplace, along with the logically inconsistent, but programmatically of a piece, praising of Hitler for his extermination of Europe's Jews. Blood libels are likewise commonplace, with Jews accused of using Moslem blood to make holiday pastries or for other ritual purposes. Jews are characterized as satanic or subhuman and their murder labeled the will of God and a religious duty.

Bernard Lewis, perhaps the West's premier scholar of Middle East studies, wrote in 1986 regarding anti-Semitism in the Arab world, "The volume of anti-Semitic books and articles published, the size and number of editions and impressions, the eminence and authority of those who write, publish, and sponsor them, their place in school and college curricula, their role in the mass media, would all seem to suggest that classical anti-Semitism is an essential part of Arab intellectual life at the present time — almost as much as happened in Nazi Germany, and considerably more than in late nineteenth and early twentieth century France."[27]

Robert Wistrich, in his monograph, *Muslim Anti-Semitism: A Clear and Present Danger*, published in 2002 by the American Jewish Committee, cites this passage and notes that since Lewis wrote it the situation has only grown worse: "In recent years . . . the anti-Semitic virus has taken root in the body politic of Islam to an unprecedented degree."[28]

A few Jewish organizations have consistently and emphatically condemned Arab governments for the promotion of anti-Semitism. But in general, except for some recent increased attention to the problem, the communal response to this "Third World" anti-Semitism, and to its embrace by the Arab world's leftist sympathizers in Europe, has been remarkably different from reaction to manifestations of right-wing anti-Semitism in Europe. The latter is, of course, no less vile, but by all measures is much less of an immediate threat. Yet American Jewish groups have routinely responded much more energetically and emphatically to the lesser threat. When Joerg Haider, leader of a far-right party in Austria with alleged ties to neo-Nazis, won for his party a place in Austria's coalition government, the outcry from American Jewish groups — understandable, given Austria's history — was loud and sharp. But Haider's appointment represented a much lesser danger than the anti-Semitic invective being spewed at the very same time by the Syrian government and echoed by other Arab regimes through their government-controlled media, yet there was no Jewish reaction of comparable breadth and intensity against the latter.

Also noteworthy, returning to the domestic scene, is the Jewish community's response to the recrudescence of populist anti-Semitism in the rhetoric of the so-called New Left beginning in the 1960s. Couched in a broader rhetoric of attacking institutionalized social injustice and championing a radically fairer and more equitable society, the new anti-Semitism elicited a generally weak response from Jewish communities and communal organizations. This remained so even after the 1967 Arab-Israeli war, when much of the New Left adopted a vehemently anti-Israel stance as well and ratcheted up its anti-Jewish rhetoric. Only the Jewish neoconservative movement, which developed largely in response to the New Left and which represented a small minority of American Jews, addressed directly and consistently this 1960s incarnation of left-wing anti-Semitism.

Indeed, as in earlier decades in Europe, many Jews, confronted with a rhetoric that characterized Jews as archetypal capitalists, exploiters of the downtrodden, a bulwark of the established system, and therefore an enemy that stood in the way of progress to a more equitable society, embraced the anti-Semitic indictment. Rather than attacking the bigots and the gross distortions of reality that they purveyed, such people often urged Jewish self-reform consonant with the bigots' indictments. Rabbi Hertzberg notes that young Jews made up a significant part of the cadres of the New Left and observes: "The adult Jewish supporters — or indulgers — of the New Left were not only some older radicals. The American Jewish establishment never really distanced itself from these young Jews."[29]

The major repositories in subsequent decades of the perspectives of the New Left have been university campuses. The widespread tolerance in campus lecture halls of anti-Jewish diatribes and bigotry couched in the language of championing the disadvantaged has likewise elicited generally weak responses from the Jewish community. So too has the broader anti-Jewish bias on campuses, which, for example, casts Jews as undeserving of protections under politically correct codes of conduct because of their supposed status as part of the dominant, white establishment.

Overall, in the decades since World War II as in earlier years, American Jewish communities and communal organizations, even groups whose mandate is to fight anti-Semitism, have been much more clear-sighted and dogged in exposing and attacking right-wing anti-Semitism than in addressing similar anti-Jewish bigotry emanating from the political Left.

AMERICAN JEWS AND THE RADICAL LEFT

The disproportionate presence of Jews in the leadership and cadres of the New Left had been noted by many early observers and was reconfirmed by the work of Rothman and Lichter in their study of the student radicals of the nineteen sixties and early seventies. That study drew on interviews and standardized tests of a wide range of university students conducted in 1971 and 1972. Rothman and Lichter compared the results from those among the students who embraced a radical political agenda to the results gleaned from testing and interviews of people who had been leaders in the radical movement in the previous decade, and they offered both psychological and social-political analyses of the place of Jews in the student radicalism of the period.[30]

In *Roots of Radicalism*, Rothman and Lichter trace the history of the new campus radicalism from the birth of Students for a Democratic Society in 1960, to the Free Speech Movement and the heyday of SDS in the mid-sixties, to the descent into violence, the penetration of the movement by the old Left, and the splintering of SDS in the late 1960s and early 1970s. Throughout the period, Jews were prominent in the Movement and at times represented an absolute majority among its leaders and even among its cadres on various campuses.

Rothman and Lichter relate this Jewish over-representation particularly to the Jews' historic marginality. They note three possible avenues of escape from marginality, consistent with what has been discussed in earlier chapters as modern avenues of escape from Jewish identity in the face of bigotry and marginalization: 1) assimilation, or immersion into the dominant identity of the surrounding society; 2) attachment to an ideology that is more universalist and redefines society and one's place within it in a way that promises to free one from his or her marginality; 3) active development of a new ideology that will likewise serve to change social situations and definitions in a way that will end one's marginality and victimization.[31] Both the second and third tack help explain the particular allure of the politics of the radical Left for those eager to shed a Jewish identity.

Consistent with this explanation is Rothman and Lichter's discovery that Jewish student radicals were overwhelmingly the children of deracinated Jews, parents who had abandoned the religion and felt little connection to the Jewish community. This also stands in contrast to non-Jewish student radicals, who commonly came from religiously observant families.

Testing and interviews also suggested that the parents of the Jewish radicals continued to feel in some ways marginalized and that they conveyed their own radical responses, their radical political views, to their children. The Jewish radicals commonly stated that their parents were more radical than they. The source of the parents' sense of marginalization is not explored, and most were successful professionals. But it can be assumed that most, given the period involved, would have been exposed in their youth to manifestations of the anti-Semitism that pervaded the country in the nineteen thirties and forties.

This parental radicalism also distinguished the new Jewish radicals from their non-Jewish peers, for whom, typically, radicalism was a rebellion against a conservative family background and a home marked by much childhood tension and conflict.

Other observations also support the comprehension of Jewish radicalism as an escape from vulnerability and marginalization, a flight to a more promising identity. For example, whereas the nineteen sixties and seventies apologists for the student radicals tended to characterize them as humanitarian champions of the weak against the strong, testing and interviews revealed that Jewish radicals actually tended to view those they championed and identified with, particularly the American black community, as powerful, as possessing a force that was going to wrest control away from the established power.

Non-Jewish radicals likewise looked at those they championed as powerful. A notable distinction, however, was that many of the non-Jews tended to view the Establishment as a paper tiger — perhaps consistent with their radicalism reflecting, as Rothman and Lichter's data suggest, a projection of struggles at home, with a father perceived as overbearing and bullying but ultimately weak. Jewish radicals, in contrast, tended to see the Establishment as likewise powerful, consistent with a Jewish perspective of being marginalized or victimized by powerful echelons in the surrounding society.

Not surprisingly, those social critics who chose to characterize the student radicals as morally exceptional individuals who had advanced to a higher plane of humanity in their attacks on contemporary social institutions and their championing of the downtrodden — a perspective shared, of course, by the students themselves, despite what the psychological testing revealed — were themselves disproportionately leftists of Jewish background.

Some of the most prominent among them, including Herbert Marcuse, who became virtually the guru of the movement, were emigrés who had been affiliated in Germany with the Frankfurt Institute for Social Research. Most of the Institute's scholars were deracinated Jews inclined to comprehend their own flight to a new identity as likewise an intellectual and moral step forward. Those among them who managed to escape Nazi Germany had typically, before being obliged to leave, dismissed the rising anti-Semitism. It clashed with their neo-Marxist analyses of the dialectic of history and their insistence on the essential inconsequentiality of religious and ethnic affiliations, and so they chose to regard it as an insignificant phenomenon unworthy of their scholarly attention. The Frankfurt Institute represented another instance in which Jews, in their flight from Jewish identity, created another identity readily recognizable as that of fleeing Jews. Thus, Gershom Scholem characterized the Institute as one of the "most remarkable 'Jewish sects' that German Jewry produced."[32]

As Hertzberg notes, the New Left received support not only from Jews affiliated with the old Left. Other Jews as well, still attached to the community, still valuing that attachment, and more mainstream in their political views, typically did not step forward to criticize the movement even when anti-Semitic themes became commonplace in its rhetoric and even when it adopted vehemently anti-Israel stances. On the contrary, many, particularly among people living their lives in a milieu in which left-of-liberal thinking, with strong elements of New Left and old Left orthodoxies, were dominant, bent to New Left arguments cast in the rhetoric of internationalism and pacifism and empowerment of the disadvantaged. In particular, they readily adopted the recasting of the Arab-Israeli conflict, the ongoing war over Israel's legitimacy and right to exist, into a struggle for Palestinian rights, and joined the chorus of criticism of Israel. This pattern in no small part reflected such individuals' eagerness to distance themselves from Israel so as not to be perceived by others in their milieu as sharing in Israel's supposed evils simply by virtue of their being Jewish or having a Jewish background.

Hertzberg's observation that the Jewish establishment never distanced itself from the New Left is underscored by the accommodation made by various mainstream Jewish organizations to Jewish groups formed around an agenda of radical-Left anti-Israel activism.

American Jews with New Left sympathies and in many instances affiliations, and often with connections to academic institutions, began in the early 1970s to create groups dedicated to indicting Israel. Some of these new organizations were conceived as exclusively Jewish, some of mixed membership, but their shared *raison d'être* was criticizing Israel and Israeli policies and promoting anti-Israel agendas in America.

One such group was the Committee on New Alternatives in the Middle East (CONAME), among whose founders, in 1970, were anti-Zionists such as Noam Chomsky. During the 1973 war, CONAME lobbied against U.S. resupply of Israel. The following year, the same year Yasser Arafat promulgated his Plan of Phases for Israel's annihilation, the organization distributed an article by one of its financial backers praising Arafat for his "moderation and pragmatism" and offering justifications for the PLO's recent massacre of more than twenty Israeli schoolchildren at Ma'alot.[33]

Some Jewish members of CONAME, believing an all-Jewish organization would have greater success in swaying elements of the broader Jewish community to their views, joined with others in 1973 to establish Breira. Breira's focus was militating for Israeli withdrawal to the pre-1967 borders and creation of a Palestinian state in the West Bank and Gaza. Issues of Israel's strategic vulnerability and the need for territorial compromises to address it, and of hostile Arab and PLO objectives vis-à-vis Israel, were essentially ignored by the group. The key to peace, it insisted, was Israeli concessions of the sort it advocated.

Breira foundered within a few years and many of its leaders moved on to establish, in 1978, New Jewish Agenda (NJA). NJA was to differ from Breira in being less narrowly focused on Israel and serving rather as a Jewish advocacy group for a broader New Left agenda in domestic as well as foreign policy. But, in fact, NJA very quickly concentrated its efforts on criticism of Israel and promotion of anti-Israel policies.[34]

In 1988, NJA lobbied heavily for planks in state and national Democratic Party platforms favoring establishment of a Palestinian state under the PLO, and it succeeded in winning such planks in six states. It consistently fought efforts by mainstream Jewish organizations to counter those resolutions.[35] In 1990, NJA's Western United States division mounted a campaign against Jewish contributions to Operation Exodus, which funded resettlement in Israel of Jews fleeing the Soviet Union. It did so ostensibly because such resettlement might be inimical to Palestinian interests. (NJA demanded a pledge from Israel not to settle any Soviet Jews in the territories, but in fact only 1 percent of former Soviet Jews were living in the territories and Israel had already agreed to American and Soviet insistence that no new immigrants be allowed to reside there.) The same year, the national NJA campaigned for a U.S. cut in funds to Israel by an amount commensurate with Israeli expenditures on settlements in the territories.[36]

Israeli strategic concerns, indeed the concerns voiced by the framers of Security Council Resolution 242 and underlying their support for Israel not returning to the pre-1967 lines, did not figure in NJA literature or activities.

Nor, except for occasional lip service, did hostile Palestinian and other Arab actions and declarations, including the ongoing murder of Israelis and insistence on Israel's ultimate annihilation.

An instance of NJA adherence to hard-core leftist orthodoxy beyond its anti-Israel agenda was its defense of the Communist regime of the Sandinistas in Nicaragua against accusations of anti-Semitism. As Rael Jean Isaac noted, "The small Jewish community [of Nicaragua] had been forced out through a combination of threats, imprisonment, confiscation of property and public humiliation — the head of the community had been arrested and forced to sweep streets,"[37] and the Sandinistas had come under intense criticism by the Anti-Defamation League and the Reagan Administration. The Sandinistas had also dispatched operatives to participate in terrorist attacks against Israeli targets. One such agent was killed while attempting to hijack an El Al plane. In 1984, NJA sent an investigatory delegation to Nicaragua. It "discovered" that the regime was beloved by the Nicaraguan people (who decisively ousted it when, in 1989, elections were finally allowed in the country), insisted that the Sandinistas did not pursue "systematic" anti-Semitism, and, in any case, blamed the regime's Jew-hatred on Israeli policies.[38]

New Jewish Agenda activists also busied themselves generating various anti-Israel spin-off organizations. In 1984 they formed "Taxpayers for Peace in the Middle East," which lobbied for linking U.S. aid to Israel to Israeli settlement expenditures six years before pushing such linkage became the policy of the parent organization. In 1989, another spin-off, "Act on Conscience for Israel/Palestine," was set up to promote a cut-off of all aid to Israel for its alleged "gross violation of internationally recognized human rights."[39]

New Jewish Agenda also allied itself in its initiatives with other anti-Israel organizations — Jewish and non-Jewish — including some groups that supported anti-Israel terror, advocated Israel's demise, and promoted anti-Semitic themes. The American-Arab Anti-Discrimination Committee (ADC) has defended perpetrators of anti-Israel terror, smearing those who criticize the terrorists as guilty of anti-Arab racism. NJA repeatedly joined with ADC in co-sponsoring anti-Israel endeavors and events and officially lauded ADC as, "a strong voice for all Americans who seek peace with justice."[40]

When an NJA leader and two other American Jews met with Yasser Arafat in Tunis in 1987, Arafat — described by the NJA representative as "warm and fatherly"[41] — suggested that what was needed was an American Jewish lobby to counter the pro-Israel AIPAC (America-Israel Public Affairs Committee). One of the other attendees obediently complied and set up the Jewish Peace Lobby to persuade Congress that many American Jews were not supporters of Israel and to promote in Congress pro-PLO and anti-Israel positions.

Yet another Jewish group that emerged during this period with a bias toward left-wing orthodoxy and an agenda emphasizing criticism of Israel is the

New Israel Fund, founded in 1979. Many of its early key figures had been active in CONAME and Breira or were also involved in New Jewish Agenda. The money raised by the New Israel Fund has been dispersed overwhelmingly to left-wing critics of Israel in the United States and in Israel. The organization has also sponsored some more politically neutral activities like rape crisis centers, and its leaders cite such sponsorship to promote its fund-raising efforts. But in fact only a minor portion of the New Israel Fund's resources have been dedicated to nonpolitical endeavors.[42]

What motivates those Jews who are active in or align themselves with these various Israel-indicting Jewish bodies and other undertakings like them? Some talk of wanting to make Israel a better place, but their kangaroo court attacks on the state, their indifference to the genuine threats Israel faces, and their association with groups that want to see Israel annihilated suggest otherwise. The most prominent common denominator among such people appears to be their cultivating as their primary identification adherence to some variation on left-wing political orthodoxy. At the same time, they retain some, however attenuated, connection with a Jewish identity as well and work to bend the latter to conform to the orthodoxy of the former. Beyond this mix of allegiances lies a wish to believe, in the face of anti-Jewish pressures, that Jewish salvation can be obtained by embrace of the wider identity of leftist acolyte and by Jewish self-reform and self-effacement in conformity with leftist tenets.

Not surprisingly, a recasting of the Jewish vocation as properly the pursuit of universalist obligations and rejection of all Jewish particularism also figures highly in the cant of the Israel-indicting Jewish organizations. A claim shared by all of them is that they are advocating universalist Jewish values against pro-Israel particularism. The theme of *tikkun olam*, healing the world, is routinely bandied about by these groups as the true, universalist, Jewish mission. A leader of the NJA declared: "New Jewish Agenda . . . draws on the Talmudic teaching of *tikkun olam*, the just reordering of the world. We work to foster justice and progressive values through social and political action."[43] Israel and Israel's interests are, from this perspective, essentially expendable. As Gordon Fellman, an NJA leader and Brandeis faculty member, stated in an interview with the pro-PLO Palestinian newspaper *Al-Fajr*: "Jews everywhere [have the] opportunity to make the choice between petty, oppressive nationalism and the universalistic, prophetic values also nurtured in the millennia of Jewish preservation of texts and traditions."[44]

Another inveterate critic of Israel, Leonard Fein, has argued that Israel cannot fully represent an end to Jewish exile because Jews will remain in spiritual exile as long as the world is disordered. "Israel . . . cannot be, quite, home, for no place can be in a world of pain." Spiritually sensitive Jews, Fein suggests, are focused on and engaged in the work of *tikkun*, repair. He writes that for Reform Judaism, as it emerged in the nineteenth century, the work of *tikkun* was comprehended as "what we now call social action." To concentrate Jewish concern on the temporal state of Israel is to focus on the geopolitical present. In contrast, the Jewish pursuit of universal healing "is wrapped up in the days that were and in the end of days, in the past and in the future. Against these, the present is empty, a burden and a bore."[45]

Fein goes further and argues, in a chapter explicating his comprehension of *tikkun olam*, that, "It is unlikely that Jews can survive, and it would be unseemly if they did, except as a community organized around values and committed to *tikun* [his spelling] *olam*."[46] One sees here in Fein the ultimate Jewish absorption of the Jew-haters' indictments. In fact, all of Jewish religious tradition, and the voice of God as conveyed in that tradition, cast the answer to Jewish fall from spiritual grace as a rediscovered piety and foresee an ultimate Jewish destiny of redemption, however long the path may be in space and time; and in this context the Jews must survive, and must exert themselves to survive, as they find their way to spiritual improvement and redemption. And Israel can with very good reason be seen as crucial to that survival. In contrast, the Jews' indicters insist, hypocritically, that the Jews' failure to conform to some standard of behavior — a standard no other people meets or is expected to meet — renders the Jews unworthy of existence; and Fein chooses to embrace and advocate that perspective.

The determination to cultivate a fealty to some universalist orthodoxy and to eschew any Jewish particularist affiliation inevitably leads the enthusiasts of such a course into moral contortions. Those contortions include a blindness to the injustice of the indictments of Israel, a numbness to the ongoing war against Israel, a tolerance not only of Israel's tormentors but of groups and individuals who go beyond anti-Israel agendas to spew frank anti-Semitism, and a predilection for offering excuses for anti-Semitic allies even while claiming to be working to save the Jews from anti-Semitism. But such moral contortions are, in fact, characteristic of those who seek to appease the haters by absorbing the haters' indictments and pursuing self-reform in conformity with those indictments.

Voices in the hierarchy of organizations such as the New Jewish Agenda and New Israel Fund have repeatedly accused Israel of causing or legitimizing anti-Semitism. They have claimed to militate for Israeli "reform" at least in part to dampen anti-Semitic sentiment by seeking to change Israel in the ways demanded by its enemies.[47] But all the while their efforts have served to legitimize anti-Semitism by making common cause with the haters and endorsing the haters' slanders.

Not surprisingly, the high profile activities of these Jewish Israel-indicting organizations provided cover for other leftist groups to attack Israel more intensely and in ways that were clearly prejudicial and bigoted. After all, there were now "many" Jews who openly agreed with them. But, in fact, Jewish activists in the Israel-indicting groups often invited and welcomed such attacks. Gordon

Fellman wrote that New Jewish Agenda was interested in gaining for the Middle East a still greater prominence in the agenda of the leftist community, which, by his lights, had heretofore perhaps been "too confused to take the issue on or too fearful of internal dissension and condemnation from outside."[48]

The activists in the Israel-indicting Jewish groups, and their membership more broadly, represented a very small part of the American Jewish community. But from the mid-1980s onward, these groups and their leaders were increasingly successful at penetrating mainstream Jewish organizations and umbrella bodies and winning from them cooperation and joint sponsorship for their activities. This success was, in fact, a major goal of some of the Israel-indicting Jewish groups. For example, one reason for NJA's encouraging the spinning off of new organizations by those of its members and leaders who were eager to promote even more extreme anti-Israel positions rather than having them do so as NJA activists was to preserve some semblance of "moderation" for NJA in order to facilitate its penetration into mainstream bodies. The Israel-indicting organizations also commonly invoked principles of "pluralism" and "inclusiveness," and the supposed legitimacy of all voices, to advance their quest for cooperation from mainstream groups.

But key to their success was the receptiveness of many leaders in mainstream bodies to appeals to *tikkun olam*, universalism and "peace." While those leaders often, indeed, attributed their responsiveness to a need for inclusiveness and for the according of legitimacy to all voices, it was in large part their own political predilections, and wish to believe that peace could be won by Israeli self-reform, that accounted for their openness to the blandishments of the Israel-indicting groups. As Rael Jean Isaac notes, "As early as 1983, Agenda expressed 'surprise' at the 'ease' with which established Jewish organizations and synagogues had offered their facilities to Agenda and conducted programs in conjunction with it."[49]

Groups that over the ensuing years jointly sponsored events with NJA included the American Jewish Congress, the Federation of Reform Synagogues, the United Synagogues of America, various Jewish Community Relations Councils, and a number of campus Hillels. The American Jewish Congress, under the leadership of Henry Siegman, was particularly receptive to the blandishments of NJA and its activists.

Even as the political orthodoxies of much of the Jewish community, including, in general, the Jewish establishment, rendered some mainstream organizations amenable to accommodating groups promoting anti-Israel programs, there were also mainstream organizations that, in their political/social agendas, typically relegated Israel to a subordinate place and that were inclined to do so still more in the late 1980s and 1990s. Perhaps these groups were influenced by attacks on Israel from the Left. But their articulated justification for further decreasing their attention to Israel tended to be less focused on expressions of unhappiness with the nation's policies than on arguments that Israel was now economically and militarily more secure and needed less attention from American Jews.

Another of their arguments was that the threat of assimilation and erosion of the American Jewish community requires that more attention be paid to Jewish education and other steps to support Jewish identity here. But even programs to promote Jewish education sponsored by these organizations tended at best to share pride of place with very different political and social efforts.

The Jewish Community Relations Council of Boston's annual report for 1997–1998, a difficult period for Israel, gave particular emphasis to reaching beyond the Jewish community to address "social justice issues" and advance "universal goals of *tikkun olam*, the repair of the world." There was nothing in what the JCRC calls its "action agenda" that entailed responding to the political and strategic challenges facing Israel. A glance at Action Alerts sent out by the JCRC over these two years — that is, calls on the community to political action, such as lobbying elected officials over some issue — reveals that virtually all those action alerts had to do with issues of support for immigrant rights, funding of welfare programs, and related matters. There was very little addressing threats to Israel, terror in Israel, and tensions in American-Israeli relations, even though these were all very live issues over those two years.

These priorities reflected a leadership that preferred that Jewish self-definition focus less on Israel than on the traditions of charity and good deeds in Jewish thought and practice and on their application to a social activist and universalist agenda. The source of this predilection is a history of such perspectives being seen as the key to acceptance in a hostile environment and therefore to Jewish well-being and survival.

But as a strategy for preserving Jewish continuity, this focus on social activism seems fatally flawed. In a hostile environment, it hardly offers something at once so valuable and uniquely Jewish as to hold people to their Jewish identity in the face of suffering for that identity; and in an essentially benign and accepting environment such as that of the contemporary United States, it does not offer enough to counter the potential allures that weigh toward assimilation.

Certainly, the promotion of Jewish literacy by the leadership of many communities is a more promising tack; indeed, Lipset and Raab argue that religious literacy and connectedness alone can preserve continuity in the long run. But just as good deeds, while a laudable element in Jewish communal exertions, are no substitute for Jewish education in the struggle for continuity, so too they are no substitute for cultivation of the bond with Israel.

The well-being of Israel, as a fulfillment of Jewish creativity, is an affirmation of Jewish vitality more compelling and more unique, and hardly less anchored in the religion, than good deeds, and more likely to bind Jews to their identity. Indeed some have argued that no other affirmation can match Israel in transmitting a sense of the continuing meaningfulness of Jewish history, tradition and peoplehood, and so in serving to hold people to valuing their Jewish identity. (And if Israel's survival and well-being are crucial for Jewish continuity, they are crucial for sustaining those commitments to charity and good deeds and "healing the world" that follow from Jewish identity, Jewish literacy, and Jewish ethics.)

Even more incisive regarding the importance of Israel for Jewish continuity is the reverse argument: that Israel's loss would have dire consequences beyond simply pushing Jews back into the corrosive, community-eroding conditions they faced before Israel's creation. Jews would have to deal as well, of course, with the overwhelmingly dispiriting fact of having regained Zion only to lose it again. This would be a defeat so demoralizing, so reinforcing of a self-perception as a people whose time in history had indeed passed, that it could only increase defections and hasten the disappearance of the Jews as a community from the world stage.

Norman Podhoretz, in a *Commentary* article in 1989 entitled "Israel: A Lamentation From the Future," considered the condition of the Jews in the wake of their acquiescing, both in Israel and the United States, to pressures for territorial and other concessions to Israel's enemies that threatened her existence and then being confronted with the consequences of their failure of will, the demise of Israel. He writes of their being "left with this burden of shame and self-disgust that is undermining our will to go on as Jews and that is dragging the glorious history of our ancient people toward an ignominious end." It is a vision of what would follow on Israel's demise that is hard to dispute.[50]

The strategy of focusing on social action and humanitarian endeavors as defining what it means to be a Jew is, of course, based largely on the assumption that this would be more ingratiating to the surrounding society than more particularist elements of Jewish identity such as the religion itself or concern with the Jewish national home. But the strategy, at least in an American context, is misconceived in ironic ways. As Hertzberg and others note, Americans are by and large a religious people, and Jews valuing and practicing their religion is perceived by many non-Jews as making American Jews more like themselves, while Jewish secularism is regarded by many as more alien.

Similarly, far from devotion to Israel being comprehended as an alien particularism, most Americans seem to regard Israel in the manner Herzl anticipated. The reestablishment of the Jewish state, of a more "normal" Jewish national life, has contributed to a positive reassessment of Jews generally as a "normal" people. Moreover, the comprehension of Israel as a pro-Western, pro-American democratic state fighting first to establish and then to sustain itself against much larger hostile and undemocratic, and often anti-Western, nations around it, fighting what most Americans perceive as the good fight, and doing so with aplomb, ingenuity, and courage, has been the dominant comprehension within the American public and has redounded to a positive comprehension of Jews generally.

Indeed, the positive impact of Israel on American perceptions of Jews and Judaism has generally been underestimated. For example, there has been a tendency in American Jewish intellectual circles to place greater emphasis on the Holocaust — on the world's coming face-to-face with the horrors that can follow on the marginalization, defamation, and dehumanization of a vulnerable minority — in fueling the positive change in the wider society's attitudes toward Jews. Revelation of the horrors of the Holocaust have been regarded as central not only to the decline of the former popular anti-Semitism but to the broader preparedness among Americans to see Jews as full partners in American society.

But there is much to suggest that, in the absence of Israel's creation, the Holocaust would have been seen as a terrible crime against a vulnerable population but a crime whose victims in any case were a vestigial people facing its demise, a people whom history was in any case passing by, and this sad tragedy would now accelerate the process. In contrast, the creation of Israel had the effect of recasting the Jews as having an ongoing place in history, a continuing legitimacy and vitality, and lent to the Jews a respect far beyond mere condolences, a respect hardly won by the slaughter of more than a third of its people.

Indeed, the advances in ecumenism, the rapprochement between Judaism and Christian churches, the recognition extended by Christian churches to the ongoing legitimacy of the Jewish faith and its positive relevance to Christianity — a centerpiece of the improved place of the Jews in American opinion — have derived in large part from the reestablishment of Israel and its comprehension as evidence of the continuing place in history of Judaism and the Jewish people. More particularly, the ecumenism has drawn much of its power from the reassessment of the Jewish roots of Christian belief, and this has in turn emanated most importantly from the recreation of Israel. The mere fact of Israel's reestablishment has fueled this reassessment, and the archaeological work done in the reestablished Jewish nation and the Biblical research carried out by its scholars have provided the reconsideration of Christianity's Jewish sources with rich and resonant content.

Indeed, the now virtually universal use of the term *Judaeo-Christian* to capture the religion-based value system of American society would very likely never have come about without Israel. In addition, not only would the demise of Israel be so dispiriting to American Jews as to make it hard to imagine long-term Jewish communal survival in its wake, but such a disaster would inexorably also entail a loss of esteem for Jews in the wider society. Israel's loss would almost inevitably engender a negative perception of Jews as a people who had squandered their national life, let it slip away, failed to muster the courage to sustain it — and it would rekindle comprehension of the Jews as a vestigial people, among history's losers, sinking toward their demise.

This chapter has considered various ways in which American Jews' sense of themselves, and the manner of their relating to the wider society, reflect the survival of stigmata of exposure to anti-Semitism even in the context of a dramatic decline in anti-Semitism in America through the last half century and widespread acceptance of Jews as equals in American society. Even more seemingly incongruous is the presence of very similar stigmata in the Jews of Israel, where national liberation, the establishment of their own "normal" state, was supposed to liberate Jews from their chronic exposure to bias, marginalization, and abuse and from the psychological scars that followed from their predicament in exile.

Section II
ISRAEL

Then did Satan say: 'How will I conquer this beleaguered one? He possesses courage, ingenuity, resourcefulness and tools of war.' And then he said: 'I'll not rob his strength, nor bridle him, nor rein him in, nor enervate his hand. But this I'll do — blunt his mind, till he forgets his cause is just.'

Israeli poet Nathan Alterman

EIGHT

Herzl and His Challengers

Innumerable objections will be based on low grounds, for there are more low men than noble in this world. I have tried to remove some of these narrow-minded notions; and whoever is willing to fall in behind our [flag] must assist in this campaign of enlightenment. Perhaps we shall have to fight first of all against many an evil-disposed, narrow-hearted, short-sighted member of our own race.

Theodor Herzl, *The Jewish State*[1]

Zionism, as conceptualized by Herzl, was an answer to both the physical threats and the ongoing civic and social disabilities confronting the Jews of Europe. The former were most notably dramatized by the assaults on the Jews of Russia, the latter were exposed when the extension of civil rights to the Jews of western Europe still left them the object of *de facto* discrimination and exclusion and of that large-scale popular hatred Herzl had seen in the anti-Dreyfusard riots in Paris and in Lueger's election as mayor of Vienna.

But Herzl intended to do more than simply provide Jews a refuge from assault and bigotry. His Zionism was quite self-consciously conceived as addressing also the spiritual wounds wrought upon Jews by their being pushed to renounce their history, people, and faith in the hope of gaining admission to the surrounding culture and their even then being rebuffed. Zionism was to be a cure for that sickness of a diminished sense of self, that poisonous imbibing of the indictments of the surrounding society, that is so often the consequence of chronic abuse. Herzl and other Zionist writers vigorously attacked anti-Semitic indictments as lies, insisted on the innate nobility of the Jewish people, and asserted that a restored nationhood would enable Jews to cultivate once more that nobility.

Yet there was also much in these writers' observations on the effects on Jews of two thousand years of exile and persecution that reflected the absorption of anti-Jewish canards. Max Nordau, for example, an articulate and impassioned ally of Herzl and defender of the Jews and the Zionist enterprise, wrote in 1902 of Jewry in exile as "physically degenerate proletarians . . . town-bred hucksters . . . "[2] Jews are variously characterized as having become too cosmopolitan, too focused on trade, too unrooted, too insular, too religious. What does "too" mean, beyond echoing anti-Jewish cant?

Or consider discussions of working the land as being in itself redeeming, as shaping a New Jew who would cast off all that has been deforming in life in the Diaspora. The concept of Redemption through working the land has both Jewish, particularly Biblical, and European, particularly Romantic, roots. But as it appears in much of early Zionist literature it also reflects an absorption of the anti-Semitic canard that Jewish concentration in occupations unattached to the land is a sign of Jewish degeneracy and unwholesomeness.

Of course the Zionists typically emphasized that the "degeneracy" of Diaspora Jews was not innate in Jews but was rather a consequence of the degradation to which Jews had been subjected in exile. But they were still repeating a bigoted characterization of Jews that had its origins in anti-Semitic cant.[3] Nordau stated at one point that, "It is the greatest triumph for anti-Semitism that it has brought the Jews to view themselves with anti-Semitic eyes."[4] The observation is at once unimpeachable and yet unintentionally ironic given that Nordau himself, like others among the early Zionists, was not immune to seeing other Jews through anti-Semitic eyes.

Herzl and his closest allies comprehended the Zionist enterprise as potentially embracing all Jews. Nordau's comments echoing anti-Semitic canards, and the use of such rhetoric by other Austrian and German Zionists who rallied around Herzl, typically appear in the context of distinguishing the low state of Jewry in exile from the potential transformation that would be wrought by the Jews' ingathering into the Jewish state. But such rhetoric is also found at times in the work of these writers, including that of Herzl himself, in the context of characterizations of Jews opposed to Zionism. This was yet another instance of cleavages in Diaspora Jewish communities leading to segments of the population seeing those from whom they are alienated at least in part through the lens of anti-Semitic caricature.

But Herzl and his associates' perception of the essential unity of the Jews, a perception to some degree reflecting their personal distance from intense communal involvement, communal politics, and communal cleavages, meant that communal divisions were of less interest to them than communal bonds. Consequently, the derogatory rhetoric that so often followed on exacerbations of and personal involvement in communal divisions was tangential to their focus and their major exertions. In contrast, eastern European Zionists were more commonly people who lived their lives immersed in the Jewish community, its politics, and its divisions; and hostile rhetoric directed against those on the other side of major communal divisions, and the embrace of anti-Jewish caricature to characterize those others, were more intense and more at the center of Zionist argument in the East.

The widespread perception among Russian Jews of distinctive Jewish peoplehood contributed to a broad receptivity to Zionism across the entire Jewish population of Russia. This was so even as Zionism encountered some resistance within various segments of the population. (For example, a number of Orthodox groups regarded Zionism as sacrilege and the Return to Zion as only to follow upon the coming of the Messiah, and some socialist circles viewed Zionism as entirely unrealistic and urged that Russian Jewish aspirations be focused on struggling for the Jews' national rights, Jewish autonomy, within the Russian Empire.) Herzl recognized the persisting strength of Jewish national consciousness in the East and its translation into broad pro-Zionist sentiment, so different from prevailing Jewish attitudes elsewhere in Europe, and he lauded Russian Jewry. He said of the Russian delegates to the first Zionist congress:

"They possess that inner unity which has disappeared from among the westerners. They are steeped in Jewish national sentiment without betraying any national narrowness and intolerance. They are not tortured by the idea of assimilation. They do not assimilate into other nations, but exert themselves to learn the best in other peoples. In this way they manage to remain erect and genuine. Looking on them, we understood where our forefathers got the strength to endure through the bitterest times."[5]

But the popularity of Zionism among Russian Jews masked deep communal divisions. The most activist Zionist groups in Russia came from the ranks of socialist workers' movements, and these groups commonly felt alienated both from traditionally religious Jews and from the Jewish *petit bourgeoisie*. They associated the former with the failed and discredited traditional leaderships, which had been unable to find effective responses to government depredations. As to the latter, the Russian government's anti-Semitic assault on the Jewish estate managers, brokers, and tradespeople of the villages and townlets, as lesser creatures pursuing unwholesome occupations, was to some degree taken to heart by many Jews. The Zionist groups formed by Jewish workers were not immune to drawing on anti-Semitic caricature in their perceptions and depictions of both the religious Jew and the *petit bourgeois* Jew. They not uncommonly comprehended the future Zion in socialist and largely secularist terms, as a utopia for the Jewish nation but one with little place for either the traditionally religious or the traditionally capitalist.

Zionism in Russia also reflected communal cleavages in other ways. Much of the articulation of Zionist arguments in the last decades of the nineteenth century in Russia was the work of former maskilim, assimilationists who were disappointed by the hostility with which their efforts at assimilation were met in the surrounding society. Many of these people were particularly affected by the wave of pogroms that the Russians unleashed in 1881 following the assassination of Czar Alexander II and the ascension of Alexander III, and they returned to the Jewish community and embraced Jewish nationalism as the only viable option for Jews. The former maskilim incorporated into their Zionist programs elements of their earlier agendas for rendering the Jews more "normal," such as an emphasis on agricultural settlement. The socialist workers' Zionist groups widely embraced this focus on agricultural settlement, although with a view toward settlement being organized on socialist principles.

But some among the former Russian maskilim, most notably Ahad Ha-Am, were dismissive of the emphasis on settlement. Ahad Ha-Am argued that the physical building of the homeland in Eretz Israel would be a slow process at best and only a small portion of European Jewry would be able to emigrate there. With European Jews spiritually adrift and being lost to the allures of assimilation, the key to "redemption," in Ahad Ha-Am's view, was the forging of a national culture based on the Hebrew language. He envisioned educating Jews in their history and their literary and philosophical heritage and building on that heritage through a Hebrew renaissance, and he looked to a reinvigorated Jewish national culture to infuse in Jews a new self-respect and serve as a spiritual counterweight to assimilationist pressures. He insisted further that the building of the national home should be pursued primarily from the perspective of reestablishing Eretz Israel as the center of the national culture for Jews everywhere.[6]

Ahad Ha-Am's cultural emphasis was dismissed by many of the Zionist socialist workers' groups, whose focus remained on pragmatic steps of land acquisition and settlement. Mitigating against fuller embrace of such a cultural agenda, even as complementing "practical" Zionism, was a prominent anti-intellectualism among the socialist workers' groups. This attitude reflected in large part popular association of intellectualism both with what was perceived as failed, anachronistic, religious traditionalism and self-abnegating and bankrupt assimilationism. This anti-intellectualism also reflected the embrace by some Jews of anti-Semitic indictments of Jews for not being sufficiently engaged in "real," that is, manual, work. Ahad Ha-Am in turn often disparaged as misguided, and doomed to failure, the narrow focus on settlement.

The divisions within Russian Jewry were exacerbated by the worsening external pressures on Russian Jews, pressures that gave life and death urgency to finding viable answers, and rejecting unworkable responses, to the problems confronting the community. The intensifying besiegement of the Jews also spurred increased embrace of anti-Jewish indictments by segments of the community in their perception and characterization of Jews on the other side of communal divisions. This reaction reflected people's wish to believe that their particular agenda was the panacea for the Jewish predicament and their fears that the formulas of contending voices would only invite continued attacks and lead to worse disaster. The widening communal fissures were mirrored in the conflicting programs of the various Zionist voices and Zionist groups that emerged from Russian Jewry, and those rifts were brought into the Zionist conferences organized by Herzl and undercut his attempts to present a united Zionist front.

HERZL AND HIS OPPONENTS IN THE ZIONIST MOVEMENT

At the first Zionist Congress, held in 1897 in Basel, Herzl succeeded in winning the attendance, and enthusiastic involvement in the proceedings, of virtually all European Zionist groups. Herzl believed that the key to turning Zionist aspirations into the reality of a reborn sovereign Jewish nation in Eretz Israel was to win Great Power support and sponsorship of the Zionist agenda, with the Zionists gaining essentially a Great Power charter for their enterprise. This strategy was endorsed and adopted by the first Congress as the "Basel program."

Herzl regarded piecemeal settlement in Eretz Israel of the sort haltingly, and generally unsuccessfully, pursued by the Russian Zionist groups as grossly inadequate and even politically counterproductive to Zionist hopes. In Herzl's view, historical precedent — the piecemeal emigration of Jews to other areas — suggested that, should such efforts in fact succeed in fulfilling the hopes of its enthusiasts and reestablish a substantial Jewish settlement population in Eretz Israel, at some point that growing population would inevitably arouse the suspicion and hostility of the controlling power, whether Turkey or a successor power. It would then trigger an anti-Jewish backlash that would bring an end to the endeavor.[7] The only way to proceed was to win the explicit approval and sponsorship of Turkey, and/or some combination of Great Powers, who would be persuaded into seeing benefit in the enterprise.

Herzl was also distrustful of the anti-intellectualism and class bias that were imbedded in the Russian socialist Zionist groups' concepts of building the Zionist state on the basis of farming settlements and manual labor. This was not only because of Herzl's wish to include all segments of Diaspora Jewry in the Zionist future. Herzl's own comprehension of the future Jewish state was also one in which Jewish intellectual capabilities would be enlisted in establishing a state as creative, as culturally and intellectually productive, as any in Europe. He saw both anti-intellectualism, the exercise in "artificially lowering the intellectual level of our masses,"[8] and class bias as counterproductive.

Herzl was similarly opposed to the anti-religious attitudes of the Russian socialist Zionists, again not simply because his Zionist vision embraced all Jews but also because he saw the religious as playing a vital role in creating the Jewish state. He wrote, in *The Jewish State*, "Our rabbis, on whom we especially call, will devote their energies to the service of our idea, and will inspire their congregations by preaching it from the pulpit. They will not need to address special meetings for the purpose; an appeal such as this may be uttered in the synagogue. And thus it must be done. For we feel our historic affinity only through the faith of our fathers."[9] And, "Thus we shall also create a center for the deep religious needs of our people. Our ministers will understand us first, and will be with us in this."[10] In 1899, Herzl argued that religious Jews would likely become "the very best Zionists" precisely because "they have not yet forgotten the national traditions and have a strong religious sentiment."[11]

At the Second Zionist Congress, in 1898, pressure particularly from the Russian Zionist groups led to an endorsement of ongoing settlement activity even in the absence of the Great Power sponsorship sought by Herzl. But Russian Zionist challenges to Herzl's program continued to grow more intense and more emphatic, making Zionist unity increasingly difficult to maintain. Russian socialist Zionists took issue with Herzl's courting of the Orthodox, of Jewish capitalists, and of the imperial powers, including the Czar.

Ahad Ha-Am, the premier advocate of "cultural Zionism," was from the beginning hostile to Herzl. Just as he was critical of the Russian Zionist emphasis on settlement, he thought Herzl's dream of mass Jewish migration to Eretz Israel and creation of a Jewish state under Great Power sponsorship was entirely unrealistic. Ahad Ha-Am maintained that Herzl's scenario, and the focus on physical threats to Europe's Jews, were a distraction from the cultural threat and the need for his envisioned Jewish cultural rebirth. He also argued that Herzl was too wedded to European culture to appreciate the cultural threat or the need for a Hebrew renaissance.

While Russian Jews from the ranks of the socialist Zionists were generally unsympathetic toward Ahad Ha-Am's cultural emphasis, and of course rejected his skepticism regarding settlement, many sided with him against Herzl. They did so in part because they sympathized with the explicitly anti-religious aspects of Ahad Ha-Am's program for a cultural renaissance, his call to win the schools away from the rabbis. In addition, Ahad Ha-Am's indictment of the acculturated Jewish middle class of central and western Europe and the earlier maskilim of Russia for their embrace of European culture and abandonment of their own cultural legacy actually converged with the socialist Zionists' antibourgeois and anti-intellectual biases. Also, Ahad Ha-Am articulated some of their own uneasiness with Herzl's pursuit of support from the Great Powers and Jewish capitalists as well as the Orthodox.

Chaim Weizmann was a member of the community of young Russian Jews who had been locked out of universities in Russia because of czarist *numeri clausi* and had gone to Germany to study. He was representative of those within that community who had initially rallied to Herzl but then, embracing the perspectives of the Russian socialist Zionists, broke with him and split the Zionist Organization. Weizmann wrote of the need to reform the Zionist Organization of "unattractive petty bourgeois, conservative, and clerical overtones."[12] In 1901, Weizmann and his circle forged within the Zionist Organization a "Democratic Faction," and Weizmann declared that his faction "will always be . . . in opposition whenever dealings with the clerical and with the bourgeoisie . . . are concerned."[13]

Herzl, worried about the potential large-scale defection of Orthodox Russian Jewry from the Zionist cause in the face of the Democratic Faction's anti-religious agenda, hurriedly organized a meeting of supportive Russian Zionists, both Orthodox and nonreligious, in Vilna in February, 1902. A religious Zionist party, Mizrachi, was formed at the meeting as a counterweight to the Democratic Faction within the Zionist Organization. Mizrachi rapidly gained the allegiance of many Zionist groups throughout Russia, which led Weizmann to declare: "The rabbinical party is organizing itself in Jesuit fashion, and I think of their machinations with disgust. Everything is vulgar and foul."[14]

However, at another conference of Russian Zionists held in Minsk in the fall of 1902, the issue of "cultural Zionism" took center stage, with Ahad Ha-Am personally promoting his agenda of "conquering the schools" and making explicit in his speech at the conference that the battle for "cultural Zionism" was a battle against the religious. The conference ultimately adopted the establishment of two separate cultural committees, one modernist and one traditional, but the unity of the Zionist Organization was shattered in a manner that would persist. Moreover, as Herzl had feared, the Orthodox population now looked upon the Zionist Organization with increasing misgivings, as seemingly representing more and more a reincarnation of the maskilim agenda of earlier decades, and anti-Zionist sentiment rapidly spread in Orthodox circles.

Fault lines within Zionist ranks widened still further upon Herzl's premature death in 1904, at age 44, and the loss of his organizational and diplomatic skills. While Herzl's political agenda of using Great Power sponsorship for a Jewish state, his "political Zionism," was kept alive by Nordau and others, it lost ground to the "practical Zionism" of those who saw the primary task as the establishment of settlements, the building of the Jewish state from the ground up. Slippage of the political program accelerated with the "Young Turk" revolution in the Ottoman Empire in 1908, consolidation of the nationalist agenda of the Young Turks, and the incompatibility of their aspirations with a Zionist charter as envisioned by Herzl.

A parallel development entailed the weakening within the Zionist Organization of those who, like Herzl, sought to establish in Eretz Israel a Jewish state, and the growing strength of those who wished to recast the Zionist goal as a more modest Jewish "national home" in Eretz Israel. This shift reflected not only the loss of Herzl's political vision and the shifting political sands with the ascent of the Young Turks. It was also a consequence of the increasingly outspoken and successful challenge within the Zionist Organization to Herzl's agenda by those who favored the "national home" concept over the pursuit of a Jewish state.

These included the supporters of Ahad Ha-Am's "cultural Zionism," those who followed Ahad Ha-Am in perceiving mass immigration to Eretz Israel as impractical and saw Eretz Israel as potentially more of a cultural center for the reinvigorated Jewish nation than as a political refuge. In addition, the "cultural Zionists" aspired to uniting Zionists and non-Zionists in advancing Ahad Ha-Am's envisioned Hebrew renaissance and did not wish to alienate the non-Zionists by pushing for a Jewish state.

The shift in emphasis from state to national home was also supported by those Russian socialist Zionists and their allies whose settlement projects were underwritten by wealthy Jewish sponsors in the West not particularly sympathetic to the concept of a Jewish state. Some among those sponsors looked upon the settlement projects essentially in nonpolitical terms, as efforts to rescue and rehabilitate refugees from Russia no different from the similar farming settlement projects for Jewish refugees that they sponsored in Argentina, the United States, and elsewhere. They did not view them as nation building and were in fact hostile to Zionism in Herzl's mode and saw it as a threat to the newly won legal citizenship status of western Jewry. (The same dynamic had prevailed two decades earlier when the Russian Hovevei Zion movement, at its creation in Katowice in 1884, had pushed Leon Pinsker to soften the pro-state message of his *Auto-Emancipation* so as not to offend Edmond de Rothschild, chief patron of Hovevei Zion's colonies in Eretz Israel.)

Herzl's aspiration to create an independent Jewish state reflected not only his capacity to appreciate the power of the idea of a reborn Jewish state both in rallying a dispirited European Jewry and in firing the imagination of potential governmental sponsors. It also reflected his ability to comprehend diplomatic paths to his goal. But, most importantly, his idea of an independent Jewish state was driven by his appreciation of the dire physical danger in which European Jewry was living and his recognition that only an independent Jewish state could provide a refuge from that danger.

Ahad Ha-Am, beyond disbelieving the feasibility of Herzl's agenda, dismissed the physical threat to Europe's Jews and saw the cultural threat as looming larger. The Russian socialist Zionists commonly viewed the nation-building project in any case not in terms of mass immigration, even if that were to be feasible. They envisioned rather the enlistment of an elite from the younger generation who would be uninfected with the dross of Jewish bourgeois capitalism or traditional religiosity and would construct a Jewish socialist utopia in Eretz Israel. This vision, again, was built in no small part on the socialist Zionists' embrace of anti-Semitic denigrations of the Jewish religion and of the Jewish commercial class. It was built on the wish to believe that the anti-Semites' ire was really directed against religious Jews and bourgeois Jews and that jettisoning traditional Jewish religiosity and Jewish involvement in bourgeois capitalism would help end the anti-Jewish assault.

An as yet unmentioned but important strain of opposition to Herzl within the Zionist movement, an opposition distinct both from Ahad Ha-Am's "cultural Zionism" and from socialist "practical Zionism" and not of Russian origin but one which made common cause with the Democratic Faction, was represented by Martin Buber. Buber initially responded with enthusiasm to Herzl's message. He spoke eloquently at the Third Zionist Congress in 1899 of the coming time when "on our own soil, from our own homes, the flag of national freedom will fly in our land,"[15] and in 1901 he became the founding editor of Herzl's Zionist weekly, *Die Welt.* But within a few months he abandoned the publication, and Herzl, and threw his support to the Democratic Faction. In subsequent years Buber's attention drifted elsewhere. To the degree that he returned to the issue of Zionism he formulated and advocated a version of cultural Zionism very different from Ahad Ha-Am's and he became an outspoken critic of the quest for a Jewish state in Eretz Israel as conceived by Herzl.

Buber, born in Vienna and reared in Lemberg (Lvov), grew up in a German Jewish cultural milieu and was a twenty-one-year-old university student when he spoke at the Third Zionist Congress. As a German Jewish intellectual, Buber was attracted to German culture and German intellectual issues and perspectives. But Jewish pursuit of assimilation was being met with the shrill anti-Semitism purveyed by the new anti-Semitic political parties in Germany and Austria and, more broadly, was receiving at best only a begrudging and limited acceptance by the surrounding society. Buber responded by perceiving the pursuit of assimilation as an untenable and demeaning Jewish self-abnegation.

He later wrote, in a 1917 essay on his "Path to Hasidism," of his early attraction to Herzl's message: "Zionism gave the first stimulus to my liberation. I can only allude here to what it meant for me: the restoration of the context, the renewed rootedness in the community. No one requires the redeeming link with nationhood as much as he who has been seized by a spiritual quest, a youth abducted by the intellect away to the skies; but among the youths of this nature and with this destiny no one needs this link with nationality as much as the Jewish youth does." This is so, Buber seems to be suggesting, precisely because the Jewish youth is reared in a culture not his own. "And for him who has disassociated himself from his society the most glittering treasure of intellect, the most prolific, illusory productivity . . . are not able to compensate for the holy insignia of humanity, rootedness, association, totality."[16]

But if Buber perceived the answer to the Jews' self-abnegating pursuit of assimilation to lie in reimmersion in Jewish peoplehood and nationhood, he did not comprehend that reinvigorated connection as Herzl did, or even Ahad Ha-Am. Herzl recognized the physical dangers facing European Jewry, saw them in the state-sponsored pogroms in Russia, in the popular support in Germany and Austria for the brutal platform agendas of the new anti-Semitic parties, and in the cries for Jewish blood of the anti-Dreyfusard mobs in Paris. He sought a haven for the Jews, and the promise of a normal life, in a Jewish state. Ahad Ha-Am gave greater weight to the cultural threat posed by the wholesale flight along the assimilationist path of substantial segments of European Jewish youth, and he envisioned a cultural renaissance, capturing the schools, as the key to a revitalized identity and reinvigorated peoplehood. Buber, seeing in the pursuit of an identity to which one is not born and is not welcome inevitable self-diminution, frustration, and loss of centeredness and yet nevertheless attracted to German culture, sought in reimmersion in Jewish peoplehood something other than a homecoming. He sought a haven from which to venture out, a path to reconciling an affirmation of Jewish identity and an embrace of the allures to which he was acculturated.

In fact, the path Buber forged was in many respects a variation on German Jewish exercises in seeking to appease anti-Jewish feeling by redefining Judaism. His course too was one of eschewing the particularist, emphasizing Judaism's universalist aspects, and presenting the Jewish community as emphatically not some exotic and alien, other-focused element within the society but rather the inventors and conveyors of a universal humanitarian ethos and sensibility.

After breaking with Herzl and making common cause with the Democratic Faction, Buber soon retreated from the Zionist Organization entirely and immersed himself in the study of Hasidism. The writings that emerged from this work place Buber among those Jews in the West who, disenchanted with assimilation, looked more and more to Eastern, Polish, Jewry, so long criticized and regarded as an embarrassment by assimilationists, as representing, for all its difficulties, a more spiritually whole and wholesome Jewry.

More particularly, Buber portrays the Hasidic Zaddik — as distinct from both secular authorities and from rabbis bound to religious formalism (Buber shared some of the anti-traditionalist perspectives of the Russian socialists and maskilim) — as "the helper in spirit, the teacher of the world's meaning, the conductor of the divine spark."[17] For Buber, the Zaddik was the conveyor of a unique, and uniquely unselfconscious, Jewish humanitarian sensibility and understanding of the world. "Here . . . was something different, something incomparable; here was . . . the living double-concern of humanity: true community and true leadership."[18] What Buber saw in reconnecting with the Jewish people was the potential to commune with that special, unique sensibility and knowledge represented for him by his Hasidic Zaddik and, drawing on that sensibility and knowledge, to venture out and relate in a special way with the rest of humanity, the surrounding German world and beyond; relate in a way that would help heal the world!

"This . . . has always been and will continue to be Judaism's significance for mankind: that it confronts mankind with the demand for unity . . . It can . . . offer, ever anew, a unification of mankind's diverse contents, and ever new possibilities for synthesis. At the time of the prophets and of early Christianity, it offered a religious synthesis; at the time of Spinoza, an intellectual synthesis; at the time of socialism, a social synthesis.

"And for what synthesis is the spirit of Judaism getting ready today? Perhaps for a synthesis of all those syntheses. But whatever form it will take, this much we know about it: it will, once again, demand unity . . . It will, once again, say to mankind: 'All you are looking for . . . is devoid of substance and meaning without unity.'"[19]

Later, Buber wrote of Jews advancing the world's oneness by acting as a link between East and West. He also went on to develop, in philosophical discourses, theories of the unifying power of experiencing the "other," of taking into oneself the sensitivities and sensibilities of the other, and of ultimately, through the cultivation of that special empathic power, achieving even unity with God: Buber's "I and Thou."

In a letter written shortly after Herzl's death in 1904, Buber asserts that Herzl possessed "nothing of an elevated Jewish nature" and contrasts him in this regard to "Spinoza, Israel Ba'al-Shem, Heinrich Heine, or Ferdinand Lassalle."[20] Ba'al-Shem was, of course, the founder of the Hasidic movement. Of the others who embody for Buber "an elevated Jewish nature," Spinoza broke with the Jewish community to immerse himself in the formulation of a rationalist universal moral philosophy. Heine converted to Christianity and frequently vilified the Jews and Judaism and asserted his attraction to Christian belief. Lassalle likewise sought to distance himself from the Jews, often invoked anti-Semitic stereotypes in his indictments of other Jews, and dedicated his energies to championing universalist socialism.

In the wake of the outbreak of World War I and Britain's subsequent assertion as one of its war aims the dissolution of the Ottoman Empire, the Zionist cause received increased attention and Zionist groups were re-energized. The sense of an approaching critical moment and a new urgency was reinforced by the assaults on eastern European Jewry that accompanied the war. In this context, Buber returned to the issue of Zionism, asserted his opposition to a Jewish state, and elaborated on his vision of what he called "true Zionism." His Zionism aspired not to the creation of a national haven and refuge for the Jewish people in the face of dire threats and assaults, not to a state that would allow Jews to defend themselves and to relate on a more equal footing with other nations. Rather, it envisioned a cultural center that would facilitate the Jews' pursuit of their universalist mission:

"For me, just as the state in general is not the determining goal of mankind, so the 'Jewish state' is not the determining goal for the Jews . . . Our argument . . . does not concern the Jewish state . . . It does not concern the addition of one more trifling power structure. It does, however, concern the settlement of Palestine, which, independent of 'international politics,' can affect the inner consolidation of the energies of the Jewish people and thereby the realization of Judaism . . . Zion restored will become the house of the Lord for all peoples and the center of the new world."[21]

The aggressive pursuit of a state by political and diplomatic means had been the essence of Herzl's response to the precarious situation of European Jewry. That effort lost ground to "practical Zionism" and "cultural Zionism" after his death and remained in eclipse through the following decade. As a consequence, the Zionist Organization was largely unprepared to advance the national cause in the new political and diplomatic landscape wrought by the outbreak of the war.

WEIZMANN, ZIONISM, AND WORLD WAR I

How far the Zionist Organization had drifted from Herzl's path, and how diminished had become its objectives, is vividly illustrated by an encounter in December, 1914, between Chaim Weizmann and Sir Herbert Samuel, a minister in the British government.[22] (Weizmann had moved to England in 1904, pursued a successful career as an industrial chemist and was ultimately responsible for the discovery of a method for synthesizing acetone that proved to be a major contribution to Britain's wartime munitions industry. He had become active in the British branch of the Zionist Organization, advancing to the position of co-vice president.)

A month before the meeting, and a few days after the British declaration of war against Turkey, Samuel, who was Jewish, David Lloyd George, then Chancellor of the Exchequer, and Foreign Secretary Sir Edward Gray had, in a meeting of the British cabinet, expressed support for the establishment of a Jewish state in Palestine. Now Weizmann, who was unaware of this earlier event, expressed to Samuel — according to Weizmann's notes on the encounter — the Jews' need for "a place where they formed an important part of the population . . . however small this place might be. For example, something like Monaco, with a university instead of a gambling-hall."[23]

Samuel, already engaged with others in advocating a Jewish state within the British cabinet, apparently, in the words of one analysis of the meeting, "tried to explain to [Weizmann] that his demands were simply 'too modest' . . . that 'big things would have to be done in Palestine.'"[24] Weizmann inquired in what ways the minister's plans were more ambitious than his own and was told by Samuel, seemingly to Weizmann's surprise, that he did not wish to go into details but that, "the Jews will have to build railways, harbors, a university, a network of schools . . . These ideas are in the mind of my colleagues in the cabinet."[25]

In effect, at this fateful time, Herzl's vision was more alive in the British cabinet than in the Zionist Organization.[26]

Weizmann was challenged by Ben-Gurion after the war on why he had not more aggressively advocated rapid establishment of a Jewish state, particularly as new successor states were being planned for, and established in, the imperial territories of all the defeated Central Powers, Germany, Austria-Hungary, and Turkey, as well as in the lost territories of Czarist Russia. Weizmann's response was that, "We didn't demand a Jewish state because they wouldn't have given us one. We asked only for the conditions which would allow us to create a Jewish state in the future. It's just a matter of tactics."[27] Weizmann had responded similarly when, at the Paris Peace Conference, Colonel Richard Meinertzhagen, a British intelligence officer in the Palestine campaign, strong supporter of the Zionist cause, and now a member of the British delegation in Paris, "urged him to strike at once and demand Jewish sovereignty in Palestine."[28]

But Weizmann's answer to Ben-Gurion and Meinertzhagen was disingenuous. Again, the 1914 conversation with Samuel shows that key elements within the British government were far ahead of him in advocating a Jewish state; Weizmann's narrow aspirations were hardly based on assessments of what was and was not likely to win British support. In fact, there is evidence that Weizmann's circumscribed aspirations led to a narrowing of the aims of Zionism's supporters inside the British government. Within weeks of the December, 1914, meeting, and in the wake of lobbying by representatives of the anti-Zionist views of much of the Jewish establishment in Britain and further conversations with Weizmann and with his colleagues in the Zionist Organization, Samuel backed away from his strong advocacy of a state. Instead he began to echo Weizmann, talking of a "cultural plan" and "a great spiritual center for Judaism in the Holy Land."[29]

Was this backing off inevitable given opposition to a Jewish state among figures in the Anglo-Jewish establishment and others of influence? Was Weizmann right that they "wouldn't have given us [a state]," even if that was not the reason for his more modest objectives? Lloyd George became prime minister in December, 1916, and Lloyd George's government went against the anti-Zionists in promulgating the Balfour Declaration and advocating a Jewish national home in Palestine — a goal consistent with Weizmann's circumscribed aspirations but no more acceptable to many British anti-Zionists than a state. There is little evidence that the wording of the Declaration, and the shift from a state to a lesser objective, were fashioned primarily to accommodate anti-Zionist opinion. There is no convincing indication that Zionist advocacy of a state charter could not have moved Lloyd George's government further in that direction in its planning for postwar dispositions.

In any case, Weizmann's narrower objective, his eschewing aggressive pursuit of statehood, appears to have been rooted in considerations other than assessment of diplomatic and political resistance.

The general shift in Zionist Organization focus in preceding years away from the diplomatic pursuit of statehood and toward "cultural Zionism" and "practical Zionism" had reflected to some degree the desire to engage anti-Zionist Jews in the work of cultural revival and Western Jewish philanthropists in ongoing efforts at settlement. Weizmann may have been concerned about alienating the anti-Zionist philanthropists if he pursued statehood.

But, again, if the worry was that the anti-Zionists would block diplomatic action, this proved not to be the case as the British government subsequently moved forward despite anti-Zionist objections. Moreover, some of the Western philanthropists pushed Weizmann to be more aggressive in pursuit of a state. A few weeks before his December, 1914, meeting with Samuel, Weizmann met with Sir James Rothschild. According to Weizmann's notes, Rothschild advised him against advocating goals that were too modest and would fail to fire the imagination of statesmen. He urged pursuing the grander vision as more likely to elicit a positive response.[30] That Weizmann chose not to do so, even when virtually invited to do so by Samuel, clearly seems to have reflected less concerns about external obstacles than his assessment of appropriate goals.

Some writers have suggested, apparently correctly, that by background, education, and temperament Weizmann was not prepared to think of state building in political and diplomatic terms in the manner that Herzl did, or even ponder the internal mechanisms of state building as Herzl had. One of Weizmann's biographers notes, "Unlike Herzl, he did not theorize in a systematic manner about the form the future Jewish state would take: its constitution, party system, administration, or army. Those questions were too abstract for his scientific mind."[31] But such disinclination, beyond reflecting limits imposed by his background and education, was also the product of active aversions and a belief that appropriate approaches to the Zionist endeavor lay elsewhere.

As noted earlier in reference to Weizmann's alliance with the Democratic Faction in the early years of the century, Weizmann actively challenged Herzl's political and diplomatic emphasis. He sided then with the "practical" Zionists' thesis of having to build Zion from the ground up on the basis of an expanding network of socialist agricultural communities. At the Zionist Congress of 1907 in The Hague, Weizmann articulated a "synthetic Zionism" supposedly integrating Herzl's political Zionism and the program of the Russian "practicals," but his focus and emphasis continued on the latter. As late as 1931 Weizmann was to state, "If there is any other way of building a house, save brick by brick, I do not know it. If there is any other way of building up a country, save dunam by dunam and man by man, and farmstead by farmstead, again I do not know it."[32]

Moreover, Weizmann shared the Russian socialist Zionists' aversion to the devoutly religious and to the *petit bourgeoisie,* the tradespeople and artisans, who comprised so large a segment of eastern European Jewry. Again, the Russian socialist Zionists, in large part under the influence of anti-Jewish prejudices, envisioned a Zionism built exclusively on socialist principles, by a new generation untainted by religious or *petit bourgeois* predilections. They certainly did not envision a mass migration to Zion of European Jews who would overwhelm the socialist experiment with European ways. They were more inclined to prefer a wandering in the desert by the Jewish masses as the younger generation built the future. In this way they were predisposed to being wary of a statehood that entailed immediate large-scale immigration, and Weizmann appears generally to have shared such predilections.

Indeed, Weizmann wrote in November, 1918, regarding the prospect of large-scale immigration into Palestine should Jews be forced out of eastern Europe *en masse*: "We shall have all the miserable refugees who will be driven out of Poland, Galicia, Rumania, etc., at the doors of Palestine. We shall be swamped in Palestine and shall never be able to set up a community worth having there."[33]

Herzl had anticipated the establishment of a Jewish military as an essential element of state building and defense of the Jewish refuge. With the outbreak of the war, some Zionist figures, particularly Vladimir Jabotinsky and Josef Trumpeldor, began pressing for creation by the Allies of a Jewish Legion to fight as a separate unit and to lay the foundation for a national military. (Jabotinsky and Trumpeldor were Russian Jews — Trumpeldor was a decorated veteran of the Russo-Japanese War — but were not aligned with the Russian socialist Zionists.) But they did so against the united opposition of the Zionist leadership, including Weizmann.

(Nevertheless, the British, early in 1915, organized the Zion Mule Corps, a supply unit recruited mainly from Jews who had fled Eretz Israel under pressure of Turkish measures against the Yishuv, the Jewish community in the Holy Land. The Mule Corps distinguished itself in action in the Gallipolli Campaign.)

(In December, 1917, British troops captured El-Arish and the following month sought to establish a foothold in Palestine. Some months later the British formed the 38th Battalion of the Royal Fusiliers, consisting mainly of Jews from London's East End. Jews were also recruited in the United States by David Ben-Gurion and others, and a 39th Battalion and later a 40th Battalion were formed. The 38th and elements of the 39th participated in the successful British campaign to wrest Palestine from Turkish forces.)

In July, 1917, Weizmann and his associates, who had been meeting intermittently with British government officials over the preceding two and a half years, submitted to the government a proposal for a British declaration favoring the reconstitution of Palestine as "the National Home of the Jewish people." On November 2, Foreign Secretary Balfour provided, in a letter to Lord Rothschild, a statement to that effect, the so-called Balfour Declaration. Balfour's letter represented a unique milestone for the Zionist cause. It gave the imprimatur of the world's major power, a power soon to be in firm control of Palestine, to Zionist aspirations. In addition, it was shortly to be the basis for the disposition of Palestine agreed upon by the victorious Allied Powers and later accepted by the League of Nations. But the path blazoned by the Balfour Declaration, and subsequently ratified by the Allies and the League of Nations in their awarding to Britain its Mandate for Palestine, fell short in crucial ways of Herzl's vision of a charter for a Jewish state. It offered a prospect more limited than did Herzl's negotiations two decades earlier with Britain and others on the possible granting of such a charter, negotiations that had elicited sympathetic responses, particularly from Britain.

The Palestine Mandate was to be a British regime, with Jews, as one writer has pointed out, having no control over "immigration, legislation, the courts and police, taxation, the governing bureaucracy, or the allocation of land."[34] Even control over security was to be in British, not Jewish, hands. This arrangement did not simply fail to meet Herzl's aspirations but represented a path that Herzl viewed as inevitably dangerous. He had argued that in situations where real authority on the ground remained in the hands of a non-Jewish regime, that regime might initially tolerate Zionist undertakings or even actively support them, but ultimately, as the Zionist foothold grew, there would be clashes of interests and the controlling regime would turn against the Jews.

Some writers have suggested that Weizmann was diplomatically naïve and, in particular, had a naïve faith in British goodwill. Certainly there is much in his writings that indicate his conviction of a comprehensive convergence of interests between Britain and the Zionists and of Britain's dedication to supporting the Zionist enterprise. But, again, beyond the limitations of his political and diplomatic acumen, it appears Weizmann actively preferred eschewing immediate statehood and embracing a gradualist approach.

In testimony before the Allied Powers in 1919, Weizmann was asked if his objective was an "autonomous government." He replied: "No, we do not demand a specifically Jewish government . . . [but] definite conditions and an administration that will enable us to send immigrants to Palestine . . . We shall make it our task to create schools where the Hebrew language would be taught and gradually to develop there a Jewish life as Hebraic as the life in England is English."[35] He envisioned that only at some unspecified future date, when the Jewish community and its institutions had been sufficiently built up in the manner prescribed by the socialist Zionists, would Jews pursue governance of the country.

NINE

The Mandate Years:
Jewish Delusions Transplanted

The Administration . . . shall encourage, in cooperation with the Jewish Agency, close settlement by Jews on the land, including State lands and waste lands.

Preamble to the League of Nations Mandate for Palestine, 1922

Through which [option] can we get in the shortest possible time the most Jews in Palestine? . . . How much greater will be the absorptive capacity without an alien, unconcerned . . . hostile administration, but with a Zionist government . . . holding the key to immigration in its hand.

David Ben-Gurion, speaking in favor of accepting the Peel Commission proposal for partition of Mandate Palestine, 1937[1]

[The Zionists are] performing the acts of Hitler in the land of Israel, for they want to serve Hitler's god [i.e., nationalism] after he has been given a Hebrew name.

Martin Buber, November, 1939, opposing the push for a Jewish state, and supporting an Arab veto over Jewish immigration[2]

BRITISH BACKTRACKING AND A WEAK ZIONIST RESPONSE, 1917–1931

In April, 1920, at San Remo, the Allied Powers formally granted to Great Britain a Mandate for Palestine, with Britain assigned the mandatory obligation to develop in Palestine the Jewish National Home as proposed in the Balfour Declaration. The Allies recognized the Zionist Organization as officially representing the Jewish community in Palestine and the Jewish effort to build the national home in cooperation with the mandatory authority. The Mandate, again incorporating the Balfour Declaration, was approved by the League of Nations in July, 1922. The preamble to the League of Nations Mandate included a statement that "the Administration . . . shall encourage, in cooperation with the Jewish

Agency, close settlement by Jews on the land, including State lands and waste lands."

But, as noted in Chapter Five, well before ratification of the Mandate by the Allies and the League of Nations, the difficulties anticipated by Herzl had already materialized. British forces had entered Jerusalem in December, 1917. The ranks of the military administration that assumed authority consisted of people for the most part indifferent to or actively hostile to Zionist aspirations. Some were animated by anti-Semitic biases. Many leading figures in the administration were drawn from the British colonial presence in Egypt, were focused on British hegemony in the region, and saw Jewish plans for Palestine as ultimately a threat to their vision of British regional domination.[3]

Soon the administration was not simply refusing to cooperate with the Zionists but also actively blocking immigration and land purchases. In 1918, the British government authorized the Zionist Organization to send an official commission to the Mandate territory; the Zionist commission subsequently clashed with the administration and had repeatedly to seek intervention of the Foreign Office in London to obtain the administration's cooperation.

At first, there was no significant Arab protest to the Balfour Declaration and Zionist intentions. On the contrary, the Emir Feisal, son of the Sherif of Mecca and putative spokesperson for the Arabs, exchanged communications with Zionist leaders in late 1918 and early 1919 and signed an agreement with Weizmann in January, 1919, giving his support to Jewish nation building in Palestine and conditioning that support only on fulfillment of his own aspirations in the region.[4] Those aspirations were based on his dealings with the British over the preceding two years and envisioned his ultimate control over all of the Middle East outside of Palestine — essentially, modern-day Syria, Iraq, and Saudi Arabia — with his seat of governance in Damascus, the major Arab city in the region.

British interlocutors did encourage Feisal in this goal, and, more particularly, some British officials were hoping to use Feisal as a means of extricating Britain from agreements with France that foresaw French control of Syria. It has often been maintained that the British made contradictory commitments to the Arabs and the Jews regarding Palestine, but there is no evidence of any commitments to the Arabs over Palestine nor suggestions of such by those Arabs with whom Britain was dealing.[5] Britain did, however, make incompatible commitments to the French and the Arabs regarding Syria.

Britain had first embraced Feisal during the war with a view toward setting him up as a rallying point for Arab deserters from Turkish ranks, to gain the deserters' enlistment in the Allied cause, and perhaps even as a rallying point for a broad Arab rebellion within Turkish territories. As the son of the protector of the holy cities of Mecca and Medina, he seemed well positioned to counter the religious prestige of the sultan and thereby more easily attract the loyalty of fellow Arabs. This tack proved unsuccessful. Through the course of the war, Feisal was able to recruit only small bands of guerrilla fighters.

But some in the British government were also eager to use Feisal to advance British interests in Syria against the French. Britain formulated a plan whereby it would facilitate Feisal's entry into Damascus with his guerrillas at the head of the Allied advance and would promote a rallying around Feisal by the local population. Feisal, whom the British perceived as their man, would then claim a preeminent position in Syria, and Britain would invoke the principle of self-determination, as articulated by Woodrow Wilson in his Fourteen Points for postwar peace, to argue that the Arabs' right of self-determination in Syria took precedence over any other claims or agreements.[6]

These machinations ultimately failed. The French consolidated their control over Syria, received a Mandate for the territory, and expelled Feisal. The British, who obtained a Mandate for Iraq as well as one for Palestine, subsequently established Feisal in Baghdad. These events had consequences for the Palestine Mandate. Feisal's older brother Abdullah had hoped to become ruler of Iraq. With Feisal's removal to Baghdad, Abdullah argued that he had been dispossessed and threatened to lead a guerrilla force into Syria to fight the French. In March, 1921, Winston Churchill, then colonial secretary, agreed to break off all Palestinian territory east of the Jordan River — amounting to about 75 percent of Palestine as then configured — and set up Abdullah as ruler of "Transjordan." (This arrangement was effectively made permanent in a White Paper in 1922.) Transjordan remained formally part of the Palestine Mandate but was now closed to Jewish settlement.

Events in Syria had other negative consequences for the Jews in Palestine. Damascus had been the major seat of Arab nationalism. With the French consolidation of control over Syria and crackdown on Arab nationalists, some of the latter, often with the support of local British authorities, fled into Palestine. There they undertook promoting opposition by the local Arab population to the Jewish presence and organizing attacks on Jewish enclaves. (Jewish casualties of Arab assaults on northern farming communities in early 1920 included Josef Trumpeldor, killed at Tel Hai in March of that year.) Britain's "loss" of Syria also further reinforced the local British administration's antagonism to Zionist aspirations. A chief aim of the British colonial leadership in Egypt and its officers in Palestine was creation of a land bridge from the eastern Mediterranean to British India. If Syria were in British hands, that goal would have been possible even without long-term British control of Palestine. But without Syria, Palestine took on increased importance in this vision of imperial necessity.

Large-scale Arab attacks on Jews in Jerusalem broke out in April, 1920, coinciding with the meeting of the Allies at San Remo that gave Allied imprimatur to the British Mandate and creation of the Jewish National Home in Palestine.

Some British officers played the role of *agents provocateurs* in encouraging these and other Arab assaults on the Jews of Palestine, and British authorities did little to stop the looting and killing.[7] The Military Administration also sought to use the riots as an excuse for curtailing Jewish immigration and other Zionist activities, arguing that local Arab antagonism would be difficult to control if such curbs were not initiated.

The British, in the postwar years, were attempting to maintain their Middle East territories with very limited forces and were indeed concerned with minimizing local unrest. But, of course, this does not account for Mandate officers working as *agents provocateurs* and stirring up anti-Jewish violence or for British authorities failing to quell Arab riots when they were fully able to do so. Nor does it explain the Military Administration's preventing local Jewish units — elements of the Jewish Battalions — from coming to the defense of the Jews of Jerusalem. Jabotinsky, who tried to organize defense, was arrested by the British and sentenced to fifteen years' imprisonment. He was soon released but only in the context of an amnesty extended also to the rioters. The British also chose to construe the Jewish units' attempts to defend the Jews of Jerusalem as an intolerable breach of military discipline and disbanded the units.

Lieutenant Colonel John Patterson, a non-Jewish British officer who had commanded the Zion Mule Corps in Gallipolli, was subsequently appointed commander of the 38th Jewish Battalion and led the battalion in the Palestine campaign. Patterson wrote extensively of the anti-Jewish depredations to which his troops, and the Jewish population of Palestine, were subjected by the British military's forces in Palestine under Allenby (the Egyptian Expeditionary Force) and later by the Military Administration. These depredations emanated both from the command structure and, in the wake of evident command tolerance, from the rank and file. With regard to Arab attacks on the Jews in April, 1920, in Jerusalem, Patterson, referring to the assault as "the Jerusalem pogrom," noted the Military Administration's encouragement of the violence, its failure to intervene to stop it, its blocking of intervention by Jewish troops, its attempts to use the Arab assault as an excuse to curb Zionist programs, and its scapegoating of Jabotinsky.[8]

Patterson wrote, for example, of the events of April, 1920, "A veritable 'pogrom,' such as we have hitherto only associated with Tsarist Russia, took place in the Holy City of Jerusalem in April, 1920, and as this was the climax to the maladministration of the Military Authorities, I consider that the facts of the case should be made public . . .

"The Balfour Declaration . . . was never allowed [by the Military Administration] to be officially published within the borders of Palestine; the Hebrew language was proscribed; there was open discrimination against the Jews; the Jewish Regiment was at all times kept in the background and treated as a pariah. This official attitude was interpreted by the hooligan element and interested schemers in the only possible way, viz., that the military authorities in Palestine were against the Jews and Zionism, and the conviction began to grow [within Arab circles] that any act calculated to deal a death blow to Zionist aspirations would not be unwelcome to those in authority . . .

"Moreover, this malign influence was sometimes strengthened by very plain speaking. The Military Governor of an important town was actually heard to declare . . . in the presence of British and French Officers and of Arab waiters, that in case of anti-Jewish riots in his city, he would remove the garrison and take up his position at a window, where he could watch, and laugh at, what went on!

"This amazing declaration was reported to the Acting Chief Administrator, and the Acting Chief Political Officer, but no action was taken against the Governor. Only one interpretation can be placed on such leniency."[9]

Patterson, as quoted in Chapter Five, wrote elsewhere of the Arab attacks, "There can be no doubt that it was assumed in some quarters that when trouble, which had been deliberately encouraged, arose, the Home Government, embarrassed by a thousand difficulties at its doors, would agree with the wire-pullers in Palestine, and say to the Jewish people that the carrying out of the Balfour Declaration, owing to the hostility displayed by the Arabs, was outside the range of practical politics."[10]

These difficulties with the Military Administration translated for Ben-Gurion into even greater eagerness to accelerate immigration and state building and quickly led to clashes with Weizmann around the latter's dedication to a slower, more deliberate pace and his confidence in the British commitment to the Zionist enterprise. For example, the Military Administration had rapidly demobilized all but one of the Jewish battalions and Ben-Gurion was eager to keep the four thousand demobilized overseas volunteers in the Yishuv. But this required that the Zionist Organization provide accommodations for their absorption, and Weizmann's representative refused to do so, placing the need for orderly and fiscally prudent absorption above the urgency of immigration and state building. The result was a heated imbroglio between Ben-Gurion and Weizmann's agent, and indirectly between Ben-Gurion and Weizmann.[11]

Later, Weizmann gave assurances to Ben-Gurion and others that the British would allow the surviving Jewish battalion to remain intact. Its demobilization shortly afterwards further reinforced Ben-Gurion's bitterness toward Weizmann's confidence in the British. It is notable that that confidence exceeded even Lloyd George's. In 1920, Lloyd George urged Weizmann to seize the moment offered by the Mandate and push aggressively for a Jewish majority before the political climate shifted: "You have no time to waste. Today the world is like the Baltic before a frost. For the moment it is still in motion. But if it gets set, you will have to batter your heads against the ice blocks and wait for a second thaw."[12] Ben-Gurion shared this perspective; Weizmann was more confident and optimistic regarding the climate.

In July, 1920, the Military Administration was replaced by a civilian authority, with Sir Herbert Samuel as High Commissioner. But Samuel, for all his Zionist sympathies, instituted a policy of consistent appeasement of Arab demands in the face both of Arab violence and the hostility of the local British military forces and civilian bureaucrats toward the Jews.

In response to widespread Arab attacks in the spring of 1921, Samuel halted Jewish immigration, a step rescinded by Churchill only under intense pro-Zionist pressure in London. Some months later Samuel issued a report encompassing political concessions to the Arabs, and the following year those concessions, as well as the *de facto* detachment of Transjordan from the Mandate, were formalized in a White Paper issued by Churchill. The Zionist Organization under Weizmann's leadership nevertheless accepted the White Paper, even as the Arabs rejected it and refused to cooperate with the new political accommodations offered them. These years also saw the Mandate administration awarding large-scale grants of public lands to the Arabs while withholding public lands from the Jews. Whatever Jewish acquisition occurred did so through private purchase.

Samuel's tenure, which lasted until 1925, was marked by additional concessions to the Arabs and further reneging on Britain's Mandate obligations toward the Jews. Samuel was replaced as High Commissioner by Lord Herbert Plumer, who generally resisted further backtracking from the Mandate even in the face of Arab pressures, and Plumer's three years in office saw a marked decrease in violence. This reflected a pattern that has been noted by a number of historians who have written on the Mandate: Appeasement tended to result in increased Arab violence as violence was perceived as yielding rewards, while a more steadfast course and rejection of concessions in the face of violence typically yielded more peaceful interludes.[13]

Throughout the decade of the twenties, Britain's reneging on its Mandate obligations, its obstructionism and appeasement of the Arabs, and the consequent slow pace of immigration and of Jewish development in Eretz Israel, resulted in widespread discontent in Zionist ranks with the leadership of the Zionist Executive under Weizmann and with Weizmann's practice of generally acquiescing to British policy. There was also unhappiness with Weizmann's consistently seeking to engage non-Zionist Jewish cooperation in institutional development in the Yishuv by de-emphasizing the goal of a state. This criticism was given particular voice at the biennial Zionist Congresses. It came not only from Jabotinsky, who resigned from the Zionist Executive in protest against the 1922 White Paper and Weizmann's acceptance of its restrictions, but also from the religious Zionists of Mizrachi and from various elements within the socialist Zionist movement in the Yishuv.

Criticism of Weizmann and the Executive reached a crescendo at the Congress of 1927, in the wake of two years that had seen severe economic setbacks in the Yishuv and Jewish emigration from Eretz Israel outpacing immigration. The failure of the so-called fourth aliyah, immigration over the preceding several years of mainly middle-class Polish Jews who had settled in urban areas and engaged in developing industrial and other commercial enterprises, was, in fact, due not only to British policy. Actions of the socialist Zionists and of their consolidated trade union, Histadrut, which encompassed about 80 percent of Jewish labor in the Yishuv, also figured in this failure. Much of the socialist Zionist leadership was acutely hostile to the new middle-class arrivals and their entrepreneurial undertakings, saw them as incompatible with its vision of the New Jew and the future Zionist state, and in various ways undermined the new arrivals' undertakings. This contributed significantly to the subsequent economic collapse, the curtailment of immigration and the increase in emigration. But British policy played a substantial part in the worsening of the Yishuv's fortunes during these years.

At the 1927 Congress, the socialist Zionist parties shared many of the criticisms of the Executive and Weizmann voiced by Jabotinsky and others. But, concerned about any strengthening of the nonsocialist opponents of the Executive, the socialists ultimately threw their support to Weizmann.

By the 1929 Congress the economic disasters had eased but criticism of the Executive, both for its accommodationist approach to British policy and for its courting of non-Zionists, was again intense and came from various quarters. For example, Rabbi Stephen Wise, representing American Zionists, attacked the Executive for its passivity in the face of Britain's violations of its Mandate obligations. The recent more vocal and outspoken stance against a Jewish state taken by the circle of "cultural Zionists" around Judah Magnes, President of Hebrew University — whose sponsors were anti-Zionist leaders in the United States and whose appointment had been supported by Weizmann — came in for particular criticism. Still, Weizmann remained in control of the Zionist Executive.

The League of Nations Mandate had spoken of "an appropriate Jewish Agency" with which the Mandate Authority was to work in advancing the development of the Jewish National Home. The composition of this "Jewish Agency" was not specified and Weizmann sought in the years that followed to construct an entity different from existing Zionist bodies and embracing an equal number of Zionists and non-Zionists, as, again, a vehicle for engaging non-Zionists in the task of building the institutions of a National Home. The Jewish Agency thus conceived and constituted met for its first session shortly after the 1929 Congress.

Also shortly following the 1929 Congress, the *de facto* leader of the Palestinian Arabs, Amin al-Husseini, Grand Mufti of Jerusalem, orchestrated large-scale assaults on the Jews of the Yishuv, attacks that began in Jerusalem and soon spread throughout the country. In Hebron, one of the hardest hit targets, more than sixty Jews were killed and the rest of the community was forced to flee. For days, British forces across the country did virtually nothing to stop the carnage. The commission appointed by then Colonial Secretary Lord Passfield to investigate the violence submitted a report that was in key respects a reprise of earlier such exercises: It acknowledged that the Arabs were fully responsible for the violence but then recommended restrictions on Jewish immigration and land purchases to placate the Arabs.

The leaders of the Yishuv and the Zionist leadership outside the Mandate protested and were supported by sympathetic segments of the British public. The League of Nations Permanent Mandates Commission also condemned the report as offering recommendations that violated Britain's Mandate obligations. Still, the Labor government in London imposed a moratorium on immigration in May, 1930, and the following fall the government issued the so-called Passfield White Paper spelling out further anti-Zionist steps. Protest against the halt to immigration and the White Paper obliged the government to lift the former and to offer some softening "clarifications" of the latter, but the White Paper was not rescinded. Nevertheless, the Zionist Organization announced it was satisfied that government pronouncements still provided a sound basis for cooperation.

At the Zionist Congress of 1931, Weizmann came under still more intense criticism for his continued soft line toward British moves inimical to Jewish development in the Mandate. This criticism again emanated not only from Jabotinsky and his supporters, the so-called Revisionists. (In 1925, Jabotinsky, in response to the Zionist Executive's refusal to demand greater authority over immigration, defense, and development in Palestine, founded the secessionist Federation of Revisionist Zionists.) It was also voiced by Mizrachi and elements of both socialist and nonsocialist secular Zionist bodies. Rabbi Wise, again representing American Zionists, attacked British policy and the Zionist Organization's passive stance toward Britain and called for Weizmann's resignation.

Weizmann was also vehemently criticized for what many perceived as the failure of his attempts to gain non-Zionist support for building Jewish institutions in the Yishuv by downplaying the goal of an independent state and by giving non-Zionists equal representation in the Jewish Agency. In the view of many, this policy had not only undermined the work of state building but had done so without actually winning over the non-Zionists. On the contrary, Jewish opponents of a Jewish state, both outside and within the Yishuv, had only become more outspoken in promoting their anti-state agenda, and had responded to the 1929 Arab riots — much to the horror of Zionists — by ratcheting up even further their public attacks on the goal of a state.

Weizmann, Non-Zionists, Binationalists, and Ben-Gurion

The anti-state circles that Weizmann had most sought to cultivate since his ascendance to a leadership role in the Zionist movement during World War I were mainly the Jewish philanthropists in the West, more particularly American Jewish philanthropists. They were typically members of the German Jewish elite in America who were involved in Jewish communal life and were often officers of major Jewish organizations. They generally supported the development of Jewish cultural institutions in Eretz Israel even as they opposed the establishment of a Jewish state. They sought to emphasize the universalist elements in Jewish belief and Jewish aspirations as, ostensibly, a more modern religious perspective. But they did so, more fundamentally, as the tack they believed would contribute to overcoming anti-Semitism in America and elsewhere and to advancing the acceptance of Jews as fully equal citizens; and they saw in any expressions of Jewish particularism, and most especially in the Zionist quest for a Jewish state, a threat to the status of Jews in America and other Diaspora countries.

The arcane philosophical pronouncements in which Martin Buber cast his "true Zionism" may appear a long way from the world of America's German Jewish philanthropists. But Buber and the philanthropists shared the same anxieties born of Western Jewish, particularly German Jewish, exposure to modern anti-Semitism, and shared the view that the proper Jewish response was to stress Jewish universalism and a Jewish mission sensitive to the needs of all and a threat to no one.

Among Jewish students and intellectuals in Germany who continued to value their Jewishness and connection with the Jewish community, many responded similarly to the intensely anti-Jewish sentiments around them. They wished for a Jewish solution but also wanted to ingratiate themselves with the surrounding society and not cut themselves off entirely from that world to which they were acculturated. And so they were likewise attracted to Judaism cast in a universalist mode and to a Zionism culturally defined, and they found Buber's formulations congruent with their personal seeking. While Buber himself preferred to stay in Germany, a number of these intellectuals emigrated in the 1920s from Germany to the Yishuv to develop Buber's brand of cultural Zionism. To the American philanthropists, these people represented the human resources through which their own vision of building institutions that would foster a Jewish cultural renaissance in Eretz Israel could be realized.

A key project that Weizmann hoped would win the support of the non-Zionists or cultural Zionists was the development of Hebrew University, for which Weizmann laid a cornerstone in Jerusalem in 1919. One of the people he courted for support was Felix Warburg, a leading figure in the German Jewish elite in America, active in Jewish organizational life and philanthropy, but an opponent of Zionist aspirations for a state. (Warburg's older brother, Max, had corresponded with Buber on the need to construct a "new Judaism" in Palestine even as he too vehemently opposed the goal of a Jewish state.[14]) In 1924, Weizmann succeeded in getting Warburg to visit the Mandate and to offer his financial backing for an Institute for Jewish Studies at the university. But Warburg conditioned his support on the appointment of American Rabbi Judah Magnes to a dominant position in the University, ultimately to the post of University chancellor, and to control of the funds.

Magnes had been an early proponent of cultural Zionism as advocated by Ahad Ha-Am. He had also embraced perspectives akin to Buber's comprehension of a spiritual Zionism congruent with Judaism's universalist mission, and he shared Buber's antipathy to political Zionism. In the wake of the Balfour Declaration and the San Remo conference, he wrote, "When I think that Palestine was conquered by force of arms and that it is made 'Jewish' by the iniquitous Peace Conference, I am reminded of the well-known Jewish description: 'Conceived and born in uncleanliness.'"[15]

In 1922, Magnes, then associate rabbi at Temple Beth El in New York, the synagogue of many of the city's wealthy German Jewish families, moved to the Yishuv to work at advancing his own vision of the Jewish National Home, which included opposition to a Jewish state. He subsequently gathered around him at Hebrew University, where he became chancellor in September, 1924, a number of the anti-state German Jewish academics who had immigrated to the Yishuv. If Weizmann conceived of the University as a tool of state building and a means of co-opting the non-Zionists into state-building endeavors, he found Magnes and his circle, and his backers in the United States, adamantly opposed to any such purpose and dedicated to using the University as a platform for attacking Zionist aspirations.

Buber, after publication of the Balfour Declaration, had likewise expressed unhappiness with the British-Zionist alliance, seeing it as a threat to his vision of a universalist, socialist, Jewish community in Palestine. In an essay written in 1919, for example, he expressed concern that the sponsorship of an imperial power would inexorably compromise "Palestinian Jewry's playing a mediating role between the Occident and the Orient" in the manner that he imagined and wished. And he asked rhetorically: "Can Jewry be truly liberated so long as Judaism's unswerving demand for justice and truth for all nations is shouldered out of the way?" as he anticipated it would be by a Zionism dependent on a Great Power.[16]

Two years later, in an address delivered in Karlsbad during the Twelfth Zionist Congress in 1921, Buber expanded on his concept of "true Zionism." He had earlier declared that the Jewish national movement must be guided by socialist principles such as those promoted by the Russian socialist Zionists.[17]

He now distinguishes between good and bad nationalism. In a formula derived in large part, ironically, from the anti-Semitic German political Romanticism first articulated in the early nineteenth century, Buber speaks of organic nationalism versus mechanical, bureaucratic nationalism. The latter is exemplified for him, as it was for German political Romanticism, by the new France created by the French Revolution. The former, good, nationalism is one that resonates with its people's sense of connectedness and shared destiny. But, Buber argues, the true, historic connectedness of the Jews is around their spiritual life, the Jewish faith, and their shared destiny is properly defined by their spiritual mission. A Zionism that is secularized and pursues nation building as an end in itself is a betrayal of "true" Jewish nationalism.[18]

In the context of these comprehensions, Buber chose to construe the Arab riots of 1920 and 1921, in which Arab mobs attacked and murdered Jews in Jerusalem and elsewhere, as confirming his fears that Jewish particularist aspirations would only reinforce hatred of Jews and that the answer was cultivation of Jewish universalism. He subsequently returned again and again to Arab hostility as evidence of the wrongness of Zionism in its current form. He argued that the Zionists needed to win Arab acceptance and insisted that the way to do so was to redirect Jewish aspirations toward his vision of a spiritual center unthreatening to anyone and also to forge an alliance with Arab workers around socialist principles.

The notion that Jewish nationalism, or Zionism, is legitimate only in a form in which it is purified of all the characteristics of petty nationalism and serves as a vehicle for advancing Judaism's universalist mission, or — a secular variation on the same theme — that all modern nationalisms are evil and Jewish nationalism is particularly sinful as Jews are properly to dedicate themselves to promoting universalism, became standard fare in the anti-state rhetoric of the German Jewish circles in the Yishuv that coalesced particularly around Hebrew University. So too did the invoking of Arab opposition as proof of the wrong-headedness of Zionist aspirations. Another popular line of argument within these circles was that Jewish efforts against traditional nationalism should also be directed to improving the lots of minorities, and so Jews in the Yishuv should focus on fashioning an ideal minority relationship vis-à-vis the surrounding Arab majority, one that could serve as a model for others, rather than seeking to build within Palestine a Jewish state with a Jewish majority.

In Germany and elsewhere, the pressures of the anti-Semitism that Jews daily encountered inspired many to embrace the indictments of their tormenters and to believe delusionally that Jewish self-reform — particularly demonstrations of Jewish benevolence and suppression of Jewish particularism — would radically transform the hostility of the surrounding society and serve as the Jews' salvation. In the Yishuv, many German Jewish academics and others continued to view the world through the prism of that delusional perspective brought with them from Europe, and the perspective shaped their response to Arab hostility toward the Jews. It inspired their view that only policies that "reassured" and satisfied the Arabs could pass muster as a righteous Jewish course, a view consonant, of course, with their predilection toward intense hostility to Jewish nationalism.

In 1925, a group of German Jewish immigrants in the Yishuv, a number of them with connections to Buber, established the Peace Association. Its members advocated abandoning Zionism for the goal of a binational Arab-Jewish state in which Jews would be a permanent minority and would, as conceived by various members, pursue with the Arabs an ideal non-nationalistic polity that would be a model for the world. Buber, still in Germany, endorsed the group and its aims. Judah Magnes also embraced it, although he expressed concerns that it was not sufficiently pacifist.[19] He comprehended the mission of Hebrew University as, first, promoting Jewish universalism and, as a corollary, advancing an anti-Zionist program for Palestine of the sort favored by the Peace Association. One writer has noted that in 1928, when Hebrew University first formally offered degree courses, a majority of its humanities and social science faculty members were also members of the Peace Association.[20]

At the 1929 Zionist Congress, Buber urged delegates to give up their pursuit of a Jewish state in favor of a binational solution. Within weeks of the speech, Magnes offered Buber a permanent appointment as dean of the faculty at Hebrew University. This did not materialize, perhaps due in part to the Arab attacks on the Yishuv that began a few days later. But the 1929 Arab assault did not lead the anti-Zionists to any modification of their views. Rather, the echelons of the Peace Association interpreted the attacks as confirming the rightness of their arguments and responded by increasing their political and diplomatic efforts to advance their program.

At a speech in Berlin in October, 1929, before local supporters of the Peace Association, and in a related article, Buber blamed the recent massacres on the Jews themselves for not having been accommodating enough of Arab sensibilities. He again argued for a binational political solution and the construction in Palestine of a cultural and political exemplar of "togetherness." He also insisted on amnesty for those Arabs convicted of murdering Jews.[21]

Also in the fall of 1929, Felix Warburg, now a co-leader with Weizmann of the newly constituted — half Zionist, half non-Zionist — Jewish Agency, perceived the massacres as an opportunity to end once and for all the pursuit of a Jewish state. He was urged on in that direction by correspondence from Magnes,[22] and he apparently considered threatening to cut off his financial support of the Yishuv if its leaders did not foreswear the goal of a Jewish state. In any case, Warburg communicated with the British High Commissioner in Palestine, John Chancellor, and Chancellor, in his report to the Colonial Office, understood Warburg to desire to negotiate with the Arabs a new political arrangement for Palestine and to be prepared to withdraw from the Jewish Agency and end his financial support if Weizmann refused to embrace, in Chancellor's words, "the policy of moderation."[23]

There is no evidence of Warburg having ever directly negotiated with the Arabs. But in late October Magnes met with an English convert to Islam and confidant of the Mufti and formulated with him a proposal for establishment of an Arab-controlled government in the Mandate and the abandonment of Jewish aspirations to a state.[24] When the leadership of the Yishuv rejected the plan, Warburg did threaten that American Jewish support for the Yishuv would be cut off if the Magnes initiative was not embraced. Nevertheless, both the elected Assembly of the Yishuv and the Zionist Executive refused to endorse it.

Magnes's meeting with a member of the Mufti's camp had been arranged by the *New York Times*' correspondent in the Mandate and avowed anti-Zionist, Joseph Levy. In the wake of rejection of his initiative, Magnes embarked on a publicity campaign to promote his views and attack the Zionists, and the *New York Times*, under the aegis of the no less anti-Zionist Adolph Ochs, gave prominent coverage and editorial support to Magnes's views.[25]

The arguments mustered by the members of the Peace Association and their sympathizers against the national aspirations of the Zionists took various forms and were often cast in moralistic terms. But beneath the various arguments lay, again, perspectives and biases shaped by Jewish experiences in the West, particularly in Germany. They were perspectives reflecting the assault of modern anti-Semitism, the absorption by many Jews of some of the canards directed against them, and their wish to believe that proper Jewish self-reform would detoxify Jew-hatred.

More specifically, the arguments of these anti-Zionists were driven by the wishful fantasy that Jews could win genuine acceptance as equal citizens of the world's states by demonstrating that they desire nothing for themselves as a people, that their faith entails essentially a universalist mission of good will that is a threat to no one and a potential boon to all. The stance of these anti-Zionists was also influenced by a related exercise in wishful thinking, the predilection of some Jews in the West to blame the nation-state for anti-Semitism and to embrace a utopian internationalism as the cure.

At the turn of the century, Herzl, whose main concern had been establishing a safe refuge for Europe's vulnerable, bloodied Jewish populations and enabling Jews to function on a more equal footing in the world, had offered a response to anti-Zionism cast in internationalist terms. He had argued that the goal of an international system transcending nation-states may have its virtues but as long as the world, and its power and defensive capabilities, were divided among nations it was reasonable and necessary for Jews to seek their own state.

Of course, the internationalists of the Peace Association directed their moral opprobrium particularly at Jewish nationalism. For most this hypocritically selective assault on Jewish nationalism reflected their underlying focus on fighting against Jewish particularism for the sake of promoting the Jewish universalist mission as the answer to Western anti-Semitism. But for some this selective critique of Jewish nationalism also reflected the belief, connected with their own image of the Jewish universalist mission, that the Jews' proper task was to lead the way to a new postnational world, to dedicate themselves as a people to building that utopian future.

In their attacks on the Zionist promotion of Jewish immigration in the context of state building, and on the League of Nations' assigning to Britain the obligation to promote "close settlement" of the land by Jews, the anti-Zionists of the Peace Association claimed that the effort to create a Jewish majority and establish a Jewish state was an immoral assault on the Arab population of the country. They argued that it was aimed at reducing the Arab population not only to a minority but to one not connected with the would-be national-ethnic identity of the state.

But there is hypocrisy here as well, as a principle accepted and promoted in international relations since the end of World War I — and widely embraced by the anti-Zionists — was the right of people where feasible to national independence, even though invariably the new states carved out for them, from, most notably, the defeated empires of Europe, contained ethnic minorities. The existence of such minorities was not perceived as undermining the legitimacy of the new states. Rather, the predicament of the minorities was seen as adequately addressed by the extension to them of internationally formulated and recognized rights. In fact various members of the Peace Association spoke of creating in Palestine a majority Arab state with a Jewish minority and did not see that arrangement as intrinsically immoral.

Of course, the explanation for this hypocrisy was, again, that the real motivation for the assault on the Zionists was an antipathy to Jewish particularism and a preference for establishing in Palestine a Jewish cultural or spiritual center based on a minority population that replicated much of the political condition of Jewish minorities in Europe. Except, according to the formulas of the Peace Association's members, the Jews of Eretz Israel would enjoy a utopian rapport with the Arab majority.

Visions of a binational state, and the variations on that theme put forward by members of the Peace Association and their supporters, reflect in other respects as well wishful glosses on the Jewish predicament forged under the pressure of anti-Semitism in the West, particularly in Germany. German Jews commonly chose to comprehend the rise of political anti-Semitism in the united Germany as due to Germans not really knowing the Jews living among them, not appreciating how much they were like themselves. Many German Jews chose to believe that the solution lay in "dialogue" between themselves and their neighbors. But this superficial and self-deluding comprehension was, of course, doomed. Its wrongheadedness was captured in Gershon Scholem's pithy comment: "To whom, then, did the Jews speak in that much-talked-about German-Jewish dialogue? They spoke to themselves."[26]

In a similar vein, the Jews affiliated with the Peace Association put forward plans for Jewish-Arab rapprochement that they regarded as so fair and equitable and conciliatory and self-effacing vis-à-vis any Jewish political aspirations that they could not help but end the Arabs' hostility, win their support, and engage them in this idealistic joint political venture. Magnes was apparently convinced that the Arabs would even agree to some modicum of continued Jewish immigration as a fair balance to continuation of the large-scale Arab immigration into Palestine that had been under way since establishment of the Mandate. But the Jews of the Peace Association had no Arab partner or interlocutor in these visions. Magnes may have had correspondence with a confidant of the Mufti in which the latter accurately reflected the Mufti's receptivity to having Jews in the Yishuv attack the Zionist enterprise, but there was no partner for the type of polity to which Magnes or his colleagues aspired. These Jews, too, were having a dialogue with themselves.

Their self-delusion was not simply a product of Arab hostility and the wish to believe that offering enough Jewish concessions could end that enmity. To be sure, it did reflect in part an impulse to comprehend the Arab attack as justified, and to indict other Jews for instigating it, in order to bolster and maintain the false belief that Arab hostility could be controlled and dampened by tempering Jewish "provocations" — a delusion at once self-effacing and arrogant in its conviction of being able to shape Arab responses. But their self-delusion also had deeper roots. It was born more fundamentally of these people's experience in Europe, where the hostility was much more ingrained and seemingly intractable and Jews were more defenseless and vulnerable and so wishful delusions of control via Jewish self-reform were more attractive.

The Jews of the Peace Association in large part simply transplanted their sense of vulnerability and their illusory answers to this new arena. In Germany they chose to believe that German anti-Semitism was really sustained by German exposure to the supposedly less civilized, more alien, Jews of the East and so the solution lay in separating themselves from the latter and attempting to refine them where possible. In Palestine they chose to comprehend the Zionists, and the Russian Jewish pioneers of the country, in the role of the Eastern Jews in Europe.

That the views of the Peace Association and its allies were shaped in large part by absorption of European anti-Semitic perspectives is indirectly if rather startlingly demonstrated by comments in a speech given by Buber in July, 1932. Buber is reiterating his arguments that Jews must remain true to their spiritual mission and must not pursue a state not founded on that mission, and he declares that if Jews stray from their proper path, if they follow the rest of the

West in segregating their spiritual life from their national life, "We shall forfeit our justification for living."[27]

Buber suggests that only Jews' devotion to their faith and to God has enabled them to survive as a people; but this concept of "justification for living" is not a Jewish concept. On the contrary, as noted in Chapter Seven with regard to similar sentiments expressed by Leonard Fein, Jewish communal lapses from spiritual and religious obligations have always been seen as a reprise of former such lapses that will inexorably involve another period of floating adrift and directionless until the community once more recovers its spiritual compass. The notion of Jews having to justify their survival, their living, does not have its origin in the history of the Jews' relationship to God but has its source rather in the history of the Jews' relationship to hostile surrounding societies and reflects absorption of hostile perspectives.

Of course, the most serious indictment of the Peace Association's program was that it entailed abandonment of the desperate Jews of eastern Europe, the Jewish masses whose rescue was an essential goal of the Zionist enterprise as conceived by Herzl. Those masses were living under increasingly stressful and intolerable pressures, most notably in reconstituted Poland but also in Hungary, Rumania, the newly created Baltic states, and elsewhere in the East. Their abandonment was a consequence of the Peace Association's members giving greater priority to visions of Jewish universalism and to the supposed morality of deracination than to rescue. But it was made easier by the sense of alienation from Eastern Jewry common within the Peace Association. Many of its members had brought with them from Germany and elsewhere in the West an antipathy toward the religiosity of much of Eastern Jewry and toward the parochial sense of Jewish group identity shared even by the anti-religious Jewish socialist labor ranks in the East, including those who had emigrated from the East to the Yishuv. This alienation and prejudice was conditioned largely by the different modern histories of Eastern and Western Jews. But it was reinforced, again, by the pressures of anti-Semitism in the West and a desire to conceive of that anti-Semitism as aroused particularly by the parochialism, religiosity, and alienness of Eastern Jews and as soluble by Jewish self-reform.

Even Buber, who saw in Eastern Hasidism preservation of the true universalist message and mission of Judaism, felt no obligation to concern himself with the plight of the Jews of the East or their rescue and was prepared to abandon them for the sake of his own vision of "True Zionism." He and his like-minded associates were willing to promote what they believed to be the properly ingratiating Jewish path even at the risk of immeasurable Jewish suffering.

Despite formal renunciation of the Magnes initiative, Weizmann in the ensuing months still sought to work out accommodations with the British and with the American philanthropists around Warburg and began to speak more of cultural Zionist goals and binationalism and to eschew reference to a Jewish state. It was this backtracking that was largely responsible for the intense and widespread criticism directed at him at the Zionist Congress of 1931. The Congress, in fact, voted to censure Weizmann and removed him, for what proved to be only a two-year interlude, from the presidency of the Zionist Organization.

The Labor Zionists continued generally to give their support to Weizmann at the 1931 Congress and helped block a declaration proposed by Jabotinsky that would have emphasized that the goal of the Zionist Organization was a Jewish state. But a number of Labor Zionist leaders, particularly the chief figure in the movement, David Ben-Gurion, saw the accommodationist path forged by Weizmann and still being followed by the Zionist Executive as disastrous.

Ben-Gurion had arrived in Eretz Israel in 1906 imbued with Russian socialist Zionist orthodoxy, including its anti-capitalist, anti-bourgeois, anti-religious, and anti-diplomatic and political, prejudices. But he had been gradually modifying his views over the past decades, in part in response to what he saw as critical weaknesses in Weizmann's tactics. In the mid-1920s, he had tried to turn the umbrella labor federation that he headed, Histradut, into a political agency that would essentially replace the Zionist Organization and work more aggressively at fostering immigration and state building. His plans in this vein were largely thwarted by his colleagues' ongoing commitment to the agenda of "practical" Zionism, their focus on expanding the Yishuv's network of socialist workers' communities and their predilection to eschew broader political-diplomatic endeavors.

In 1927, in the wake of the faltering and ultimate reversal of the recent large-scale immigration from Poland, an immigration spurred by the increasing intensity of assaults and other depredations against Polish Jewry, Ben-Gurion became more impatient with socialist orthodoxy. He recognized the need to transcend its antipathy toward bourgeois immigrants and capitalist investment if the Yishuv was to build up its economy and properly promote and support immigration. He could see that these goals would not be achieved by the insistence on socialist structures and by that dependence on philanthropy that he believed Weizmann was perpetuating. But here, too, Ben-Gurion ran up against the resistance of his Labor Zionist colleagues.

Ben-Gurion was bitterly disappointed by the outcome of the 1931 Congress and understood that the situation of the Jews of Europe was becoming ever more desperate. (In July, 1932, he wrote of Diaspora Jewry facing the possibility of "physical and spiritual annihilation, of decline and destruction."[28]) During this period, he embarked on seeking to gain control of the Zionist Organization and redirecting its efforts toward an intensive political campaign to open the way for large-scale immigration into the Mandate. Hitler's rise to Chancellor of Germany early in 1933 reinforced, of course, Ben-Gurion's sense of urgency in pursuing the course he envisioned. (In January, 1934, he told the Histadrut Council that "Hitler's rule imperils the entire Jewish people."[29])

Ben-Gurion succeeded in the 1933 Zionist Organization elections to win the control he desired and soon began to move various operations of the Zionist Executive and the Jewish Agency (the Executive plus the non-Zionists that Weizmann had added) from London to Jerusalem. But many of Ben-Gurion's colleagues in the Labor Zionist leadership still resisted his wish to launch an aggressive political program to promote immigration. They still preferred to use the Zionist Organization to advance "practical" rather than diplomatic initiatives and many remained focused on concerns that large-scale immigration would undermine their agenda of building a New Jew to people a socialist utopia.

Seeing his efforts falter, Ben-Gurion in mid-1934 sought to join forces with Jabotinsky to pursue a political-diplomatic offensive promoting immigration and the establishment of a state. This was a major change of direction, as he had for years been battling Jabotinsky and the Revisionists to advance Histadrut's monopolistic control of the labor force in the Yishuv. But over numerous meetings, the two men forged agreements to advance their shared objective.

But again key figures in the Labor Zionist hierarchy balked at any cooperation with the Revisionist "capitalists." Ben-Gurion at one point responded, "I am sorry to see that our party does not adequately appreciate . . . that in its hands rests the fate of the Jewish people at one of the most grave . . . moments in our generation."[30] His opponents, however, insisted that the issue of cooperation with the Revisionists be decided by a Histadrut referendum, and Ben-Gurion's undertaking was rejected. The Zionist Organization remained ineffectual vis-à-vis the immigration issue and continued to cede critical authority to the Jewish Agency, half of whose members were categorically opposed to large-scale immigration and state building.

In the three years after the Nazi seizure of power in Germany, the British did ease to a degree their policies restricting Jewish immigration. About 100,000 Jews entered the Mandate over this period (some of that number consisting of "illegal" immigrants). But this immigration obviously still fell far short of the need. In March, 1936, Ben-Gurion urged a high profile campaign in Britain and the United States demanding support for immigration to the Yishuv of a million Jews. Again he was unable to muster sufficient support among his colleagues.

THE ARAB REVOLT, THE WHITE PAPER, AND JEWISH DIVISION

The following month, Grand Mufti al-Husseini unleashed another wave of Arab massacres of Jews as well as attacks on Jewish farms that entailed wide destruction of crops. He also orchestrated a general strike that was to last six months and crippled the economy of the entire Mandate. Magnes in Jerusalem and Warburg in New York, together with the American Jewish Committee, perceived the new upheavals in the Mandate as another opportunity to pursue their own negotiations with the Arabs based on Jewish acceptance of curtailment of immigration and of establishment of an Arab-dominated government in Palestine.[31] Weizmann once more took the path of acting to placate the anti-Zionists as well as the British by eschewing pro-immigration initiatives, much to Ben-Gurion's disgust.

The British yet again appointed a commission to investigate the unrest and formulate recommendations, and the Peel Commission in 1937 — informally early in the year and officially and publicly in July — proposed partition of the Mandate into independent Jewish and Arab states. The Jewish state would consist of about 4 percent of the original Palestine Mandate. The League of Nations objected to the proposal, insisting that it violated Britain's obligations to the Jews under the Mandate. Ben-Gurion, however, agreed to the recommendation, focused as he was on the looming catastrophe in Europe and his recognition that even this mini-state would offer the Jews a refuge. He argued: "Through which [option] can we get in the shortest possible time the most Jews in Palestine? . . . How much greater will be the absorptive capacity without an alien, unconcerned . . . hostile administration, but with a Zionist government . . . holding the key to immigration in its hand."[32] Weizmann, too, endorsed the partition plan, although it is noteworthy that even at this late date he did not support immediate mass immigration.[33]

Meanwhile, anti-Zionists, including Buber, Arthur Hays Sulzberger of the *New York Times* dynasty (who succeeded Adolph Ochs as publisher in 1935), and Warburg, vehemently denounced the partition plan. Warburg declared that acceptance of the Peel proposal reflected a Zionist "lust for power" and "a concept of Jewish life which is abhorrent."[34] This rhetoric of hyperbolic vilification, and its cold indifference to the desperate plight of Europe's Jews, seem, again, incomprehensible unless recognized as emanating from exposure to anti-Jewish pressures and as representing a learned response of detaching oneself from certain other Jews and of pursuing self-abnegation and accommodation as the proper path that will win relief from the surrounding hostility.

At the Zionist Congress in August, 1937, Warburg again argued for his binational solution and for limits on immigration and suggested that the mini-state proposed by the Peel commission would, in any case, also have to limit immigration or face being "overrun" by Jews. Ben-Gurion's response was to attack those who "view a Jewish state as jeopardizing their property, status, rights, and influence." He emphasized the dire situation of Europe's Jews and insisted that, "We must not consider endangering in the least the possibility of establishing a Jewish state in exchange for the donations of Warburg and his associates."[35]

Ben-Gurion prevailed at the Congress, but the Arabs rejected the Peel proposal and the British quickly backtracked on it, with Prime Minister Chamberlain insisting on another investigatory commission and conveying to the new body his disapproval of the partition recommendation. Shortly afterwards, the Arabs, under the Grand Mufti and with Nazi encouragement, initiated open rebellion in the Mandate. They targeted Jews, British officials and troops, and Arabs considered too accommodating of the Jews. Over the next two years, the Mufti's forces killed more than four hundred Jews and several thousand Arabs.

The British ultimately put down the rebellion. But in 1939 they adopted new anti-Zionist policies, restricting Jewish immigration to a total of 75,000 over the following five years and committing Britain to the transformation of Palestine into an independent Arab state within ten years. This policy, published in a new White Paper in 1939, once more elicited opposition from the League of Nations as a violation of Britain's mandatory obligations to the Jews. But the League of Nations, having failed to muster a forceful response to fascist aggression in the preceding years, was now a dying organization with little left even of its formerly limited authority.

Within the Zionist community, the Chamberlain White Paper was, of course, viewed as an outrage, and, with war obviously approaching in Europe, a likely death warrant for much of European Jewry. The anti-Zionists and "cultural Zionists" continued, however, to see things differently. Buber had finally left Germany for Jerusalem in March, 1938. There he reinvigorated the binationalist camp and helped found the "League for Jewish-Arab Rapprochement and Cooperation" the following spring, shortly after Britain's announcement of its new policy. The League campaigned in support of limits on Jewish immigration and insisted that there should be no Jewish immigration without Arab consent.

Buber also launched into public attacks on the Zionists in speeches and print. In an article in *Haaretz* in November, 1939, two months after the start of World War II, he argued not only that Zionism was an immoral cause but, since all nationalisms were in his view intrinsically and equally morally bankrupt, it was "performing the acts of Hitler in the land of Israel, for they (i.e., the Zionists) want to serve Hitler's god (i.e., nationalism) after he has been given a Hebrew name."[36]

It is not clear that any Jewish actions in the wake of the Chamberlain White Paper would have altered Britain's subsequent policy vis-à-vis Jewish immigration to the Mandate. That policy was one of vigorously blocking immigration even in the face of the Nazi genocide; of, indeed, obstructing all efforts to rescue any European Jews out of concern that the more Jews that survived the war, particularly as refugees, the more postwar pressure there would be on Britain to alter its Mandate objectives. But it was hardly insignificant that, as White Paper writ was first being translated into British Colonial Office, Foreign Office, and military procedure and execution, an outspoken circle in Jewish Palestine, a circle able to mobilize influential allies in the United States, likewise supported limits on Jewish immigration and opposed immigration without Arab consent. The fact that Jews were unable to muster a united front in the face of the British blockade against Europe's Jews made it easier for Britain to adopt and enforce its policy of preventing rescue and immigration.

Revelation of the genocide in Europe, and of Britain's obstruction of rescue and heavy-handed closure of the Mandate to Jews, significantly eroded the ranks of the anti-Zionist and "cultural Zionist" camps in the United States. But in the Yishuv the "cultural Zionist," or "true Zionist," forces continued their anti-state campaign and their support for limits on Jewish immigration. In the summer of 1942, a new Peace Association, "Ihud" ("Union Association"), was established with Buber and Magnes as its leaders and aggressively pursued attacks on the Zionists. Also in 1942, American anti-Zionists formed the American Council for Judaism, which lobbied intensely against the Zionists. Magnes worked to coordinate Ihud's efforts with those of this American group. In 1943, Magnes published articles in England, in *The Economist* and *The Times*, and in the United States, in *Foreign Affairs* and *The Nation*, urging that Britain and the United States support Ihud's anti-state agenda. The *New York Times*, following Arthur Hay Sulzberger's instructions that editorial policy on the Mandate "be predicated on the Magnes point of view,"[37] actively promoted that agenda in both editorials and news stories.

In May, 1944, Buber again published an article advocating a binational state and insisting that levels of immigration be determined by agreement with the Arabs.[38] A month later, in response to publication of a statement by Weizmann supporting Jewish control over immigration to the Yishuv, Buber attacked this "maximalist" position and argued that immigration must be sensitive to the views of others and be based on an "objective criterion."[39] In August, 1944, replying to some criticism of his position, Buber reiterated his stance and declared that Jews had no right to unilateral actions that might result in their becoming a majority in Palestine.[40]

Britain's postwar policy was to keep the Mandate virtually closed to displaced Holocaust survivors in Europe, this despite the urging of humanitarian and other groups that entry be relaxed and a declaration by President Truman in support of immediate admission of 100,000 survivors. The British stance led to further defections from anti-Zionist ranks in the United States. Still, many prominent anti-Zionist Jews in the States persisted in their anti-state campaign and the *New York Times* criticized Truman for his advocating the admission of 100,000 refugees to Palestine.[41] During this period, the *Times* also refused to publish an advertisement by the pro-Zionist American League for a Free Palestine. Publisher Sulzberger asserted that the paper was doing so in part because it disagreed with charges in the ad critical of Britain and it feared stirring up ill will between Britain and the United States. Moreover, Sulzberger declared, "We happen to believe that the British are acting in good faith and not in bad faith."[42]

In the Yishuv, Buber and his circle still campaigned in this period against large-scale immigration of refugees. Testifying before the Anglo-American Inquiry Commission in March, 1946, Buber resuscitated an old socialist Zionist argument against such immigration as a companion piece to his plea that immigration be permitted only to the extent agreed upon by the Arabs. He suggested immigration should be limited to a level consistent with an agriculture-based economy; that is, with the Yishuv's building the National Home by working the land. There is nothing in his testimony on the predicament of the refugees, the survivors of European Jewry, and the need to provide a safe haven for them. There is no recognition of their having any moral or ethical claim to admission to the National Home.[43]

(Amazingly, Buber in his later writings would return to defending the agrarian rationale for limiting immigration and defining acceptable immigrants. In a piece written around 1950, he argues that all was well in Palestine until the fourth Aliyah of 1924–1928, when middle-class Polish Jews came in, and then the arrival in the 1930s of middle-class German Jewish refugees fleeing Hitler. Both, Buber maintains, threw off the organic, gradual development of the Yishuv exclusively according to socialist agrarian principles and, in his view, also somehow thereby compromised the potential for rapprochement with the Arabs.[44] He reiterates this perspective in 1956 when he regrets that history obliged the Yishuv to replace "careful selection and training of immigrants" with mass immigration. He does not mention how he and his allies fought that mass immigration and how those who actively opposed it contributed to the loss of myriad lives that could have been saved.[45] Buber also states that Israel's proper role in the world is as a model of communitarian socialism as exemplified in the agrarian kibbutzim.[46])

In the summer of 1946, Ben-Gurion signaled his support for a partition of Western Palestine that would give the Yishuv control over immigration in the territories allocated to the Jews. A few weeks later Joseph Proskauer, head of the traditionally anti-Zionist American Jewish Committee and himself a major figure in anti-Zionist circles, articulated a change of policy by the Committee in the direction of support for large-scale refugee immigration into Palestine by any means, including partition and establishment of a Jewish state.

In October, 1946, Truman extended his support to partition and "creation of a viable Jewish state in control of its own immigration and economic policies in an adequate area of Palestine."[47] The following February, Britain referred the issue of the future of the Mandate to the United Nations. A United Nations investigatory commission, after visiting Palestine, recommended partition into a Jewish state and an Arab state, and the General Assembly, on November 29, 1947, ratified the partition plan.

Still, Buber, Magnes, and their allies in the Yishuv and in the United States fought against the proposed Jewish state. Magnes accused those former sympathizers who had defected to the Zionist cause of having "left the Jewish tradition of piety and holiness."[48] He came to the States at the urging of State Department officials opposed to partition and a group of anti-Zionist American Jews and lobbied for abandonment of the partition plan in favor of a United Nations trusteeship over Palestine.[49]

Why Buber, Magnes, and their circle believed that a "binational" state dominated by an Arab majority was desirable but a Jewish majority state was intrinsically impure and unholy is, again, difficult to fathom without recognizing behind this vehement preference the anxiety of European and American Jews in the face of anti-Jewish pressure and the fantasy nurtured by some of their number of easing that pressure by embracing universalist aspirations and renouncing all Jewish particularist reaching for power, even for the power of self-defense. Before and even during the war they were prepared to sacrifice the desperate Jews of Europe to what they perceived as the higher ground of the renunciation of state power, and after the war they were no less prepared to sacrifice the interests of those who had survived the Holocaust.

Part of their vision of the proper Jewish path was of a Jewish cosmopolitanism and intellectual integration into the West, and into the world as a whole, that they feared would be sacrificed if Jews became merely parochial citizens of a Jewish state, people like any other people. But this of itself could not have accounted for their vehement hostility to creation of a Jewish state, as they would still have been free to live their lives elsewhere and as they chose. Rather, it was the fear that the world would become even more hostile to the Jew and would use the Jewish state to strip Jews elsewhere of their still fragile and incomplete status as equal citizens that drove these people's vehement hostility to a state, for all their invocation of supposed higher ideals.

In some of their statements in support of "binationalism," Ihud's members and their sympathizers particularly attacked the Zionists' aspiration to a state with a Jewish flag, Jewish army, and other accoutrements of Jewish national power and identity, including the state's defining as one of its duties and responsibilities the ongoing free immigration of Jews from elsewhere. They condemned Zionist intentions as an intolerable injustice to the Arab inhabitants of the country, even in a partition state where the Arab minority was relatively small. Here again there was talk of an ideal binationalism with no cultural, ethnic, or national bias.

But, in fact, the norm on the continent from which most of these people had come was of nations virtually all of which, including the strongest democracies, did have a particular dominant culture and ethnicity despite sizable minorities. This truth was not regarded even by those around Buber — at least was not attacked — as rendering those states illegitimate, nor as something they should abandon to accommodate their Jewish and other minorities. Moreover, as noted, in the wake of World War I, in the political milieu in which Zionism was given its international legitimacy, there was a broad consensus that right and fairness demanded subject peoples, where feasible, be given sovereign lands in which to live and cultivate their linguistic, cultural, religious, and historical national heritage and in which to defend themselves, even if there were — as was everywhere the case — sizable minorities within their borders. The only proviso was that those minorities should enjoy a proportional role in democratic governance of the countries in which they lived and that their own religious and cultural freedoms and rights should be respected and protected.

If, in the abstract, Ihud and its sympathizers were critical of the state system wherever it existed, it was, again, particularly, and vehemently, toward the Jewish state that they directed their hostility and their attacks. They did so employing a rhetoric that would cast those Jews who wanted to create a nation like other nations as evil in a way the champions of other nations were not. They pursued their bigoted offensive against the Zionists' aspirations to a state even though recent and current history had demonstrated for much of the rest of the world that Jews, simply to survive, were in need of a state of their own as few other peoples were.

TEN

The Labor Decades:
New Country, Old Pathology

I saw that the root [of Ben-Gurion's course for the nation] was in a dis-
tortion of the soul . . . in the tyranny of the dead over the living. Because
this very idea means that through it the dead send messages and com-
mandments to the living, and these messages may very well be murder-
ous ones . . . There, in Ben-Gurion, I saw the black demon-fire . . . He
embodied in himself the entire Jewish mystique.

Amos Oz[1]

BEN-GURION VERSUS THE ACADEMICS

The attacks of Buber, Magnes, and their associates on the Zionist enterprise
did not end with the founding of Israel. Even as the new state was struggling
to fight off invading Arab armies, Buber was haranguing the Jews of the land
for their supposedly evil embrace of "sovereignty"[2] and Magnes still communicated with the State Department on plans to undo Jewish independence in
favor of an Arab-Jewish confederation. Nor did they shrink, in their hostility
to the state, from any rhetorical excess. Thus Ben-Gurion and his associates were
repeatedly compared, in their focus on state building, to Mussolini and Hitler.

It was obviously not simply utopian visions of internationalism that
prompted this vituperative ire; Buber and Magnes did not voice the same spleen
toward all national leaders, toward Churchill or Roosevelt, for example, or even
Stalin. What spurred them, rather, was their utopian vision of Jewish universalism and self-effacement and cultivated powerlessness. Any other Jewish path,
even in the service of saving lives, was viewed by them as the worst of crimes
and abominations. State power and spiritual integrity, Buber argued, are irreconcilable for Jews.

Magnes died in late 1948, but Buber and his circle, centered mainly around
the humanities and social science faculties at Hebrew University, continued their
assaults on the Jewish state in the years after Israel's founding. It is a common phenomenon that those convinced of the essential value and rightness of an endeavor

will regard what they perceive as flaws in its execution simply as problems that must be addressed in more properly advancing the effort. In contrast, those who take a more jaundiced view of the enterprise will more likely interpret such flaws as confirming their comprehension of the entire undertaking as misconceived. So, too, did Buber and his allies not simply find fault with aspects of Israeli policy in the years after the nation's founding. They did not merely attack Ben-Gurion and the Israeli government for such steps as the military responses to Arab terrorism, the cultivation of an alignment with the West, the development of a nuclear program, and the kidnapping, trial, and execution of Adolph Eichmann. Rather, they interpreted these policies and actions as evidence that Israel should not exist, as proof of its essential sinfulness.

Obviously, others in Israel did not endorse every aspect of Israeli governance. But most Israelis would respond to policies and actions of which they were critical by advocating reforms that would bring state policy more into congruence with their vision of how the Jewish state ought to function. If they disagreed with elements of foreign or domestic policy such as aspects of the treatment of immigrants or of state policy toward the nation's Arab minority, those Arabs who had stayed in Israel or had been readmitted and become citizens, they would view proper relief to lie in the government's modification of its position. For Buber and his circle, in contrast, virtually every point of perceived state misbehavior was interpreted as confirmation that the entire national enterprise was indeed a horrible mistake.

Various writers, most systematically and comprehensively Yoram Hazony, have written about the ongoing domination of Hebrew University, particularly the humanities and social science faculties, by associates and students of Buber and Magnes, people with similar views and a similar animus toward the Jewish state, in the years after Israel's founding. They have also traced how these people directed much of their "academic" work toward indictments of the Zionist enterprise and how these academics became the chief educators of Israel's intellectual elite and inculcated in that elite their own jaundiced perspectives toward the Jewish state.

An example cited by Hazony of prominent "scholarly" themes developed in this vein at the University is that of Messianism.[3] To the outside observer, Buber's own agenda might seem ostentatiously redolent of Messianism, and more particularly of Messianism conceived in Christian terms, with the Jewish vocation defined as a universalist mission of powerlessness, self-effacement, and self-sacrifice to redeem the world.[4] But Hebrew University scholars and Buber allies such as the historian Jacob Talmon argued that the Zionist effort to "redeem" the Jewish people through state building was itself a false "messianism" and compared Ben-Gurion and the Zionists to the false messiahs and their followers of earlier eras. (In effect, these academics proffered arguments very similar to those of the small Orthodox sect Naturei Karta, which likewise inveighed against Zionism as a false messianism and declared the state the worst of sacrileges in its daring to reestablish a Jewish commonwealth before the Coming of the Messiah. Naturei Karta has over the years paid homage to the PLO and Yasser Arafat and advocated Israel's destruction and the establishment of Arab authority over all of Palestine as the way to cleanse the land of the Zionist sacrilege.)

Hazony attempts to account for the success of these Hebrew University academics in winning so many of their students from among the Israeli intellectual elite to their perverse views of the state and to their universalist perspectives and philosophy. He argues that much of the explanation for this success lies in the failure of the Labor Zionist movement to construct any substantive countervailing intellectual edifice in support of the Zionist enterprise.[5] Certainly, an aversion to intellectualism was part of the world view of the Russian socialist-Zionist circles that had founded the Yishuv's collective farms and formed the early political parties and governing institutions of Labor Zionism. Their anti-intellectualism derived not only from socialist ideology but also from the effort of Russian Jewish labor circles to shape a "New Jew" who would be redeemed by working the soil. They wished to separate themselves from what they perceived as the failed intellectualism of the European Jewish elite and the failed intellectualism of much of the leadership of Jewish Orthodoxy.

This anti-intellectualism has been the theme of myriad anecdotes told of the early Zionist settlers. For example, the poet Avraham Shlonsky related the negative reaction of his fellow kibbutzniks on their learning that he was writing for a literary magazine; they viewed that sort of endeavor as representative of the sterile, bourgeois exertions of Diaspora Jewry and something to be avoided by the pioneers in Zion.[6] *Haaretz* wrote in 1920 of immigrants that were coming with intellectual aspirations and declared, "There is space in Palestine for a thousand philosophers, no more. No more! The rest — if they wanted to live and build — need not a mind but a pair of hands."[7] Even Weizmann, in a 1919 letter, complained of too many intellectuals among the immigrants.[8] The same anti-intellectualism figured in the socialist Zionists' distrust of Herzl's emphasis on pursuing diplomacy and on developing and promoting the idea of the state, as against their own focus on building facts on the ground farm by farm, worker by worker, and constructing the state by creating a critical mass of homesteads, labor projects, and workers.

In addition, what there was of ideology vis-à-vis statehood within socialist ranks in the Yishuv was in part hostile to the push for statehood. Elements of the socialist Left and the kibbutz movement adhered to anti-nationalist socialist tenets. (They had in some measure been drawn to those tenets by the same historical-psychological factors, the chronic besiegement of Europe's Jews, that had figured in shaping the internationalism of the German Jewish academics at Hebrew University.) Some among them — including the Hashomer Hatzair kibbutzim — favored binationalism. These contingents also served as a source of critiques of the state in the wake of independence; indeed, some would argue that their critiques of the state were politically much more significant than were the indictments of the academics.[9]

It is also noteworthy that whatever urgency in state building had been felt by Labor Zionist leaders in the half century prior to the founding of the state and immediately thereafter was based on considerations that were largely irrelevant by the mid-1950s. To the degree that Ben-Gurion's sense of urgency had been shared by his colleagues, they had been driven by the wish to save who could be saved from among the embattled millions of Jews in Europe and then, after World War II, from among the remnant who had survived and the besieged Jews of the Arab world. Most of European Jewry had been annihilated and the survivors in Europe and in the Arab world who could be brought to Israel had already been settled there by the time those who attended university in the nineteen fifties came of age. And the aspirations that continued to animate many of the older Labor Zionists, visions of constructing, on the foundations of working the soil and the factories, a model socialist state in Zion, were perceived by more than a few of their children as sterile, gray, and intellectually uninspiring.

Moreover, the comprehensions that gave the Zionist enterprise deeper and more compelling significance for many people struck no chord in much of the younger generation. For others the Return meant reestablishing their long-exiled and downtrodden nation within the family of nations, reclaiming their history, fulfilling their faith, and opening up the potential of a new, in many respects liberated, Jewish creativity, a picking up of creative threads put aside with the hardships of exile. But these were perspectives bound up with a religious-historical connectedness of the sort widely denigrated by the militant secularism of large segments of the Labor Zionist camp and so were typically not a source of inspiration extended to the children on the kibbutzim. It was not something to which they were acculturated or which they were reared to value, a circumstance that further reinforced the sterileness of the Labor Zionist milieu for many of its children.

There were, of course, some among the older generation of Labor Zionists who had in large part freed themselves of much of the narrow socialist parochialism and associated biases of the Labor pioneers, Ben-Gurion being the most notable example. Having arrived in Palestine as a Labor Zionist zealot, he was within a few years disenchanted with the exaltation of working the land as the highest good and with the anti-intellectualism that was another pillar of Labor Zionist creed. In 1909, at age twenty-two, he wrote to his father, "I have no desire . . . to be and remain a farmer . . . I hate being possessed by the earth, which binds its owners to itself and enslaves them."[10] Later he went off to study law in Istanbul and to immerse himself in intense self-education, which over time encompassed extensive studies in Jewish as well as general history and in Jewish religious literature. He also gradually came to appreciate Herzl's emphasis on diplomacy and on promoting the idea of the Jewish state. In addition, while Ben-Gurion continued to adhere to socialist visions of proper Zionist institutions, he learned to appreciate as well the shortcomings of the focus on communal organization and state building in the Labor Zionist mode.

But how exceptional Ben-Gurion and his allies were among the leadership and ranks of Labor Zionism is demonstrated by how much resistance he encountered, and how little headway he was able to make, through the nineteen twenties and thirties in his efforts to forge a more aggressive diplomatic and political stance in the face of the dire threats confronting European Jewry. His efforts to push for some Jewish control over immigration, some elements of state authority to promote immigration and absorption, were largely stymied by the adherence of those around him to socialist Zionist orthodoxies concerning the proper way to build the Yishuv. So too were, latterly, his attempts to effect an alliance with the nonsocialists and Jabotinsky to advance the cause of immigration and state building as the situation in Europe deteriorated even further.

Ben-Gurion, as he educated himself in Jewish history and in the literature of Jewish peoplehood and belief, found additional inspiration, beyond his early Labor Zionist perspectives, for the task of nation building and drew closer to Herzl's comprehension of the Jewish state, foremost as a safe refuge but also as a place of spiritual healing for souls diminished by the vagaries and abuses of life in exile. He came to comprehend such healing as built on something richer and more profound than simply the balm of labor, the healing of working the soil — as built also on a reconnection with a nurturing culture and nurturing faith. He drew upon this broader, deeper vision of the Zionist endeavor as he helped shape the new state's institutions and define its meaning and mission, its aspirations and its obligations.

But for many of the pioneers' sons and daughters, or grandsons and granddaughters, who responded to the prevailing Labor Zionist ethos of the kibbutzim with a sense of suffocation in the face of its intellectual aridness, the militant anti-religious bias of the kibbutzim in which they were reared served effectively to cut them off from Ben-Gurion's course of liberation, from his intellectual rebellion via immersion in Jewish history and the literature of Jewish peoplehood and faith.

But Hazony and others are not simply interested in accounting for the defection of so many among the brightest children and grandchildren of Israel's Labor Zionist pioneers, in the years after the state's independence, to the internationalist and anti-state perspectives of their teachers at Hebrew University, or to similar views within the far Left ranks of Labor Zionism and the kibbutz movement. Rather, they are seeking to explain more than such defections. They are most concerned with exploring the seemingly ever-increasing penetration of those anti-state perspectives, over the ensuing decades, to the point where they not only prevail almost without challenge among large segments of the academic and artistic elites in Israel but also have attained a significant popularity within the governing elites and among the Israeli electorate. But there are difficulties with explaining this disaffection vis-à-vis the Zionist enterprise mainly in terms of the failure of the Labor Zionist elite and of nonsocialist constituencies in Israel to construct countervailing intellectual edifices, for all the genuine impact of this failure.

In the earlier years of the state, in fact, more of the children of the pioneers followed the course proffered by Ben-Gurion, and by those of his associates who had navigated a similar intellectual odyssey away from the stultifying elements of Labor Zionism, than embraced the views of Buber, Magnes, and their circle. The prevailing anti-religious sentiment of the kibbutzim and other Labor Zionist bastions did not preclude their doing so, despite its influence. Nor did the socialist convictions of the Labor Zionists prevent them from following Ben-Gurion's lead, which was hardly surprising. If those convictions helped render the children of the pioneers more receptive to the internationalism purveyed at Hebrew University, Ben-Gurion's image of the state likewise incorporated much of the socialism of the Labor Zionists.

Some might argue that the increasing popularity of internationalist and anti-state perspectives among the academic, artistic, and political elites of Israel in subsequent decades, and the decline of the hold of Ben-Gurion's vision on these elites, demonstrate, in fact, the importance of intellectual edifices. They might contend that it was the control of Hebrew University and its daughter institutions over the higher education of the nation's elite, and their control in turn by Buber, Magnes, and their associates and protégés, that accounted for the ever-widening influence of their views. They might claim that it was the circumstance that Ben-Gurion's perspectives were not developed and propagated by any comparable institutions that accounted for their ultimately losing ground among the elites, a process perhaps reinforced by the attenuation of that desperate practical urgency to state building and ingathering that had dominated Ben-Gurion and his allies' thinking in the 1920s, 1930s, and 1940s.

But the popularity, through the state's first decades, of Ben-Gurion's alternative views, that perspective that he and some of his colleagues arrived at after their own rebellion against many of the austere verities of Labor Zionism, clearly suggests that the competitive dissemination of such views is not entirely dependent on the work of the academy and intellectual institutions. It indicates as well that additional factors beyond the weight of intellectual institutions may play a role in determining victory and defeat in such competitions.

A look at the influence elsewhere of academic institutions espousing, defending and disseminating a particular political philosophy supports this view. Such comparisons suggest that indeed an academically championed political philosophy, particularly one purveyed under conditions where no alternative voices enjoy the same place of privilege in a society's intellectual arenas, will commonly sway at least transiently large numbers of those who pass through the centers of learning. But consideration of such circumstances elsewhere also suggests that for this sort of inculcation to have a more pervasive impact on the later thinking of students, on the views abroad in the society more generally, and on societal policy, the philosophy being pushed must answer some need beyond simply the attraction experienced by many to intellectual formulas.

In the United States, in the context of the turmoil of the nineteen sixties, more particularly in the context of opposition to the Vietnam War, internationalist and anti-state, and to some degree socialist, views that had long had a presence in academia suddenly enjoyed a much expanded popularity. The espousers of these views and their acolytes have largely dominated American university campuses, at least elite campuses, since then. (In fact, some critics of Hazony have argued that, in his tracing of the current pervasive embrace of internationalist and anti-state sentiments by Israel's academic and cultural elites to the influence of Buber, Buber's colleagues and their protégés, Hazony erroneously ignores the prevalence of similar views among American and European academics in the last three decades and the eagerness of Israeli intellectuals to emulate their American and European colleagues.[11])

But while the preeminence of such perspectives on American university campuses has had at least a transient impact on the thinking of myriad students, and while similar views have come to prevail among the artistic elites in the States much as they have in Israel, the penetration of these views into American governance, into the shaping of policy in the United States, while not insignificant, has been quite circumscribed. This is particularly so when compared to the dramatic influence of such perspectives on policy making in Israel. In addition, popular espousal of such views in America, including their long-term retention even among those attracted and influenced by them as students, is likewise quite limited. On the contrary, even among many erstwhile student enthusiasts of those perspectives of their college professors, there is more commonly a substantial return to the different opinions abroad in the country.

It could be argued that at least part of the explanation for this lies in the fact that in the United States, unlike in Israel, there were indeed countervailing intellectual institutions. Conservative and neoconservative think tanks, for example, while not enjoying a strong presence in the universities comparable to that of their intellectual rivals, nevertheless challenged the other side in the arena of public discourse, in journals of ideas and in books and lectures. One could maintain that these competing institutions provided an intellectual foundation for resistance to the deeper penetration into the society and into policy of the verities in vogue on the nation's campuses.

This is certainly true. But it is also true that there was a broad popular resistance to, for example, arguments that claimed a moral equivalence between the Soviet Union and the United States in the Cold War, let alone arguments that laid the greater blame on the United States or indicted the United States as the more reprehensible — both internationally and internally — of the rivals. There was a broad conviction that American democracy and its associated freedoms and the national institutions that flowed from them placed the nation, for all the room for improvement, on an incomparably superior moral plain than its Communist rival. This view was overwhelmingly embraced, even among those beyond the reach of the conservative and neoconservative think tanks, and even among those whose university professors had told them otherwise or who were told otherwise in the movie theaters. This resistance, among the shapers of policy and among the voters who place them in office, to the verities dominant on the campuses, not only prevailed in the 1970s and 1980s but has also done so in the years since the end of the Cold War.

One factor that has likely contributed to the different penetration into policy in the United States as compared to Israel of the perspectives dominating the campuses is the difference in the two countries' electoral systems. The Israeli system — which has a very low threshold of votes needed to win parliamentary representation — is much more open to the views of small constituencies and gives such constituencies much greater representation and influence. It thereby places less of a premium on ideological compromise for the sake of attracting a threshold constituency and abets the penetration of idiosyncratic ideological views, whether of the Right or the Left, into policy making. Also significant is that candidates for parliament are not directly elected by constituents but rather run on party lists and are elected according to their place on the list and the number of votes garnered by the party. Candidates therefore must appeal primarily to their party hierarchy rather than to a constituency for political advancement, which facilitates enforcement of ideological conformity and thereby further reinforces the sway of ideological orthodoxies in parliament and policy.

IMPACT OF THE ARAB SIEGE

But a much more substantive factor in shaping the different response to the dogma of the universities in Israel and America concerns the reality that Israel has been for all its existence a state under siege. It has been if not actively at war nevertheless challenged, rejected, and potentially threatened by virtually all of its neighbors. Some in its citizenry have inevitably perceived the siege as unending; and some — as within all besieged populations, as within Jewish communities vulnerable and under attack in the past — have responded by comprehending the solution to lie in assigning the sin to one's own community and seeking salvation in self-reform.

In the context of the distress associated with the siege, the views proffered by Buber and his associates and protégés, views that asserted the essential sinfulness of the state-building enterprise, were particularly attractive to some. For many of the children of the pioneer elite, the alienation from Jewish history, culture, and religion in which they were reared made it all the easier to embrace, when faced with the pressures of the siege, the perspectives of their university professors. While for others who may have been less thoroughly alienated and more open to Ben-Gurion-type comprehensions as counterweights to the corrosive effects of the siege, the absence of intellectual institutions articulating, defending, and disseminating such views loomed increasingly large and contributed to drift toward the dogma of the universities.[12]

Moreover, the popularity of these views and their impact on policy grew with the persistence of the siege. Perhaps also contributing to this phenomenon was the increasing exposure of much of the population to images of alternative lives free of besiegement, which further stoked impatience to attain such lives. But another, and likely more important, factor in fanning the popularity of indictments of the state was the growing definition of divisions within Israeli society, such as secular versus religious splits. These divisions, as in European Jewry, allowed the elite to place the "sin" on those across the divide, to recast the genuine vying for political power among competing camps in Israel by painting those "other" Jews as the enemy and the obstacle to peace and reconciliation. This tack resonated with many within the elite's own camp and so made the accommodationist and anti-state and internationalist perspectives more appealing to many.

But the key element remains the siege itself. Consider, for example, the views of one artist, Amos Oz, perhaps Israel's most eminent novelist and an influential spokesperson on public policy. Oz left his home in Jerusalem at age fourteen (his mother had committed suicide two years earlier) and moved to Kibbutz Hulda. He later wrote of the kibbutz — generically, not just Kibbutz Hulda — as the "least bad place I have ever seen,"[13] described its attractions to him, including its socialist values, but also noted its "suffocation . . . depression, petty jealousies, the various pressures of convention, and so forth."[14]

Oz traced his intellectual escape from the negatives of the collectivist mentality, and the negatives of the Labor Zionist institutions of the state, in large part to Pinhas Lavon, a founder and resident of Kibbutz Hulda and ideologist of the particular branch of socialist Zionism that had established the kibbutz. But it is very likely that his education at Hebrew University also played a substantive role in that "escape."

Lavon seems a curious hero for Oz; he had been a supporter of binationalism for a time in the 1920s but as Israeli defense minister in the early 1950s he had charted an aggressive military course in response to Arab attacks, pushing steps beyond what other elements of the leadership as well as the IDF believed prudent, and had been the central figure in a scandal involving the employment of *agents provocateurs* in Egypt. Lavon lost his post over the affair but he subsequently claimed that he had been the victim of a cabal involving Ben-Gurion and key IDF figures and that this cabal was moving the country toward a military dictatorship. It was these accusations that appear to have particularly endeared him to Oz.[15] Lavon's assertions and their fallout were in the limelight around the same time that Oz, as a student, was encountering the anti-state sentiments so prominent at Hebrew University, where there was much militating by faculty and students in support of Lavon and against Ben-Gurion.

Oz's writings suggest that his animus toward Ben-Gurion was a response both to Ben-Gurion's religious-historical comprehension of the Zionist enterprise and to elements of Ben-Gurion's communal view of the state. They also suggest that his hostility was shaped by his exposure to the anti-religious biases of Labor Zionism and to anti-state ideology in the university as well as by his personal experience of negative aspects of communal living. But it is also clear in his writing that the heat of his rage toward Ben-Gurion and Jewish history, Jewish culture, Jewish ties to the land, derives from the siege, from the surrounding hostility that prevents him from living a "normal life" in the land.

Oz wrote of his views in the late 1950s: "I saw that the root [of Ben-Gurion's course] was in a distortion of the soul . . . in the tyranny of the dead over the living. Because this very idea means that through it the dead send messages and commandments to the living, and these messages may very well be murderous ones . . . There, in Ben-Gurion, I saw the black demon-fire . . . He embodied in himself the entire Jewish mystique."[16] One sees here of course a crude caricature of what it means to value ties to one's history, people, culture, faith — a dismissing of all such ties as "the tyranny of the dead." One can detect also the influence of Oz's having been educated in anti-state and anti-religious dogma. But again the key element, the source of the heat, can be discerned in the phrase: "these messages may very well be murderous ones . . . "

It is the threat posed by the siege, the threat of having to kill or be killed, that shifted Oz's alienation toward history, culture, faith, from an abstract intellectual accoutrement into a crusade, indeed, in various ways an anti-Zionist crusade in the Buber mode. It is most reminiscent of nineteenth-century Jewish intellectuals in Europe who railed against the curse of the Jewish, of Jewish history and Jewish identity (often doing so — as Oz does — while professing individualism or universalism as more noble and high-minded than any narrow ethnic or religious or national identity), but whose indictments of all things Jewish were a response to Europe's besiegement of the Jews and their own eagerness to escape the siege. Recall, for example, Berlin salon mistress Rachel Levy's complaints, cited in Chapter Three, about being treated poorly by the surrounding society because she was a Jew, and her solution: "The Jew must be extirpated from us."

There are, to be sure, ambiguities in Oz's positions and significant distinctions between his articulated stances and those of Buber and his circle. Oz, neither in the 1950s nor since, would have characterized himself as anti-Zionist or characterized Israel's creation as intrinsically sinful. On the contrary, he has viewed himself as a defender of Israel and has attacked the Arab refusal to accept Israel's existence. But in his insistence on being liberated from Jewish history, from the "Jewish mystique," in his demand for "normalcy," he is demanding relief from the stresses that are bound up for him in the Jewish. Foremost is the stress of being an Israeli in an Israel defined as a Jewish state, the stress of the siege perpetuated by those who will not tolerate such a state, and the hope for resolution by shedding at least elements of the Jewish.

The centrality of the siege in shaping Oz's indictments of the state can also be seen in his defenses of Zionism. He has written at various points, in keeping with the internationalist bent of sections of the socialist camp in Israel and of elements of Israeli academia, that he is against the institution of the nation-state and sees it more as a tool of evil than of good. "Nationalism itself is, in my eyes, the curse of mankind."[17] He would prefer to have the world consist of "only spiritual civilizations tied somehow to their lands, without the tools of statehood and without the instruments of war."[18] He is a Zionist only because of absolute necessity, because Israel is necessary to protect the lives of Jews: "I am forced to take it upon myself to play the 'game of nations' . . . because existence without the tools of statehood is a matter of mortal danger."[19]

But Oz's impulse to define this utility of the state so narrowly and so starkly — saying nothing, for example, of cultural, ethnic, and religious values and their free cultivation — is in large part a reaction to the siege and a reflection of the wish that claiming little more for the state, eschewing everything that he chooses to perceive as going beyond the basic protection of life, will placate Arab hostility. Oz writes at one point, "Our justification vis-à-vis [the Palestinians] cannot be based on our age-old longings . . . The Zionist enterprise has no other objective justification than the right of a drowning man to grasp the only plank that can save him."[20] But what nations are driven to define "objective justifications" for their existence — or, at least, in what nations does the drive for such definition resonate with significant segments of the population — other than nations under siege?

There are elements of Ben-Gurion's leadership in defining and building the state, beyond his emphasis on Jewish historical and religious bonds with Eretz Israel, that likewise alienated some children and grandchildren of the Labor Zionist camp and, as alluded to, apparently figure in Oz's resentments. Ben-Gurion emphasized communal obligations and responsibilities not only for defending the new state against external threats but also for building the state. He stressed shared obligations and responsibilities vis-à-vis, for example, settling the remnant of European Jewry and the hundreds of thousands of Jewish refugees from the Arab world. Ben-Gurion constructed a system commonly referred to as "statism" in which the population was called upon to make sacrifices and exert itself to communal ends, and the population generally rose to the challenge. Israelis' standard of living actually dropped significantly over the first decade of the country's existence in response particularly to the costs of absorbing an immigration that nearly tripled the country's population, but this did not spark any major rebellion against that undertaking.

Ben-Gurion's "statism" had, of course, much in common with socialist communitarianism and was, in many respects, a putting into effect of Labor Zionist policy. On the other hand, the defining of all Jews as potential citizens of Israel, and, more importantly, the priority given to bringing Jews to Israel and sacrificing in the service of their absorption, was for some old-line Labor Zionists counter to their preferred policy of giving priority — as they had urged in the 1920s and 1930s as well — to absorbing those who would contribute to constructing the socialist utopia. Still, the most common view was that, if many of the new immigrants brought in by Ben-Gurion, such as the traditional Jews of the Arab world, were stuck in atavistic ways, their children and grandchildren would be molded into Labor Zionists. But for some, particularly among the younger generation, the entire concept of communal sacrifice for Jewish communal goals, the whole concept of giving priority to state, and Jewish, objectives, was comprehended as an intolerable intrusion on individual freedom. This was particularly so for those divorced from broader Jewish religious bonds and from the earlier desperate need for communal action in the context of a threatened European Jewry. Ben-Gurion was perceived as the villain curtailing their freedom, and this also figures in Oz's antipathy.

Communal goals and communal sacrifice versus individual freedom might have been an issue under any circumstances; indeed it is so in every state for some individuals and has been a live source of contention in Western democracies throughout the centuries of modernity. But it is also true that the government of Israel was for the most part not actually intruding on individual freedom beyond imposing taxes to support immigrant absorption and other state-building programs, and these monetary intrusions were not the target of Oz's hostility or that of others in the socialist Labor camp who were hostile to Ben-Gurion. It is likely that the communitarianism and dedication to absorption and other state goals would not of themselves have stirred this animosity were it not that the state enterprise was under external siege, were it not that the surrounding Arab states comprehended every immigrant, as every other state-building project, indeed every "Jewish" project, as an act of aggression. Again, Oz's balking at having forced upon him a communal identity, and communal obligation, that "may well be murderous" captures the centrality of the siege in his grievances against Ben-Gurion.

But those who shared Oz's views in the 1950s were then an exception among the children of Israel's Labor Zionist elite. Most sympathized with Ben-Gurion's course. They did so in part because the horrors of the genocide in Europe, and the *raison d'être* for a Jewish state as endorsed by the League of Nations and then the United Nations, were still fresh enough in many people's minds. So too was the flush of Israel's postindependence achievements, its survival against the Arab onslaught of 1947–48 and its ingathering, however difficult, of the remnant of European Jewry and of the approximately 800,000 Jewish refugees from the Arab world.

But another reason most in the Labor Zionist camp supported Ben-Gurion's course was that it was in fact children of the Labor Zionist pioneers — people with whom most of those on the Left identified and sympathized — who were running the country with Ben-Gurion. They were the people who were managing the practical necessities of dealing with ongoing Arab hostility, settling and rehabilitating the immigrants, navigating all the other work of nation building. This sympathy and identification helped to override for most on the Left any allure of hostile internationalist utopian reveries or hostile individualism.

In addition, there was then a widespread — if, in retrospect, seemingly naïve — optimism, particularly among some of the Labor Zionist elite, that the Arab siege would be short-lived, that it was driven by factors that would soon be ameliorated and so it, too, would ease and end. There were theories early on that Arab hostility was fueled by colonial manipulation and would dissipate when European colonialism retreated from the Arab world. After all, had not Britain, for its own ends, exacerbated Arab antagonism to the Jews in the Mandate, even employing *agents provocateurs* to do so? British officers had led Transjordan's Arab Legion against Israel in 1947–48 even as King Abdullah had been lukewarm about the war. This theory drew strength, of course, from socialist inclinations to view the world in terms of colonial abusers and colonized victims, a variation on the class struggle.

Others argued that the Arab war against Israel was propelled by the machinations of conservative Arab monarchs and would end as new, reformist forces rose to power. Indeed, many saw the coup in Egypt that catapulted Gamel Abdel Nasser to power in 1952 as a harbinger of peace. They construed Nasser's declarations of a socialist domestic policy to rehabilitate Egypt — declarations that struck a more than sympathetic chord in the breasts of Israeli socialists — as signaling a sober turning inward by Arab regimes to address their severe domestic problems and so the beginning of the end of their use of war against Israel as a distraction from domestic woes. In a similar vein, it was maintained by some that hostility to Israel was fed by pan-Arabism and so would inevitably ease as the various Arab nations redirected their attention to their own people and their internal development. Others suggested that Arab enmity was encouraged and sustained by Arab despots of various stripes but would disappear with what they believed to be the impending democratization of the Arab world.

Of course, the Arab siege continued, and chronic terrorist assaults and vocal support by Arab governments for an ongoing campaign to destroy Israel dissipated much of the earlier optimism. Finally, the events immediately preceding the 1967 Six Day War, the virtually universal Arab rallying around Nasser's declaration that the time had come to annihilate Israel, largely disabused Israelis of whatever still remained of their earlier convictions that internal changes within the Arab world would soon work to defuse anti-Israel hostility. But Israel's rapid and overwhelming victory in the war inspired a new optimistic theory regarding Arab opinion: That Israel's demonstration of its determination to survive and of its ability to defend itself and to inflict punishment on those who attack it would oblige the Arabs finally to reconcile themselves to Israel's existence.

In addition, some events in the immediate wake of the war were interpreted in a manner that reinforced this optimism. For example, the Arab side had ostentatiously initiated and prosecuted a buildup to war in the weeks preceding hostilities. This process had included declarations of an imminent campaign of extermination against Israel, vast mobilization and movement of forces and armaments to Israel's borders, imposition of a blockade against Israel's port of Eilat, and forced removal of United Nations troops stationed as a buffering presence on the Israeli-Egyptian border. These Arab actions rendered the subsequent conflict, in the view of most of the world outside of the Arab states and their Communist allies, certainly in the view of most in the West, a defensive Israeli war against Arab aggression.

The Security Council's Resolution 242 that emerged after the war reflected this understanding of the conflict and rendered the return of Arab territory contingent on Arab recognition of Israel and abandonment of rejectionist policies. It did so in its insistence that a peace be negotiated between Israel and its Arab neighbors and that "secure and recognized boundaries" be agreed upon bilaterally in the context of such negotiations, and in its refusal to demand that Israel return to its prewar lines.

The Arab states and the Soviet Union had fought for wording demanding a return of "the" territories or "all" territories captured by Israel from Syria, Jordan, and Egypt in the course of the war. But the wording finally agreed upon in the resolution calls only for a return of "territories," to be negotiated by the Israelis and their neighbors; and the framers of the resolution made clear that they regarded a return to the prewar boundaries undesirable and an invitation to further instability and conflict.[21] President Lyndon Johnson, shortly after the war, stated that Israel's retreat to its former lines would be "not a prescription for peace but for renewed hostilities"; and he advocated new "recognized boundaries" that would provide "security against terror, destruction, and war."[22]

Israelis then anticipated that the eagerness of Arab regimes to regain at least some of their lost territories would be a spur to their reconciling themselves to Israel's presence sooner rather than later.

Again Israeli optimism was proven wrong. In August, 1967, the Arab nations, meeting at Khartoum, agreed unanimously on a policy of "three no's" — no recognition, no negotiation, no peace. Within months, Egypt was conducting occasional military operations against Israeli forces. In 1968, with Soviet support, Egypt launched a "war of attrition." This entailed persistent attacks, mainly artillery bombardments along the Suez Canal, aimed at imposing ongoing losses on Israel in men and materiel that would ultimately force the country to withdraw from captured territories without the negotiations, recognition, and peace called for in Security Council Resolution 242. These hostilities continued until 1970 and ended without the Arabs achieving any of their objectives but with peace no closer.

Hostilities also occurred on another front. In 1964, Palestinian Arabs had founded the Palestine Liberation Organization with a charter whose clauses were focused on the pursuit of Israel's annihilation. Particularly after the 1967 war, the various constituent organizations of the PLO undertook armed attacks against Israel that continued over the ensuing decades. These were essentially terrorist forays against civilian targets in Israel and abroad, incursions launched at first primarily from Jordan and later, after the PLO was expelled from Jordan in a 1970 civil war, mainly from Lebanon. This war too, while exacting a toll in Israeli dead and wounded, failed to attain Arab objectives. But it was a constant reminder to Israelis of their besiegement.

During these postwar years, the Israeli government continued to be controlled by the Labor Zionists, their factions now largely merged to form the Labor Party. The initial postwar period saw continuation of the emergency national unity coalition that had been established during the May, 1967, Arab buildup to hostilities. This was the first Israeli government to include right-of-center representation, in the form of the Gahal bloc, but the government was dominated by Labor. (Gahal had been established in 1965 by the merger of the Liberal Party, a centrist party whose agenda was focused on liberal opposition to the socialist economic policies of the Left, and the Herut Party, heirs to Jabotinsky's political legacy.)

In 1970, Gahal withdrew from the coalition over disagreement with the government's acceptance of American Secretary of State William Rogers's disengagement plan for ending the war of attrition along the Suez Canal. (Many Labor leaders shared the concerns on the Right that Egypt would use the ceasefire to bring anti-aircraft missile batteries to the banks of the canal, thereby threatening Israeli air support for its forces on the other side. The United States committed itself to assuring that Egypt would not do so, and Labor then accepted the disengagement. In fact, within two days of the cease-fire the Egyptians did bring their missiles to the canal, and the United States did nothing. Israel considered attacking the batteries but ultimately decided against this step. The Egyptian missiles subsequently played a key role in Israel's initial setbacks and losses in the 1973 Yom Kippur War.) With Gahal's withdrawal, Labor led a government that included only minor coalition partners.

ISRAELI VIEWS AFTER THE SIX DAY WAR AND EMERGENCE OF THE PEACE MOVEMENT

Despite the official Arab rejectionist stance, the war of attrition, and the terror attacks, Israeli leaders still anticipated there would eventually be negotiations and an exchange of territory in return for a formal peace.

Soon after the 1967 war the Israeli government informally defined areas of the captured territory that it believed were vital for the country to retain in order to diminish the nation's earlier strategic vulnerability, as exemplified by its previous nine-mile width in virtually the center of its most densely populated region. On the West Bank, these informal plans entailed retaining the sparsely populated Jordan Valley, key east-west mountain passes leading to the valley, and the eastern slopes of the Judaean and Samarian hills — likewise sparsely populated — overlooking the valley, as well as the immediate vicinity of Jerusalem. (Yigal Allon, deputy prime minister at the time, drafted a proposal for disposition of the West Bank, and most subsequent formulas for territorial compromise there have been variations on the "Allon Plan.") But Israel anticipated that the balance of the West Bank, including areas home to the vast majority of the territory's population, would be returned to Jordan in the context of a peace agreement, and that most of the territory taken from Egypt would likewise be returned as *quid pro quo* for recognition, negotiations, and a formal peace. (The Golan Heights was almost universally believed to be strategically vital, and its control by Syria too dangerous, leaving Israel too vulnerable as demonstrated by past experience, to contemplate substantial territorial concessions on that front. The fact that the Heights had been maintained by Syria essentially as a closed military zone and was very sparsely populated rendered more feasible the prospect of Israel's retaining control of it.)

As time passed with persisting negative, rejectionist signals from Arab governments, and long periods of open hostilities, Israeli leaders generally believed that the country had no choice but to remain in all the captured territories until Arab opinion changed and moves toward peace were possible. They also generally believed there was little problem in doing so. The most troubling aspect of ongoing retention of all the territories was its perpetuation of Israeli control over, and responsibility for, the large Palestinian Arab population of the West Bank and Gaza, numbering in excess of a million people.

Shortly after the end of the Six Day War, on June 27, 1967, the Knesset approved incorporation into the Jerusalem municipality of East Jerusalem — covering an area of six square kilometers — and some of Jerusalem's environs, consisting of another sixty-four square kilometers, most of them beyond Israel's prewar lines. The Knesset act entailed extension of Israeli law, jurisdiction and administration to these areas. But beyond this virtual annexation of East Jerusalem, the Israelis did not seek to change the legal status of the territories, and Moshe Dayan, then Defense Minister, formulated a policy of minimal intrusion into the lives of the Palestinian Arabs. Day-to-day administration of the territories continued largely in the hands of the former Arab bureaucracy.

In the West Bank, for example, Jordanian law remained in effect and local bureaucrats attended to most civic matters and often stayed on the payroll of the Jordanian government. Jordanian currency continued to be legal tender. Jordanian school curriculum was employed in the schools — with Israel even allowing the continued use of some school texts only partially expurgated of virulently anti-Israel and indeed frankly anti-Semitic material — and was taught by Jordanian-paid teachers. Jordan River bridges were opened by agreement of Israel and Jordan to facilitate contacts between residents of the territories and the wider Arab world. The Temple Mount was left under the control of the Moslem Waqf headed by a Jordanian-appointed mufti. These measures were adopted with the aim of minimizing friction, demonstrating Israel's willingness to negotiate a return of most of the territory to Arab sovereignty, and, it was hoped, facilitating negotiations and peace.

Other steps taken by Israel were intended to decrease friction and smooth relations by improving the quality of life in the territories. Among those steps were enlargement of the electrical grid and its extension to areas of the territories, including many villages, that had been without electricity; improvement in schooling; establishment of a modern health system; and modernization of the water system, with provision of running water to regions of the territories previously dependent on well water.

Of course, none of this changed the reality that the Palestinian Arabs were living in political limbo, with few political rights. While one can note that the population had not had any greater political rights under the Jordanian government or, in Gaza, under Egypt, and that indeed populations throughout the Arab world typically enjoyed no greater political rights, the political limbo in which the Palestinian Arabs were now living was not viewed by either them or Israel as a desirable situation. On the other hand, Israel believed, and the United Nations affirmed, that the status quo should be changed only in the context of negotiations on the basis of Security Council Resolution 242, which in turn required the appearance of as yet absent Arab interlocutors.

Moreover, the steps taken by the Israeli government to ameliorate the living conditions of the Palestinian Arabs while they remained under Israeli jurisdiction reflected an Israeli administrative regimen very different from its typical characterization by Arab voices and those of the Arabs' allies. According to Hanan Ashwari, for example, in a speech at the infamous Conference Against Racism in Durban, South Africa, in August, 2001, "Those of us who came under Israeli occupation in 1967 have languished in the West Bank, Jerusalem, and the Gaza Strip under a unique combination of military occupation, settler colonization, and systematic oppression. Rarely has the human mind devised such varied, diverse, and comprehensive means of wholesale brutalization and persecution."[23] Of course, Arab voices, and their European, and indeed Israeli, sympathizers have not hesitated to compare Israeli policies in the territories even to Nazi policies and conditions of Nazi occupation. Yet the facts tell a very different story.

For example, after dramatic growth in the number of school classes in the territories during the Israeli presence, by the early 1990s illiteracy had dropped to 14 percent of adults over fifteen (compared to 69 percent in Morocco, 61 percent in Egypt, 45 percent in Tunisia, and 44 percent in Syria). Per capita GNP grew between 1968 and 1991 from $165 to $1,715 (compared to $1,440 in Tunisia, $1,050 in Jordan, and $600 in Egypt). Life expectancy rose from 48 in 1967 to 72 in 2000 (compared to an average of 68 in 2000 for all of the Middle East and North Africa). Infant mortality dropped under Israeli health programs from 60 per 1,000 live births in 1968 to 15 per 1,000 lives births in 2000 (compared to 40 in Egypt, 23 in Jordan and 22 in Syria), and Israeli inoculation programs eradicated polio, whooping cough, tetanus, and measles. The percent of the population with round-the-clock electricity expanded from 20.5 percent in 1967 to 92.8 percent in 1986. The percent of Arabs in the territories with running water in their homes increased from 16 percent in 1967 to 85 percent in 1986. Possession of electric or gas ranges for cooking rose from 4 percent in 1967 to 83.5 percent in 1986. There were comparable increases in ownership of refrigerators, televisions, and automobiles.[24]

The worst living conditions among the Palestinians at the time of Israel's entry into the territories were those of Palestinians living in the refugee camps. This was particularly so in Gaza, where the camps housed a much larger proportion of the total Palestinian population than in the West Bank and where the Egyptians had allowed no electricity or running water in the camps and forbade residents to work outside the camps. Under Israeli administration, camp residents, as well as the general population, had virtually universal access to employment, as even the UNRWA, invariably hostile to Israel, acknowledged: "If it were possible for the Agency to investigate need properly, it seems reasonable to suppose that many refugee families in . . . the West Bank and the Gaza Strip, where full or virtually full employment prevails . . . would be transferred from R category (eligible for all services) to N category (not eligible)."[25]

The Israelis also sought to alleviate the squalid living conditions in the camps. They built new housing units outside the camps for residents and also provided building lots, infrastructure, and subsidies for those who wished to build their own houses, with, in either case, ownership being transferred to the residents. By 1983, over 3,000 Palestinian families had moved into Israeli-built houses and about 3,500 families had moved into houses they had built themselves on lots prepared and provided by Israel.

It is noteworthy, however, that the PLO and the Arab states vehemently opposed these housing programs, perceiving the provision of better living conditions to the refugees and their descendants as undercutting both the push for these people's return to Israel and the efforts to recruit them into PLO cadres. In addition, various arms of the UN embraced the Arab stance. In 1985, shortly after Israel opened up new housing constructed with support from the Catholic Relief Agency, the UN General Assembly passed a resolution condemning Israel's efforts to relocate refugees to better housing as a violation of the refugees' "right of return" to their former areas of residence in pre-1967 Israel.[26]

Whatever the difficulties in terms of political limitations endured by the occupants of the territories, it obviously requires a particularly ugly anti-Israel animus to proclaim the conditions of life under the Israelis comparable to a Nazi occupation.

The Israelis also, early in their administration of the West Bank, had explored the possibility of themselves setting up a Palestinian Arab government in the area that might ultimately achieve independence in some sort of alliance with Israel. In the summer of 1967, government officials interviewed eighty-eight West Bank notables for their views on the pursuit of such a plan. But there was little agreement among the interviewees and, in the face of opposition particularly from militantly rejectionist Palestinian forces outside the territories, the effort came to nothing.[27]

During the immediate postwar years, the Israeli government established some settlements in the West Bank, in locations consistent with the Allon Plan's designation of strategic areas vital for Israel to retain in order not to recreate that pre-1967 vulnerability acknowledged by the drafters of Security Council Resolution 242. Beyond this, Israel essentially waited for Arab interlocutors with whom it could negotiate. Meanwhile, public opinion on how to deal with the territories that had fallen to Israel in the war varied widely and in significant ways cut across traditional party lines.

Among some acolytes of Buber and his circle, Israel's control over the West

Bank and Gaza triggered a renewed militating for a "binational state," a single entity encompassing all of the area west of the Jordan and stripped of any formal Jewish identity. Such a state would be stripped as well, of course, of the Law of Return, the Israeli legislation allowing Jews to come to Israel virtually at will and receive immediate Israeli citizenship. The PLO charter likewise demanded a single state west of the Jordan, insisting not only on the annihilation of Israel but also — as its charter spelled out — the return to Europe and elsewhere of all Jews who had immigrated to Palestine since 1917 (the date of the Balfour Declaration) together with their descendants. PLO operatives and spokespeople now often echoed the binationalists' calls for one "democratic" state spanning all of western Palestine and downplayed for Western audiences their demand for the departure of most of Israel's citizens and their calls made elsewhere for establishment of an "Islamic republic" in Palestine.

But very few Israelis, even within socialist Labor circles, embraced the concept of binationalism, just as few had done so during the Mandate. The general assumption even on the far Left was that the Palestinian Arabs would eventually follow a separate national course, perhaps again as part of Jordan, at least half of whose population consisted of families that had moved to Jordan from western Palestine between 1947 and 1967.

In contrast to the few "binationalists," there arose in the wake of the war a more popular Land of Israel Movement, which advocated retention by Israel of all the captured territories and which drew its leadership mainly from Labor Zionist ranks. The demands to retain the Sinai, or at least part of it, and the Golan, were based mainly on security considerations. Many also saw retention of the West Bank and Gaza as a strategic necessity; supporters of the Land of Israel Movement argued that while an Allon Plan-type arrangement might gain Israel a defensible border along the Jordan River, the enclave on the West Bank that would be returned to Arab sovereignty would still present a potentially catastrophic threat. But some within the Movement also argued, with regard particularly to the West Bank, that a basic tenet of Zionism was a return to the Jews' ancestral home as the foundation for building the Jewish state and that it would be unconscionable for Israel to give up not only a part of that ancestral home of which it had now gained control but indeed the places historically and religiously most significant to Jews — Hebron, Rachel's Tomb near Bethlehem, Shechem, and other locations like them.

But while some Laborites in government posts shared at least in part the views of the Land of Israel Movement, the unofficial policy of the Labor Party, and therefore the government, remained to seek a settlement in the West Bank along the lines of the Allon Plan. A fundamental consideration was, of course, the demographics, the presence of a large Palestinian Arab population that most of the party leadership believed Israel could not and should not absorb. (The government also continued to anticipate a territorial compromise in Sinai, even though the peninsula was unpopulated, as strategic considerations offered latitude for compromise there. With regard to the Golan, the government continued to view the potential for returning any of the plateau as narrowly circumscribed by strategic necessity.)

The Gahal Party, while in the government, did not forcefully advocate a separate policy. But during and after its participation in the government, much of its leadership was sympathetic to the Land of Israel Movement. Many leaders of the political Right tended, however, to be more forthcoming than Labor leaders with regard to prospective concessions in the Sinai, largely because the Sinai had not been part of Mandate Palestine nor did it have the same religious-historical significance as the West Bank.

The religious parties in Israel varied widely in their perspectives on disposition of the territories. Non-Zionist parties were indifferent or hostile to retention of the captured areas. The National Religious Party, which left the government coalition in 1970, split over the issue. Some of its former echelons supported the Land of Israel Movement while others aligned themselves with the opposite end of the spectrum, joining the Peace Movement, which also emerged in the wake of the 1967 war.

The Peace Movement was more an umbrella of disparate groups with different perspectives, less unified than the Land of Israel Movement. The common thread was advocacy of a return of all, or almost all, the captured territories and conviction that embracing and pursuing that step were the key to attaining the peace that still eluded Israel. Some in the Peace Movement, typically people associated with the old hard-core ideological Left, or the New Left, or old academic anti-Zionists who were not advocates of binationalism, saw Israel as the source of the conflict and wanted the government to return all the captured land as an act of atonement. Also, since it was Zionism in their view that was an affront to the Arabs and aroused their hatred, they often argued as well for stripping the state of its Jewish and Zionist accoutrements — revoking, for example, the Law of Return. Others perceived Israel as the victimized target of Arab aggression but maintained that Israel ought to show itself to be a special state unlike other states by being fully forthcoming with regard to disposition of the territories. They were generally convinced that this gesture would win peace.

Some of those involved with the Peace Movement were dissatisfied with Israel insisting on Arab interlocutors coming forward and wanted the government not just to offer to withdraw from all the captured areas but to do so unilaterally. Some advocates of this position militated for Israel to set up a Palestinian state in the West Bank and Gaza, while others feared such a state would be a source of instability and danger and proposed that the government take unilateral steps to return at least the West Bank to Jordan.

Other groups prominent in the ranks of the Peace Movement, in addition to hard-core leftists, and academics of both the ideological anti-Zionist and the radical accommodationist mold, were artists, journalists, writers, and students. Members of these latter groups were almost invariably university-educated, and the students, of course, were presently in university, and their views at least in part reflected the influence of the academic critics of the state. Another potential factor in shaping the views of circles associated with the Peace Movement, a factor discussed by various writers, is what has been characterized as the particular sensitivity of these circles to reference groups outside of Israel, reference groups whose own political predilections would strongly incline them to favor the politics of the Peace Movement.

Rael Jean Isaac, in discussing the influence of reference groups, notes that academics, artists, writers, journalists, and students "are particularly open to the communication channels built up by associational rather than communal structures . . . Those in the intellectual and artistic professions in a country like Israel, at once small and seeking Western standards of excellence, inevitably turned to the intellectual and artistic world of Europe and the United States for styles and fashions"[28]; and the political fashion of that world in Europe and America was very much in the mode of the Peace Movement. (The ideological Left in Israel was likewise sensitive, one might say exquisitely sensitive, to the views of its ideological colleagues in Europe and elsewhere, and of course that sensitivity would again have weighed strongly toward criticism of the Israeli government and support for the Peace Movement.)

Perhaps the influence of professional reference groups outside Israel was indeed substantial for many supporters of the Peace Movement. But however much an artist or writer or university professor might turn for professional standards and professional fellowship to colleagues outside the country, for him to take his political cues as well from those sources, rather than from an assessment independent of such influences, still entails a choice. It requires that, in the face of the real struggles confronting Israel, one choose to waive independent assessment and value professional identity above communal identity; it involves the person's choosing to disconnect himself in this regard from the community in the face of the siege.

The common assumption among those drawn to the Peace Movement, that peace could be had if the nation would only make the accommodations they recommended, was a conviction essentially unsupported by evidence. On the contrary, there were very strong indications that the Arab states were unprepared to offer Israel a comprehensive peace even in exchange for full return of the captured territories. The "three no's" of Khartoum were a blanket rejection of recognition and peace, not an offer of peace in exchange for complete Israeli withdrawal and rejection of peace if Israel balked at these terms.

Moreover, there were many indications that perpetuating the state of war with Israel served the interests of Arab regimes in terms of both their domestic politics and their jockeying with other Arab governments, and that these regimes did not perceive the potential gains of peace with Israel, even the retrieval of territory, as worth foregoing the benefits of the state of war. The scenario envisioned by the followers of the Peace Movement, that if Israel only demonstrated sufficient generosity and goodwill, the Arabs would be obliged to acknowledge that goodwill and reconcile themselves to Israel's existence, was a scenario to which its adherents clung in defiance of, rather than in response to, any evidence-based assessment of Arab attitudes and aspirations.

By the Peace Movement's own reckoning during this period, it had the support of only 5 percent of Israelis, and most of that support was for the proposals of its most cautious and moderate voices.[29]

Although opinion polls are notoriously difficult to interpret, and results are very much influenced by the framing of questions, polls of Israeli opinion regarding the captured territories in the period 1967 to 1973 do reveal consistent patterns.[30] A huge majority of Israelis, in excess of 90 percent, consistently opposed return of the Golan Heights. This seems to have reflected the political and military echelons' stance regarding the Golan and also people's memory of attacks from the Golan, both of which underscored the strategic importance of retaining the area. The public held similar views of Sharm el-Sheikh in the Sinai (Egyptian blockade of Eilat via Sharm el-Sheikh was a *causus belli* in both the 1956 and 1967 wars), although a majority of Israelis was amenable to territorial compromise in the Sinai. This was again consistent with the position of most of the political leadership. People generally believed that a territorial compromise that yielded an effective disengagement even short of full peace might be feasible in the Sinai since the territorial expanse was such that, should Egypt embark on a new military campaign, Israel would still have time to mobilize, as it did in 1967.

As to the West Bank and Gaza, very large majorities supported retaining at least most of these areas, but fewer Israelis favored keeping control of them in their entirety than favored doing so with the Golan or Sharm el-Sheikh. This reflected on the one hand a response to the strategic, historic, and religious significance of these areas and, on the other hand, a sensitivity to the demographic issues and the desirability of ultimately relinquishing control of heavily populated regions in any future settlement.

In the years immediately following the 1967 war, the Israeli government established significant contacts with the Jordanian regime. (As King Hussein himself acknowledged, he had ordered the initiation of hostilities against Israel at the start of the war and had continued to pursue his attack even though Israel urged him to remain out of the conflict and promised it would refrain from action against him if he did so. Israel nevertheless, in the wake of the war, supported Hussein's maintaining involvement in the affairs of the West Bank.[31]) These contacts were not only on the level of the myriad Jordanian officials who lived and worked in the West Bank and others who regularly traveled back and forth between Jordan and the territory but also entailed the highest echelons of the two governments. But Jordan balked at negotiating a territorial compromise along the lines envisioned in the Allon Plan. Indeed it is likely that Jordan would have demurred even if Israel had offered to return the entire West Bank in exchange for peace, as King Hussein clearly regarded a separate peace with Israel as too much of a risk, a step that would place him too far at odds with the Arab consensus and would invite potentially devastating Arab retribution.

There were also informal contacts with Egypt during these years, although less consistent and much cooler than those with Jordan. Some were initiated by Egypt, some by Israel, and all did little to thaw relations between the two countries.

The 1973 Yom Kippur War, launched in a surprise attack by Syria and Egypt, caught Israel largely unprepared and, while the country's forces ultimately recovered and gained the upper hand in the fighting, cost nearly three thousand Israeli dead. The war was followed by much soul-searching and recrimination about Israel's lack of readiness. Confidence in the government dropped significantly, and basic confidence in the country's security and prospects for the future also decreased. But there appears to have been relatively little shift in attitudes toward the territories, with the various camps interpreting the war in ways that reinforced their earlier perspectives.[32]

Those generally against territorial concessions looked at the war as a continuation of the Arab campaign of annihilation against Israel. The Egyptians might claim that they only wanted to push Israel back from the Canal and trigger international intervention and pressure on Israel to negotiate a withdrawal from the Sinai; but Israel had indicated earlier it was prepared to offer a unilateral withdrawal from the Canal as a prelude to bilateral talks. As to Syria's war aims, they clearly went beyond regaining the Golan and included sweeping into the Galilee and the heart of Israel, and many Israelis argued that, particularly given the precarious state of Israel's predicament at the start of the war, the same assault from the pre-1967 boundary with Syria would likely have led to the country's annihilation. The war therefore underscored the need to maintain defensible buffer zones.

Some in this camp also argued that the complacency in the military that contributed to Israel's being taken by surprise and suffering its initial disasters was not simply a matter of overestimates of Israeli military strength. They maintained that it also reflected a politicization of the military leadership, many of whose members were from kibbutzim and whose ranks were overwhelmingly affiliated with the Israeli Left. The general staff, in this view, had been influenced by Peace Movement arguments that the initiative was all Israel's, that Arab hostility was reactive and circumscribed, and that that hostility could be resolved by the right package of concessions and sufficient demonstration of Israeli good-will.

In contrast, for those in the Peace Movement and their supporters, it was Israel's failure to make sufficient offers of concessions — or, as many of their number advocated, to undertake concessions unilaterally, even without Arab in-terlocutors — that had heightened Arab frustration and led to the war, and so the war demonstrated the rightness of their arguments.

If the war largely reinforced people's prior opinions vis-à-vis the territories, it changed opinion in terms of a real increase in pessimism in the war's wake. Eighteen thousand people left Israel in 1974, the highest number since the War of Independence, and immigration dropped precipitously.[33] A postwar poll showed that 83 percent of Israelis expected another war in one to two years.[34] *Davar*, the Labor Party newspaper, ran an article arguing that Jews were giving too much weight to Zionism and that Judaism could survive without the state.[35]

This pessimism appears to have translated into a leftward shift within the Peace Movement and in left-wing ranks generally. A greater number of Israelis now questioned the legitimacy of the Zionist enterprise. More significant in terms of numbers was the evolution of that political and "academic" writing, art, and literature that in the preceding decades — largely under the influence of the anti-Zionist academics — had promoted anti-state views. Its creators had chafed at the burden of Jewish history and identity in Israel, had cast it as con-fining, deforming, diminishing, and potentially killing, and had advocated lib-eration from all that. Their message now found new purveyors and new sympathetic audiences. This was so even if those new admirers were generally unprepared to reject entirely the state, or Zionism, or to see the Arabs as the abused victims and the Jews as victimizers, as some of the academics, artists, and writers chose to see them. But even as many in Israel were dispirited by the war and by the failures and ongoing threats that it revealed, those who conse-quently felt their nation an intolerable burden or embraced Arab indictments or believed that dramatic unilateral Israeli concessions and demonstrations of goodwill would assure peace were still a minority even within socialist Labor circles.

In a poll of public opinion a year after the war, 75 percent of Israelis sup-ported increased Jewish settlement in the West Bank, while a poll commissioned by *Haaretz* some months later indicated nearly half of Israelis were prepared to return virtually to the pre-1967 borders in exchange for peace.[36] Although these results seem to demonstrate that Israelis were voicing inconsistent opinions, they actually do not, but they do illustrate other points. The question regarding peace was cast in ideal terms: What would you give up for genuine peace? In fact, the vast majority of Israelis saw absolutely no prospect for such a peace in the real world. The maximum that seemed attainable out of negotiations — and the population overwhelmingly supported negotiations — was an armed "peace" with some mutually agreed upon steps toward enforcement but with hostilities ever looming. Those hostilities could potentially be sparked by new perceptions of Israeli vulnerability by the "peacemaking" Arab regimes, or by new pressures on those regimes leading them to change policies, or by change in the leadership of these generally unstable, certainly undemocratic nations, with successor regimes not feeling obliged to adhere to the policies of their predecessors. The overwhelming consensus among Israelis was, therefore, that any "peace" would require vigilance and security measures and defensible borders, elements that might be foregone in an ideal world.

But the "peace" question in the *Haaretz* poll also reveals the perspective of the Peace Movement, with which the staff and management of *Haaretz* generally sympathized and identified: That genuine peace was attainable were Israel prepared to make sufficient concessions to win it. The question was formulated by the newspaper to demonstrate underlying support for the Peace Movement demands for greater Israeli concessions, while the dissonance between the two polls indicated that the majority of Israelis, including those in the Labor Zionist camp, comprehended the question as representing a utopian ideal divorced from the realities of Israel's predicament.[37]

ELEVEN

Demonizing the "Other Israel," 1977–1988

Itzhak Ben Aharon, former Labor Member of Knesset and head of the Histadrut Labor Federation, on the election of Israel's first non-Labor Zionist government, June, 1977: "The results are a mistake."
Television interviewer: "But Mr. Ben Aharon, this is a democracy and the people have spoken."
Ben Aharon: "The people are wrong."[1]

An event that in many respects initiated a much more profound shift in opinion within Labor Zionist ranks than the Yom Kippur War occurred four years after the war. This was the election of June, 1977, and the formation of the first non-Labor Zionist government in Israel's history, under the premiership of Menachem Begin.

Various factors contributed to Begin's victory. Labor Zionist leaders, who had formed a number of unifying as well as splinter dissident political parties since the establishment of the state and most of whom in recent years had run under the umbrella of a unifying Labor Coalition, were still tainted by the trauma of the Yom Kippur War and the intelligence failures and lack of preparedness that had preceded it. Public confidence in Labor was further eroded by a skein of revelations of malfeasance involving Labor figures, abuses of power of a sort that are perhaps inevitable when one party has governed for thirty years. These scandals included, in the two years before the election, the suicide of the housing minister, who was being investigated for allegedly embezzling Labor Party funds, indictment of the head of the Histadrut health insurance plan on bribery charges, conviction of the former manager of the state oil corporation on embezzlement charges, indictment of a former head of the state-run Israel Corporation for embezzlement of corporation funds, indictment of the director of customs for illegally waiving customs fees of business friends, arrest of a high official of the Bank of Israel for illegal activity related to his office, and disclosure that Prime Minister Rabin's wife was maintaining an illegal overseas bank account.[2]

Some observers have argued that the perception, widely held since the 1973 war, that any peace with the Arabs was likely far off may also have figured in Labor's election defeat. They note that widespread grievances with domestic government policies had existed for years, but there had also been a popular sentiment that Labor, with its vision of territorial concessions in exchange for peace arrangements with Jordan and Egypt, was the party best equipped to pursue negotiations and achieve a resolution of the conflict, at least with these neighboring countries. According to this argument, as such negotiations and resolution appeared ever more remote, some of the electorate became more prepared than previously to vote their domestic grievances and against Labor.

(A variation on this view involves American President Jimmy Carter. Some people have pointed to Prime Minister Rabin's visit with Carter in Washington in March, 1977, at which Carter essentially rejected Labor's stance regarding territorial compromise as a foundation for negotiations. They have suggested that this contributed to Israeli public perception that the Labor formula for peace had no hope of making progress and so helped undermine Labor's position with the electorate.[3])

But the biggest single factor in Labor's defeat was that a large percentage of Israel's majority Sephardic population rallied to Begin. These were Jews who had come to Israel as refugees mainly from Arab countries. Many of them and their descendants believed they had always been patronized and treated with disdain by the European Jews who made up the country's ruling Labor Zionist elite. Certainly they had been settled in disproportionate numbers in "frontier" towns away from the nation's metropolitan core, in areas that were chronically short-changed in terms of educational resources, employment opportunities, and government investment generally. Many of them, together with their children and grandchildren, now expressed their resentment at the ballot box.

The children and grandchildren of the country's socialist Zionist elite, and devotees of Labor Zionism more generally, widely perceived the defeat as more than an election reversal. They saw it as a national catastrophe. It seemed the fruition of what so many of the Labor Zionist pioneers had most feared: the overwhelming of the great socialist experiment by an influx of Jews too religious and too bourgeois. Indeed, Laborite hostility was directed no less at Begin and his supporters of European origin, often descendants of early nonsocialist Zionist immigrants, than at the Sephardim. The former were often religiously observant and were indicted for their religiosity and their nonsocialist predilections in much the same way as the Sephardi were.

The tenor of some of the extreme response by the Left to the election results was captured in remarks made on Israeli television the night of the election by Itzhak Ben Aharon, a former Labor Member of Knesset and former head of the Histadrut Labor Federation. Ben Aharon declared to his interviewer, "The [election] results are a mistake." When the interviewer noted, "But Mr. Ben

Aharon, this is a democracy and the people have spoken," his interlocutor responded: "The people are wrong."[4] Ben Aharon was also quoted as saying, "The country won't take this lying down."[5]

Shulamit Aloni, founder of the Civil Rights Movement party and head of its small Knesset faction, declared that the election results demonstrated the nation had become "less rational, more nationalistic, more mystical, less governed by common sense." Nor was she alone on the Left when she concluded that one consequence of the election was that "war is at the gate."[6]

The hostility voiced by elements of the Left toward Likud's constituency reflected not only the anti-capitalist and anti-religious parochialism of much of the Left and its disagreements with the prevailing views of the Likud constituency vis-à-vis the territories and issues related to the siege. That hostility also entailed a long-standing pattern of frankly bigoted attitudes toward the Sephardim. It is worth noting in this regard the discrepancy between concerns expressed by voices on the Left with respect to the problems faced by Israeli Arabs versus their very different response to the problems of the Sephardim.

Many on the Israeli Left had long been attentive to the difficulties confronted by Israel's Arab citizens (a separate group, of course, from the Arab residents of the territories acquired in the 1967 war, who were not Israeli citizens). They pointed, for example, to the funding of Arab village and town services at a lower level than that of other jurisdictions in the country. Indeed, some critics construed this lower level of government support not simply as a public practice that had to be redressed but as additional evidence of the essential evil of the Zionist endeavor.

(In fact, various observers have noted that the residents of the Arab villages and municipalities have been, since the founding of the state, essentially non-compliant in property tax payments to the government, with commonly under 30 percent of taxes due collected. In 1999 in Um El Fahum, for example, just over 27 percent of residents paid their property taxes. This compares to in excess of 80 percent property tax compliance overall in the nation. All Israeli governments have tolerated this state of affairs for the sake of domestic tranquility. Consequently, according to such arguments, the payment of revenues by the government to Arab municipalities and villages, even when lower on a per capita basis [that is, per municipal or village resident] than revenues to predominantly Jewish jurisdictions, is actually much higher than payments to Jewish municipalities and villages if calculated as the ratio of per capita government payment to per capita revenue collected from residents. Moreover, payments by the government to Arab villages and municipalities have at times exceeded payments to the Jewish sector. In 1999, for example, Arab town councils, whose constituents represented 10.4 percent of Israel's population, received 24.3 percent of the total allocations to local councils throughout Israel.[7])

(On the broader economic conditions of the Israeli Arab community, recent statistics point to a dramatic narrowing of the gap in standard of living between Israeli Arabs and Israeli Jews. Even some prominent voices on the Israeli Left, such as Amnon Rubinstein, stalwart of the left-of-Labor Meretz Party, have cited this evidence as giving the lie to claims by ideologues of the Left that Israeli institutions confine the Arab community to the status of a permanent underclass.[8])

But the inequitably low provision of government services and support to the towns whose populations were predominantly Sephardic was typically not of interest to these left-wing critics of the government, presumably because it did not serve their ideological arguments. While one might have expected such critics' socialist egalitarian predilections to have led them to sympathize with the rebellion of the Sephardim against the government's seemingly discriminatory treatment, that rebellion failed to evoke any such response. Instead, it elicited condemnation, often, again, in the harshest and crudest terms.

Amos Oz provided some of the most vitriolic responses to the 1977 election. Virtually from the end of the 1967 war, Oz had opposed any Israeli territorial claims on the West Bank, whether those advocated by the Land of Israel Movement or those envisioned by the Allon Plan and whether based on security or religious-historical considerations. He had, of course, no sympathy for the views of the Right vis-à-vis the territories. But his animus toward Likud's supporters went beyond this. For he also embraced the perspective held by many of the old Labor Zionist pioneers and expressed by Buber that the Right's religious and bourgeois constituency had prevented Israel from realizing its socialist ideals: "Why didn't Israel develop as the most egalitarian and creative social democratic society in the world? I would say that one of the major factors was the mass immigration of Holocaust survivors, Middle Eastern Jews and nonsocialist even anti-socialist Zionists who ached for 'normalization.'"[9]

With his various resentments of the Likud constituency, Oz declared in the wake of the election: "Evil days are upon us . . . [The] petit bourgeosie [credo] . . . will become the official doctrine: 'Catch as catch can.' This will now be accompanied increasingly by the tom-tom beat of latent, cultic tribalism, blood and soil, intoxicating slogans, Betar [the pre-state Revisionist youth movement] and Masada . . . the variety of wars of purity and impurity, fanaticism with dark fears, suppression of reason in the name of exhilarating visions . . . "[10]

Oz actually suggested that Labor youth ought to arm themselves to fight the Likud in the streets. "If, indeed, the Likud-NRP government encourages the growth of the Gush Emunim [religious settler movement] in paramilitary form — sort of falanges with weapons arsenals and staffs and communications equipment — then our youth movement will have to respond to this frightening challenge." Oz went on: "If the Likud starts silencing 'defeatists,' if they purge the [state-controlled] radio and television of 'troublers of Israel' and 'morale destroyers' — we shall have to react in the manner of a fighting workers' movement: in the streets . . . "[11]

But more consequential among the reverberations of the 1977 election than the release of leftist vitriol was a change in the impact of some of the arguments of the ideological Left on the broader Israeli public.

The internationalist, anti-Zionist academics were inclined, of course, to comprehend Arab hostility, its eruptions into wars against Israel, and the absence of moves toward peace, as Israel's fault and the fault of Zionism. Their acolytes among Israeli teachers, artists, writers, and others were likewise inclined to view the perpetuation of hostilities as somehow Israel's, and Zionism's, fault. But prior to 1977 these views were not shared far beyond some very limited circles, mainly within the academic and artistic elites.

There were also people within the Peace Movement who, like Oz, regarded themselves as Zionists but, often at least in part under the influence of the anti-Zionist academics, believed Israel was not being forthcoming enough in concessions toward the Arabs, was being too narrow and nationalistic and atavistically attached to the land. They argued that Israel should be prepared to return virtually to its pre-1967 borders and that doing so would inexorably elicit peace. But such people likewise represented a very small portion of the population.

Even among those in the broader public with socialist Labor sympathies, the perspective was typically that the Labor-dominated governments since 1967 were prepared for a fair peace but that there were no Arab interlocutors with whom Labor could negotiate such a peace, that Arab leaders still found it more politically expedient to perpetuate the war against Israel. If some Israelis had been so disheartened by the 1973 war that they had lost hope of the conflict being resolved and were pushed by their pessimism to embrace Arab indictments and look to Israeli self-reform as the only hope, this was still the response of a relatively small minority.

But the election of 1977 resulted in a situation in which many of those in the broader public with Labor Zionist roots and sympathies viewed the government as now in the hands of people they regarded as alien "others," elected by a constituency of alien "others." This opened the way to Labor supporters being more receptive to arguments blaming Israel for perpetuation of the conflict with the Arabs. The election, in fact, had no real impact on Arab policy toward Israel and provided no objective reason for anyone to reevaluate earlier assessments of the conflict and what drove it. But the emergence of an Israeli government from which these people felt alienated made it progressively easier for them to respond to the ongoing, seemingly intractable, war by placing the onus for continuation of the conflict on Israeli government policy.

Was there a change in Israeli policy by the new government? To be sure, many in the leadership ranks of Begin's Likud Party, and in the party as a whole, were critical of Labor preparedness to return much of the West Bank to Arab sovereignty. (Likud had been formed in 1973 by the merger of Gahal with several small parties on the Right and had subsequently been embraced by a number of those Laborites who were associated with the Land of Israel Movement.) They opposed this Labor stance for both strategic reasons, as representing too great a danger to Israel's security, and religious-ideological reasons, as entailing an intolerable retreat from key Jewish religious sites and the heart of Biblical Eretz Israel.

The Likud platform evolved into advocating that future negotiations regarding the West Bank be pursued on the basis of establishing Palestinian Arab autonomy under Israeli sovereignty rather than ceding the areas that Labor had been prepared to cede. Certainly this represented a policy change, and one could argue, whether correctly or incorrectly, that at some future point at which the Arab side became prepared to negotiate peace, this Likud stance would make achieving a resolution of the conflict more difficult than it would be under Labor policy.

But there had been over the previous decade no interlocutor among the Arabs for negotiations and an agreement of the sort endorsed by Labor. Indeed, such an agreement was becoming in important ways more unlikely. For example, the Arab League in 1974 declared the PLO the only representative of the Palestinian people, rendering Labor's plan of a territory-for-peace deal with Jordan increasingly remote. Consequently, claims generated on the ideological fringe of the Labor Party that peace was being blocked by Likud extremism and intransigence had no real basis in fact. But such claims now won ever widening acceptance among Labor sympathizers. It did so both because they were eager to believe, in the face of persistence of the Arab siege, that peace was attainable, and because they viewed the new government and its policies as separate and alien from themselves and so were more prepared to indict it.

In reality, autonomy versus Arab sovereignty for populated areas was not as much a divide between Labor and Likud supporters as widely presented, and the gap would likely have shrunk further in the event of actual negotiations. Polls of Likud voters have consistently indicated overwhelming concern with security as compared to religious-historical considerations, the same priority as Labor supporters. When, in a 1984 poll, Israelis who favored Likud's position of autonomy for the territories were asked whether, were autonomy impossible, they would prefer annexation or territorial compromise, 52 percent chose the latter and only 10 percent annexation. When asked if they would agree to territorial concessions in the context of a full peace agreement with Jordan — essentially Labor's position — two-thirds said they would.[12]

A major factor in the alienation and distaste felt by so many Labor stalwarts toward Likud and its supporters, both Sephardi and Ashkenazi, was, again, the anti-religious sentiment so long ingrained in Labor Zionism and the jaundiced and generally negative views held by its followers toward the religious traditionalism of much of Likud's constituency. This religious divide also had an impact on Labor-Likud differences vis-à-vis territory captured in 1967. Likud's greater interest in retaining sites of religious significance did figure substantially in its preference for negotiating Arab autonomy under Israeli sovereignty in the West Bank rather than ceding areas there to Arab sovereignty. This sentiment led to arguments from the Left that the religious traditionalism of Likud and its followers and religious claims to West Bank sites were another obstacle to peace. But these arguments were overstated for several reasons.

The capture of eastern Jerusalem and the West Bank from Jordan in 1967 placed under Jewish control for the first time in nearly two thousand years not only the Temple Mount, Judaism's holiest site, but those areas that were the heart of Biblical Israel and Judah and the scene of many of the chapters of Jewish history discussed in the Bible. This development struck a chord in both religious and many "secular" Zionists. Over the ensuing decades, as Labor governments established settlements in those parts of the West Bank that they believed were strategically necessary for Israel to retain in the context of peace agreements, they drew upon the sense of connection with these areas felt by many within both the religious and secular communities in recruiting for building and populating the settlements. It would have been curious had they done otherwise, as the leaders of those Labor governments were in large part followers of Ben-Gurion, whose conviction it was that the validity of the Zionist enterprise was rooted in the Jews' historical and spiritual connection with Eretz Israel.

After 1977 the Likud government did allow greater latitude for the establishment of settlements at Biblical sites close to Arab population centers in the West Bank. This was something that Labor had generally eschewed with a view toward returning those locations to Arab sovereignty in the context of a negotiated peace, and Likud came under attack for thereby creating additional obstacles to peace. But, of course, there was still no partner for peace, whether on Labor's terms or Likud's. Moreover, Likud's change in settlement policy was largely a difference of degree rather than of kind.

For example, in 1968 a group of religious Jews had moved into temporary quarters in Hebron, where essentially no Jews had lived since the Arab massacre of 1929 and the British evacuation of the survivors. Those who went there in 1968 had done so with the intention of reviving the community in what is the second most sacred city in Judaism and establishing a presence near the religiously revered Tomb of the Patriarchs. The response in the Labor Zionist leadership had been mixed. Some, including Dayan at the time, saw the move as simply creating friction. Deputy Prime Minister Yigal Allon, a Labor Zionist although not then a member of the Labor Party, supported their presence, even though Hebron, as a populated Arab area, was not part of the land that Israel was to retain according to his peace plan. A number of Labor leaders felt that Jews should not be stopped from living in areas that they supported returning to Arab sovereignty, just as there were large numbers of Arabs living in Israel.

In 1970, Allon won approval for the Jews in Hebron to establish the new town of Kiryat Arba just east of the city.

In 1974, in the wake of the Yom Kippur War, a group of mainly young religious Israelis from the ranks of the National Religious Party (which, as noted, was split on the territorial issue) broke away from the party and established Gush Emunim, dedicated to aggressive settlement of Judea and Samaria. Over the next three years, prior to the Likud victory of 1977, the group succeeded in establishing settlements near Ramallah (Ofra) and Nablus (Kadumim) and another just east of Jerusalem (Maale Adumim). Only the last was consistent with Labor visions of territory Israel would need to retain. Yet the Labor government acquiesced to all three. Dayan, reflecting an important strain in Labor opinion, had urged in 1969 the establishment of urban settlements near Ramallah, Jenin, Nablus, and Hebron.[13]

It is, again, also noteworthy that Likud supporters, when asked about what criteria ought to guide government compromises in any future peace negotiations with the Arabs, joined their Labor compatriots in giving overwhelming emphasis to security-related, rather than religious-historical, considerations. Likewise significant is that Begin was prepared to dismantle settlements in the context of a peace agreement with Egypt and Israel's return of the Sinai. While some have argued that this was because those settlements had been established by Labor and were not at sites of religious importance, it is nevertheless true that doing so entailed reversing previously established policy regarding settlements when an opportunity was presented for a negotiated peace.

In effect, differences in policy between Likud and the preceding Labor governments regarding settlements were not as extreme as often portrayed. Of course, academics and the ideologues of the Left who questioned the Zionist enterprise, or at least put the onus on Israel and Jewish nationalism for the ongoing Arab-Israeli conflict, condemned the settlement policies of both parties and rejected security as well as religious-historical considerations as a legitimate basis for Israeli actions. But among the broader population of Labor Zionist adherents, there had been, during that postwar decade of Labor Party rule, wide endorsement of the view that security considerations required Israel to retain areas of key strategic importance even in the context of a peace agreement and that those areas ought to be settled. The ascension of a Likud government, however, rendered many of those same Labor supporters more receptive to the idea that government settlement policy was an untenable obstacle to peace and even to arguments, despite the absence of any viable Arab interlocutor for an agreement involving the West Bank and the Palestinian Arabs, that peace would be forthcoming were it not for Israeli state actions.

Other, similar shifts in Laborite attitudes toward government stances likewise followed the Likud victory, even though, again, those stances reflected no substantive change from the positions of previous governments. For example, the extreme rhetoric that had characterized anti-state, anti-Zionist ideologues, such as rhetoric comparing Israelis to Nazis because Israeli governments insisted on having an army and on fielding it when they believed the nation was threatened, had persisted into the years of statehood, and had been hurled with renewed enthusiasm by its devotees in the post-1967 context of Israel holding sway over an alien population. Both before and after the 1967 war such rhetoric had elicited wide public condemnation across the political spectrum. But even that extremism enjoyed a greater tolerance, at least was less universally condemned, within the ranks of Labor supporters when the government came into the hands of people outside the Labor Zionist fold. This was so even though policies affecting the day-to-day lives of the Palestinian Arabs remained essentially the same under the Likud government, as did Israel's military policies.

The changes in perspective in the Labor Zionist camp that followed the Likud victory could be seen very early on in aspects of the public's response to developments with Egypt. Those developments included Anwar Sadat's groundbreaking offer to Israel of a peace treaty in exchange for a full return of territories and acknowledgment of Arab "rights," his subsequent visit to Israel in November, 1977, and the negotiations that followed. Begin embraced Sadat's offer of negotiations toward peace and welcomed him to Jerusalem, and opinion throughout Israel anticipated the dawning of a new era. But much of the Zionist Labor camp was inclined to credit the breakthrough entirely to Sadat and to dismiss Begin's role. Likewise, when negotiations bogged down in the months after Sadat's visit, many on the Left chose to put the onus entirely on the Israeli government.

In March and April of 1978, some circles within the Labor Zionist camp began to articulate demands for rapid Israeli concessions and to stigmatize Israel as the obstacle to peace. The Peace Now organization was born in this context, as a broad association of old and new "peace" activists, the latter much more numerous, and was able to rally tens of thousands to anti-government demonstrations. The organization formulated tenets as common denominators with which all of its followers could agree. Among them were:

"The security of Israel depends on peace, not on territories . . .

"The government should reach peace with Egypt based on the principle of 'territories for peace' as determined by UN resolution 242 . . .

"Israel should stop all settlement in the occupied territories. Settlements are an impediment to peace and push the Arabs away from the negotiating table."14

There are a number of particularly notable aspects to these tenets. The government was, of course, negotiating on the basis of territories for peace, in keeping with UN Security Council Resolution 242. Why then did Peace Now make a point of this, unless it was really insisting that all territories be given up. That this was in fact the case is reinforced by the first item, which offers a false dichotomy. Indeed, the thinking in Labor since 1967 had been that peace required some retention of territory by Israel and that a return to the pre-1967 lines would be incompatible with peace. Similarly, settlements had been established by Labor because it deemed retaining the settled areas vital to achieving an enforceable peace. Peace Now was articulating a blanket condemnation of settlements, which placed it at odds with Labor's strategic assessments and long-standing Labor policy.

Why were these anti-Labor views gaining such support now, support of a sort they did not attain when Labor governments were in power? The change could not be ascribed to the shift in Egyptian policy, as Peace Now's tenets were not addressed simply, or even predominantly, to Israeli negotiating positions regarding the Sinai, and Sadat's initiative had altered nothing vis-à-vis the other administered territories. Egypt did put forward demands concerning the West Bank and Gaza but made clear it would not on its own negotiate over them, and Israel still had no other Arab interlocutors.

Despite the absence of any other Arab negotiating partners, the Peace Now view of the world was that the Arabs were ready to offer Israel peace if only Israel would give back all territories, and therefore Israeli refusal to do so was the chief obstacle to peace. The burgeoning popularity of this opinion on the Israeli Left was essentially another reaction by the Left to the government's now being in the hands of the "Other Israel."

Begin did succeed in negotiating a peace treaty with Sadat, and he gave up all of the Sinai, including settlements, to do so. But many on the Left chose to give credit for the accord entirely to Sadat and to charge Begin with having failed to attain a broader peace because of his eagerness to maintain Israeli control of the West Bank. Indeed, they accused Begin of having pursued the agreement with Egypt not because he wanted peace but because he believed he could achieve through the agreement a somewhat more secure hold on the West Bank. These critics pointed to Egypt's having endorsed, as part of the Camp David accords, pursuit of an interim autonomy plan for the West Bank and Gaza (Sadat's cover to avoid appearing to have abandoned entirely broader Arab interests in his negotiation of a treaty with Israel). They claimed that Begin felt he had thereby strengthened his position on the West Bank.

In fact, Labor, in its policy statements over the preceding years, had been less forthcoming regarding disposition of the Sinai than Likud had been. Begin did give the entire Sinai back, even dismantling the settlements there. While being attacked by the Peace Movement for not offering still more concessions, he was criticized by many in the Labor leadership for having given too much. They accused him of increasing the risks to Israel and of doing so because he made too light of security considerations and overemphasized religious-historical significances, which entailed attaching comparatively less importance to the Sinai.

In the months after negotiation of the Camp David accords, Israel pursued a dialogue with Egypt on autonomy for the West Bank and Gaza. Other Arab states, along with the Palestinian leadership, condemned the talks. But as time passed with no progress, many, perhaps most, in the Labor Zionist camp blamed the Begin government for the lack of progress.

Were more Israelis on the Left flocking to the Peace Movement now because they perceived Sadat's change of policy as marking an opening to other peace accords, even if the rest of the Arab leadership still condemned Sadat's actions? In fact, nothing in the developments with Egypt countered Labor's long-standing arguments concerning either Israel's need to retain strategic areas or Israel's greater latitude for negotiations with Egypt (even if less latitude, in the eyes of many Labor leaders, than Begin took) because of geostrategic considerations. Those considerations referred to the breadth of the Sinai and its translation into Israel's having some time to mobilize in the event of an Egyptian shift toward hostilities, a latitude increased by the demilitarization scheme for Sinai negotiated with Egypt and overseen by the United States.

Moreover, Sadat's assassination not long afterward, which many feared would lead to the unraveling of the peace and could well have done so if a leadership more hostile than Mubarak had succeeded Sadat, underscored Labor's long-standing insistence on the retention of defensible borders even in the context of peace treaties. So, too, did the incessant harangues against Israel, and indeed against Jews, that remained a staple of government-controlled media in Egypt despite the Camp David treaty.

It was not the breakthrough with Egypt that drew people to the Peace Movement. Rather, it was frustration with persistence of the siege despite that breakthrough, together with the circumstance of Likud having replaced a leadership with whom much of the Labor Left identified. Both factors rendered easier the embrace of indictments of Israel that promised peace if only Israel were more forthcoming.

THE LEFT, THE "OTHER ISRAEL," AND THE LEBANON WAR

This dynamic, in which the indictments of Israel purveyed by its enemies, and by anti-Zionist Jews both within and outside the country, gained greater currency across the Israeli Left in the context of the rise to power of "other" Jews and the establishment of a nonsocialist government, reflected, in fact, a familiar pattern. The targeting of both the government and its supporters as the offending party, as the perpetuators of the Arab-Israeli conflict, without whom peace would be at hand, was a reprise of a pattern recurrent in Diaspora history and fostered by the twin factors of sharp splits in the Jewish community and intense anti-Jewish pressures from surrounding populations.

An obvious modern parallel was the indictment of Eastern Jews by many German Jews for refusing to acculturate to the surrounding European society, refusing to adopt modern European ways, and thereby supposedly perpetuating anti-Semitism. That indictment was fostered by the sharp differences between German Jews and Eastern Jews and the intense anti-Semitic pressures to which European Jews were being subjected. (Those differences between the two communities were in turn born of different communal histories in recent centuries and of the anti-Jewish pressures on German Jews yielding efforts at assimilation that were unlike the Eastern Jews' responses to such pressures.) Many German Jews chose to comprehend anti-Jewish hatred in German society as actually directed against Jews in the Eastern mold and chose to endorse the canards of the haters and to see them as understandable and appropriate responses to these parochial, alien, "primitive," Eastern Jews. They chose to believe that reforming Eastern Jews, making at least those who came to Germany into assimilated Jews like themselves, or, short of that, distancing those "other" Jews from themselves, would reassure the surrounding society and stanch its hatred. Many Jews in Germany cleaved to this comprehension despite being constantly bombarded with counterproofs to its premises and assumptions.

The socialist Zionist pioneers of Israel aspired to shape in the country a New Jew, whose attributes were defined in large part by these early Zionists taking to heart the indictments of the anti-Semites, seeing the Old Jew of anti-Semitic caricature as the problem, and imagining their New Jews would be the answer that would end the hatred. Not only would they have their own nation and therefore, as Herzl and other Zionists anticipated, be perceived as more of an equal to other people, and so be more respected by them. Not only would they also be in a position to defend themselves. But they would work the land and so would not be tied to supposedly demeaning, soul-eroding and deforming vocations in commerce, and would be liberated from a primitive religiosity. They would be freed from the Jewish capitalist ways and Orthodox religious ways that were the target of so much of anti-Jewish caricature.

How then were the children and grandchildren of these pioneers, and those among their fellow Israelis who likewise embraced that comprehension of the New Jew and the new Zion, to understand the persistence, despite their remaking of themselves, of unmitigated anti-Jewish and anti-Israel hatred in the surrounding Arab societies? How were they to construe the sympathy with that hatred, and with the Arabs' ongoing war against Israel, expressed by much of the rest of the world, and even by international bodies such as various arms of the United Nations?

The anti-Zionists among the academic and artistic elites of the country proffered the explanation that Israelis' self-reform had not gone far enough, that socialist and anti-religious feeling were not enough. They argued that Israelis had to be more self-effacing, that they had to divest themselves of their atavistic

Jewish nationalism, be more accommodating of Arab sensibilities and more a model of anti-nationalist universalism.

But most in the Labor Zionist camp were not buying this. Most saw the Jewish state, its rebirth in Eretz Israel, and its capacity to defend the people and to enable them to live relatively normal lives, as an essential good. If they were perplexed by the persistence and murderous intensity of Arab enmity, by its failure to be resolved with the demise of European colonialism or with any of those other changes that Israelis in earlier years had imagined would resolve it, and by this enduring hatred being directed even toward the New Jews into whom they had molded themselves, they were inclined to live with that perplexity. They were predisposed to follow the pragmatic course blazed by Ben-Gurion and still pursued by his heirs in leading the country, politicians who were people like themselves, drawn from the ranks of Labor Zionism. Indeed, they overwhelmingly endorsed that course, which entailed maintaining the nation's strength and its sense of its own righteous mission in the face of Arab enmity. They regarded that enmity and hatred and dedication to Israel's destruction — the PLO's covenant and all its clauses, for example, that demanded the nation's dissolution and the dispersion of its people, and the active terrorist war incessantly directed against the country — as the essential wrong. They saw as right the path of remaining steadfast until changes within the surrounding societies would render peace possible.

But when the government passed into the hands of people outside the Labor Zionist fold, people whose constituency was likewise generally outside that fold and, moreover, was generally religious, so that both leaders and constituents were more in the mold of Labor Zionism's "Old Jew," the Labor Zionist camp became increasingly amenable to a radical reassessment of the Arab siege. It became dramatically more receptive to arguments that ascribed the persistence of the conflict with the Palestinians, and with Arab states other than Egypt, and the coldness of the peace with Egypt, not to Arab bigotry, nor to the political utility of the war against Israel for many Arab leaders, nor to Arab extremism, nor the persistent influence of pan-Arab nationalism and Islamic fundamentalism, but to the policies and the supposedly atavistic views of Likud and its constituency, to these "other" Jews, and, by extension, to Israel.

The Labor Zionist constituency became more open to arguments that Israeli self-reform was the key to achieving acceptance by the Arabs and the peace that Israelis desired. It did so despite all evidence to the contrary; despite the reality that Arab hostility and rejection of Israel had been as intense during thirty years of Labor control as it was now, in the term of the new Likud government, and despite the fact that the Likud-led coalition had forged the first peace treaty with an Arab state and made extensive concessions to do so. It embraced this distorted perspective just as many German Jews, despite all the evidence to the contrary, clung to acculturation and assimilation as the answer to anti-Semitism and blamed those who resisted both or were slow to them, especially the Jews of the East, for anti-Semitism's persistence.

To be sure, only relatively few within the Labor Zionist camp accepted arguments purveyed by the anti-Zionist professors and their protégés or the far Left to the effect that the Zionist enterprise, the Jewish state, was intrinsically sinful and the source of all difficulties. But more and more Israelis in that camp were now receptive to indictments of Israel. The absence of alternative intellectual institutions offering different perspectives loomed larger in the context of the twin factors of deep division in the community and incessant besiegement. The intense and unmitigated hostility of the surrounding societies pushed the objects of that hostility toward entertaining — in the modern Diaspora mode and in the abused child mode — wishful images of self-indictment and self-reform as the answer, as the route to extracting acceptance and peace from Israel's neighbors; and the ascent to governance of Jews perceived as "others" allowed the "self-indictment" to be directed at those "others" and therefore rendered it easier to embrace.

The change of government also distanced the Labor Zionist constituency from connection with the path of Ben-Gurion and his protégés, who did not have their academies, their intellectual institutions promoting and perpetuating their vision of the nation. That vision had derived its strength from its pragmatic building of the country and rallying of the people to it under Ben-Gurion's premiership and subsequent governments with which Labor's constituency identified, and so it suffered loss of cogency and loss of following when Labor lost power.

In addition, if the Labor Zionism of Ben-Gurion, infusing historical and religious content and meaningfulness into the nation-building enterprise, held its own against the anti-Zionists largely because of its pragmatic leadership of the state, its expression in action, the Labor defeat meant more than simply the loss of that powerful platform for Ben-Gurion's model. The ascension to government of people from whom the Labor Zionists felt alienated also led many in the Labor Zionist camp who may otherwise have embraced Ben-Gurion's model to begin to link with the incumbent Right those perspectives that were common to both Ben-Gurion's brand of Labor Zionism and the nonsocialist parties and their constituencies. Such areas of overlap included valuing historical and religious attachments to the land and valuing the Jewish accoutrements of the state. Many on the Left increasingly came to connect such perspectives with those alien others now leading the government, and consequently to look more askance at them than they had when Labor in the Ben-Gurion mold governed. In this way too, they grew more receptive to the jaundiced views of the anti-Zionists vis-à-vis historical and religious connections to the land and vis-à-vis the Jewish accoutrements of the state.

Changes in perspective in the Labor Zionist camp related to the perception of Likud and its constituents as an alien "Other Israel" can also be seen in the public's response to Israel's invasion of Lebanon in 1982, a year after formation of a second Likud government as successor to the first.

Israel undertook the invasion to dismantle the mini-state that the PLO, after its expulsion from Jordan in 1970, had established in the southern part of Lebanon. Israel had mounted earlier forays into southern Lebanon in response to terrorist attacks by the PLO across the Lebanese border. A Palestinian raid in March, 1978, in which terrorists hijacked an intercity bus north of Tel Aviv and ultimately killed 34 passengers, had triggered a large-scale Israeli incursion. But after Israel's withdrawal, the PLO had quickly reestablished itself and had done so in even greater strength in terms of the forces and materiel at its disposal.

In 1982 the IDF swept all the way up to Beirut and remained there until the PLO leadership and about 14,000 members of its military cadres departed Lebanon for Tunisia and elsewhere. Only then, and then only gradually, did Israel withdraw to what became for nearly two decades Israel's "security zone," an occupied buffer region in the southern 10 percent of Lebanon. This buffer was intended to defend Israel proper from Palestinian and other armed groups operating in Lebanon under the aegis of the Syrian forces that occupied the rest of the country.

Some of the sharp debate in Israel over the conduct of the Lebanese War concerned its scope. A number of people argued that the threat posed by the PLO could have been addressed by a more limited incursion targeting the PLO's mini-state in the south. They maintained that it was wrong to go all the way to Beirut, which entailed confronting PLO cadres there in a heavily populated urban environment, inevitably resulting in substantial civilian casualties, and which in any case, in their view, served no strategic aim. Some conjectured aloud that the only purpose of the advance to Beirut was to strengthen Lebanese Christian forces in the country's ongoing civil war, which pitted mainly Christian militias against the PLO and its Lebanese Moslem and Druse allies, and to help install in Lebanon a sympathetic, predominantly Christian, government.

In fact, Israel's aid to the Christian militias and its support of the chief Christian figure, Bashir Gemayel, failed dramatically when Gemayel, weeks into the campaign, was assassinated by Syrian agents and when Christian forces subsequently collapsed. These events led various Israelis who had seen the alliance, and promotion of Christian interests, as the central aim of the march to Beirut to feel vindicated in their criticism of the advance. The massacre at the Sabra and Shatila refugee camps in Beirut, not far from Israeli positions, of several hundred Palestinians by Christian forces — a reprisal for the assassination of Gemayel and for massacres of Christians by the PLO in recent years, most notably the slaughter perpetrated in the Christian town of Damur — was also seen as a terrible but allegedly predictable outcome of a wrongheaded Israeli policy.

Others in Israel defended the advance to Beirut by noting that more limited incursions had been tried in the past, as in 1978, and had failed. PLO forces would merely flee north to safety in Beirut and then return to their former positions in the south when the Israelis left. Only pursuit of the enemy to Beirut held out any hope of success. Moreover, Israel had worked to minimize civilian casualties in the city, even as the PLO used the civilian population for cover, as the organization had done in the south as well; and accounts from Lebanese sources on the level of civilian casualties, about one-tenth the figures given out by the PLO and its sympathizers, were consistent with Israeli caution.[15]

Supporters of the campaign also argued that it was a perfectly reasonable policy to extend what aid Israel could to those Lebanese Christians who wanted to ally themselves with Israel and seemed in a position to contribute to the struggle against common enemies. Nor should Israel be held responsible for a reprisal attack of undisciplined troops not under its control; and if the attempt to aid the Christians failed miserably, the primary purpose for advancing to Beirut resulted in success: The PLO leadership and thousands of its forces were obliged to leave the country, the previous pattern of PLO regrouping in southern Lebanon as soon as Israel terminated an incursion was finally broken, and the organization no longer had a nearby territorial base from which it could attack Israel.

But beyond such sharp arguments over the conduct of the campaign, there was another, overarching, level of criticism triggered by the Lebanon War. Many of the leaders of Labor and other left-wing parties, and their constituents, maintained that this was an unnecessary war. They alleged that for the first time in Israel's history the nation had initiated a war and had done so for no compelling security reason. They asserted that, in fact, Israel's northern border had been relatively quiet in the months immediately preceding the incursion and so the campaign could not be justified as a response to PLO attacks. They noted that an immediate provocation cited by the Likud government was the attempted assassination by the PLO of Israel's ambassador in London, but argued that this act hardly warranted large-scale hostilities.

The notion that the Lebanon War was unique in Israel's history, unjustified, and therefore, in effect, an act of aggression, a betrayal of Israel's use of its military purely for defensive purposes, became very popular. Labor and its political allies were able to muster an estimated 400,000 people, virtually 10 percent of the nation's Jewish population at the time, in a demonstration against the war.

But the rhetoric of the Labor indictment, the argument of the war's uniqueness, is not supported by closer scrutiny. In fact, the Lebanon War in many respects closely resembled the 1956 Sinai Campaign. At that time Israel had endured years of terrorist attacks across its border with the Gaza Strip, then under Egyptian control; attacks mounted by groups that Nasser's government financed, armed, trained, and directed. In addition, Israel's southern port of Eilat was effectively blockaded by Egypt's control of the Gulf of Aqaba through its Sharm el-Sheikh strongpoint, at the southern tip of the Sinai peninsula, which closed the Straits of Tiran to ships bound to and from Eilat. The primary goals of Ben-Gurion's war plan were to destroy the terrorist bases and establish conditions that would mitigate against a subsequent resumption of cross-border raids into Israel, as well as to lift the blockade of Eilat. These aims were comparable to those of Israel in Lebanon in 1982.

If in the latter case the level of cross-border attacks had decreased in the months immediately preceding the war, nevertheless the threat posed by the growing military capability of the PLO in its mini-state meant that the entire northern section of Israel was hostage to PLO artillery and rockets and constrained to live on a siege footing. The citizenry was frequently forced to retreat to underground shelters, economic development in the north had come virtually to a stop, people were leaving the region for safer areas. In fact, the impact of the PLO threat from Lebanon was in many respects greater than had been that of the terrorist presence in Gaza prior to 1956, in that the region near the Lebanese border was much more heavily populated and developed than Israeli areas adjoining Gaza. In this regard, the economic costs of the status quo on the Lebanese border prior to the 1982 war could be compared to the economic costs of the blockade of Eilat in the 1950s. The situation in northern Israel in 1982 was one that few countries, certainly few Western countries, would tolerate.

In 1956, as in 1982, Israel coordinated its attack with outside belligerents. In 1956 it did so with France and Britain, who wished to reverse Nasser's nationalization of the Suez Canal and conspired to use an Israeli advance to the canal as an excuse to intervene and seize control of the waterway. In 1956, as in 1982, this coordination with outside forces failed. Under pressure from the United States as well as the Soviet Union, England and France were obliged to retreat from the canal and Israel was forced to withdraw quickly from the Sinai and Gaza. But the Sinai Campaign, through its clearing of terrorist camps and its demonstration to Egypt of Israeli capabilities, did yield some respite from cross-border attacks, as did the Lebanon campaign. The 1956 war also gained Israel relief of the blockade of Eilat, while the 1982 war and establishment of the security zone in southern Lebanon effectively ended the siege conditions that had prevailed in northern Israel.

Given the similarities of the two campaigns, why the very different public responses in Israel? To be sure, for a number of anti-Zionist academics and their protégés, and for Israelis on the extreme Left of the political spectrum, particularly those inclined to follow Moscow's line on Middle East affairs, there was no great difference in reactions to the two events. They had responded to the Sinai War by inveighing against Ben-Gurion's supposed fascist militarism and by arguing that Israel's collusion with imperialist powers England and France demonstrated the rightness of their condemnations of the entire Zionist enterprise as likewise inherently colonialist, imperialist, and corrupt; and such voices interpreted the Lebanon War in much the same way.

But relatively few Israelis, including within the ranks of Labor Zionism, followed the anti-Zionist ideologues and the extreme Left in their attacks on the Ben-Gurion government in 1956. The public generally shared the view that the cost in Israeli lives of the ongoing terrorism was intolerable and that forceful action was necessary to stop it, and most Labor Zionists were part of this consensus. They typically sympathized with Ben-Gurion, still perceived him as very much one of their own, their leader, and were more than prepared to endorse his policies.

But in 1982, the predilection in Labor Zionist ranks was, again, to regard the Likud government as a reactionary force alien to the ideals of Labor Zionism. This, coupled with people's eagerness to find solutions to the Palestinian Arab thorn in Israel's side and the seemingly intractable Arab antagonism, inclined many on the Israeli Left to put aside their previously more open-eyed perception of the threats against Israel and the nature of those threats, put aside also their prior willingness to support government policies to contain the threats, and to shift instead to a discounting of the dangers confronting the nation. They were now inclined to look with jaundiced eyes at government stances and initiatives and to construe them as overreactions and, in fact, as the source of ongoing Arab enmity and the chief obstacle to peace. So the PLO threat was dismissed by many and the Lebanon War became for them an unprovoked war, indeed Israel's first war undertaken not out of necessity but by choice.

One enthusiastic purveyor of this characterization of the Lebanon War as Israel's first optional war was Amos Oz,[16] which was somewhat curious in that he had been highly critical of the Sinai Campaign, had described it as an "evil" act,[17] and obviously had not seen it as necessary. Oz got around this contradiction in part by changing his assessment of the Sinai War. He argued at one point that there was no real threat to which the Lebanon War could be construed to be a response, whereas in 1956, in contrast, Nasser was preparing to destroy Israel and was close to achieving the strength to do so.[18] Elsewhere, Oz simply omitted reference to the Sinai War. He stated in a 1990 interview: "No one debates the fact that the wars . . . in 1948, 1967 and 1973 were a matter of life and death. . . . By contrast, the Lebanon War was optional."[19]

Some Laborite critics of the war went so far as to argue that, since the PLO mini-state in Lebanon was essentially harmless, the government's campaign to eradicate it must have been driven by considerations other than Israel's security. They maintained that the real reason for the war was to strengthen Israel's hold on the West Bank and Gaza by undermining the Palestinian leadership.

Another notable facet of this predilection to perceive the PLO threat, and that of the broader Arab world, as overblown, and to regard the Likud government as the real enemy, was the growing popularity in the late 1970s and early 1980s of the theme of the supposed "Holocaust syndrome" of the Right. Some Western critics of Israel had long purveyed the argument that, because of the Holocaust, Israelis harbored baseless, paranoid fears of others wanting to annihilate Israel and, in particular, confounded Arabs with Nazis. This theme was now increasingly invoked by Israelis on the Left in their critiques of the Likud government and its supporters. Voices on the Left began to appeal to this "syndrome" as an explanation of the Right's distrust of, and militant stance toward, the Arabs states and the PLO. They did so even as the PLO and its allies in the Arab world were openly calling for Israel's annihilation, declaring Israel's demise their sacred and unwavering goal, incorporating Nazi demonizations of Jews into their media programming and their school curricula to advance their agenda, and assiduously seeking to back up their words with actions.[20]

THE NATIONAL UNITY GOVERNMENT

Begin, under incessant pressure related to the Lebanon War, resigned as prime minister in August of 1983 and was succeeded by Yitzhak Shamir. The withdrawal of a small party from the ruling coalition in March, 1984, triggered elections later that year.

The country was still riven by widespread unhappiness with events in Lebanon, particularly with the IDF's remaining bogged down there and taking a continual stream of casualties in the many months since the departure of the PLO from Beirut. In addition, Israel was suffering from major economic problems, including hyperinflation. Conditions consequently seemed ripe for Labor to do very well in the elections. But the balloting yielded what was in effect a dead heat. Neither major bloc was able to form a ruling coalition, and Labor and Likud ultimately established a National Unity Government with plans for a rotating premiership. Labor's Shimon Peres would hold the office for the first twenty-five months while Shamir would serve as foreign minister, they would then exchange portfolios, and Labor's Yitzhak Rabin would be defense minister for the entire life of the government.

During the next several years, diplomatic initiatives, including one boosted by a meeting between then Prime Minister Peres and Jordan's King Hussein, ultimately got nowhere, and a common attitude among Labor Zionist followers — indeed, an attitude promoted in various ways by the Labor leadership — was that progress toward peace was attainable but the Likud presence in the government prevented positive movement.

During the last year of the government's four-year tenure, in December,

1987, an outburst of widespread and persistent rioting in Gaza triggered the start of the Palestinian "Intifada." The initial events of the Intifada were essentially spontaneous. These occurrences, and the subsequent perpetuation, in both Gaza and the West Bank, of the rioting and violence and of what increasingly became also a pattern of civil disobedience, were fed by widely shared frustration and anger with Israeli administration of the territories. They were also spurred to no small degree by resentment over the failure of the PLO and of the Jordanian presence in the territories to achieve any progress toward an end to the status quo. With regard to the former, Israeli commentator Amos Elon observed, "The intifada was an uprising . . . also against the sterility of PLO rhetoric and terror."[21] Others have made the same point.[22]

The Palestinian Arabs had been living at this point for just over twenty years in political limbo. In addition, while Israeli governments had largely continued to follow Dayan's policy of minimal interference with life in the territories, the impact of Israeli administration on conditions in the territories, including economic conditions, was nevertheless substantial. The economy of the territories had become closely bound to that of Israel. Indeed Dayan, while urging minimal administrative interference, sought to encourage an intertwining of the economies, believing that growing interdependence would bode well for genuine peace in the wake of a political settlement. This situation, although leading to remarkable economic expansion in the territories, also became a major source of friction. As has been argued by authors highly critical of Israeli policy in the territories prior to the Intifada, it was not so much a matter of malign Israeli intent vis-à-vis the territorial economy and related aspects of life there but rather the impact of a vast, slow-moving, often redundant, and typically user-unfriendly Israeli socialist-style bureaucracy.[23]

Israelis themselves incessantly complained of that bureaucracy as a constant frustration and bane of their existence, and some actually left the country to escape it. But average Palestinians had, of course, even less resources to cope with it than did most Israelis. In addition, if Israelis ultimately tolerated the heavy hand of the bureaucracy as a price to be paid for life in Israel, for Palestinians it was perceived simply as a demeaning foreign imposition backed up by a foreign military. Also, while Israel might point to the far-reaching gains in the territories in such areas as literacy, life expectancy, infant mortality, access to electricity and plumbing, and economic status generally, gains greatly surpassing those in surrounding Arab countries, the Palestinians themselves were comparing their situation to life in Israel, behind which they were substantially lagging.

The prospect of ongoing perpetuation of the political and economic status quo also figured significantly in triggering and sustaining the Intifada. The Labor Party might look to Jordan as Israel's hoped-for interlocutor in a land for peace settlement, but Jordan had been rejected for this role by the Arab

League in 1974 and, in addition, had been consistently losing authority and credibility among the populace in the territories. The Palestinian Arabs increasingly regarded Jordan as only having helped, through its representatives in the territories and its financial infusions and economic relations, a relatively small cadre of loyalists, and as representing the interests of an older, traditional segment of society disconnected from the greater part of the population.

Loyalty to the PLO had, in contrast, been growing for many years in the territories. But the PLO had rejected the proposals for autonomy talks included in the Camp David agreements between Israel and Egypt and also seemed to be offering no prospect of a change in the status quo. In addition, many in the territories were aggrieved by PLO corruption and by PLO interventions in the territories that, like those of the Jordanians, benefitted only selected cadres. (In fact, substantial segments of the population in the territories had prospered as a result of Jordanian, PLO, and Israeli policies, including segments of the refugee population, and these groups largely distanced themselves initially from the Intifada. But many among them became increasingly drawn into the uprising, some by choice and enthusiastically so, others in response to threats and fears of reprisal.)

The fundamentalist Islamic organizations, with their growing social service networks, were winning increasing numbers of adherents in the territories, in large part in response to disillusionment with the PLO's corruption and its failure to use its extensive financial resources to address basic needs of the people. But the fundamentalists were likewise not perceived as offering an end to the status quo.

An indigenous Intifada leadership did ultimately evolve in the territories. It was comprised typically of people who were affiliated with one of the various branches of the PLO or, to a lesser extent, with one of the Islamic groups, but who saw themselves as much more attuned to the needs of the population and conditions on the ground than was the Palestinian leadership in exile. But these indigenous figures sought to walk a fine line between initiating policy and bowing to the directions given by the external hierarchy. They feared retaliation from the PLO under Arafat, who, with his associates, was clearly hostile to the emergence of an independent leadership in the territories and was prepared to act harshly to quash any challenges to his authority. By the summer of 1988, those within the territories were no longer able to sustain their semi-independent position and Arafat and his agents had effectively taken control of the Intifada.

(While Israeli governments, in exploring avenues for an agreement with Arab parties over disposition of the territories, had since 1967 looked particularly to Jordan or to Palestinian leaders within the territories as potential interlocutors, Israeli policies had actually fostered the growth of PLO influence. Even as the nation defined the PLO, with its terror campaign and its goal of

Israel's annihilation, as the enemy, Israel's *laissez-faire* predilections had translated into tolerating pro-PLO activities in the territories, such as publication of pro-PLO editorials, as long as those activities did not entail direct incitement of violence. Most significantly, Israel had allowed free entry of PLO funds that were used to buy influence and recruit agents. Then Minister of Defense Ezer Weizmann stated in 1978: "It does not matter that they get money from the PLO as long as they don't build arms factories with it."[24])

Also in the summer of 1988, King Hussein renounced all claims to the West Bank and to representation of the Palestinian Arabs. Some observers saw this move — which entailed as well cutting off the salaries of civil servants in the territories and stopping Jordan's other infusions of money and support — as a ploy by the King to reverse his declining fortunes in the West Bank. They suggested Hussein was anticipating that the residents of the territories would ultimately regret the loss of his aid and involvement, would recognize that the gulf between the PLO and Israel was unbridgeable and his exit made the conflict more intractable, and would turn to him for reengagement and help. Other observers insisted that Hussein simply saw that his standing in the territories had largely evaporated, feared the unrest might spread to the majority Palestinian population in his remaining kingdom, and so felt disengagement prudent. In any case, Hussein's move hammered yet another nail in the coffin of Labor's Jordan strategy.

The Israeli leadership of both blocs initially disbelieved that the Intifada entailed, as it did at least in its first stages, a spontaneous uprising. The government looked upon it rather as another Arab attempt — like the war of attrition or the PLO terror campaigns — to win Israeli concessions without negotiations or compromise. The government was also at a loss for how to end the uprising. It used the military to control the violence and curb its spilling out beyond Palestinian enclaves, to maintain some level of Israeli presence and authority within those enclaves, and to uncover and harass the indigenous leadership. But it quickly concluded that there was no military solution to the uprising or — amounting to the same thing — it was culturally and ethically unprepared even to contemplate employing the level of force that likely would have been required to end the confrontation. At the same time, it perceived no political solution.

Both political blocs in Israel were reluctant to acknowledge that the Palestinian population overwhelmingly saw the PLO as its representative. Both blocs attached undue significance to PLO cadres' widespread use of brute force and threat to extract cooperation from other Palestinians; both chose to interpret this phenomenon as indicative of a pervasive alienation from the PLO; and Labor still clung to the hope of engaging Jordan as a partner for negotiations on the territories even after King Hussein had renounced playing any such role.

To the extent that the Labor and Likud leaderships were forced to recognize the status of the PLO in the territories, they were stymied. Both looked at the PLO's terror agenda, and the PLO charter with its focus on destroying Israel, and Arafat's Plan of Phases, and saw negotiating with the PLO and the granting of any authority in the territory to the organization as inevitably creating a revanchist entity in the heart of Israel, one that would bring its terror virtually to every Israeli doorstep and introduce myriad intolerable and potentially insoluble security threats.

The Israeli election of November, 1988, again resulted essentially in a dead heat between the two major blocs and yielded another National Unity Government. Likud had achieved sufficient marginal gain to win Shamir the premiership for the duration of the government, with Peres as foreign minister and Rabin as defense minister. Shortly after the vote, Rabin proposed that elections be held in the territories to empower a local leadership with whom Israel would enter into negotiations on the fate of the territories. Members of the local leadership of the Intifada requested Arafat's permission to pursue the overture but, predictably, Arafat would not authorize their doing so.

Meanwhile, the United States, the only potential mediator between Israel and the Arabs, had begun in the summer of 1988, in the wake of Hussein's renunciation of responsibility for the territories, to explore the possibility of opening a dialogue with the PLO. Its conditions for doing so, conditions consistent with past American commitments to Israel, were that the PLO renounce terrorism, accept unreservedly UN Security Council Resolutions 242 and 338 (the Security Council resolution that followed the 1973 war), and recognize Israel's right to exist in peace and security.

In November, 1988, a meeting of the Palestine National Council in Algiers recognized the original 1947 UN resolution (Resolution 181) calling for creation of Arab and Jewish states in Palestine, and in the following month Arafat made a number of ambiguous statements seemingly directed toward satisfying the Americans. Finally, on December 14, under much pressure and a day after offering more ambiguous declarations before the UN in Geneva, Arafat finally made a statement that conformed to the wording the United States demanded. Secretary of State George Shultz then announced America's preparedness to engage in a dialogue with the PLO.

Prior to the Intifada, most Israelis believed it was in Israel's interest that the country ultimately negotiate a political separation from the Palestinian Arabs. They also believed, however, that Israel had to await a negotiating partner, and that the country would need to, and could, tolerate the wait. The Intifada, and the many clashes between the IDF and the civilian population of the territories which were a part of it, entailed scenarios that were widely perceived as corrosive for those Israelis engaged in duty in the territories. The confrontations of the Intifada were also seen by many as corrosive for Israeli society at large. In addition, both soldiers and the military leadership were unhappy with their task in the territories and regarded it as compromising and undermining what ought to be the IDF's primary role, preparing to defend the country in war. All of this served to promote among Israelis the view that the status quo more broadly, even without the uprising, the circumstance of Israel controlling an alien population in political limbo, was intrinsically corrosive and something of which the nation had an interest in divesting itself as soon as possible.

But if the Intifada rendered many Israelis all the more impatient to effect a political disengagement from the Palestinian Arabs, it offered Israel no solution to the problem that had prevented movement toward a resolution through the prior two decades. This remained the absence of an interlocutor with whom Israel could negotiate a compromise in the territories that would win the Palestinians political separation while allowing Israel to retain areas vital to its security. If anything, such negotiations appeared more remote, as Jordan had now emphatically disengaged from the territories.

In the context of this unpromising reality, the delusions purveyed by the Peace Movement widened still further their hold on the Israeli Left.

TWELVE

Delusions Ascendant:
The Peace Movement Up to Oslo

*We have not conceded and will not surrender any of the existing com-
mitments that have existed for more than 70 years . . . We have within
our Palestinian and united Arab society the ability to deal with divided
Israeli society . . . We must force Israeli society to cooperate . . . with our
Arab society, and eventually to gradually dissolve the 'Zionist entity.'*
Palestinian "moderate" Faisal Husseini, November, 1992[1]

*A new generation of Palestinian leaders was emerging . . . Younger peo-
ple like . . . Faisal Husseini . . . Most of the peace groups on the Israeli
side maintained contacts with these new leaders and tried to persuade
Israelis that these Palestinians could be partners in negotiations.*
Peace Now activist and historian of the peace movement,
Mordechai Bar-On[2]

THE PEACE MOVEMENT AT THE TIME OF THE INTIFADA

For many Israelis, the Intifada and the violence that accompanied it reinforced
both their desire for disengagement and their conviction that disengagement
must leave Israel in control of strategic areas that would allow it the capacity
to defend itself. But for some, the television tapes of ugly clashes, the persistent intensity of the confrontation, and the widespread condemnations of Israeli
actions and demands for Israeli concessions overrode all else. These people's response to the Intifada was to demand retreat and to insist that Israel seek less
a negotiating partner than an agent to whom it could hand off the territories.
Their stance was also very often to dismiss strategic considerations and potential threats as irrelevant once the territories were disposed of, as, they argued,
there would then inevitably be "peace." In the face of confrontation and with,
again, no prospect of an end to the struggle, the ranks of those who reacted by
choosing to put the onus on Israel and to see the solution as Israeli self-reform grew
once more. The "peace" organizations won new adherents and, by the summer of

1988, even before the United States had extracted verbal concessions from a reluctant Arafat, they were urging that Israel talk to the PLO.

Peace Now, in its declarations during this period, attempted to blur differences between those of its followers who wanted to return to the 1967 lines and were sure peace would then ensue and those who still thought Israel would need to retain crucial areas and win some concessions from the Arabs. But the camp that saw giving everything back as inevitably assuaging all Arab hostility, and perceived Israel's reluctance to do so as the major impediment to peace, was clearly growing. In addition, many of those within the Peace Movement who thought Israel's security did require retention of key strategic areas believed that the PLO would inevitably accept such territorial compromises. Indeed, they had found prominent Palestinians who assured them this was so. They therefore joined the chorus of voices insisting that it was Israeli reluctance to talk to the PLO that was the obstacle to peace.

That the PLO was the dominant political force among the Palestinian Arabs was, of course, true. That its prospective role as a negotiating partner for Israel was highly problematic was also true, but not to the growing ranks of the "peace" camp. The dangers of negotiating with an organization that was still engaged in terror and still directed by a charter whose focus was Israel's annihilation were manifest. To do so entailed implicitly acquiescing in Israel's legitimacy and right to exist being a subject of negotiations, not something to which sovereign states typically bow. In addition, the prospect of handing control of any part of the territories to such an organization — one that had even articulated, and whose leader was constantly reiterating, a plan to gain a foothold in the territories by negotiations and to use that foothold as a base for pursuing Israel's annihilation — was so fraught with obvious difficulties as to lead most Israelis to regard the PLO as far from a fit partner. But, again, this was not the view within the ranks of the Peace Movement.

One argument mustered by some in the Peace Movement, beyond their conviction of the PLO's sincere desire for peace, was that Israel had no choice but to talk to the PLO as the organization was the dominant political force among the Palestinian Arabs and there was no other potential interlocutor. The obvious counter-argument was that, whatever its prominence, the organization, unless it underwent some dramatic and substantial metamorphosis, was still unfit to be a negotiating partner. Short of such a transformation by the PLO, if the Palestinian Arabs wanted to negotiate their way to political separation from Israel they would have to find other representation.

This tack, clearly one open to Israel, would, however, entail a test of wills, and for many in the "peace" camp that prospect was untenable. The persistence of the other side in sustaining the conflict, most recently via the Intifada, was a demonstration of will before which they preferred, in their desire for "peace" and "normalcy," to give ground unilaterally. They preferred to embrace the perspectives of the other side and to convince themselves of the reasonableness, even the moral superiority, of doing so, to cast doing so as wiser and more ethical; and they chose not to think about, or simply to deny, the dangers of their stance.

Those in the Peace Movement often sought to bolster their position by claiming that the PLO had indeed changed. In the November, 1988, meeting of the Palestine National Council in Algiers, at which the Council declared the establishment of the State of Palestine with Arafat as its President, the PNC also proclaimed that it was doing so on the basis of UN Resolution 181. This was the General Assembly resolution in 1947 that called for the creation of two states in the Mandate, one Jewish and one Arab, and that the Palestinian Arabs had rejected at the time. Resolution 181 entailed for Israel territories that were much less, and much less viable, than Israel's pre-1967 domain. (In its re-grouping and responding to the war waged against it in 1947–48 by the Palestinian Arabs and subsequently by the surrounding Arab states, Israel had gained control of additional land.) It was hardly a basis for negotiation now. But many involved with the Peace Movement hailed the PNC's Algiers declaration as implicitly recognizing Israel's right to exist. When, in the following month, Arafat, with obvious reluctance, acquiesced to American demands that he state unambiguously a renunciation of terrorism, a recognition of UN Security Council Resolutions 242 and 338, and acknowledgment of Israel's right to exist with peace and security, those within the Peace Movement embraced his doing so as additional proof of the rightness of their views and confirmation that a new era had indeed dawned.

Were these steps by the Palestinian leadership worthy of note? Of course. Did it make sense for Israel to try to discern their significance? Again, of course. It was obviously in Israel's interest to learn whether these moves represented a genuine new agenda, with new objectives, for the PLO, or were simply made in the context of the Plan of Phases, steps to win legitimacy and recognition by the United States without any intention of altering the PLO's revanchist and annihilationist goals. Or — a third possibility — were they something in between, perhaps representing a power struggle within the organization over which of two directions it should follow?

But for many in the Peace Movement, such questions, if considered at all, were quickly dismissed. In their eagerness to interpret evidence in conformity with their desires, they could see these events as only meaning that the PLO had indeed decided to pursue genuine peace and now all that was required was a reciprocal Israeli response. Counterevidence included statements by PLO leaders, in communications with their constituents, of the organization's continued dedication to the PLO covenant and its focus on Israel's annihilation. But this was disregarded.

An example of such statements was the declaration by senior PLO member Ahmad Sidqi Dajani on November 22, 1988, that, "We in the PLO make a clear distinction between covenants and political programs, whereby the former determine the permanent strategic line while the latter are tactical by nature. We would like some of our brothers to take note of this difference, that is, of our continued adherence to the Palestinian National Covenant."[3] Another example was the comments of Arafat's second in command, Abu Iyad, some days later: "The borders of our state noted [by the PNC Algiers declaration] represent only a part of our national aspirations. We will strive to expand them so as to realize our ambition for the entire territory of Palestine."[4]

Similarly ignored by the true believers of the Peace Movement were Arafat's own assurances to his people of his steadfast allegiance to the Plan of Phases, and evidence of continuing PLO involvement in terrorist attacks on Israel.

Mordechai Bar-On, a founder of Peace Now but someone more sober-minded than many of his associates, has written the most definitive history of the Peace Movement.[5] This 470-page book, much of it devoted to the peregrinations of the PLO, never even mentions Arafat's Plan of Phases. Bar-On apparently did not want it to exist and so he simply ignored it.

This predilection to embrace positive or potentially positive evidence and ignore or dismiss counterevidence in the service of supporting desired scenarios, supporting the wish that Israel need only be more forthcoming and peace would be at hand, had served to render many in the Peace Movement devotees, in effect, a form of Whig history. Whig history — deriving its name from late eighteenth- and early nineteenth-century liberal optimism as embodied in the rhetoric of Whig political parties — entails a comprehension of history as moving consistently and inexorably toward improvement in humanity's condition.

One might think that Jews would be particularly unreceptive to this gloss on events, given the repetitive recurrence over several millennia of history unfolding in catastrophic reverses for them. Indeed, the worst debacle ever visited upon the Jewish people was not long ago initiated and executed by a German government only decades after Jews had been granted full citizenship and *de jure* equality in Germany. Yet the very circumstance of the Jews' subjection to so much abuse assured that, in any period of relatively better conditions, part of the community, desperate to escape that painful history, would eagerly interpret the improved conditions as evidence that a new day had dawned and the horrors of the past had finally been left behind. Even as others in the community would be attuned to Jews having been at such a better place many times before and to such current conditions being no guarantee of what the future would hold, some would choose to embrace self-deluding Whiggish perspectives. The fact that comprehensions of history as circular and recurrent have widely given way in the modern era to a more unidirectional view of history has only made such Whiggish interpretations easier for Jews to adopt.

Israel itself, in its relations with other states, even with other states in the

Middle East, had in its short history notable experiences of conditions going from better to worse. For example, in trying to cultivate counterweights to the hostility of the Arab states around it, Israel had sought to develop close relations with non-Arab nations in the region, most notably Turkey, Iran, and Ethiopia; and, from the nineteen fifties onward, it enjoyed considerable success in this endeavor. But the revolution in Iran in 1979 turned a virtual ally into a regime that is one of the most intransigently hostile to Israel in the world, a government that has pursued a campaign of terror against Israel, and against Jews elsewhere, that is the envy of Arab terrorist groups. (Its involvement in bombings of the Israeli embassy in Buenos Aires and of that city's headquarters of Argentine Jewish communal organizations were only the most spectacular of such acts of terror.) Indeed, Iran, with its declared intent to pursue Israel's annihilation and its aggressive and technologically sophisticated programs for developing weapons of mass destruction and the missile capacity to deliver them, has become the state that presents perhaps the greatest existential threat to Israel. While in Ethiopia, the coup against Haile Selassie in 1974 and the emergence of a pro-Communist regime under Mengistu Haile Mariam saw for Israel the transforming of what had been an important friendship into a more ambiguous relationship and ultimately into one marked largely by hostility.

Yet many in the Peace Movement, in their eagerness to believe that peace was at hand were Israel only forthcoming enough, chose to embrace every positive step by an Arab party vis-à-vis Israel as part of an irreversible progression that would inexorably turn enemies into negotiating partners and negotiating partners into friends in the building of a pacified and prosperous Middle East. They chose to see Israel as therefore obliged not only to respond generously to every gesture along the way but to decrease its preoccupation with strategic concerns such as defensible borders. Such concerns, they argued, would soon, with the coming peace, be passé and represented atavistic thinking that only inhibited Israel from making the concessions that would finally elicit peace.

Another self-delusion likewise common among Peace Movement enthusiasts and somewhat paralleling the Whig fallacy — and once more symptomatic of the eagerness to put aside coherent reflection for the sake of sustaining fantasies that "peace" and a "normal" life were genuinely at hand if only Israel would grasp them — was what might be called the fellowship fallacy. Activists in the Peace Movement maintained ongoing dialogues with prominent figures in the territories with ties to the PLO. These figures would seem to their Israeli interlocutors to be quite reasonable. They would, in informal conversations and even at times in public forums, make statements about their images of the contours of a negotiated settlement much more measured and accommodating than the hard-line declarations of the PLO leadership; and the Israelis involved in these conversations chose to comprehend such statements as representing positions which the PLO was prepared to adopt in negotiations with Israel.

Again, it was certainly in Israel's interest to explore such statements and to evaluate their significance. They could indeed reflect positions that the PLO was informally putting forward to test Israel's response and was prepared to embrace in the context of negotiations. Or they could simply be a device for luring Israel into negotiations and winning concessions without representing policies that the PLO had any intention of actually adopting. Or they could be something in between; for example, stances that some within the PLO leadership were prepared to endorse while others rejected, so that their significance depended on the relative strength of competing PLO factions.

But to many "peace" activists such overtures — put forward in informal talks by, for example, Faisal Husseini, at the time perhaps the most prominent PLO surrogate in the territories — were undoubtedly the genuine article, the PLO's true position, and further evidence that a real peace was attainable were Israel only to grasp it. When, at an October, 1989, peace rally, Husseini declared, "The Palestinian Peace camp has won, and now leads the PLO and the Palestinian people,"[6] many in the Israeli Peace Movement were inclined to embrace the statement as authoritative and impeccable proof of a further advance in the inexorable march toward peace.

Not surprisingly, when those same Palestinian interlocutors made, as they often did, very different, hard-line, statements, their Israeli associates simply discounted such declarations. Faisal Husseini, in a November, 1992, speech before an Arab youth organization in Amman, declared that, "We have not conceded and will not surrender any of the existing commitments that have existed for more than 70 years . . . We have within our Palestinian and united Arab society the ability to deal with divided Israeli society . . . We must force Israeli society to cooperate . . . with our Arab society, and eventually to gradually dissolve the 'Zionist entity.'"[7] Even more explicit remarks in the same vein were made by Husseini after the initiation of Oslo, including statements in which he insisted that the Palestinian goal was still a Palestinian state "from the river to the sea" and suggested that the Oslo agreements were a Trojan horse through which the Palestinians will ultimately achieve that end.[8] Yet his Israeli friends persisted in viewing him as their partner in the quest for an equitable and durable peace.

This attitude toward Husseini's utterances reflected not only an overvaluing of the positive and undervaluing or discounting of the negative by the peace activists. It also — amounting virtually to the same thing — represented an overvaluing of what was said personally to them and undervaluing of anything contradictory said to others. In subsequent years, the same calculus applied when Israeli peace activists met with high PLO officials, including Yasser Arafat himself. Arafat's assurances to them about his desire for peace would, amazingly, be valued more highly than his statements to his media, and his speeches to his people, and his instructions to his educators, to the effect that Israel was an illegitimate usurper of Palestinian rights and the Palestinian patrimony and must be destroyed. Arafat's messages to his own people were consistently ignored and his message to the Israeli Left was embraced as reflecting his true feelings and intent.

If there seems a certain arrogance to this self-delusion, that arrogance is, in fact, an intrinsic aspect of people's assuming responsibility for intolerable situations over which they have no real control for the sake of staving off despair by imagining control. Consider again the paradigmatic situation of the abused child: He chooses to feel responsible, to see himself as "bad," in order to sustain the fantasy that if he becomes "good" enough his father will stop beating him, or his mother will no longer neglect him, or whatever other type of abuse he has been subjected to will end. Intrinsic to the fantasy is the delusional belief that his actions will control and determine the parents' behavior, an arrogating of delusional power to himself.

A similar dynamic prevails for those who, in the face of the seeming intractability of Arab hostility, have responded by embracing Arab indictments of Israel and choosing to believe that if only Israel would be more forthcoming, would become "good," Arab hostility would dissipate and peace would be won. Intrinsic to that delusion is the belief that Israeli actions can control Arab actions. Inherent in the delusion, for those who embrace it, is a conviction that their own formulas for Israel being good, formulas that they believe to be self-evidently reasonable and fair, cannot help but elicit in Arab interlocutors genuine and heartfelt commitments that the Palestinian people and its leaders will respond as these reformist peace-loving Israelis would want them to respond. So they were convinced that, whatever Arafat said to others, he must have been telling his Israeli interlocutors the truth when he claimed to desire genuine peace and vowed to reciprocate Israel's becoming "good" by providing that peace.

Of course, other Israelis challenged the peace activists' benign interpretations of PLO intentions and their seeming arrogant and narcissistic conviction that forthcoming PLO declarations made to them should be given greater weight than any more militant and hostile statements by the organization, and even by the same individuals, made in other venues. But a common retort by the peace activists was a global and moralizing attack on these challengers. They as peacemakers, they argued, are only seeking a better, peaceful life for their children and grandchildren, and in their dialogues they had seen the humanity of the other side — in some instances had even exchanged photographs of children and grandchildren with them. How could anyone doubt that these individuals, and the PLO leadership they represented, and the constituency they represented, wanted the same things, peace and prosperity, for themselves and their children and grandchildren?

Those who challenged this, they insisted, were in effect denying the humanity of the other side, denying the other side had the same feelings and aspirations as themselves. They were bigots and racists; perhaps narrow-minded because of benighted upbringing and insufficient education, but nevertheless bigots and racists. Bar-On, again far from the most doctrinaire of the peace activists, noted that the Sephardic Jewish community in Israel tended to be more distrustful of Arab intentions and added that this seemed, in surveys, to be related to educational level and level of religious traditionalism. He also made the point that segments of the Ashkenazi community that were less educated and more traditional were likewise more distrustful of the possibilities for genuine peace than were Israel's elites. Bar-On concluded: "Higher learning, it is believed, exposes individuals to a wider variety of opinions, trains them in new analytical and flexible modes of thought, and enables them to relate to issues in a less emotional and more self-critical way, which leads to greater tolerance and understanding of the 'other' and of the complexity of the issues."9

Entirely missed by the "peace" activists in this comprehension was, of course, the narrow-mindedness of their own assumption that their interlocutors, and the Palestinians generally, must think as they do and subscribe to their values and perspectives. This assumption is another facet of that seeming arrogance born of their desire to believe that Israeli action will determine Arab action and that Israeli reform will inevitably yield the wished-for Arab response.

Obviously, one can appreciate that others are as human as one's self and harbor many of the same feelings and sensibilities as oneself and at the same time also recognize the possibility of dramatic differences in aspirations, perspectives, and priorities. Palestinian leaders may be personable and forthcoming in dialogues and may sincerely be prepared to pursue compromise and a viable peace, or they may engage in dialogue and strike a forthcoming pose in the interest of advancing a less pacific agenda. A Palestinian leader may love his grandchildren and also believe that he owes it to the Palestinian refugees and their descendants to pursue Israel's annihilation, that to do otherwise would be a betrayal of that obligation and perhaps of religious duty as well. One can appreciate the humanity of the Palestinian people but also recognize that their leaders have conveyed to them in their media and their schools and their houses of worship the message that they have been stripped of their patrimony by rapacious invaders who have no legitimate right to any part of Palestine and that only the extirpation of the Zionist state will satisfy the demands of justice and so they must dedicate themselves to that end.

Even while recognizing the humanity of the Palestinians, and appreciating their love of their children, one can still be legitimately concerned about how much these messages from their leaders will shape their actions. Or one may see signs that many Palestinians are indeed prepared for a peaceful resolution of the conflict, are even prepared to resist exhortations by their leaders to the effect that they are obliged to pursue Israel's annihilation; an observer may see evidence of this and still be wary. For he can at the same time be cognizant of the fact that in the past as well, even in the nineteen twenties and nineteen thirties, there were many Palestinians who were prepared to live peacefully with the Zionists and who resisted calls for violence, but in the face of a leadership bent on pushing out the Jews — as in the 1936 to 1939 uprising or again in 1947 to 1948 — these people's desire for peaceful coexistence was swept aside. Such individuals were often cowed to silence or, if they resisted being silenced, often paid with their lives for their resistance. They accounted, for example, for many of the hundreds of Arabs killed by the Mufti's forces during the 1936 to 1939 uprising.

There was and is, therefore, more than sufficient reason behind the desire of some Israelis to be cautious: to seek to facilitate the two peoples' pursuing separate political lives, but to proceed in a way that maximally allows Israel to defend itself against potential, indeed even likely, revanchist agendas. The dismissal of such caution, and of the reasoning behind it, as racist and bigoted is, at the very least, intellectually dishonest.

Again, many in the Peace Movement chose to construe their impatience with concerns about secure borders, their faith that Israeli withdrawal would lead to a peace that would make security concerns passé, as a product of their education and sophistication, which supposedly enabled them to appreciate the "other" and see his hopes and dreams as no different from one's own. This pose was bogus in various ways. Not only was their seeing the "other" in this manner, as a mirror of oneself, a product not of sophistication but of a narcissism born of wishful thinking, but the correlation of their concept of "liberal" thinking with education was also a distortion.

A key facet of this argument was that their Arab interlocutors were also well-educated and cultured, like they, and so must think the same liberal way and want the same liberal things. But in fact, when aggressive policies are ideology-driven, it is very often those with the most extensive formal education who have been most schooled in the ideology and who therefore most subscribe to its aggressive tenets. In Egypt, for example, even decades after the peace treaty with Israel, the most educated sectors of the population have been the ones that have spawned the most vehement hostility to Israel and have led the opposition to normalization of relations. In fact, the Israeli Peace Movement itself in some ways reflected this phenomenon. Many in its ranks were indeed drawn from the most educated, and their education had in no small part been education in the ideology of self-indictment, the ideology of comprehending the war against Israel as a war that can be ended only by embracing the enemy's claims and answering them with self-reform.

Not infrequently during those years of the Intifada, and in the years since, Peace Movement activists did have the experience of discovering that their Palestinian interlocutors were making demands on Israel that went beyond what they had previously stated, or what the Israelis thought they had heard; and occasionally in such instances the "peace" activists would express a sense of betrayal. But there was also a pattern of their ultimately embracing the new demands as reasonable and as worthy of serious Israeli consideration and acquiescence for the sake of peace. The investment in the belief that peace could be had by immersing oneself in the perspective of the other and maximally accommodating that perspective exerted too much psychological force to allow them to draw hard lines and to sustain a sense of indignation and a commensurate rethinking of their premises.

This accommodationist mode has essentially entailed a stark bias in favor of the Palestinian "other" and against the Israeli "other," those within Israeli society who have disagreed with the Peace Movement's perspectives. The former have in a sense been forgiven everything, the latter nothing. For example, if Peace Movement activists have tended to give short shrift to security concerns, it is hardly surprising that they have responded to expressions of a need to retain certain territories because of their religious and historical significance as outrageous, virtually barbaric, an inconceivable willingness to risk young Israeli lives for the sake of some primitive, atavistic attachment. Surely, they would argue, the strength of a people is to accommodate the past to the needs of the living. But when the Arab side has put forth demands that they couched in religious significances and obligations, these same critics would insist on the necessity of Israel attuning itself to the cultural sensitivities of the other side and seeking to accommodate those sensitivities.

A statement by Mordechai Bar-On in the introduction to his history of the Peace Movement precisely captures the mind-set of many of those who subscribed to the movement's perspectives. Bar-On writes that it is "a moral obligation — for Israel to resolve the hundred-year conflict with its Arab neighbors."[10] The statement is remarkable for its lack of qualification. It does not say that it is Israel's moral obligation to be alert and responsive to possible opportunities for diminishing or resolving the conflict, or even that Israel must not only react to such potential opportunities but must actively explore for them and seek to promote them. Rather, it implies that Israel is capable by its own actions of bringing about peace and that if the conflict remains unresolved it is because Israel has failed to meet its moral obligation.

The statement succinctly articulates that determination — under the pressure of ongoing enmity and hostility and in a desperate desire to end the assault — to ascribe to oneself or one's own camp the capacity to bring about the wished-for resolution through a self-reform that answers the other side's indictments. It captures the corollaries to that mind-set noted previously. One is the wishful casting of the actions of the other side as entirely determined by one's own, in effect the quite arrogant discounting of the capacity of the other side for independent action shaped by independent motives and calculations. Another is the bias against those in one's own camp who resist conforming to the author's desired program versus the indulgence of those in the other camp who offer such resistance. The impulse to discount the independent will of the other side, to see the other side's perspectives as reasonable demands that Israel must accommodate, and to see failures to elicit positive responses from the other side as necessarily due to Israel's falling short, obliges the author to indict any Israelis who are recalcitrant by his standards and to exonerate any Arabs who might be construed as recalcitrant.

There is an obvious irony in the attempt to comprehend Arab actions as entirely determined by Israeli actions, in that Israel is in fact able to exert remarkably little influence on the calculations and actions of its neighbors. Yet, of course, it is that very circumstance, the capacity of the Arab world to pursue policies of vilification and delegitimization of Israel irrespective of Israel's actions, the circumstance of Israel's essential helplessness in this regard, that inspires the reaching by some Israelis for delusions of control. The reality is that the vast Arab world does not need peace with Israel. Whatever benefits might accrue to the Arabs through peace — regaining of territory, economic benefits from trade and joint projects with a prosperous Israel — tend, not surprisingly, to count for relatively little in the calculation of Arab leaders and peoples. Arab leaders have found hostility to Israel a useful tool in distracting their populations from domestic grievances, and useful as well as a tool in inter-Arab rivalries, and this continues to be the case. Israel's economic strength, and the gains to be had from ties with Israel, are too insignificant to offset such calculations.

The situation with Egypt is instructive. Egypt has entered into a formal peace with Israel, and the Camp David accords entailed numerous agreements related to trade, all of which, if implemented, would have brought gains to Egypt. Moreover, Egypt is the strongest and most populous Arab state and the one most able to resist pressure from the rest of the Arab world. Yet, both to satisfy opinion elsewhere in the Arab world and to serve calculations of domestic challenges and the weighing of domestic forces, Egypt has essentially failed to implement these economic accords, has chosen to forego their benefits and keep Israel at arm's length. (A few joint endeavors, mainly farming projects in Egypt entailing the introduction of sophisticated Israeli agricultural techniques, have gone forward, and Egypt has derived benefit from these undertakings. But both the projects and Egyptian gain from them have proceeded under a virtual news blackout in Egypt and their existence is unknown to the vast majority of Egyptians.) In addition, Egypt's state-controlled media, despite the formal peace, daily pours out a litany of hatred and antagonism against Israel and, indeed, against Jews generally.

The Syrian government has wanted the Golan Heights returned. But it has rated hostility to Israel as of such importance in maintaining the minority Alawite dominion in the country and in justifying heavy-handed domestic policies that it has been willing, for the sake of such domestic considerations, to forego steps to reacquire territory and to reap as well the economic benefits of peace, including Western aid. (The impotence of Western, essentially American, aid as an inducement to Arab states to establish peace with Israel is amplified by the fact that for some key Arab states American support is attainable — because of oil and other strategic considerations — even without their acceptance of Israel. The United States will support Saudi Arabia no matter what its policies toward Israel, just as it supports Saudi Arabia no matter what its policies toward internal democratic reform. Egypt's cold peace and even hostility toward Israel has cost it virtually nothing in terms of U.S. support and aid, including military aid, on a grand scale. For European nations, of course, the attitude of the Arab states toward Israel is of essentially no significance in determining levels of support.)

Jordan is the state that has the capacity to benefit most from normalization of relations with Israel, and its leadership has generally been the most interested in pursuing such a peace. But it long hesitated, being vulnerable to military and other pressures from its neighbors and to the sentiments of a population with largely Palestinian roots and intensely hostile to Israel, and formally maintained a distance from Israel for many years. Even after signing a formal peace, Jordan has held off fully cultivating economic opportunities out of calculation of the sentiments of the Arab states and of much of its own population. Indeed, professional organizations in Jordan, led by the most educated segments of the population, have mounted aggressive and effective anti-normalization campaigns opposing trade and professional relations with Israel, campaigns that have included retaliation against individuals engaged in contacts with Israel.

Israel is a regional military power, and this no doubt has acted at times as an effective deterrent against military assault. But Israel's military might has essentially no impact on the calculations that underlie the hostility of the surrounding states toward Israel, as none of those states feels threatened by Israeli power. That is, none feels obliged to weigh Israeli power in its calculations of the stance to take toward Israel, because none expects that its hostile stance, as long as not turned into overt military action, will elicit any military moves by Israel that might threaten its regime.

In reality, by virtue of the relative size and strength, in population, wealth and territory, of the Arab world versus Israel, Israeli actions have been and continue to be reactive to Arab initiatives rather than vice versa. But, again, it is this very lack of control — these real limits on Israel's ability to bring about the acceptance in the region and normalization of relations that it desires — that has been a key factor in driving some Israelis to delusions of control.

This does not, of course, mean that the peace with its neighbors that Israel desires can never be had. (A common element of the rhetoric of the "peace" camp has been the illogical, and ahistorical, claim that anyone who does not subscribe to the camp's dogma must believe that peace is impossible.[11]) It simply means, rather, that if and when such a peace comes about will be determined primarily by decisions and actions of the Arabs and not by Israel, and that Arab decisions and actions are shaped by political and social dynamics whose evolution is, and will remain, essentially impervious to Israeli influence.

ISRAEL, THE PEACE MOVEMENT, AND THE PLO, 1988–1992

The leadership of neither of the major parties in Israel's National Unity Government shared Peace Now's sanguine view of negotiations with the PLO in the summer of 1988. Both saw the PLO as a revanchist organization still dedicated to Israel's destruction and both believed that its legitimization through recognition as a negotiating partner would only strengthen the organization. Nor did their views change in November and December with Arafat's reluctant steps toward meeting the United States' prerequisites for an American-PLO dialogue. In April, 1989, Shamir offered a plan for moving forward worked out with Rabin: Israel would agree to pursue negotiations as envisioned by the Israeli-Egyptian Camp David Accords but would not negotiate with the PLO. Israel was prepared to enter into immediate direct talks with the Arab states, to support elections in the territories for selection of Palestinian delegates to negotiations, to work with these delegates along with Jordan and Egypt toward establishment of an interim autonomy in the territories, and at the end of the interim period to negotiate a final status accord for disposition of the territories.[12]

Shamir appears to have had profound reservations about his own plan. All parties anticipated that anyone running for a delegate post in the territories would have to pass PLO muster and, if elected, would take his or her marching orders from Arafat; and Shamir believed that Israel would inexorably be pushed into the disastrous position of negotiating with the PLO. But he offered no other plan for moving from the status quo to a more stable accommodation with the Palestinian Arabs. Rabin seems to have been more sanguine about the proposal. Perhaps he hoped that, while the Palestinian delegates would in fact be essentially agents of the PLO, the stature and legitimacy that would accrue to them by virtue of their victory in Palestinian elections and their participation in negotiations would ultimately allow them to act more independently as representatives of the population in the territories and so increase the possibilities of reaching a stable and viable accord.

In the ensuing months, American Secretary of State James Baker pressed Shamir for elaborations of his plan that would make it more acceptable to the PLO. He also pushed for an end to all Israeli settlement activity, making no distinction between settlements in strategically vital and unpopulated areas that had been established largely under Labor and had broad Labor as well as Likud support and settlements near Palestinian population centers. Peace Now essentially endorsed Baker's position, likewise calling for an end to all settlement activity and aggressively campaigning against any construction in the territories. Rabin and the Labor leadership were eager to chart a path that would placate the Americans. In April, 1990, when Shamir essentially rejected Baker's demands, Labor withdrew from the National Unity Government, which was then replaced by a narrow coalition under Shamir.

In June, 1990, a PLO faction closely associated with Arafat attempted a seaborne terrorist attack against Tel Aviv. Arafat refused to condemn the attack, and Secretary of State Baker, under pressure from Congress, reluctantly broke off the U.S.-PLO dialogue. The PLO fell into further disfavor when Arafat openly supported Saddam Hussein's invasion of Kuwait in August, 1990, and then sided with Iraq against the American-led coalition mustered to oust the Iraqis from Kuwait. Palestinians in the territories endorsed Arafat's stance, widely hoped Saddam Hussein would fulfill his threats to "burn half of Israel," and cheered the missile barrages launched by Iraq against Israel in the ensuing Gulf War — an assault which the Israelis, under intense American pressure, refrained from answering.

Many in the Peace Movement, invested in their own comprehension of Palestinian attitudes and aspirations, were, in Bar-On's words, "profoundly disturbed and confused" by Arafat and his people's rallying to Saddam.[13] Even the prominent West Bank figures with whom they held dialogues and socialized and exchanged family photographs, people they saw as nurturing hopes that converged with their own and as the exemplars and proofs of Palestinian moderation and commitment to peace, people like Faisal Husseini and Sari Nusseibeh, endorsed Arafat's pro-Saddam stance. Some in the Peace Movement reacted with bitterness.

In an article entitled "Don't Call Me," Yossi Sarid, a leading peace activist, wrote that, "The hugging and kissing between Arafat and Saddam Hussein are disgusting and frightening . . . [When the crisis is over] nobody will hurry to invite the junior lackey of Saddam to the negotiating table." Sarid went on that, "until further notice the Palestinians can count me out."[14]

An Israeli television celebrity sympathetic to the Peace Movement, Yaron London, noted that Palestinian support for Saddam, and for Saddam's aspirations to a pan-Arab empire, raised questions about Palestinian demands for self-determination. London's statement touched on an old controversy. Since 1967 and Israel's attaining control over the West Bank and Gaza, the Palestinian leadership had been asserting that their constituency represented a distinct people with a right to national self-determination and that Israel, including those Israelis who wanted to negotiate the Palestinian Arabs' fate with Jordan, was depriving them of that right. But during the British Mandate, it was common for Arab leaders and academics opposed to the Zionist enterprise to argue that there was properly no such thing as Palestine, that the concept was a Jewish invention, and that the territory called "Palestine" was really part of the greater territorial patrimony of the entire Arab nation, of which the non-Jewish inhabitants of the territory were a part.

As noted in Chapter Seven, the Arab historian Philip Hitti testified in 1946 before the Anglo-American Committee of Inquiry that "There is no such thing as 'Palestine' in history, absolutely not." Earlier, in 1937, a local Arab leader appearing before the Peel Commission similarly declared, "There is no such thing [as Palestine]. 'Palestine' is a term the Zionists invented."[15] (A variation on the same theme was the insistence that Palestine is properly part of Syria. A meeting of Arab leaders in Jerusalem in 1919 convened to select Palestinian delegates to the Paris Peace Conference declared: "We consider Palestine as part of Arab Syria, as it has never been separated from it at any time. We are connected with it by national, religious, linguistic, natural, economic and geographical bonds."[16]) During the Jordanian occupation of the West Bank and the Egyptian occupation of Gaza, the Palestinian Arabs had not claimed a distinct peoplehood or sued for self-determination. Similarly, when the PLO was founded in 1964, it focused its founding charter not on achieving Palestinian self-determination and independence but on destroying Israel. In addition, the covenant, both in its 1964 iteration and its 1968 revised version, characterizes Palestine as "an inseparable part of the greater Arab homeland."

It was against this background that, for example, Golda Meir was inclined to see the post-1967 emphasis on Palestinian nationhood as a ploy to win the world's support for the war against Israel by turning it from an Arab-Israeli conflict into a war of national liberation. But in his endorsement of Saddam, Arafat was essentially reverting to that earlier Arab stance and saying much the same thing as Golda Meir had. Arafat justified Saddam's invasion and annexation of Kuwait by arguing that all the borders of the Middle East are artificial constructs imposed on the Arabs by Western colonial powers, that there are properly no Iraqis or Kuwaitis or Jordanians or Palestinians or Syrians or Saudis, but that they are all one Arab nation and all the territory of the Middle East is their common national patrimony.

Thus London observed: "Most [Palestinians] want a modern Saladin who will unify the Arab world and expel all non-Arabs from the Middle East . . . Therefore, goodbye Husseini, goodbye Nusseibeh . . . When you come back to ask for my sympathy for your 'legitimate rights' you will find that your pro-Saddam screams have deafened my ears."[17]

Not everyone in the Peace Movement experienced even a temporary disenchantment with the Palestinians as peace partners. Some immediately characterized Palestinian enthusiasm for Saddam as an understandable consequence of their frustration and desperation. A not uncommon argument was that, as the support for Saddam was so illogical, it must reflect desperation; "illogical" meaning here, of course, that it did not conform to what those in the "peace" camp thought the Palestinians ought to want. Others in the Peace Movement actually expressed sympathy with the Palestinians' stance, arguing that the American-led coalition against Saddam was a resurrection of Western imperialism trying to impose its will on the region and that the Palestinians were right to oppose it. The disenchantment with the Palestinians and their leaders, however, was very widespread. But, perhaps not surprisingly, it was also short-lived.

Peace Now declared during the crisis that, "there is no other option but to conduct a dialogue with [the Palestinians] and thereby attempt to resolve the Israeli-Palestinian conflict."[18] This is an obviously valid statement; movement toward resolution of the conflict would require dialogue with the Palestinians. What is remarkable is the rapidity with which the Peace Movement broadly reverted to perceiving Arafat's PLO as a fit partner for that dialogue. For example, Yossi Beilin, leader of the dovish camp in the Labor Party, wrote an article criticizing Yossi Sarid's "Don't Call Me" piece. Beilin insisted that, while Arafat's behavior might be regrettable, Israel still had to negotiate with the PLO.[19]

Other elements of the "peace" camp's response were even more remarkable. The crisis dramatically demonstrated the dangers entailed in Israel retreating to its vulnerable pre-1967 borders and its nine-mile width. It underscored the wisdom of pursuing a resolution in which Israel retained the sparsely populated Jordan Valley and related strategic areas as a vital buffer against attacks from the east, or against a joining of Palestinian forces with eastern forces in an assault on Israel: the logic that had driven Allon's plan and Labor's settlement policy. Yet the Peace Movement reverted almost immediately to condemning all Jewish settlements and advocating a withdrawal virtually to the pre-1967 lines.

The Peace Movement also returned to insisting that genuine peace could be assured if only Israel were sufficiently forthcoming in its concessions, and to casting not Arafat and his coterie but rather the Israeli government and its supporters as the obstacles to peace. Thus, Peace Now accused the government of seeking "to manipulate the political mistakes which the Palestinians and the PLO have made in order to advance" its own, less forthcoming, policies.[20] Notable also in this statement is the whitewashing characterization of the actions of the PLO and its supporters as "political mistakes," a depiction reflecting the wish to blur the Palestinians' eagerness for a Saddam-led war of annihilation against Israel into something less threatening and more in keeping with what the "peace" camp wanted to be the aspirations of the other side. "Political mistakes" suggested Arafat and his followers were in fact seeking a resolution along the lines proposed by the Peace Movement but had simply gone about pursuing it in the wrong way.

In the wake of the Gulf War, the United States — having, by its success in executing the war, achieved a new pinnacle of influence in the region — sought to organize an international conference on the Arab-Israeli conflict. It proposed that opening ceremonies be followed by direct bilateral negotiations between Israel and Syria and between Israel and a joint Jordanian and Palestinian delegation as well as by negotiations on regional cooperation involving Israel and all the states of the Arab Middle East.

The PLO, its support of Saddam Hussein having resulted in both diplomatic and financial reverses (Kuwait and Saudi Arabia cut off their former subsidies to the organization), acquiesced in having the Palestinians represented by figures from the territories, although it was tacitly understood that these figures would be functioning according to directions from the PLO. It also agreed to talks being limited to pursuing interim autonomy arrangements as envisioned by the Camp David accords. The Palestinians acceded as well to being formally part of a joint Jordanian-Palestinian delegation. Israel, for its part, reluctantly yielded to the Palestinian contingent being led by someone from Jerusalem, Faisal Husseini. (Israel had been concerned that such a step would undercut its claim of sovereignty over reunited Jerusalem.)

The conference convened in Madrid at the end of October, 1991, and was followed by the planned bilateral negotiations, held in Washington, and by regional negotiations at various venues around the world. The bilateral talks soon bogged down, and this was the state of affairs when, in June, 1992, Israel held Knesset elections. Labor, under the leadership of Yitzhak Rabin, emerged victorious from the elections and formed the new government, ending fifteen years of Likud's either controlling or participating as an equal partner in Israel's government.

By some measures, the inroads of the Peace Movement and its arguments over the previous fifteen years on Israeli public opinion, and more particularly on the ranks of those traditionally in the Labor Zionist camp, might appear to have been quite limited. For example, opinion polls even at the end of Likud's tenure showed that a majority of Israelis supported the view that Israel must retain control of most if not all of the West Bank in any settlement, and also believed that Israel would need to hold onto the Golan Heights[21] — results that clearly revealed substantial percentages of Labor Zionist followers holding these views. Of course, these majorities did not reflect commensurate support for Likud and its positions. Rather, at this time the official stance of Labor was that Israeli security, the ability of the nation to defend itself, required that it keep control of key strategic areas in the West Bank and of the Golan and the poll results reflected the extent to which public sentiment followed the official views of Labor and Likud, which converged on these matters.

If increasing numbers of the higher echelons of Labor were being won over to the Peace Movement's perspectives, it was acknowledged in the party that the public mood even among Labor supporters was less sanguine about the possibilities for genuine peace and still leaning to Labor's traditional positions.

Indeed, Labor's choice of Rabin over Shimon Peres to lead the party in the 1992 elections, and the campaign's emphasis on security, were intended to reassure those Labor sympathizers who were uneasy with the drift of some of Labor's key figures toward the Peace Movement. Rabin had the image of a military man who would ensure Israel's security interests in any negotiations, and during the campaign he made explicit promises to retain key strategic areas in the West Bank and never to negotiate away the Golan Heights. In addition, the Labor Party platform stressed the party's adherence to long-standing Labor positions vis-à-vis the territories, including its traditional stance on potential negotiating partners:

"Israel will continue and complete negotiations with authorized and agreed-on Palestinians *from the territories occupied by Israel since 1967* [emphasis added]. . . . There is a need for an agreement in a Jordanian-Palestinian framework . . . and not a separate Palestinian state west of the Jordan. . . . Jerusalem will remain united and undivided under Israeli sovereignty. . . . The Jordan Valley and the western shore of the Dead Sea will be under Israeli sovereignty. . . . In any peace agreement with Syria, Israel's presence and control, both military and in terms of settlements, will continue [on the Golan Heights]."[22]

This Labor gambit of emphasizing traditional party stances on security issues and the territories seems to have played a substantial role in the party's subsequent election victory.

But events in ensuing months would show that electoral support for Rabin's traditional Labor message, and signs generally of discomfort among Labor Party constituents with the drift by some leaders and spokespeople away from the party's long-standing positions on peace and security, were misleading. The Peace Movement had offered a steady drumbeat of reassurances that genuine peace, along the lines of relations among states in western Europe and not simply a more secure armistice or a cold and tenuous "peace," was possible. It had offered assurances that the PLO was a partner with whom such a peace could be negotiated. It had argued that, in the coming peace, concerns about the retention of defensible positions in "Palestinian" territory would be moot and passé. It had insisted that those who disagreed with this conviction were not people with reasonable concerns about Israel's security and survival but rather, in Bar-On's words, "diehard chauvinists and religiously motivated expansionists."[23] It had maintained that it was such people, not the PLO and its followers, who were the obstacle to the peace all right-thinking Israelis desired. The true inroads of this drumbeat on the ranks of Labor Zionist sympathizers were revealed a year after Rabin's election.

Those inroads were born of weariness and eagerness to end the seemingly interminable Arab war against Israel and to attain "normal" lives. They were born of the wish to believe that the right steps by Israel could win what was desired, and the associated willingness to demonize Likud and its followers, the Sephardim and the religious, those "other" Jews, to cast them as the enemies of "peace," in the service of such fantasies. The actual impact of the Peace Movement and its dogma was revealed when, in 1993, Rabin capitulated to the "peace" camp's program and abandoned traditional Labor positions on security and peace and his campaign promises of the 1992 election. Labor's constituency offered essentially no resistance but rather capitulated with him.

THE PEACE MOVEMENT AND THE NEW HISTORIANS

The Peace Movement's recasting of the Arab-Israeli conflict as a readily soluble dispute with a willing peace partner, a dispute that would be brought to an end once Israelis reconciled themselves to reasonable concessions and reached out for the extended hand of peace, had been buttressed during the decade or so preceding Rabin's capitulation by several complementary "movements" within Israeli society. These latter were in turn inspired in large part by a wish to bolster the "peace" camp's perspectives, and their evolution and growing popularity within Labor Zionist circles and beyond paralleled that of the "peace" camp and reflected the burgeoning eagerness to embrace the Peace Movement's self-delusions.

One of these complementary "movements" emerged, as did a significant segment of the leadership of the Peace Movement, from Israeli academia and was inspired in part by anti-Zionist circles in Israeli universities. It has become known as the New History, its practitioners as new historians. The stated aim of the new historians has been to debunk Israeli national "myths": more particularly, to cast a critical eye at Israel's pre-history, birth, and early development that would yield a supposedly more "honest" understanding of the country's past. But most of these historians have also had a political aim, not infrequently explicitly acknowledged, of offering historical support for the Peace Movement's comprehension of the Arab-Israeli conflict and winning adherents to that perspective, lessening people's fears and rendering them more amenable to concessions for "peace."

The implicit logic of this political aim of Israeli revisionist history is straightforward. If Israelis could be made to see Israel's birth as sinful, as an unfair assault on the Palestinian Arabs and perhaps others of the Jews' neighbors, or at least as a morally ambiguous undertaking that involved a greater blurring of right and wrong, of aggressor and aggrieved, than is generally recognized, then the Jews of Israel would become more sympathetic to the perspectives of their Arab neighbors. They would also be less inclined to view their neighbors as irreconcilable foes bent on Israel's destruction and more willing to see them as people like themselves who simply want — have always simply wanted — a fair resolution of the conflict. So they would be prepared to be more forth-coming, to make painful concessions, to achieve that fair resolution.

Aside from its echoes of the "Zionism is sinful" tradition long ensconced in the social science faculties of Israeli academia, the work of the new histori-ans no doubt also received some inspiration from politically correct revisionist history as practiced with substantial popularity throughout Western academia. An example is the writings of American revisionist historians who would place the lion's share of the blame for the Cold War on the West, particularly on the United States. It is also likely that the warm reception accorded the Israeli new historians on Western campuses contributed more than a little to their own en-thusiasm for their reinterpretations of the historical record.[24]

One can debate the relative weight of such considerations, versus the new historians' genuine devotion to the Peace Movement and its perspectives, in serv-ing as extraneous, nonscholarly influences on the shaping of their revisions of history. But the explanation for the remarkable reception accorded their writings by the Israeli popular media and public at large, particularly by the con-stituencies of Labor Zionism, is the same as the explanation for the contem-poraneously burgeoning popularity of the Peace Movement. The warm reception given the new historians in Israel had seemingly no parallel in any other Western nations vis-à-vis their own revisionist historians and was all the more remarkable given, as shall be seen, the shoddiness of most of the New History as history. That enthusiastic response was spurred, again, by the ea-gerness of Israelis, in the face of interminable hostility and vituperation, to see the Palestinian-Israeli, and broader Arab-Israeli, conflict as indeed soluble and to see Israeli behavior as the key to a solution, with Israel but having to change its ways and make the right concessions to elicit its desired peace.

Bar-On, in his history of the Peace Movement, sets truth on its head by dismissing the generally more accurate nonrevisionist literature on Israel's early history and embracing the "new historians" as "objective." But in doing so, he illustrates the convergence of the perspectives of the New History with those of the Movement:

"A highly subjective and selective interpretation of the history of the con-flict [i.e., the earlier, nonrevisionist history] has posed a significant psycholog-ical obstacle to reconciliation. Recently several Israeli historians have reexamined this history in a more objective and self-critical manner [Bar-On, in a footnote here, cites Benny Morris's *Birth of the Palestinian Refugee Problem*]; such re-assessments may help Israelis to better understand all sides' responsibility for the human tragedy of the Israeli-Palestinian conflict, and may contribute to ef-forts to address a judicious and mutually acceptable resolution of the strife."[25]

Morris's book, published in 1987, is one of the seminal works of Israel's New History. The author argues that, while the great majority of Palestinian refugees from the 1947–48 fighting left of their own volition to get out of harm's way, some were driven out by the Israelis and — the more revisionist claim — that Ben-Gurion and his associates were in fact eager for the Palestinian Arabs to leave and regarded their doing so as an important aim of Yishuv policy.[26]

Another prominent work in the new-historian mode is Avi Shlaim's *Collusion Across the Jordan: King Abdullah, the Zionist Movement, and the Partition of Palestine* (1988).[27] Shlaim asserts that Abdullah and Ben-Gurion conspired, with British support, in Transjordan's seizing the West Bank territories that were to be given to the Palestinian Arabs under the United Nations partition plan, with the *quid pro quo* being that Transjordan acquiesced in the establishment of Israel. He claims, in effect, that Israel worked with Transjordan to strangle the nascent Palestinian state, in contrast to popular belief that Israel was the victim of an onslaught by the Palestinians and surrounding Arab armies. Another corollary of Shlaim's thesis is that the Israelis, having secured the support of Transjordan and Britain, were never really threatened with annihilation in the 1947–48 war.

Ilan Pappe's *Britain and the Arab-Israeli Conflict, 1948–1951* (1988),[28] likewise promotes the thesis of Transjordanian-Israeli collusion with British approval. Pappe is particularly insistent on the supposed benevolence of the British toward the Israelis and on the absence of any real threat to Israel's survival in the 1947–48 war. In another vein, Tom Segev, in *The Seventh Million* (1991), claims, against overwhelming evidence to the contrary, that Yishuv leaders were cool to the plight of European Jews during the Holocaust and failed to pursue opportunities to rescue them.

All these authors have published prolifically over the subsequent years on related themes or other aspects of Israel's early history and have been joined by numerous other "new historians." Together they have generated a large outpouring of literature elaborating themes to the effect that the Zionist enterprise has been a morally more ambiguous undertaking than it has generally been portrayed to be and that the Palestinian Arabs were indeed victims of Israeli policy. Additional recurrent elements of the revisionist claims are that Arab hostility has not been as annihilationist as it has been depicted, that Israel's existence has never really been threatened, that Israel has in fact been the villain in much of its dealings with the Arabs, and that Israel has failed to grasp various opportunities for peace. The overall thrust of this literature is that the Palestinian Arabs and the Arab states should be seen in a more benign light than they have been and, extrapolating from this to a frequently implicit and indeed often explicit conclusion, that Israelis should be more prepared to see a fairness in Arab indictments and demands and should not be so concerned about what has seemed to them existential threats or so fearful of what they have hitherto perceived as risky concessions.

The last decade and a half have also seen the publishing of an extensive literature debunking much of the New History, including those works noted above. This literature has revealed in detail the tendentiousness endemic in the writings of the new historians: Their consistent ignoring of vital primary sources and gross distorting of those sources that they do invoke; their sacrificing of basic principles of historiographic scholarship and academic integrity to an often openly acknowledged political agenda; their — in the words of one critic — "fabricating" of Israeli history in the service of that agenda.[29]

Critiques of Morris's *The Birth of the Palestinian Refugee Problem* provide an illustration of this distorting of the historical record.[30] Morris is in many ways the leading figure among the new historians. He is the one most touted by those who invoke the new history for political purposes, either as part of a broader indictment of Israel or in the context of supporting particular policies such as those advocated by the Peace Movement. In addition, whereas some new historians such as Ilan Pappe acknowledge that their interpretations of the historical record are filtered through a political bias (and argue that this is inevitably the case in the writing of history), Morris rejects this relativist thesis and insists that he is offering an objective and impartial analysis.[31] Consequently, the overwhelming evidence of his distortions of the archival data is all the more devastating to his assertions and to his claims of how he arrived at them.

A pretense commonly put forward by the new historians is that their revisionist histories are based on newly available information and so they are able to offer a truer picture of the past than that provided by their predecessors. Morris asserts this as well, but scrutiny of the arguments of his 1987 book and of his other work reveals less paradigm-shifting use of new material than tortured interpretations and misrepresentations of old information; and this is true generally of the New History.

The observation has been made against the new historians that those elements in their theses that are true are, in fact, not new, and those elements that are new, typically the most dramatic and damning claims, are not true. This, too, applies as well to Morris's arguments in his 1987 book. That some relatively small portion of the Palestinian refugees were forced out of their homes by the Israelis had been noted by Israeli historians at least since the 1950s.[32] Suggestions by Morris and others that earlier historians had insisted no Arabs had been forced out are simply untrue. In contrast, Morris's broader and most damning thesis, that Ben-Gurion and his associates desired to clear the areas under their control of Arabs and that this was an aim of Yishuv policy, is new but not true.

A review of Morris's use of the historical record is damning for him and not for Ben-Gurion. What follows are two related examples taken from Efraim Karsh's *Fabricating Israeli History.* Morris claims that Ben-Gurion wrote to his son, Amos, in 1937, "We must expel Arabs and take their places."[33] Karsh notes: "This rang a distant bell . . . I recalled the letter as saying something quite different. Indeed, an examination of the Hebrew text confirmed my recollection.

It read as follows: '*We do not wish, we do not need* to expel Arabs and take their places . . . "' (italics are Karsh's).[34]

More broadly, while Morris acknowledges that Britain's Peel Commission had recommended transfer of populations as part of its 1937 partition plan, he suggests that the idea came from the Zionists. This is likewise a distortion of the actual record.

In a similar vein, Morris cites a speech by Ben-Gurion delivered on December 13, 1947:

"Ben-Gurion starkly outlined the emergent Jewish State's main problem — its prospective population of 520,000 Jews and 350,000 Arabs. Including Jerusalem, the state would have a population of about one million, 40 percent of which would be non-Jews. 'This fact must be viewed in all its clarity and sharpness. With such a [population] composition, there cannot even be complete certainty that the government will be held by a Jewish majority . . . There can be no stable and strong Jewish State so long as it has a Jewish majority of only 60 percent.' The Yishuv's situation and fate, he went on, compelled the adoption of 'a new approach . . . [new] habits of mind' to 'suit our new future. We must think like a state.'"[35]

Morris insinuates that the speech suggests Ben-Gurion's support for re-solving the demographic difficulties by forced transfer of Arabs out of Israeli territory. But Karsh points to elements of the cited text that Morris omits (omit-ted sections italicized):

"There can be no stable and strong Jewish State so long as it has a Jewish majority of only 60 percent, *and so long as this majority consists of only 600,000 Jews* . . .

" . . . We must think in terms of a state, *in terms of independence, in terms of full responsibility for ourselves — and for others* . . . "[36]

As Karsh notes, who were these "others" that Ben-Gurion was referring to if not the Arab minority in the state? More significantly, Ben-Gurion's refer-ence to "only 600,000" Jews makes clear that Ben-Gurion looked to Jewish im-migration as the solution to the demographic problem. Morris's omission of these lines was a distortion of his sources in support of his insinuated gloss on Ben-Gurion's meaning.

But Morris's unconscionable misrepresentation of Ben-Gurion's speech went beyond these omissions. Morris, for all his claims of making more thorough use of primary sources than his predecessors, in fact in this instance, as Karsh demonstrates, did not use the primary source for the speech, but rather an edited version of Ben-Gurion's war diary. The unedited speech, readily available to Morris, even more thoroughly renders his thesis untenable. There, Ben-Gurion, after noting the demographic difficulties "so long as the majority consists of only 600,000 Jews," states,

"In order to ensure not only the establishment of the Jewish State but its existence and destiny as well — we must bring a million-and-a-half Jews to the country and root them there. It is only when there will be at least two million Jews in the country — that the state will be truly established . . . A Jewish government whose concerns and actions will not be predominantly geared to the enterprise of aliya and settlement that will increase our number in the Land of Israel to two million in the shortest period of time — will betray its foremost responsibility and will endanger the great historical achievement gained by our generation."[37]

This fuller quote from the speech obviously demonstrates even more clearly that in Ben-Gurion's thinking the answer to the demographic threat was Jewish immigration, not expulsion of the Arabs. There is absolutely no hint of the latter in the speech, but Morris edited Ben-Gurion's words to make the true focus of the speech less explicit.

There is still more to Morris's distorting omissions. In fact, Ben-Gurion believed it was in Israel's vital interests that the country retain a substantial Arab minority, anticipating — naïvely so, given all that has ensued — that the nation's Arab minority would serve as a bridge for Israel to the surrounding Arab world; and he explicitly asserts this in the speech. Following his reference to thinking "in terms of full responsibility for ourselves — and for others," Ben-Gurion continues:

"In our state there will be non-Jews as well — and all of them will be equal citizens; equal in everything without any exception; that is: the state will be their state as well. . . . The attitude of the Jewish State to its Arab citizens will be an important factor — though not the only one — in building good neighborly relations with the Arab states. If the Arab citizen will feel at home in our state, and if his status will not be in the least different from that of the Jew, and perhaps better than the status of the Arab in an Arab state, and if the state will help him in a truthful and dedicated way to reach the economic, social, and cultural level of the Jewish community, then Arab distrust will accordingly subside and a bridge to a Semitic, Jewish-Arab alliance will be built . . . "[38]

This, and more in the same vein, were omitted by Morris in his mangling of Ben-Gurion's words for the sake of presenting them as offering hints of a supposed predisposition toward a policy of expulsion. In addition, Morris then, through the rest of his book, treats Ben-Gurion's supposed support for transfer as a given,[39] and he ascribes the absence of documentary evidence of this support to Ben-Gurion's caginess, his not wanting to leave a paper trail.[40]

Beyond those distortions of fact that provide the underpinnings of Morris's major thesis, the book also contains many small misrepresentations which likewise serve to cast the Israeli case and Israeli actions in a negative light. For example, Morris writes at one point, "In 1947, Jews . . . owned some 7 percent . . . of Palestine's total of 26.4 million dunams of land. The Partition resolution had earmarked some 60 percent of Palestine for the Jewish State; most of it was not

Jewish-owned land. But war was war and, if won, as Ben-Gurion saw things, it would at last solve the Jewish State's land problem."[41]

Morris is clearly seeking to convey the impression that the vast majority of Mandate land was Arab-owned and that what became Israel consisted mainly of Arab real estate seized in the war. But over 70 percent of Mandate Palestine, and of the area that comprised Israel in 1948, was public, or state, land. Both Arabs and Jews were in the position, in areas they subsequently controlled, of taking possession of land the vast preponderance of which they had not previously owned. Of the territory that became Israel in 1948, in fact 8.6 percent was owned by Jews, 3.3 percent remained in the possession of Arabs who stayed and became Israeli citizens, and under 17 percent belonged to Arabs who had fled.[42]

Other examples of the same sort can be given to illustrate further Morris's dishonest methodology in his 1987 book. Morris employs a similar *modus operandi* in his later work, as in *1948 and After: Israel and the Palestinians* (1990), in which he expands on some of the themes of his 1987 book.[43]

Bogus scholarship also characterizes Ilan Pappe and Avi Shlaim's development of their thesis concerning supposed collusion between Israel and Transjordan in the 1947–48 war and supposed British participation in the collusion and support for the establishment of the Jewish state. The distortions and misrepresentations in their work have been well-documented by various historians.[44]

Tom Segev's at once vicious and absurd claims regarding Ben-Gurion and his associates' attitudes toward the plight of Europe's Jews, in *The Seventh Million: The Israelis and the Holocaust,*[45] represent another genre of the "Israel as born in sin" or "Zionism as illegitimate" literature. Various themes in this other genre include assertions that the Yishuv's leaders ignored the plight of Europe's doomed Jews, or that they callously exploited the disaster, or that they mistreated the survivors, or even that they were somehow guilty of contributing to the catastrophe. While Segev's book is not the ugliest or most outrageous example of this pseudo-history, it is perhaps the most significant of the genre in that his prominence in Israel as a journalist won the work particularly wide attention.

One striking feature of the book is its myriad contradictions. Segev repeatedly acknowledges that there was virtually nothing the Yishuv could have done to rescue Europe's Jews, or even to save many additional individuals. He reinforces this by noting that, in the three years between the end of the war and the creation of the state, as the Yishuv was pursuing illegal immigration without the obstacle of a Nazi-dominated Europe, with various European governments sympathetic, and with only the British as enemy, it was able to achieve public relations successes but almost invariably failed to overcome the British blockade. Yet this does not keep Segev from faulting Ben-Gurion and the Yishuv leadership for not doing more to save European Jewry before and during the war. He acknowledges the deep sorrow and sense of guilt felt by the Jews of the Yishuv over the martyrdom of Europe's Jews and recognizes that the feelings of guilt were in some respects psychologically more tolerable to them than full recognition of their helplessness, than full acceptance that the New Jew they were trying to mold was incapable of saving his brethren. Yet Segev still uses that sense of guilt against the Yishuv, as somehow a measure of actual dereliction. He also accuses the Yishuv leadership of not feeling enough sorrow and pangs of conscience.

Elsewhere, Segev's arguments, if not strictly self-contradictory, are nevertheless illogical. A major theme of the book is his attack on Israel's characterizing itself as the heir of the Holocaust's victims and appropriating to itself their legacy; and he points out that most of those killed were not active Zionists. But the truth remains that the Yishuv was the only political entity in the world that wanted Europe's Jews and that if it had not been obstructed by British quotas and blockades it would have been able to save many more both before and during the war. Segev goes further and states that the failure of rescue was a failure of the Zionist enterprise, as the Zionists had promoted their quest for a state as necessary in order to provide a refuge for the world's Jews. But the terrible dimensions of the failure were, of course, due to the fact that the Yishuv was not an independent state free to set its own immigration policy. To this obvious rejoinder that things would have been different had the Yishuv been an independent state, Segev responds with the ludicrous non-response that the claim is an ideological argument and not an historical one.

The socialist Zionist leadership in the Yishuv could be faulted in that, through the decade before the war, its consensus was still in favor of the limited and selective immigration that it saw as most conducive to constructing its socialist utopia. The leadership consistently ignored Ben-Gurion's warnings of impending catastrophe and rejected his efforts to push, even in alliance with Jabotinsky and the Revisionists, for immediate large-scale immigration. But Segev never really considers this failure.

Segev also casts as somehow nefarious Israel's pointing to the Holocaust as demonstrating the necessity of a Jewish state, its using the Holocaust to call upon the conscience of the world to support the Zionist enterprise. But he never makes clear, for all the heat he generates in discussing the matter, what is wrong or illegitimate about this invoking of the Holocaust. In addition, Segev elsewhere endorses the view that "the right of self-determination is a universal right of every nation,"[46] albeit he does so in the context of a reference to the Palestinians' predicament. One would think then that he would be offended by Israel's being put into a position of having to argue its right to exist. But, on the contrary, his focus is on what he sees as the inadequacy of Israel's arguments.

Similarly, Segev gives two explanations for Israel's being obliged to justify its existence: the Arab siege, and the fact that most Jews do not live in Israel. The second "explanation" is silly. Most Irish do not live in Ireland, most ethnic Italians do not live in Italy, and most Anglo-Saxons do not live in Britain; this hardly puts those states in the position of having to defend their right to exist. It is the Arab siege that accounts for Israel's being pushed into that position; and, again, one might expect Segev to be exercised by the unfairness of Israel's having to justify its existence. But instead he joins with the besiegers to scrutinize critically the arguments the state has mustered as it has faced its kangaroo court.

The hypercritical attitude toward Israel at the heart of Segev's formulations is captured in his reference to a more contemporary issue. He notes that during the Gulf crisis and Gulf War of 1990–1991 there were revelations of German contributions to Iraq's programs for developing weapons of mass destruction, particularly its chemical weapons programs, and that, as Israel braced for and confronted missile attacks, there was much media coverage in Israel of this German role, with all its reverberations with memories of the genocide. Segev's gloss on the episode: "It was . . . used to revive animosity toward Germany, now reunited Germany."[47]

What accounts for Segev's jaundiced perspective? Why does he take offense at Israel's arguments defending its existence rather than at the Arab siege that has obliged the state to defend its existence? The answer becomes clearer in his sharp distinction between what he sees as improper versus proper lessons to be drawn from the catastrophe in Europe: the lesson of the need for Jewish self-defense versus supposedly broader-spirited universalist conclusions. Segev casts these two perspectives as alternatives, with people having to choose one or the other, when of course both are legitimate. The Holocaust points to the need both for Jews to be able to defend themselves and for Jews to join in broader struggles against hatred and bigotry.

But Segev frames them as sharp alternatives because of the siege. He chooses to believe — again, despite all the evidence to the contrary — that if Jews would only make the "right" choice and eschew the "wrong" they would undergo a self-reform that would end the siege. Nowhere in the book does Segev attempt to assess what threats the Arab assault actually poses, or what Arab objectives are. Nor does he ever refer to the genocidal agenda propounded routinely in Arab media, Arab schools, Arab mosques. Yet he nevertheless speaks censoriously of Israelis confounding Arabs with Nazis and seeing an existential threat from the former. He declares his fear that comprehending the Holocaust in terms of Jewish nationhood and the necessity of Jewish self-defense inclines Israelis to "limit their willingness to take the risks involved in a compromise peace settlement."[48]

Once more, a supposed work of history is shaped less by an interest in historical inquiry per se than by frustration with the Arab siege and embrace of the delusion that sufficient Israeli self-effacement, self-indictment, and self-reform can end the siege.

There have been a number of devastating critiques of Segev's book by other historians.[49] But, as noted, there has also been a skein of additional publications indicting Israel in more extreme terms for its supposed nefarious use of the Holocaust and indeed of the Holocaust's survivors. Amnon Rubinstein, a leading figure in the far left Meretz Party and hardly associated with the supposedly narrow-minded Israeli Right, offers a scathing review of this "academic" literature, particularly its effort to portray the Holocaust as not a Jewish catastrophe but a universal catastrophe that has been misappropriated by the Zionists. Rubinstein states at one point, after citing a representative passage, "This is no parody. These words were written with abysmal serious-mindedness. They intend to prove yet again that the memory of the Holocaust is another Zionist-Jewish myth and that postmodern man must eschew this myth, adopting the ostensibly scientific, universalistic explanations as his new bible."[50]

But such explanations — the sharp contrasting of "Jewish" versus "universalistic" interpretations of the Holocaust and the delegitimizing of the former and apotheosing of the latter — have encountered a receptive audience in Israel beyond the narrow confines of self-reinforcing and mutually congratulatory academics. These perspectives also continue to recruit acolytes within academia. That they do so is, again, in large part a direct consequence of the siege and the wish to believe that proper obeisance to the universalist message will win peace.

As suggested, the writers of the New History have varied somewhat in their depiction of their aims and intentions. But virtually all, like Segev, have given clear indications that they regarded their work as weapons in the struggle to move Israel toward peace through self-reform.

The first author in the New History vein to attain some prominence was Simha Flapan, whose book *The Birth of Israel: Myths and Realities* was published in 1987.[51] Flapan had been for many years a leading figure in Israel's Mapam Party, ideologically to the left of Ben-Gurion's Mapai, and an outspoken critic of Israeli policy under Ben-Gurion and his Labor Zionist successors. Flapan states in his introduction that his intention in writing the book was to "undermine the propaganda structures that have so long obstructed the growth of the peace forces in my country."[52] His aim is to do so by supposedly refuting what he calls the Zionist "myths" surrounding Israel's founding and the 1947–1948 war. Elsewhere in his introduction he reiterates his goal even more explicitly: "It is the purpose of this book to debunk these myths, not as an academic exercise but as a contribution to a better understanding of the Palestinian problem and to a more constructive approach to its solution."[53]

Benny Morris, reviewing in 1990 seminal texts of what he first labeled the

New History (or New Historiography), acknowledges that Flapan's work "is not, strictly speaking, a 'history' at all but rather a polemical work written from a Marxist perspective . . . Politics rather than historiography is the book's manifest objective."[54] But Morris nevertheless embraces Flapan's formulation of the alleged "myths" of Israel's founding. Pappe endorses Flapan's arguments even more categorically,[55] and Shlaim too associates his own perspectives with Flapan's.[56]

Morris, as noted, has insisted he is simply seeking to provide in his histories objective and impartial analysis and has striven to distinguish himself from those "who use history to prove political points and buttress contemporary political positions" or "who would brandish history in the service of present-day peacemaking."[57] But in an article in 1988, not long after he published his first book, Morris notes that the "old" or "official" history of Israel's war of independence "has significantly influenced the attitudes of Diaspora Jews, as well as the attitude of European and American non-Jews, toward present-day Israel — which affects government policies concerning the Israeli-Arab conflict."[58] This suggests that, at the least, he was not unmindful of contemporary political implications of his revisionist history. He concludes the same article by expressing, albeit coyly, the hope that the New History of Israel's founding will have a contemporary political impact; that it "may also in some obscure way serve the purposes of peace and reconciliation between the warring tribes of that land."[59]

Shlaim, in *Collusion Across the Jordan*, does not explicitly relate his history to contemporary politics. But, in language very often more polemical than historiographic, he does wield his fatally flawed scholarship to cast Israel and its policies in 1947–1948 as the primary villain of the piece. Shlaim softened his polemical language somewhat for the abridged, paperback version of the book,[60] but the anti-Israel slant of the work remained essentially intact. Elsewhere, his relating of his skewed version of the history of 1947–1948 to contemporary politics is quite explicit. In a later book, Shlaim declares, "The establishment of the State of Israel involved a massive injustice to the Palestinians. Half a century on, Israel still had to arrive at the reckoning of its own sins against the Palestinians, a recognition that it owed the Palestinians a debt that must at some point be repaid."[61]

Ilan Pappe, as indicated, has acknowledged that his interpretations of history are filtered through a political bias. (Morris, asserting his own distance from such bias, writes disapprovingly of Pappe's "views on the historian's craft . . . that historians have political attitudes and beliefs, and should give them free rein in their works, even using these works to promote current political agendas."[62]) For Pappe, that political agenda goes beyond even the Peace Movement's stance that sufficient Israeli concessions will inexorably elicit peace and that a return essentially to the pre-1967 lines is the crux of the required concessions. Pappe, long active in Israel's Hadash (Communist) Party, has advocated some compromise in Israel's sovereignty, and even at times the dissolution of the Jewish state, as the path to peace. More particularly, he has been a vigorous advocate of the Palestinians' "right of return" as a necessary element in bringing about peace by rectifying "the horrendous crime committed against the Palestinian people in 1948."[63]

But whatever the various nuances of the new historians' own relating of their work to the search for peace, the warm reception accorded their theses within Israel has been very much tied to attitudes toward the Arab-Israeli conflict. As noted, the "New History" quickly won, and has since sustained, an enthusiastic following not only among Israel's academic and artistic elites but also well beyond those elites, a following that includes a substantial portion of the general public. The reason for this enthusiastic reception has been that the distortions of the New History converge with a political message that significant portions of the Israeli public have been eager to hear: The message that Arab enmity is simply a response to Israeli misdeeds and so if Israel would only make proper amends the enmity would cease, the long siege would end, and peace would prevail.

THE PEACE CAMP, POST-ZIONISM, AND ISRAEL'S LITERARY ELITE

Another of the movements complementing the Peace Movement likewise emerged in large part from Israel's university campuses, was also inspired to no small degree by anti-Zionist circles in Israeli academia, and has been widely referred to by the rubric "post-Zionism." *Post-Zionism* is a term that has been used over the years in a number of different contexts. But in this context it refers to arguments that Israel's aspirations to be a democratic state and also a Jewish state are irreconcilable; that, in addition, the state's Zionist, and Jewish, accoutrements are an intolerable insult to Israel's Arab citizens; and that Israel ought to divest itself of its official Jewishness for the sake of embracing a new universalist and democratic ethos.

An earlier and different use of the term *post-Zionist* and synonymous expressions was a descriptive employment of such terms in the 1950s and 1960s by people, particularly veteran Labor Zionists, who regretted what they saw as the loss of Zionist communitarian commitment and dedication in favor of a decadent Western individualism. Indeed, many of the Labor Zionists who led the Land of Israel movement in the post-1967 period were motivated in large part by the hope that the effort to establish more secure borders and reclaim the historic Jewish heartland would bring about a reinvigorating of earlier Zionist commitment. In contrast, the anti-Zionism or post-Zionism of the academics, writers, artists of the 1980s and 1990s is, of course, prescriptive, an arguing for "liberating" the state and its citizens from a collective identity on historical and religious grounds; that is, from a Jewish identity.

Again, themes of the supposed moral turpitude of creating a Jewish state harken back to the anti-Zionist arguments of, for example, Buber and his associates in the pre-state era. It might be argued that the academic literature in this vein of the years immediately preceding the 1992 election should be viewed essentially as a continuation of that earlier academic anti-Zionist campaign and does not really represent a new efflorescence of these themes at this time. Such might be said of, for example, philosopher Joseph Agassi's comparisons of the Jewish state to Nazi Germany and the Soviet Union, in *Who Is an Israeli?*[64] (1991). Indeed, whereas the New History had evolved largely in the mid-eighties, quickly gained popularity and helped, with the Peace Movement, to prepare the groundwork for the capitulations of the 1990s, the burgeoning of anti-Zionist/post-Zionist themes complementing the Peace Movement was essentially a post-1992 phenomenon. The anti-Zionist/post-Zionist literature dramatically expanded then and its acolytes attained important government positions and played substantive roles in influencing and shaping national policy.

Certainly, there was an explosion of such literature and a popularization of its themes after 1992, driven by a belief among some on the Left that it was Israel's official Jewishness that accounted for its hostile rejection by its neighbors. According to this perspective, Israel's reforming itself into a more "universalist" state, liberating itself from its supposedly too parochial, too narrow Jewish accoutrements, would help win it acceptance from its neighbors, would be another reaching out to grasp the peace attainable if Israel were only sufficiently forthcoming.

But if there was no great academic expansion of this literature in the preceding years that served to prepare the way for these post-1992 phenomena, there was in those years a significant expansion of what might be called "counter-Zionist" themes in Israeli fiction, poetry and other arts, and a dramatic popularization of such views through the vehicle of the arts. These popular artistic expressions of such perspectives worked, like the New History, in tandem with the Peace Movement to prepare the ground for what followed, for large-scale acquiescence in, indeed embrace of, the post-1992 capitulations.

It should be noted in this regard that leading Israeli cultural figures, particularly fiction writers, enjoy the status of intellectual icons in the country. Their views on politics, foreign and domestic policy, morality and religion are freely offered, widely respected in the nation, and sought out and attended to by large segments of the population.[65]

In artistic critiques of the Jewish state and of the pervasiveness of Jewish themes in Israeli national life, one hears echoes, of course, not only of the long tradition of academic anti-Zionism but also of earlier elaborations by writers and artists of such themes, as in Amos Oz's early demands to be liberated from Ben-Gurion's concept of the Jewish. But Oz's stance in the 1950s and 1960s was one eschewed at that time by the vast majority of Labor Zionist constituents; Ben-Gurion had many more followers than Oz. But by the 1980s such views, indeed outlooks even more consistently hostile to Zionism, even more closed to recognition of any redeeming virtue in the Zionist enterprise, were the standard fare of Israeli writers and artists and enjoyed wide popularity. In addition, the Jews and their Zionist state were now consistently and explicitly portrayed in the works of Israeli writers and artists as the villains in the Arab-Israeli conflict.

Oz himself, in his nonfiction writing in the years after the 1967 war, did not quite subscribe to radical post-Zionist or anti-Zionist agendas. But he continued to develop his earlier negative perceptions of the state as imposing an unfair burden of Jewish history, Jewish religiosity, and Jewish peoplehood on its citizens. He now focused on arguments to the effect that peace could be had from the Arabs were Israel only forthcoming enough and that it was atavistic Jewish zealotry, Jewish parochialism, and Jewish paranoia that prevented Israel from doing the right thing. His writings in this vein in the postwar decades are representative of perspectives that, in even more radical form, came to dominate the work of Israeli novelists, poets, and artists by the 1980s.

Oz has consistently acknowledged that Israel was genuinely threatened in 1967 and that its actions then were justified. He has even suggested at some points that Israel may have to retain for security reasons various areas that came under its control in the war.[66] Some of his attacks on Gush Emunim and the religious settler movement might almost be construed as reflecting the traditional post-1967 Labor distinction between strategic areas and strategic settlements versus "ideological" settlements and the Land of Israel Movement's program of retaining control over, in particular, all of the West Bank. But elsewhere during this period Oz clearly expressed his opposition to all settlements and was dismissive of the Allon Plan and its variations.[67] The thrust of his rhetoric was that virtually all of "Palestinian territory" should be given back and that returning it would bring peace; and he suggested that all resistance to that agenda was representative of an extremist tribal mentality infused with the worst elements of the Jewish legacy. (Oz offers a curious logic in this context: Any impulse to retain any of the territory must reflect a tribal, parochial turning away from the world because Israel's neighbors and much of the rest of the world are against Israel doing so. In effect, the measure for Oz of proper Jewish behavior is Jewish accommodating of the world's demands, which are assumed to be fair and just and humane and forward-looking.)

Oz never genuinely addressed the grave strategic risks that returning to the pre-1967 borders would entail; the closest he came to doing so was to assure his readers that the Palestinians could never represent an existential threat to Israel.[68] But this assertion, the truth of which he was apparently convinced, was sufficient in his view to warrant full withdrawal. Just as he argued that Israel's only justification for being is that it is a life raft for drowning people, he suggested that any policy that cannot be defended as necessary for sustaining that raft is illegitimate, and this is how he viewed the continued Israeli presence in the territories.

A corollary of his conviction that the Palestinians represented no real threat is that Israel could therefore take the risk of major concessions even if the Palestinians' intentions might not be entirely pacific. But the latter possibility is not one Oz seemed seriously to entertain. On the contrary, the ambiguous statements and actions of Arafat and his Palestine National Council at their 1988 meeting in Algiers were embraced by him as a definitive turning point for the Palestinian leadership that opened the door to peace. For its part, Israel needed only to speak to the PLO and cede it control over the territories to obtain that peace. Oz repeatedly cast Israel's situation as having to choose between territory and settlements or peace, doing so at times by means of assertions that settlements are not worth going to war over; as though that "choice" actually captured Israel's predicament and completely foregoing territory would completely assure peace.

In lieu of rational evaluation of his thesis, a thesis he clearly wished to believe true, the bulk of Oz's nonfiction writings on the subject consisted of rhetorical claims of the "rightness" of Israel retreating from all the territories, of the land's proper ownership by the Palestinians, accompanied by rhetorical salvoes savaging those who think otherwise. Oz's rhetorical promoting of Arab claims takes some strange turns. He asserts, for example, that declarations by some to the effect that areas of Eretz Israel were "liberated" in the 1967 war are absurd because land, as an inanimate object, cannot be liberated.[69] By the same token, of course, the land itself, as an inanimate object, cannot be "occupied"; yet Oz does not hesitate to characterize not just populated areas but even empty stretches of West Bank land, including those sectors long viewed strategically vital by Labor, as "occupied."[70]

Indeed, Oz goes further and — falling deeper into the literary device known as the "pathetic fallacy," the attributing of animate and human qualities to the inanimate — suggests the land itself is "Arab" or "Palestinian." The rhetorical argument goes on in such flourishes as depicting Palestinian homes and communities as fitting into the landscape, even as being an organic part of the landscape, whereas Israeli houses or villages in the territories do not belong and are scars on the terrain.[71]

Of course, the same rhetoric is used by anti-Zionists, and anti-Semites, who maintain that Israel should not exist at all, that all the land is naturally Arab and that the Jewish presence on any of it is unnatural, a violation of the land. The borders between that rhetoric and Oz's are obviously arbitrary. But Oz does want Israel to exist and is employing his rhetoric in the service of the wish to believe that, if he can convince Israelis of the rightness of being forthcoming enough, and if Israelis act on that conviction, the other side will be forthcoming enough in return.

A recurrent theme in Oz's essays, and in the writings of other Israeli literati who share Oz's perspectives, a theme likewise intended to convince Israelis of the necessity and propriety of full withdrawal, in the expectation that this will win full peace, is the casting of the conflict as a tragedy of two rights in one land. "The confrontation . . . [is] like a Greek tragedy. It is a clash between right and right . . . "[72]; "Many of the best poets and writers see the Israeli-Palestinian war . . . as a Greek tragedy: right against right . . . "[73]; and so on.[74]

But there are several glaring problems with this rhetoric. Yes, there are two peoples living between the Jordan and the Mediterranean, and certainly both have a right to be there. But to characterize their conflicting claims as somehow representing an exceptional and unique tragedy is a gross distortion of reality. In addition, the recognition that both peoples have a right to be where they are casts absolutely no light on the task of sorting out their conflicting claims and fashioning a secure peace.

The international legitimacy and support given to the Jewish people's quest for a National Home in its ancestral homeland came about in the context of the dissolution of empires in World War I. A number of states, in addition to the mandated Jewish National Home in Palestine, were formed or reconstituted then, including Finland, Poland, Lithuania, Latvia, Estonia, Czechoslovakia, and, in the Middle East, mandated Arab states in Syria and Iraq; and virtually every one of these states included at least two ethnic groups there by right. The principles for establishing these states and helping define their borders were the principles proposed by Woodrow Wilson. Foremost was that of the creation of national homes for previously disenfranchised peoples. But it was widely recognized that ethnic and religious populations were very much interspersed in the former empires, and so another principle was to guarantee the rights of the minorities that would inevitably people the new states. Additional considerations that ultimately influenced the disposition of territories as the new states emerged included concerns for their economic viability and their strategic capacity to defend themselves.

An example of the application of these various factors was the reconstitution of Poland. It was broadly felt that the Poles, disenfranchised for a century and a half, were a people who deserved a national home. As noted earlier, the territories allotted to them included large numbers of ethnic Russians, Lithuanians, Germans, and Ukrainians, representing together some 25 percent of the total population, as well as Jews, who were another 10 percent of the population. In some local areas these other groups were majorities. A substantial portion of the German, Lithuanian, Russian, and Ukrainian populations were averse to Polish sovereignty and many, at times joined by forces from the sovereign states with which they had ethnic ties, offered armed resistance. Still, the sympathy of the world at large was with the previously disenfranchised Poles, and no one not invested in the conflict saw anything particularly unique or tragic in this creating of a Polish state on land belonging to at least *six* peoples. The claims of the minority groups were thought adequately satisfied as long as their pre-scribed minority rights were maintained.

The Israeli-Palestinian situation would appear in some respects to be more easily resolvable than the parallel conflicts in a number of those other states. The Palestinian Arabs do not want to be part of Israel, and Israel does not want them to be a part of the state and is willing to cede areas that are home to the vast majority of Palestinian Arabs to facilitate their pursuing a separate politi-cal course. This is unlike other situations where minorities have wanted to break off but the dominant nationalities have been unprepared to cede any territory to accommodate such a move. The issues that obviously have stood and con-tinue to stand in the way of a settlement between Israelis and Arabs are Israel's insistence that borders accommodate vital Israeli security requirements and that the devolved Palestinian entity not pose any threat to the state, versus the other side's demands for a return to the pre-1967 borders as well as freedom to pur-sue an agenda in which those boundaries are only a first step to the annihila-tion of Israel.

Mere recognition of the fact that both peoples can claim to be in the land "by right," no matter how often and how solemnly that fact is repeated, adds nothing in terms of pointing the way to a resolution of these conflicting agen-das. Yet Oz and others have adopted the mantra of "two rights" as a tool to focus Israeli attention away from legitimate security concerns and genuine threats and to promote the notion that a return to the pre-1967 borders would be a fair and just recognition of the other "right" and would unlock the door to gen-uine peace. They also use that mantra to suggest that for Israelis to do anything less, to persist in laying claim to part of the territories, is unfair and unjust and makes Israel responsible for perpetuating the conflict.

This rhetoric that castigates Israel, assigns to it the onus for continuation of the Arab-Israeli conflict, and whitewashes Arab, particularly Palestinian, ac-tions and intentions, figures also, of course, in Oz's fiction, as it does in that of Israel's other leading novelists. In an essay written in 1972, Oz notes the com-plaints of "ideologues and politicians" against Israel's fiction writers and poets for their constant excoriating of the Zionist endeavor. His response is that great literature by its very nature must focus on the "gloomy, ugly, ignoble"; that ren-dering the negative in people's lives, and the accompanying paroxysms of their souls, in original and moving language is literature's royal road.[75]

But this explanation is disingenuous at best. Certainly there is a long tra-dition in Western literature of examining the darker sides of the human soul; and the twentieth century saw in addition the apotheosis of a more universal literary gloom, a literary rhetoric of existential angst, of the ultimate futility and meaninglessness of all striving, of the ultimate lie and emptiness in all assertions of transcendent meaning and value. But Oz and his literary fellow travelers in Israel do not write about inexorable existential loneliness or the falseness and hypocrisy of all claims of higher meaning. They write about what they assert to be the illusions and hypocrisy in Zionist claims of higher meaning and noble endeavor. Rather than seeing value in nothing, they very commonly see all value residing in the perspectives and strivings of Israel's enemies.

In the universe of this Israeli literature, if Israeli lives are empty it is because they are overshadowed by the burdensome lies of Zionist dogma. In Oz's early novel, *My Michael* (1968), the ennui of the heroine is relieved by her emotional connection with two Palestinian terrorists.[76] In A.B. Yehoshua's early story "Facing The Forests" (1963), the protagonist, living an isolated life as a fire ranger in a Jewish National Fund forest, is alienated from what are depicted as the callow Jewish visitors. He emotionally identifies with an aged Arab who smolders over the destruction of his village in the 1947–48 war, its remains now blanketed by the woods. The Israeli ultimately acquiesces to the Arab's torching and destroying the forest.

Yehoshua, in his nonfiction writing, has at times taken strongly pro-Zionist stances much freer of ambivalence and much less receptive to hostile indictments of Israel than the views expressed in Oz's essays. In a collection of such writings published in English in 1981 under the title *Between Right and Right*, Yehoshua faults Diaspora Jewry for not trying harder over the course of the last 2,000 years to get back to Eretz Israel. He argues more particularly that Jews should have done more to immigrate and establish the state in the 1920s and 1930s. He attributes the Jews' reluctance to give up their exile despite its tribulations largely to the allure of the abnormality of the Golah, or Diaspora, its rendering the Jews in their own view special, unique, and — living essentially free of temporal and territorial power — purer in their religious devotion and relationship to God. Yehoshua sees the Holocaust as ultimate proof of the bankruptcy of this sentiment and the ultimate failure of the Diaspora.[77]

Consistent with this perspective, Yehoshua argues that the Jews have a transcendent moral right to their state and that it is wrong for Israelis to set unique and unrealistic goals for themselves to justify the state's existence or to try to justify its existence in other ways. Indeed, to do so is simply internalizing the indictments of the nation's enemies and can lead only to self-blame. In a similar vein, he writes of Israel's right to defensible borders, to be in a position to preserve itself.

Touching more broadly on the self-doubt generated by the siege and that self-doubt's delusional nature, Yehoshua at one point speaks of protracted attack engendering both self-righteousness and self-hatred. Certainly, while resistance to chronic besiegement is laudatory, the mere circumstance of being under attack does not of itself make the victims better people and any predilection of such victims to so construe their situation is itself, as Yehoshua suggests, divorced from reality. At the same time he notes that other delusion: "Self-hatred, an attempt to identify with the enemy, to elude him by adopting his positions . . . What emerges, then, is total criticism of everything done in Israel; everything appears to be faulty and futile."78

Given these views and insights, what could have led Yehoshua to his own shrill indictments of Israel and vocal championing of the positions of Peace Now? The explanation seems to be related to his determination to comprehend Israel as properly rendering Jews a "normal" people. As reflected in his indictment of the Diaspora, which is in fact overstated and ahistorical, he wants to believe that Jews have, indeed have long had, the capacity to make their circumstances more normal if only they are determined enough to do so. Normality requires peace, and he states clearly that he chooses to believe that Israel by its own self-reform can go a long way to achieving the peace that is necessary for normality and that those who think otherwise have, like Diaspora Jews, some aversion to Jews becoming a normal people.79 He wishes to believe that peace and normality could be had if Israel is only sensitive enough to the other side and makes sufficient concessions.

It is in the context of this wish that Yehoshua suspends his best judgment regarding security and viable peace partners and embraces the delusions of the Peace Movement. That same eagerness for normality seems to have spurred his echoing at one point Diaspora Jews broken by the animosity of surrounding societies; his declaring, in the face of the seemingly unending siege, that it would be better if Jews converted to Christianity and Islam to propitiate their neighbors.80

Oz and Yehoshua continued to incorporate perspectives popular in the Peace Movement — indictments of Israel and rhetorical embrace of Arab positions — into their fiction, and in the decade before Oslo they were joined by younger writers in a flourishing of such fiction. The major distinction was that the younger writers were generally still more shrill and venomous in their attacks on Israel and promotion of those hostile to her.

Perhaps no one better exemplifies this strain in the younger cohort of Israeli fiction writers in the decade before Oslo than David Grossman. Grossman actually made his first big splash in the Israeli literary scene with a work of mainly nonfiction, *The Yellow Wind* (1988). The book is devoted to discussing what the author perceived as the evils of Israel's presence in the territories and is in various ways reminiscent of Oz's *In the Land of Israel,* except still more vituperative and intellectually dishonest.

On one level, Grossman's core thesis in the book is not only true, it is obvious: Israeli control over an alien and hostile population in political limbo is inexorably corrosive and not in the nation's long-term interest. Indeed, despite political differences within the country, a substantial majority of Israelis agreed on the desirability of a resolution that allowed Israel to separate itself politically from the Arab population of the West Bank and Gaza while retaining control of those largely unpopulated areas necessary for Israel's defense and while assuring that the Palestinians' pursuit of a separate political course would not translate into an existential risk to the state. But, of course, Israel still had no partner for such a resolution.

Yet the readers of *The Yellow Wind* are told none of this, nor anything else of Israel's preparedness for compromise or of the difficulties of finding a path to genuine peace. The bulk of the volume is devoted to reporting examples of the deleterious impact of Israel's control of the territories, examples embellished by what Grossman acknowledges to be fictionalized depictions of that impact where he feels the factual instances do not suffice.[81] The implicit subtext is that it is Israeli moral bankruptcy that allows the situation to continue and that if Israelis would only come to their senses, do the ethical thing, and end their presence then peace would follow. Grossman brooks no challenge to his thesis that the whole of the territories are properly Palestinian and that any Israeli claim vis-à-vis the territories is illegitimate and an obstacle to peace. In this context, he mimics Oz's invoking of "pathetic fallacies" and insists that the Israeli presence is a violation of the land; that, for example, "the architecture of [the settlers'] villages is strange to the landscape, proud and overbearing."[82] This sort of mindless purple prose permeates the book, along with Grossman's pervasive indictment of Israel.

Grossman does express distaste for Arab terror but insists Arab hatred and the impulse to terror are responses to Israel's control of the territories — history, in *The Yellow Wind*, begins in 1967 — and so Israel's perpetuation of its control is the ultimate driving force behind the continuing terror. Further, he tends to divide all Palestinians into those who are passive in the face of the Israeli presence and those who actively oppose it, and he sympathizes with the latter and is condescending of the former, suggesting that they are spiritually broken people. Palestinians who cooperate with or aid Israeli authorities, presumably even in fighting terror, earn not only Grossman's disapproval but his hostility.

When confronted with an Islamist rally and its chanting of "anti-Israel" slogans, slogans likely calling for Israel's annihilation, Grossman is surprised and wonders whether, if he were attacked, or his child were, he would revise his opinions and "begin to surrender to hate."[83] But, in fact, Grossman reserves his hatred for the settlers and their supporters, whom he perceives as playing a key role in perpetuating Israeli control and therefore in preventing the peace that he so desires and chooses to believe is readily available.[84]

The themes of *The Yellow Wind* figure prominently as well in Grossman's fiction. *The Smile of the Lamb* (1983) features a young Israeli who embraces a West Bank Arab as his mentor and is sympathetic when his mentor murders an Israeli military administrator of the territories. Grossman said of the book in a dust-jacket blurb: "It is . . . a story of the Jewish people in Israel, champions of humanistic morality and justice turned subjugators of another people, causing the erosion of their own values."[85] In his other novels, those who harbor universalist sensibilities and embrace pacifism are good and those who are stirred to defend embattled Jews and an Israel at risk are cast as darker souls who have forfeited something of their humanity.[86]

If Grossman's focus is particularly on Israel's culpability in recent decades vis-à-vis its presence in the territories, other young Israeli writers during these years offered broader indictments of the Zionist enterprise. One of the most celebrated novels of the pre-Oslo period was Meir Shalev's *A Russian Romance* (1988; published in English as *The Blue Mountain*), a book peopled by characters whose devotion to Labor Zionist endeavors — working the land, defending their homes — is depicted as callous, shallow, hypocritical, and insensitive to the terrible costs. The only characters with a touch of the noble and heroic about them are figures indifferent or hostile to, or rebelling against, the efforts of the Zionists.

Of course, any political endeavor, no matter how noble, can and will be subverted by some to callous and ignoble actions and purposes, and in free societies it is common for such patterns of behavior to be the target of the rhetorical barbs of essayists and fiction writers. But if that were the intent of Shalev and his contemporaries, they would have allowed for a redeeming of those ideals in portrayals of people who lived them honestly and admirably. Or if their grievances were with a Zionism whose communitarian strains stifle individuality, their rhetoric would have allowed for some vision of a salutary compromise between communal obligations and cultivation of individuality. But what characterizes so much of the celebrated Israeli fiction produced during the 1980s is the blanket indictment of Zionism, the general absence of Zionism in a different perspective, a Zionism embraced nobly. Indeed, there is an absence even of the possibility of such a Zionism.

The Zionism of individuals genuinely, generously, honestly dedicating themselves to the task of redeeming a people from persecution and restoring their dignity through national independence, a Zionist idealism that for many transcended narrow personal pursuits and gave a higher meaning to their lives, simply does not exist in this literature or exists only to be bowdlerized, satirized, and debunked; and the same perspective and rhetorical bias came to dominate the other arts — poetry, theater, film, the plastic arts — during these years.[87] A measure of the extent of this dominance of the Israeli cultural scene by purveyors of anti-Zionist themes is that over the last two decades of the century virtually all the authors awarded the Israel Prize in literature by the Ministry of Culture were such writers. "Only two prizes," notes Hazony, "to Haim Guri and Moshe Shamir (1988) — stand out as representatives of the older Labor Zionist literary tradition."[88]

The explanation for the wide and unprecedented recruitment of young writers and artists to this rhetorical perspective, and for the remarkably warm reception accorded their work by the Israeli public, cannot lie simply in popular rebellion, in the name of individuality, against early Zionist communitarianism. Nor do these phenomena reflect secular rebellion against the role of the Orthodox in Israeli civil life, itself hardly a major theme in the literature. If these were the issue, the rhetoric would point to some alternative equilibrium or resolution between society and individual, historical-religious culture and the culture of personal self-definition. Moreover, the rhetoric would not be so dominated by the constant cloud of the Arab siege and the equation of liberation from Zionism with escape from or transcendence of the siege.

What has generated and sustained these literary conventions, what has attracted the young to practice them and so much of the nation to embrace the art they have produced, is the wish by so many Israelis to see that rhetoric as truth. They have wished to believe that it is what the literature identifies as the Zionist perspective — a community seeing itself as at risk, perceiving itself as surrounded by people who still desire its annihilation, working to be constantly girded for battle to defend itself — that is the source of Israel's difficulties and the obstacle to a "normal" life. They have wished to believe that that perspective is based not on reality but on a distortion of reality by historical memory and the weight of millennia of painful Jewish experience. They have wished to believe that if only the nation would transcend the Zionist mind-set, see that the greater humanity lay not in Zionism's dictates but in the views of its Jewish and Arab critics, then Israel would rethink its stances, reform its nationalist zeal and preoccupation with defense and security, and make the concessions that — the wish goes on — would inevitably win it peace.

The writers and artists who worked the anti-Zionist themes during these years, and their fans and followers, often cast their arguments in terms of searching for normalcy, in terms of desiring to make Israel a "normal" state, without explicit reference to the conflict with the Arabs. They did so as though they were simply measuring Israel by some general standard of "normal" to which other states adhere. But having a dominant historical-religious culture and identity is, in fact, the norm for states in the world, including democratic states. Once more, the "normality" Israelis were seeking was the normality of peace and it is in the context of eagerness to end the Arab siege that the desire to de-Zionize and de-Judaize the state must be understood.

Those who chose to believe that de-Zionizing and de-Judaizing the state would win the wished-for peace found it easier to embrace such beliefs during these years because, again, they saw as the chief constituents of the Zionism they were repudiating that "Other Israel" that had been leading the nation for the past decade and from which they felt so alienated.

Amos Elon, perhaps Israel's most prominent political essayist, certainly the best known internationally, wrote in 1971 of the early work of Yehoshua and Oz (work written before the 1967 war and capture of the territories), "When openly political, their writing leans to a tormenting sense of guilt, which in extreme cases takes the form of a gnawing complex of legitimacy."[89] Elon notes that this literary-political perspective did not begin with Oz and Yehoshua; he cites the novels and stories of S. Yizhar (Yizhar Smilansky) set in the War of Independence. Yizhar's fiction features protagonists "harassed by debilitating doubts and morose moral agony."[90]

Elon recognizes that this self-doubt and moral agonizing were in large part a reaction to the early idealism of the Zionist enterprise — the visions of creating, by the sheer willpower of Zionism's New Jew, a socialist, egalitarian utopia. They were a response to those utopian expectations being compromised by the exigencies of the real world. But Elon is inclined to compare the Zionist enterprise in this respect to the course of all utopian revolutions. In fact, the self-doubt and moral agonizing he is discussing is quite particularly a phenomenon of revolutions born in reaction to chronic, debilitating abuse, and even more particularly a Jewish phenomenon. This is so because the early Zionists, in response to the indictments of the Jews' tormentors in Europe, chose to endorse elements of the indictments, chose to see European Jewry as misshapen and as remiss in its eschewing of spiritual transformation, and chose to believe that sufficient willpower and determination could achieve that transformation. So their heirs and protégés were particularly vulnerable to self-doubt when they were not able to attain their idealized vision of the New Jew in his New Society.

But the intensity of this moral agonizing was not simply a matter of Zionist theories encountering quotidian realities. It was much more a consequence of the siege, of the indictments of the Zionist experiment by the surrounding societies and their supporters, which resonated with the Zionists' predilection to see besiegement as a product of Jewish spiritual failure. This is recognized in part by Elon. He states at one point, "The art of Oz, Yehoshua, or Yizhar cannot be viewed in isolation. It must be seen within the general frame of their lives — perpetual siege and endless war . . . "[91]

Yet Elon seems to miss the full impact of the siege. He sees the elite elements of Israeli society, including many of its artists, still measuring life by the Zionist ideal and bumping painfully against the siege. He writes, for example, that Zionist idealism leads such people to empathize with Arab pain and "in their empathy with the Arabs, those afflicted with the [moral] malaise occasionally find themselves in a moral cul-de-sac. Bound as they are to moral principles, they are unable — because of the ferocity of Arab opposition and the absence of any significant reciprocity — to put those principles into practice."[92]

And elsewhere: "Among some intellectuals, university people, and artists, a vague if persistent predilection for self-censure has survived the vicissitudes of war and threats of annihilation from the Arab side."[93]

But, in fact, it is the chronic vicissitudes of war and threats of annihilation that have led some Israelis to cultivate that self-censure and morose ruminating. They have done so in the service of fantasies that sufficient self-indictment and self-reform will placate the other side and end the siege and open the way to the Zionist utopian ideal. Israeli writers have cultivated self-censure in the service of fantasies that their holding up to the Israeli public fictionalized mirrors of Israel gone wrong will effect a broader self-indictment and inspire that self-reform that will bring peace.

Elon again sees the idealism driving the fantasies of peace in this passage: "The ardent hope for peace that powerfully pervades Israeli literature and public opinion is genuine and sincere . . . [But] there is a dreamlike, unrealistic quality in the current Israeli ideal of peace. Under its spell the conditions of peace are set so high that they can hardly be realized. The Israeli ideal of peace is a product of historical experience. It is another reflection . . . of the original ideology of Zionism that was committed to an idealistic assumption of man's perfectibility; it testifies to the lingering strength of that ideology. In the aftermath of the 1967 war the Israeli ideal of peace occasionally exuded an almost religious, Manichean air."[94]

But, once more, in accounting both for the Zionists' early embracing of idealistic fantasies and for Israelis' subsequent measuring of themselves, and their national life, by unreal standards, it has been Jewish/Israeli conditions of besiegement that have been the cause and the fantasies and self-censure that have been the consequence. As the siege persisted beyond 1967, as hopes for peace were dashed, more and more Israelis were inclined to adopt those visions, previously the preserve particularly of Israel's artists and academics, of peace achieved through self-indictment and self-reform.

It is noteworthy in this regard that there have been many Israelis who have not responded to chronic besiegement with self-indictment and with fantasies whose theme is that peace requires only self-reform. Many people, likewise imbued with values drawn from Zionist ideals, have regretted that those values have been compromised by exigencies of the real world but have done so without the morbid self-censure and moroseness of which Elon writes. As Elon notes, Israel's first law of conscription stipulated that inductees would serve one year in the army proper and a second year in public service in the agricultural sector; an accommodation, without despair, of Zionist agrarian ideals to necessity.[95] And Moshe Dayan stated in an interview: "In one important way my life has been a failure . . . I set out to be a farmer — and I think I made quite a good farmer. Yet I have spent most of my adult life as a soldier, under arms . . . Farming, for me, is not only a means for living but also a [moral] concept."[96] Not caught up in fantasies that peace could be had merely by sufficient concessions, Dayan could have regrets about the course of his life, the lapse from the ideal, without self-indictment.

Interestingly, Elon, for all his insights into Israeli hopes and Israeli self-censure divorced from reality, embraces many of the same delusions noted in Oz and others among Israel's elites, delusions whose shared logic is that enough Israeli empathy, self-blame, and territorial withdrawals will inexorably win peace. From shortly after the 1967 war and over the subsequent decades, despite his references to Arab extremism and annihilationist agendas, the thrust of Elon's observations has been that Israel's ceding the land captured in the Six Day War will indeed elicit peace. He has chosen to construe the major obstacle to peace to be Israeli sentiment — particularly what he characterizes and deplores as retrogressive religious-nationalistic sentiment — that seeks to retain control of the territories, most notably the West Bank. Elon does distinguish at times between what he calls "legitimate security settlements" and other settlements,[97] and he appears at points to recognize the serious security risks that would be posed by full withdrawal. But more typically he is supportive of Israel's return virtually to the pre-1967 borders, is critical of those who oppose this, and treats as an established fact the notion that Israel's giving up the territories will win genuine peace.[98] A recurrent theme in Elon's writing is that Israel must choose between territory and peace,[99] as though it is a law of nature that fully foregoing the former will fully gain the latter.

Elon also joins those who cite what they see as Israel's abuse of the Palestinians in the territories as an argument for full withdrawal. He writes at one point of how an occupation that had started out liberal had become illiberal. Certainly, the status quo in the territories entailed all sorts of problems and certainly there were good reasons for Israel to seek a separation from the Palestinian Arab population. But, again, citing those problems casts no light on finding a trustworthy interlocutor with whom Israel could deal in pursuing separation. Nor does it help toward establishing agreed upon borders that would take account of Israel's genuine security needs (the "secure and recognized borders" referred to in Security Council Resolution 242), or toward negotiating enforcement mechanisms for any agreement. Noting the problems of the status quo could be useful in the context of prodding the Israeli administration in the territories to ameliorate those problems while Israel pursued the quest for a more comprehensive answer through a viable separation mechanism, but it added nothing to the resolution of these other issues. Yet Elon and others cited the difficulties of the status quo in the context of assertions that, despite overwhelming evidence to the contrary, giving up the territories would resolve everything.[100]

Nor did Elon shrink from distorting and exaggerating the problems of Israeli administration. In April, 1982, he issued false claims of Israel banning books in the territories. When challenged on his assertions, Elon held fast and even insisted, "It's all part of the preparations for a fascist regime! Soon we'll have it all, concentration camps as well as the burning of the books."[101] Some years later, in an article about a visit to Amman in 1994, Elon wrote that in recent decades Jordan had forged ahead in all areas, including education and health care, while the territories had stagnated under Israeli control.[102] But in fact the opposite was true. To cite but a few relevant statistics, by the early 1990s illiteracy in the territories had dropped to 14 percent of adults over fifteen; the level of illiteracy in Jordan was about 15 percent in 1998. Infant mortality in the territories fell under Israeli health care programs from 60 per 1,000 live births in 1968 to 15 per 1,000 live births in 2000; in 2000 infant mortality stood at 23 per 1,000 live births in Jordan. Life expectancy in the territories rose from forty-eight in 1967 to seventy-two in 2000, in comparison to a life expectancy of sixty-one in Jordan in 2002.[103]

Elon has used other rhetorical tacks as well to excoriate Israel, downplay the threat to the nation, and bolster the argument that Israeli concessions would win peace. He repeatedly echoes the revisionist historians' unsupported and widely refuted claims that Israel missed various earlier opportunities for peace, and he asserts this categorically, without citing the revisionists' dubious evidence for their claims or the counterevidence. He argues also that Israelis' fears of Arab intentions are paranoid, reflect the legacy of Jewish history, particularly the Holocaust, and entail an irrational conflating of Arabs with Nazis[104]; this even as he acknowledges elsewhere the depths of Arab anti-Semitism and genocidal sentiment.

Vis-à-vis the Palestinian-Israeli aspects of the conflict, Elon speaks in the familiar language of "two rights." Again, such references, while having some validity, offer — like the citation of problems with Israeli administration of the territories — nothing in the way of finding a path to resolution of the struggle. Yet they are put forward as though Israelis need only recognize the "right" of the other side and a peaceful resolution will follow.

In a similar vein, Elon at various points seeks to sensitize his readership to his view that the Arabs were made to pay the price of Europe's crimes against Jews and that this "must burden the conscience of Israelis for a long time to come."[105] Like many of Elon's Israel-indicting assertions, this is stated categorically, without explanation or qualification. Elon appears to be referring, at least at some points, to European abuse of the Jews over the centuries, the Jews' consequent pursuit of an independent national life, and Europe then helping Jews establish that national life at, supposedly, the expense of the Arabs. It is worth noting, of course, that most of Israel's Jewish population is descended from people driven to embrace a Jewish national life by abuses suffered in Moslem, mainly Arab, countries, not in Europe.

In addition, virtually all post-World War I nation building could be construed as European powers redressing their crimes at the expense of others. European powers had deprived Poles of their national life; was the reestablishment of Poland a matter of ethnic Germans, Ukrainians, Russians, and Lithuanians in the new Poland being made to pay for the crimes of those Powers? Was the creation of Czechoslovakia a case of ethnic Hungarians and Germans in Czechoslovakia being made to pay for the crimes of the European Powers? Were the Lapps and ethnic Russians in the newly established Finland similarly victims of those Powers? And if it is a matter of Europe creating new realms, rewarding some and depriving others, if that is the European crime, then the Arabs largely benefitted from the "crime," as in the creation of the Arab states of Syria, Transjordan, and Iraq, and later the Sudan, with the Arabs profiting at the expense of, for example, the Kurds of Iraq and Syria and the blacks of the southern Sudan.

Or perhaps Elon is referring, as others have, to the European crime of the Holocaust and the sympathy it created for the Zionist cause in the wake of World War II. But if Israel's cause was advanced by that sympathy, in fact the march of fascism and Nazism in Europe in the nineteen thirties actually interfered in important ways with the building of the Jewish national home. Anti-Jewish sentiment in British ranks became even more popular, and it was translated more emphatically into policy, as Britain began to anticipate a war, saw fascist propaganda penetrating the Arab world, and swung more determinedly to placating Arab opinion. While the League of Nations had worked effectively in earlier years to counter British steps to renege on Britain's obligations to the Jews under the Mandate, the rise of fascism resulted in the destruction of the League of Nations and freed Britain's hand to act against the Zionists. If the Arabs were in some respect the victim of European policy, it can be said with at least equal veracity that the Zionists and many of the Jews killed in the Holocaust were victims of Arab and British policy.

But Elon's entire concept of the creation of Israel having to "burden the conscience of Israelis" is, like the "original sin" arguments of others, less a statement reflecting historical analysis than a polemical flourish relating to advocacy of the Peace Movement's stance on proper current policy.

The "counter-Zionist" rhetoric of Israel's writers and artists, like the New History of its academics, worked in symbiotic rapport with the Peace Movement — at once being fed by the Peace Movement and reinforcing the Movement — to promote and solidify the conviction of much of the electorate, particularly the constituencies of Labor Zionism and the other parties of the Left, that peace could be had if Israel only reformed itself. In the months and years after the 1992 election, the drumbeat of that literary-artistic rhetoric, of the New History, of the anti-Zionist/post-Zionist academic writings, and of the Peace Movement grew ever louder in its promotion of new directions, new soul-searching and self-indictment and self-reform, that would lead to the national self-abnegation and concessions that its purveyors chose to believe could not help but assure peace.

A writer of an earlier generation, a writer in that Zionist mode whose themes were now eclipsed, the novelist Aharon Megged, looking at the embrace of Arab perspectives in art and literature, and also in the New History, in academic anti-Zionism, and in much of the rhetoric of the Peace Movement, wrote in 1994:

"We have witnessed a phenomenon which probably has no parallel in history: An emotional and moral identification by the majority of Israel's intelligentsia, and its print and electronic media, with people committed to our annihilation."[106]

Of course, Megged was essentially correct. But, predictably, those he was speaking of rejected his indictment. They did so not least because, even though the Palestinian leadership was continuing to call for Israel's ultimate annihilation and to promote that end among its followers, those whom Megged was attacking refused to hear this Palestinian message. Rather, they insisted — out of exhaustion with the siege, out of desperation for "normalcy" — on seeing the Palestinian leadership and constituency as they wanted them to be, as no less eager than themselves for compromise and peaceful resolution of the conflict. They insisted on believing that what they themselves regarded as fair concessions could not help but be seen as fair by the Palestinians as well, could not help but lead to peace. So the obstacle to peace was not Palestinian annihilationist policies but, rather, Israelis who — either out of nationalist fervor, or a morbid and benighted preoccupation with security and defense, or an atavistic and superstitious religious attachment to particular sites — refused to make the peace-winning concessions. In their eyes, their "emotional and moral identification" was not with people committed to their annihilation but with the Palestinians of their imagination, created largely in conformity with what they wished the Palestinians to be, which is to say essentially like themselves. Among the intelligentsia of whom Megged spoke, and their enthusiastic followers, were people who, soon after the 1992 election, became key shapers of Israeli policy.

In the wake of his election victory in June, 1992, Rabin sought to continue negotiations under the so-called Madrid formula, with Israel meeting bilaterally with a joint Palestinian-Jordanian delegation in talks that excluded direct PLO representation. He also apparently continued to hold out hope for pressing into effect his earlier proposal to arrange direct elections in the territories for Palestinian representation, a process that he anticipated would give legitimacy to a leadership within the territories and undercut the influence of the PLO.

But Arafat was, of course, no more prepared to countenance elections in the territories now than he had been earlier. While he tolerated Madrid formula bilateral meetings in Washington between Israel and Palestinian delegates who clearly answered to him, he increasingly put up obstacles to progress in this arena as well. As the talks dragged on for months without notable advancement, the constituency of the Peace Movement, which had grown so dramatically during the years of Likud ascendancy, with large numbers of Israelis drifting away from traditional Labor positions on peace and security, turned its wrath on Rabin. Peace Now embarked on a campaign demanding greater progress and largely blaming Rabin for having failed to fulfill his promise of a quick interim agreement with the Palestinians. It also again urged direct negotiations with the PLO. In addition, the organization actively campaigned against all settlement construction activity.

In the summer of 1993, in response to a number of attacks on Israel from across the Lebanese border, Israel retaliated with a large-scale bombing campaign. Peace Now added this as well to its list of grievances against Rabin's government and insisted that security along Israel's northern border can only come from a "breakthrough in the [Madrid formula] peace negotiations with Syria."[107]

Rabin, in insisting in his election campaign that, consistent with long-standing Labor Party policy, he would retain vital strategic areas in the West Bank, had made an implicit distinction between settlements in those areas and settlements elsewhere, the latter established in large part on the basis of historical and religious considerations and often close to Palestinian population centers. He had also made the same distinction explicitly, contrasting security settlements to ideological settlements and declaring his support for the former and negative views of the latter. But in the months after his election, Rabin took steps, congruent with Peace Now demands, to limit the financing and further development of settlements throughout the West Bank, making no such distinction. In other respects, however, he seemed over the first year of his government's tenure to resist the vocal demands for policy changes coming from Peace Now. But, in fact, as would soon be revealed, his government was in the process of secret negotiations that entailed radical breaks with earlier policy, and with campaign promises, and drew Rabin's government dramatically closer to the positions of the Peace Movement.

THIRTEEN

Oslo: Rationalizing the Irrational

On September 4, 1993 [with public announcement of the Oslo agreements], a festive crowd poured into the Tel Aviv central square by the tens of thousands to celebrate . . . The traditional site of the peace movement's demonstrations and protests for the past fifteen years now witnessed an entirely different event. 'This was a real happiness. People cried of joy,' wrote Yael Gvirtz, a journalist who had attended many of the peace movement's activities . . . The ecstatic crowd cheered Minister Shulamit Aloni when she said, 'No more parents will go weeping after the coffins of their sons.' Amos Oz closed his remarks by saying, 'And death shall rule no more.'[1]

BEILIN'S CONVICTIONS AND RABIN'S RATIONALIZATIONS

Secret, unofficial talks between PLO representatives and Israeli academics with government connections had begun in Norway in December, 1992. They proceeded under the guiding hand, on the Israeli side, of Yossi Beilin, deputy foreign minister in the Rabin government and protégé of Foreign Minister Shimon Peres. The following April, Peres informed Rabin of the talks and their progress and won Rabin's approval for continuing to pursue them and for having Israeli officials join the negotiations.

In meetings over the next several months, a Declaration of Principles was hammered out as a blueprint for steps toward resolution of the Israeli-Palestinian conflict. The Declaration was predicated on Arafat's commitment, on behalf of the PLO, to recognize Israel's right to exist in peace and security, to accept UN Security Council Resolutions 242 and 338, to pursue peaceful settlement of the conflict and agree that all issues will be resolved by negotiations, to renounce the use of terrorism and other acts of violence, to assume responsibility for compliance with these commitments by all PLO elements, to declare that those articles of the Palestinian Covenant that call for Israel's destruction or are otherwise inconsistent with these new commitments are inoperative and no longer valid and to have the changes in the Covenant ratified by the Palestine National Council. These points were agreed to by Arafat in a letter to Rabin on September

9, 1993. Rabin, in his response, recognized the PLO as the representative of the Palestinian people.

The Declaration of Principles itself, signed by Arafat and Rabin in a ceremony on the White House lawn on September 13, called for establishment of a Palestinian Interim Self-Government Authority, election of a Palestinian council, and an initial Israeli withdrawal in the coming months and ceding to the Palestinian Authority control over most of Gaza and over Jericho in the West Bank. It also addressed the beginning of negotiations both on an Interim Agreement governing the Palestinian Authority's assumption of additional jurisdiction and development of additional institutions in the territories and on a Permanent Status accord to be based on Resolutions 242 and 338 and to be in force in no more than five years. Much of the Declaration of Principles is devoted as well to delineating areas of future Israeli-Palestinian cooperation in economic and development programs and to establishing mechanisms to promote additional progress.

In the wake of revelation of the Oslo talks and the signing of the Declaration of Principles, Rabin and those around him sought to argue that what had occurred was not as dramatic a break with past policy, or with Rabin's campaign pledges, as might first appear. Yes, Israel had negotiated and come to an agreement with the PLO, moves that Israeli governments had previously perceived as entailing intolerable dangers, bringing a revanchist force with a bloody terrorist history and long-standing commitment to Israel's destruction into the heart of Israel and likely soon within shooting range of most of Israel's population. But, it was argued, the PLO had now radically reformed itself, as attested to by those undertakings made by Arafat as prelude to the agreement. Also, the five-year interim period envisioned by the Oslo accord was consistent with the interim autonomy proposals that had been a part of the Camp David agreements with Egypt and that both Labor and Likud governments had thereafter officially supported. (The Camp David autonomy proposals, however, had not entailed ceding extensive and virtually exclusive control over specific territories, as was effected by the Oslo accord, and this was a difference with obviously far-reaching implications.)

The government argued additionally that the interim agreements were a period of testing and, should the PLO and its forces revert to their old ways, Israel would be free to reenter the ceded areas and expel them. Furthermore, it was claimed, the Declaration of Principles did not prejudice ultimate outcomes, did not preclude Israel's long-term goal of retaining control of strategically vital areas and of a unified Jerusalem (even though negotiations on Jerusalem were agreed to by Israel as a final status issue). Nor, the government insisted, did it commit Israel to recognition of an independent Palestinian state or preclude final arrangements in which the Palestinian entity retained a status that was more one of autonomy, or of some kind of condominium association with Jordan or with both Israel and Jordan, than of sovereignty.

Rabin and his allies also pointed out that the major territorial concession thus far was the ceding of Gaza, and who among Israelis was not pleased to be rid of responsibility for Gaza? Moreover, they noted, there was a general consensus among Israelis that it was in the country's national interest to divest itself of areas of dense Palestinian population; and now, with the Jordan option gone, and no viable moderate alternative to the PLO, with whom was Israel to negotiate?

In a related vein, the government noted that Israel was confronted with the increasing influence in the territories, at the PLO's expense, of the Islamic fundamentalist groups Hamas and Islamic Jihad. Those organizations, it was argued, articulated positions even more intransigent and less amenable to any political dialogue than the PLO and were responsible for the killing of mounting numbers of Israelis; and so the chance for any kind of political settlement might have been lost if Israel had not acted as it did. (The rising influence of the Islamic groups in the territories and the concomitant slippage of his own position likely figured in Arafat's accepting at Oslo terms that fell short of what he would have preferred. It was another factor that weighed in his calculations, along with his difficult straits in the wake of his ill-conceived alliance with Saddam Hussein during the Gulf crisis and the promise of Oslo bringing him a dramatic rehabilitation.)

Others in the Israeli government, perhaps most notably Shimon Peres, promoted the accord by pointing to the tremendous economic benefits, themselves of strategic significance, that would accrue to Israel as, for example, countries that had previously eschewed relations with Israel in deference to the Arabs and to Arab support of the Palestinians would now feel free to reverse such policies when the PLO itself had entered into a peace accord with Israel. (In fact, Israel's major political gains in this particular sphere, such as the establishment of new diplomatic and economic relationships with India and China, had already occurred in the wake of the Arab states' sitting down with Israel at Madrid.)

For all the government's promoting of the Oslo agreement, the accord was barely ratified by the Knesset. It gained sixty-one votes in the 120-member parliament, with those sixty-one including all the Arab members. (Israeli law does not require Knesset approval of a treaty or peace agreement, but submission of important initiatives to the Knesset has become an accepted tradition and an expected step in establishing such an initiative's legitimacy.) Also, a poll conducted after publication of the accord and before the White House signing ceremony revealed 53 percent in favor and 45 percent opposed.[2]

For the half of Israel opposed to the agreement, that leap of faith that transformed Arafat and the PLO into peace partners seemed a potentially suicidal delusion. They hardly thought it prudent to trust a "partner" who not only had devoted his life to pursuing the destruction of Israel but, in addition, had a long record of violating his bilateral agreements even with states toward which he had no comparable animus, as he had done most notably and with bloody consequences in Jordan and Lebanon. Moreover, the Oslo agreement appeared to point to Israel ceding to the PLO virtually all the territory beyond the pre-1967 lines. Rabin seemed in effect to have abandoned all his promises regarding security and secure borders and to have capitulated entirely to the prescriptions of the Peace Movement. In the view of many, this would create conditions that would leave Israel fatally vulnerable. Among those who shared such concerns were many Israelis of the Left who remained convinced that keeping to traditional Labor positions on territorial compromise and the retention of key strategic areas was vital for Israel's survival. (Rabin indicated as well his preparedness to return the Golan Heights to Syria in exchange for a peace treaty; this despite campaign promises to the contrary and long-standing Labor assertions of the strategic necessity of retaining the Golan.)

How did Rabin himself comprehend Oslo? There is no clear answer to this, although myriad answers have been offered by pundits. It does seem clear that if Rabin trusted Arafat and believed at all in his reform, it was hardly an unalloyed and doubt-free trust. Perhaps he was truly convinced that Arafat, whatever his intentions, could be contained, that the obligations of governing his people and of having necessarily to work with Israel to make his Palestinian entity economically viable would restrain his bloodier, more annihilationist impulses. Perhaps Rabin also truly believed that if this proved after all to be a false expectation, if the Palestinian territories became a base for those revanchist policies so many predicted, the IDF could indeed simply return and retake the ceded territories. He may also have been convinced that if, on the other hand, the process went forward without mishap, Israel could in fact achieve a final status agreement that would allow it to retain control of all of Jerusalem and of those areas in the West Bank that Israeli Labor leaders, including himself, had always regarded as vital to the nation's defense and survival. Perhaps Rabin even expected that Israel could arrive at a final status accord that would grant the nascent Palestinian entity something short of full sovereignty and so render it less of a threat whatever the predilections of its future leadership.

On the other hand, Rabin seems to have displayed at various times in his life a deep-seated pessimism, and he spoke frequently of the looming threats of advanced missile arsenals and weapons of mass destruction being deployed by Iran, Iraq, Syria, and other hostile states. He may have felt, despite grave doubts about Arafat and Assad, that Israel had no choice but to cut any deal with them that offered the possibility of diminished and presumably containable risks at least from the Palestinians and the inner circle of Arab nations, those immediately adjacent to Israel. He may have believed that such a course could also serve to undercut the belligerency of the outer circle of threatening states. There are statements by Rabin that suggest this line of thought.

No doubt some Israelis accepted the arguments of Rabin and his allies that Oslo did not compromise the foundations, including the key territorial foundations, of Israel's long-standing strategic calculations, that Israel would retain the areas necessary for its defense and would not allow the emergence of a fully sovereign and strategically threatening PLO state. No doubt some Israelis completely trusted Rabin in this. But the slim majority of Israelis who supported Oslo was not simply comprised of such people who believed Rabin. A great many of those supporters were, rather, people who — eager for "peace," desperate to see an end to the war — had been won over by the Peace Movement and had convinced themselves that there was no Palestinian threat. They were people who chose to believe there was no need to worry about strategic areas in the West Bank, and no reason not to go back to the pre-1967 borders, as sufficient Israeli concessions would inexorably elicit a genuine and enduring peace with the other side.

Indeed, the course of the secret negotiations in Oslo and the contents of the accord that emerged from those talks clearly demonstrated — as the large majority of Israelis, both the nearly 50 percent who opposed the accord and a substantial portion of those who welcomed it, recognized — that Oslo represented the victory of the program of the Peace Movement. This was perhaps hardly surprising to anyone who looked at the gestation of Oslo, given that the chief government nurturer of the negotiations and the accord was Yossi Beilin, himself a fierce devotee of the Peace Movement.

Insight into Beilin's views is offered by, among other sources, his book *Israel: A Concise Political History*, published in the year preceding the Oslo agreement. In the book, Beilin paints an idealized picture of Israel before the 1967 war, claiming that the country was developing and prospering and that 1957 to 1967 were the nation's "finest years."[3] In contrast, Israel's 1967 victory was a "curse" that brought an end to the good times.[4] Beilin argues that the victory led to a large expansion of Israel's defense expenditures that has undercut the nation's development.[5] (Elsewhere in the book he does acknowledge some of the overwhelming evidence that contradicts this picture.)

Beilin characterizes Israel's presence in the West Bank as a Pandora's Box and advocates as desirable going back to the Israel that existed before the 1967 war. He downplays there having been any existential or even very serious military threat to Israel in its war of independence or in the years that immediately followed, and he generally ignores subsequent threats as well. He never mentions the Arab buildup to the 1967 war, or Arab declarations that the time had come for Israel's annihilation, and he understates or entirely omits later threats to Israel, including that posed by Palestinian terrorism. The toll in lives taken by Palestinian terror is entirely absent. Beilin also declares without any qualifying statement that the PLO had in 1988 proclaimed itself reconciled to a peaceful resolution of the conflict with Israel,[6] even though Arafat was at the time reaffirming his commitment to Israel's ultimate destruction.

Beilin builds on this downplaying of threats to support the view that Israeli defense expenditures in the post-1967 era were an unnecessary burden on the state. He ignores the fact that, given increased technological challenges from its neighbors, Israeli defense costs would inevitably have had to expand greatly in any case, and that the strategic advantages offered by some of the territory captured in the war has actually allowed the nation, even in the face of threats from its neighbors, to defend itself at lesser expenditure than would otherwise have been necessary. Nor does he acknowledge that a return to the pre-1967 lines now would, at best, confront Israel with strategic challenges requiring a large-scale expansion of defense costs, and that those expenditures, no matter how great, could not compensate for the loss of strategic territories.

Beilin's thesis that increased defense budgets after 1967 would have been avoidable if the war had not occurred, and his parallel argument that going back to the pre-1967 boundaries would allow Israel to divert defense costs to education and other good uses, are built on the premise that Israel behind its pre-1967 lines was not genuinely threatened in the spring of 1967 and would not have faced military threats thereafter. It assumes that those threats that have confronted the nation since 1967 are due entirely to Israel's control of the territories, and that such challenges, and Arab hostility generally, would end if only Israel returned to its pre-1967 lines. But Arab statements, Arab strategic planning, Arab political and military actions, and the statements, planning, and actions of Arafat and his PLO, as well as of the so-called rejectionist Palestinian groups, were all evidence of the falseness of Beilin's premise.

Beilin, however, chooses to ignore all this. A telling illustration of his mindset is that nowhere in his book, as nowhere in Bar-On's, is there mention of Arafat's Plan of Phases.

Beilin's book, with its highly distorted recasting of Israel's past, captures the premises of his Oslo strategy and, indeed, was an effort to garner support for his vision of Israel's future. One would have difficulty finding another example of strategic, life-and-death policies being put forward by individuals in positions of power that have been based on premises as divorced from reality as Beilin's "peace" assumptions and "peace" proposals.

Consistent with his advocacy of a return to the pre-1967 boundaries, Beilin paints Israel's choices in terms of extremes: Either it retains all of the West Bank and perpetuates its intolerable control over the area's Palestinian population or it withdraws to the pre-1967 lines. The Allon Plan is barely mentioned and never described. What had been Labor Party policy since 1967 and was supported also by much of the Israeli electorate beyond Labor's constituency — the ceding of those territories where the overwhelming majority of the

Palestinian population live and the retention of strategically vital, sparsely populated areas such as the Jordan Valley — does not exist in Beilin's book.

Beilin's insistence that Israel faced no existential threat in its war of independence or in the early years of its nationhood, that all the fighting in that
period was simply over borders, converges, of course, with the arguments of
the new historians. So too does his implicit message that Israelis' fears then and
indeed subsequently during periods of threat and war were overwrought, as well
as his use of this as a foundation for dismissing present fears of the Arab threat.
Beilin has been a devotee of, in particular, Benny Morris's version of history,
and he is reported to have insisted that the Oslo negotiators read Morris and
absorb his supposed lessons.[7] (Beilin does state that after the 1956 war Nasser
"sought to transform the Arab-Israeli conflict from a dispute over the fate of
refugees and permanent borders into an existential conflict."[8] But he clearly indicates that he does not believe Israel's existence has ever actually been challenged by the Arab states.)

Beilin describes his secret choreographing of the Oslo talks in his later book
Touching Peace (1999). He reports in the book that, as a Labor Party activist,
he had been meeting with Palestinians since 1983 seeking to promote an Israel-
PLO accord and that Oslo gave him the opportunity to turn his vision of peace
into reality. Beilin also reveals in the book that, in pursuing his agenda of an
Israeli-PLO peace, he has not had much patience with the niceties of democratic governance. Thus, in December, 1992, he did not hesitate to urge
American officials to enter into a dialogue with the PLO even though his doing
so ran counter to what were then the policies of the Israeli government in which
he was deputy foreign minister.

Beilin's depiction of the Oslo negotiations reveals as well that security issues figured very little in his thinking. At no point in the talks did he seek the
input or advice of the military; and while he does declare repeatedly that the
Palestinian state would have to be demilitarized, he never sought any mechanism for enforcing demilitarization. He mentions that, in early broaching of a
Gaza-Jericho First plan, Arafat wanted to be given control of the Jordan River
bridges as well, and he notes that this was problematic because it would have
entailed early transfer of too much land to be acceptable to the government.
But there is nothing to suggest he saw any potential security problems with
Arafat's controlling the bridges. Beilin indicates in various passages that his blithe
unconcern with security matters was due to his conviction of his Palestinian
interlocutors' "sincere commitment to peace."[9] But behind this conviction lay
his trust that, as peace would, in his view, be of such obvious and enormous
benefit to the Palestinians as well as to Israel, the Palestinian leadership must
see things as he does and so it only requires sufficient Israeli concessions to assure a genuine peace.

When questioned at various times, in the wake of the Oslo agreement, about the fears of many in Israel that he was pushing for a return virtually to the pre-1967 boundaries and even conducting discussions with the Palestinians toward this end, Beilin adamantly denied his doing so. Yet it was clear from his writing at the time that he supported such a territorial resolution, and it seemed equally clear from news leaks that discussions along such lines were in fact occurring. Beilin acknowledges in *Touching Peace* that this had indeed been the case.

Starting in September, 1994, what became known as the Stockholm talks were undertaken between Israeli and Palestinian emissaries under the guidance of Beilin and, on the Palestinian side, Mahmoud Abbas (often referred to also by his *nom de guerre*, Abu Mazen). In arranging these talks, Beilin was pursuing after Oslo a *modus operandi* for which Oslo itself was a paradigm: engaging in informal, unofficial, and essentially secret talks with Palestinian interlocutors, which allowed the obfuscation, should the talks be discovered, that anything discussed did not represent government policy, that the conversations were simply academic exercises without policy significance. Should, as at Oslo, these informal discussions lead to some substantive agreement, he could present the public — again as at Oslo — with a *fait accompli*, which would then be particularly difficult for the Israeli people to reject. For it would place them in a take-it-or-leave-it situation and, if they saw the agreement as too dangerous and turned it down, would put the onus on Israel for rejecting "peace."

In this instance, it was not only the Israeli public that was kept in the dark but also, as Beilin admits, Peres and Rabin. Beilin accounts for his not informing them by explaining that, if he had told Peres, Peres would have been obliged to tell Rabin and "I reckoned Rabin would be reluctant to embark upon discussion of the permanent settlement at such an early stage. I decided to keep the business under wraps, pending some really significant development in this track."[10] Of course, a major consideration for Rabin was to have a testing period to assess the Palestinians' compliance with their Oslo commitments, particularly with regard to security issues. But, again, Beilin had few concerns in this regard.

The Stockholm talks produced, in October, 1995, a final draft agreement for a permanent settlement. Beilin does not report its provisions but it is clear that it called for Israeli withdrawal virtually to the pre-1967 lines and creation of a Palestinian state in the ceded territories. Beilin writes that he had arranged to reveal the negotiations and their results to Peres upon returning from a trip to the United States. But while in the United States, on a day when he discussed the talks and their outcome with Amos Oz and Oz offered to help him win Rabin and Peres' support, everything was suddenly thrown into turmoil by the assassination of Prime Minister Rabin.

Beilin's method of seeking to create *faits accomplis* irrespective of public opinion or indeed government policy pioneered, or at least epitomized, what became in the course of the 1990s virtually standard Labor Party operating procedure. It entailed employing the subterfuge of denying, in election campaigns and in ongoing articulations of policy, any intention to pursue concessions outside the national consensus or established Labor Party positions, while seeking to negotiate in secret on such compromises of long-standing policy and to present the public with *fait accompli* agreements incorporating those concessions. This methodology not only became standard procedure for the Labor leadership but was hailed in statements and discussions by party leaders as a legitimate, even necessary and desirable, form of statecraft. The argument became: If most Israelis still lagged in their understanding that peace could readily be had were they only to break out of old thinking about defensible borders and security and threats posed by their neighbors, then it was the obligation of leaders to do that breaking out for them, to turn such concessions into established facts, despite the public's resistance.

Beilin defends this perspective in a discussion of his decision, shortly after the PLO's 1988 Algiers meeting, to bring Faisal Husseini, whom he viewed as a sincere partner in advancing the cause of peace, to a Labor Party caucus. Beilin notes that the move aroused much indignation in the party and explains that, "Plotting a course against the tide, knowing from the start that one's actions or words are sure to be unpopular, and, in spite of that, creating a fact that cannot possibly be ignored — this was my *modus operandi* [italics in original]. My objective at this stage was to increase as far as possible the number of 'kosher' interlocutors, to identify possible common denominators and arrive at informal accords with the Palestinian leadership, thus proving to Peres, Rabin and the institutions of the Labour Party that agreement really was attainable."[11]

Of course, all Beilin was proving throughout his career as negotiator was that agreement on a document was attainable. But the difference between a "peace" agreement and peace was something he chose not to recognize, preferring to believe that the second would follow inexorably from the first. The peace he wished for made so much sense to him, had such an irrefutable logic in his eyes, that he simply dismissed the doubters, and similarly ignored even his "peace partners" when they plainly declared that they viewed things otherwise. He knew better.

Shimon Peres, a politician of an older generation and one who appeared to have harbored very different strategic views earlier in his career, was not only won over to the perspectives of the "peace" camp but also became an enthusiast of Beilin's form of statecraft. At one point during this period, Peres declared with regard to public attitudes and government policy, "A leader must be like a bus driver . . . He cannot turn his head all the time to see how the passengers feel."[12] While this seems a particularly incommodious metaphor given his meaning, as, presumably, passengers do have some say in where their fare is to take them, Peres' intent is clear enough.

Hillel Halkin, a prominent Israeli translator and commentator whose own political sympathies had been distinctly on the Left, was nevertheless angered by announcement of the first Oslo agreements because of their flagrant betrayal of campaign promises by Labor. Halkin wrote of the Labor leadership's recent conviction that intentional misleading of the public is high statesmanship:

"Such a view, which is almost universally held today on the Israeli Left, strikes me as cynical beyond bounds. Of course politicians frequently lie to the public, although those who lie least and with the uneasiest conscience are the ones who look best in the history books. But it is one thing to lie about ordinary matters of political expediency, another to lie about a momentous decision that will profoundly affect the future of one's country for as long as it continues to exist. If the question of Israel's borders, of their location and defensibility, of who lives and rules on either side of them, and of their relationship to the claims of thousands of years of Jewish history is not something about which to consult the Israeli public within the framework of democratic politics, what is democracy for?"[13]

Beilin's belief that peace with the Palestinians was readily attainable if only Israel committed itself to sufficient self-reform and concessions, and his willingness, in the service of that belief, to deceive the Israeli public, to pursue policies beyond what the public was prepared to countenance and then to force acceptance of those policies as a done deal, were the dual foundations of his diplomatic and political maneuverings. They in turn rested on his conviction of the benign nature of Palestinian intentions and the immutability of those intentions. They rested as well on his certainty that Israeli concern with strategic territories and self-defense was misguided. He was convinced that Israel's maintaining a posture that would allow it to respond effectively, to protect its citizens and preserve itself, should the nascent Palestinian entity turn hostile, was essentially unnecessary. Given that available information hardly supported Beilin's understanding, much less his certitude, it appears that, once more, the explanation for both lay in wishful thinking. They were the product of an eagerness to see an end to the siege and a wish to believe that the steps he was promoting would, if properly executed, inexorably bring about the denouement he desired.

Some years later, as Beilin continued to cling to the same perspectives and policies even as much additional evidence had accumulated indicating the wrongheadedness of his comprehensions, he was asked in an interview about his stance. Beilin responded that, "I want to live in a world where the solution to an existential problem is possible. I have no proof that this is really the case . . . I am simply not prepared to live in a world where [problems] are unsolvable."[14]

One can imagine hearing very similar words from a moral crusader, someone who devotes himself or herself unreservedly to changing the world for the better by fighting the forces that promote hatred and war. But this has not been

Beilin's course. On the contrary, when Arafat and the Palestinian leadership have, for example, taught in their schools that all of what was Mandate Palestine properly belongs to the Arabs, that the Jews are usurpers with no legitimate claim to any part of the land, and that Palestinian children have not only the right but the obligation to pursue Israel's annihilation, and when they have used their media and their mosques to purvey the same message, Beilin has ignored the incitement and its implications or made excuses for it. Confronted with the reality that Israel faces problems it cannot resolve by its own action, that it cannot simply by unilateral concessions win its neighbors to the peace it desires, Beilin has wished not to believe that reality, and so he has simply closed his eyes to it. Being " not prepared to live in a world where [some existential problems] are unsolvable," Beilin has consistently chosen to embrace the delusion that, despite all the evidence to the contrary, the other side desires what he desires and the world can be rendered what he wants it to be if only Israel is sufficiently forthcoming.

THE SPOKEN PREMISES: A CRITIQUE

The essentially surreptitious agenda pursued by Yossi Beilin in his choreographing of the Oslo process, including Israel's ultimate return virtually to its pre-1967 boundaries, with all the strategic dangers that would entail, was supported by many in Israel's governing coalition. These supporters included not only Beilin's allies in the Labor Party but also, and more emphatically, members of Labor's chief coalition partner, the Meretz Party. Meretz's policies were essentially to the left of Labor and very much aligned with the Peace Movement, in which many of its leaders were long-standing activists. But Beilin and his allies' unspoken agenda was not all that was wrong with Oslo. Even if one looks at Israel's publicly articulated, "official," objectives as put forward by Rabin and his associates and at their arguments defending Oslo as consistent with those objectives, there were many immediately obvious and dangerous difficulties with their stance.

A common theme in defense of Oslo by Israeli leaders around Rabin was that there was no alternative to Arafat as a negotiating partner. It was certainly true that all potentially more moderate interlocutors in the territories had been cowed into silence by Arafat's forces. As government spokespeople emphasized, the only organized alternative Palestinian leadership consisted of militant Islamic rejectionist groups that had been responsible for many recent attacks in Israel and that openly declared their opposition to peaceful resolution of the conflict. Government spokespersons also argued that the Islamic groups were gaining ground in the territories against Arafat's forces and so the possibilities of some negotiated agreement would likely diminish over time.

But, of course, while there was some validity to government claims that Israel had no political alternative to the PLO as a negotiating partner, it hardly followed from this that the PLO was itself a viable partner. Yes, Arafat had signed statements declaring his peaceful intentions. But, again, he had a long record of breaking agreements he had solemnly undertaken and unleashing bloody conflict against his erstwhile partners in those agreements, as in his ventures in Lebanon and Jordan. Moreover, he had declared a policy — and continued to restate that policy in speeches in Arabic — of gaining what territory he could from Israel by negotiations and using that territorial foothold as a base from which to pursue Israel's destruction. There was, therefore, additional good reason for skepticism about Arafat's conversion to the path of peace. Israel's readiness nevertheless to take his signed assertions of peaceful intentions at face value essentially reflected an embrace of the Peace Movement's conviction, despite all evidence to the contrary, that the Palestinians were offering genuine peace in return for sufficient Israeli concessions.

Another assumption explicitly articulated by the government was that Arafat would control and dismantle the violent, rejectionist Islamic fundamentalist groups who were his main competitors for influence in the territories, thereby enhancing Israeli security. But it was far from clear, particularly given the record of his tactics over the years, that Arafat would not seek, rather, to co-opt the fundamentalist groups or attain some other *modus vivendi* with them and even use them as a tool for putting ongoing military/terrorist pressure on the Israelis while having the deniability of his own hands being clean. Indeed, precedent pointed to the likelihood of his at once continuing to compete with the fundamentalists while cooperating with them in actions against Israel. The expectation that Arafat would confront and dismantle the fundamentalist organizations was founded on conviction of Arafat's conversion to co-existence with Israel, which in turn was, again, based much more on wishful thinking than on available evidence.

No less dubious an articulated premise of the Rabin government was that of the potential reversibility of Israeli concessions should the Palestinians, despite the government's expectations, fail to fulfill their obligations under Oslo. Israeli concessions, as conceived by Oslo, would, of course, primarily entail the ceding of territory. While this might be "reversible" in terms of Israeli military capability should, for example, ceded territories become staging grounds for terror, it was predictable that taking such military steps would be very problematic for several reasons. To do so would likely entail significant loss of life and would also inevitably elicit worldwide condemnation no matter what the provocation.

Moreover, it is an almost invariable pattern in accords between democratic nations and nondemocratic parties that the former feels constrained against forcefully addressing violations by the latter, however egregious. This is largely because to do so would be to acknowledge to the electorate that the leadership had exercised poor judgment and had been misled or duped into entering into a flawed agreement. As a result, the democratic side very typically becomes an apologist for the accord violations of the co-signator. Indeed, the more the democratic side has given up of important assets in the agreement the more reluctant it is to acknowledge to the electorate problems with compliance and the more it becomes a defender of the other side. This dynamic, too, could be expected to inhibit any Israeli move to reenter ceded territory in response to the Palestinian leadership's violations of its Oslo obligations.(This factor obviously becomes less significant in the event of a change of government, with the successor administration not having been responsible for the accords and therefore not having the same vested interest in defending them despite evidence of problems. But the Rabin administration's spokespeople who assured the public of Oslo's reversibility in the event of Palestinian violations clearly were not thinking in terms of potential steps by a successor administration led by Labor's political competitors.)

As noted, another argument put forward by Rabin and his associates was that the step-by-step approach of Oslo safeguarded Israel's territorial claims. That is, as the accord deferred negotiation and agreement on ultimate disposition of the territories, Israel could, and definitely would, insist upon retaining strategic areas vital to its security, such as the Jordan Valley, certain high ground, and areas necessary for the defense of Jerusalem — those portions of the territories that Labor had always insisted must be retained in a final agreement in order for the state to be able to defend itself. But, of course, the Oslo agreement also left the Palestinians free to insist on a full Israeli retreat to the pre-1967 lines — or even further. Moreover, an obvious problem was that to the extent that Israel ceded parts of the territories in Oslo-prescribed interim agreements, it was depriving itself of bargaining chips and undercutting its position in attempts to negotiate a territorial compromise of the sort that had since 1967 been the Labor Party's objective.

Again, it is unclear how much Rabin himself believed Oslo would indeed lead to that sort of compromise, a denouement he insisted was still his objective; and it is clear that some important figures in his government were more than prepared to return virtually to the pre-1967 borders. But whatever Rabin's intentions or expectations, the Oslo accord in fact substantially undercut Israel's ability to achieve its long-standing, and publicly still embraced, aims.

Yet another major premise invoked in support of the Oslo process, one apparently endorsed by virtually everyone involved in shaping government policy, was that arrangements for economic benefits to accrue to the Palestinian population as part of Oslo would have the effect of giving the Palestinians a greater vested interest in peace and would undercut Palestinian support for violence. The Oslo agreements also foresaw joint Israeli-Palestinian economic projects that, it was anticipated, would improve relations between the two populations and further win Palestinians to peaceful co-existence rather than violent rejection of Israel. Perhaps Rabin anticipated that improvement in the economic lot of the Palestinians, including gains from joint projects with Israel, would help render territorial compromise along the lines of traditional Labor policy more acceptable to the Palestinians and more achievable. Others in the government no doubt foresaw Palestinian economic gains and concomitant investment in peace as further rendering Israeli concerns about defensible borders moot, as strengthening the peace that they anticipated would inevitably follow on sufficient Israeli concessions such as full withdrawal. But everyone in the government seems to have believed that Palestinian economic gains would inexorably be translated into a more secure peace.

In addition, the Madrid conference in 1991 had initiated not only bilateral talks between Israel and several Arab parties but also a series of international meetings aimed largely at promoting regional cooperation involving Israel and Arab countries. In the wake of Oslo there was also much optimism within the Israeli government that concessions to the Palestinians and efforts to improve the economic lot of the Palestinian population would yield a greater willingness within the Arab states to put aside their long-standing vilification of Israel and join in mutually beneficial bilateral and regional projects, thereby promoting and cementing a wider peace. Perhaps the leading Israeli champion of such possibilities was Shimon Peres. In his book *The New Middle East*, published the year of the initial Oslo accords, Peres talks of a utopian reconciliation between Israel and her neighbors not only as possible but as virtually inevitable, the irresistible direction of history.[15]

Peres had come to favor territorial concessions to the Palestinians generally consistent with those promoted by the Peace Movement. He invoked his vision of a New Middle East in large part to advance the argument that old concerns about defensible borders are outmoded and Israelis need to move beyond such thinking. In his book, he advocates a confederation between the emerging Palestinian state and Jordan, with the area west of the Jordan River demilitarized.[16] But the thrust of the work is promotion of the thesis that former comprehensions of borders, security, and sovereignty have become irrelevant. In terms of warfare, he argues that the ubiquity of missile technology and weapons of mass destruction has rendered state boundaries and "strategic territory" insignificant. (Once more, this is hardly a view many military experts would endorse.) The increasing globalization of trade has also diminished the significance of national borders. Both security and economic well-being now require regional relationships and accommodations that transcend borders and traditional concepts of sovereignty. Peres anticipates Israel and its neighbors forming a prosperous economic union along the lines of the European Union, with issues of national borders becoming moot in this coming era of interdependence, peace, and cooperation.

Peres' vision of the world as interconnected by trade to such a degree that former concepts of sovereignty have lost their meaning, while cast by Peres as an avant-garde, forward-looking insight, is actually a century-old perspective going back to early socialist internationalism. Peres' argument against Israelis concerned with borders and security is reminiscent of an exchange in 1890 between the Russian Jewish Marxist Alexander Helphand and the Zionist Nachman Syrkin. Helphand declared, "Today nationalism is meaningless. Even the manufacture of my coat demonstrates the international character of the world: the wool was taken from sheep in [Turkey]; it was spun in England; it was woven in Lodz; the buttons came from Germany; the thread from Austria." At which point Syrkin interjected: "And the rip in your sleeve comes from the pogrom in Kiev."[17]

There is obviously some truth to arguments that straitened economic conditions — for example, conditions under which people are without resources, without jobs, without opportunities to improve their situation — can translate into an environment breeding extremism. Similarly, economic circumstances that offer people hope for improving their lot and a material interest in maintaining social stability can serve as a disincentive to extremism and destabilizing violence. But there are limits to the applicability of these generalizations and much that weighs against their utility as a basis for Israeli policy. An equally valid generalization is that the force of economic inducements as counterweight to deeply ingrained and widely promoted ideological convictions — such as the widely held Palestinian, and broader Arab, conviction that Israel has no right to exist — is questionable at best. Not infrequently, the opposite has been the case, with economic gain having the effect simply of providing ideologically aroused militant populations, or militant segments within a population, with more means to pursue their violent agendas.

In addition, neither Israel nor the Western contributors to proposed joint economic projects or to exclusively Palestinian projects designed to improve the Palestinian economy had any effective means of assuring that their efforts would actually benefit the Palestinian population. Indeed, half a century of Western investment in attempts to moderate Arab politics by bolstering Arab state economies and the economic lot of those states' populations had largely failed. They had foundered not just on the obstacle of pervasive government corruption that diverted such Western investment away from the benefit of the wider population. They had foundered also, and perhaps even more fundamentally, on the obstacle of government policy that used financial reward, including license for corruption, to buy and retain the loyalty of key segments of the population and that was therefore invested in preserving a highly centralized and controlled economy in order to be able to go on implementing this system of rewards and incentives. Governments also sought to maintain such control, and to limit economic opportunities outside of government management, out of fear that the development and expansion of a potentially independent and affluent middle class would ultimately translate into political challenges to the status quo.

Arafat's PLO was known to be highly corrupt and its agents in the territories were likewise viewed as corrupt and as having, over the years, diverted Palestinian assets away from the people and to their own lavish use. Indeed, a major reason for the growing popularity of the Islamic organizations in the territories was that they were regarded as much more honest and attentive to the needs of the population than were the PLO and its minions. There was no reason beyond wishful thinking for Israel to believe that this pattern would change with implementation of the Oslo agreements. On the contrary, Arafat could be expected to establish in the territories yet another regime that would use financial rewards, including license for corruption, to buy and retain loyalty and that would work to prevent the evolution of a free market and the potential growth of a politically independent middle class.

Another factor that had frustrated Western governments in their efforts to see economic aid to Arab regimes translated into material improvements in the lives of their citizens was the very high birth rate in Arab countries. This had recurrently resulted in population increases that outpaced and swamped whatever expansion there had been of national economies. (Estimates have indicated that the Egyptian economy, for example, would have to sustain virtually impossible rates of growth to keep up with the nation's increases in population.) But the birth rate in the West Bank and Gaza has also been very high, with that in the latter often ranked as the highest in the world. There was little reason to expect that an Arafat regime would seek to encourage a lowering of family size for the sake of more readily translating economic gains into material improvement in people's lives. On the contrary, the Palestinian leadership regarded population growth as a weapon against the Israelis, creating demographic pressures in what had been Mandate Palestine, the land from the Jordan to the Mediterranean, that would cause increasing problems for Israel. The leadership encouraged large families as patriotic. This factor of population growth should have been yet another obvious check on sanguine Israeli assumptions that economic aid to the Palestinians would be readily translated into improved lives for the Palestinian population and a concomitant moderation of attitudes toward Israel.

The entire concept of seeking to improve people's lives through economic aid and of thereby moderating militant attitudes is, in fact, much more meaningful when applied to populations within an aid-giving country rather than to foreign populations. In the former case, where a government is attempting to help a subgroup of its own citizens, the government is in a position to address effectively problems of corruption and to counter directly the promotion of militant ideologies. It can even have an impact on such matters as family size. It can educate the population on the relation of family size to financial well-being. Even more importantly, it can extend improved educational and employment opportunities to women, improved education of women being, according to various studies, the chief factor in reducing the norms of family size within a society. Assumptions about the potential effectiveness of aid aimed at benefitting a foreign population always have to take into consideration the inevitable impact of factors outside the donor nation's control. This reality ought to be a check on overwrought optimism in all such situations, including those much more promising than that confronted by Israeli policy makers seeking to improve the economic lot, and thereby moderate the politics, of the Palestinians.

Israeli government aid and infusion of money into the Palestinian economy in the wake of Oslo were to come particularly in the form of government financial support for joint economic projects and, most importantly, Israeli payments to the nascent Palestinian Authority of various taxes collected in Israel from Palestinians. Many in the Israeli government seem to have genuinely convinced themselves that funds paid to the Palestinian Authority by Israel and by various donor states and international organizations would be used to improve the lives of the Palestinian population. Others anticipated a continuation of PLO corruption and diversion of much of these collected funds to the personal coffers of PA officials. But they convinced themselves that the flow of so much money, particularly the tens of millions of dollars paid monthly by the Israeli government in tax remittances, would at least have the effect of giving PA officials a vested interest in maintaining their Oslo commitments. Certainly, if Western aid aimed at improving the lot of populations had a very dicey record, there was substantial precedent for Western aid to strongman regimes helping to sway favorably the policies of those regimes.

But such precedents were typically in situations where leaders were not ideologically hostile, as Arafat obviously was to Israel, and this optimistic if cynical assessment by some Israelis was again self-deluding and failed to take account of ideological commitment. It was at once cynical and naïve, and perhaps once more reflected an eagerness by some Israelis to see the other side as like themselves and so as inevitably sharing their own lack of ideological fervor. Arafat and the PLO had long had access to vast wealth and there was little evidence that this had moderated dedication to their anti-Israel agenda. The assumption that the promise of additional wealth through Israel would do so was a very weak premise indeed.

No less dubious were the Israeli government's expectations that steps toward reconciliation with the Palestinians would yield a dramatic positive change of attitude toward Israel throughout the Arab world. Some Israeli leaders were convinced it would open the way to bilateral and regional cooperation with Arab states, to which the latter would be attracted in no small part by opportunities to avail themselves of Israeli expertise. Such expectations were most sanguinely articulated, again, in Shimon Peres' concept of a New Middle East. But the ongoing hostility of the Arab states toward Israel over the preceding decades had hardly been predicated exclusively or even primarily on sympathy for the Palestinians. The ill-treatment of the Palestinian Arabs by those same Arab states was just one indication of the limits of any such "sympathy." Rather, that hostility was predicated on the perceptions of Arab regimes regarding the utility of anti-Israel policies in advancing their own domestic and international, particularly inter-Arab, interests. There was therefore no reason to expect that any accommodation with the Palestinians would translate into a dramatic change of heart by Arab rulers in their attitudes toward Israel.

Indeed, some Arab governments might seize on Israeli-Palestinian accommodation to effect a warming of relations with Israel in ways they saw to their advantage. But others could as likely be expected to retain their former hostility and, by way of justifying their doing so, to criticize Israel's Palestinian interlocutors for compromising the Palestinian and broader Arab "cause."

There might be a high likelihood of some peripheral Arab states taking the former course. More importantly, the Jordanian regime, which had long had substantive informal contacts with Israel but, given its vulnerability to and dependence on stronger Arab states, had been afraid of getting too far ahead of other Arab governments by dealing with Israel more openly, could be expected to take advantage of Israeli-Palestinian agreements to pursue more aggressively its own relations with Israel. But even the Jordanian leadership would likely be constrained in how close it drew to Israel, and how much it pursued potentially very beneficial bilateral ties, by countervailing considerations. These include a population in which people with Western Palestinian (that is, the part of post-World War I Palestine west of the Jordan) connections were a majority and would very probably respond to any PLO dissatisfaction with the pace and extent of Israeli concessions by opposing the normalization of Jordanian-Israeli relations. As to the other Arab states, there was little reason indeed — given, again, the place of anti-Israel policy in their domestic and inter-Arab calculations — to expect any dramatic change of heart or policy.

More particularly, the notion that the economic advantages to be gained by relations with Israel, including access to Israeli expertise, would be a strong inducement to Arab states — in the wake of steps toward an Israeli-Palestinian accommodation — to put aside their hostility, cultivate ties, and pursue bilateral and regional projects with Israel, was entirely unrealistic. It was another manifestation of that hubris born of the wish to believe that peace could be bought if only Israel pursued the proper policy of accommodation; that Israeli steps would determine Arab steps. As indicated earlier, Israeli economic strength and expertise simply do not weigh that significantly in Arab calculations as an inducement to peace. Indeed, the absurdity of this particular version of the delusional hubris shared by so many in Israel had already been amply demonstrated by relations with Egypt since the Camp David treaty. Egypt, for reasons of domestic and inter-Arab policy, had chosen to forego implementation of virtually all the many agreements on economic ties and cooperation written into the treaty. It had chosen to violate the accords, even though implementation would undoubtedly have brought it useful economic benefits.

There is another body of evidence that runs counter to the Oslo optimism regarding both opportunities for peace and Israel's capacity to engineer that peace. This relates to attitudes prevalent in the Moslem Arab world toward other religious and ethnic minorities living within that world.

Certainly popular hatred of Israel, fanned by governments, by government-controlled education systems and media, and by Moslem clerics, runs deep in Arab opinion. But it is also true that there has been a widespread animus against other minorities — both religious and ethnic — within the region. That animus has in many respects grown worse, particularly on the religious level, and has been fueled by the rise of Islamic fundamentalism in recent decades, but it is not exclusively attributable to this.

Bias toward religious minorities, including the "tolerated," *dhimmi,* minorities — Christians and Jews — with their subjection to chronic discrimination and recurrent episodes of murderous assault, has been a feature of the Arab Moslem world since the earliest days of the faith. Ethnic bias directed against non-Arab Moslems has also been a recurrent phenomenon.

These prejudices, with the minorities regarded as inferior beings, have been further fed in the modern era by the widespread belief among those in the Islamic-Arab world — likely induced and amplified by state and religious education and consequent cultural convention — of having been stripped of their proper place in the sun by the ravages of colonialism and as still suffering from colonial depredations. From the perspective of that comprehension, minorities within the bounds of the Moslem-Arab world — in popular thought, an illegitimately shrunken Moslem-Arab world — are often seen as alien intruders, or as one-time subject populations, whose present positions are vestiges of those same colonial depredations and whose presence in the Arab states is less than legitimate. Indeed, the popular comprehension of Israel as a vestige of European colonialism should likewise be seen in this context.

The cumulative resentment and hatred have manifested themselves in pressure on Christian minorities throughout the Arab world since the retreat of the colonial powers. Examples of that pressure include draconian legislative measures against, and repeated violent attacks upon, the large Coptic Christian community (perhaps 15 percent of the national population) of Egypt, the most cosmopolitan of Arab states; the decimation of the Christians of Lebanon; and sharp declines in Christian populations elsewhere. Such attitudes have found expression also in attacks on Kurdish populations — a Moslem but non-Arab people — in Syria and Iraq, attacks prosecuted with virtual silence from the rest of the Arab world. These assaults include the murder of up to 200,000 Kurds by Saddam Hussein in what appears to have been early steps in a plan for genocide prior to Saddam's diversion of his forces to the conquest of Kuwait in 1990, as well as his resumption of assaults on the Kurds, until countered by Western air power, after the Gulf War.

Popular Moslem Arab hostility toward the region's minorities has also led to pressures on the Berber populations — another Moslem but non-Arab people — in the Mahgreb, particularly Algeria. Algerian Berbers played a disproportionately large role in the fight for Algerian independence, yet virtually from the time independence was achieved they were subjected to a campaign of "Arabization," with Arab-dominated governments seeking to eradicate Berber language and culture. A largely secularized population, they have been victimized, since the outbreak of the Algerian civil war in 1992, both by the government and by Algeria's Islamist insurgents.

But the most horrendous example of delegitimization of ethnic and religious minorities in the Arab world has been the on-and-off genocidal war pursued by the Arab governments of Sudan since Sudanese independence in the mid-nineteen fifties. This has been a campaign with both racial and religious dimensions, prosecuted against the black, and mostly Christian or animist, population of the southern Sudan. The assault has escalated in recent decades and has killed over two million Sudanese blacks. This genocide, too, has proceeded with virtual silence and tacit, and at times even explicit, support from the rest of the Arab world. More recently the Sudanese government has launched murderous attacks, and what some have characterized as another genocidal campaign, against the Moslem black population of its region of Darfur, doing so again largely with at least the tacit support of its fellow Arab nations.

Of course in all these instances the distressed populations were not living in their own sovereign states, were not being attacked because they possessed a sovereignty that somehow intruded on Moslem-Arab rights and proper Arab preeminence. They were all populations living within states in which Moslem Arabs were the dominant constituency.

Yet the Israeli government was convinced that, in return for territorial and other concessions, the Arab world would make an exception for the Jews. It would not only accept the Jews as it has done no other minority but was prepared to reconcile itself to, and even embrace, in a genuine and enduring peace, a sovereign Jewish state.

A vivid illustration of the disconnect between Israeli assumptions, at the time of Oslo, of a coming peace bought with Israeli concessions and bolstered by economic bonds, and Arab perceptions and attitudes toward Israel, was the Arab response to Shimon Peres' vision of a New Middle East. This vision was conceived by Peres, and touted by his allies, as a road map to an inevitable halcyon future of mutually beneficial Arab-Israeli interdependence and cooperation. But indicative of reaction to the book in the Arab world is the introduction to the Arabic translation, published in Egypt and distributed by an Egyptian government-owned company. It casts the work as part of a Jewish campaign for world domination, declaring: "Peres's book is nothing but an additional step toward the implementation of the dangerous plots [of the *Protocols of the Elders of Zion*]."[18]

Obviously one could then, and can now, discern differences of nuance, and at times of more than nuance, between regimes and between Arab sub-populations in terms of their expression of the negative, intolerant, and chauvinistic, attitudes that are so dominant in the Arab world, and it is the duty of Israeli leaders to be alert to these differences. Indeed, it is — to use Bar-On's term, but in a more appropriate way — the "moral obligation" of Israeli governments to explore and cultivate any opportunity offered by developments in the Arab world to move relations forward, if not toward genuine peace, if that remains impossible, at least further away from potential hostilities and toward a more stable and secure armistice. A preparedness to offer some concessions, including territorial concessions, particularly in the context of separation from the Palestinian Arabs, in pursuing such goals has long enjoyed the support of an overwhelming majority of Israelis.

But to construe enemies who had a history of terror spanning decades, and whose commitment to accommodation and co-existence was dubious at best, as negotiating partners, to give them land and guns within shooting distance of most of Israel's population, to see them, moreover, not only as interlocutors in moving toward some more secure armistice but as trustworthy partners in fashioning a genuine and durable peace, was not "moral." Nor was it moral to refuse to countenance debate about the Palestinian leadership's commitment to such an outcome, or even to tolerate any doubt about the durability of that outcome when these interlocutors — assuming that they, despite all odds, remained true to their negotiated pledges — were no longer on the scene (succession being always a very dubious proposition with nondemocratic regimes). Nor was it moral to be prepared to hand over to these people's control areas strategically vital to the survival of the state on the assumption that survival would no longer be an issue of doubt in a durable peace, betting the very existence of the state not only on the trustworthiness of these interlocutors but on the irreversibility of any "peace."

This skein of actions based on one highly dubious and dangerous premise after another was, in fact, an abdication of "moral obligation" on the part of the Israeli framers and ratifiers of Oslo. It was an abandonment of their moral responsibility to protect the lives and well-being of Israel's people — and it was driven, above all else, by spiritual exhaustion with the siege, a wish to believe they could end it by the right concessions, and a self-deluding embrace of will-o'-the-wisp visions of peace.

FOURTEEN

Oslo Underway: Encountering, and Ignoring, Reality

We should be honest with ourselves and admit that Israel is the principal enemy of the Palestinian people. It was the enemy in the past, it is the enemy in the present, and will continue to be the enemy in the future.

Yasser Arafat, May, 1995[1]

There are enemies of peace who are trying to hurt us, in order to torpedo the peace process. I want to say bluntly that we have found a partner for peace among the Palestinians as well: The PLO.

Yitzhak Rabin, November, 1995[2]

INCITEMENT, TERROR, AND THE ISRAELI RESPONSE

What, in fact, followed on the initial Oslo accords was essentially what the doubters anticipated.

On May 4, 1994, Israel and the PLO signed the Gaza-Jericho self-rule agreement (sometimes referred to as the Cairo Agreement) spelling out the first stage of implementation of the understandings outlined in the September, 1993, Declaration of Principles. Issues covered in this nearly 300-page document include the structure and composition of the Palestinian Authority, definition of the territory being transferred to the Authority, security arrangements, details of the Palestinian Authority's assumption of responsibility for civil affairs within the territories coming under its control, issues of legal authority, and protocols concerning economic relations between the PA and Israel.

The various elements of the Cairo Agreement represent a first fleshing out of the "land for peace" premise of the Declaration of Principles. Israel was ceding most of Gaza as well as Jericho and parts of its environs to the Palestinian Authority. The Palestinians in turn reiterated and expanded on anti-terror and anti-violence commitments they had made in the September 9, 1993, Arafat letter and the Declaration of Principles. The PA undertook to "take all measures necessary in order to prevent acts of terrorism," to "abstain from incitement, including hostile propaganda," and "to take legal measures to prevent incitement by any organizations, groups, or individuals within [its] jurisdiction." Among other PA obligations under the Cairo Agreement were that the PA would pursue no independent foreign policy and would take no steps that would prejudice the ultimate status of the territories or Jerusalem.

The agreement also authorized creation of a Palestinian armed force — explicitly defined to be a police force and not a nascent military — with responsibility for executing customary policing functions as well as preventing terrorism against Israel. The force was to number no more than 9,000 members, of whom 7,000 could be drawn from PLO cadres outside the territories, and to be equipped with limited weaponry as likewise defined by the agreement.

The end of terrorist acts against Israel was particularly touted by Rabin and his colleagues as one of the major benefits that would accrue to Israel as a result of the Oslo process. Arafat and his allies had foresworn in the 1993 accord their own engagement in terror and were now committed to acting against others responsible for attacks on Israel, particularly the Islamic fundamentalist groups. Moreover, Rabin emphasized that negotiations could not proceed in an atmosphere of violence, that ongoing anti-Israel terror would be a violation both of the agreements and of their spirit, and a cessation of violence would be a test of the Oslo process and a condition for its continuation. An end to incitement to violence was similarly characterized as a key test of the Palestinian Authority's compliance with its obligations under the accords and so of the viability of the Oslo process.

But anti-Israel rhetoric and incitement by Arafat and his associates did not end. Indeed, as noted in the Introduction, on the evening of September 13, 1993, just hours after his signing of the DOP and his handshake with Rabin on the White House lawn, Arafat, in a broadcast on Jordanian state television, assured his followers and the Arab world generally that the events of the day, rather than representing a shift in policy toward reconciliation with Israel, were simply steps in the first stage of his 1974 Plan of Phases for Israel's destruction.[3] In September, 1993, alone, Arafat referred to the Plan of Phases more than a dozen times in statements to Arab media.[4] In the ensuing months, allusions to the plan were a staple of Arafat's speeches before Palestinian and other Arab audiences. So also were comparisons of the Oslo agreements to Mohammed's treaty with the Quraysh tribe, an accord terminated when Mohammed was strong enough to defeat the Quraysh.[5] Still another recurrent Arafat theme was calls for Jihad, or Holy War, against Israel.[6]

Arafat also at times stated his agenda even more explicitly, referring, for example, to areas within Israel that the Palestinians would ultimately possess. In a speech in 1995, he declared, "Be blessed, O Gaza, and celebrate, for your sons are returning after a long celebration. O Lod, O Haifa, O Jerusalem, you are returning, you are returning."[7] In a speech broadcast in November, 1995, Arafat assured his audience, "The struggle will continue until all of Palestine is liberated."[8]

The Israeli government's response to this and other incitement by Arafat and his associates was muted. Most often, the incitement was entirely ignored. Israeli media, both government-controlled and independent, likewise tended to ignore it. This was no doubt in part because the incitement was embarrassing and called into question government policy and the new-found faith in Arafat. But in addition to this, there seemed to be an assumption among many in government circles, and among those in the media sympathetic to government policies, that the incitement did not really matter, that the assurances of peaceful intent that Arafat and his lieutenants were conveying to Israeli officials were more important than the incendiary messages they were giving to their own people.

This attitude had been common among leaders of the Peace Movement vis-à-vis their Arab interlocutors during the preceding years. Then too they had given greater weight to what was said to them than to what their interlocutors were saying to Palestinian audiences. The overarching rationale behind this narcissistic comprehension seems to have been, again, a conviction that their Palestinian opposite numbers must desire the peace they themselves desired. Therefore, all that was required for peace was sufficient Israeli concessions, and the assurances given them by their Palestinian interlocutors that this was indeed the case must be those interlocutors' true feelings.

From these premises it was only a short leap to construe Arafat's incitement-laden speeches as merely reflecting his assessment of what was politically expedient but as something that should not be given any great weight. Nissim Zvilli, a Labor MK (Member of Knesset) and member of the Knesset's Foreign Affairs and Defense Committee at the time, subsequently acknowledged, "I remember myself lecturing in Paris and saying that Arafat's double-talk had to be understood. That was our thesis, proved [later] as nonsense. Arafat meant every word, and we were naïve, thinking that he is doing it to overcome the resistance to the agreement among his public."[9]

One problem with the benign comprehension of Arafat's incitement that should have been obvious was that even if Arafat were indeed genuinely committed to peace but simply felt unable to convey that message to his people, even if the situation were that he sensed they wanted to hear something more bellicose from him and felt obliged to accommodate them but did not really mean what he was telling them, his incitement was still undermining the prospects of peace by failing to reconcile his people to it. He was instead stirring them to the opposite of peace. Indeed, the need to promote reconciliation, and concerns about the effects of bellicose messages, are what had prompted Israel's insistence on the anti-incitement clauses in the Oslo agreements.

But here again a common assumption within the government was, in effect, that if preparing the Palestinians for peace, and avoiding incitement, were desirable, they were not really *necessary* for peace. The execution of sufficient Israeli concessions would inexorably dampen Palestinian belligerence and win the Palestinians to reconciliation.

From this perspective, many construed the Palestinians' receptiveness to incitement as a consequence of their not yet experiencing the full benefits of peace, and they saw the solution to Palestinian hostility in more rapid implementation of Israeli concessions. Indeed, if the step-wise nature of the Oslo process and of Israeli withdrawals was presented to the Israeli public by the government as a mechanism for testing Arafat's, and the Palestinians', intentions and trustworthiness, some in the government, particularly those Laborites around Yossi Beilin and ministers drawn from the Meretz Party, appear to have seen no such need for testing. They unequivocally trusted both Arafat and the Palestinians to give Israel full peace for full withdrawal, would have preferred to institute territorial concessions much more rapidly, and saw utility in gradual withdrawal only as a device for acclimating the Israeli public to the new realities the government was creating and thereby diminishing the likelihood of the public's balking.

In addition to the persistence of incitement, acts of terror likewise continued apace even after the signing of the Declaration of Principles. From September, 1993, until July 1, 1994, when Arafat entered the territories, fifty Israelis were killed in terrorist attacks, including thirteen in two bus bombings in April, 1994. Supporters of the accords looked to Arafat to condemn these attacks and typically got lukewarm condemnations at best. Nevertheless, they noted that the perpetrators of these murders were overwhelmingly agents of Hamas and, to a lesser extent, Islamic Jihad. They argued that Arafat, in keeping with his Oslo commitments, would control and stifle these fundamentalist groups once he was established in the territories; indeed, he would do so more effectively than Israel could.

However, in the fifteen months between Arafat's establishment in Gaza and the signing of the next accord, Oslo II (September 28, 1995), another ninety people were killed in Palestinian attacks. By way of comparison, Palestinian terror had taken about 400 lives in the twenty-six years from the 1967 war and Israel's entry into the territories to the inception of Oslo.[10] The dead since Arafat's arrival included eighty-seven Israelis and three visitors to Israel. Sixty-four of the dead, among them the three non-Israeli Jews, were killed in bombings. This was virtually the same pace of murders as in the preceding months. Nineteen of these killings occurred in Gaza and were perpetrated from areas now under Arafat's control. In addition, many of the other attacks, including all the bombings, were the work of groups whose infrastructures and training facilities were in Gaza, and they were often carried out by people recruited in Gaza.

Again, if Arafat offered any condemnation at all, it was lukewarm and couched in statements that such attacks were against Palestinian interests. Even these pinched declarations were typically pried from him only after bombings that killed large numbers of Israelis and only when international attention was turned to Arafat's response. Moreover, such statements invariably avoided condemning Hamas and Islamic Jihad — the perpetrators of the bombings — by name. On the contrary, Arafat at times praised the terror groups, their leaders, and their operatives.[11]

Arafat also praised the methods of the terrorists and hailed their operations as models for others to emulate. In a speech in Gaza on January 1, 1995, after a series of deadly suicide bombings inside Israel, Arafat told his audience: "We are all seekers of the path of martyrs. And I say to the shaheeds [martyrs] who have already died, on behalf of the shaheeds who are still alive, that our vow remains, and our commitment remains, to continue the revolution." Some months later, in another forum in Gaza, Arafat again told his audience, "We are all seekers of the path of shaheeds, in the way of truth and rights, the way of Jerusalem, capital of Palestine . . . We will continue this long and difficult jihad, the way of martyrdom, through sacrifice . . . on this difficult jihad, through the fallen, through victory, through glory, not only for our Palestinian people, but for our Arab and Islamic nation."[12]

Not surprisingly, Arafat did nothing to disarm Hamas and Islamic Jihad or dismantle their infrastructures. While he did occasionally arrest members of these organizations and murderers of Israelis, detainees were often soon released or given furloughs. This pattern quickly became known as "revolving door" imprisonment, and some such "prisoners" were even recruited into the Palestinian police.

Despite the Cairo Agreement's obligating the Palestinians to extradite murderers of Israelis to Israel for trial, Arafat rejected all requests for extradition, and Palestinian officials declared categorically that no one would ever be handed over to Israel.[13] They asserted that alleged murderers of Israelis would instead stand trial in Palestinian courts, but what ensued for those brought to court was typically a bogus trial and the same pattern of, at most, a brief incarceration.

In addition, PA officials routinely praised the Islamic fundamentalist organizations and asserted that they and the PA shared common interests and aims, with Israel their common enemy. For example, PA Justice Minister Freih Abu Medein declared: "The PA and the [Hamas] opposition complement each other . . . We regard Hamas and Islamic Jihad as national elements . . . The main enemy, now and forever, is Israel."[14] The supposedly moderate PA Cabinet Minister Hanan Ashrawi insisted that, "It is not up to Israel to decide or define who is our enemy. Hamas is not the enemy, it is part of the political fabric."[15]

Even Yossi Beilin had declared, shortly before the signing of the Declaration of Principles (DOP) in September, 1993, that the Oslo agreements were contingent on an end to terror. The *Wall Street Journal* reported on September 1, "Mr. Beilin . . . said that the [DOP plan] is conditional on the Palestinians being able to prevent Islamic fundamentalist groups who oppose the peace talks from carrying out terrorist attacks against Israel . . . Mr. Beilin continued, 'As in any other agreement, there is the belief that both sides will be able to implement it and can be trusted, but if there is a clear violation, it will be more than understandable that we cannot adhere to it.'"[16] But neither Beilin nor anyone else shaping the policies of the Rabin government called for a halt to Oslo in the face of the terror assault and the PA's collusion in it.

In these fifteen months between Arafat's arrival in Gaza and the signing of the next accord, Oslo II, the initial Israeli government stance, that terror and the peace process were incompatible and that continuation of the former would mean termination of the latter, was effectively abandoned. The Israeli government's response to the ongoing violence, and to Arafat's failure to fulfill his Oslo obligations vis-à-vis terrorism and his, instead, lending support to the terrorist groups, was muted at best and frequently even protective of Arafat.[17] Indeed, the government even cast Arafat and his Palestinian Authority as an ally against the terrorism despite the overwhelming evidence to the contrary. For example, in August, 1995, addressing the issue of recent terrorism and the challenge it presented to Israel, Rabin declared: "This is a war against the enemies of Israel and the enemies of peace. It is a war which we are waging today, to some extent, together with the Palestinian Authority, whose enemies they are also."[18]

On occasion, in response to public outrage, government officials would angrily demand more effective action by the Palestinian Authority to quell the terrorism. But no reassessment or reevaluation of policy ever ensued.

An excuse offered by some in the Israeli government on behalf of Arafat was that he did not clamp down on the fundamentalist organizations because he was not politically strong enough to do so. There was, in fact, much evidence that contradicted this claim regarding Arafat's strength. But, in any case, the explanation raised obvious questions concerning the wisdom of the government's negotiating "peace" with someone whom it perceived as not strong enough to assure his constituency's adherence to any agreements.

But the Peace Movement's supporters in the government, the dominant voices in Rabin's coalition, had an answer to such questions: more Israeli concessions. Picking up on a theme played upon by the Palestinian leadership, a theme that converged with Peace Movement rhetoric, these officials argued that the Palestinian people were frustrated by the pace of Israeli concessions and by their not seeing quickly enough the dividends of peace, and so speeding up the process would strengthen Arafat's hand and weaken support for the terrorist organizations. A variation on this theme soon became the government's overarching rhetorical response to the recurrent terrorist atrocities: The primary target of the terrorists, it was argued, was not the Israelis who were their victims but rather the peace process itself; it was not Jews or Israelis *per se* they sought to kill, but the "peace." So the proper Israeli response would be to accelerate the process and the pace of concessions and thereby frustrate the terrorists.[19] For some in the government, this line of argument, and the protection of Arafat, were no doubt motivated by a desire to defend the government, to cast its Oslo gamble in a positive light despite the terror and Arafat's recalcitrance. But many in the coalition sincerely believed this rhetoric.

Of course, as was entirely obvious to numerous observers, this Israeli response essentially rewarded the Palestinians for terror. The more terror, the more the government urged a speeding up of the "peace process," whose most tangible elements were Israeli withdrawals and other concessions. Not surprisingly, the terror did not diminish and Arafat continued on his course of tolerance toward and tacit, and at times explicit, cooperation with the terrorism's perpetrators.

FATHOMING ARAFAT'S STRATEGY, AND THE ISRAELI DEBATE THAT WASN'T

That Arafat remained true to his goal of destroying Israel and supplanting it with a Palestinian Arab state in all of Mandate Palestine is clear from his public statements, in Arabic, to Palestinian and other Arab audiences, from the message conveyed by the media, schools, and mosques under his control, and from the statements and writings of his lieutenants. These sources, and Arafat's actions in the territories, also yield clues to his understanding of Israel and its vulnerabilities and to the strategy and tactics by which he would seek to execute his Plan of Phases and achieve his objective of Israel's dissolution.

In fact, Arafat had long believed, even before his official elaboration of the Plan of Phases in 1974, that a terror war prosecuted from bases in the West Bank and Gaza could fatally undermine Israel. He stated in 1968 that such a strategy could have the effect of "preventing immigration and encouraging emigration . . . destroying tourism . . . weakening the Israeli economy and diverting the greater part of it to security requirements. Creating and maintaining an atmosphere of strain and anxiety that will force the Zionists to realize that it is impossible for them to live in Israel."[20]

The intervening years appear only to have strengthened Arafat's conviction of Israel's vulnerability and the wisdom of his war plan. At the time of Oslo's inception, he saw Israel as a state in retreat and suffering from a loss of nerve.

It was unwilling to endure casualties, as amply indicated, in the view of many in the Arab world, by the Israeli public's response to losses in the Intifada and in Lebanon. It had grown accustomed to Western-style wealth and comfort and was no longer prepared to accept hardship or sacrifice. It was essentially suing for peace. Arafat believed that his own people's willingness, in contrast, to tolerate sacrifice, as demonstrated in the Intifada, gave him an edge over Israel. He seems clearly to have expected that under pressure, including the pressure of terrorist violence, there were virtually no limits to the extent of the retreat he could force upon Israel.

Early in 1996, reports circulated that Arafat, in a recent visit to Stockholm, had told an audience of Arab diplomats, "We plan to eliminate the state of Israel and establish a purely Palestinian state . . . We will make life unbearable for Jews by psychological warfare and population explosion . . . They will give up their dwelling and leave for the U.S. We Palestinians will take over everything . . . I have no use for the Jews. They are and remain Jews."[21] Arafat's reported statement in Stockholm did not explicitly include military pressures among his means for effecting Israel's disintegration. But elsewhere he clearly referred to such pressures, and a few months after his visit to Stockholm he remarked to Israeli interlocutors, "Are you Israelis capable of sustaining 500 fatalities? We can readily sacrifice 30,000 martyrs, or more. And let there be no doubt that we know what your main weakness is: [sensitivity to] human life."[22]

From his arrival in Gaza, Arafat cultivated contacts with the Israeli Arab community, seeking to strengthen further its already very strong identification with the Palestinians in the territories and to encourage its perception of him as its true leader, as prelude to his making future territorial demands on pre-1967 Israel. In a speech on July 1, 1994, the day of his first coming to Gaza, Arafat promised to "liberate" Israel's Arabs: "I am saying it clearly and loudly to all our brothers, from the Negev to the Galilee, and let me quote Allah's words: 'We desired to be gracious to those that were abased in the land, and to make them leaders, and to make them the inheritors, and to establish them in the land.'"[23]

Israeli Arab rebellion would be one more pressure he would bring to bear on Israel to hasten its demise. As for those Israelis who did not leave in the face of the multipronged assault, internal cohesion would inexorably unravel and — whether Arafat imagined a regional war as part of the *coup de grace* or the end coming simply from Palestinian efforts — the Jewish state would ultimately collapse.

(Notable in the context of this scenario was the response of Israel's tourism minister, Uzi Baram, in a television interview in November, 1994, when he was asked, in effect, what he would do if the Palestinians continued to attack Israel after gaining the accommodations envisioned in the Oslo accords. Baram answered: "I'll go to the American Consulate and apply for a visa."[24] Not long

afterwards, Baram was the top vote-getter in the Labor Party primary that preceded the May, 1996, Israeli election.)

That the terror Israel experienced in the months after Arafat's coming to
Gaza elicited from the government the response it did — reluctant bluster, demands that quickly dissipated, no change in policy but, instead, calls for a speeding up of the process of concessions — served, as did many other Israeli actions
as well, to reinforce Arafat's assumptions of Israel's weakness and ripeness for
defeat and his pursuit of tactics consonant with those assumptions.

The Islamic terrorist groups became a tool for applying the very sort of
stresses Arafat believed would undermine Israeli national morale and cohesion.
Under no real pressure from the Israeli government, he was consistently able
to avoid cracking down on the terrorist organizations, could allow them significant rein, and could use their terror to extract more Israeli concessions; and
he could all the while preserve, with the government's support, deniability of
complicity. Whatever limited and short-lived pressure was applied to him in
the wake of terrorist atrocities was quickly defused by Arafat with the fig leaf
of temporary arrests and occasional condemnations. Such steps, together with
his assurances of his pacific intentions and dedication to a "peace of the brave,"
assurances given in speeches in English and especially in conversations with
Israelis, proved to be more than sufficient for the Israeli government to maintain its defense of the peace process and of Arafat as a partner and to keep the
train of Israeli concessions essentially on track.

Representatives of the government repeatedly argued, against skeptics who
decried Arafat's failure to dismantle the infrastructures of the terrorist groups,
that Arafat and the fundamentalists obviously had conflicting and competing
interests. The one, in the government's view, was against peace; the other for
peace, as Arafat repeatedly averred in English; and so the government was right
in seeking to strengthen Arafat against his competitors. But recognition that
Arafat and the Islamic fundamentalist organizations were not one, were in some
respects competing with each other for the loyalty of the Palestinian population and supremacy in the territories, hardly represented a rebuttal to claims
that they shared an agenda directed toward Israel's destruction and were col-
luding, at times tacitly, at times explicitly, in pursuit of that agenda. Recognition
of their competition was even less persuasive as such a rebuttal when there was
so much evidence of their collusion in terror for those who bothered to look
and were willing to see.

Among the pieces of evidence that Israeli leaders had in hand during this
period but were unprepared to "see" was intelligence information about an operational agreement forged between the PLO and Hamas in meetings in Cairo
in December, 1995. A military intelligence report to the government in March,
1996, stated: "Arafat believed the genie would stay in the bottle as long as it

suited the interests of the PA. The understanding his representatives reached in December 1995 with Hamas representatives — though it never became a formal agreement, but actually determined the behavior of Hamas and the PA ever since — symbolizes [Arafat's belief] more than anything. Within the framework of this understanding, Hamas implicitly committed itself not to act against Israel and Israelis from areas under PA jurisdiction until the end of the IDF redeployment and the elections of the PA council. Arafat has done practically nothing since to fight the operational infrastructure of Hamas and Islamic Jihad while they exploited that to prepare a series of terrible attacks. A close examination of Arafat's behavior and that of his people enables us to see clearly that this is not merely a policy that began in recent months. It is the conception that has guided him since he entered the territories."[25]

After the outbreak of violence in September, 2000, and the unraveling of the Oslo accords, various senior officials in military intelligence and other Israeli intelligence services pointed to reports such as the one cited here to argue that they had informed the government of Arafat's noncompliance with Oslo's security provisions and of his continued commitment to a belligerent agenda but that government leaders chose to ignore the warnings. But the reality appears to have been more complicated. The deluded conviction that, despite all appearances to the contrary, Arafat and the Palestinians were prepared to give Israel genuine peace in return for sufficient concessions, swept over the leaders of Israel's intelligence community — a significantly politicized leadership — as well as the nation's elected officials. While the various branches of Israeli intelligence were providing the government with evidence of Palestinian malfeasance and commitment to terror and ultimate confrontation, the leaders of the intelligence community were submitting contorted and hedged interpretations of the evidence that sought to reconcile it with the possibility of Arafat still being a genuine "peace" partner. It may well be that this reflected in part the intelligence leadership's simply providing the political echelon with what it knew the latter wanted to hear — a not uncommon phenomenon even though a dereliction of duty. But it seems that also at work here was an embrace by the intelligence community of the Oslo *zeitgeist* that blinded it to the full import of its own data.[26]

Also noteworthy in this regard was the failure of the intelligence services to monitor aggressively Arafat's speeches and other activities for clues to his intentions. Indeed, some of the crucial intelligence gathering during this period, such as recording of Arafat's May, 1994, speech in Johannesburg calling for Jihad against Israel as well as some details of the Cairo meeting between Hamas and Arafat's representatives, were acquired by private parties, not by the intelligence services.

Arafat, even as he was making use of the terror and its perpetrators, was all the time strengthening his own armed cadres and likely believed that he could and would deal decisively with the fundamentalist groups if and when they were no longer useful to him or offered too much of a challenge to his authority. The fundamentalist groups no doubt were not pleased by Arafat's constant expanding of his armed forces and saw them as ultimately a threat to themselves, but they were also hardly displeased by the wresting of territory and other concessions from Israel. Indeed, in tandem with their ongoing acts of terror, they were able to claim to the Palestinian public that it was their pressure on the Israelis, and not Arafat's negotiating, that was the real generator of Israel's concessions. They also likely believed that in the end, however much Arafat might build up his "police," the Palestinian population's disgust with the corruption of PA officials and operatives and with their general indifference to the public's needs, together with people's greater respect for the Islamists, would enable them eventually to wrest control of Palestine. But Arafat and the fundamentalists' conflicting and competing versions of eventual denouements were hardly obstacles to cooperation in steps aimed at undermining Israel's morale and cohesion and ultimately challenging her survival.

The Israeli government's ignoring or downplaying of Arafat's repeated calls for Holy War, his assurances to his people of his dedication to Israel's ultimate dissolution, and his other exercises in incitement, and the government's continually responding to terror not as a violation of Oslo commitments but as a reason to hasten forward into additional "agreements," were accompanied by other government failures as well. There were additional examples of the Rabin administration refusing to allow Palestinian flouting of the first Oslo accords to halt or even slow more than briefly the parade of more concessions and more "peace" ceremonies.

Arafat quickly established armed forces substantially exceeding those allowed under the Gaza-Jericho accord, and his agents lost no time in organizing smuggling operations to bring into the territories weapons banned by the agreement. All this occurred with the full knowledge of Israel but with no impact on Israel's eagerness to pursue accommodation. The Palestinians' failure to extradite murderers of Israelis again caused barely a ripple.

Despite Oslo commitments protecting Palestinians who had cooperated with Israeli intelligence prior to the agreements, Arafat's forces immediately embarked on a series of "collaborator" murders that killed dozens. This too elicited hardly a murmur of protest from the Rabin administration. In addition, the Oslo accords included arrangements for cooperation between PA and Israeli security services, and Israel repeatedly passed on to the PA information about terrorist activities; but this very often led not to any significant moves by the PA against the terrorists but rather to the PA using the information to track down possible Palestinian sources of the Israeli intelligence and to attack them, once more with little Israeli reaction. But it should hardly be surprising that Israel was virtually silent about the murder of so-called Palestinian collaborators when it was so supine in its responses to the murder of Israelis.

Arafat's brutal style of governance at once victimized many Palestinians and boded ill for the peace process, yet it too aroused little protest from the Israeli government or its supporters. Indeed, when voices on the Israeli Right criticized Arafat's regime, they were attacked by their political opponents for supposedly making an issue of Arafat's less than democratic methods in order to advance their "anti-peace" agenda.

While not all the steps taken by Arafat to impose his dictatorial control entailed violations of Oslo, some did; and insofar as the Israeli government acquiesced to those violations, its stance represented not simply passivity in the face of Arafat's course but virtual collusion in it. As noted, Israel did nothing about Arafat's creating security forces far larger than those allowed by Oslo, forces that not only posed a threat to Israel but became Arafat's chief tool for intimidating and controlling any challenging elements among the Palestinians. (According to Amnesty International, Arafat established "possibly the highest ratio of police to civil population in the world."[27])

Oslo stipulated that elections for a Palestinian Council should be held in July, 1994, two months after the signing of the Gaza-Jericho accord. But Arafat wanted time to establish his control and intimidate any potential dissident elements that might vie for council seats, and Israel acceded to extending the period before the elections from two months to twenty months, allowing them to be rescheduled for January, 1996.

Arafat's assumption of control in the territories has been best described by Daniel Polisar, who at the time headed Peace Watch, the only Israeli group accredited by the PA to be an observer of its 1996 elections. Polisar documents "the rise of a regime characterized by a massive police force whose specialty was intimidation of political opponents; an executive branch in which Arafat alone made all major decisions and in which the civil service was reduced to a corrupt patronage machine; the institutionalized absence of the rule of law, and a judiciary that lacked any independence; and the intimidation of the media and human rights organizations, to the point that it became virtually impossible to transmit any message other than one personally approved by Arafat."[28]

Arafat rewarded some supporters with monopoly control over essential goods and services and allowed others to extract shakedowns from independent entrepreneurs, all of which led to a dramatic shrinking of the private sector. This was not a violation of Oslo but obviously dealt a blow to hopes that foreign infusion of money would lead to the growth of an independent middle class invested in peace. Yet Israel was silent. (Amotz Asa-El, then financial columnist for the *Jerusalem Post*, was an early Oslo enthusiast and attended international donors' meetings that had pledged almost a billion dollars to create industrial parks in areas controlled by the PA and potentially provide a tremendous boost to the Palestinian economy. In 1996, Asa-El wrote of the Palestinian Authority's failure to do its part to establish the industrial parks and its instead allowing the plans to wither. Asa-El attributed this in part to Arafat's unhappiness with the fiscal transparency demanded by international donors. However, Arafat was also unwilling to foster economic development along the lines intended by the donors because he was not prepared to allow the rise of a politically independent middle class.[29])

Arafat and his PA associates diverted a large percentage of the PA budget, much of it consisting of foreign contributions, to personal accounts and private use. A comptroller's report on PA finances for 1996 stated that $325 million out of a budget of $800 million had disappeared, either to "waste" or embezzlement by PA officials. This, too, dramatically undermined hopes that foreign aid would foster economic development and political stability. Israel was not only silent on PA corruption but actually contributed to it. In a protocol ancillary to the Oslo accords, Israel had agreed to reimburse the PA for taxes collected on imported goods destined for areas under Palestinian governance. Arafat insisted that the taxes be placed in accounts personally controlled by him, and Israel agreed to this. The transfers, until interrupted upon Arafat's launching of his terror war in September, 2000, amounted to about $2.5 billion.[30]

The Palestinians had developed, under Israeli administration, the freest press in the Arab world; Arafat established PA-controlled newspapers to overwhelm the independent papers, and he ultimately intimidated and crushed the latter. A story in *Columbia Journalism Review* noted in early 1996, "Since Arafat assumed power . . . in May, 1994, the security forces have made more than thirty arrests of journalists and editors . . . Reporters Sans Frontiers, a watchdog group based in Paris, released a report at the end of 1995 deploring the Palestinian Authority's policy of suspending newspapers and employing threats and violence against journalists."[31] Arafat also imposed a government monopoly on broadcast media, and he used all the media organs under his control for incitement against Israel. Again, Israel was silent.

A number of human rights groups had flourished in the territories during Israel's control. Either out of "nationalist" sentiment or because of Arafat's pressure, all retreated from high-profile human rights monitoring. The few individuals who refused to bend and chose instead to criticize PA practices were threatened, arrested, and accused of being Zionist agents. Not only was the Israeli government silent, but the Israeli Left in general was mute. B'tselem, an Israeli human rights group that had reported on alleged Israeli human rights violations in the territories but had always been essentially a conduit for claims against Israel made by Palestinian field workers, now abandoned its chief field operative, Bassem Eid, who had sought to report on PA abuses and was labeled a collaborator for his efforts.[32] B'tselem subsequently took much of its information from the former human rights group al-Haq even though the group, always a major source of B'tselem claims and never very reliable in its anti-Israel assertions, had now been reduced virtually to a PA house organ.[33]

Again, when voices on the Israeli Right complained that only a democratic Palestinian entity offered the possibility of an enduring peace and that Arafat's regime could not be trusted as a partner, the government and its supporters attacked those voices as seeking to use the democracy issue to obstruct progress toward "peace."

The prevailing government opinion, despite all the countervailing evidence, continued to be that sufficient Israeli withdrawals and other concessions would lead to peace, indeed not only to a cold peace but to a reconciliation and subsequent relations comparable to those of the states of western Europe. This opinion manifested itself in the government's interpretation of all Palestinian violations of current agreements, however bloody, as mere bumps along the way to the beckoning peace. It was also reflected in the virtual absence of any serious debate in the Israeli public arena — beyond the protests of those who opposed the Oslo accords and saw them as leading inevitably to disaster — concerning the balance of risks and benefits for Israel entailed in the Oslo process, the potential dangers they posed to the country, and how those dangers might be addressed.

For example, among those within the government, while the dominant opinion appears to have been the Peace Movement position that Israel could safely return virtually to its pre-1967 lines, others still seemed to believe that Israel must retain some strategic positions in the territories for its security. Yet there was no serious debate among supporters of the accords on the territorial issue and security. More remarkable still, even assuming that Arafat were a trustworthy peace partner, one would expect a responsible government to take into consideration issues of the difficulties that might confront the country if, after its territorial withdrawals, Arafat were overthrown by a rejectionist coup. Or what if he were simply succeeded by a regime hostile to Israel, or — even if the peace with the Palestinians held — if hostile regimes in neighboring states mounted an attack and Israel had to defend itself without control of the territories it had ceded? Virtually none of this was discussed or debated in the public arena.

Where were the sober analyses and discussions by supporters of the accords of what land Israel could cede without undermining its capacity to defend itself? Where were the careful considerations of issues such as possible Palestinian use of terrorism as an instrument of state after a final accord and possible Israeli responses? Where was discussion of the logistical problems posed by policing greatly extended borders and doing so having foresworn options of preemption and response in force? Where was discussion of the strategic consequences of Israel's losing its intelligence-gathering capacities in the territories, the strategic significance of greatly decreased freedom of mobility following territorial concessions, and the strategic threat posed by greater exposure of Israel's population centers to terror and other attacks?

Again, questions such as these are relevant not only to the possibility of hostilities emanating from within the lands ceded to the Palestinians but to hostilities emanating from neighboring states as well. Yet questions of the implications of Israel's contemplated territorial concessions for its ability to respond to threats of the latter sort were likewise not analyzed, discussed, debated. More particularly, during these same months between the two Oslo accords, Rabin indicated his willingness to negotiate a peace agreement with Syria under which — despite his campaign promises to the contrary — he would concede all of the Golan to the Syrians. Yet there was no public discussion, aside from that emanating from voices vehemently opposed to such a step. That opposition, in fact, included a majority of Israelis; and a hunger strike by nineteen Golan activists in September, 1994, elicited visits to the Golan by an estimated 250,000 people, 5 percent of the nation's population, in a show of solidarity with the strikers. But there was no serious analysis or debate by the government's supporters of the strategic significance of loss of the Golan Heights, or of the threat to Israel's water supply that retreat from the Golan would entail, and of how Israel might possibly offset the various risks and threats posed by ceding of the Golan.

On the contrary, the prevailing assumption within the government, and among its supporters, was the Peace Movement assumption that such public discussions were unnecessary because the basis of all Arab-Israeli conflict was Arab grievances that could be comprehensively addressed by Israeli self-reform and concessions. Once Israel had appropriately reformed itself and made sufficient concessions, an era of peace and goodwill would ensue that would render those strategic concerns moot.

THE TREATY WITH JORDAN: REALITIES AND DELUSIONS

Notable also as an expression of the Rabin government's self-deluding mindset were the significances attached by many in the Israeli government to the peace treaty negotiated with Jordan during this same period and signed on October 26, 1994.

The treaty with Jordan was to many observers the one and perhaps only positive consequence likely to emerge from the Oslo process, and its achievement came as no surprise. King Hussein had for more than two decades maintained substantive positive contacts with Israeli leaders, and Israel and Jordan had long cooperated on some important security matters. These relations had never been formalized because Jordan, economically weak compared to the Arab oil states and somewhat dependent on the latter for financial support, militarily weaker than her often hostile and aggressive neighbors Syria and Iraq, and having a population whose majority had Western Palestinian connections and closely identified with the Palestinians in the territories, was afraid of getting too far ahead of the Arab consensus vis-à-vis Israel. It did not see itself as able to take the step that Egypt had taken in forging its own treaty with Israel. But the events of September, 1993, the mutual recognition and negotiated agreements between Israel and the PLO, provided the cover for King Hussein finally to follow Egypt into a formal peace with the Jewish state.

The treaty fell short, of course, of what had for decades been at least Labor Party hopes of the Jordanians negotiating a territorial compromise on the West Bank and taking formal responsibility for and control of those areas that would revert to Arab sovereignty. But the agreement did have the potential of heralding for Israel the first genuinely "normal" peace with an Arab state. It held the promise, for example, of mutually beneficial trade relations and of cooperation in many other areas as well, in contrast to the "cold" peace with Egypt. By any measure, the treaty with Jordan was an important achievement.

But at least some influential voices in the Israeli government insisted on attaching to it significances that the treaty could not support and that ran counter to all sober assessment, significances consistent however with the comprehensions of the Peace Movement. At around this time, reports emerged of Yossi Beilin, Deputy Foreign Minister and chief architect of Oslo, being engaged in secret "informal" discussions with a high-ranking Palestinian official on future Israeli territorial concessions that would entail virtually a return to Israel's pre-1967 borders.[34] The reports of the Beilin meetings and their drift concerning future Israeli concessions led some in official positions to defend more openly such concessions and even to invoke the Jordan agreement in support of them.

An example was the response of a senior foreign ministry official when asked, a few months after the signing of the Jordan treaty, about the reports and, in particular, about the dangers of Israel ceding to Palestinian control the Jordan Valley.[35] The valley had long been regarded as strategically vital to defend Israel from assault from the east. Its loss as part of a redeployment from the West Bank would reduce the country to a width of nine miles at its most heavily populated areas on the coastal plain, and Arab forces would have ready access to the heights dominating the plain. This would be true not only of Palestinian forces, which would control the heights, but of any Arab army advancing from the east.

The senior official answered by denying there had been any "formal" offer of such a withdrawal. (The reports at the time said Beilin had proposed an interim period of some years during which the Israeli army would remain in the valley and after which it would evacuate, leaving the valley fully under Palestinian control and sovereignty.) But he added that in any case the Jordan Valley was no longer of such strategic significance, as the treaty with Jordan meant that the important border between Israel and any potential aggressor from the east was now Jordan's border with Iraq!

Such a statement, divorced in so many respects from responsible risk-assessment and policy making, provides a particularly dramatic illustration of the government's investment in delusions regarding the new conditions that would ensue were Israel to make sufficient concessions. Those conditions, they insisted, would translate into an inexorably firm and durable peace.

The list of reasons why the treaty with Jordan, for all that was positive about it, in no way altered the strategic significance to Israel of the Jordan Valley, is a long one indeed. It includes numerous potential scenarios that a responsible government was obliged to consider in its policy making and that rendered control of the Jordan Valley as vital as ever.

First, there was much opposition to the peace within Jordan, including opposition emanating from the majority of its population descended from Palestinian refugees. These people would likely continue to be, at best, a source of hostility to the treaty as long as the Palestinian Authority was not maximally satisfied with Israeli concessions (and, for many, as long as so-called rejectionist groups such as Hamas and Islamic Jihad remained viable and hostile to any accord). Israel had to consider the possibility that hostile groups might at some point force a reversal of Jordanian policy or seize control of Jordan. To put it bluntly, a single bullet could nullify the treaty.

Also, Jordan's neighbors Iraq and Syria were much stronger militarily than Jordan, and Israel had to take into account the possibility of Jordan being overrun by an assault from one or both of its neighbors, an assault that could bring hostile armies to the Jordan River. (One could argue that an assault on Jordan by Iraq would give Israel at least some time to muster its forces, and so in this regard the situation on the eastern front would be comparable to the demilitarized Sinai, where a hostile Egypt mustering its forces would give Israel time to mobilize. But, aside from the fact of Israel having at least a peace of sorts with Egypt, Israel has a common border with Egypt on which it could mobilize in a crisis. In contrast, after ceding the Jordan Valley, Israel, in order to face a hostile army moving to the Jordan, would have to cross the territory of a likely sovereign and potentially hostile Palestinian state. The ceding of the Jordan Valley is precisely what would, in this context, make the situation in the east different from that on the Sinai border and much more dangerous.)

What should have been another key consideration is that Israeli withdrawal from the Jordan would in itself create threats to the Hashemite throne and to the peace that Israel had negotiated with King Hussein. Yasser Arafat, from his entry into Gaza in July, 1994, cultivated increased contacts with Israeli Arabs and took steps to establish himself not only as leader of the Arabs in the territories but of those in Israel as well. So too Arafat had always viewed himself as the proper leader of the Palestinian population in Jordan, and he began, with his presence in the territories, to cultivate more vigorously his position among them and his competition with King Hussein for their loyalty. If Israel retained the Jordan Valley, it would serve as a geographical buffer between Jordan and the emerging Palestinian entity and represent an obstacle to Palestinian designs on Jordan. Alternatively, Israel's ceding the valley would give Arafat and his circle much greater ability to exploit their challenge to King Hussein or his successor and would directly threaten the Hashemites and the viability of Jordan's peace with Israel.

Israeli withdrawal from the Jordan Valley would threaten the peace with Jordan in other ways as well. King Hussein had always favored close ties with the West, but he had felt threatened enough by Iraq and Syria at times to seek to placate his stronger Arab neighbors even when doing so ran counter to his connections with the West. His support for Saddam Hussein in the wake of Iraq's invasion of Kuwait and in defiance of the American-led anti-Saddam coalition is perhaps the most dramatic example of this. While the Oslo agreements provided some cover for Hussein's treaty with Israel in the wider Arab world generally, that cover did not mollify Syria and Iraq, both of which were critical of Oslo as well as of the Jordan-Israel pact. That King Hussein would risk antagonizing his rejectionist neighbors to the extent that he did was due in significant part to Israel's unwritten provision of a security umbrella for Jordan against attack by either Syria or Iraq, just as Israel's aerial buzzing of Syrian forces when they invaded Jordan in 1970 played a pivotal role in Syria's decision to retreat.

But Israel's capacity to intervene effectively in Jordan in the face of whatever military challenge to the Hashemites might arise is dependent not only on the ability to utilize its air power but also its ability to introduce ground forces if necessary, and this in turn requires Israel's control of the Jordan Valley and free access of its forces to it. Israel's ceding the Jordan Valley, and the passes leading to it, to the Palestinians would almost inevitably push the Hashemites to reassess their strategic position and to distance themselves from Israel and draw closer to and seek to mollify Iraq and Syria. They would do so both because they would feel more vulnerable to Iraq and Syria and because they would feel more in need of Arab counterweights to a threatening Palestinian presence in the Jordan Valley. This strategic shift would, of course, have the effect of increasing the threats to Israel.

For obvious reasons, the Jordanian leadership would never say publicly that it wants Israel to retain control of the Jordan Valley and not cede it to a Palestinian state, that it regarded Israel's giving up the Jordan Valley as creating grave threats to its own well-being and survival. But Jordan's views on this, and the strategic issues involved, were clear and well-known. That influential elements of the Israeli government were nevertheless prepared to have Israel withdraw from the Jordan Valley is — aside from the direct threats doing so would present to Israel — another example, like the abandonment of so-called Palestinian "collaborators" to Arafat's death squads, of Israelis betraying parties with which they have forged genuinely positive relationships in their headlong delusional rush to placate Israel's enemies.

The depth of Jordanian concerns over apparent Israeli preparedness to cede the Jordan Valley to Palestinian control, and to a lesser degree over other elements of Israeli policy in the context of Oslo, was demonstrated in indirect but fairly dramatic fashion in early, 1996, in the course of the run-up to the Israeli election that May. The election, occurring in the wake of Rabin's assassination the previous November, pitted Shimon Peres against Likud leader Benjamin Netanyahu. Various Arab leaders, in an effort to support Peres, repeatedly insisted that they would not deal with Netanyahu if he won and that the peace process would be halted. Jordan, two months before the vote, abruptly invited Netanyahu to meet with Crown Prince Hassan in Aqaba, undercutting the Arab pro-Peres strategy and bolstering Likud's chances. In addition, Jordan's leading newspaper, *Al Aswaq*, published an editorial in favor of Netanyahu's candidacy just days before the balloting. These steps no doubt reflected in large part King Hussein's belief that Netanyahu was much less likely than Peres to yield the Jordan Valley to Arafat and would generally pursue policies toward Arafat that would better serve Jordan.[36]

THE OPPOSITION AS THE ENEMY

As noted in previous chapters, when Jewish constituencies have responded to their tormentors by embracing the enemy's indictments and pursuing self-reform and concessions as the path to relief, those constituencies have very often targeted as the "true" enemy other Jews. They have done so by, for example, casting those other Jews as the actual object of the tormentors' wrath and so the "true" source of the community's difficulties, or by castigating them for refusing to accommodate the tormentors' indictments and thereby perpetuating the community's grief. In this instance, the major targets of the government's animus were those Jews who saw the self-delusion and terrible dangers in the Oslo path and voiced their opposition to it.

The government and its supporters wrapped themselves in the characterization of the Oslo accords as a "peace process," and all challengers were now attacked as "enemies of peace," often as the Jewish equivalent of those Arab "enemies of peace" who were perpetrating the terrorist attacks against Israel.[37] This was so whatever the basis of people's questioning of the accords, whether they did so out of distrust of Arafat or out of concern that, irrespective of Arafat's intentions, the concessions the government was prepared to make would gravely undermine Israel's capacity to defend itself. Those who voiced doubts were enemies of peace.

Again, there was virtually no public discussion or debate among supporters of Oslo addressing the extent of concessions Israel could safely make. Nor was there public consideration of the strategic challenges Israel would confront in response to the territorial withdrawals it was contemplating and of how it would meet those challenges. It was perhaps not surprising then that the government and its supporters were not prepared to respond seriously to the critiques of Oslo put forward by its opponents, that it limited its reaction almost exclusively to smears and name-calling. But its doing so was another mark of its eagerness to put aside all measured consideration in its embrace of the faith that sufficient concessions would inexorably yield a durable peace.

After the initial wave of popular enthusiasm by large segments of the Israeli public in response to the first Oslo accords, support for the agreements began to erode. This was no doubt due in large part to the ongoing terrorist violence and to popular impatience and discontent with the government's efforts to exonerate from responsibility Israel's "peace partners," Arafat and the Palestinian Authority. In March, 1995, a poll of Israeli Jews revealed that 45.9 percent believed the Oslo process entailed more dangers than potential benefits for Israel and only 22.5 percent believed the opposite; 62.4 percent were dissatisfied with the process and only 10.9 percent expressed satisfaction with it; 64.4 percent felt personal security had deteriorated while only 8.9 percent thought it had improved.[38] This dramatic and persistent decline in popular support for Oslo seemed only to make the government and its supporters more shrill in their vilification and demonization of their opponents.

Not surprisingly, a major source of opposition to the Oslo accords was the population of the settlements. This was a disparate group of people. Some, with their roots in secular Labor Zionism, had joined those settlements that had been established by Labor governments with a focus on reinforcing claims to sparsely populated strategic areas. Others were religiously motivated people who were determined to secure a presence particularly in religiously and historically significant locations. Still others had moved to settlement communities for the sake of better living conditions at more affordable costs than they could find in, for example, Jerusalem or Tel Aviv.

The intensity of their opposition to government policy also varied substantially. For instance, many who lived in areas of generally recognized strategic importance and whose political affiliation had long been with the Labor Party were less intense than others in their criticism of the government. They often cited Rabin's earlier distinction between "strategic" and "ideological" settlements and still hoped, despite indications to the contrary, that he remained committed to Israel's retaining at least the former. But Rabin was no longer emphasizing such distinctions among settlements even as he continued to speak of areas in the territories vital to Israel, and he responded to criticism from settlement groups with harsh blanket condemnations. He even suggested that the settlers, and their supporters in opposition to Oslo, were not true Israelis.[39]

The delegitimization of critics took other forms as well. Illustrative is the government response to a terrible event in the spring of 1994. Baruch Goldstein, an Israeli physician living in the territories, was attending Purim services at the Tomb of the Patriarchs in Hebron and allegedly overheard from adjoining Moslem services and the mosque's loudspeakers calls to "kill the Jews" — long a staple in the sermons of some Palestinian clergy. The next day Goldstein entered the mosque and shot dead twenty-nine Arab worshippers before he was himself slain.

This horrible act was immediately condemned in the most damning terms by all Israeli parties and virtually the entire Jewish population, including the settlers and their leaders. While Goldstein had his apologists and defenders, they did not number more than a few hundred at most. For most Israelis there seemed to be a natural coming together in revulsion over the massacre. This re-action stood in sharp contrast to widespread Palestinian support for the terrorist killings of Israelis, and to the Palestinian leadership's silence, or ambiguous criticism at best, in response to anti-Israel terror.

Yet voices within the Israeli government and among its supporters, then and in the ensuing months, sought to tar much of the opposition with Goldstein's crime. They advanced the argument that such an event would likely not have occurred had the opposition not been painting in falsely dire and threatening terms the dangers posed by the agreements with Arafat. They accused those unhappy with Oslo of fanning anti-Palestinian hysteria. This argument appeared, in the view of many observers, perniciously hypocritical, not least because the same pro-government voices were silent on Palestinian promotion of terror. Palestinian terrorism was not the work of individuals but of organizations operating freely under Arafat's jurisdiction, often with his support and encouragement, and again with much demonstrable public support as well. Yet members of Rabin's government and other Oslo enthusiasts not only refused to condemn this state of affairs but routinely argued that Palestinian terror had no significance as a reflection of Palestinian opinion or of the intentions and trustworthiness of Israel's Oslo partners and the viability of the Oslo process.

Every subsequent act of anti-Arab violence or incitement by an Israeli became likewise a weapon for attacking the entire opposition. In contrast, acts of Palestinian violence elicited perhaps occasional demands that Arafat do more to crack down on the perpetrators of the violence but more typically exonerations of Arafat, the Palestinian leadership, and Palestinians at large.

The government went still further in its delegitimizing of the opposition and grossly violated democratic norms by employing *agents provocateurs* in its anti-opposition campaign. It used such agents to promote, and themselves engage in, extremist anti-Arab statements or anti-government attacks, such as holding aloft portraits of Rabin dressed in a Nazi uniform at opposition rallies and elsewhere. The intent of these dirty tricks was clearly to discredit further anti-Oslo opinion and win back public sympathy.[40]

Government-controlled media were also enlisted in this campaign to delegitimize the opposition. The extremist chanting and banners generated by the *agent provocateur* campaign almost invariably found their way onto Israeli television as representing the views of the opposition and its constituency. Nongovernment media, which were overwhelmingly supportive of the Peace Movement agenda and current government policy, likewise joined in vilification of the opposition.

At the same time, the government, in its eagerness to pursue the Oslo process and to bolster public support, sought to conceal from the public anti-Israel incitement by Palestinian officials and clerics and in Palestinian media and schools as well as evidence of Arafat's tolerance of and cooperation with Islamic fundamentalist and other groups perpetrating anti-Israel terrorism. Notable in this context was an episode in 1994 in which Shimon Peres, meeting with Arafat at the Erez checkpoint on the border of the Gaza Strip, was unknowingly picked up by the microphone of a French filmmaker threatening to end this concealment and make public Arafat's violations of his Oslo commitments.[41]

In effect, government leaders saw themselves not as the public's servants but as paternal guiding figures, as philosopher kings, who could legitimately withhold information from a too benighted and emotional public in the interest of cultivating accommodation with Arafat and his associates and achieving "peace."

Both state and independent media followed the government in this as well. They generally all but ignored such stories as anti-Israel incitement by Palestinian officials and institutions, the Palestinian leadership's tolerance of and cooperation with the terrorist groups, and other violations by the Palestinians of their Oslo commitments. Indeed, so little was any of this covered in the Israeli media that citizens' groups emerged to do the job: to monitor, for example, official Palestinian media, statements by Arafat and other Palestinian leaders, Palestinian school texts, and sermons by Arafat-appointed mullahs, and to inform the Israeli public and the wider world of their venomous anti-Israel, anti-peace, and often anti-Semitic and annihilationist content.[42]

Israel's Elites Join in Attacking the "True" Enemies of Peace

Israeli cultural elites beyond media and journalistic circles also tended to sympathize with the government's agenda and, in their professional work, to lend support to that agenda.

Additional publications in the vein of the so-called New History elaborated further on themes of Israel's early and persistent culpability and, in particular, its supposed failure to grasp earlier opportunities for peace. No less tendentious and distorting of the historical record than earlier forays into the genre, these works were nevertheless received with critical enthusiasm and wide popularity. They served to reinforce the government's insistence that Arab hostility could be comprehensively mollified and peace assured by Israeli self-indictment and self-reform and far-reaching concessions, and that the doubters and critics of Oslo were simply seeking to perpetuate old Israeli moral and political errors.

Writers from other fields of academia pursued their own assaults on the Zionist enterprise and the state of Israel, frequently challenging, in the vein of the early anti-Zionists, the very concept of a Jewish state and the philosophical premises of Israel's institutions. Meanwhile, the artistic elites in the country continued to devote themselves most often to depicting Zionism and the state it created as crushing, disfiguring, potentially deadly weights on the lives of Israel's citizens. These various efforts all reinforced still further government promotion of self-reform and far-reaching concessions as the way out of the siege and as the path to peace.

Nor did this synergy between the exertions of the nation's cultural elites and those of the political leadership brought to power in 1992 simply entail the former offering support for the latter. It also involved the former providing guidance to the latter and influencing the government in its undertaking of reforms of national institutions, perhaps most notably the national education system. These reforms were primarily aimed at making the state and its institutions less Jewish and less Zionist, weaning the public away from Zionist perspectives and Zionist verities and rendering it more accepting of radical concessions as its leaders pursued their delusions of peace.

Among leading new historians, Benny Morris expanded his thesis of Israeli misdeeds in *Israel's Border Wars, 1949–1956* (1993).[43] He argues in the book, along with other claims, that after 1948 Israel's neighbors were much less threatening and more amenable to accommodation than has been previously acknowledged and that Israel's overly harsh military responses to Arab incursions poisoned the atmosphere, undercut Arab openness to reconciliation, and widened and intensified the conflict. As in his earlier works, Morris builds his assertions of Israel's culpability on misrepresentations of archival data and unsupported dark inferences regarding the aims and calculations of Ben-Gurion and other Israeli leaders.

Critics of this book, as of Morris's earlier works and indeed the work of the other leading new historians, in addition to discrediting these authors' indictments of Israel, have faulted them for their failing to make use of available Arab sources. As one reviewer notes of *Israel's Border Wars*, "Arabs are virtually nonexistent"[44]; that is, there is no serious consideration of Arab decision-making and the shaping of Arab policy. It has been suggested that for some, like Morris, this failure reflects at least in part their limited command of Arabic. But it is also a reflection of the rhetoric of the new historians. All are intent on "revealing" Israel's transgressions, and more particularly on demonstrating that Israeli actions and policies sabotaged opportunities for peace. All are invested in believing that the right policies pursued now by Israel would win peace. Consequently, each has a rhetorical interest in portraying Arabs two-dimensionally, as essentially reactive and as responding in predictable ways to Israeli moves, with Israeli aggressiveness inexorably perpetuating conflict and Israeli reform the key to peace.

In numerous journal articles and newspaper pieces during this period, Morris,[45] Ilan Pappe,[46] and Avi Shlaim[47] worked to popularize further their claims of Israeli culpability and also to rebut their critics. But they did so without seriously addressing or countering evidence of both their blatant disregard of large bodies of archival material that challenged their arguments and their misuse and distortion of those sources that they did invoke.

Other Israeli historians during these years joined the ranks of the self-styled slayers of Zionist "myths." Some among them attacked the Zionist enterprise not just for supposed transgressions during Israel's founding and the early years of the state but for perceived sins involving much larger swathes of the Jewish past. For example, Moshe Zimmermann, a historian at Hebrew University, argued that there is no such thing as a Jewish people or Jewish nation with its own distinctive history, and so the entire premise of Zionism, as representing the aspirations of the Jewish people and a solution to the difficulties that have dogged and ravaged the Jewish nation, is based on a lie.

Zimmermann's argument pulled together a number of anti-Zionist themes, some old and others of more recent vintage. The early fears of some Jews that Zionism would compromise the citizenship status recently won by Jews in various countries of the Diaspora, particularly in the West, and the concomitant insistence that Jews were a religious community and not a people or a nation, are echoed in Zimmermann's assertion that the world's Jewish communities were more fundamentally a part of their local societies than part of a distinct Jewish people sharing common values and longings. The early anti-Zionist, or "true" Zionist, theme, promoted particularly by the German Jewish academics around Buber, that Jews should consider themselves primarily in terms of universalist values and their place in universal history and eschew particularist self-definitions, which these people considered vestiges of a primitive past, is also echoed in Zimmermann. He argues, for example:

"The point of departure is no longer . . . the *a priori* distinctiveness of Jewish history, but rather of 'universal history' . . . From the moment that the premise of Jewish or Israeli distinctiveness is no longer axiomatic . . . all of history looks different."[48]

Zimmermann also invokes in his attack on Zionism the ahistorical notion of a direction to history, and a Whiggish direction at that. Zimmermann foresees a postnational future, as popularized in Israel by Peres; with Europe leading the way to "post-sovereignty," offering a vision of the coming postnatonalist world and demonstrating the error of Israeli ethnocentricity and focus on nationhood.[49]

Of course, all of Zimmermann's arguments are vulnerable to myriad devastating rebuttals. The idea that Jewish communities shared much with their local societies is hardly a retort to their sharing values and aspirations with each other as well, or hardly negates historical truths of shared vulnerability and victimization. In any case the identification with Zion and immigration to Israel were not something imposed on Diaspora Jews by Zionist mythmakers but were chosen by Jews, at times under the pressure of external tormentors but still chosen. It is those who would deprive Jews of those choices who could more properly be seen as the culpable ideologues.[50]

Moreover, virtually all modern nation-states, including Britain and France as well as Israel, were created by the amalgamation of populations diverse in important ways, and typically by coercion being a much more important part of the mix than in Israel's history. To argue that the disparate cultural strands of the Israeli population somehow delegitimizes the Zionist enterprise or the state is itself a narrow anti-Jewish bias. Indeed Zimmermann's is an anti-Jewish bias of a particularly crude sort, as when he compares education in Israeli history and Zionism not to education in national history, and the passing of national ideology from adults to children, in Britain or France or the United States, but to the education of Hitler Youth.[51]

Zimmermann's work explicitly connects historical revisionism with the advancement of a post-Zionist agenda. According to Zimmermann, as there was no Jewish nation or people to provide a foundation for a legitimate national liberation movement, Zionism is bogus and, in any case, passé, and so it ought to be discarded into the trash bin of history. Academics from other disciplines were also often invoking at this time historical revisionism in support of post-Zionism. For example, Baruch Kimmerling, a sociologist at Hebrew University, likewise maintained that the early Zionists "invented" Jewish peoplehood to legitimize a national liberation movement. He argued that they then nefariously wielded this false peoplehood as a weapon against the Arabs and as justification for Zionism's supposedly militaristic and "racist" policies, and he concluded that the Jews of Israel must now mend their ways.[52]

In fact, the invoking of quasi-historical arguments to challenge Jewish peoplehood, Zionism and Israel became virtually a model of interdisciplinary cooperation in Israeli academia. Joseph Agassi, a professor of philosophy at Tel Aviv University, wrote that Israel, having established itself on the basis of a misconceived "phantom nation" (i.e., the Jewish people), is consequently similar to the Soviet Union and — the reader might well have guessed — Nazi Germany. Agassi also argued against the Law of Return for presumably reinforcing the illegitimate concept of Jewish peoplehood and all the supposedly terrible things that have flowed from that concept.[53] The caliber of Agassi's thinking is captured in his argument that the fact that Israel allows Arabs to be elected to the Knesset but does not draft them into the army demonstrates Israel is a militaristic state. His reasoning: As Israel defines itself as a Jewish state, it by definition discriminates against its non-Jewish citizens; and, therefore, its allowing those citizens into the Knesset while not drafting them into the army must reflect the state's valuing the army more than the Knesset and its viewing weapons as more powerful than words![54]

Ze'ev Sternhell, a professor of political science at Hebrew University, argued in *The Founding Myths of Israel* (first published 1995) that the founders of the state, while proclaiming socialist and liberal principles, lacked proper universalist sensibilities and were really driven first and foremost by nationalism. Even worse, their nationalism was imbued with religious meaning. According to Sternhell, Israel's difficulties have essentially flowed from this.

Sternhell acknowledges that "the Israeli version of nationalism was unusually moderate."[55] But he poses the question of whether the state's founders could not have endeavored to attenuate it even more and "thus establish a liberal, secular, and open society, at peace with itself and its neighbors?"[56] In Sternhell's formulation, sufficient Zionist self-effacement would have inexorably translated into a Zion accepted by its neighbors. It is actually not clear if Sternhell's preferred alternative vision includes a Jewish state.

The writings of some other academics during this time focus less on details of the alleged misbegetting of Zionism and simply emphasize Zionism's sinfulness or, at best, its obsolescence. Menaham Brinker, a professor of Hebrew literature at Hebrew University, declared in a *Jerusalem Post* article in September, 1995, that Zionism is a "totalitarian" concept that "has outlived its usefulness and will ebb away in time."[57] Hebrew University anthropologist Danny Rabinovitch joined those urging that such insights be translated into policy. He advocated government confession of "the original sin of Israel" and establishment of a day of mourning to "mark the suffering of the Palestinians during the rise of Israel."[58]

Many within Israel's artistic elites — painters, novelists, poets, filmmakers, playwrights — likewise continued to devote their efforts largely to excoriating Israel and Zionism, while others became enthusiastic advocates of the Oslo process and reserved their venom for those who challenged Oslo.

That Amos Oz would be an outspoken supporter of the path taken by the Labor-Meretz coalition is hardly surprising, but there are noteworthy elements of Oz's support that reflect particularly clearly the mind-set of the "peace" camp during this time. In his advocating, in previous years, withdrawing virtually to the pre-1967 borders and ceding the territories to the PLO, Oz would also occasionally suggest that the Left should be mindful of the fears of those Israelis who distrust the Palestinians. He also expressed the view that it was the moral obligation of the "dovish Left" to be in the forefront of demanding Palestinian compliance with any agreements and to be "the first to take up arms" if the Palestinians continued to pursue a "phase-by-phase strategy" against Israel.[59] In September, 1993, just prior to the signing of the first Oslo agreements, Oz wrote, "The Israeli doves, more than other Israelis, must assume, once peace comes, a clear-cut hawkish attitude concerning the duty of the future Palestinian regime to live precisely by the letter and the spirit of its own obligations."[60]

But when, in the months and years that followed, the Palestinian Authority routinely violated virtually all its security-related obligations, incited its constituency to ongoing battle against Israel and colluded in a campaign of terror that matched the worst Israel had ever endured, Oz, like the ministers in the government and like almost everyone in the peace camp, chose to ignore the violations. Rather than respond as he had insisted the Israeli Left must, he instead remained a cheerleader for continuing the process of Israeli concessions for "peace." If now and then he expressed some brief, perfunctory unhappiness with Arafat and his associates, he hardly adopted the "hawkish attitude" that he had earlier urged and that the government had promised.

Oz's sacrifice of his declared principles in the service of pursuing "peace" can be seen also in the fate of another of his pre-Oslo pronouncements. Oz observed in a 1986 article, "The tragedy of history . . . is the perpetual cowardice of relatively decent societies whenever they confront the ruthlessness of oppressive ones."[61] Yet as Arafat, upon his arrival in the territories, rapidly imposed what has come to be known as his "thugocracy" on the population under his control, Oz, again along with virtually the entire peace camp and the Israeli government, was silent.

The blithe indifference of much of the journalistic and literary elite to Palestinian incitement and terror, the uncritical embrace of Arafat as peace partner, is captured in an article written in April, 1994, by Amos Elon. Referring to the massacre two months earlier by Baruch Goldstein of Palestinians at the Tomb of the Patriarchs in Hebron, Elon wrote, apparently without irony: "[Goldstein] had derailed the ongoing peace talks and damaged, perhaps irreparably, the excruciatingly slow process of reconciliation between Palestinians and Israelis that was started in 1993 in Oslo and on the White House lawn."[62] Thus according to Elon, reconciliation had been proceeding more or less smoothly until this terrorist attack by an extremist Israeli. Elon fails to note that between the handshake in Washington and the horror in Hebron twenty-seven Israelis had been killed in twenty-one terrorist attacks by Palestinians, and that the reason those attacks had not derailed anything was because the Israeli government chose essentially to ignore them. He too chooses to ignore that terror, its significance, and the dangers of the government's passivity in the face of it.

Not all of Israel's artistic elite became during this period cheerleaders for Oslo or subscribed to variations on the thesis that Israel had sinned and that peace is at hand if only the state and the society would sufficiently reform itself. As noted earlier, in June, 1994, Israeli novelist Aharon Megged published a blistering attack on Oslo and its supporters, declaring that some of the steps they were pursuing "seem animated by a subconscious suicidal drive."[63] He pointed out the dissonance between the Palestinian leadership's statements in English, with their conciliatory messages, and its inflammatory, war-mongering exhortations to its constituents in Arabic, and he excoriated Israel's political elite for ignoring or downplaying the latter.

Megged took to task Israel's artistic and academic elites, including the purveyors of revisionist New History and the post-Zionist ideologues, for their distortion of the past and their fraudulent indictments of Zionism and Israel. He cited, as ominous prophecy of the current intellectual atmosphere in Israel, Nathan Alterman's poetic lines: "Then Satan did say: 'How will I conquer this beleaguered one? He possesses courage, ingenuity, resourcefulness and tools of war.' Then he said: 'I'll not rob his strength, nor bridle him, nor rein him in, nor enervate his hand. But this I'll do — blunt his mind, till he forgets his cause is just.'"

Megged acknowledged that obviously the Zionist movement and the state of Israel have at times made mistakes, as all national revolutions and all states have. But he pointed to the dishonesty inherent in the academic critics of Israel taking events out of context in order to smear the movement and the state. He noted: "A history of World War II could be written focusing on the suffering of Germans from Allied bombings and invasions — and it would all be based on facts, for the Germans really did suffer terribly. All one need do is distort proportions."

In a summarizing statement quoted earlier, Megged criticized particularly "the majority of Israel's intelligentsia, and its print and electronic media" for identifying morally and emotionally "with people committed to our annihilation; people who openly declare their intention to expel us from this land." He cited as an additional example of this mind-set action by the group "Women in Black," an Israeli organization that had been demonstrating for years at major intersections in Israel militating for withdrawal from the territories. Megged noted that "'Women in Black' decided in February of 1990 to wear the colors of the PLO, whose charter calls for the annihilation of Israel, that is — their own annihilation." (Amos Elon, in contrast, characterized "Women in Black" thus: "Their declared wish is to be guided by moral principle and a concern for human rights rather than political opportunism . . . In their somber dignity . . . their lament is marked by a silent, timeless eloquence."[64])

Megged further observed: "Whoever researches the dimensions of this pathological phenomenon, possibly rooted in the Diaspora proclivity for self-abasement and sycophancy toward Jew-haters, would have to go through enormous quantities of material." He concluded the piece with the statement: "If the rising tide of self-doubt fails to subside, if the self-denial of our right to be here continues to enfeeble us, the 'Satan' of Alterman's poem will triumph, and we shall lack the strength to resist dangers to our very existence."

As already noted, Megged was almost universally attacked by his fellow writers and artists.

TRANSLATING POST-ZIONISM INTO POLICY (IN THE CAUSE OF "PEACE")

The actual translation into policy of the anti-Zionist or post-Zionist polemics emanating from Israel's cultural elites, particularly its artists and academics, was undertaken by various arms of the coalition government brought to power in 1992. The new government's minister of education, Meretz Party head Shulamit Aloni, sought to end student trips to Auschwitz because, she declared, the trips stirred up in the students Jewish "nationalistic" sentiment.[65] They entailed, in her view, "Too much manipulation of us into seeing ourselves as victims who must be strong."[66] Aloni also insisted that the victims of the Holocaust were not so much "Jews" as simply "human beings" and the latter identity ought to be the one emphasized.[67]

Among Aloni's vocal supporters was Tom Segev, who again promoted the false dichotomy that the lesson of the Holocaust could be either one of Jews needing to defend themselves against threatening forces in the world or one of Jews needing to champion democracy and fight racism. In Segev's view, Israelis should forego the former and embrace the latter.[68] Amos Elon supported Aloni's stance in similar terms.[69]

Another campaign undertaken by the Education Minister was for the removal of references to God from IDF memorial services. Meanwhile, Aloni's deputy, Micha Goldman, called for changing the text of "Hatikva" because, he asserted, the national anthem was too Jewish. It focused too much on the Jewish Return and Jewish redemption and so was not appropriate for a state that included non-Jewish citizens.[70]

Another Meretz Party member, Amnon Rubinstein, succeeded Aloni as education minister in 1994. Rubinstein, a former Dean of the Law School at Tel Aviv University, has often articulated perspectives very different from those characteristic of his Meretz colleagues. He has been a harsh critic of the revisionism of the new historians, arguing that the leaders of the Yishuv made all sorts of efforts to reach some accommodation with the Arab population in the pre-state years but were met only with rejection and violence, and that this pattern continued after statehood. He has even quoted approvingly comparison of Israeli attempts to win over the Arabs to some rapprochement, and the negative Arab response, to German Jewish efforts to win acceptance in Germany and the negative response of the surrounding society.[71] Rubinstein has also written of the betrayals of the British during the Mandate, which the new historians are likewise inclined to prettify.

Rubinstein is critical as well of the post-Zionist academics, pointing out the intellectual dishonesty that is characteristic of their arguments. He notes the predilection of many post-Zionists and new historians to criticize the concept of objective history and talk of competing narratives. But, he observes, they then dismiss the Jewish narrative and accord legitimacy only to the Arab version of truth, while typically omitting information that might cast a negative light on the Palestinians and other Arabs.[72] Rubinstein refers also to their inclination to judge Israel by an impossible standard that no polity could meet.

Speaking more broadly of secular, Left-leaning Israelis, Rubinstein has stated they have had difficulty coping with the animosity directed against them as Israelis and Jews, confronted as they are not only with Arab hostility but also the bigoted animosity to which they are subjected in the United Nations, in Europe, and elsewhere. He has suggested that this has driven them to close their eyes to the truth of Arab hatred and intransigence and to embrace as reality fantasies of a benign Levant that does not exist.[73]

Yet despite his awareness of and insights into many of the distortions of the new historians and the post-Zionists and his understanding of the psychology behind the embrace of those distortions by much of the Israeli Left, Rubinstein has endorsed some of those distorted perspectives. He chose to believe that Arafat and the Palestinians truly gave up their annihilationist agenda in 1988, and that Rabin, through Oslo, seized a genuine opportunity for peace. The vast majority of Israelis who favored holding onto parts of the territories viewed doing so in terms of security requirements, with an outlook akin to that traditionally advanced by Labor. Yet Rubinstein has chosen to see the religious-nationalist camp as it evolved after the 1967 war and its theological claim on the territories as the real source of resistance to not returning to the pre-1967 lines and therefore as the primary threat to peace and the state. Much of Rubinstein's book *From Herzl to Rabin* is devoted to tracing extremist elements within the religious-nationalist camp and their uncompromising territorial agenda. There is no shortage of citations he can offer from some rabbis and others within the camp that are inflammatory in the extreme and at times overtly racist.

It appears to be in the context of these perspectives on the opportunity for peace and the threat from within facing Israel that Rubinstein associated himself with Meretz and with its efforts to counter what it regarded as negative religious inroads into policy making. But even beyond his embrace of Oslo's rationales, there have been inconsistencies in Rubinstein's positions. He states that the overwhelming majority of Israelis want to maintain their, and their children's, Jewishness, and he obviously includes himself within that majority. That aim is hardly consistent with the radical excising of Jewish content from school curricula, yet he promoted such excision.

Apparently Rubinstein's concerns about religious-nationalist intrusion into policy, and his perception that this intrusion was an obstacle to the peace now genuinely available from the Arabs in return for sufficient concessions, led him to believe that curricula should be amended to preclude any encouragement of religious-nationalist sentiment. He writes of the prospects of peace, "Suddenly, it appeared as if [through Rabin's Oslo policy] the old vision of abolition of hostility [between] Jews and their immediate surrounding — the Arabs, and their more remote surroundings — the international community, could perhaps be realized."[74] He construed his education reforms as advancing that vision.

Upon succeeding Aloni as education minister, Rubinstein quickly undertook revising State Education Law so as to shift the focus of Israeli education more exclusively toward the universal and away from the Jewish and Zionist. The proposed law did not simply emphasize universalist values and principles to be promoted by the education system but sought to eliminate the Jewish national values that were so central to the education law being replaced. As Yoram Hazony notes of the prospective legislation, the Jewish national aims of the school system until that point — teaching "the value of Jewish culture," "love of the homeland," and "loyalty to the Jewish people" — were rather pointedly removed.[75]

A slightly revised version of the proposed law passed a preliminary Knesset vote but was dropped after the change of government in 1996. But the education ministry enacted curriculum revisions in the vein of post-Zionist agendas despite the failure of the proposed legislation. In 1994 a new curriculum for high school civics emphasized five "Goals Concerning Values": four entailed respectively the promoting of democratic values, support for human and civil rights, fulfillment of civic duties, and citizens' engagement in public affairs. The fifth was cast in the neutral wording of teaching students "to understand the fact" that Israel is the state of the Jewish people, with no positive value being attached to this fact.[76] The new civics curriculum also delineated nine "Goals Concerning Knowledge and Understanding"; none referred to Israel's connections with the Jewish people, Jewish history, the Jewish faith, or Jewish values.[77]

While texts reflecting the new civics curriculum took some years to develop, its post-Zionist biases were quickly reflected in teacher enrichment courses and in the thrust of national matriculation exams. Not only were questions pertaining to the Jewish character of the state virtually dropped from the exams, but those questions that did appear tended to stress alleged negative consequences of Israel's being a Jewish state. For example, the only germane question on the 1995 exam asked students to "explain two difficulties with which Arab-Israelis must grapple because of the fact that Israel is the state of the Jewish people."[78]

A new archaeology curriculum for high school students, formulated by a committee under the chairmanship of Hebrew University archaeologist Yoram Tzafrir and introduced in 1995, reflects, like the new civics curriculum's goals concerning values, neutrality toward the Jewish state. While Israeli archaeologists have assiduously explored the physical record of all the civilizations and cultures that have left their mark on the history of Eretz Israel, in Israeli schools that part of the record pertaining to Jewish history in the land had been given particular attention as an element in the comprehending and teaching of Jewish history. But in the new curriculum's introductory description of its aim, there is not a single reference to Jews, Judaism, the Jewish people, or Jewish history. The emphasis is again on the universalist or transnational. Students are to learn and appreciate the record of the past exclusively as part of the heritage of "world civilization," not at all from the perspective of Jewish civilization, or Jewish history, or Jewish culture. In one startling statement, the introduction declares, "The proper reconstruction of cultures of the past will assist the student in understanding the roots of the culture of our age, and in uprooting fundamentalist beliefs" — meaning, presumably, any Zionist or Jewish particularist allegiances.[79]

The education ministry sought to revise the history curriculum along similar lines. The first part to be completed, in 1995, was the curriculum for middle schools, by a committee under the leadership of Moshe Zimmermann. Zimmermann's attitudes on Jewish nationhood and Zionism have already been discussed, including his comparison of the teaching of Zionist "ideology" to the education of Hitler Youth. The old curriculum had begun with the Biblical period and had taught Jewish history as a core focus. The new curriculum eliminated the Bible, began with the conquests of Alexander the Great and the rise of Hellenism, and first considered the Jews as one of the subject peoples affected by Hellenic civilization. The focus was on "universal history," as represented especially by the rise and decline of world civilizations, with the Jews and Jewish history pushed to the periphery. In an interview in *Haaretz*, in February, 1994, Zimmermann declared, "Learning about the [Jewish] people and the state [of Israel] appears in the program, but certainly not as a subject of primary importance."[80]

These same years saw the rise of an assault on Zionism and the idea of a Jewish state by Israel's judiciary, especially its Supreme Court under Chief Justice Aharon Barak.

The right of the Jewish people to establish Israel as their state was not only asserted by Israel's Declaration of Independence but affirmed by the United Nations. At the same time, Israel, in its Declaration of Independence and in all its political traditions, declared itself to be a democracy, and the state explicitly recognized the equal civil and human rights, under the law, of non-Jewish minorities in the country. But throughout the history of the nation some voices have argued that Israel cannot define itself as both Jewish and democratic.

In new Basic Laws enacted in 1992, the Knesset asserted that, indeed, Israel is "a Jewish and democratic state." But since 1992 claims of the impossibility of Israel being both Jewish and democratic have become commonplace, as have efforts to divest the nation of its Jewish self-definition and identity, including judicial efforts in this direction.

The thrust of the judiciary assault has entailed assertions by Supreme Court justices, among them Chief Justice Barak, that Israel can be a "Jewish" state only to the extent that "Jewish" is defined exclusively in terms of the universalist principles embodied in Jewish thought, such as principles of the dignity of the individual, privacy, freedom; that is, those universalist elements of Judaism that are identical to democratic principles and reflect no Jewish particularism. Barak wrote in a paper in 1992:

"The content of the phrase 'Jewish state' will be determined by the level of abstraction which shall be given it. In my opinion . . . the level of abstraction should be so high, that it becomes identical to the democratic nature of the state . . . The values of the state of Israel as a Jewish state are those universal values common to members of democratic society."[81]

From this perspective, Israel is to be a post-Zionist democratic state with no distinctive Jewish identity beyond the fact that, at least currently, the majority of its population has Jewish roots.[82]

In the same paper, Barak declared that the new Basic Law of 1992 conferred upon the Supreme Court the right to strike down any legislation it considers "unconstitutional." But Israel has no formal constitution, so in effect Barak is claiming for the Supreme Court the right to nullify any law it deems in violation of its own concept of a proper Israeli constitution.

(Similarly, with no constitution, there is no constitutional system of checks and balances. The legislature has no right of "constitutional" amendment that could provide mandatory new ground rules for Supreme Court decisions. In addition, unlike the practice in virtually all other democratic nations, and the practice in Israel in the early years of the state, the Israeli executive and legislature have no right of judicial appointment and confirmation. Rather, appointments to the bench are controlled by the Supreme Court itself. This not only allows the Supreme Court to be self-perpetuating in ideology, it also stymies cultivation and articulation of alternative perspectives by anyone in Israel's legal "food chain" who might aspire to achieving ultimately an appointment to the nation's highest court.[83])

In effect, Israel is confronted with a virtual dictatorship of the judiciary. Indeed, former Israeli Supreme Court Justice Moshe Landau, who was also president of the Supreme Court for some years, has stated with regard to the Court's arrogating to itself additional power and authority, "I think that Supreme Court President Aharon Barak has not, and does not, accept the rightful place that the court should have among the various authorities in our regime." Landau sees Barak striving "to interject [into all areas of Israeli life] certain moral values as he deems appropriate. And this amounts to a kind of judicial dictatorship that I find completely inappropriate."[84]

Barak has demonstrated his preparedness to use his arrogated power to undermine the Jewish foundations of the state.

One illustration of this has been Barak's instructions to Israeli jurists, in his *Interpretation in Law* (1994), that when confronted by what seems to them a conflict between democratic and particularist Jewish values, the judge "should act as the enlightened community would." Barak then explains: "The metaphor of the 'enlightened community' focuses one's attention on a part of the public. One's attention is turned . . . to the educated and progressive part within it. What distinguished the enlightened community from the rest of the public? . . . The enlightened community represents that community whose values are universalistic, and which is part of the family of enlightened nations."[85]

In effect — even putting aside the boldly elitist, anti-democratic thrust of the assertion that the views of only a particular segment of the population should shape legal interpretations — Barak is instructing jurists to be guided in their rulings by those Israelis who embrace the anti-Zionist or post-Zionist agenda and are eager to strip the nation and its institutions of all Jewish particularist meaning and content.[86]

Former Supreme Court Justice Landau also notes the Barak court's effort to use its appropriated powers to advance elements of the post-Zionist agenda, and he sees the impetus to these judiciary exertions as derived largely from the stresses of the siege and, again, the wish to believe that Israeli self-reform and self-effacement will resolve the conflict. Landau expresses fears that this mindset, propagated in the courts, in the media, and in academia, is putting at risk the survival of the state. He argues that, "It's a kind of self-hatred. And it causes weakness, fatigue, self-deception and a lack of preparedness to fight [for survival]."[87]

Another assault on the Jewish nature of the state that grew in intensity and in its progress toward shaping policy during these years, and that has been closely related to the judicial campaign against Zionism and the concept of a Jewish state, involved attacks on the Law of Return. Israel enacted the Law of Return, actually two laws, almost at the very inception of the state, giving Jews everywhere the right to come to Israel (1950) and attain immediate citizenship (1952). Critiques of the law have been put forward on various grounds over the years. There have been complaints about the costs of open immigration, particularly the costs of supporting elderly or ill immigrants. Other criticisms have focused on the possible inundation of the country by people who convert simply to escape difficult conditions in their homelands. Still others have been centered on concerns about the potential swamping of the country by the "wrong kind" of immigrants, those not to the political or cultural or religious taste of the complainers. Some Israelis have voiced fears about immigration contributing to the ecological degradation of the country through population growth. But among anti-Zionist and post-Zionist groups the criticism has been particularly that the Law of Return is racist and undemocratic, and this theme was advanced with growing intensity during the early 1990s.

For example, an article by Ran Kislev in *Haaretz* in July, 1990, called the Law of Return "reminiscent of the Nuremberg Laws." Another by Danny Rubinstein (July, 1991) declared it the kind of discrimination that "was the basis for the apartheid regime in South Africa." In yet another, Tom Segev (October, 1995) maintained that it "contradicts the essence of democracy."[88]

While some of these statements emphasized that the supposedly racist and undemocratic Law of Return was incompatible with universalist principles, others also argued more specifically that it was unfair to Israel's Arab minority. David Grossman (in *Yediot Acharonot*, September 29, 1993) insisted that it is an obstacle to "full equality" for Israeli Arabs. Haim Ganz, on the law faculty of Tel Aviv University, described it as "depriving the Palestinians . . . of rights parallel to those that this law accords to Jews . . . " Yael Tamir, then on the philosophy faculty of Tel Aviv University, maintained that the Law of Return constitutes "a violation of the right of national minorities to equal treatment." The absorption of post-Zionist arguments into national policy was, again, widespread in the period immediately after the 1992 election, and in 1994 and 1995 voices within the governing coalition were beginning to militate for changes in the Law of Return.[89]

The penetration of the anti-Zionist and post-Zionist perspectives so common among Israel's cultural and academic elites into national policy during these years extended even to the military. Asa Kasher, professor of philosophy at the University of Tel Aviv, went beyond the harsh critiques of the state offered by so many of his colleagues to criticize the very existence of Israel. Kasher declared in a 1992 article, "I am much closer to the feeling that from the point of view of values, and from a social point of view, the state is a lost cause. The clearest symptom of normalization that I can think of is emigration from Israel."[90] Yet such views did not preclude his being selected by Ehud Barak, then chief of staff of the IDF, to chair a committee to develop a new code of ethics for the Israeli military. Not an especially modest man, Kasher described the resulting document, *The Spirit of the IDF*, as "one of a kind . . . the most profound code of ethics in the world of military ethics, in particular, and the world of professional ethics, in general."[91]

The "values" and "basic principles" laid out in the code are generic universalist ones that might apply to any military. An IDF soldier's loyalty is to be to the state, its citizens and the principles of democracy. Nowhere among its values and principles is there any reference to the Jewish state, the Jewish people, or the land of Israel. As Yoram Hazony notes, the extensive missions undertaken by the IDF to rescue Ethiopian Jews and to help persecuted Russian Jews escape the Soviet Union — as well as other missions on behalf of Diaspora Jews in distress — would be inconsistent with *The Spirit of the IDF*. For they were not undertaken in defense of the state, its citizens or democracy but rather out of loyalties and a sense of obligation and responsibility not to Kasher's taste. Despite its radical redefinition of the proper role of the IDF and its soldiers, *The Spirit of the IDF* was adopted by the defense establishment in 1994 virtually without protest or dissent.[92]

THE *KULTURKAMPF* AND THE SIEGE

Clearly, the early 1990s saw an acceleration of the *Kulturkampf* waged by much of Israel's academic and cultural elites against Zionism and the concept of a Jewish state. The same years witnessed — an even more dramatic development — the infiltration of the perspectives of these elites into state policy by the Labor-Meretz coalition brought to power in 1992. All of this coincided with the new government's adoption of the Peace Movement's perspectives on the Arab-Israeli conflict and the proper path to peace. In addition, the government used the anti-Zionist or post-Zionist revisions in the education system and in other arms of governance in large part to counter public resistance to and promote support for its Oslo agenda.

Nevertheless, one might argue, this pattern of events does not necessarily mean that the *Kulturkampf* itself, or even the steps by leaders of the new government to translate "post-Zionist" perspectives into policy, can be attributed simply to the siege and to the eagerness of many war-weary Israelis to believe that proper self-reforms and concessions would bring peace.

One might offer as counterevidence the fact, for example, that those same elites, and much of the Israeli population that was inclined to embrace their views, had long-standing grievances against the religious establishment in the country and its constituencies, against their political power and how they wielded it. One might argue that those grievances, which had little to do with the siege, played a significant role in spurring efforts to make the nation and its institutions more "universalist" and less "particularist."

But a closer look at this and other counter-arguments supports rather than refutes the importance of the siege in fueling, sustaining, and more recently intensifying the anti-Zionist and post-Zionist enthusiasms of the cultural and academic elites and of those similarly inclined in government and in the public at large.

With regard to the secular-religious divide in Israel, in fact the most enduring legal intrusions of the religious establishment into people's lives are relatively limited. They entail control over Jewish marriages, divorces, conversions, and funeral rites. With occasional exceptions, they have typically inspired relatively limited opposition. (The complaints by Reform and Conservative Jews in the West, particularly in the United States, concerning the Orthodox legal monopoly over such matters in Israel, have found little supportive resonance among Israelis.) Sabbath restrictions have caused widespread discontent at times but have largely been rolled back, as have other legal intrusions into daily life.

The biggest remaining popular grievances against the religious establishment revolve around two issues. One concerns what many see as disproportionately large public funds allocated to religious schools and other religious institutions. But this situation is typically perceived, among those troubled by it, as requiring solution via legislation and curtailment of the power in the Knesset of the religious parties, not through altering the fundamental principles of the state. The other source of popular grievance concerns the exemption of large numbers of ultra-Orthodox citizens from military conscription. This, of course, is an issue of such intense resonance precisely because of the siege. But it is also a matter widely viewed by the secular community as requiring legislative remedy, not revision of the basic principles of the state.

In addition, while the academic, cultural, and left-wing political elites of Israel no doubt overwhelmingly share the broader secular population's unhappiness with aspects of the political muscle flexing of the religious establishment, that unhappiness had for a long time not figured significantly in these elites' anti-Zionist and post-Zionist rhetoric or agenda. Indeed, the *bêtes noires* of that rhetoric and those agendas had been primarily Ben-Gurion, his allies, and philosophical heirs, and their religious-historical comprehension of the state, not the Orthodox community and its, in fact, widely diverse views of the state. (It is noteworthy in this regard that some of the most radical anti-Zionist and post-Zionist rhetoric had come from individuals who were themselves Orthodox Jews.)

The intensity of the anti-Zionist and post-Zionist elites' antagonism toward those others — toward Ben-Gurion, his allies, and his like-minded successors — had, indeed, been directly related to the siege. The elites had viewed those "nationalists" as the enemy whose supposedly atavistic attachment to the land, resistance to concessions, and distrust of Arab intentions were an intolerable obstacle to the peace and "normalcy" that, they insisted, would readily be achieved were Israel only to offer sufficient concessions.

Moreover, the Orthodox community became a central target of these elites precisely when elements of the community swung toward more aggressive religious-nationalist stances, militated for Israeli retention of the entire West Bank and pursued Jewish settlement throughout the area. This focus on the Orthodox evolved in the context of a Peace Movement rhetoric that ignored Israel's well-founded security concerns and largely rejected the legitimacy of any Israeli claims on parts of the territory such as those traditionally put forward by Labor. It was part of an effort to cast Israel's choice as between holding onto all the West Bank for the religious reasons propounded by some in the Orthodox community or giving up virtually all the territories in the supposedly liberal and open-minded spirit of secular modernity and thereby winning peace. The siege, and visions of ending it, have been at the heart of the post-Zionists and anti-Zionists' post-1967 attacks on the Orthodox and have likewise been the key to widespread public endorsement of those attacks.

The history of militant advocacy of "universalism" and antipathy to so-called Jewish particularism is, of course, also suggestive of the connection of such sentiments to the siege. Again, Jewish anti-Zionism in the late nineteenth and early twentieth centuries was fueled by fears that Jewish nationalism would fan anti-Jewish sentiment in surrounding societies in the Diaspora and instigate a rolling back of *de jure* gains by Jews toward civil equality in the West. Insistence on "Jewish" being comprehended as representing exclusively a religious identity and vocation with an exclusively universalist message and meaning, an identity having no national or other particularist significances, was likewise inspired by the wish to placate anti-Jewish sentiment.

No doubt the German Jewish academics around Buber or sympathetic to his views were also moved in part by their own enchantment with the intellectual life they had known in Europe and fears of being cut off from the European intellectual mainstream in a Zionist state. But these fears of ostracism and exile themselves reflected a sense of Jewish vulnerability and a perception that only Jewish self-abnegation and rigorous eschewing of anything suggestive of Jewish particularist sympathies would be tolerated by that European cultural mainstream.

Of course, promoting international understanding and international cooperation in humanitarian endeavors are laudable undertakings. But it is bigotry to insist that Jews must choose between commitment to such efforts and pursuit of the freedoms and protections potentially accorded them in an independent Jewish national life, freedoms and protections widely available to other peoples. To insist that Jews alone, who have, in fact, pledged themselves in their faith for millennia to precepts entailing moral, ethical obligations both to their own people and to all of humanity, be proscribed the right of independent national life in the name of a universalist agenda, is anti-Jewish bias and reflects the contorting of oneself to accommodate anti-Jewish indictments. Casting such a universalist agenda in moral terms, as representing some higher, more liberal, more humane sensibility, and refusing to acknowledge the underlying fear of anti-Jewish sentiment, largely reflects a cultivating of intellectual dishonesty and self-delusion in the service of that fear.

In the context of such predilections, the Arab presence in Eretz Israel, and antagonism on the part of some Arabs to the Zionist enterprise, were seized upon by the anti-Zionists and "true Zionists" initially as an excuse, an argument in support of their anti-state agendas. Arab hostility was also highlighted as a harbinger of the terrible antagonisms and setbacks that they feared would inevitably ensue should Jews rally to the nationalist cause. These sentiments evolved into that self-serving moralizing that sympathized with Arab grievances, even the Arab war against the Zionists, and that chose to believe that Arab hostility could be assuaged and a "cultural" Zionism could flourish and Jews live in peace were the Jews only to forego their insistence on sovereignty, on a nation of their own.

Of course, this pre-state history does not "prove" that the recent popularity of "universalist" anti-Zionist and post-Zionist sentiment also has its roots in fears of the siege and of anti-Jewish hostility in the Arab world and beyond. In fact, even if one can trace, at least in the Israeli academic world, a continuity of teachers and students between the early anti-Zionist intellectuals and their present-day acolytes, there was in the immediate postindependence period a sharp decline in the popularity of such sentiments. Consequently, their present prominence must at least to some degree be seen as a new phenomenon.

But the marginalization of anti-Zionist sentiment in the early postindependence period was in large part a product not just of the state's having become a *fait accompli* but also of people's anticipation of impending acceptance by the surrounding world and the state becoming "normal." It was the endurance of the siege, and loss of hope in its ending, that inspired the resurgence of "universalist" sentiment and delusions of solving the Jews' problems by self-abnegation and self-reform.

In addition, the current academic and cultural elites in Israel have demonstrated exquisite sensitivity to opinion in the West and in the wider world generally, particularly a fear of ostracism because of Arab-inspired, siege-inspired anti-Israel sentiment in the wider world and an eagerness for acceptance by their cultural and academic peers. Many members of these Israeli elites have conspicuously enjoyed the accolades won by their personal criticisms of Israel; and it is overwhelmingly the anti-Zionist writers and artists who are the darlings of the world media, as it is the new historians and other academic critics of Israel who receive the visiting lectureships and professorships in western Europe and the United States. Clearly, a significant part of these Israeli elites' comprehension of "normalcy" is such acceptance, which can be won fully only with an end of the siege; and so their desire for that acceptance is another spur to grasping at straws for relief from the siege.

The concept of embracing individual identity over Jewish group identity, of liberating oneself from the Jewish, like the concept of universalist versus Jewish particularist sensibilities, also has its roots, as noted earlier, in the nineteenth- and twentieth-century eagerness of many Jews to escape anti-Semitism; in this instance by shedding the Jewish for the "individual." Here too the path of escape has often been defended by moralistic posturing. Assertions were made of the individual being one's essential identity, with all else, all group affiliations, serving mainly as dead weight on the soul. Significantly, the very notion of militant individualism free of cultural identity was widely seen as a peculiarly Jewish phenomenon; and, of course, most Jews who pursued this tack to escape the Jewish just adopted another culture as their own in their eagerness to be "individuals." In the Israeli context, following this path of self-defined individuality has likewise been a reaction to besiegement, to the life-narrowing, potentially deadly, antagonism of the surrounding world toward the Israeli group identity.

But what of arguments that the endorsement and promotion of an anti-Zionist or post-Zionist "universalism" are simply the expression of a desire that the state be more like other Western democracies, more "democratic" and less parochial? The obvious problem with such arguments is that the post-Zionist reforms actually put forward by the academic and other elites and supported by significant segments of the Labor-Meretz government were, in fact, less emulations than caricatures of policies and institutions in the Western democracies.

Consider the education reforms undertaken by the post-1992 government. Does any western European government not teach, as a major focus of its history curriculum, its own national history, including the cultural and social history of the nation's "people" as defined by the ethnic group most associated with the state? Does any forego such teaching in deference to the large minority ethnic populations that have become citizens of those states? Has any eradicated that history or pushed it to the periphery in favor of "universal" history, rendering the latter not simply a complementary curriculum but the dominant and virtually exclusive curriculum?

Have the British stopped teaching British history, or the French expunged French history from their school curricula, now that a substantial percentage of both country's citizenry consists of recent immigrants from Asia and Africa? Have any of those western European states whose national flags include a cross — Switzerland, Britain, Norway and the other Scandinavian states, for example — considered changing their flag, as some in and out of the Israeli government have suggested changing Israel's flag, in deference to the growing Moslem population in their state? Or has any changed its national anthem because the minorities in the nation cannot relate to the history reflected and invoked in that anthem?

Amnon Rubinstein, a stalwart of the Meretz Party and someone whose dedication to assuring equal rights for Israel's minorities has been steadfast and a central tenet of his political agenda, has observed that flags and national anthems are typically rooted in a national and religious tradition. Rubinstein argues that "this connection seems to be conventionally accepted even in the most enlightened countries — countries where Jews live under flags adorned with crosses without feeling that their rights have been compromised."[93]

Such observations apply also to criticism of Israel's Law of Return. The Law of Return touches on the very *raison d'être* of the state of Israel and reflects, as do League of Nations and United Nations declarations, international recognition of the need of the Jews for a state of their own. Yet it is declared by post-Zionist elites to be somehow undemocratic and even racist and unfair to the Arab minority citizenry in Israel because it gives immigration preference to Jews. Among the obvious rebuttals to this claim is the fact that a number of states often put forward by the Israeli post-Zionists as democratic models for Israel give immigration and citizenship preference to those with ethnic ties to their countries, do so without these groups having the horrendous histories of forced exile and persecution that the Jews do, and obviously do so without regarding the relevant policies and laws as undemocratic.

European states that give such preference include Denmark, Italy, the Federal Republic of Germany, Greece, and Poland.[94] Amnon Rubinstein notes the preferential repatriation laws of various countries, including the Federal Republic of Germany, and observes, "In spite of the existence of the European Convention on Human Rights and the European Court for Human Rights, Germany has never been called upon to annul its own 'Law of Return' on grounds that it harms the universal principle of equality . . . [Moreover,] the right of a state to differentiate between groups of potential immigrants and citizens was expressly recognized in the United Nations Convention on the Elimination of All Forms of Racial Discrimination, ratified in 1965."[95] In addition, the legitimacy of state policies of preferential repatriation was affirmed by the Council of Europe in 2001.[96]

In seeking to strip Israel of its Jewish identity, post-Zionist voices have also argued that Israel's claim to be not only a Jewish state but "the state of the Jews" and to have an interest in and responsibility for the Jewish Diaspora is another characteristic that sets the nation apart from normal states and undermines its legitimacy. But here again, Israel's stance is not as unique or "abnormal" as its critics would suggest. On the contrary, Rubinstein observes that in Europe there has been a trend toward increased recognition of the right of states to assert an interest in and responsibility for their kin living elsewhere, with "kin" meaning, of course, those with ethnic ties to the major group within states. Rubinstein points out that, "Nine European countries — Austria, Bulgaria, Greece, Hungary, Italy, Rumania, Russia, Slovakia, and Slovenia — have even passed laws granting official status to the connection between the nation and its ethnic or national brethren living abroad." The legitimacy of such legislation and related state policies was asserted by the Council of Europe's Venice commission in 2001 and endorsed by the Council in 2003.[97]

Nor does the judiciary in any western European country, in any of those nations that the post-Zionists hold up as models for Israel, feel obliged to cleanse its legal system of all elements reflective of the particularist cultural and ethnic traditions of its nation in deference to some model of "universalist democracy." The standard that is, in fact, embraced in the Western democracies, and that generally prevails in them, even if too often breached, the standard for their judiciaries as well as for their other governmental institutions is the standard of equality of all citizens before the law and equal treatment of all citizens by all the state's institutions. And those Israelis whose true intent is that Israel conform to other Western democracies will measure Israel's doing so by that standard.

But, of course, it is that standard that was consistently promoted and embraced in speeches and actions by Ben-Gurion and his allies and supporters, by the earlier *bêtes noires* of the anti-Zionists and post-Zionists. It is that standard that was advanced by them as the ideal Israel must strive for. If actions have at times fallen short of that ideal, that too is not unlike other Western democracies and ought to be addressed by greater efforts in the spirit of that ideal.

There is no inconsistency between Israel's embracing that standard and also defining itself as the national home of the Jewish people, the Jewish state, or teaching Jewish history as a key curriculum in its schools. (In fact, the Arab population by its own choice has always had a separate school system and has never been obliged to study Jewish history.) Nor is Israel's retaining its flag and anthem, and prescribing an ethical code for its military that refers to the Jewish people and the Land of the Jews and Jewish ethical teaching, and preserving the Law of Return, inconsistent with that standard.

So it is hardly unreasonable to see in the advocacy of radical anti-Zionist or post-Zionist reforms an agenda other than the bogus one of making Israel more like the other Western democracies. Nor is it unreasonable to perceive in claims that the Jewish accoutrements of the nation's institutions are unfair to the Arab minority something other than a desire to mirror other Western states vis-à-vis accommodation of minorities. Rather, there is much reason to see in such claims a reprise of the old binationalism promoted by some between the world wars and, like that political movement, an effort to render Jews more accommodating of anti-Jewish demands in the hope of thereby winning over the haters.

To assess from another vantage the centrality of the siege in this advocacy of radical "universalism" and "post-Zionism," consider how prominent such arguments would be in an Israel that was, in fact, living in genuine peace with its neighbors. Imagine, for example, if after 1967, or 1973, the Arab countries had given up their quest for Israel's destruction, truly reconciled themselves to recognizing Israel as a legitimate state in the region, and turned their energies to internal reform to build their own nations and succor their own peoples. Imagine if the Arab states had allowed, even encouraged, Jordan and the Palestinians to join together and had supported redefining the conflict as simply one of establishing equitable and secure boundaries between Jordan-Palestine and Israel. Imagine if they had endorsed the conflict's being settled by territorial compromise, with the Arabs of Jordan, and of those territories ultimately ceded by Israel to Jordan-Palestine, resolving among themselves issues of Palestinian versus Jordanian identity and of the parameters of governance within a unified state, a state at peace with Israel.

No doubt there would still be some voices in Israel, particularly among the academic and cultural elites, promoting universalist agendas and decrying whatever in the society and culture reflects particularist ethnic, religious, and national allegiances. There are such voices, especially among the comparable elites, in all the Western democracies. But it is extremely unlikely that under conditions of genuine peace the pursuit of radical reforms in the name of "universalism," or in the false pretense of achieving an improved "democracy," would have reached that intensity or popularity or penetration into government policy that it has, in fact, achieved in Israel.

In an Israel at peace, there would not be the same perceived need by so many to strip Jewish history out of the education of Israel's youth in favor of "universal" history, or to falsify Jewish history in order to render Israelis more self-critical and more sympathetic to the hostility and assaults of its Arab neighbors, or to change the national anthem and national flag, or to excise the Jewish and Zionist content from the IDF's code of ethics, or to do away with the Law of Return — to render the state, by these various steps and others like them, less Jewish and less Zionist. Under conditions of genuine peace, the percentage of Israelis desirous of such steps would no doubt be very similar to the percentage of like-minded souls in other Western democracies, a small minority indeed, and the place of such agendas in the national discourse would likewise be very similar, vanishingly small. Israel then truly would be much more like other Western democracies than it currently is.

But Israel's national life, and national discourse, are distorted by the siege. The popularity and penetration into policy of "universalist" reforms, of the campaign to make Israel less Jewish and less Zionist, are driven by the desire to render Israel more acceptable to its neighbors. They are embraced, like territorial concessions, in the spirit of wishful belief that self-reform and concessions will inexorably win Israel peace and end the siege. The purpose of the reforms in this context is two-pronged: to appease the Arabs directly by rendering Israel less Jewish, and to wean recalcitrant Israelis from supposedly parochial Jewish and Zionist sentiments and concerns and make them more receptive to territorial and other concessions.

Many of the purveyors of the New History and of post-Zionism and advocates of radical "universalist" reforms have actually acknowledged the connection between their programs and the search for peace. Certainly, a number of new historians have stated their desire to have their revisionist renderings of Israel's past make Israelis more amenable to concessions; and figures in the post-1992 education ministry such as Shulamit Aloni explicitly characterized the reforms they advocated as an effort to render Israelis less "nationalistic" and, again, more amenable to concessions.

The writer David Grossman has frequently promoted "universalist" reforms to make Israel less Jewish and Zionist, such as revision of the Law of Return, and he has done so in the name of democratic ideals.[98] But elsewhere he acknowledges that he regards the reforms he favors as part of the concessions necessary for Israel to win the peace that he believes is attainable in exchange for sufficient self-reform.

Shortly after the start of the Oslo process, Grossman declared that to see the process to its fruition in peace Israelis must concede to the Arabs not only geographic territories but territories of the soul. They must surrender their belief that it is of overriding importance for the Jewish people to have the military capacity to defend itself in its own land, the belief that the Holocaust was further evidence of the necessity of this, and the belief that the willingness of Israelis to sacrifice for the defense of the country, and to want to take an active role in that defense, is a virtue. They must also give up the belief that the creation of Israel represents a national return for the Jews from a long and too often horrifyingly painful exile. They must yield even their belief in the value of Jewish peoplehood.[99]

In this statement about the need for such concessions of the soul in the service of the Oslo process, Grossman takes steps toward setting aside the lie that his and others' advocacy of these concessions really represents some single-minded striving for "universalist" and "democratic" ideals. But the statement still, of course, perpetuates another lie, the delusion — based on exhaustion with the siege and a desperate and overwhelming desire for its end — that the right self-abnegations by Israel, the right mix of territorial and spiritual retreat, can win Israel the peace it desires no matter how much the objective evidence of words and deeds by the other side indicates otherwise.

OSLO II, RABIN'S ASSASSINATION, AND THE SYRIAN FRONT

On the second anniversary of Oslo, in September, 1995, Israelis could look back at two years of increased terror and at Arafat having consistently refused to take steps against the infrastructure of the terror groups but rather, according to much evidence, having actively cooperated with those groups. Israelis had also witnessed over those two years ongoing incitement by Arafat and his allies, with calls to Jihad, declarations of Israel's illegitimacy, promises of her ultimate destruction, and praise of the terrorists and their "successes." Indeed, Israelis had seen the Palestinian Authority violate virtually all of its commitments under Oslo regarding mutual recognition and reconciliation as well as security. Nevertheless, the Rabin government on September 28, 1995, signed a second interim agreement with the Palestinians, so-called Oslo II. The new accord essentially entailed further Israeli territorial concessions in exchange for a recommitment on the Palestinian side to security steps and moves toward reconciliation to which it had pledged itself in the prior agreements but had as yet failed to fulfill.

The Israeli territorial concessions under Oslo II involved an initial land transfer of specified areas and an Israeli commitment to additional withdrawals in ensuing months of as yet generally undefined dimensions. In the first transfer, Israel was to cede to the Palestinian Authority control of all municipalities in the West Bank except for Hebron, which was the only city in the territories with a Jewish community. Israel also committed itself to reaching an agreement with the Palestinians regarding Hebron and handing over most of the city to Palestinian control by March 28, 1996.

Oslo II established a system of three categories of jurisdiction in the West Bank: Area A, land under full Palestinian control; Area B, in which all civil authority was ceded to the PA while Israel retained responsibility for security; and Area C, which consisted of territory remaining at least for the present under full Israeli control. The first Oslo II transfers, in which the municipalities except for Hebron became parts of Area A, also entailed the shift of lands encompassing some 450 towns and villages to the status of Area B. These first transfers occurred within weeks of the signing of Oslo II, and Areas A and B then comprised 27 percent of the West Bank. The remaining 73 percent included the Jewish settlements and, beyond this, mainly unpopulated areas. The locations comprising Area A contained 26 percent of the Palestinian population while those comprising Area B contained 70 percent, so that 96 percent of the Palestinian population of the West Bank was now living in areas under PA administration.

Oslo II's provisions were again presented to the Israeli public as a *fait accompli* for which there had been very little forewarning by the government. In addition, those provisions seemed to point to Israel's eventual return virtually to its pre-1967 borders, although this was not explicitly stated.[100] Between the signing of the accord and the first withdrawals, Rabin sought Knesset ratification of Oslo II. In a speech to the Knesset on October 5, he acknowledged that Arafat and the PA had failed to fulfill their obligations under earlier agreements regarding measures against terrorist organizations, extradition of terrorists, and amendment of the Palestinian National Charter to remove the sections calling for Israel's annihilation. He failed to mention other violations, including evidence of cooperation between Arafat and the Islamic fundamentalist groups, incitement to violence, and praise for the terrorists voiced by Arafat and his associates. Rather, Rabin sought to exonerate Arafat from the violence. He was clearly unprepared to allow Palestinian Authority violations of earlier accords, whether those violations he did not acknowledge or the ones he enumerated, to stand in the way of further Israeli concessions.

Consideration of the accord in the Knesset was choreographed by the government in a manner consistent with its policy of ramming through Oslo-related agreements virtually as *faits accomplis*, with a minimum of public and even Knesset scrutiny. Knesset members were allowed only three hours to study the accord, a document of over three hundred pages, before casting their votes.[101] The agreement was endorsed by a two-ballet edge, 61 to 59. (If one subtracts the votes cast by the five Knesset members representing anti-Zionist Arab parties, the count was a three-ballot margin against ratification.) In the ensuing weeks, as the first territorial transfers under Oslo II were taking place, public opinion against the accord remained intense and polls measuring support for potential prime ministerial contenders consistently showed Likud leader Benjamin Netanyahu beating Rabin.

At a government-organized rally in support of Oslo on November 4, Rabin was shot and killed by Yigal Amir, a law student from the Orthodox community. As with the Goldstein massacre a year earlier, the crime elicited revulsion across the political spectrum. But, again as in the wake of that earlier horror, the government and its supporters sought to use the event to delegitimize the opposition. In this case, they blamed the entire opposition as complicit in the murder, as having sown the seeds of violence and assassination through their attacks on Rabin's policies.

Government spokespeople and supporters pointed to reprehensible rhetoric, such as characterizations of Rabin's policies as treasonous, which did come from some voices within the opposition but from far fewer and more peripheral voices than the government would suggest. Government supporters also cited, more particularly, the appearance at opposition rallies of highly inflammatory posters depicting Rabin in Nazi uniform.

What was revealed only later was that those posters were the work of a government-employed *agent provocateur*, who also orchestrated media attention to them. They were part of the government's use of *agents provocateurs* to discredit the opposition. Still more troubling was the gradual revelation that the same *agent provocateur* working for the state security service had actually been involved with the assassin, seemingly goading the assassin and his friends to increasingly aggressive behavior, presumably with the intention of using such behavior to further damage the opposition.

One would have thought that Rabin's colleagues and supporters would have

taken the lead in demanding and pursuing investigation of the role of government agencies in *agent provocateur* adventures and especially the role that this
agent's connections with Yigal Amir may have played in the assassination. But
the government leadership for the most part demurred from aggressive pursuit
of such inquiries, and the Israeli media, which overwhelmingly supported
Rabin's policies, likewise desisted from giving prominent attention to the *agent
provocateur* issue or pushing for intensive investigation. Nor did demands for
such investigation become a prominent cause among Rabin's supporters in the
general public.

Certainly, some on the Left were very troubled by the government's employment of *agents provocateurs*. As one longtime Labor sympathizer wrote: "The
Machiavellian use, by a secret service controlled by the Rabin government, of
agents provocateurs . . . to foment and aggravate such violence as a means of discrediting the opposition to the peace process is no less frightening than the violence itself."[102] But this was a rare statement for voices in the Labor camp.

Rather, the government leadership and its allies in the media and supporters
in the public at large seemed most interested in pursuing the campaign to delegitimize the opposition by broad-brush staining of all critics of Rabin's policies
with responsibility for the assassination. They chose to maintain the focus on
this attack campaign and not allow it to be diverted or diluted by attention to
the role of government "dirty tricks" in the events leading up to the assassination. Indeed, they preferred to sustain this focus on the attack campaign even
at the cost of allowing crucial aspects of the assassination, and the events leading to it, to escape scrutiny and understanding. Also noteworthy in this regard
is that commentators discussing the assassination from the perspective of broadly
indicting the opposition continued routinely to cite the posters of Rabin in Nazi
uniform as an example of the unconscionable rhetoric that supposedly led to
the murder and routinely failed to mention that those posters were the work
of a government-employed *agent provocateur*.[103]

The individual in question, Avishai Raviv, was indicted for his possible involvement in Rabin's murder but was not put on trial until more than seven
years after the assassination. He was then acquitted of any responsibility for
Rabin's death.

The wholesale smearing of the opposition as responsible for Rabin's assassination and the intensified delegitimization of anti-Oslo voices was accompanied by increased harassment of anti-government meetings and demonstrations
and by efforts to quash criticism of the government as "incitement." Hillel
Halkin, writing two months after the murder, observed, "Since the assassination there have been signs that the Labor government has embarked on a wor-
risome policy of using rarely invoked anti-'incitement-to-rebellion' laws in order
to intimidate forms of protest and criticism that would be permitted, or at least
considered less severe legal offenses, in most democratic countries."[104]

Broad public revulsion over the assassination and sympathy for Rabin led to a tidal shift in public sentiment in favor of the government, whose standing in opinion polls now rose dramatically. The Labor leadership under Rabin's successor as prime minister, Shimon Peres, decided to try and capitalize on this shift, which they feared might well be temporary, by advancing the date of national elections from the fall of 1996 to May 29. But a number of subsequent events undermined this tack.

Most significant was a dramatic increase in terrorist assaults in early 1996. In a nine-day period, from February 25 to March 4, fifty-nine victims died and hundreds were injured, almost all in suicide bombings. The onslaught turned the majority of the public back toward grave misgivings about Oslo. Another factor in this swing in opinion was wide public awareness, despite the government and media's muting of the story, of the Palestinian Authority's role in either encouraging and collaborating with the terror or, at the least, tolerating it, failing to act aggressively against it, and using it for Arafat's own ends. Public opinion was also put off by Arafat's cynical and outrageous claims that Israel had armed Hamas and Islamic Jihad to carry out the bombings of Israeli civilians.[105] At the same time, PA officials were declaring that, if Israel did not proceed with meeting Palestinian demands, the Palestinians would resort to force and now had the military capabilities to so so. They also acknowledged that they had both armed forces and weaponry beyond what was allowed them by the Oslo accords.[106]

The shift in Israeli mood was reflected in the popular replacement, on bumpers stickers and elsewhere, of the invocation "*Shalom, Chaver*" ("Goodbye, friend"), President Clinton's farewell in homage to Rabin made famous at his funeral, with the bitterly ironic variation, "*Shalom, Chaverim*," ("Good-bye, friends"), in homage to the victims of Rabin's Oslo process.

Peres responded to the terror by demanding stronger action by Arafat against the Islamic fundamentalist organizations and their terror infrastructures, such as training, bomb building, and other facilities. He also froze negotiations with the Palestinians on plans for the withdrawal from Hebron and for further territorial concessions. But these steps had only limited impact on public opinion.

Other notable events around this time that had a negative effect on Peres' electoral hopes included clashes on Israel's northern border and in Lebanon. In April, 1996, in response to Hezbollah rocket attacks on northern Israel, the government unleashed artillery barrages against targets in southern Lebanon and strikes against some elements of economic infrastructure elsewhere in the country. In one of the artillery assaults on what was thought to be a Hezbollah position, the IDF accidentally killed 102 Lebanese civilians who had fled from elsewhere into the target area. Anger over the deaths led a portion of Israel's Arab community, which overwhelmingly supported the government and its Oslo policies, to threaten a boycott of the coming election. At the same time, northern Israel's vulnerability to attack, and the government's failure to respond effectively, raised additional doubts about government policies for some Israelis, especially among those living in the north.

The events in Lebanon in April, 1996, are also noteworthy from another perspective. As already suggested, the Labor-Meretz coalition that came to power in 1992 embraced, not surprisingly, delusions about potential peace with Syria very similar to those it nurtured regarding the Palestinian leadership. That is, it believed sufficient Israeli concessions would inexorably lead not only to an agreement with Syria but to a peace so solid and durable that Israel could cede territories previously regarded as vital to the state's defense and survival. In the spirit of this faith, the governing coalition soon opened negotiations with the Syrians in which it offered to hand over the entire Golan Heights, although, as was typical for this government, it obfuscated in informing the Israeli public of the concessions it was prepared to make and did not do so until August, 1995.

Despite the scope of the Israeli offer and intense shuttle diplomacy by U.S. Secretary of State Warren Christopher acting as intermediary between Israel and Syria, Hafez Assad demurred. The Israelis had chosen to believe that concessions on their part were all that was required for peace, another instance of the intense desire for a solution leading to delusional overvaluation of one's own control of the situation. But Assad was also weighing the importance to his regime of the conflict with Israel in terms of internal Syrian political dynamics, and he decided the Golan was not worth the domestic risks associated with ending the conflict.

Nevertheless, throughout the life of the Labor-Meretz coalition government, policy in the north was shaped by the intense desire for an agreement with Syria and the belief that an accord based on Israeli concessions was still attainable. Indeed, Peres, on ascending to power, pushed for resumption of talks with the Syrians in hopes of quickly negotiating a peace. Through American intercession, he restarted meetings with Syria at Wye Plantation in November, 1995. The talks were suspended in response to the terrorist bombings of February and March, 1996, and Syria's refusal to condemn the attacks. But even after the subsequent Hezbollah katyusha barrages on Israel in April, an offensive that could not have been launched without Syrian approval and support, Peres still maneuvered for a quick pre-election agreement with Assad.

One consequence of this perennial courting of Syria was that, in responding to attacks on Israeli forces in Lebanon or rocket barrages on northern Israel, assaults perpetrated by Hezbollah guerrillas under Syrian and Iranian sponsorship, the government would pull its punches. It would, for example, fire at supposed Hezbollah strongholds, an ineffective riposte as Hezbollah could anticipate it and take defensive measures such as evacuating vulnerable positions. Or on occasion, after attacks on Israel proper, the government would undertake actions striking at the economic stability of Lebanon, actions that it argued would put pressure on the Lebanese government and indirectly on the Syrians, whose army controlled Lebanon and whose economy fed in crucial ways off that of Lebanon. Such responses included instigating large-scale movement of population from the south and striking economic infrastructure targets like power-generating plants. But Israel would not strike at the Syrian occupation forces in Lebanon.

In effect, Israel allowed Syria to conduct a proxy war against it at virtually no cost. It did so in order, in the government's thinking, not to upset the Syrians and muddy the opportunity for "peace." As in other elements of the government's policies shaped by its "peace" strategies, there were victims of this tack. They included Lebanese civilians caught up in the strikes against Lebanese infrastructure or injured or forced to flee their homes due to futile artillery barrages aimed at Hezbollah targets. This occurred in Rabin's response to attacks on northern Israel in 1993 and again in Peres' actions in April, 1996. There were also Israeli victims of the government's Syrian strategy, the soldiers in Lebanon and civilians in the north of the country who were subjected to Hezbollah assaults while their government refused to use the strongest weapon at its disposal, attacks on positions in Lebanon of Hezbollah's Syrian suppliers and sponsors, to force a reining in of Hezbollah by Syria. Once more, Israelis were left vulnerable and lives were lost in the government's pursuit of delusional visions of advancing a fantasied peace with "partners" who were not interested in peace.

FIFTEEN

The Netanyahu Interlude: A Bump on the Road to Self-Immolation

There is a deeper motive for the hatred we feel for Benjamin Netanyahu . . . In the early 90s . . . we, the enlightened Israelis, were infected with a messianic craze . . . All of a sudden, we believed that . . . the end of the old Middle East was near. The end of history, the end of wars, the end of the conflict. Like the members of any other messianic movement, we decided to hasten the end, and anointed Yitzhak Rabin as our Messiah . . .

Hatred of Netanyahu enables us to conveniently forget that before the bubble burst, we acted like fools. We fooled ourselves with illusions. We were bedazzled into committing a collective act of messianic drunkenness. Hatred of Netanyahu also gives us a chance to forget that it was not the rise of Netanyahu that brought on the paralysis of Oslo but the paralysis of Oslo that brought on the rise of Netanyahu. The hatred permits us to keep harboring the notion that everything is really much more simple, that if we only pull back, if we only recognize Palestinian statehood . . . we would be able [once again] to breathe in that exhilarating, heady aroma of the end of history, the end of wars, the end of the conflict.

Haaretz columnist Ari Shavit, December, 1997[1]

VICTORY AND A DIFFICULT START

Public apprehension about the government's "peace" policies was heightened by the terror bombings of late February and early March, 1996. Events along the Lebanese border the following month further eroded public confidence in the government's Oslo course and also alienated segments of the Israeli-Arab population. Nevertheless, Shimon Peres was expected to win the May election easily. Among the advantages for Peres was having the support not only of government media but also of Israel's essentially pro-government and pro-Oslo independent media. In addition, Peres enjoyed the explicit endorsement of the Clinton Administration, an unprecedented phenomenon as the United States usually did not meddle directly in Israeli politics.

The Clinton Administration had not been party to the original Oslo negotiations of 1993, but it had quickly become an enthusiastic backer of the Oslo process. President Clinton, not a strong chief executive on foreign policy, was more than prepared to follow Peres and Rabin's lead in embracing Arafat as a peace partner, likely more so as many of his most generous contributors were Jewish enthusiasts of Oslo. The potential blow to American strategic interests represented by a weakened and more vulnerable Israel did not seem to concern him.

However, despite pre-election expectations, Benjamin Netanyahu won the Jewish vote by 55 percent to 45 percent and emerged the overall victor by a narrow majority of about 1 percent.

In the months that followed, voices within the Labor and Meretz leaderships, as well as their supporters, commonly explained their loss as due to the benighted nature of the Israeli electorate and the failure of the defeated government to educate the nation properly on the peace process. Yossi Beilin, in the prologue of his book *Touching Peace* (1999), states that the government had been misled by the public's enthusiastic response to the Declaration of Principles in the fall of 1993 and did not appreciate the need to exert itself to mold "public understanding."[2] He expounds on the same theme in the book's epilogue.[3] In contrast, Beilin barely speaks of the impact of the ongoing terror on public understanding and on the election results. Indeed, he acknowledges its import only on page 185 of his book and even then tries to minimize the terror's dimensions. Nowhere does he mention PA involvement in the terror.

Beilin's self-delusion with regard to the Labor-Meretz failure is compounded by intellectual dishonesty. In elaborating on the government's not properly educating the public, he states, "We were also mistaken in that we didn't show the public what we envisaged at the end of the process, and we thereby exposed ourselves to unnecessary accusations and questions."[4] But, of course, this was not a mere oversight or mistake. The heart of Beilin's *modus operandi* was to keep the public in the dark about the vision of a settlement that he promoted in negotiations. He employed this strategy because he anticipated the country would regard his concessions as too dangerous and he wanted to present the nation with *faits accomplis* that would be very difficult to reject.

No less dishonest and disconnected from reality are Beilin's repeated references in the book to Palestinian negotiators proposing the development of programs that would educate the two peoples for peace,[5] and his regret that this was never pursued. In fact, Israel, in efforts never mentioned by Beilin, had almost immediately after the signing of the first Oslo agreements introduced into its schools an extensive peace curriculum designed to promote understanding of the other side. The government also mounted a public relations campaign to the same end. But the government's efforts were overtaken by the public's exposure to the PA's obviously pursuing an agenda different from peace and reconciliation.

Beilin, as he talks of Palestinian proposals for "peace education," also omits mention of the fact that the curriculum the PA purveyed in its schools emphasized Israel's illegitimacy and the necessity of its destruction and that this was also the dominant message of PA-controlled media.

The Israeli public voted in 1996 against Palestinian terror and Palestinian incitement. Beilin chose to ascribe that vote to ignorance, and he distorted reality to fit his construction.

Similar explanations for the election results were offered by Oslo negotiator Uri Savir, in *The Process* (1998). Again, the government's failure is construed as not having adequately educated the people. Like Beilin, Savir notes that his Palestinian negotiating partners spoke of needing to educate the people for peace; and, like Beilin, Savir omits any mention of the Palestinian leadership's subsequently educating its children, and its population generally, for war and the pursuit of Israel's destruction.

Savir is avid in his depiction of the personal rapports that he developed with his Palestinian interlocutors, and his book contains many homey photographs. He suggests that the Oslo process would have stayed on course if only the warm feelings he shared with his Palestinian counterpart had filtered down to the people. That Arafat and the PA might have a hostile agenda, or even that Palestinian incitement and terror might suggest a hostile agenda, is never considered by Savir. He does not mention the terror until page 148, consistently exonerates Arafat and the PA from responsibility for it, and is critical of those who would implicate them in it. Moreover, Savir suggests that Israel could have been more forthcoming to Arafat and that this might have precluded the terror by strengthening Arafat and enabling him to act more forcefully against it. Throughout the book, virtually every reference to Palestinian transgression is balanced by an evenhanded claim of failure by both parties.

The supposedly benighted Israelis who opposed talks with the PLO are variously characterized by Savir as extreme rightists who harbored exaggerated and irrational fears for Israel's security, people who wished to annex all the territories, nationalists who believed that the hostility of the other side was immutable and eternal, those Israelis who "still wanted to rule the Palestinians," and those who "failed to see that economics, technology, science, and international relations determine the real power of countries, more than land."[6] According to Savir, Netanyahu was elected by these people, together with others whose vote, in Savir's formulation, was not an expression of revulsion over Palestinian incitement and terror and a consequent loss of any faith they may have had in Oslo. Rather, it was an expression of ignorance, a reflection of the fact that Oslo's "message did not filter down enough to the people."[7]

Nor were such distortions of the reality behind the 1996 election results simply the purview of figures in the Rabin and Peres administrations such as Beilin and Savir. Ehud Sprinzak, a Professor of Political Science at Hebrew University, wrote of Netanyahu's constituency in an article published in *Foreign Affairs* in the summer of 1998.[8] According to Sprinzak, that constituency consisted of "Israel's nationalist right, its radical right, and its soft right,"[9] the last composed of groups that embrace no intense ideological position on the territories but "whose stock in trade is intense mistrust of and hostility toward Arabs."[10]

The terrorism that had wracked Israel over the years since the start of Oslo is first mentioned by Sprinzak on page seven of his eleven-page article and is then characterized as simply something that reinforced the biases of Netanyahu's constituency. Sprinzak makes no mention of Arafat and the PA's involvement in the terror or their incitement of their public to ongoing war against Israel.

Sprinzak did discuss the terrorism some months earlier in a piece published in the *Washington Post*.[11] There he ascribes it primarily to Hamas but does not condemn that group. On the contrary, Sprinzak insists that such Hamas tactics as suicide bombings are simply a response to "humiliating Israeli actions." He cites approvingly Hamas statements to this effect, and he criticizes both Netanyahu and Peres for seeking to "demonize" Hamas. In Sprinzak's view, sufficiently forthcoming steps by Israel will likely lead to Hamas joining Arafat as Israel's peace partner: "A significant improvement in the political and socioeconomic conditions of the Palestinian masses . . . will reduce Hamas's incentives to commit atrocities against Israeli civilians and drive its pragmatic leaders to greater cooperation with the Palestinian Authority."

Hamas's explicitly declared objective of pursuing to the end Israel's destruction, and Arafat's promotion of the same agenda — the agenda that, with its accompanying terror, had elicited the Israeli electorate's rejection of the Labor-Meretz coalition — are realities that simply did not exist in Sprinzak's universe within the Political Science department at Hebrew University.

The balloting that gave victory to Netanyahu produced other unanticipated results as well. It was the first Israeli election conducted under new rules that mandated the casting not of the previous single vote for one's favored parliamentary slate but rather of two votes, one for a parliamentary slate and another for a prime ministerial candidate. This election reform was initiated to stabilize governments by giving greater independence and authority to the prime minister in an arrangement falling somewhere between a straightforward parliamentary system and an American-style executive and legislative split. But the separate ballot for prime minister meant that voters were no longer constrained to vote for one of the two major parties if they wished to influence directly the selection of the prime minister. Many Israelis, in this debut of the new system, took the opportunity to abandon the major parties and vote for one of the smaller lists whose platforms more closely fit their own political predilections. The result was a Knesset much more fragmented than at any earlier time in the state's history, one hardly conducive to more stable government but rather presenting daunting obstacles to the formation and maintenance of a governing coalition.

Netanyahu's relative inexperience in government (the highest offices he had previously held were deputy foreign minister and UN ambassador) and his personal clashes with colleagues led to strained relations with many erstwhile and potential allies and exacerbated even further the difficult task of building a coalition. It was not until June 18 that he finally had a government in place, and the coalition under his leadership continued throughout its existence to be fractious and unstable.

As to the policies he hoped to pursue with his government, Netanyahu had given mixed signals during the campaign. It was clear that he fully appreciated the severe flaws in the Oslo process and the dangers they posed to Israel; indeed, no Israeli better articulated these problems. At a few points in the campaign he had indicated he intended, consistent with the views of those in the Likud leadership who believed Israel must retain full control over all of Eretz Israel, to roll back the territorial concessions made by the previous government. Moreover, he had implied he saw doing so as justified under Oslo by virtue of the PA's failure to fulfill any of its Oslo obligations.

More typically, however, Netanyahu had suggested that he would honor the concessions Israel had already executed but would continue to freeze the process and would insist on the PA's fulfillment of its earlier commitments as a prerequisite for further negotiations and further movement by Israel. A stance of maintaining Peres' discontinuation of negotiations and making Palestinian compliance a prerequisite for further talks and further steps by Israel no doubt resonated well with the skepticism about the Oslo agreements shared by most Israelis. It also rendered Netanyahu's victory more than just a protest vote against the failed policies of Rabin and Peres.

But from the moment of his government's taking office, Netanyahu was subjected to myriad, intense pressures to resume negotiations despite Arafat's flouting of his earlier commitments. The leadership of Labor and Meretz and their supporters, minimizing in their arguments the significance of Palestinian noncompliance and ignoring the fact that it was their own government that had initiated a freeze in response to Palestinian terror and Arafat's refusal to address it, excoriated Netanyahu. They asserted that his continuation of the freeze reflected a desire to perpetuate the "occupation" and was a rejection of "peace." The Israeli media echoed this rhetoric, and foreign governments and press —

most shrilly, of course, Arab governments and press, but hardly less so those of Europe — and indeed the American media and to some degree the American administration, did so as well. Netanyahu's demands for PA compliance with the obligations it had repeatedly undertaken in the various Oslo agreements, demands that were hardly unreasonable, were portrayed as a nefarious ploy to scuttle Oslo.

The most significant for Netanyahu of the pressures to resume negotiations despite PA noncompliance were those coming from domestic sources and from the Clinton Administration. At the same time, Netanyahu had measures available to him to try and counter both. He could potentially have used his exceptional oratorical skills to go over the heads of political foes and even a hostile Israeli media and effectively present the merits of his positions directly to the Israeli public. In addition, his insistence on PA compliance enjoyed extensive support in the American Congress, which — although there is always some risk in an Israeli government possibly antagonizing an Administration by turning to Congress to counter Administration pressures — was certainly available as a potential ally in advancing Netanyahu's case in Washington. But he did not act effectively to ease either the domestic or foreign pressures, and, on August 14, 1996, he reentered negotiations with Arafat without having made any headway on the compliance issue.

Perhaps Netanyahu saw this step as simply a tactical retreat and believed that resuming negotiations would itself drain some of the intensity from the attacks to which he was being subjected and he could still make PA compliance a condition for progress in negotiations. But the voices that had demanded of him a return to the negotiating table despite PA noncompliance merely proceeded to demand of him "progress" in the negotiations despite PA noncompliance.

Arafat, meanwhile, was no doubt unhappy with Israel's shift away from its earlier pattern of yielding a rapid succession of unilateral concessions. But, while he had used the terror card extensively in that earlier period to push forward the process of Israeli concessions, he now largely clamped down on terror. In the six months from the last of the bombings of late February, early March, 1996, until early September, seven people (six Israelis and one Jewish American teenager studying in Israel) were killed in terror attacks emanating from the territories. In contrast, 152 had been killed in the preceding twenty months since Arafat's arrival in Gaza.

Some in the new Israeli administration preferred to attribute this decline in terror to heightened and more effective government security measures. But what there were of these measures could not have had such a dramatic impact on the level of terror as long as the terrorists had available to them a free base of operations in the territories. The decline was much more due to steps taken by Arafat.

Nor were Arafat's likely motives for this reining in of the terror difficult to discern. In the initial three months after the February-March bombings, he had to deal with Peres' freeze of negotiations but knew that, given the mood of the electorate and Peres' concerns about the upcoming election, he was hardly likely to extract more concessions at this time through more terror. In any case, he did not want to do anything that would almost certainly redound to Netanyahu's gain at the polls. In the wake of the election, Arafat was confronted with a prime minister who was not going to respond to terror as his predecessors had, by invoking it as a reason to speed up Israeli concessions. Rather, he would use it as a justification for keeping negotiations and Israeli concessions on hold. Arafat therefore had good reason to continue his moratorium on terror. (Arafat's drastic curtailing of terror attacks during these months served parenthetically to give the lie to those Oslo enthusiasts who argued that Arafat had always been opposed to the terror but was incapable of stanching it, that it was out of his control, or that only more, and quicker, Israeli concessions would give Arafat the popular support he needed to clamp down on terror.)

In late August and early September, Arafat attempted to employ a different tactic to pressure Netanyahu. He called on several occasions for massive attendance and demonstrations at Moslem religious services to protest Israeli policies. But the Palestinian public largely shunned these calls and the planned demonstrations fizzled. However, a new opportunity presented itself to Arafat in late September.

Israel had some years earlier cleared a tunnel along the outside of the Temple Mount's Western Wall, at a depth of what two thousand years ago had been approximately street level. The tunnel, which ran north from the plaza and Jewish prayer area at the southern end of the Western Wall, had then been opened to tourists. But access was limited by the necessity of those entering having to trace their steps back to exit the same way they had come in, near the prayer area and plaza. The previous government had reportedly discussed with the Moslem Waqf, which, in keeping with Moshe Dayan's policies, still served as custodian of the Temple Mount, opening an exit at the far end of the tunnel as *quid pro quo* for Israel's acceding to the Waqf's request to open an additional mosque on top of the Mount and to clear an underground area known as Solomon's Stables for use as the mosque.

Waqf construction in Solomon's Stables had already begun. But when Netanyahu opened the new exit to the tunnel on September 24, 1996, he was attacked by Arafat and the Palestinian Authority for allegedly acting unilaterally and seeking to undermine Moslem holy places. Arafat literally claimed that Israel was tunneling under the Temple Mount and that the Mount was about to collapse,[12] even though the tunnel was outside the Temple Mount's walls and had been there for years. The new exit was also, of course, outside the Temple Mount's walls. The Palestinian Authority also claimed that the Israeli action was a violation of the Oslo II agreement, but there is in fact nothing in Oslo II supportive of this claim.

Arafat issued an urgent call to his people to defend the holy sites on the Mount, and he succeeded in triggering widespread rioting, initially in Jerusalem and then elsewhere as well. In addition, he unleashed his armed forces, including snipers, to attack Israeli soldiers in what became known in Israel as the "Checkpoint War." In the ensuing four days, fifteen Israeli soldiers were shot dead by Palestinian police and about sixty Palestinians were killed.

In the public relations war that accompanied the battles on the ground, Arafat again bested Netanyahu as he had done vis-à-vis the resumption of negotiations. The Israeli Left attacked Netanyahu for allegedly having acted provocatively by opening the tunnel exit and having thereby triggered the violence. The Israeli media echoed this view. Most foreign governments and foreign media took the same stance, with many in the media claiming that Israel had dug a tunnel under the Temple Mount. Again, as any of their correspondents in Jerusalem could have ascertained for themselves, Israel had not dug a tunnel nor was the existing tunnel under the Temple Mount.

The Checkpoint War demonstrated once more Arafat's continued commitment to using violence and terror as weapons against Israel. But most observers outside the country, and indeed half of Israel, chose to ignore this and to continue perceiving Arafat as Israel's "peace partner."

The Checkpoint War also demonstrated another negative truth that should have been obvious. Oslo enthusiasts maintained that the ties with Arab states that emerged in the wake of Oslo would be a force for moderation and serve to push recalcitrant Palestinian opinion toward reconciliation. In fact, the opposite was true. Agreements with Arab states, even the formal peace with Egypt and Jordan, remained hostage to Israel's satisfying the Palestinians. The Jordanian regime was, again, the Arab party most interested in peace with Israel; but, given the Palestinian connections of Jordan's population and the sentiment of its people, even King Hussein felt obliged to respond to the mini-war by declaring that his peace with Israel was "definitely in danger."[13]

The Arab states that had more limited relations with Israel, and that were invariably less invested in those ties than was King Hussein in his, could be expected to retreat from their connections with Israel even more readily in response to Palestinian dissatisfaction. Indeed, Oman, for example, froze its new relations with Israel in December and stated that it would continue the freeze until Israel "fulfills its obligations to the Palestinian leadership."[14] Oman renewed its ties to Israel in January, 1997, after the Hebron agreement,[15] but then severed them again two months later in a show of solidarity with Palestinian complaints over settlements.[16]

The mini-war did, however, have one consequence that could be construed as positive from an Israeli perspective. The upper echelons of the IDF had become, in the view of many observers, increasingly politicized in recent years. (Considerations of political affiliation in appointments to the Israeli general staff had always been a problem; officers with Labor Zionist credentials traditionally enjoyed a distinct advantage. But this pattern, and the divergence from straightforward merit criteria, seemed to many people to have become more blatant and more entrenched.) As a result, the IDF leadership consisted predominantly of individuals inclined to the perspectives of the Peace Movement, now the perspective of the Labor Party as well, that a genuine peace was at hand. The IDF was largely caught by surprise by the circumstance of Arafat's police turning their automatic weapons and sniper rifles on Israeli soldiers and police. It was abruptly disabused of its overly sanguine assumptions and thereafter reassessed the strategic predicament into which the Oslo process had led the nation and began to plan in a more realistic way how to cope with that predicament.

HEBRON, THE "NOTE FOR THE RECORD," AND RECIPROCITY

Netanyahu, failing to counter effectively the increased pressure on him mounted in the wake of events around the tunnel opening, responded to the pressure by reentering negotiations with the PA, briefly terminated in the context of the fighting, and by agreeing in the ensuing weeks to terms of withdrawal from Hebron. He did so despite his still not having secured any reversal of the PA's pattern of noncompliance with its Oslo obligations.

The emerging Hebron accord generally followed the 80:20 division of Hebron (80 percent to Arafat, 20 percent to continue for the time being under Israeli control) envisioned in Oslo II. By early November Israel was beginning to transfer authority in the city to Arafat's forces even though a full agreement had not yet been concluded. The last elements of an accord were in place by the end of November, but Arafat then balked at signing. He seemed to view his endorsement of the agreement as likely to ease the pressure on Netanyahu and deferment of completion of the accord as providing a means of sustaining the pressure and as a potential tool for extracting more concessions from Netanyahu. While this ploy initially met with some success, it soon became clear even to many of Arafat's supporters in Israel and abroad that it was he, not Netanyahu, who was obstructing completion and enactment of the agreement, and Arafat was then prevailed upon to abandon the tack. The last details were resolved in early January and the accord signed on January 15; it was approved by the Knesset the next day.

The signing of the Hebron agreement was accompanied by United States Middle East coordinator Dennis Ross's submitting to both parties a "Note for the Record," which summarized the accord. The "Note for the Record" reiterated Israel's commitment to three additional redeployments as specified in the Interim

Agreement (Oslo II), the first to take place in early March. It also referred to Israel's undertaking a prisoner release, resolution of other Interim Agreement issues, and resumption of permanent status negotiations. The "Note" restated the Palestinians' commitment to those measures regarding revising the Palestinian National Charter, fighting terrorism, and addressing other security-related matters to which the Palestinians had committed themselves in the various earlier Oslo protocols.

The opening paragraph of the "Note for the Record" also refers to the two leaders implementing the Interim Agreement "on the basis of reciprocity." Netanyahu would subsequently point to this as evidence that he had achieved for the first time explicit and formal recognition that Israel's concessions were tied to Arafat's fulfillment of the Palestinians' Oslo obligations. This recognition, he declared, marked the end of unilateral Israeli concessions. In the Cabinet meeting of January 15, which took up approval of the Hebron accord, he argued that the "Note for the Record," and also a letter from Secretary of State Warren Christopher that was to accompany the accord, established clearly the United States' recognition of the principle of reciprocity and linkage between Palestinian compliance with prior obligations and additional Israeli withdrawals. But Netanyahu's negotiation and conclusion of the Hebron accord still contradicted his previous declarations that Palestinian compliance with what had already been agreed upon was a prerequisite to further Israeli concessions. Moreover, the accord, like previous Oslo agreements, provided no mechanism for measuring, monitoring, or enforcing reciprocity.

Another issue that surfaced in the January 15 Cabinet meeting on the Hebron accord concerned determination of the nature and extent of the three further Israeli withdrawals called for under the Interim Agreement and alluded to in the "Note for the Record." Netanyahu maintained that Israel would unilaterally decide the scope of the withdrawals and that the United States recognized this, and he indicated that this would be confirmed in Warren Christopher's letter. But an Israeli television report during the Cabinet meeting suggested that this was not the State Department's view. The meeting was then recessed to await American clarification. In fact, the Christopher letter offers no entirely clear-cut acknowledgment of Israel's right to determine unilaterally the scope of further withdrawals. But the State Department at this point issued a statement that, "The guarantor's [i.e., the United States'] letters [one to Arafat, one to Netanyahu] which Secretary Christopher intends forwarding to both sides also relates to the process of further redeployments as Israel's responsibility . . . "[17] This clarification helped secure the Cabinet's narrow endorsement of the accord.

The Israeli army completed its withdrawal from the ceded areas of Hebron within hours of the Knesset approval of the agreement on January 16. Almost immediately, the PA initiated harassment of the Jewish enclave in Hebron, with rioting, stone throwing, firebombing, and gunfire. This continued on and off thereafter. The government added the events in Hebron to its list of talking points on the Palestinian Authority's violations of its Oslo commitments and frequently reiterated its demand for reciprocity. But it nevertheless went ahead and offered on March 7 to hand over another 9.1 percent of West Bank territory to the Palestinians as the first of those "further redeployments" called for in the Interim Agreement. (The "Note for the Record" specified, at the time of the Hebron accord, that the first redeployment should occur in the first week of March.)

As it happened, this withdrawal did not occur, but not because of Israel's holding out for Palestinian compliance. Rather, the Palestinians rejected as inadequate the 9.1 percent scope of the offered retreat. The ensuing stalemate persisted for more than a year and a half, and during this time the Netanyahu government, in speeches and statements by the Prime Minister and other government officials at home and abroad and in press releases by the foreign ministry, hammered away at Palestinian noncompliance.

Also during this time, additional incidents of violence, in many instances perpetrated by Palestinian "police," including terrorist attacks initiated by Palestinian armed forces, added further to the violations invoked by the Netanyahu government in its demands for Palestinian compliance. Among such incidents were the murder of another thirty-eight Israelis, injury of hundreds more, many aborted terrorist attacks, and myriad stonings, firebombings, and acts of arson.

Representative of the government's campaign regarding Palestinian violations is a Special Report issued by the Foreign Ministry in July, 1997, documenting the PA's failure to fulfill its Oslo-related commitments as enumerated in the Hebron protocol and the "Note for the Record." The document touches on security violations of the Hebron protocol itself, among them the PA's paying Palestinian youths to riot and attack Israeli soldiers and Jewish residents of Hebron and the PA's deploying in Hebron nearly four times the number of policemen allowed by the accord (1500 rather than the allowed 400).

But most of the Special Report is devoted to PA violations of those earlier commitments reiterated in the Note for the Record. As noted in the Report, the PA had failed to change the PLO Covenant. (The PA was to submit to the Palestine National Council for ratification a new version of the Covenant free of those clauses calling for Israel's annihilation, but had yet to do so.) It had failed to fight terror and prevent violence. (On the contrary, as the document cites, officers of the PA "police" had themselves been involved in organizing and perpetrating terror attacks.) It had failed to halt incitement to violence against Israel. (Enumerated points in the Report include PA officials and media praising the terrorists and their actions, threatening Israel with war, accusing Israel of supposedly trying to poison Palestinians or infect them with AIDs through injections and contaminated food, and myriad other instances of slander, incitement, and war-mongering.[18]) It had failed to dismantle the terrorist organizations' infrastructures. It had failed to apprehend, prosecute, and punish terrorists. (The document notes "revolving door" incarceration policies and the fact that many members of terrorist organizations had been inducted into the Palestinian police.) It had failed to transfer terror suspects to Israel as called for under Oslo. (For example, on March 31, 1997, Israel had submitted to the PA a request for extradition of thirty-one Palestinians involved in the terrorist murder of Israelis — eleven of the requests were new, twenty involved people whose extradition had been petitioned earlier as well; no extraditions ensued.) It had failed to confiscate illegal weapons. It had failed to keep PA police forces at levels agreed upon in the accord. (Over thirty thousand men were under arms, while only 24,000 were permitted.) It had also failed to restrict PA activity, including quasi-police activity, to areas under PA control.

In January, 1998, the Cabinet unanimously passed a resolution linking further redeployment to PA fulfillment of commitments made or reiterated as part of the Hebron agreement.

But despite Netanyahu's efforts to give prominence to Palestinian noncompliance, particularly regarding security matters and incitement, and to the principle of reciprocity, he did not succeed in gaining substantive traction for these themes in either the domestic political sphere or the diplomatic realm. On the contrary, Israel's political opposition and media continued to urge his government to move forward with territorial concessions, to advance the "process," and the Peace Movement held rallies protesting the government's alleged foot-dragging. To the degree that the government's arguments regarding Palestinian noncompliance and the importance of reciprocity were noted at all, they were characterized as ploys being used by Netanyahu to obstruct "progress."

In December, 1997, Ari Shavit, a columnist for *Haaretz* — the newspaper of Israel's elites and the most ideologically driven of the nation's nongovernmental media — wrote a remarkable and in many respects milestone article in which he broke ranks with his colleagues in the peace camp to critique their vilifying of Netanyahu.[19] In his irony-laden piece, Shavit contrasts the Israeli Left's hatred of Netanyahu with its enthusiasm for Rabin and Peres' governments. That enthusiasm, Shavit notes, ignored those governments' undemocratic and heavy-handed methods, which the Left ought to have abhorred, because Rabin and Peres had wielded such methods in the service of "peace": "So do we hate Benjamin Netanyahu because his government hastily and recklessly adopted irreversible historic decisions with blatant disregard for proper procedure, not bothering to take account of the feelings of half the country, only bothering to receive Knesset approval after the fact? Oops. That would be the Rabin and Peres governments. As for ourselves, we simply remained silent.

We did not feel that proper procedure and fair democratic rules and proper public debate were so important."

Shavit goes on: "So why do we hate him so much? . . . [Because] despite our determination not to hold an open democratic referendum on the question of peace, opting instead to make it a retroactive vote on facts that had already been set in motion — the moment of truth came. And when the long-overdue plebiscite on the peace process was finally held . . . the Israeli public told us no. The Israeli public said Netanyahu . . .

"But there is a deeper motive for the hatred we feel for Benjamin Netanyahu . . . In the early '90s . . . we, the enlightened Israelis, were infected with a messianic craze . . . All of a sudden, we believed that . . . the end of the old Middle East was near. The end of history, the end of wars, the end of the conflict. Like the members of any other messianic movement, we decided to hasten the end, and anointed Yitzhak Rabin as our Messiah . . .

"Hatred of Netanyahu enables us to conveniently forget that before the bubble burst, we acted like fools. We fooled ourselves with illusions. We were bedazzled into committing a collective act of messianic drunkenness. Hatred of Netanyahu also gives us a chance to forget that it was not the rise of Netanyahu that brought on the paralysis of Oslo but the paralysis of Oslo that brought on the rise of Netanyahu. The hatred permits us to keep harboring the notion that everything is really much more simple, that if we only pull back, if we only recognize Palestinian statehood . . . we would be able [once again] to breathe in that exhilarating, heady aroma of the end of history, the end of wars, the end of the conflict."

In a follow-up article published two weeks later, Shavit related how he had been excoriated in the intervening days by many of his fellow Peace Movement devotees within Israel's elites, attacked as a quisling for daring to criticize Oslo's True Believers. But he notes the great and in some ways growing threats to Israel posed by her neighbors and asks how the nation and its people will be able to go on living under those threats. Shavit observes: "One thing is certain . . . We can't [adjust to the threats in a viable way] as long as the almost sole contribution of the veteran Israeli elites to the public discourse is automatic applause for any withdrawal, and automatic catcalls against any pause in withdrawal. We can't do this as long as the Israeli elites continue to behave as if the Jewish-Palestinian conflict . . . will be resolved the moment the Israeli Defense Force withdraws to the border of June 4, 1967."[20]

But Shavit's was a rare voice of self-criticism and moderation among Israel's Oslo enthusiasts, especially among those cadres of enthusiasts that comprised the largest part of the nation's elites.

As in the domestic sphere, so too internationally Netanyahu continued to be portrayed most often, by governments and media, as the villain who was holding back progress; a depiction reflecting in no small part, at least in Europe and the United States, the influence of the Israeli political opposition and Israeli media. A measure of the extent to which the Clinton Administration adopted the stance of the Israeli Left, even in its giving a pass to Arafat's noncompliance in security matters, was the State Department's policy regarding American victims of Palestinian terror.

The State Department had for some years posted rewards for help in apprehending and prosecuting terrorist killers of Americans and had maintained a public information program to bring attention to American victims of terror and to the reward process. But American victims of Palestinian terror — mainly American Jews who had been living in Israel or visiting and studying there — were excluded from the program. This was apparently in an effort to avoid attracting public attention to the fact that their killers were typically living at liberty in Arafat-controlled areas, or living under some loose "arrest" regimen, or were even serving in Arafat's police forces. The policy was intended, more fundamentally, to avoid bringing pressures to bear on Arafat or raising public awareness of the issue of Palestinian noncompliance. It is unlikely that the administration and the State Department would have made the same exemption for Palestinian terror had the Israeli Left joined with Netanyahu in seeking to press Arafat to end his collusion with the terrorists.[21]

In addition, the Clinton Administration, again largely under the influence of the Israeli opposition and its American Jewish supporters, effectively rejected Netanyahu's demands for reciprocity. Indeed, it not only pushed Israel to proceed with territorial concessions without Palestinian compliance but insisted that the next round of territorial concessions exceed the dimensions proposed by the Israelis in March, 1997. Early in 1998, the State Department came up with the figure of 13 percent as the proper size of the next West Bank withdrawal, based not on any consideration of Israel's strategic position and defense needs but simply on the fact that an additional 13 percent would place the nice round number of 40 percent of the West Bank under Arafat's control. In effect, the administration reneged both on its formal endorsement of the reciprocity principle in the "Note for the Record" and on its acknowledgment at the time of the Hebron accord that Israel had the right to determine the dimensions of the further interim redeployments.

Once more, there appear to have been steps Netanyahu could have taken to counter both domestic and American circles that were undermining his stance on Palestinian noncompliance. At home, he could have done more to go over the heads of the opposition parties, the media, and even elements of his fractious coalition who did not fully share his jaundiced views of Oslo. He could have addressed the Israeli public more directly and more forcefully on the dangers posed by Palestinian policies and evasions.

With regard to the United States and the issue of the next interim withdrawal, Netanyahu initially balked at Administration demands, stating that it would be militarily too risky, especially given Arafat's failure to comply with his security obligations and his obviously keeping alive an option of violent confrontation. When Secretary of State Madeline Albright, in the spring of 1998, imperiously, and with veiled threats, summoned Netanyahu to Washington to finalize a 13 percent withdrawal plan, Netanyahu chose to remain at home. In response to this confrontation, many members of Congress publicly and forcefully sided with Netanyahu, arguing that it was Israel that was taking the security risks and that the Israelis had the right to decide what steps were prudent and tolerable and what were not.

Congress had also recently become more aware of the extent of PA anti-Israel incitement when a number of members attended screenings of tapes of incitement-laden Palestinian Authority television broadcasts, including children's programming that featured little girls singing of wanting to become suicide bombers in Jerusalem. Netanyahu could have built upon Congressional support to continue to counter pressures on him and keep the administration at bay and to buttress his demands for Palestinian compliance and reciprocity.

Awareness in the United States of PA incitement, including through children's television, was increasing among the general public as well as in government circles as a result of some, albeit limited, media coverage. A story in the *Philadelphia Inquirer* in September, 1997, reported the following PA broadcast segment: "A schoolgirl, perhaps 8 years old and all nervous giggles, stands before a television camera and sings in a squeaky voice: 'I am a daughter of Palestine . . . Koran in my right hand, in my left — a knife.' A slightly older girl with her ponytail wrapped in a checkered kaffiyeh gives an emotional recitation of a poem for Palestinian leader Yasser Arafat: 'I am finished practicing on the submachine gun of return . . . We swear to take vengeful blood from our enemies for our killed and wounded. We will board a bustling boat which will take us to Jaffa [an Israeli city].' The girl approaches Arafat, who plants congratulatory kisses on her cheeks."[22] Netanyahu could have cited such stories in the American media to bolster further his insistence on an end to Palestinian Authority incitement and other violations of Oslo as a precondition to further Israeli concessions such as additional withdrawals.

But he failed in both the domestic and American arenas to utilize effectively the resources available to him. Domestically the pressures for more unilateral Israeli concessions persisted unchecked. With the United States, Netanyahu simply yielded and acceded in October, 1998, to attending a summit with Arafat and Clinton at Wye Plantation in order to hammer out a redeployment agreement that was obviously to be based on the American proposals of Israel ceding an additional 13 percent of the West Bank.

Netanyahu may have anticipated that the summit would end in deadlock and collapse. But with the president's prestige on the line, the prime minister was clearly placing himself in a difficult position of potentially having to reject presidential proposals and thereby to incur even greater Administration wrath, or capitulating. In the event, he capitulated, and in doing so not only failed to make effective use of congressional backing but undercut those in Congress who most firmly supported him and had most vociferously argued, with Netanyahu, that a withdrawal of the dimensions prescribed by the administration, at least under current circumstances, posed too great a threat to Israel.

WYE RIVER AND AFTER

The Wye River Memorandum, signed on October 23, 1998, indeed called for Israeli transfer of 13 percent of the West Bank to Palestinian administration (that is, transfer of territory until then in Area C to either Area A or Area B status). It also mandated transfer of 14.2 percent of West Bank land from Area B to Area A status, from partial to full Palestinian control. The Memorandum also referred once more to "reciprocal responsibilities" and enumerated yet again the security-related obligations the Palestinians were to fulfill, including "outlawing and combatting terrorist organizations," "prohibiting illegal weapons," and "preventing incitement." But such reiterations had obviously become hollow. The same can be said of Wye's stipulations that the Palestinians provide Israel a list of its policemen, yet another repetition of a prior commitment never fulfilled. Likewise hollow was Wye's spelling out of steps the PA was to take to revise at last the PLO charter.

The only potentially significant innovations of the Wye agreement in relation to old and as yet unfulfilled Palestinian commitments were the establishment of bilateral, American-Palestinian, and trilateral, U.S.-Palestinian-Israeli, committees to monitor Palestinian compliance. The first were to scrutinize the actions taken by the PA to dismantle terrorist cells and the infrastructures of the terrorist organizations and to review prosecution and punishment of those involved in anti-Israel violence and terror. The trilateral committees were to deal with the smuggling and possession of unauthorized weapons and explosives and to monitor and address PA incitement. The PA also agreed in the Wye Memorandum to issue a decree against incitement and establish a mechanism for rendering the decree comparable to Israeli laws on the subject. These various committees, with their American complement, were obviously created at Israel's behest and reflected Netanyahu's efforts to put teeth into calls for Palestinian compliance, particularly regarding security matters and incitement.

The issue of PA incitement, while remaining largely ignored by Israeli media and, of course, American media, was receiving increased attention in the United States not only in Congress but also among some mainstream Jewish groups, and this likely also figured in the administration's willingness to give the subject more attention at Wye. An example of greater American Jewish monitoring of PA incitement was the report published by the Anti-Defamation League in October, 1998, the month of the Wye Agreement, entitled "Anti-Semitism in the Palestinian Authority: Fall 1997–Fall, 1998." The report cited numerous anti-Semitic statements and claims made in official PA media.

Perhaps Netanyahu entertained genuine hopes for the efficacy of the new bilateral and trilateral committees and did not regard them merely as something to show to his constituents as proof that Wye had not simply been an exercise in Israeli capitulation. He seems to have harbored at least some such positive expectations. But there were reasons to be less than sanguine.

An American staff consisting of people with backgrounds in dealing with terrorism — the American representatives to the relevant committee were drawn from the CIA — could well help monitor PA steps vis-à-vis the terrorist organizations, and even help gauge the PA's own involvement with terrorism, and could push Arafat toward compliance with relevant Oslo commitments. But the CIA, as an arm of the American government, could also be expected to bend its activities to the will of the U.S. Administration, to accommodate Clinton's eagerness to see the "process" move forward untrammeled by too many embarrassing revelations about or confrontations with Arafat's regime. It could be expected to follow the course of the State Department in reporting to Congress on the PA's compliance with its Oslo and other obligations as a prerequisite to Congressional approval of additional U.S. funds for Arafat. The State Department routinely whitewashed the Palestinian regime's incitement to and involvement in anti-Israel violence as well as its iron-fisted, corrupt, and largely lawless style of governance. Expectations that the American involvement would adequately address Israel's concerns about Palestinian noncompliance on security matters should have been slim indeed.

American participation in the trilateral committee on incitement — where each party was to be represented by a media specialist, a law enforcement representative, an education specialist, and a current or former elected official — could likewise potentially have had some salutary impact. In fact, the American representatives emerged from early committee meetings genuinely shocked and outraged by the defamation of Israelis and Jews, delegimitization of Israel, encomiums to terror and martyrdom, and calls to Jihad that they discovered to be permeating Palestinian school texts and media. But the Palestinians stonewalled, manufactured excuses and "explanations" and refused to undertake changes, and the United States backed down, ultimately allowing the committee to lapse rather than confront Arafat and aggressively push for changes. (Israel's election to power in 1999 of another Labor-led coalition, under Ehud Barak, a government once again, like the Clinton Administration, less interested in Palestinian compliance than in advancing the "process," contributed to the lapsing of the committee on incitement, or at least enabled the administration to allow its demise without any significant opposition.)

The Israeli government ratified the Wye Memorandum on November 11, subject to a number of stipulations: that the Palestinian National Council repeal sections of the PLO Covenant calling for Israel's annihilation; that the third and last redeployment under the Interim Agreement — a redeployment not covered by Wye — not exceed 1 percent of West Bank land; that the PA rearrest thirty terrorists it had previously incarcerated and then released from jail; that Israel retain the right to annex West Bank land if the PA were to declare a state unilaterally (as it was threatening to do by May 4, 1999); and that Israel's obligations under Wye would be suspended if the PA failed to comply with its commitments. Those stipulations relating to Palestinian compliance and reciprocity had, of course, no more enforcement teeth to them than did the various Oslo documents in which the Palestinians had solemnly pledged themselves to their obligations or those documents which explicitly referred to the necessity of reciprocity.

Netanyahu's acceptance of the Wye Agreement alienated various elements of his coalition. These included not only those who were inclined to offer no additional territorial concessions under any circumstances, a small minority, but also people who were prepared for some additional land transfers but not without a turnaround in the PA's wholesale violation of its commitments and particularly its ongoing involvement in incitement and violations of security obligations. In December, a number of erstwhile supporters and members of the government joined with the opposition to vote for early elections.

Some who were opposed to Oslo and saw it as exposing the state to intolerable dangers argued to like-minded colleagues that, whatever their anger and frustration with Netanyahu, support for new elections, with the possibility of a Labor-Meretz victory, was self-defeating and likely to speed Oslo concessions. But others countered that Israel was presently in the worst possible position. It was making the concessions that the Labor-Meretz opposition would make and yet receiving only opprobrium from the opposition and — in large part because of Labor and Meretz's stance — from the world at large, which continued to cast the government as an obstacle to peace no matter what Netanyahu did. Moreover, many on the Right were convinced that — given Arafat's warmongering in the Palestinian media and schools, smuggling in of arms and expansion of his "police force," and general preparation of his people for confrontation and war, and his obvious lack of interest in genuine reconciliation — war was inevitable; and they believed it would be better if it were to come on Labor's watch, when the country might be united in response. They anticipated that if war were to break out when the Right was in power, the Peace Movement and its allies in the opposition, whatever the circumstances of the explosion, would put the onus on the government and dangerously divide the nation.

In January, 1999, the Knesset, by a large majority, voted to set elections for May 17, seventeen months early.

Throughout his months of governance, Netanyahu, for all his awareness of the terrible strategic risks posed by Oslo, proved unable to ameliorate even the most egregious problems of the Oslo process. He also failed to shape a new direction vis-à-vis Syria. On the contrary, he largely followed his immediate predecessors' policies, seeking to reach accommodation with Syria based on Israel's essentially ceding the entire Golan Heights. Like them, he did not appreciate the nature and depth of Assad's opposition to a formal peace with Israel even if that peace would win him back the Golan. Netanyahu also followed his Labor predecessors in allowing Syria — for the sake of keeping illusory possibilities of an agreement "alive" — to continue to prosecute its proxy war against Israeli forces in Lebanon at no cost.

Consequently, Israelis continued to be killed while assaults on Israeli forces, and even rocket attacks on northern Israel, were answered by, at most, essentially ineffectual air strikes and artillery bombardments of presumed Hezbollah positions. Occasionally, emplacements of other militant groups, such as Syrian-sponsored rejectionist Palestinian forces, were also targeted. In the thirty-five months from Netanyahu's formation of his government until his electoral defeat by Labor's Ehud Barak in May, 1999, seventy-eight Israelis died in Lebanon and hundreds more were wounded.

It is hardly clear why Netanyahu, given his awareness of the grave dangers that withdrawal from the Golan would pose to Israel, nevertheless was prepared to cede that area. There are some indications that he saw loss of the Golan as a lesser danger than wholesale retreat in the West Bank and imagined an agreement with Assad would relieve the pressure he was under vis-à-vis the Palestinians and potentially improve the contours of a territorial resolution in the West Bank. But for him to anticipate that Golan concessions would buy him gains in terms of world or even American or leftist Israeli pressures in negotiations with Arafat would obviously have been self-deluding. In any case, either ceding of the Golan or loss of strategic positions in the West Bank would pose grave threats to Israel's survival and well-being. To yield in one sphere to gain in the other, even if those gains were to be had, would still have been extremely dangerous, a road that one could anticipate would inevitably end in disaster.

SIXTEEN

Ehud Barak and Oslo's Collapse: End of a Fantasy

Let us all look at it together . . . A drawing of Palestine. It is so beautiful. There is Acre, Haifa, Jaffa, Tiberias [all Israeli cities] . . . You can see how pretty our land is, how very pretty it is. And to all of our loved ones, who are on the map, whether they are from Acre, Haifa, Jaffa, or Nazareth . . . we bid everyone a welcome.

Children's show on Palestinian Authority television, September, 2000[1]

[Arafat still] doesn't accept the legitimacy [of Israel].

Shlomo Ben-Ami, Israeli foreign minister under Barak

NEGOTIATIONS UNDER BARAK

Ehud Barak, who had been chosen to lead the Labor Party in the wake of Shimon Peres' 1996 loss to Netanyahu, was a former chief of staff of the IDF and Israel's most decorated soldier. Despite the policies pursued by his party over the preceding seven years, Barak was able to project in the election campaign an image much like that of Rabin before the 1992 balloting, as a no-nonsense, clear-thinking and tough-minded soldier who would take no step that would compromise the nation's security.

Indeed, among reporters, columnists and other writers who covered strategic and military issues, the common wisdom was that the territorial compromise that Barak would be prepared to negotiate as part of a final status agreement with the Palestinians would be not very different from that to which Netanyahu was believed to have aspired. It would entail Israel's retaining the Jordan Valley and other key strategic areas and transferring to the Palestinians a total of some 60 to 70 percent of the West Bank. That is, Israel would cede an additional 20 to 30 percent beyond the territories that would be within areas A and B after completion of the withdrawals specified in the Wye Memorandum.

On other military-strategic fronts, Barak promised in his election campaign to withdraw all Israeli forces from Lebanon within a year of his election. He also pledged to seek aggressively to do so in the context of a peace agreement with Syria that would entail a formal peace as well with Lebanon, whose policies were, of course, essentially dictated by Syria. With regard to how much of the Golan he would offer Syria, Barak's statements during the campaign were ambiguous. But he clearly sought to convey that he would be more security-conscious and less forthcoming than Netanyahu had been in his backdoor negotiations with Assad.

At the time of Barak's accession to the premiership, Israel had carried out the first of the three withdrawals specified in the Wye Memorandum as constituting redeployments one and two of the three redeployments prescribed by the Interim Agreement (Oslo II). Israel had, in that first withdrawal, ceded 2 percent of area C, of the total of 13 percent to be transferred from area C over the three withdrawals detailed in the Wye Memorandum.

Barak, in the months after coming to power, indicated that he would prefer to skip over the remaining interim withdrawals, both those specified by Wye and the third redeployment prescribed by the Interim Agreement and whose contours were yet to be defined, and move directly to a final status accord. He argued that each previous interim transfer had entailed much dispute and wrangling and had generated additional ill feeling. Advancing immediately to negotiation of a final status agreement would potentially serve to avoid protracting this pattern of negative interactions and its corrosive effects on relations between the parties. Barak offered, as compensation for the Palestinians' foregoing of the interim transfers, to accelerate the timetable for achieving a final status accord.

If Israel was going to be pushing ahead with the Oslo process despite the Palestinians' noncompliance with their obligations under earlier agreements, Barak's pursuing a comprehensive accord had a certain logic to it. The Oslo model of interim agreements and interim withdrawals was predicated on the assumption that a gradualist, step-by-step process would allow for the building of mutual trust as a foundation for further accords and concessions. More particularly, it would allow Israel to test Palestinian intentions and compliance before she ceded additional lands. (This was the articulated rationale. To the true believers within Israel's leadership, the process of step-wise accords was intended more to get Israelis acclimated and reconciled to the dramatic concessions these leaders intended to offer the Palestinians, concessions far beyond the prevailing national consensus.) But the approach of interim accords had thus far hardly built trust or established a more substantive foundation for peace. Israel was simply squandering assets that it could use in final status talks, a circumstance that, in fact, made it ever less likely Israel could negotiate a final status agreement that met its vital, existential needs. (At least this was the view of those within the government whose perspective was more measured. To Beilin and his like-minded associates, the issue of weakening Israel's negotiating position was of little concern, as they were interested in returning in any case virtually to the pre-1967 lines and were convinced that peace would then inexorably prevail.)

The Palestinians, however, wanted to have as much territory as possible in hand before the sides advanced toward a final status accord. This would have been true in any case, for just as the interim transfers weakened Israel's negotiating position they strengthened Arafat's. But having prior control of maximum territory was even more important for Arafat as — from all the available evidence — he was unprepared to sign away the option of future Palestinian demands on Israel and so had no intention of concluding a final status agreement.

Of course, even if Arafat signed a comprehensive accord, he would not definitively be foreswearing the option of future additional claims against Israel. Indeed, as already noted, Arafat's career was marked by a trail of solemnly sworn agreements, most with fellow Arab leaders, which he subsequently broke. But he had built his career on demanding the annihilation of Israel, was still educating his youth to that goal, was also conveying it to his entire constituency through his media and speeches, and repeatedly insisted that Oslo was only phase one of his Plan of Phases. He was, by most evidence, unprepared to give even the appearance of "betraying" the Palestinian national program, the program he had cultivated, by signing a document that declared itself a final settling of all issues. There were many indications that Arafat's intention was to oversee a breakdown of the Oslo process. He was therefore even more eager to have as much land in hand as possible prior to that denouement and the acceleration of hostilities that would follow.

Barak ultimately gave in and acceded to continuing the step-by-step approach. In September, 1999, he negotiated at Sharm el-Sheikh a new timetable for the remaining withdrawals called for in the Wye Memorandum; most significantly, the transfer of 11 percent of the West Bank from full Israeli control to Palestinian jurisdiction. Israel completed these withdrawals in March, 2000.

This sequence of events — Barak's seeking to effect a change in the direction of negotiations, a shift that made vital sense from Israel's perspective, but then capitulating on the endeavor — may appear to be a continuation of the pattern discerned in Netanyahu's diplomacy. But there were crucial differences. In particular, the constant if unenforced concern with Palestinian noncompliance and the need for reciprocity that had been at the center of Netanyahu's approach to Oslo had now disappeared. It was no more an issue than it had been in the Rabin and Peres governments of 1992–1996. The focus was once again on pursuing visions of a final accord with Arafat and simply choosing to believe that peace would inexorably ensue when that imagined end point was reached, however much Arafat's incitement to war and his security violations, including tolerance of and even complicity in terror, might suggest otherwise to some.

Various observers in Israel chose to see Barak's wanting to go directly to a final status agreement as reflecting his awareness that Arafat was not a peace partner and would not agree to an accord definitively declaring all issues resolved. According to this view, Barak preferred to have the process break down before Israel made further territorial concessions. But Barak's policies over the course of his tenure as prime minister, particularly the concessions he offered at Camp David and Taba and his pursuit of an agreement based on those concessions even in the face of Arafat's balking, do not support this formulation but rather render it untenable.

With regard to Syria, Barak essentially followed the path of his three predecessors, soon making clear that he was prepared to return the entire Golan to Syrian sovereignty in exchange for "peace." He apparently did so, again like his predecessors, with the full expectation that Assad would ultimately accept Israel's offer. Once more the Israeli leadership refused to recognize that Arab adversaries might weigh the prospect of peace differently from how Israel would want them to weigh it.

(To questions about how Israel would defend itself against a subsequent surprise Syrian assault if Syria did accept return of the Golan in exchange for a peace agreement, Barak either focused on peace also benefitting Syria, precluding such a threat — a claim in line with Peace Movement rhetoric — or spoke of Israel's offsetting the loss of territory through early warning technology. The latter argument represented a grossly unrealistic expectation according to most strategic and intelligence experts. In their view, no technology could compensate for the strategic losses entailed in ceding the Golan, and Israel would inexorably be left dangerously vulnerable.)

In December, 1999, Barak began American-mediated negotiations with Syrian foreign minister Farouk al-Shara in Washington. The talks ended without a breakthrough, but over the following weeks Israel continued to pursue a Syrian agreement. The major territorial point of contention, according to news leaks, was whether Israel, in descending from the entire Golan, would withdraw only to the international border or, as Syria demanded, also leave those areas along the Sea of Galilee that Syria had seized prior to the 1967 war and that Israel had then retaken.

Even many supporters of Oslo and of return of the Golan to Syria balked at Assad's demand for more. They did so in part for pragmatic reasons, in particular because the additional territory potentially to be ceded, by extending Syrian control to the shores of the Sea of Galilee, would present critical difficulties such as compromising this key source of Israel's water supply. But there were also issues of principle. The Arabs were demanding the return of all territory taken by force of arms and yet they were in this instance insisting that Syria be given territory it had taken by force of arms prior to the 1967 war. Nevertheless Barak, with the support of most of his government, indicated a readiness for additional concessions.

Still the Syrians would not budge, even refusing to resume direct negotiations. In February, 2000, President Clinton met with Syrian President Assad in Geneva to test Assad's intention and effect what he anticipated would be a major breakthrough. In the event, Assad indicated that he was unprepared for a full peace with Israel no matter how forthcoming Barak was on ceding territory. Only in the wake of this denouement in Geneva did Barak and the Clinton Administration begin to awaken to the fact that Assad did not regard peace with Israel as worth the domestic risks it would entail, however much land on and beyond the Golan peace would bring him.

Barak's courting of Assad over the preceding months, like the steps toward Syria taken by his recent predecessors, had involved the sacrifice of both principle and pragmatism to deluded policy. This was true not only with regard to negotiations over the Golan and concurrent Israeli actions in Lebanon. Also notable in this vein was the contrast in Israeli responses to events in Syria and Austria during those months.

In Austrian elections in October, 1999, Joerg Haider's far right Freedom Party did unexpectedly well, and Barak expressed concern and called for a struggle against fascism and neo-Nazism. Four months later, when Austria's president agreed to the formation of a coalition government that would include Haider's party, Israel recalled its ambassador from Vienna.

During these same months, Syria's state-controlled media ran several stories with anti-Semitic themes. One such, in late November, regurgitated the blood libel, the claim that Jews use the blood of gentiles for their religious rituals, which was also the theme of a popular book by Syria's defense minister, Mustafa Tlas (*The Matzah of Zion*, 1984).[2] An editorial in late January in Syria's leading newspaper, *Tishreen*, a mouthpiece for the Assad regime, focused on denial of the Holocaust while insisting that Israeli policies are worse than those of the Nazis.[3]

By any measure, Arab anti-Semitism is a much greater threat to Israel, and to Jews generally, than the Freedom Party in Austria. Yet Barak remained silent on the Syrian libels. His most notable comments regarding the Syrian government during this period was his characterization of Assad as "a courageous leader" (November 9, 1999).

As one Israeli columnist, contrasting Barak's responses to events in Austria and in Syria, observed: "[Barak] is afraid of reminding the Israeli public about the nature of the regime to which he proposes yielding the strategic Golan Heights in exchange for a peace likely to be as trustworthy as *Tishreen's* sense of history."[4]

The writer goes on to suggest that to be silent with regard to Syrian anti-Semitism for the sake of a deal to surrender the Golan just makes Israel's Syrian gambit all the more untethered from rational policy. The author could, of course, have said much the same of Israel's pursuit of a deal with Arafat and its silence regarding anti-Semitism in official Palestinian Authority media.

The collapse of the Syrian track still left Barak with having to address his campaign promise of an IDF withdrawal from Lebanon within a year, a withdrawal that now was clearly not going to come about in the context of Barak's preferred scenario, a peace agreement with Assad. Major left-wing constituencies continued to demand an Israeli pullout whatever the status of negotiations. In contrast, the predominant opinion on the Right was that unilateral withdrawal would be a prescription for disaster. In this view, the IDF's presence in the security zone, while having entailed a cost in the lives of military personnel, had worked to protect Israel's civilian population in the north, where terrorist raids in the years before 1982 had taken a high toll of Israelis.

Voices on the Right, and indeed some on the Left, argued that a unilateral pullout would not end the violence, as others maintained, but rather would bring Hezbollah and its allies to Israel's northern border and again render the civilian population of the north vulnerable to attack. They noted that Hezbollah's leaders openly declared their intention to prosecute their campaign to destroy Israel and "liberate" Jerusalem. They also pointed out that, in view of the level of Hezbollah armament, future attacks on the north after withdrawal could be on a much wider and more intense scale than anything experienced before. Moreover, unilateral Israeli withdrawal would be seen by the Arab world and its allies as a Hezbollah victory, an Israeli retreat in the face of force, and would invite more, not less, aggression. Some also observed that the Israeli military toll in Lebanon could well be reduced if Israel stopped allowing Syria to run its proxy war against the IDF cost-free.

But in the months after Barak's election, a number of voices on the Right also began to support unilateral withdrawal. This came about because Barak was clearly bent on using the public's eagerness for extrication from Lebanon as a lever to increase public support for ceding the Golan to Syria. Since the post-1992 Rabin administration, there had been a commitment from Israeli governments to submit any agreement with Syria to a referendum. Polls showed that most Israelis still viewed giving up the Golan as too dangerous, too great a threat to the country's survival. But it was widely believed that if the government presented the public with a negotiated "peace" accord that entailed full withdrawal from the Golan, another *fait accompli*, along with the threat that Israel would be seen by the world as "anti-peace" if it rejected the accord, it might well win a referendum. Many government figures also thought that a referendum victory would be even more likely if the accord was presented as providing as well a mechanism for a negotiated withdrawal in Lebanon.

Some Israelis who opposed giving up the Golan agreed with this assessment. They therefore began to favor unilateral withdrawal from Lebanon as a means of depriving Barak of use of the Lebanon situation to garner public support for ceding the Golan.

In the wake of Assad's Geneva meeting with Clinton and his blanket rejection of a deal, Barak declared that he would indeed pursue a unilateral withdrawal from Lebanon. He appears to have harbored hopes that announcing this would prompt the Syrians to reconsider their negative stance, as, he believed, the Syrians too realized that after a unilateral IDF pullout the Israeli public would have less incentive to approve any agreement with Syria that entailed giving up the Golan. However, no evidence of such a Syrian reappraisal ensued, and, in May, 2000, Israeli forces abruptly and unilaterally abandoned the security zone in southern Lebanon.

In doing so, Israel also abandoned the South Lebanese Army that it had created and supported in the security zone, and the SLA quickly disintegrated. There had been signals that Israel would continue to aid the SLA after withdrawal, but it did not sufficiently prepare the organization for going forward without an IDF presence. Barak seems to have preferred that the SLA cease to exist rather than have it carry on with Israeli backing and have the Lebanese, Hezbollah, the Syrians, and their allies claim that this support represented continued Israeli intervention in Lebanon and justified ongoing military action against Israel.

Barak was meticulous in insuring that Israel relocated all its troops and positions behind the international border. Moreover, prior to withdrawal he had obtained confirmation from third parties that the Lebanese army would enter the erstwhile security zone to prevent cross-border guerrilla/terrorist attacks on Israel. He also had declarations from the United Nations that, in keeping with the relevant Security Council resolutions (425 and 426), UN forces would monitor the border and assist Lebanon "in ensuring the return of its effective authority in the area."[5] (Some in the Israeli government had absolute faith in Lebanese and United Nations intentions. Yossi Beilin, in particular, asserted that Israel need not worry, that the Lebanese army and UN forces would indeed move into the abandoned security zone and guarantee its pacification.[6])

In the wake of the pullout, the UN certified that Israel had indeed withdrawn to behind the international border. This step was to trigger the promised pacification intervention. But Hezbollah quickly entered the abandoned security zone in force. The UN, in turn, increased its presence only temporarily. It did not confront the Hezbollah cadres but rather allowed them to occupy those fortified installations near the border that Israel had left intact because the UN had agreed to take possession of them and use them for their promised monitoring force. The Lebanese army likewise did not fulfill its commitments.

The aftermath of the withdrawal was therefore the presence of Hezbollah in force on Israel's northern border, as the skeptics had anticipated. In addition, Hezbollah soon received hundreds of more advanced and longer range missiles and other improved weaponry from Iran and deployed them along the border. Relative quiet, punctured by occasional cross-border attacks and shelling by Hezbollah, has prevailed in the Israeli north since the withdrawal, but northern Israel, down to Haifa and beyond, now lives under the threat of potentially devastating missile bombardment. Once again an Israeli government had rendered the country more vulnerable, and in the process of doing so had abandoned friends, for the sake of imagined, illusory gains vis-à-vis placating the nation's enemies.

The skeptics were also right in another regard: The withdrawal was perceived by the Arab world and its allies as a victory of Hezbollah over the vaunted Israeli army. Moreover, voices among the Palestinians, including in the PA media and within the leadership, quickly began to argue that if Hezbollah could force the Israelis back so could they and that the PA ought to abandon negotiations for a military campaign emulating Hezbollah's.

Arafat had always regarded violent confrontation as a necessary tack for gaining his ultimate objectives. Now, among those around him and within the Palestinian population more generally, events in Lebanon had rendered the prospect of such confrontation more attractive and promising.

CAMP DAVID AND BEYOND

With collapse of the Syrian track in February, 2000, and Israel's completion of the last of the Wye redeployments the following month, attention had turned to what would come next in the "peace process" with the Palestinians. Arafat demanded a large Israeli withdrawal in the third redeployment prescribed by the Interim Agreement and threatened unilateral declaration of a state if his demands were not met. The Israelis reiterated that they had the right to determine the extent of an additional withdrawal and alluded to old Israeli threats to annex territory still under Israel's control if Arafat proclaimed a state unilaterally.

Amid this sparring, Barak again floated the idea of moving directly to final status negotiations, and reports surfaced in the media of secret talks between the parties in which the Israelis indicated the extent of the territorial concessions they were prepared to make as part of a final agreement. Those concessions, according to the reports, encompassed more and more territory as the weeks passed and soon far exceeded what any of the military commentators thought feasible from a strategic perspective, even in the context of a genuine peace. However, the fact that Yossi Beilin, Justice Minister in the Barak government, was one of the Israelis allegedly engaged in these talks lent credence to media claims of wholesale territorial concessions, as such a negotiating stance seemed to conform to the territorial offers Beilin had apparently made to the Palestinians during the previous Labor-Meretz government.[7] News leaks triggered rising anticipation of the country again being presented with a Labor-Meretz *fait accompli.*

These reports of secret talks were surfacing against a background of information that one might have thought would have given the government pause in its proffering of additional concessions. Intelligence assessments provided to Barak in the preceding months informed him that the intensity of Palestinian incitement was increasing and was having an impact in stoking anti-Israel sentiment not only in the territories but also among Israeli Arabs and throughout the Arab states. Moreover, intelligence reports spoke of seeing this sentiment already being translated into increased violence in the territories and within Israel. Barak chose essentially to ignore the import of these assessments, remain silent on the incitement, and press on for an agreement.[8]

In March, 2000, the Foreign Ministry did issue a bulletin expressing concern over increased anti-Israel "incitement, hostility and demonization," much of it with anti-Semitic content, emanating from official state media in the Arab world, including official Egyptian media.[9] But the government did not consistently press its concerns, nor did it amend policy in response to this dangerous development.

Also in 2000, media monitoring organizations such as Middle East Media Research Institute and Palestinian Media Watch reported on anti-Semitism and delegitimization of Israel not only in Palestinian media and in statements by PA officials but also in the new curriculum and textbooks introduced by the Palestinian Authority for the 2000–2001 school year. For example, Jews are mentioned in the new texts almost exclusively in negative, derogatory terms, and maps consistently omit Israel, depicting all of the land between the Jordan and the Mediterranean as "Palestine." But this latest chapter of the campaign waged in Palestinian classrooms against Israel and the Jews had no impact on the government's pattern of ignoring Palestinian incitement and violence and pushing ahead with offers of concessions in exchange for "peace."

Despite Barak's blandishments, however, Arafat, according to media reports, was balking at concluding a final status agreement. Some argued he was holding out for yet more concessions; and various Israelis aligned with the Peace Movement, including members of the government, urged Barak to provide those concessions. But as Arafat made clear in speeches to his own constituency and the wider Arab world and in his actions, he was not interested in signing any final accord.

Arafat's preferred scenario seemed to be, rather, to declare a state unilaterally, however Israel might respond (and he likely did not believe that a Labor-Meretz government would annex the territories remaining under its control or take any strong measures against the Palestinian Authority). The scenario entailed winning the support of the world, in particular the Europeans, for his state and his claim to all the territories still in Israeli hands. Arafat would then seek to leverage that support to force an Israeli withdrawal and achieve his state in all of the West Bank and Gaza without Israeli approval, without conceding to Israel a final resolution of the conflict, and without precluding, even on paper, his pursuit of additional claims. The major inhibiting factors to his pushing forward with unilateral declaration of a state appeared to be American pressure not to do so and indications from the Europeans that they would not support such a step in the face of American opposition.

Seeing Arafat continuing to balk despite all his blandishments, and expecting that sufficient pressure from Clinton would change Arafat's stance, Barak began to urge on Clinton a three-way summit to conclude a final settlement. But Arafat's regime released repeated statements to the effect that there had been insufficient preparation for such a meeting and conditions were not yet ripe, and the American administration initially seemed unenthusiastic about the proposal given the Palestinians' obvious coolness. The president was reluctant to put his prestige on the line in an exercise that was so uncertain of success.

But Barak continued to push the plan. More importantly, Clinton faced the deadline of only another few months in office and was eager to have a final Israeli-Palestinian agreement as the jewel of his foreign policy legacy. He was apparently impervious to the inevitable fragility of any accord that might emerge and the likelihood of its being a prelude to future disaster. Clinton ultimately arranged for a summit with Barak and Arafat at Camp David starting July 11, 2000, for the purpose of hammering out a final status agreement.

As additional leaks emerged of what Barak was offering Arafat in pre-summit meetings, elements of Barak's coalition began to abandon the government. But the summit was to take place during the Knesset's summer recess and there was no decisive move to bring the government down prior to the recess or, subsequently, to recall the Knesset for that purpose.

The rapidly declining support at home for his government, and in particular the very meager public backing for the wholesale concessions he was evidently prepared to make, did not inhibit Barak. He went to Camp David and put on the table, according to what could be gleaned from media reports (there was no official revelation of the proposed Israeli concessions), the transfer of about 95 percent of the West Bank, as well as all of Gaza, to Palestinian sovereignty. This included the Jordan Valley and other territory long deemed vital to Israel's security and survival, as well as parts of Jerusalem, among them sections of the Old City and perhaps even the Temple Mount. The offer envisioned Israel retaining major settlement blocks by annexing the remaining 5 percent of the West Bank, but proposed transferring to the Palestinians some pre-1967 Israeli territory as compensation for that 5 percent.

The summit continued for seventeen days. But, despite the dimensions of the Israeli offer and intense pressure from President Clinton, Arafat demurred. He apparently was indeed unwilling, no matter what the Israeli concessions, to sign an agreement that declared itself final and foreswore any further Palestinian claims.

In addition, Arafat demanded at the summit that Israel accede to the Palestinians' so-called right of return, the claimed "right" of all Palestinian refugees from the 1947–48 war and their descendants not only to move to the nascent Palestinian state in ceded territories but to "return" to "homes" within Israel's pre-1967 lines. This is, of course, a claim to the right to dismantle Israel. While the Palestinians had raised this issue throughout the Oslo years, their Israeli interlocutors, consistent with their embrace of other distorted visions of reality commensurate with their wishes, had chosen to construe such demands as not serious. They had chosen to see them as simply a *pro forma* stance that would be abandoned by Arafat once Israel, via sufficient concessions, had demonstrated its fairness and goodwill and eagerness for peace. Even the Palestinian Authority's repeated declarations, from the time of its initial establishment, that it would do nothing to improve the housing conditions of the refugees because they would be "returning" to homes in Israel, and the PA's indeed taking no step to ameliorate housing in the refugee camps,[10] failed to dent the Israelis' wishful thinking.

But the Israeli negotiators at Camp David were soon proven wrong; the Palestinian demand for the "right of return" was not abandoned. Israel apparently responded by offering to take in tens of thousands of 1948 refugees and their descendants. But this did not satisfy Arafat, and the issue of the "right of return" and its supposed sanctity were given extensive play by the Palestinians in the wake of the breakdown of the Camp David summit and in the subsequent Taba talks.[11]

But if Arafat's rejection of Barak's offers and Clinton's urgings left his long-term strategy still intact, Arafat also faced difficulties after Camp David. His preferred scenario, again, was to be in a position to declare a state unilaterally in the face of supposed Israeli intransigence and to win extensive international recognition and support, particularly in Europe and perhaps from the United States as well, including support for his claims to territories still under Israeli control. But most of the European states followed Clinton in seeing the Israeli offers as very forthcoming and placing the onus for the summit's failure on Arafat, and he was as far as ever from having European or American support for unilateral action. Nor did his regime's post-Camp David complaints regarding Israel's not recognizing the Palestinian refugees' "right of return" win over the Europeans or Americans.

According to various sources, including members of his government, Arafat quickly embarked after Camp David on plans for initiating confrontations with the Israelis.[12] These were to involve both mass "demonstrations" — that is, marches against Israeli emplacements, mainly by Palestinian youth — and armed attacks by his numerous militias and security services entailing a shooting component to the mass demonstrations as well as other assaults against the Israelis. The apparent aims of the policy were manifold. They included potentially forcing Israel to withdraw from some strategic positions and perhaps even to abandon one or more vulnerable settlements, and potentially extracting from the Israelis additional concessions as well. The objective of the "demonstrations" was seemingly also to push the Israelis to retaliation that would cause casualties among the Palestinian youth taking part, an eventuality that would be virtually inevitable with Palestinian shooters placed among the demonstrators and certain to draw return fire. Such casualties, it was anticipated, would win back world sympathy lost in the wake of Camp David. This could translate into support for the unilateral declaration of a state, or at least for an international presence on the ground that would likewise serve Arafat's aim of extrusion of the Israelis without a conflict-ending agreement.

Those who monitored Palestinian Authority media through the summer of 2000 saw signs of preparation for war even before and during the Camp David talks. Palestinian Media Watch, in a report released on August 3, 2000, cited statements by Palestinian officials to the effect that agreement to anything short of maximal Palestinian demands would be a betrayal of the national cause. In addition, "along with the calls not to compromise, threats of violence continued at an unprecedented pace, creating an eve of war atmosphere . . . Palestinian TV contributed to [this] atmosphere, by its repeated broadcast of military parades [and] video clips of violence against Israeli soldiers."[13]

There were other indications as well during the summer that the Palestinian Authority was gearing up for war. Media reports in July, 2000, told of Palestinian forces shifting to a war footing. On the instructions of the Palestinian ministry of supplies, wholesalers greatly increased purchase orders for key commodities, and soon the public began stockpiling basic products. Preparations also extended to emergency services, in anticipation of war casualties.[14]

Arafat used a September, 2000, visit to the Temple Mount by Ariel Sharon (who had replaced Netanyahu as head of Likud after Netanyahu's 1999 election defeat) as the occasion to unleash his campaign of violence. News stories that Barak had offered Arafat control of the Temple Mount in their Camp David negotiations had triggered a firestorm in Israel, with the public overwhelmingly condemning such a move, and Sharon's visit was no doubt intended in part to assert Israel's claim to the Mount. But it was portrayed by Arafat and his colleagues as more than that, as a desecration of Islamic holy sites. The ensuing violence was cast as Israel's fault, as having followed inexorably from Sharon's trespass.

Much of the media, both in Israel and abroad, not surprisingly parroted this slant, labeling Sharon the cause of the violence and claiming such absurdities as his having entered Islamic shrines on the Mount or his having violated long-standing prohibitions against Israelis visiting the Mount. (In fact, Sharon had not gone into either the Dome of the Rock or the Al-Aqsa Mosque. In addition, since 1967 the Mount had been open to all people, including Israelis, and was frequently visited by Israelis, among them Israeli politicians.) These distortions, and the blaming of Sharon for the violence that followed his visit, continued in the world media even after Palestinian leaders acknowledged that the violence had been planned in advance and that Sharon's visit was not its cause.

(For example, in March, 2001, Palestinian Authority Communications Minister Imad Al-Faluji stated in a speech in Lebanon: "Whoever thinks that the Intifada broke out because of the despised Sharon's visit to the Al-Aqsa Mosque, is wrong . . . This Intifada was planned in advance . . . "[15] Arafat advisor Mamdouh Nofal offered similar testimony around the same time. Nofal, in an interview with the French weekly *Le Nouvel Observateur*, reported: "A few days before Sharon's visit to the Mosque, when Yasser Arafat demanded that we be ready to go into battle, I pleaded . . . against the use of arms. . . . Jibril Rajoub . . . also tried to warn Arafat against the danger of a military confrontation. In vain."[16])

The violent demonstrations accompanied by shooting at Israeli forces from the crowds and sniper fire from fixed positions, the explosives and sniper attacks elsewhere against Israelis, and Arafat's release of imprisoned Hamas and Islamic Jihad operatives and his recruitment of those organizations into his campaign of violence, initially elicited from Barak the declaration of a freeze on negotiations until the assaults stopped. Barak also alluded to taking retaliatory measures if the attacks continued. They did continue, but there was no substantive retaliation and in short order Barak was again pursuing negotiations with Arafat despite the ongoing violence.

The weight of public opinion was against his conducting talks while hostilities persisted and Israelis were being killed. It also objected to his resuming negotiations in view of the fact that his government had collapsed and he had the support of less than a third of the Knesset and so had no mandate for negotiations. In addition, most Israelis were dissatisfied with Barak's Camp David concessions, which were to be the basis for new talks. But Barak apparently remained convinced that a final status agreement could yet be achieved and, in keeping with Peace Movement dogma, that, whatever the current state of affairs, peace would inevitably reign in the wake of such an agreement. He was so eager to arrive at that point that he was willing to cross all earlier red lines regarding Israel's territorial needs and claims, to take extreme strategic risks, and to do so despite the collapse of his government and the continuing murder of Israelis in hostilities initiated and choreographed by Arafat.

In November, 2000, about two months into the mini-war, the government prepared a White Paper documenting Arafat and the PA's violations of Oslo agreements and encouragement of incitement and violence, including Arafat's repeated assurances to Palestinian audiences that Oslo was merely a step in the Plan of Phases and that his goal was still the destruction of Israel. Among the allegations made in the White Paper were that the PA "has directly sponsored violence, has adopted an ambivalent attitude toward terrorism while condoning Hamas extremism, has not collected illegal firearms, has sponsored violent incitement, has conducted foreign policy in violation of interim agreement obligations, has infringed economic agreements . . . [and] has condoned large-scale criminal activities."[17]

But elements of Barak's rump government opposed release of the document and successfully lobbied to have it watered down, and the foreign ministry did not aggressively pursue its dissemination.[18] Most importantly, the material in the White Paper did not stop Barak from offering still more concessions to Arafat and insisting that if an agreement were signed peace would ensue.

In early December, 2000, it became clear the government was about to be formally brought down and, as an alternative to facing a vote of no confidence, Barak resigned. A date was set for election of a successor prime minister, with Barak serving, in effect, as head of a caretaker government in the interim. Yet even at this juncture, Barak pressed on with his Camp David path. Negotiations continued at Taba in the Sinai until about a week before the scheduled election, with Barak's representatives reportedly making yet more concessions and Arafat still refusing to conclude an agreement.

That Barak, at various points in the talks, was prepared to cede sovereignty over the Temple Mount — not just control over the Moslem religious sites, which were, of course, already in the hands of the Waqf, but sovereignty over Judaism's holiest place — brought the policies of the Israeli government, under the influence of the Peace Movement, in line in an important symbolic way with the thinking of the anti-Zionist "universalists."

The anti-Zionists, under pressure of anti-Jewish sentiment, eager to placate that sentiment by self-abnegation, and at the same time seeking to cast their capitulation as a noble tack, asserted that Jews had somehow evolved spiritually beyond needing a state of their own. They had developed to the point of comprehending and embracing a universalist sensibility and universalist vision, and a Jewish state represented regression to a lower form of national-religious existence. So, too, Barak was now asserting that no place on earth should be so precious, sacred, or meaningful to Jews as to preclude its being ceded for the sake of placating Israel's enemies. Barak's supporters in this stance insisted that to believe otherwise represented an atavistic overvaluation of the concrete, the physical, the territorial, and a retreat from the supposed spiritual essentials and higher morality that ought to be the people's focus.

In fact, there had been, even before the Camp David negotiations, governmental compromising of Israeli and Jewish interests vis-à-vis the Temple Mount, particularly under Barak. As previously noted, the Moslem Waqf, per a policy initiated by Moshe Dayan in the wake of the 1967 war, had remained official custodian of the Temple Mount, but prior to Oslo there was considerable cooperation between the Waqf and Israeli authorities. For example, any renovations undertaken by the Waqf were cleared and overseen by the Israeli Antiquities Authority, the Temple Mount being not only Judaism's holiest site but an area of premiere archaeological significance, generally considered one of the most important in the world.

Shortly after the establishment of the Palestinian Authority, Arafat replaced the Jordanian-appointed Waqf with his own appointees, and the new Waqf began to diminish cooperation with Israeli officials. The Waqf did inform Israel in 1996 of its intent to renovate a subterranean area known as Solomon's Stables to serve as a new mosque, and Israel agreed to this in return for supposed Waqf agreement to the *quid pro quo* of Israel's opening an exit to the Hasmonean tunnel that ran along the outside of the Mount's western wall. When Netanyahu opened the exit, of course, Arafat denied any such prior agreement and launched his Checkpoint War; and the Waqf virtually ended all contact and cooperation with Israel, including with the Antiquities Authority.[19]

Subsequently, the Waqf, having cleared and renovated additional subterranean areas near Solomon's Stables without any coordination with Israel, informed the Barak government of its intent to open another exit to the now enlarged mosque for safety purposes. The government acquiesced, and again the Waqf undertook construction beyond what it had mentioned to Israel. But most significantly, in December, 1999, the Waqf brought large earth-moving equipment onto the Temple Mount and, on this most sensitive of historical sites that archaeologists would excavate only with small and precise tools, began digging up tons of material and trucking them to dumps outside the Temple Mount.[20]

The Waqf's actions caused an uproar even among many nonreligious Israelis and Israelis from the ideological Left, as the excavation not only offended religious sensibilities but the sensibilities of people concerned with the historical record and the sanctity of archaeological sites. A Committee Against the Destruction of Antiquities was formed, whose members included Amos Oz and A.B. Yehoshua.

Adding to the widely shared outrage in Israel was the conviction that the Waqf's behavior represented more than simply callousness to Jewish religious as well as broader, scholarly, interest in what happens on the Temple Mount. As an editorial in the *Jerusalem Post* stated, "It is fair to assume that bulldozers were used not just out of archaeological boorishness but in a deliberate attempt to hinder the recovery of artifacts that it finds ideologically inconvenient."[21] Indeed, the Waqf spokesman, Adnan Husseini, insisted at the time, "We don't need to have contact with anyone. Every piece of stone on the Temple Mount is Islamic property."[22] The Arafat-appointed mufti of Jerusalem, Ekrima Sabri, already notorious for his violent anti-Israeli and anti-Jewish sermons, subsequently declared, "There are no historical artifacts that belong to the Jews on the Temple Mount."[23]

But the government, fearful of arousing Palestinian ire, did nothing to interfere with the Waqf's actions or even to impose some monitoring. It was pointed out that the government's policy was in violation of Israeli law, which requires that excavations and construction anywhere in the country must be done in consultation with the Antiquities Authority. Moreover, construction on sites with religious significance must be approved by representatives from the Education, Religious, and Justice ministries.[24] But Barak acted without any such consultation, and he refused to change his stance.

A year later, the Waqf embarked on more digging, and again the Barak government did nothing. In addition, in the wake of Sharon's visit to the Temple Mount in September, 2000, and Arafat's launching of his terror war, the government acquiesced to Palestinian demands that Moslems have exclusive access to the Mount and barred Jews from visiting it, and Barak subsequently rejected recommendations from the security services and petitions by others to rescind the ban.[25]

As reports leaked of the government's evolving negotiating position in the weeks and months after Camp David, a large majority of Israelis did not follow Barak and the hard-core Peace Movement enthusiasts in their willingness to extend the territorial capitulations even to the Temple Mount. As the violence persisted, with episodes perpetrated by Hamas and Islamic Jihad in collusion with Arafat but most often by Arafat's own militias and security forces, as the riots and sniper killings and bombings took an increasing toll of Israeli lives, and as Arafat refused to make any effort to rein in his forces, fewer and fewer Israelis saw Arafat as a "peace partner," or the Palestinian Authority as interested in peace; and fewer and fewer, even among former Oslo enthusiasts, continued to believe that a genuine peace could be had if only Israel made sufficient concessions.

Israelis were confronted with Arafat not only refusing to act against the violence, to tell his forces to stand down, but his seeking instead to extend the violence beyond Israel's borders, to bring the Arab states into a confrontation with Israel, indeed to widen the conflict even further by casting it as a Holy War for the defense of sacred Islamic sites. (In early September, Arafat told the Islamic Conference's Jerusalem committee that Israel was planning to destroy the Dome of the Rock and Al-Aqsa Mosque and build a Third Temple.[26]) Israelis also saw Arab media inveighing against them and arguing that Israel was ripe for attack, that Hezbollah in Lebanon had demonstrated her weakness. They witnessed mass demonstrations on the streets of Arab capitals calling for Israel's blood. They, or at least most of them, awakened to the truth that their Oslo exercise had brought them not peace but vulnerability, had led them to the brink of war on a scale they had not seen for decades. Most Israelis now recognized that the path forged by the Peace Movement had led them potentially to national disaster.

It was this public assessment that underlay Sharon's landslide victory over Barak in the February, 2001, election, by a margin unprecedented in Israel's history (63 percent to 37 percent).

Still, at the time of the election, there were those who remained invested in the delusions of the Peace Movement and of Oslo. There persisted a constituency, including people within the leadership ranks of the Labor Party and, of course, of Meretz, and among the editorial voices of Israel's Hebrew newspapers, and from the academic and cultural as well as the political and journalistic elites, who continued to insist that the Peace Movement was still right and that peace was at hand if only Israel would make sufficient concessions.

Many refused to recognize Arafat and his minions as the source of the violence, blamed Israel instead, and even shifted their indictments of Israel in tandem with Arafat's rhetoric *de jour:* First, it was Sharon's visit to the Temple Mount that was at fault for the explosion; then it was the IDF's overly harsh reaction to the "demonstrators"; next it was the "collective punishment" imposed by Israel in response to the violence; and after this it was the ongoing presence of the settlements that was the central problem. (This even though Barak had offered to remove settlers from all of Gaza and about 95 percent of the West Bank and to compensate the Palestinians for the remaining approximately 5 percent with land from pre-1967 Israel, and even though the Palestinians themselves had declared that the sides had been close to an agreement on borders.[27]) According to the Peace Movement's true believers, Arafat and the Palestinians were still extending their hand in peace if only Israel would properly reach for it.[28]

THE ACADEMIC AND CULTURAL ASSAULT, AND GOVERNMENT ACCOMMODATION, UNDER NETANYAHU AND BARAK

During the governments of Netanyahu and Barak, Israel's academic and cultural elites continued to promote a gloss on Israel's past and present and a formula for Israel's future that converged with and buttressed the rhetoric and agenda of the Peace Movement. They elaborated and purveyed through their various disciplines themes of a troubled Zionist past as defined by the New History, Zionism's problematic present, and its cure in self-reform and a post-Zionist future. Also during these years, government ministries, even under Netanyahu, persisted in efforts to translate those jaundiced interpretations of Israel's past and post-Zionist formulas for Israel's future into national policy.

The overall thrust of the Israeli media — newspapers and both government and nongovernment electronic media — continued to be cheerleading for Oslo and for the agenda of the Peace Movement and denigrating of any criticism of Oslo as atavistic, anti-peace, and bigoted. The major media also continued to serve as virtual censors, typically eschewing coverage of violations of Oslo by Arafat and the Palestinian Authority. Stories that received scant coverage included security violations and the incessant incitement of Palestinian children and the population at large — through school texts, newspapers, television, and mosques — to Jew-hatred and Holy War against Israel. Israel's leading Hebrew papers, and Israeli television and radio, remained steadfast in their embrace of the delusion that peace could be had by concessions and self-reform, in their willful blindness to countervailing evidence, and in their promotion of that delusional vision. Consistent with this, the media persisted in lionizing the new historians and the promoters of post-Zionism and in supporting government reform in post-Zionist veins.

The Israeli literary scene also remained dominated by themes of the perniciousness of Zionism. These themes were as always swathed in much self-righteous, moralizing rhetoric, but they were fired, as was often transparently clear, by the siege and by the desperate desire to escape its threats. Leading literary figures such as Oz and Grossman continued their writing and commentary in this vein and younger writers joined in.

A poem by Nathan Zack, "A Small Song for the War Dead," (1996), conveys the poet's hostility to the state. It also conveys the obvious truth that his ire is rooted in the burden of the siege and reflects his responding to that burden by choosing to turn critical opprobrium away from the besiegers and onto the besieged. It reflects feeling trapped, in the age-old manner, by the weight of Jewish identity and accompanying Jewish victimhood, desiring to be free of that weight, and justifying this desire by indicting the besieged identity:

> *In whose throat is the grandeur of the future, . . .*
> *While she with her steel foot tramples,*
> *Each whom she finds in her way,*
> *Each who chances upon her,*
> *Each who was among her sons,*
> *How good it is that I have died, am rid of you, my homeland.*"[29]

The wishful inversion of besieged and besieger, the casting of Israel as the villain who stands in the way of peace, and in many instances the casting of the Arabs as innocent victims and heroic defiers of Israeli evil, continued also as dominant themes in the visual arts in Israel during these years. The Israeli photographer Micha Kirschner published a collection in 1997 in which, as Hazony writes: "Scores of Jewish public figures, representing all parties and points of view, are portrayed as crucified and drowned and hanged, or standing naked with machine guns, or slashing themselves with razor blades, or touched up to look like demons and ghouls and practitioners of the occult. In Kirschner's Israel, it seems that Jews have built a life of unmitigated decay, an entire nation of ruin and death. The Arabs, however, are a different story. Kirschner's Arabs (as portrayed in the same volume) are like creatures from a different universe: real human beings, crying, resisting, comforting their loved ones in the face of the scourge. A portrait of Arab member of the Knesset Hashem Mahmid shows him standing heroically against a gang of white-robed Jewish klansmen, as a large Star of David aflame behind him spells out the Jews' message of hatred and murder."[30]

In the academic sphere, works in the New History vein continued to be churned out, including new books by Benny Morris[31] and Avi Shlaim[32] in which the authors, both for the first time, offer their respective formulations of the entire history of the Zionist-Arab confrontation. Both authors repeat the major anti-Zionist and anti-Israel distortions and misrepresentations of their prior writings and extend the same biases to those earlier and later chapters of the conflict that they had not previously addressed. In both, Israel is depicted at virtually every turn as the party bearing the burden of fault. Arab misdeeds, when acknowledged, are characterized as simply reactions to Israeli provocations. Responsibility for perpetuating the conflict, and indeed for instigating it in its present form, is laid primarily at Israel's door.

In looking at more recent years, Shlaim hails the initial Oslo agreements as representing an "historic reconciliation," but argues that, due primarily to Israeli policies, the subsequent unfolding of the Oslo process was a "bitter disappointment" to the Palestinians.[33] Israeli disappointment is not addressed. Shlaim says little about Palestinian terrorism during the Oslo years and when he does mention it he typically characterizes it as a response to supposed Israeli depredations.[34] The only party he explicitly credits with playing a positive role in reaching the peace treaty with Jordan is King Hussein, and the failure to reach agreement with Syria during these years is blamed primarily on Israel.

Shlaim portrays Netanyahu as simply determined to end the Oslo process and undermine the march toward reconciliation and peace. He dismisses Netanyahu's arguments regarding Palestinian noncompliance and his insistence on reciprocity as merely excuses for sabotaging the Oslo agreements. Shlaim insists that, in contrast to Netanyahu's nefarious role both before and after the Wye memorandum, "The Palestinians scrupulously adhered to the course charted at Wye."[35] Elsewhere he declares, "If Peres was a dreamer, Benyamin Netanyahu was the destroyer of dreams."[36]

It is in his epilogue to this book that Shlaim claims Israel's founding was a "massive injustice" to the Palestinians and Israel has yet to atone for its sins.

Morris's rendering of the Oslo years is quite similar to Shlaim's. He makes greater note of Palestinian terror and acknowledges that Arafat's "unwillingness or inability to control the terrorism" was a contravention of the Oslo agreements, but he balances this by immediately adding that "Israel too violated a number of important provisions and certainly acted in a manner contrary to the spirit of the accord."[37] He, like Shlaim, writes evenhandedly of "extremists in both camps." He too lays the blame for failure to reach an agreement with Syria primarily on Israel. Morris likewise excoriates Netanyahu, dismisses his insistence on Palestinian compliance and reciprocity as dishonest and hypocritical, and portrays Netanyahu as seeking to undermine movement toward peace.

In his Conclusion, Morris reviews the failure, over the decades, to achieve peace. He ascribes it largely to Israel's refusal, in the 1950s, to be conciliatory enough, then to Israel's "territorial greed" after the 1967 war, and, in the 1970s and 1980s, to Israel's failure to match what he characterizes as the PLO's evolution toward a "conciliatory stance."[38]

Efraim Karsh, in a review of the two books, writes that Shlaim and Morris, while espousing Arab perspectives, give no voice to the Arab protagonists (a criticism made also by numerous reviewers of the authors' earlier works). They offer instead only one-sided, jaundiced interpretations of the words and actions of Israelis as gleaned almost exclusively from Israeli sources. Karsh concludes that by ignoring Arab/Palestinian sources and by "reducing Palestinian/Arab behavior to a corollary of Jewish/Israeli conduct, [Morris and Shlaim] have reaffirmed the Orientalist image of the Arabs as passive, apathetic and lacking a sense of national purpose."[39]

But, again, the political creed that underlies the theses of the new historians, and that accounts for the warm reception accorded their work within Israeli elites and by the Israeli public more broadly, is the belief, the wishful anticipation, that sufficient Israeli self-reform and concessions will inexorably win peace from the Arabs. A corollary of that faith is a comprehension of Arab behavior as indeed passive and reactive, as determined by Israeli behavior. It is a wishful choosing to believe that the endurance of the siege has been simply a reflexive Arab reaction to Israeli missteps and that sufficient Israeli self-reform cannot fail to elicit a reflexive Arab peace.

Yet another tendentious and profoundly dishonest work in the new historian and post-Zionist mode published during these years was Tom Segev's *One Palestine Complete: Jews and Arabs Under the British Mandate*, which appeared in Hebrew under a different title in 1999 and in English translation in 2000. The thrust of the work, as is typical of the genre, is jaundiced reexamination and indictment of the Jews, generally positive reassessment of their adversaries, and more particularly a bolstering of claims against the Yishuv and Israel.

Segev seeks to rebut the extensive evidence that the British administration in Palestine typically favored the Arabs and ultimately sought to prevent the emergence of the Jewish state. He argues that, on the contrary, the British primarily supported the Zionists and it was the Arabs who got treated badly. Indeed, while acknowledging that Britain never promised the Arabs control of Palestine, Segev nevertheless talks of the Mandate as "twice promised,"[40] with the British then ostensibly reneging on their pledge to the Arabs. In Segev's rewriting of the history of the Mandate, the aggrieved Arabs understandably fought back against both the biased British and the pushy Jews, and the Arab revolt ultimately led the British to give up on maintaining their presence in Palestine; but, in large part because of British favor, the Zionists emerged victorious in the ensuing struggle.

Segev advances his revisionist thesis in part through his use of "slice of life" passages, stories of supposedly representative individuals based largely on diaries and other personal papers. Much of the book is devoted to this, and the British and Arab protagonists are generally sympathetic figures or are cast in a sympathetic light while the Jews are less attractive or are thus portrayed by the author.

But the burden of Segev's thesis is conveyed by the book's more straightforward history writing, and these passages offer a peculiar legerdemain. Segev tells the reader very early that the British administrators in Palestine, from the beginning of the military administration in 1917, were in general positively predisposed toward the Jews and the Zionist project. His evidence for this claim is very thin and he omits much counterevidence. For example, he does not inform the reader of Churchill's estimation in 1921 that 90 percent of the British army in Palestine was against the Balfour Declaration or of similar observations by other British officials.[41] Segev does subsequently cite myriad examples of anti-Jewish animus on the part of British officials starting from the early years of British control; but, having declared that the British favored the Jews, he then interprets that animus as largely a reaction to Jewish pushiness and related provocations. Kinder observations regarding the Arabs by British officials are explained as a consequence of the Arabs being less irritating than the Jews.

This line of argument and the accompanying distortions are purveyed throughout the book. An illustrative instance is Segev's reference to a later statement from Churchill, dating from the 1940s, in which he observes that most British officers in Palestine were strongly pro-Arab. Segev insists that this bias was a response to Jewish "terror" and poor British morale in the face of the conflict with the Jews. But the statement by Churchill dates from 1941, well before the confrontation between the Yishuv and the British turned violent.

Segev's book is riddled with other omissions and distortions that flow from his promotion of an insupportable thesis. His claims of overarching British sympathy and favoritism toward the Zionists lead him, for example, to omit any mention of the various complaints lodged by the League of Nations against Britain for its betrayal of its mandate obligations to the Jews.[42]

A pervasive misrepresentation that follows from Segev's core thesis is his claim that the British had no coherent reason to be in Palestine. Segev musters a number of quotes by British officials questioning the wisdom of the British presence. But he omits mention of high-level documents that did formulate a coherent case for the importance of Palestine to British imperial interests.[43] Segev advances his claim in part to argue that the British were there mainly to help the Jews. But he does so more basically because to accept genuine British interest in holding onto Palestine runs counter to his thesis of Britain happily playing midwife to a Jewish state. It also opens the door to one of the major reasons why the British in fact favored the Arabs, beyond simply the anti-Jewish prejudice revealed in myriad quotes from British officials and noted as well by many other officials. British administrators believed that the Arabs were more pliable and that giving the Arabs the upper hand in local affairs would better serve the goal of perpetuating the British presence.

Segev is also interested in puffing up the Arab role in ultimately getting the British to leave and in diminishing the role of the Jews and the post-World War II struggle of the Yishuv against the British. He argues that, since the British saw no good reason for being in Palestine anyway, the Arab revolt of 1936–1939 convinced them to leave and they only delayed their departure because of the war. But, as the weight of historical documentation overwhelmingly demonstrates, British interest in staying in Palestine, always intense, grew with anticipation of the war and with the war itself and persisted after the war, not least out of a desire to defend British interests in Arab oil. Britain's postwar policies in Palestine, including its continued favoritism toward the Arabs, were propelled by its drive to perpetuate its presence. It was indeed the confrontation with the Jews that obliged Britain to abandon Palestine. Segev's contrary revisionist claim leads him to such silliness as the statement: "The Soviets, surprisingly and rather inexplicably, supported the Zionist movement [in 1947]."[44] The Soviets' support was not inexplicable at all. They wanted to pry the British out of the area and saw backing the Zionists as serving that objective.

Of course, there were some British officials in Palestine, by all evidence a distinct minority, that did favor the Zionist enterprise. But it is noteworthy that in speaking of those individuals most known for their pro-Zionist sympathies and activities, Orde Wingate and Richard Meinertzhagen, Segev disparages them. He tells us, for example, that Meinertzhagen, in his writings on Palestine, "sounds like something of a lunatic"[45] and that Wingate was described behind his back as "mad."[46] No comparable denigrations are offered of the Arabs' many partisans in the British ranks. It is as though Segev believes that anyone genuinely sympathizing with the Zionists must be crazy.

In his whitewashing of British policies toward the Yishuv, Segev further distorts the historical record by downplaying the significance of Britain's White Paper of 1939 that severely limited Jewish immigration over the ensuing years with the intent of then ending Jewish immigration altogether; this as the Jews of Europe were, of course, desperate for places of refuge. Segev assures his reader that "the White Paper's role in the Holocaust is, in the end, relatively small."[47] But in fact, just the documented record of those Jews who had access to ports that would have allowed transit to Palestine but were blocked from making their escape by British obstruction offers strong evidence that at least several hundred thousand could have been saved had the British allowed Europe's Jews admission to Palestine.[48]

Segev also uses the book to repeat those accusations against the Yishuv's leadership that he had made in his earlier work, *The Seventh Million*, to the effect that Ben-Gurion and those around him did not do enough to rescue Europe's Jews. It is inconsistent, to say the least, to insinuate that the leaders of the Yishuv, possessing no sovereign power, could have saved substantial numbers of Jews had they worked harder at it, while at the same time claiming that the anti-rescue policies of the people who did have the sovereign power in Palestine had no significant impact on the loss of life.

Segev, in addition to purveying his thesis of British favoritism toward the Jews and the consequent unfair treatment meted out to the Arabs, also more directly recasts the Arab position in a more sympathetic light. Recurrent Arab terror through the years of the Mandate is described at times in some detail, but Segev then offers rationales for it. He also insists, against much counterevidence, that it was generally spontaneous and was not supported or condoned by the Arab leadership, and he offers false equations of Arab terror with much rarer Jewish acts of terror, acts that truly were not supported by the Jewish leadership.

Segev also consistently equates the leaders of the two communities. He repeatedly points out, for example, what he sees as similarities between Ben-Gurion and the Palestinian Arab leader, Haj Amin al-Husseini, Grand Mufti of Jerusalem. In addition, his depiction of Haj Amin is generally sympathetic. He is portrayed as a reasonable and moderate man who resisted violent confrontation with the Jews and British but was forced into it by events, a portrait that offers little resemblance to the one that emerges from the extensive available documentation on him. Among other omissions, Haj Amin's activities during World War II, much of which he spent as Hitler's honored guest in Berlin, are essentially ignored by Segev. His recruitment of European Moslems for the SS, his many other pro-Nazi exertions and his praise of the Final Solution — as in his declaration of November 2, 1943, that "the Germans know how to get rid of the Jews" (the same day he received a congratulatory telegram from Himmler reminding his Arab friend that the Nazi Party had inscribed on its flag "the extermination of World Jewry") — do not fit Segev's narrative agenda. Haj Amin, who in a broadcast on Radio Berlin in March, 1944, called upon Arabs to, "Kill the Jews wherever you find them; this pleases God, history and religion," is drawn by Segev as at least Ben-Gurion's moral equal and in various respects his better.[49]

Additional elements of Segev's sympathetic recasting of the Arab situation during the Mandate include his commenting extensively on the impact of Jewish immigration on the status quo but his absolute silence on the immigration of tens of thousands of Arabs into the Mandate during these years and their impact on the political dynamics. In writing of the 1947–48 war, Segev claims that about half the Arabs who fled were expelled and he references Benny Morris[50]; but even Morris, in the book cited, suggests that expulsion accounted for a much smaller percentage of the refugees.

Segev's book is an exercise in contorted reasoning, omission of vital information, and distorted representation of other data, all in the service of indicting the Yishuv and bolstering its adversaries, with the ultimate aim being, once more, the promotion of a reformed Israel more self-effacing and more accommodating of Arab demands.[51]

The popularity of indictments of Israel inspired a cadre of New History acolytes who published extensively during these years. In keeping with the cavalier attitude toward the historical, archival record exhibited by figures such as Morris and Shlaim, if Israeli "sins" could not be found in the record one simply invented them. Thus, a masters degree in history was awarded Teddy Katz by Haifa University on the basis of a thesis in which he supposedly demonstrated that in May, 1948, the Haganah's Alexandroni Brigade massacred about 200 residents of the Arab village of Tantura. Veterans of the brigade subsequently sued Katz for libel, and Katz then retracted the claim and issued a statement that, "having looked again at the evidence, he was convinced beyond a shadow of a doubt that there was no basis to allegations that a massacre was carried out."[52]

Perhaps not surprisingly, Katz had his defenders even after his retraction. New historian Ilan Pappe, writing in the *Journal of Palestine Studies*, argued essentially that even though Katz had fabricated his massacre story, his thesis captured a higher truth of Palestinian victimhood.[53] Journalist and revisionist historian Tom Segev made much the same argument. Segev's main complaint against Katz is that his actions would delay the day when Israel accepts what he sees as its moral and political responsibility for the future of the Palestinian refugees.[54]

Of course, the fault for Katz's invented history lies not just with him but with the professors at Haifa University who taught him how to do history, who not only approved his thesis but lauded it with a grade of 97, and who granted him his degree. This is what had come to pass for academic integrity in Israeli universities. Intellectual honesty and academic integrity, like those hundreds of Israelis killed by Palestinian terrorists in the years of Oslo, became, in the pro-Oslo jargon of the time, "sacrifices for peace."

As in the preceding years, academics from other disciplines joined the assault on Israel under the guise of historical analysis, often employing the tack of using such "analysis" for an indictment, in the post-Zionist vein, of the entire concept of a Jewish state. Not infrequently, they were quite explicit in indicating that the impetus to their attack on the state was the siege and that they were prepared to support the dissolution of Israel for the sake of ending the siege.

Adi Ophir, a philosophy professor at Tel Aviv University, made critiques of Israel with a "New History" facade the centerpiece of articles published in *Theory and Criticism*, a journal that he edited for the Van Leer Institute and that was subsidized by the Education Ministry.[55] In an essay he co-authored and published in 1998, Ophir opines that Jewish "nationalist sovereignty" is the root of what he characterizes as the "Palestinian-Jewish conflict" and that the solution lay in a "state that will not be a nation-state." His proposed alternative is some variation of early visions of a binational entity, one that will be free of "the unholy coupling of nationalism and political sovereignty." In the new state, "the borders would be open and naturalization would be regulated on a universal, not national basis." But, Ophir and his co-authors inform us, "the state would need a strong police force to act against any violent attempt [of those groups within it] to undermine [its] universalistic structure."[56]

Other academics outside the history departments offered critiques of Israel similar to Ophir's. While perhaps not explicitly calling for dissolution of the state, they likewise suggested that the state as it has thus far evolved has been the cause of the siege and that a dramatic reconfiguration is the key to placating Israel's enemies.

There were still other academics who insisted during these years that Israel was responsible for perpetuating the siege and that Israeli self-reform was the key to peace but who definitely did not advocate Israel's dissolution. Their work is no less intellectually dishonest and chilling for that, however; and they probably had an impact on fellow Israelis eager to embrace delusions of peace greater than the impact of those who called for Israel's demise. A notable example is Yaron Ezrahi, another professor of political science at Hebrew University, who, in *Rubber Bullets* (1997), takes as a given that Israel has no legitimate claim on the West Bank and that its presence there is entirely "senseless" and "sinful." He acknowledges at a few points that Israel does have legitimate security concerns, but he repeatedly insists — without any attempt to support the assertion and in contradiction of the view of, for example, the framers of Security Council Resolution 242 — that the pre-1967 borders sufficiently address all of the nation's security needs. Ezrahi further takes as a given — again without evidence — that Israeli willingness to end entirely its presence in the West Bank would inexorably yield peace. Ezrahi clearly wants to believe this and so he simply assumes it.

Building on these premises, Ezrahi sets out to explain why Israelis have chosen a senseless and sinful occupation over peace. He discusses what he perceives as a clash in Israel between "nationalistic" and "liberal-democratic" conceptions of power, or, alternatively, a clash between two "Jewish world views": "one, founded on a long memory of persecution, genocide, and a bitter struggle for survival, is pessimistic, distrustful of non-Jews, and believing only in Jewish power and solidarity. The other, nourished by . . . the Enlightenment idea of progress, a deep sense of the limits of military force, and a commitment to liberal-democratic values, is . . . confident in the possibility of Arab-Israeli coexistence and a future Israel as an open and advanced society unthreatened by war."[57]

Of course, Ezrahi sees the former camp as irrationally aggressive and against peace, the latter as prepared to forego "Jewish fantasies of empire" — Ezrahi's term[58] — and grasp the peace that is readily available. But the whole formulation is based, again, on premises he is never willing to examine, such as the interest of the other side in establishing a genuine peace in exchange for territorial concessions, and the ability of the state to defend itself behind its pre-1967 lines. Ezrahi's formulation is a castle built on very loose sand indeed.

Beyond the "nationalistic" versus "liberal-democratic" and other, related, dichotomies with which Ezrahi constructs his thesis, there is an additional dichotomy that enjoys his special attention: the collective versus the individual. Ezrahi elaborates on old themes concerning the collectivist perspectives of Labor Zionism, their reinforcement by Jewish religious-national tradition, the preeminent role of those collectivist predilections in shaping the state, and the consequent slow and belated emergence of the centrality of the individual in Israeli consciousness and Israeli society. He argues that the collective focus predisposed the state to a preparedness to sacrifice the individual to state goals and so to a readiness to perpetuate the occupation and forego peace, whereas proper valuing of the individual would mitigate against such sacrifice and place a greater value on peace. According to Ezrahi, it is those Israelis who have come to appreciate the life of the individual that have led the drive to give up the territories and thereby end the siege and win peace.

An obvious rejoinder to this argument is, of course, Oslo's death toll. Indeed, of all the political and military blunders that the Israeli polity has made since its founding and that have resulted in loss of life that could have been avoided, few if any have been responsible for a more predictable and wanton casting away of lives of individual Israelis than the Oslo process and the belief that bringing into the territories Arafat and his cadres and setting them up as a neighboring government would bring peace.

But beyond this, Ezrahi's presentation of the relationship between "collectivist" versus "individualist" perspectives and peace policy is insupportable because it is again based on false assumptions. Ezrahi refers to the emergence of the "individual" in Western social-political history. But the evolution of a sense of individual identity as distinct from social-political collective identity occurred, and that sense persists, in the context of a perception of individual interests at variance with collective interests. An Israeli may decide that he is unwilling to risk his life to maintain the Israeli presence in the territories if he sees his own interests as unconnected with the collective interest as reflected in government policies that seek to maintain that presence. If, however, he agrees with the policy and its premises, if he believes that his own life and the lives of those dear to him would be endangered by allowing the territories to pass into the hands of, for example, Arafat and his associates, the distinction between "individual" and "collective" will be largely irrelevant to him vis-à-vis serving in the territories. The distinction as used by Ezrahi is predicated on his unquestioned and essentially false assumptions that the Israeli presence in the territories is illegitimate and that ending it will inexorably bring about a stable peace and save lives.

One can, of course, believe that Israeli policy is well-founded, that it is indeed necessary to protect the lives of the nation's citizens, and still not want to risk one's own life in its execution. Indeed, people have left the country because of exactly that mind-set, even if they have very often justified their doing so *post facto* by finding fault with Israeli policy. They have emulated in their actions those many Diaspora Jews who, in the face of anti-Jewish pressures from surrounding societies, sought to unburden themselves of what they experienced as the painful and potentially deadly weight of the Jewish predicament, of Jewish history, and did so by fleeing it; and Ezrahi makes clear that his championing of the "individual" is likewise very much in the tradition of such people.

Ezrahi states at several points his desire to escape Jewish history, complains that he cannot enjoy nature properly in Israel because every place in the country is too suffused with that history, and observes that he only truly finds peace and escape when he is on vacation out of the country. He speaks of his recurrent nostalgia for a childhood moment that was for him "a seductive invitation to a trip outside the Jewish-Zionist epic."[59] Ezrahi certainly does not indicate an interest in shedding his Jewishness, or his connection to Israel. But he makes clear that he is desperate to have the binding of his individuality to the Israeli/Jewish collective rendered safe, "normal," and he is willing to embrace delusions of peace through Israeli self-reform in his eagerness for that safety.

The true dynamic of Ezrahi's argument is revealed when he discusses his trepidation as his son approached induction into the army in 1991. Ezrahi states he felt obliged to convey something of his concerns to his son but was unsure what to say. He also sensed that the setting for the discussion would be significant, and he decided to take his son on a pre-induction trip to the American

West. He opened the conversation as the two of them sat beside the rim of the Grand Canyon.

Of course, that in itself is a message to his son. He is conveying that there is a huge world out there free of the Jewish-Israeli predicament and its dangers.

If Ezrahi truly felt obliged to open his heart to his son, the forthright thing for him to have done would have been to reveal his fears for his son's safety and acknowledge that there was a part of him that even wished his son would leave Israel and free himself of the risks of being there and sharing in its predicament. Instead, he turned his fears, and his anger over his son's situation, into an indictment of Israel. He argued that his son, and all Israelis, would be safe if only Israel would make enough concessions, go back to the pre-1967 borders, satisfy Arab demands. In part, as he indicates, he hoped that his son would agree and become a conscientious objector.

His son, however, would have none of it. He insisted that withdrawal would be too dangerous, and that in any case Israel had no reliable, stable partner with whom to negotiate a peace agreement involving the territories.

These were valid enough observations. But Ezrahi dismissed them as simply the thoughts of a boy not yet mature enough to break from the herd mentality of his peers and his society, not yet grown enough to cultivate his individuality as distinct from the collective.

In turning his understandable fears for his son into an indictment of Israel, in giving free and uncritical rein to his investment in the delusion that peace could be had if only his son's countrymen would see the light and reform themselves, in confounding the wish with reality, and in refusing to give an honest hearing to his son's more than reasonable rejoinders, Ezrahi not only does a disservice to Israel but does a disservice, indeed in a real sense betrays, his son.

Ezrahi's son apparently confronted contorted challenges not only from his father but also from his mother. She was likewise an Israeli academic, a professor of comparative literature, who around the same time articulated similar reality-distorting indictments of Israel but in more bizarre form. For example, Sidra Dekoven Ezrahi wrote, in *Beginning Anew: A Woman's Companion to the High Holy Days* (1997), a gloss on the story of Abraham, Sarah and Isaac, Hagar and Ishmael, which figures in the first of the Torah readings on the High Holy Days. During the preceding years, Palestinian terrorist attacks had led on various occasions to Israel imposing a closure in the territories, not allowing Palestinians to enter Israel proper — hardly an unreasonable security measure. According to Ms. Ezrahi's gloss, however: "Every time we would impose a closure on the West Bank and Gaza, we would cast Ishmael out, sealing him off hermetically from our sight and sending him to the wilderness to die of hunger and thirst . . . When Israeli Jews are finally prepared to acknowledge in the Palestinians a significantly different set of . . . competing claims to Abraham's inheritance, they will also be prepared to give up the idea of the whole that

swallows all of its parts . . . It is what may save the youngest of Abraham's progeny, that fragile child of Isaac and Ishmael called the Peace Process, from being
sacrificed, yet again, in our lifetime."[60]

The Netanyahu and Barak years also saw continuation of demands by elements of Israel's academic and cultural elites for post-Zionist revamping of the
state's institutions, including alteration of the national flag and anthem and legislative changes to de-Judaize Israel. Amos Elon, for example, argued in 1996
that Israel had to move beyond citizenship related to "history, culture, race, religion, nationality, or language," and that the process might well entail the "Law
of Return" being perceived as expendable.[61]

A key arena during these years for the interjection of post-Zionist perspectives into government policy continued to be the education ministry. The
ministry introduced during this period new textbooks reflecting the curriculum reforms of the early 1990s and their post-Zionist biases. Among the most
notable was *To Be a Citizen in Israel: A Jewish and Democratic State*, produced
by the ministry and brought into the schools in the 2000–2001 academic year
as the only approved text for the year-long citizenship course mandated for all
Jewish high schools. The book emphasizes supposed conflicts between the Jewish
and democratic foundations of the state and omits both the history and significance of Israel's Jewish roots and the historical and philosophical background
of the modern democratic nation-state.[62]

As one observer has noted, at the founding of the Jewish state "it was also
widely accepted among Jews and non-Jews alike that Israel's political institutions should be modeled on those of Britain, Western Europe, and Scandinavia,
whose national states were steeped in the history and symbolism of the national
groups that founded them."[63] But the rhetoric of *To Be a Citizen in Israel* teaches
students that the Jewish accoutrements of the state are a taint on its democratic character. The book depicts such national institutions as "Hatikvah" and the
"Law of Return" as controversial, despite the citizenry's overwhelming support
for both, and suggests to students that a recasting of the state in a post-Zionist
mold would be preferable to its present form. A section of the book focuses on
Israeli Arab grievances against the state as presently constituted and was authored
by an Israeli Arab who has supported anti-state violence by the nation's Arabs
unless Israel voluntarily sheds its Jewish identity.[64]

The education ministry also approved and introduced for the 2000–2001
academic year a number of history texts reflecting the revisionist glosses, distortions, and biases of the new historians. The academic rigor of the new texts
is suggested by such errors as the misreporting in one of the books of the founding of the PLO and promulgation of its charter as having occurred not in 1964
but in 1967. The absence of commitment to accuracy complements the text's
commitment to the delusions of the peace movement; the misdating of the PLO
charter to 1967 is consistent with the argument that the root of Arab hostility

is Israel's presence in the territories and that retreat from the territories would inexorably win peace. This particular work is a text for ninth graders entitled *The Twentieth Century*, and its author, Eyal Naveh, wrote that he hoped, "the views of the nationalist Right . . . would be shoved to the margins and relegated there forever. My book's objective is to contribute to this goal."[65]

Naveh's book was produced privately, as was another history text for ninth graders also adopted by the education ministry as meeting its new, essentially post-Zionist guidelines. A third ninth-grade history text in the same vein, entitled *A World of Changes,* was published by the ministry itself.

The ninth-grade history curriculum is devoted to the events of the twentieth century. It is particularly in this year that students are to learn about the history of Zionism and Israel, and so the revisionist, post-Zionist slant of the approved texts is all the more significant. The Shalem Center published an in-depth comparison of the education ministry's own book, *A World of Changes,* to the earlier texts used for the ninth-grade history course, and the study dramatically demonstrated how the history of Zionism, the Holocaust, and Israel had been drained of much of the crucial content formally taught.[66]

But, as Hillel Halkin has pointed out, the cumulative impact of the new texts transcends withholding from students particular information on these subjects or imparting to them the revisionist slant given to what content remains. Halkin writes: "What [students] hear and study tells them nothing of what the declaration of a Jewish state in 1948 meant to Jews in Israel and all over the world: nothing of the excitement, the tremendous emotion, the joy and the tears; nothing of the dizzying sense of a dream unbelievably come true; nothing of the fear that this dream might soon perish in yet another annihilation of Jews; nothing of its roots in history, of *all* Jewish history suddenly focused by the moment as though by a burning glass; nothing of the thoughts and feelings of the young men and women who went into battle bearing this history on their backs; nothing at all . . . What can one say of such textbooks? That they do not attempt to create in the young Israeli the slightest identification with his people or his country? That they make no connection between this country and 3,000 years of Jewish history? That they do not explain in any meaningful way why . . . the Arab claim to it is not better than the Jewish one? All of the above is true. . . . This is the real damage inflicted on the new textbooks by the 'new history' and the cultural trends it represents . . . It is a process of numbing and emotional divorce."[67]

But, of course, that is the intent of those who crafted the new curriculum and its texts. If Israelis are numbed and emotionally divorced from their history, their people, their country, then they will more readily surrender elements of all for the sake of "peace."

These years also saw continued heavy-handed suppression, during Netanyahu's tenure as well as Barak's, of dissent from pro-Oslo positions. (Even during years of Likud-dominated governments, Israel's large state bureaucracy has remained essentially in the hands of Labor-affiliated functionaries, and state policy on the bureaucratic level has continued to reflect primarily the political predilections of these operatives.)

In January, 2001, in the fourth month of Arafat-incited violence, the Labor Party demanded that "Women in Green," a grassroots organization opposed to Oslo and to Barak's concessions, be banned for sedition and for incitement against Barak. Women in Green's crime was that it had distributed bumper stickers with such slogans as "Barak is tearing out our heart."[68] At the same time, numerous groups and individuals within the Israeli Arab community were voicing their support for Palestinian actions against Israel and urging that their community join in what Arafat had labeled the "Al-Aksa Intifada," but neither Labor nor its allies were calling these voices seditious or advocating bans or indictments.

The predilection to use the criminal justice system in partisan ways had been a recurrent fixture of Labor Zionist governance, but this proclivity seems to have reached a new intensity in the context of Labor's promotion and defense of the Oslo process. Notable in this regard was the aggressive prosecutorial pursuit of Netanyahu, after he had left office, for his allegedly having used state employees for personal projects and having kept gifts received while in office that properly belonged to the state. In contrast, pursuit of Ezer Weizman, then President of Israel, for allegedly having received large payoffs to advance left-wing political goals — with the amounts involved being much larger than those entailed in the allegations against Netanyahu — was much less vigorous.

The blatant political use of prosecutorial actions prompted Alan Dershowitz, Professor of Law at Harvard, to address the matter in a letter to Haaretz in August, 2000. Dershowitz noted "Israel's long history of prosecuting, often unsuccessfully, some prominent public officials, while foregoing prosecution of others." He went on: "Even those who want to see Benjamin Netanyahu prosecuted appear to acknowledge that if the same test that was applied to Ezer Weizman were to be applied to Netanyahu, there would be no prosecution"; and he warned: "It would be discriminatory in the extreme to apply a less demanding evidentiary and prosecutorial standard for Netanyahu than has been applied to other political figures in the past . . . Any less demanding standards would reasonably raise the specter of political partisanship and discrimination."[69]

But, again, the political use of the criminal justice system by Labor loyalists only escalated during the Oslo years as the Left chose to see itself as the keeper of the path to peace and to see its opponents as against peace and therefore free game for virtually any attack that could be mounted against them.

It is also noteworthy in this regard that throughout these years, as the Left continued to smear the entire anti-Oslo Right with responsibility for Rabin's assassination, the trial of Avishai Raviv, the *agent provocateur* who had been involved in anti-Rabin incitement with the aim of discrediting the Right and had worked with Rabin's assassin, continued to be postponed. The nature of his collusion with government agencies out to discredit the Right had yet to be publicly examined.

In addition, Israel's major media, government-controlled and private, continued during these years not only to promote pro-Oslo policies but also to ignore both PA violations of Oslo commitments and Israeli critiques of Oslo. Indeed, the voices of critics of Labor and Meretz orthodoxies, whether Oslo-related or pertaining to other issues, were all but absent from major Israeli media. This bias reflected what even Meretz MK Amnon Rubinstein observed to be "a unitary choir with a collectivist taste lacking a critical polyphony" that held sway over Israeli intellectual discourse.[70]

THE INTERNAL ASSAULT AFTER SEPTEMBER 2000

Arafat's unleashing of violent confrontations and terror in September 2000, and his refusal over the ensuing months, despite intense international pressure, to call a halt to the onslaught, led many previous supporters of the Oslo process to rethink their position. Indeed, many even from the ranks of the Peace Movement finally opened their eyes to the realities that they had until then assiduously shunned and began to appreciate the dangerous delusions at the heart of Israeli embrace of the Peace Movement agenda and of Oslo.

But, as noted, there were still those true believers who remained unswayed. Among them were members of the media and of the cultural and academic elites and politicians of the pro-Oslo Left who continued to insist on the rightness of their vision of peace through Israeli self-reform and concessions and on the preparedness of the other side for reconciliation were Israel only forthcoming enough. Such people also persisted in denigrating the doubters as enemies of peace or at best plodders still stuck in old modes of thinking. If Israelis were now convinced that Arafat was not a partner for peace and that Arab hostility had not fundamentally changed, voices among the undaunted peace visionaries simply argued that those sentiments spoke ill of Israel and not of Oslo or the Peace Movement.

In November, 2000, Israeli journalist Nahum Barnea, writing in the *Seventh Eye,* a magazine published by The Israel Democracy Institute, referred to the "lynch test." This was shortly after, in one of the more gruesome acts of Palestinian violence that marked the early weeks of renewed hostilities, two Israeli reservists strayed inadvertently into Ramallah, were arrested by Palestinian police, and then were handed over to a mob that slaughtered and mutilated them. Barnea cited as failing the "lynch test" those Israeli journalists who, even in the face of this savage episode, remained uncritical, knee-jerk apologists for the Palestinians and indicters of Israel.

Barnea noted in particular *Haaretz* writers Gideon Levy, Amira Haas, and Akiva Eldar. All three writers largely devoted their energies to castigating Israel for supposed crimes against the Palestinians, ignored or rationalized Palestinian incitement and violence, and promoted radical Israeli "reform" as the path to peace. All gave preference to their accusations against Israel over factual accuracy.

Levy, a few days before the lynchings, insisted that the Palestinians were right to resort to violence because only in the face of violence had Israel ever made concessions to the Arabs. Barak's offers at Camp David — only one of many possible counter-examples to this assertion — are not even mentioned by Levy. The reason for the omission is indirectly made clear in the article; nothing counts as a concession in Levy's view unless it entails full capitulation to Arab demands, and so Israel's offer of anything less warrants Palestinian terror. "Only after the next great bloodletting will we allow them to establish a state in the 1967 borders, as is their right."[71]

Three days after the lynchings, Levy was writing in the same vein. The real obstacle to peace, he declared, was that Israel was not a peace partner. He mentioned the lynchings only to dismiss them as paling in significance beside the difficulties of the Palestinians. The standard Israeli and American view, as well as the stated claim of various Palestinian officials, was that Arafat — in not only rejecting Barak's proposals but also offering no alternative plan and instead walking away and resorting to violence — chose war. But Levy informs us that, no, Barak's proposals were not generous enough and therefore it was Israel that chose war.[72]

Akiva Eldar likewise consistently cast Israel, both before and after the lynchings, as the villain in the conflict. He, too, insisted, as in an article published in December, 2000, that Barak was not being forthcoming enough. Eldar wrote that IDF intelligence had informed Barak before Camp David of its assessment that "his generous proposals would not satisfy Arafat," and therefore, in a strange twist of logic, Eldar placed the onus for the subsequent deterioration of the situation on Barak for having gone ahead and presented the proposals anyway. Again, there is no criticism of Arafat and the Palestinians either for their rejection of Barak's offers or their resort to violence.

Amira Haas, the third *Haaretz* reporter mentioned as having failed the "lynch test," was fined for slander by an Israeli court in June, 2001, for having claimed that Jews in Hebron had kicked, spat upon, and danced around the body of a Palestinian wanted for involvement in terrorism and killed in an encounter with Israeli troops. The army and the Hebron Jewish community denied the story, and television file footage supported their version of events.[73] This was merely a particularly egregious example of what has been common practice for Israeli media ideologues of the Left: inventing "facts" to fit their anti-Israel and pro-Palestinian apologetics.

Barnea's piece on the "lynch test" was a rare instance of Israeli media self-scrutiny. But Barnea himself, an Oslo enthusiast throughout the preceding years, even when his son was killed by Palestinian terrorists operating under an Arafat green light in 1996, joined many other journalists in only partially acknowledging the problems of Oslo and the Peace Movement agenda. He and others of similar predisposition now exhibited a vacillating attitude in the face of Arafat's war. They would recognize and articulate the fatal flaws in the "peace" process after some new terrorist atrocity or other act of Arafat-sponsored violence but then retreat into old patterns of thought when there was a respite from the bloodletting.

A clearer picture of the political and strategic realities facing Israel was offered by Ari Shavit in an article that once more broke from the received wisdom of his pro-Oslo *Haaretz* colleagues. Writing on January 15, 2001, about the upcoming election for prime minister, Shavit decried the rapid succession of prime ministers in recent years and attributed it in part to the blunder of Israel's having instituted direct election for the office. But he also perceived the turnstile succession of prime ministers as reflecting "a profound existential crisis" brought on by a decision "produced and directed by Justice Minister Yossi Beilin . . . who had Israel sign an illusory document [the Oslo accords] which undermines the foundations of its existence." Shavit suggested that the nation is rapidly rejecting its prime ministers because "not one of them is capable of defending the country after Beilin entrusted its security to the hands of its enemies."[74]

As in the media, so too in Israeli academia, not surprisingly, there were those who continued to blame Israel for the absence of peace. Shortly after the outbreak of the violence, Tanya Reinhart, a linguist on the faculty of Tel Aviv University and frequent indicter of Israeli policy under both Likud and Labor governments, posted an article on an Internet Web site in which she insisted that Barak's concessions at Camp David and afterward at Taba still reflected an effort to subjugate the Palestinians and impose a form of perpetual imprisonment on them. She writes at one point that, "[The Palestinians] are given one choice: accept prison life, or perish."[75]

Reinhart was particularly bitter at Barak's post-Camp David reluctance to cede control of the Temple Mount to Arafat. She also castigated him for allowing Sharon to visit the Temple Mount. These steps, she insisted, had the effect of "turning the conflict into a religious one." Despite the acknowledgment by Palestinian officials that Arafat had planned and choreographed the outbreak of armed clashes, Reinhart still blamed Israel for the violence. Reinhart was critical of Arafat, but not for his rejection of Israeli concessions or for his use of violence and pursuit of his annihilationist agenda. Rather, she attacked him for his not being anti-Israel enough. Arafat, to Reinhart, had fallen from leadership of a "national liberation movement" into "collaboration" with Israel.[76]

Many within the leadership and ranks of Peace Movement organizations also put the onus for the mini-war on Israel. Even though the Palestinians had unleashed the violence after rejecting Israeli offers to hand over at least 95 percent of the West Bank and all of Gaza to Arafat's control and to give territory in pre-1967 Israel in compensation for the percentage of the West Bank retained by Israel, Peace Now continued to blame the settlements for the violent turn of events. The organization published an open letter to Prime Minister Barak declaring that "the settlements . . . are the main obstacle to the achievement of an agreement with the Palestinians," and urged Barak to take steps against them. Peace Now also published the open letter ad in the Palestinian paper "Al Ayam," even as that paper was praising the violence, lionizing its agents, and purveying anti-Israel and anti-Jewish screeds.[77]

Key figures in the Barak government also continued to insist that peace could still be won if Israel only made sufficient additional concessions. They supported the government pursuing further negotiations at Taba even while Arafat waged his war, and they urged Barak to be more forthcoming. Some criticized him for not having been accommodating enough of Palestinian demands thus far. The talks at Taba continued until January 27, 2001, a week before the election for prime minister, and the mind-set guiding the Israeli delegation is captured in comments several months later by Shlomo Ben-Ami.

Ben-Ami was a professor of history at Tel Aviv University in civilian life, Barak's foreign minister, and a leader of the negotiating team at Taba. Looking back in June, 2001, at Arafat's rejection of what Ben-Ami states was an offer of all of Gaza and 97 percent of the West Bank, and additional land from pre-1967 Israel as compensation for the other 3 percent, he conceded that Arafat was only pretending to endorse a two-state solution but in fact still "doesn't accept the legitimacy" of Israel. (A few months later, he elaborated on his new insight: "For Arafat, Oslo was a sort of huge camouflage act behind which he was exercising political pressure and terror in varying proportion in order to undermine the very idea of two states for two peoples."[78]) But despite his recognition of Arafat's ongoing rejection of Israel's right to exist, and even after vivid demonstration of the strategic dangers that Israel now faced and those still greater dangers that would prevail in the wake of additional land transfers to Arafat, Ben-Ami still held to the delusions of the Oslo enthusiasts. His answer to the current predicament was for the world to "force Israelis and Palestinians to accept the same solution [i.e., the Camp David and Taba formulas that would give Arafat virtually the entire West Bank and east Jerusalem, including most of the Old City] that seemed so close a few months ago."[79]

At Camp David and Taba, Ben-Ami was prepared to ignore all strategic risks, and all evidence of Arafat's hostile agenda, in his desperation for "peace" and "normalcy" — and apparently nine months of explicit and bloody demonstration of the true consequences of Oslo had not dampened his enthusiasm for that deluded and disastrous course.

SEVENTEEN

American Jews and Oslo

Arafat is not going to be happy with that.
Sara Ehrman, board member of Americans for Peace Now,
complaining that dovish American Jewish leaders had failed
to press Secretary of State Madeleine Albright to treat Israel,
led at the time by Ehud Barak, more harshly in order to
extract additional Oslo-related concessions. (August, 1999)[1]

To fully grasp the history of the delusions that were the "peace process," the response of the American Jewish community to Oslo must also be considered. By far the largest Diaspora community in the world, American Jews, as already noted, have long been deeply involved with events in Israel and very concerned about the nation's well-being.

Wide sectors of the American Jewish public greeted revelation of the first Oslo agreements in September, 1993, with at least some modicum of hopefulness and, in some quarters, wild enthusiasm. Polls of American Jewish opinion in the months and years that followed tended to show a consistent if seemingly contradictory pattern of support for Oslo but also distrust of Arafat, reservations about Israeli territorial concessions, and expectations that those concessions were more likely to compromise Israel's security than bring Israel closer to genuine peace. This backing for the Oslo process even in the face of distrust of Arafat and skepticism regarding territorial concessions reflected in part the widely held "liberal" predisposition among American Jews to approve of anything with the word *peace* in its title. It also reflected an inclination among American Jews to follow the lead of Israeli governments with regard to defining proper Israeli policy, so that embrace of the "peace process" by Israeli governments also inexorably elicited support for Oslo among American Jews despite their misgivings.

Those reservations were deprecated and dismissed by Oslo's enthusiasts in Israel and in the States as representing old, knee-jerk, "right-wing" convictions out of touch with the current realities of life in Israel and the Middle East. But the persistent skepticism among American Jews could more justifiably be laid to the Palestinians' campaign of terror waged against Israel during the Oslo years and to Arafat's ongoing calls for Jihad, refusal to dismantle the terror organizations, frequent collusion with and praise of the terrorists, myriad exercises in incitement, and other violations of Oslo.

There were differences, however, between the views of the general American Jewish population, as measured in polls, and those of the leaders of many American Jewish organizations, including mainstream groups. The latter were typically more enthusiastic and less ambivalent in their support of the "peace process."

In looking at the response to Oslo of American Jewish organizations, those bodies will be considered under three headings: groups that had been formed to oppose Israeli government policies, entities spawned by Oslo, and mainstream organizations.

THE RESPONSE TO OSLO OF ISRAEL-INDICTING JEWISH GROUPS IN AMERICA

Some of those organizations discussed in Chapter Seven that had come into being essentially to attack Israel and its policies were still operating in 1993. Not surprisingly, they remained focused on criticizing Israeli positions and indicting the state for not being forthcoming enough vis-à-vis its Arab neighbors. The Jewish Peace Lobby after 1993 consistently argued that Israel would have to offer the Palestinians more and that peace would ensue once Israel had made concessions along the lines the Lobby demanded, including the division of Jerusalem.[2] It persisted in lobbying Congress for support for its stances.

Leaders of the New Israel Fund continued to direct most of the Fund's resources to groups in Israel advocating Arab views and opposing and challenging government positions. In 1997, the Smithsonian Institution planned a lecture series on "Israel at 50" and agreed to have the New Israel Fund formulate the program. The scheduled list of speakers consisted overwhelmingly of critics of Israel, such as Azmi Bishara, an Arab member of the Knesset who had recently paid homage at the grave of an Islamic Jihad murderer of Israelis; Ehud Sprinzak, whose defense of Hamas was noted in Chapter Fifteen; Yaron Ezrahi, the author of *Rubber Bullets*; and Tom Segev. When the program was canceled because of protests against its bias, Norman Rosenberg, New Israel Fund's executive director, declared that the complaints, "[were] driven by right-wing extremists who wish to stifle any open commentary about Israel."[3]

A common thread of the Israel-indicting groups had been that Israel was strong and secure, that it faced no real strategic threats, and that its invoking of security concerns was simply an excuse to avoid making those concessions that, in the view of these groups, were the Arabs' due and would ensure peace. After September, 1993, even as these organizations sustained their attacks on

Israel for not being forthcoming enough, they also used the Labor-Meretz government's about-face on Israeli strategic redlines, and its downplaying of the risk of territorial and other concessions, to support and justify their own dismissing of Israeli security concerns.

Another group in the Israel-indicting mold is Americans for Peace Now (APN), set apart by its affiliation with an Israeli organization. An earlier iteration, American Friends of Peace Now, had formed at the beginning of the 1980s to support Israel's Peace Now. At that time, the membership of the Israeli group had still represented a range of positions on territorial concessions, with many members believing Israel had to retain some areas of the West Bank for security reasons, while American Friends of Peace Now had advocated more radical, maximal territorial concessions and downplayed security concerns. Early in its existence, the group had published an ad in the *New York Times* essentially characterizing Israel as the impediment to Middle East peace.[4]

The successor body, Americans for Peace Now, opposed all Israeli settlements, testified in Congress against loan guarantees for Israel unless Israeli government support for settlements ended, fought against transfer of the American embassy to Jerusalem, advocated division of Jerusalem and expulsion of Jews from parts of the Old City, and continued to dismiss Israeli security concerns.

Leadership of both Americans for Peace Now and its predecessor organization overlapped with the leadership of such groups as the New Jewish Agenda, the Jewish Peace Lobby, and CONAME (which had lobbied against U.S. arms shipments to Israel during the Yom Kippur War). Gail Pressberg, for a time president of APN and then director of APN's Center for Israeli Peace and Security, had a long history of involvement with anti-Israel organizations and events, including some marked by frank anti-Semitism, and in her earlier career had not notably demonstrated any concern for Israel's security. Pressberg's Israel-related activities have been documented by Rael Jean Isaac. In the late 1970s, as director of the American Friends Service Committee's Middle East "Peace Education" Program, Pressberg had organized anti-Israel conferences and called for a halt to U.S. arms shipments to Israel. Pressberg had also signed ads making wildly untrue and defamatory claims about Israeli actions in Lebanon, opposing relocation of the U.S. Embassy to Jerusalem, and demanding Israel's return to its pre-1967 borders. From the 1970s onward, she was a consistent promoter of and apologist for the PLO. When, in September, 1986, terrorists killed twenty-one Turkish Jews at sabbath prayer in their Istanbul synagogue, Pressberg characterized the slaughter as due to "the humiliation and dispossession felt by Palestinians" and used the occasion to urge again U.S. negotiations with the PLO. In 1988, Pressberg co-authored a "guide" to the Middle East conflict for American high school students. It slandered Jews — declaring, for example, that "in Jewish eyes, the Arab is dirty, lazy, thieving, incompetent . . .

and uppity" — and was designed to encourage students' identification with and support for Arab positions.[5]

During the years of Oslo, Americans for Peace Now welcomed Israeli concessions to the PLO but consistently pushed for still more concessions and faulted Israeli governments for not offering more. A December, 1998, APN fund-raising letter signed by Leonard Fein attacked Israel's "Judaizing" of Jerusalem. (In point of fact, Jerusalem had become less Jewish since 1967, with Arab population growth outpacing Jewish growth proportionally and Arab housing construction outpacing Jewish construction proportionally.)

Those organizations such as Americans for Peace Now that had been founded to attack Israeli government policies and promote accommodation of Arab, particularly Palestinian, positions invoked the Oslo agreements as vindication of their agenda, evidence that Israel had finally awakened at least partially to the wisdom of what they had always demanded of it. They also enlisted the Oslo accords as a tool to demonstrate to American Jews the validity of their stances in the hope of thereby winning additional support and legitimacy. Their success in this latter endeavor was by some measures very limited, in that their positions remained well outside the predominant contours of American Jewish opinion. But some groups, particularly Americans for Peace Now, did win greater acceptance by mainstream American Jewish organizations as the latter, for reasons that will be discussed, embraced more wholeheartedly than the American Jewish public the shift in policies introduced by the 1992 Rabin government and reflected in the Oslo agreements.

AMERICAN JEWISH GROUPS SPAWNED BY OSLO

A somewhat separate category of American Jewish organizations, distinct from both the Israel-indicting groups and the established, mainstream bodies, were those that either came into being to support Oslo or had been founded to pursue some relatively benign activities intended to advance peace and reconciliation and, after September, 1993, became supporters and promoters of Oslo. Particularly prominent among the former is Israel Policy Forum (IPF), created in 1993 at the behest of Israel's Labor-Meretz coalition government and placed under the leadership of a former APN president, Jonathan Jacoby, who had earlier in his career signed a *New York Times* ad accusing Israel of "state terrorism."[6]

One of IPF's early efforts, intended to convey to the American public and American leaders an impression of wide American Jewish enthusiasm for Oslo, was its sponsorship of a poll that ostensibly showed 87 percent of American Jews supporting the "peace process." The poll was grossly skewed in the framing of its questions, as, for example, in its asking: "As you may be aware, Israel agreed to recognize the PLO as the official representative of the Palestinian people after the

PLO renounced terrorism, removed the clauses from its charter which called for the destruction of Israel, and formally recognized Israel's right to exist. Do you approve or disapprove of the Israeli government's decision to recognize the PLO as the official representative of the Palestinian people?" Not surprisingly, 82 percent approved. The poll did not ask, for example: "Do you trust the PLO's renunciation of terror?" Also, it was, of course, dishonest in its assertion that the PLO charter had been changed. The Anti-Defamation League, which had been reported to have co-sponsored the poll, disassociated itself from it.[7]

A subsequent Israel Policy Forum poll, conducted in the spring of 1994, used the tack of a skewed sample of the Jewish community — 65 percent stated they did not belong to any Jewish organization and 63 percent did not even regard themselves as Zionists — to increase the likelihood of pro-"peace process" responses.[8] The poll also underrepresented Orthodox Jews in its sample.[9] Other IPF initiatives included mailing packets to rabbis promoting pro-Oslo sermons for the High Holidays, offering a sample sermon, and urging rabbis to organize pro-Oslo letter-writing campaigns to Congress to demonstrate Jewish support for the "peace process."[10]

IPF also began issuing quarterly reports on the status of the Oslo process. But these reports, following the lead of the Rabin and Peres governments, downplayed Palestinian incitement and violence. The fall, 1997, issue, which covered the period of the shootings and killings that followed the Netanyahu government's opening of the Western Wall tunnel exit, failed to identify the initiator of the violence and noted only that "violence is up." Similarly, nothing is said of Palestinian incitement. Rather, the report speaks evenhandedly of "the perils of confrontational modes of behavior as practiced by Netanyahu and Arafat."[11]

Not surprisingly, during the Netanyahu government the organization assumed an oppositional stance and continued to promote Labor-Meretz positions. When, in the spring of 1998, Secretary of State Albright issued an ultimatum to Netanyahu concerning the Clinton Administration's demands vis-à-vis the size of the next Israeli withdrawals, IPF joined Americans for Peace Now in lobbying Congress in support of the administration's position.

Even after Arafat's initiation of his mini-war in September, 2000, Israel Policy Forum hewed to its Oslo-promoting mission. It remained evenhanded on the violence and its sources and intimated that those who disagreed with its pro-Oslo stances were anti-peace, as in a March 2, 2001, letter to the *Forward* by IPF's then president, Judith Stern Peck.

A similar group, Project Nishma, actually created in 1988 as a venue for what it characterized as "security-minded doves," likewise became a cheerleader for Oslo. It lobbied Congress in support of the Labor-Meretz agenda and sought to depict that agenda as enjoying wide American Jewish grassroots backing, with the skeptics among American Jews being a minority. Once more, those who challenged Labor-Meretz policies were smeared as opponents of peace. In 1997, Project Nishma merged with Israel Policy Forum.

Many of those in the American Jewish community who became pro-Oslo activists focused on advancing economic ties between Israel and the Arab states, Israel and the Palestinians, and American Jews and the Arab states, as a tool for establishing peace. They saw the promise of beneficial economic opportunities as a powerful incentive for the Arab states and the Palestinians to pursue peace. Perhaps the highest-profile organization emphasizing this course was the Center for Middle East Peace and Economic Cooperation. Founded in 1989 by successful American Jewish entrepreneur S. Daniel Abraham and a friend, former Utah Congressman Wayne Owens, the Center sought to cultivate contacts with Arab governments and serve as a bridge between Arabs and Israelis, including their leaderships.

Weaknesses in the arguments that economic incentives can help secure Israel peace with its neighbors are discussed elsewhere, but key echelons of the Labor-Meretz coalition believed in the power of such incentives to assure realization of their objectives for Oslo. The Center for Middle East Peace and Economic Cooperation, whose leaders shared that faith and enthusiasm, quickly allied itself to the Israeli coalition's pro-Oslo endeavors. The Center also became, regrettably, a venue for attacking those who were troubled by the Palestinian Authority's violations of its Oslo obligations and skeptical of Palestinian intentions toward Israel; and the Center's leaders served as apologists for Arab officials and their policies.

In December, 1996, during the premiership of Benjamin Netanyahu, the Center held a conference that was billed as a "Retrospective on the Peace Process" but proved to be mainly, according to media reports, a sustained attack on the Netanyahu government. Guest speakers included PA general secretary Ahmed Abdul Rahman, former Secretary of State James Baker, and columnist Thomas Friedman. Rahman excoriated Israel and its policies and insisted there were no Palestinian violations of Oslo. On the issue of Arafat's agreement in several of the Oslo accords to change the Palestinian charter and its calls for Israel's destruction, Rahman said, "We don't want a new charter." Baker urged greater pressure on Netanyahu and suggested the United States had to get tougher with Israel. Friedman similarly advocated the administration forcing Israel to be more forthcoming and praised Baker and former Secretary of State Kissinger for having aggressively pressed Israel while they were in office.[12]

Most of the other speakers as well focused their remarks on criticizing the Netanyahu government or Israel in general. Interestingly, the speaker apparently most willing to address Arab shortcomings vis-à-vis peacemaking was the Jordanian ambassador.[13]

The Center also involved itself in promoting Syrian-Israeli peace, and the

Center's founder, S. Daniel Abraham, a frequent visitor to Damascus, became something of an apologist for Hafez al-Assad. In an interview in July, 1997, Abraham declared that Assad "wants to make peace with Israel . . . I believe he would love Syria to join the global economy." Abraham went on to observe, "Not all dictators are terrible people, and not all dictatorships are terrible forms in which to live." He added that most Jews in Syria live freely and "there was no anti-Semitism to speak of"; this after the great majority of Syrian Jews had fled the country and Secretary of State Warren Christopher had some months earlier protested "an anti-Semitic article published in the semi-official *Syrian Times*."[14] A 1999 ad by the Center proclaimed, "President Assad has scrupulously kept all of his commitments in earlier disengagement accords with Israel. He possesses both the will and the ability to make peace with Israel and implement it throughout Syria." In contrast to his warm feelings for Assad, Abraham is reported to have asked President Clinton, "Do you really think Netanyahu wants peace?"[15]

The efforts by the Center and its key figures to whitewash and promote Arab leaders and their policies and to advance the Labor-Meretz agenda, indeed to advocate at moments an even more radical course, resulted in other strange and at times embarrassing episodes. One involved an August, 1999, conference call between Secretary of State Albright and Jewish leaders. Sara Ehrman, a board member of Americans for Peace Now who had been hired by the Center as a "senior advisor," was accidentally caught on tape complaining to another Center employee over the failure of the doves among the Jewish leaders to press Albright during the conference call to treat Israel more harshly. (This even as Israel was now again led by a Labor-Meretz coalition, under Ehud Barak.) Ehrman added: "Arafat is not going to be happy with that."[16]

Ehrman also commented on a complaint to Albright in the course of the call to the effect that the Secretary seemed to be suggesting a moral equivalence between Israeli construction at Har Homa and a recent terrorist attack at the Mahane Yehuda market in Jerusalem. Ehrman remarked to her co-worker: "What the hell is this question of moral equivalency? You mean provocative acts that are responded to with desperation are a question of moral equivalency?" Her colleague actually put the greater onus on the Israeli leadership, declaring: "Arafat didn't decide to put a bomb in Mahane Yehuda. Bibi [Netanyahu] did decide to build at Har Homa."[17]

In November, 1999, Hillary Clinton attended an event in Ramallah at which Arafat's wife, Suha, absurdly accused Israel of daily poison-gas attacks that were causing cancer in Palestinian women and children, and Mrs. Clinton responded initially by saying nothing and kissing Mrs. Arafat. Reports at the time averred that Ehrman and Center executive director Jon Gersten had arranged the Clinton visit and that, while Mrs. Clinton had wanted to issue a swift and strong statement condemning Mrs. Arafat's remarks, Gersten had helped dissuade her.[18]

In March, 2000, a story in the *Forward*, under the title "Toasting a Tyrant," told of another fiasco involving the Center. At a lunch that the Center hosted in honor of the president of Yemen, S. Daniel Abraham praised the honoree for his "actively supporting a comprehensive regional peace," a very dubious claim. Abraham also lauded President Ali Abdullah Saleh for "the democratization of his country," even though Saleh had been reelected the previous year with 96.3 percent of the vote, was grooming his son as his successor, controlled virtually all of Yemen's media and intimidated those outlets not directly under his control, and had been cited by the State Department for policies abusive of women.[19] A last question addressed to the president by invited guests after the lunch was whether Israelis would be allowed to travel to Yemen on Israeli passports. Saleh refused to respond and abruptly left the event, ducking a planned meeting with the media and with potential investors.[20]

Another set of undertakings by American Jews in support of the "peace process" entailed pursuit of what might be seen as a variation on the "economic bridge building will promote and secure peace" theme. These were initiatives predicated on the assumption that person-to-person bridge building would inexorably promote and help secure peace. Organizers of perhaps the best known effort in this vein, Seeds of Peace, which brought together Israeli and Palestinian children at a Maine summer camp, eventually found themselves engaging in and defending the indefensible, much as Abraham and his Center did.

Efforts in the direction of person-to-person bridge building had long been undertaken in Israel itself, on the initiative of Israelis. A well-known example, and a recipient of substantial New Israel Fund support, was Neve Shalom, an Arab-Jewish village in Israel set up to promote Arab-Jewish co-existence. Obviously, the promotion of peaceful co-existence is a worthwhile endeavor, but at Neve Shalom the effort had degenerated into something different. It routinely entailed encounters in which the Arabs verbally attacked the Jews for alleged Israeli crimes against Palestinians and other Arabs, and the Jews willingly took on the mantle of sinners ready to repent. They embraced all manner of distortions of past history and present reality and responded to the indictments and vituperation of their Arab neighbors with a steady stream of *meae culpae*, doing so in the service of delusions that acknowledging their supposed sinfulness and reforming would usher in the age of peace.[21]

Moreover, the Jewish residents of Neve Shalom were educating their children in the same mind-set. A reporter who attended a weekend encounter session involving Arab and Jewish students from the eleventh and twelfth grades wrote of the final session in which counselors guided the students through exercises in role-playing. All the roles were either Jews who were abusing Arabs or Arabs who were being abused by Jews. Jewish victims of Arab abuse, or any other interaction between the communities, did not exist in the world of the Neve Shalom pedagogues and their charges.[22]

The Seeds of Peace endeavor enjoyed much fanfare. The first contingent of student campers, in the summer of 1993, was invited to the September signing of the Oslo Declaration of Principles on the White House lawn, subsequent groups were feted at the State Department, and the undertaking gained laudatory media coverage worldwide. But Seeds of Peace degenerated under its sponsors' guidance in a manner paralleling the Neve Shalom phenomenon. As reported in the *Jerusalem Post* in January, 2000, "A recent film called 'Peace of Mind,' produced by Seeds of Peace and intended for theater and television screenings around the world, casts doubt on the organization's motives. It is so tilted in favor of Palestinian arguments, so unquestioningly sympathetic to Palestinian grievances, that it becomes a propaganda instrument rather than an ode to young friendship."[23]

The film, in explicating the Arab-Israeli conflict as background to the students' encounters at the camp, presents a doctored and bogus past and a similarly distorted present. While the film states that it was produced by the Arab and Israeli campers, three of the four Israeli students featured in it wrote to Seeds of Peace to protest its bias and to assert that "we did not make the movie, as the movie claims . . . The movie was only shot in part by us, and most of our footage, including its most significant statements from our point of view, were discarded."[24]

The mind-set of the camp's organizers was further revealed in an incident recounted by the father of one of the camp's Israeli students in a letter to the *Jerusalem Post*. "One morning, the camp assembly was told by the founder, John Wallach, that that morning a Palestinian had run down two Israelis and killed them and that he was subsequently killed. He asked for a moment of silence for the Israelis and the Palestinian. The Jewish campers immediately objected and refused to stand for the Palestinian. Apparently no one could explain to Mr. Wallach that there is no moral equivalence between terrorists and their victims."[25]

MAINSTREAM AMERICAN JEWISH ORGANIZATIONS AND OSLO

Those organizations that had come into being to attack Israeli policies and that inevitably continued after Oslo to focus their efforts on criticism of Israel were the voices of distinctly minority constituencies in the American Jewish community. So too were those groups that were either created after September, 1993, to support the Labor-Meretz coalition's Oslo policies or had existed as some relatively politically nonpartisan, peace-promoting endeavor and had subsequently enlisted to cheerlead for Oslo. Most American Jews, while eager for Middle East peace and generally supportive of negotiating efforts, remained highly distrustful of Arafat and anticipated that continuing Israeli territorial concessions was much more likely to bring the nation peril than peace.

But as suggested earlier, even the leadership of many of the long-established, mainstream American Jewish organizations embraced Oslo with an enthusiasm substantially greater than that of American Jewry generally and often even that of their own rank and file. Various factors contributed to this phenomenon. Certainly an eagerness to keep in step with the Labor-Meretz coalition and its policies for the sake of Israeli/American-Jewish solidarity, and also for the sake of maintaining their own relations with Israeli leaders, figured in the thinking of some American Jewish groups. An organization like AIPAC — the America-Israel Public Affairs Committee — a broadly supported fixture of the American Jewish community whose mandate is to lobby Congress in support of the U.S.-Israel relationship, was obviously under tremendous pressure to fall in line with the dramatic shifts in Israeli policy represented by Oslo. AIPAC was soon lobbying Congress to provide, for example, aid packages to the PLO, despite the loathing for Arafat and skepticism regarding the PLO of many in Congress, and despite the ongoing terror and Arafat's continued incitement to Jihad and to Israel's ultimate dissolution. AIPAC did so largely because the Labor-Meretz coalition believed economic support would co-opt PLO militancy and revanchism and help secure peace.

A predilection to follow the Israeli government's lead could not, however, explain entirely the breadth and depth of the American Jewish leadership's signing on to Oslo. Those looking open-eyed at the reality of Israel's situation and the delusions that underlay its Oslo policies might well have chosen on principle to distance themselves from the folly of such policies even if that would have meant organizational and personal estrangement from the Labor-Meretz government. (Indeed even in AIPAC, while some in the professional echelon of the organization seemed not only to embrace the Oslo agenda but to do so with conviction and aplomb, there were members of the lay leadership, the highest level of AIPAC's financial supporters, who were unhappy with the organization's stance, and many longtime contributors were so put off by AIPAC's pro-Oslo activities that they withdrew their support.)

Moreover, much of the American-Jewish leadership was cool to the Netanyahu government's skepticism regarding the premises of Oslo. This is further evidence that the leadership's enthusiasm for Oslo could not be explained simply as reflecting a predilection to fall in line with Israeli government positions.

The explanation for why criticism of Oslo, or at least skepticism of it, was not more widely voiced by the American Jewish leadership was that much of the leadership actually welcomed the Israeli shift in policy. Those in the leadership generally shared the American Jewish community's leftward political sympathies. Many of them were predisposed to desiring a convergence of high-profile "Jewish" stances with so-called liberal opinion (reflecting a largely idiosyncratic but currently popular version of what constitutes liberalism) and to emphasizing, in any defining of what is "Jewish," the universal and universally lauded. Many of them traveled in circles of the country's "liberal" elites, were sensitive to what they took to be the sentiments of those elites, and were particularly likely to be among those Jews who responded to anti-Israel distortions in the "liberal" media with embarrassment rather than outrage and resentment. So they were in some respects more predisposed than most Jews to welcome any Israeli shift in policy that played well in the "liberal" media and appealed to "liberal" sentiments, and seemingly to do so without looking too closely or concerning themselves too much with the implications of those policies for the state's well-being.

The same sentiments rendered many of them receptive to the claims — based on an eagerness for peace rather than rational assessment — that the other side, the Palestinian and broader Arab leadership, inevitably, unquestionably, wanted what they wanted — prosperity and peace. They were therefore predisposed to construe Israeli self-reform, concessions, and promises of cooperation aimed at mutual prosperity as leading inexorably to the desired peace.

Indeed there were some segments of the mainstream Jewish leadership whose focus — not entirely unlike that of the Jews who had founded the peripheral groups that had come into being to "reform" Israel and its policies — was primarily on conforming to some "liberal" agenda. They directed their efforts mostly to espousing, and mustering and leading Jewish community support for, what were viewed as "social action" causes in America, and on building connections with other "liberal" and minority communities. Such people were likely to react to "liberal" criticism of Israel by choosing not to exert themselves to question negative glosses on Israeli policy or to invoke countervailing information to critique such glosses but rather to accept indictments of Israel at face value. They were very often people who reacted further by preferring to distance themselves from Israel; people who, striving in any case in their organizational work to draw the community more fully toward "social action" causes, sought at the same time to draw it away from the cause of Israel; and they often chose to justify their doing so by arguing that Israel was now strong enough that its security and survival were assured, and it had come so far economically that it no longer required the same financial support from American Jews, and so it was right and appropriate that the community turn its attention more fully to other causes. Such leaders welcomed Oslo not only because it promised to reduce their embarrassment over Israel but also because the stances and arguments of the Israeli government now supported their own assertions to their constituencies that Israel's safety was assured and so it was reasonable to focus communal energies elsewhere.[26]

But there was a notable gap between those in the Jewish leadership shaping such agendas, seeking to de-emphasize Israel and justifying their stances by arguing that Israel was secure and peace was at hand, as well as others in the leadership who embraced Oslo and Labor-Meretz policy, and, on the other hand, broader American Jewish opinion. Evidence of that gap was offered by a poll conducted by the Indianapolis Jewish Community Relations Council (JCRC) in 1996.

The poll showed that while JCRCs across America, including the one in Indianapolis, together with the JCRC national umbrella group, the National Jewish Community Relations Advisory Council, were all promoting an agenda emphasizing social action in a "liberal" vein, the Indianapolis Jewish community held markedly different views and had different priorities. With regard to Israel, while the JCRCs were typically claiming not only that Israel was now safe but that American Jews overwhelmingly concurred with this view and also overwhelmingly supported Oslo, the Indianapolis JCRC poll indicated otherwise. Almost 80 percent of those questioned believed, for example, a Palestinian state would be a threat to Israel's security. Less than half felt that Israel should give up Judea and Samaria, even with a viable peace. More than two-thirds said Arafat could not be trusted.[27]

But if some mainstream Jewish leaderships used Oslo to justify their organizations' disengagement from Israel, there were others, as suggested, that remained highly engaged and concerned with Israel and at the same time embraced Oslo with an enthusiasm that could not be explained simply as their choosing to follow the Israeli government's lead. Their sentiments seemed to reflect rather a pursuit of political concerns and predilections, concepts of proper Jewish and Israeli behavior, that trumped careful examination of the implications of Oslo for Israel's well-being and survival. The results were actions by various American Jewish leaders that hardly served their constituencies well.

The Anti-Defamation League (ADL) is a venerable Jewish organization that has obviously done important work over almost a century in fighting not only anti-Semitism in America but racial and religious bigotry of all sorts. At the same time it has also tended to be more alert and responsive to hatred and anti-Semitism emanating from the Right of the political spectrum than from the Left, even though the latter has often been as vicious and dangerous — some would argue in recent decades more dangerous — than the former.

However much this political predilection figured in the leadership of the ADL's general enthusiasm for Oslo, the fact is that Yasser Arafat, from his entry into the territories in 1994, orchestrated a campaign of defamation and vilification against Israelis and Jews. He promoted in PA schoolbooks and media, over which he always maintained tight control, denigration of Jewish belief, classic anti-Semitic caricatures of Jews, claims of Jewish perfidy and godlessness, blood libels against Jews, assertions that Jews have no historical connection with the land of Israel, denial of any Jewish religious ties to the Temple Mount, denial of the Holocaust, and much else in the same vein. Yet the ADL's response was ambiguous at best. In the fall of 1998 it published a report on anti-Semitic statements proffered by the Palestinian Authority over the previous year, and at various times it would put out press releases urging Arafat to change his ways. For example, one such release in November, 1998, called upon Arafat to remove anti-Semitism from official PA airwaves.[28] Yet Arafat's anti-Jewish campaign did not keep the head of the ADL, Abraham Foxman, from leading American Jewish delegations in pilgrimages to the PA chairman or proffering Arafat "gifts of Jewish art."[29]

At a meeting in Ramallah in September, 2000, Foxman presented Arafat with a letter regarding recently introduced PA school texts. The letter expresses concern over the books' failure to mention Israel on maps of the region, but praises them for excluding "the anti-Israel and anti-Semitic passages prevalent in the previous textbooks and curricular material."[30] But, in fact, as noted in Chapter Sixteen, the new books denigrate Jews and Judaism and continue to teach that all of Israel rightly belongs to the Arabs.

In an even stranger vein, voices within the leadership of United Jewish Communities, whose chairman at the time was Charles Bronfman, apparently sought in 1999 to have that organization present to Arafat its Isaiah Peace Award for outstanding service to humanity. The group ultimately decided against the proposal. (Not surprisingly, an official of Americans for Peace Now, when asked about the plan, did not see any problem with recognition of what he characterized as Arafat's "important contributions to the peace process.")[31]

THE AMERICAN JEWISH LEFT, THE PRESIDENT, AND OSLO

Beyond an eagerness to maintain ties with the Labor-Meretz coalition government and its leaders, or a predilection to give greater weight to their own investment in fashionable left-wing orthodoxies and to their standing among the constituencies of those orthodoxies than to any rational assessment of what Oslo was likely to mean for Israel, there was another factor that weighed on the side of American Jewish leaders' embrace of Oslo. This was the enthusiastic adoption of the Oslo process, and its aggressive cultivation, by President Clinton and his Administration and the interest of many in the Jewish leadership in maintaining and buttressing their connections with the White House.

How much did the Jewish leaders harbor views and sympathies that converged in any case with those of the president or how much did they bend their views for the sake of presidential access? Among those who became cheerleaders for Oslo, whether the first or the second characterization is the more apt no doubt varies significantly from one to another. But the seductiveness of access should not be underestimated. The long history of Jewish minority communities sending delegations to represent their interests in the halls of power is replete with instances in which maintaining their position before the powerful became a higher priority for those delegations than serving their communities.

The impact of the president on the American Jewish leadership's stance vis-à-vis Oslo went beyond likely inclining some among the mainstream leadership to be more outspoken in favor of Oslo or less vocal about misgivings than they might otherwise have been. A number of Clinton's close political friends and supporters, people who in fact may have helped shape his views of Israel and his enthusiasm for Oslo, were American Jews whose own perspectives on Israel were well to the left of the American Jewish consensus. Peter Edelman, a close personal friend of the Clintons who in 1992 headed Clinton's transition team for the Justice Department (and later served as assistant secretary of Health and Human Services) was then Chairman of Americans for Peace Now (APN) and submitted memos to the transition team on behalf of the organization. Eli Segal, chief financial officer in the Clinton transition team, was also a board member of APN. Samuel Berger, who through much of Clinton's presidency was his national security advisor, was likewise a supporter of APN.[32] Sara Ehrman, yet another APN board member and mentioned earlier in the context of her post with the Center for Middle East Peace and Economic Cooperation, was also a Democratic Party fund-raiser, senior political advisor to the Democratic National Committee, senior campaign operative for Clinton and a Clinton family friend. Center founder S. Daniel Abraham was a major Clinton contributor and booster. These people's connections with the president meant that the organizations with which they were affiliated were given a higher profile in American Jewish organizational life and accorded increased deference by the mainstream organizations.

For example, in March, 1993, the Conference of Presidents of Major American Jewish Organizations, the national umbrella group for major organizations, after much internal debate voted to admit Americans for Peace Now as a constituent member. It did so despite APN's history of militating against Israeli policies whatever party was in power in Israel, promoting Arab — particularly Palestinian — positions, ignoring or discounting threats to Israeli security and Israeli strategic concerns, and routinely demanding maximal Israeli concessions. Media commentary on the Conference's step attributed it to deference to the close ties between the White House and a number of APN founders and leaders.

There was some broader discussion in American Jewish media regarding the impact of the president's connections with people whose views on Israel and the Middle East and whose affiliations with Jewish organizational life reflected mainly one end of the spectrum of American Jewish opinion and were generally outside the American Jewish consensus. Some voices questioned whether Clinton was getting a false impression of what American Jewish attitudes regarding Oslo actually were and whether this influenced policy decisions. The issue was raised, for example, in the context of Sara Ehrman's accidentally recorded complaints that the dovish Jews on a conference call with Secretary of State Albright had not pressed Mrs. Albright to treat Israel more harshly, and Ehrman's statement that, "Arafat is not going to be happy with that." Seth Gittell, writing of the episode in the *Forward*, noted, "Some see the taped remarks as evidence that the coterie of dovish American-Jewish advisors surrounding Mr. Clinton are preventing him from obtaining a full picture of public opinion regarding the peace process."[33]

Of course, others as well were promoting Oslo to the president, including, at the start, the Rabin government, and also important echelons of the State Department. It is also not hard to see how Oslo might well have appealed to his own predilections. But at the same time the president was highly sensitive to constituent opinion, and to the views of his contributors, who were likewise disproportionately — very disproportionately — from the American Jewish Left. If they were the people who had his ear and if they conveyed to him that their views were the views of American Jewry, one cannot easily dismiss the suggestion that this may have contributed, for example, to Clinton's hostility to Netanyahu and his general indifference to Netanyahu's concerns.

Natan Sharansky attended the Wye Plantation negotiations in the fall of 1998 as a member of Netanyahu's cabinet. Sharansky has written that President Clinton at Wye concurred with him in a conversation that the success of any agreement hinged on supervising an end to incitement, including incitement in Palestinian school curricula.[34] Yet Clinton ultimately refused to support Netanyahu's demands that further Israeli concessions should be conditioned on the Palestinian Authority's compliance with its earlier obligations such as an end to incitement in Palestinian media and school texts. Could Clinton's pushing for additional Israeli concessions and withdrawals irrespective of Palestinian violations of earlier agreements have been determined in some part by a belief that this is what not only portions of the Israeli population wanted but also what most American Jews wanted? Although hard to answer, and not to be overstated, neither can the possibility be dismissed out of hand.

Leaders of mainstream American Jewish organizations and other American Jews who embraced Oslo often did so at least to some degree out of embarrassment and unease with negative images of Israel conveyed in much of the American media and with criticism of Israeli policies emanating particularly from some

Left-leaning American groups. They did so anticipating that the Oslo process and concomitant Israeli concessions would improve Israel's image in the United States and thereby erase the sources of their discomfort. But there were once again ironies in this phenomenon of Jews embracing Jewish self-reform to ingratiate themselves to critics in the surrounding society.

Polls of American opinion, which have consistently shown strong support for Israel, have also indicated some of the foundations of that support, and those foundations are consistent with more general criteria for American sympathy. For example, Americans tend to side with those they perceive as sharing their principles, and Israel is regarded as a fellow democracy in a sea of autocrats. It is also seen as gutsy and self-sufficient in a dangerous neighborhood, reflecting qualities Americans value in themselves and in their own history. Pacifism is not valued as an absolute good by most Americans; nor is moral relativism, an inclination to bend over backwards to find the virtue in all sides. Nor does the perception of who is David and who Goliath in a conflict rank that highly in shaping American sympathies, although much is made of this in Jewish assessments of public opinion. Certainly it counts for less than the principles that are being fought over. Nor should this be a surprise, since Americans have seen themselves as at once the Goliath in various conflicts and also the party in the right.

From the perspective of such valuations, Israel's pro-Oslo and related policies were in a number of ways more likely to diminish than to reinforce popular support for Israel in America. Such was the likely impact, for example, of the whitewashing of Arafat, not a popular figure in America, and associated Israeli breast-beating even as hostile messages continued to emanate from the other side. A similar reaction could be expected to Israel's apparent bending and retreating in the face of terrorist assault out of exhaustion and fear of additional casualties or fear of unleashing wider conflict or undermining the "peace" process, whether with Arafat or with Syria. Nor was the looking to America to financially underwrite Oslo with aid to Arafat, or to place American troops in harm's way in the Golan Heights and provide aid to Assad in the context of a possible agreement with Syria, likely to improve Israel's standing in American opinion. Nor was the willingness to cede to Arafat sites of central historical and religious importance to Judaism and to downplay connections with the land in the service of accommodating the Arabs through territorial concessions; the preparedness to give up even the Temple Mount, to agree in essence that there was little worth fighting for, no concession worth resisting. (Retreats before unsavory enemies and hostile "partners" are likely to be perceived in the States in negative terms in any case, but even more so given many Americans' own religious feeling for those sites and inclination to see the Jews of Israel as their proper custodian and then being confronted with Israel seeming to casually surrender them.)

All this was much more likely to diminish Israel in the eyes of many Americans than enhance it. Indeed it was becoming commonplace to hear admirers of Israel seem puzzled and offer delicately worded but clearly pointed questions that asked, in effect, what had become of the country's spirit, its will to look honestly at its predicament and stand up to its enemies rather than shrink into self-deceiving and self-defeating accommodations.[35]

Similar ironies surrounded relations between Israel and the United States at the governmental level. Pro-Oslo Israelis and their American Jewish colleagues were inclined to take at face value blandishments from the State Department and the White House, and indeed to conceive parallel arguments on their own, to the effect that Israel's disregarding PA violations and pushing forward with Oslo concessions, and also pursuing ceding the Golan Heights to Syria in exchange for "peace," would reinforce American support for Israel. In fact, the opposite would inevitably be true.

As already noted, Americans have always been sympathetic to Israel, but an alliance evolved only after Israel demonstrated its capacity to defend itself. If Israel sacrifices territories vital for its defense and renders itself vulnerable — and it has been the repeatedly reaffirmed opinion of American military leaders that ceding the Golan, the Jordan Valley, and other key areas in the West Bank, would inevitably compromise the state's ability to defend itself — ultimately the alliance will rupture. United States policy will inexorably come to reflect Pentagon opinion that Israel will have become a strategic liability; a state whose vulnerability might drag the United States into a war, and very likely an unwinnable war, in its defense; and this will result in a strategic distancing from Israel, a loosening of the strategic ties, to avoid possibly being drawn willy-nilly into an Israeli defeat.

In effect, those enamored of Oslo were not only undermining Israel directly but undermining its strategic relationship with the United States as well.

EIGHTEEN

A War of Terror
and Israel's Awakening

The heroic martyrdom operation [of the man] who turned his body into a bomb [is] the model of manhood and sacrifice for the sake of Allah and the homeland.
> Yasser Arafat in a letter to the family of the terrorist who killed 22 people, mostly teenagers, at a Tel Aviv disco, June, 2001[1]

A . . . poll conducted last week showed Israeli Jews solidly united in the view that . . . Arafat will not fight terror seriously (82 percent); is not interested in real peace with Israel (87 percent); cannot be trusted to keep agreements (90 percent); and cannot be believed when he condemns terror (98 percent).
> Yoram Hazony, "Israel's Right and Left Converge," April, 2002[2]

Even if Arafat will sign an agreement, I find it hard to believe, in view of his behavior during the last two years, that he or his successors will abide by it.
> New historian Benny Morris[3]

I supported Oslo. I supported talking with Arafat. The greatest disappointment was to discover that despite everything I believed, everything I've promulgated, that asshole never gave up terror.
> Israeli journalist and commentator Hirsh Goodman[4]

I think I can say there is a type of mutual trust. To a very great degree I do trust [Arafat].
> Yossi Beilin, cited in *Haaretz,* June, 2001[5]

In the wake of his landslide election to the premiership on February 6, 2001, Sharon sought to woo the Labor Party into a broad-based coalition government. Such a coalition made sense from the perspective of the balance of power in the Knesset. The recent election had not involved balloting for a new legislature; the election law that had separated the prime minister's race from Knesset balloting had allowed for an election for the former without voting for a new legislature, and the Knesset had chosen not to dissolve itself. Consequently, the composition of the Knesset was still that created at the time of Barak's 1999 victory over Netanyahu and did not reflect the shift in public sentiment away from Labor since the start of the Palestinians' terror war. This posed difficulties for Sharon, and many commentators predicted that, given the balance of power in the Knesset, his government would be short-lived and within a few months there would be yet another election for prime minister. There were obvious political reasons for Sharon to want to include the large Knesset Labor bloc in his government coalition.

Yet Sharon may well have been able to maintain a government without Labor, particularly as shortly after his victory the Knesset enacted a reversion of the election process to a single ballot system. This meant that a prime minister could no longer be ousted without triggering balloting for a new Knesset; and both the parties of the Left, given the mood of the nation, and the smaller parties, given that the single ballot arrangement put them at a disadvantage and favored the major parties, would be loathe to call a general election. Moreover, Sharon's energetic efforts to win over an ambivalent and internally divided Labor Party, and the high price he was willing to offer it in terms of ministerial portfolios, suggested that his motivation went beyond simply the calculus of Knesset politics. Nor were the broader considerations behind his strategy difficult to discern.

All evidence indicated that for the foreseeable future Arafat would continue, and even escalate, his war, and Sharon could anticipate that, in the vein of the Labor Party when previously in opposition and of the Oslo-related formulations of the Israeli Left, a Labor Party in opposition would choose to blame his government for the persistence of hostilities, would accuse it of not being forthcoming enough, and would thereby divide national opinion and hobble his policies. Sharon could foresee that even though a large majority of Israelis would likely continue to urge strong measures in response to Palestinian terror and would reject Labor formulations, attacks by Labor would still have the effect of fracturing national consensus and undermining his government.

A further consideration concerned international opinion. Despite the limited dimensions of Barak's response to terrorism in the preceding months, Israel had been severely criticized abroad. When, in the wake of the murder of Israelis, Barak directed the IDF to attack PA "police" installations, after first warning the PA in order to allow evacuation and so usually causing no loss of life, the focus of comment abroad, including from the United Nations and the European Union, was typically condemnation of the Israeli response rather than of the Palestinian terror. When Israel tracked down and killed a terrorist leader in the territories, the nation was attacked for its use of "assassination." When it sought to limit Palestinian access to pre-1967 Israel as a security measure, or took other steps to impede the free movement of terrorist cadres, it was condemned for "collective punishment." At times even voices in the American administration, particularly in the State Department, joined in the chorus of anti-Israel indictment. Sharon faced the prospect of Israel enduring continuing and even escalating terror assault and of having to fashion a more effective response in the face of a hostile international climate. He may well have anticipated that he might be able to cultivate overall American support and manage criticism from other nations with Labor as a partner and that both would be significantly more difficult with Labor attacking him.

In addition, the Palestinian leadership was working hard to instigate an expansion of the conflict into a broader war, and many observers believed there was a high likelihood, in particular, of Hezbollah attacking Israel across the Lebanese border and triggering hostilities between Israel and Syria. Sharon no doubt viewed this prospect and his ability to respond effectively as likewise greatly enhanced by national unity, anticipated a Labor Party in opposition undermining that unity, and was driven all the more by the possibility of a wider war in his determination to forge a coalition with Labor.

Sharon's pursuit of Labor elicited criticism from many Likud colleagues. The party as a whole looked upon the Labor leadership not only as bearing responsibility for the Oslo debacle but as having learned little from its past errors and more likely to hinder than to help confront the challenges now facing the nation. Also, ministerial appointments given to Labor meant, for the most part, depriving Likud leaders of those portfolios. But criticism of Sharon's assiduous courting of Labor went beyond the ranks of Likud loyalists and other voices on the Right of the Israeli political spectrum. Many other Israelis as well now saw Labor leaders primarily as the architects of dangerously misguided policies and did not want them to continue in important policy-shaping positions.

Sharon nevertheless persisted in his course and, a month after the election, a government that included Labor was sworn in, with Shimon Peres as foreign minister and Labor's Benjamin Ben-Eliezer as defense minister.

Meanwhile, the terror continued. Most of those who had so far lost their lives to Palestinian attacks had been killed in shootings, some by bombs. March, 2001, saw the first deaths to suicide bombings. In the initial months of the new government, the Israeli response to the terror continued much as it had been; some targeted killing of terrorist leaders and operatives, attacks on mainly empty PA buildings and related infrastructure, and blockades of PA areas from which attacks had emanated. In addition, the government withheld tax funds usually reimbursed to the PA and refused to resume negotiations while the terror continued.

All of Israel's measures continued to be condemned internationally, most notably by the European Union, individual European states, and the United Nations. At best, these critics would talk of a "cycle of violence" that must end; but this itself was a distortion as there was no cycle but rather Palestinian initiation of terror and Israeli responses. No one could doubt that if the terror ended the Israeli actions would end as well.

As in the first months of the terror war, the United States, especially the State Department, joined in the chorus of indictment. In March, the State Department berated Israel for "extrajudicial killings" and also insisted it resume money transfers to the PA, even though this would obviously entail Israel providing Arafat with funds he could use to support his terror campaign. In the same month, the United States called upon Israel to end its blockade of Palestinian towns on the West Bank. In April, 2001, Secretary of State Powell complained that Israeli measures were "excessive and disproportionate." (Voices in the United States as well as in Israel noted an inconsistency between such statements and Powell's earlier elaboration of a war-fighting doctrine, the "Powell Doctrine," that called for the application of overwhelming force. Of course, Israel's responses to the terror fell far short of overwhelming force.) At the end of April, when Israel briefly reoccupied a section of Area A in Gaza, this too earned it American criticism. In May, the State Department, in a mandatory report to Congress, continued its pattern of whitewashing Palestinian Authority involvement in terror, merely noting Israeli allegations of such involvement.

On June 1, 2001, the worst terrorist attack to date, a suicide bombing at a Tel Aviv discotheque, killed twenty-two Israelis, mostly teenagers. (Under pressure from Western diplomats, Arafat issued a *pro forma* condemnation of the slaughter, but a month later a German television network displayed and read from a congratulatory letter sent by Arafat to the parents of the bomber.[6]) Many observers thought that this would trigger a large-scale action to dismantle Arafat's regime and eradicate both PA and fundamentalist cadres involved in terror; an action much of Israel regarded as inevitable at some point and as necessary to end the terror war. But Sharon held back. He had declared a unilateral cease-fire on May 22 and he insisted he would maintain the cease-fire.

Sharon's restraint was attacked not only by many in both the leadership and rank and file of his Likud Party and others on the Right but also by a large part of the wider population. Even Chemi Shalev, very much a voice of the Israeli Left and a perennial critic of the state, spoke not long afterward of Sharon's "policy of restraint" and noted that it was "extremely unpopular in the Israeli public."[7]

Sharon himself offered relatively little explanation for his stance. He did speak of "strength in restraint" and said that he did not want to trigger a wider war, but he did not elaborate on his thinking or his strategy for ending the terror. Commentators gave various rationales. Some said Sharon was seeking mainly to sustain his coalition government and so was holding back in order to accommodate Labor sentiment. Others said he truly was wary of setting off a wider war and wanted Israel to be better prepared for such a possibility before he moved into the territories in greater force.

Still others suggested that Sharon was most concerned with avoiding introduction of an international force into the territories — something Arafat was eager to see and for which he had much support in Europe, the United Nations, and elsewhere — and did not want to take any action that would increase the likelihood of such intervention. (There was much evidence Arafat was hoping an Israeli misstep would greatly increase the loss of Palestinian life and this in turn would lead to international intervention, and evidence that his terror campaign was intended in part to bait Israel with the aim of triggering such a misstep. He was reported to have told his entourage, "The Jews will yet make the fatal mistake; all that is required is patience. A bomb that misses its target and hits a concentration of people, or some other operational hitch. Something will happen to turn the tables and what now looks like an unprofitable investment will yet be converted into a successful gambit."[8])

Another view was that Sharon did not want to dismantle the PA in a large-scale attack because it was not in Israel's interest either to be itself responsible for civil administration of Palestinian population centers or have the international community assume that responsibility. Yet another theory emphasized Sharon's relationship with President Bush: For all the criticism coming from the State Department, and occasionally from the president, Bush was clearly distrustful of Arafat and sympathetic to Sharon and to Israel's plight, and the prime minister wanted to cultivate this relationship and not take any measure that might alienate the White House.

Some Sharon supporters maintained that the IDF's fighting ability had been so compromised over the years of the "peace process" that rebuilding was necessary before it could either take on a full-scale assault against the terrorists or be properly prepared for the wider war that such a step might trigger and so the time was not ripe for more forceful action. Other supporters argued that Sharon's main interests were indeed to maintain his coalition government and to cultivate his relationship with the American administration and that these were the right priorities; that internal unity and American support were important for the struggle ahead and would allow Sharon to expand gradually the range of his responses to continued terror.

Sharon's critics took a darker view of his policies and of the various explanations offered for them. Some on the Right suggested that Sharon was most concerned with establishing himself as a statesman and reforming his widely held image — the product of popular glosses on his military career and his role in the Lebanon War — as a trigger-happy warrior too ready to seek military solutions to political problems; and they argued that he was reshaping his legacy at the expense of the nation's security. Others complained that he was bending too much to accommodate Labor; that, in any case, Labor was discredited and the public overwhelmingly supported stronger action. Still other voices on the Right noted that there was wide support for Israel in Congress and Sharon could act more forcefully without endangering the relationship with America. Also, it was argued, the IDF was prepared to take on the terrorists and at the same time to respond as necessary to any hostile action from elsewhere.

The overarching criticism from the Right was that, even if Sharon thought he could gradually enlarge his actions against the PA and the Islamist groups to dismantle their terror infrastructures, the approach was misconceived. Not only did it entail tolerating ongoing losses to terror. It also failed to provide sufficient disincentive to Arafat's continuing his terror war. On the contrary, by all evidence Arafat still thought he had a winning strategy. He held the world's attention on the conflict and had the Europeans and even the Americans eager for its resolution; he had them viewing him as an indispensable party; he had the Israelis at bay and taking constant casualties; he had discredited Sharon's election promise of a plan for security; he could sacrifice much of his infrastructure and even his manpower and, as long as he survived and could still cause mayhem, he was ahead. He still believed that in the end either the Israelis would cave in and accede to peace on his terms or the festering conflict would trigger intervention of an international force that would allow him to establish his state based on the pre-1967 lines, to do so without agreeing to a formal end to the conflict, and to continue to undermine Israel with further claims and further terror. Israel might think it was depriving him of crucial assets but he thought differently and that was what mattered. Moreover, Israel might believe that his population, paying the cost of his war, would eventually turn against Arafat, and it could point to some signs of Palestinian discontent with his leadership. But the PA's media and mosques and schools were telling Palestinians their problems were all Israel's fault, and Arafat's "police" could control those who might turn against him, and, in any case, the preponderance of evidence, including polls of Palestinian opinion, suggested the population was remaining overwhelmingly loyal to him and supportive of his war. Therefore, these critics of Sharon argued, the only way out was to sweep Arafat and his associates aside along with their terrorist cadres.

Critics on the Left, in contrast, insisted that Sharon should be negotiating with the Palestinians, offering them incentives to stop the terror; that the refusal to enter into talks while the terror continued was a reflection of Sharon's militaristic mind-set and he ought to be more forthcoming. They argued that he had no strategy for peace or security.

Despite the criticism at home and abroad, Sharon persisted over the subsequent months in essentially the same pattern of responses to terror, seeking to enlarge only incrementally and gradually the scope of IDF activity. This did not succeed in stemming the terror; on the contrary, whereas in the eight months of Arafat's war that had preceded the discotheque bombing of June 1, an average of twelve people a month were killed in Palestinian attacks, over the next eight months the number of murdered increased to twenty-one per month. Nor was there any indication that Arafat, for all his promises to Western diplomats to rein in the terror, felt obliged to rethink his terror strategy.

On the other hand, Sharon was able to increase the latitude of IDF responses with little interference from outside, and his supporters chose to see this as carefully calculated movement toward an ultimate victory. This greater military latitude, such as progressively more extensive incursions into Palestinian cities, proceeded despite on and off criticism from the American administration, especially the State Department.

For many Americans, the terror attacks on New York and Washington on September 11, 2001, led to stronger identification with and sympathy for Israel's struggle against Arab terror, and this was true particularly among those already inclined to be supportive of Israel. But in anti-Israel circles, and among some elements of the government, fashioning an American response to September 11 not only required constructing an international alliance but, more specifically, winning over Arab states and appeasing Arab opinion by pressuring Israel for concessions to Arafat. The State Department seemed, in fact, to increase its criticism of Israel in the weeks that followed, prompting Sharon to declare in early October that Israel would not play the role thrust upon Czechoslovakia in the 1930s and the West should not seek to propitiate the Arabs at Israel's expense. The Bush Administration took umbrage at the statement, the media generally, including in Israel, berated the prime minister, and Sharon offered "clarifications." But the speech likely served a salutory purpose domestically in its articulating what many Israelis felt regarding Western, particularly European, government and media commentary on the nation's war against Palestinian terror.

In addition to generally increasing the already substantial support for Israel in the United States, the events of September 11 and their aftermath had the effect as well of bringing into clearer focus the hypocrisy of State Department criticism of Israel's anti-terror measures. Many American columnists and commentators noted that State was indicting Israel for steps that the United States itself was taking, often in much more draconian fashion, against sources of anti-American terror.

An event that in some respects had a more straightforward impact on the American approach to Palestinian terror was the Israeli capture of the ship the *Karine A* in the Red Sea on January 3, 2002. The *Karine A* carried large amounts of sophisticated weaponry provided by Iran to the Palestinian Authority and its cargo would have dramatically increased the PA's capacity to wreak havoc in Israel. Arafat personally assured President Bush that he knew nothing about the weapons purchase, but irrefutable intelligence evidence proved otherwise. Bush, aware, of course, of Arafat's long involvement in terror, already had a low opinion of him and had refused to meet with him; but he seems to have believed that, with sufficient pressure and incentives, Arafat could be persuaded to work to end the terror war. Moreover, the administration wished to win Arab support for the broader war against terror — even more so as the administration began to look beyond the campaign against the Taliban regime in Afghanistan and to lay the groundwork for a military confrontation with Iraq — and this had reinforced its preparedness to assuage Arab opinion by attempting to work with Arafat.

In any case, that was the approach President Bush's administration had consistently pursued in addressing the Israeli-Palestinian conflict. But the *Karine A* affair and Arafat's lying to him about it seems to have played a significant role in Bush's gradually shifting to declaring Arafat an unfit partner and insisting that new Palestinian leadership was necessary for there to be movement toward peace.

General Anthony Zinni, who had been working with the two sides in an open-ended fashion to achieve some progress on the so-called Tenet Plan (named for CIA chief George Tenet, it called for the Palestinians to end terror, dismantle the terror infrastructure, and halt incitement and for Israel to stop military responses and pull back to its September, 2000, lines) was recalled to Washington in the wake of capture of the *Karine A*. Zinni told Arafat he would return only if Arafat implemented particular steps against terrorism and incitement and also took responsibility for the *Karine A*. On January 27, Vice President Cheney spoke of the seriousness of the *Karine A* affair and of his disbelief of Arafat's claims of innocence, and the next day President Bush told President Mubarak of Egypt that he had thought Arafat was willing to fight terror and was "disappointed" by the *Karine A* interception.[9]

In March, under pressure from Arab states, the administration sent General Zinni back to the area, and to meetings with Arafat, despite Arafat's not fulfilling Zinni's earlier preconditions. But when Vice President Cheney visited the Middle East the same month, he refused to see Arafat and indicated he would meet with him only when Arafat had taken some meaningful step toward ending the terror.[10] Secretary of State Powell met with Arafat in April but was reported to have conveyed to him a "last chance" message.[11] In May, the administration was still urging Israel to deal with Arafat, but on May 6, President Bush stated that "[Arafat] has disappointed me"[12] and a month later, on June 24, in a televised address, the President insisted that a change in Palestinian governance to a democratic leadership untainted by involvement in terror was a necessary precondition to peace.[13]

(President Bush subsequently articulated as a major policy goal the promotion of democracy throughout the Middle East. He noted that democratization had expanded in virtually every other region — in South America, Africa, eastern Europe, East Asia — with the Arab world standing alone as a solidly nondemocratic bloc while its people were no less deserving than others of the fruits of democratic governance.[14] This stance marked a dramatic shift from what had long been United States policy and American foreign service orthodoxy to the effect that, both for assuring access to Middle East oil and for other geostrategic reasons, the United States must support Arab strongman regimes and that to do otherwise — including to encourage democratization — could lead either to chaos or the rise to power of hostile forces and, in either case, a severe compromising of American interests.)

(The terror attacks of September 11, 2001, underscored the shortsightedness of that orthodoxy. American support for regimes such as those in Saudi Arabia and Egypt meant that the United States was targeted by the aggrieved, anti-government populations of such countries for its buttressing of their oppressors and was attacked as well by those nations' state-controlled media, which America's supposed allies were happy to have excoriate the United States as an enemy in their efforts to divert popular discontent away from themselves. In addition, Saudi Arabia financed and otherwise supported a worldwide campaign by Wahhabi clerics to promote their aggressive, Jihadist brand of Islam and incite attacks on the non-Moslem world and its institutions, with the Saudi government using this anti-Western, particularly anti-American, campaign as *quid pro quo* for Wahhabi support for the regime and, again, as a tool to counter discontent at home.)

(Of course, efforts to bring democratization to the Arab world will inevitably be fraught with problems and dangers. While Arab populations may be eager to be rid of their oppressors, they do not necessarily look to Western-style democracy as their preferred alternative. Some Arabs long for that, and more than a few very brave souls in Arab states have sought actively to promote liberal government and have all too often endured terrible abuse and hardship for their efforts; yet this is far from a widely endorsed goal. Events in Algeria in 1992, where relatively free elections were about to hand governance to radical Islamist forces until the transfer was thwarted by government cancellation of the polling, are but one illustration of the potential pitfalls of steps toward democratization.)

(Even the achieving of a truly democratized Middle East, marked not simply by the introduction of elections and popular government but embracing liberal democratization with all the constitutional protections that characterize modern Western states, would be no guarantee that Middle Eastern Arab nations would, for example, become more accepting of their non-Arab neighbor states, including Israel, or give up their use of Israel and the United States as distractions from and scapegoats for domestic ills. Democratization does not necessarily translate into tolerance, particularly in foreign policy. Still, if no panacea, democratization of the region would in all likelihood be such a boon to the citizens of the Arab nations and to the world at large — not least, to the besieged minorities in the Arab states, from the Christians of Egypt and the Berbers of Algeria to the targets of Arab genocide like the Kurds of Iraq and the blacks of Sudan — that the articulation of its pursuit as American policy and as the touchstone for American efforts in the region must be viewed as a most important and positive turn in the direction of American diplomacy.)

Meanwhile, March, 2002, saw a quantum increase in Palestinian terror, with 133 people killed, including 29 murdered in the worst single terror attack to date in Arafat's war, the suicide bombing of a Passover seder in Netanya on March 27. The onslaught triggered the IDF's ratcheting up its actions against Palestinian cadres, including, under the rubric Operation Defensive Shield, sustained raids into terrorist bastions in Palestinian areas previously left largely unscathed, as in the Jenin refugee camp.

This more aggressive policy continued over the months that followed. The wider world's response both to the increased terror and to Israel's actions recapitulated earlier patterns. The United Nations issued repeated condemnations of Israel. On April 15, The United Nations Human Rights Commission, under the presidency of Syria, passed a resolution supporting the "right" of Palestinians to use terror against Israel; six European members of the commission — Belgium, Sweden, Austria, Spain, France and Portugal — voted in favor of the resolution.[15] The UN also accused Israel of perpetrating a massacre in Jenin in its incursion there in April; only in August, after long availability of evidence to the contrary, did the UN clear Israel of the charge.[16]

European states individually and the European Union likewise continued their biased attacks on Israel, even as more information was emerging of European Union funds being used to finance Palestinian terror. The State Department issued repeated demands for Israeli "restraint" and State persisted in releasing reports whitewashing the Palestinian leadership's involvement in terror despite myriad proofs of that involvement.[17] President Bush's statements on Israeli actions were at times critical, at times supportive, emphasizing Israel's need to take steps to protect its population.

Israel, in any case, largely kept up its IDF operations at a higher level in the ensuing months and was doing so when, at the end of October, 2002, the Labor Party withdrew from the government.

The increased aggressiveness of IDF actions did not end the terror. In the first four months of accelerated IDF activity, April through July, 2002, terror claimed an average of forty-two lives per month; in the last five months of the year, the terror organizations were still killing twenty people monthly. Rightwing Israeli critics of the Sharon government argued Israel was still holding back too much and, by not pursuing all-out war against the terrorists, was squandering Israeli security and Israeli lives. As evidence of the failure of Sharon's policies, they pointed not only to ongoing terrorist attacks but also to continued PA incitement and determination to pursue the terror war, and high Palestinian support for the terror (as indicated by Palestinian polls such as that in September, 2002, showing 80 percent of Palestinians favoring continuing the terror[18]). Left-wing critics persisted in demanding Israeli concessions as the answer.

But government supporters argued that the increased operations after the Passover massacre in Netanya marked a turning point in the war and the beginning of a consistent wearing down of the Palestinians' terrorist resources and capabilities. Moreover, they maintained, the Israeli public's broad endorsement of this more aggressive policy demonstrated Sharon's success in uniting public opinion behind him and boded well for his being able to take what additional steps were necessary to win the war that Arafat had launched.

THE PEACE CAMP AND ARAFAT'S WAR, 2001–2002

The broad national unity that coalesced in response to the terror war reflected essentially the Israeli public's looking in a more clear-eyed way, without delusions, at its adversaries' intentions and at the challenges and dangers confronting the nation. The molding of this unity entailed, of course, a substantial shift of opinion by many earlier supporters of the "peace camp" and Oslo. But both the hard core of some "peace" groups, such as Peace Now, and elements of the political, journalistic, academic, and cultural elites in the country, despite the war launched against Israel in September, 2000, remained true believers in their vision of peace through Israeli concessions.

Another sign of a hard-core constituency clinging to the delusions of the "peace process" was the refusal by some IDF reservists during this period to serve in the territories, based on their conviction that Israel's presence there was the major cause of the conflict's persistence and that Israel had no right even to respond militarily in the territories to terror attacks. In January, 2002, fifty reserve officers signed a letter of refusal to serve. Soon the officers' list had tripled, and about 400 reservists told Yesh Gvul (an Israeli group to the left of Peace Now) that they, too, would not serve in the territories.

Some of the so-called refuseniks emphasized in their comments that they had witnessed abuses by soldiers in the territories. But, obviously, if they had seen abusive behavior their first obligation was to report it and push for such conduct being stopped, and it seemed relatively few people had taken that step. Moreover, if one recognized that Israel had legitimate, vital interests in the territories, efforts to stop inappropriate behavior would be one's only response to witnessing violations of proper conduct. Even if a soldier believed that the Israeli presence rendered such episodes inevitable, that there was an unavoidable morally corrosive dimension to that presence, the response would still be to seek out how the nation could best address that problem while defending its vital interests. The refusenik response that the only proper course was total Israeli withdrawal was predicated on the deluded conviction that withdrawal was not only compatible with peace but was indeed the path to peace. It is noteworthy in this regard that some refuseniks described and comprehended the violence of recent years not as a terror war initiated and prosecuted by Arafat and his cadres with the ultimate aim of challenging Israel's existence but rather as "the war for the peace of the settlements."[19]

Peace Now officially opposed soldiers' refusing to serve, yet some Peace Now activists endorsed the movement. Around the same time, a so-called Peace Coalition, comprised of "peace" activists from Peace Now, Meretz, and the Labor Party, launched a campaign entitled, "Out of the territories, back to ourselves." It advocated unilateral withdrawal from Gaza and most of the West Bank and resumption of negotiations based on retreat virtually to the pre-1967 lines.[20]

Israelis were dying in the war; the Israeli media and others were finally reporting on the incitement to terror and to pursuit of Israel's annihilation that had always been a feature of Palestinian media, mosques, and schools; scholars such as Bernard Lewis and Robert Wistrich were writing of the genocidal anti-Semitism purveyed by the Palestinian Authority and by other Arab governments through recent decades and unmoderated by Oslo; and organizations such as the ADL were likewise taking up the issue of genocidal anti-Semitism. Wistrich, in his 2002 report on Moslem anti-Semitism written for the American Jewish Committee, observed, "Such anti-Semitic incitement and falsifications [in statements by PA officials and in material broadcast on PA television] should not be trivialized or reduced to a mere annex of the Palestinian political struggle against Israeli occupation, as the conventional wisdom usually presents it. The latest intifada has made it transparently clear that Palestinian, Arab, and Muslim grievances against the Jewish state cannot be satisfied simply by Israeli territorial and political concessions."[21] But the true believers in the Peace Movement, along with many from Israel's political, journalistic, academic, and cultural elites, still held to the conviction that they knew better and that sufficient Israeli concessions would suffice to win peace.

The Labor Party, senior partner in the governments that had initiated and pursued the path of Oslo, suffered deep divisions and substantial constituent defections in the wake of the Palestinians' unleashing of their terror war, and party fissures became even more sharply defined in the context of Labor's joining Sharon's government after the February, 2001, election, with a number of Labor leaders opposing the move.

Those against participating in the government were generally those Laborites who, even five months into the war, were still enthralled with the delusions of Oslo, continued to look upon Arafat as their "peace" partner, and viewed Sharon as an impediment to their envisioned resolution of the conflict. But the Labor leaders who supported joining Sharon's governing coalition were hardly free of such delusions.

Labor's presence in the government through the twenty months from early March, 2001, to the end of October, 2002, likely did bolster national unity and also helped contain — to the degree that it was contained — anti-Israel sentiment and measures emanating from European leaders. At the least, Labor was not stirring up anti-government sentiment abroad and in effect giving foreign governments freer license to condemn Israel, as it had done at other times, and Peres as foreign minister at various points defended Israeli actions in European and other forums.[22] In October, 2002, Sharon credited Peres with having prevented European sanctions against Israel.[23]

But at the same time, Peres persisted in regarding Arafat as a "peace partner," someone with whom Israel could still fashion a genuine resolution of the conflict.[24] He continued for much of the period to pursue meetings with Arafat and to offer apologies for him, such as suggesting that Arafat did not have sufficient control to end terror, rather than acknowledging the Palestinian leader was not interested in stopping the terror and in fact was using all his resources to perpetuate it.[25] Peres also remained convinced the Oslo accords provided the foundations for an ultimate peace and insisted his vision of a New Middle East was still viable.[26]

Other Labor ministers clung to similar delusions. Defense Minister Ben-Eliezer declared in August, 2002, that the Palestinian leadership sincerely wanted to end the terror but was unable to do so.[27] Transportation Minister Ephraim Sneh, in April, 2002, after the murder of 133 people in March and another 37 since the beginning of April, threatened that Labor would bolt the coalition if the government sought to exile Arafat.[28]

Those Laborites who had opposed the party's joining Sharon's government were even more adamant in insisting upon the continued viability of Oslo and suitability of Arafat as a "peace partner." Despite all the terrorist atrocities and the overwhelming evidence of the PA's involvement in the terror, as well as the PA's promotion of its annihilationist agenda, many in Labor did not shrink from blaming Sharon for the absence of peace. The chief voice in this camp was the main architect of Oslo, Yossi Beilin. Various members of Arafat's regime acknowledged Arafat had chosen the path of war in the summer of 2000 and American negotiators such as Dennis Ross asserted that Arafat had no intention of coming to an agreement with Israel.[29] Yet Beilin insisted, in articles and speeches in 2001 and 2002, that an accord was within reach at Taba and that Sharon's election had destroyed the opportunity for peace.[30]

Beilin also faulted Barak and his foreign minister, Shlomo Ben-Ami, for not being forthcoming enough to complete an accord before the election,[31] and he attacked Peres for joining Sharon's government and supposedly thereby help-ing to snuff out the peace that was at hand.[32] In the midst of the carnage of Arafat's war, Beilin asserted that the concept of defensible borders was anachro-nistic and if Israel returned virtually to its pre-1967 lines in the context of a signed agreement with the Palestinians all would be well.[33] He berated Sharon for making the manifestly obvious assertion that there was, under present cir-cumstances, no chance for genuine peace and the most that could be hoped for was the more modest achievement of a stable armistice.[34]

Beilin evenhandedly characterized the terror war as the consequence of "mu-tual lack of trust and mutual violations."[35] He acknowledged that it was a mis-take not to address Palestinian incitement during the Oslo years but persisted in refusing to see the import of the PA's constant use of its media, mosques, and schools to denigrate Israel and Jews and to push Palestinians to pursue Israel's destruction.[36] For Beilin, such incitement neither called into question the PA's interest in peace nor dampened his conviction that sufficient Israeli con-cessions would be rewarded with resolution of the conflict. While labeling Sharon a racist who is against peace, Beilin said of Arafat, "I think I can say there is a type of mutual trust. To a very great degree I do trust him."[37]

Beilin was active in distorting the descent into war in other ways as well. Barak had offered at Taba to withdraw virtually to the pre-1967 lines and dis-mantle most settlements and to cede pre-1967 Israeli lands to the Palestinians in compensation for the small areas of the West Bank to be retained by Israel; and the Palestinians themselves indicated at Taba that the territorial disputes were largely resolved and that the crucial outstanding issue was the so-called right of return. But Arafat and those around him, starting a few months after the collapse of the talks, sought to shift the focus of diplomatic attention and public perception, particularly in America, away from the PA's rejection of a deal, and they did so by claiming that Barak had actually not been that forth-coming and the real impediment to an agreement was the settlements.[38] Arafat's own earlier statements contradicted this ploy. For example, he said after Camp David, "We told the Israelis: [We demand] not only al-Haram al-Sharif, the Holy Sepulcher, or the Armenian quarter, but the whole of Jerusalem, the whole of Jerusalem, the whole of Jerusalem"; and, "The return of the refugees to their homeland and their dwellings [in Israel] . . . is sacred."[39] But much of the "peace camp" embraced the Palestinian revisionism.

As noted, Peace Now, during the first months of war, asserted that the prob-lem was the settlements. It subsequently ignored events in Taba, and intelligence about the Palestinian agenda, and continued focusing on the settlements as the supposed obstacle to peace.[40] Various Labor leaders, including Beilin, joined in emphasizing the settlements as a factor at least equal to Palestinian incitement and terror in accounting for the collapse of talks.[41]

Even Peres rejected this disingenuous emphasis on the settlements. Indeed,

Peres went further; early in 2001, he joined Sharon in voicing concerns about an American plan that prescribed a total settlement freeze as *quid pro quo* for ending terror (the so-called Mitchell Plan). As Peres pointed out in a letter to Secretary of State Powell, a settlement freeze had not been part of Oslo — Rabin had informally agreed not to start new settlements but would not end the growth of established ones — and so the Mitchell Plan amounted to rewarding terror with political gains.[42] Yet Beilin continued to insist that settlements were the most important issue and ending settlement activity was the key to peace.

Some in the Israeli media, including erstwhile supporters of Oslo, now excoriated Beilin for his having corrupted the political process in his pursuit of "peace" — as in his repeated attempts to engineer in secret, and without authority, *faits accomplis* — and for his willful distortion of the truth. Ari Shavit did so in an article in November, 2001, entitled, with reference to Beilin's record, "A Direct Threat to Democracy."[43] The *Jerusalem Post's* Amotz Asa-El was an early Oslo enthusiast and had, as he reported, "praised Beilin as an influential visionary." In December, 2001, he described the Labor Party's ongoing defense and promotion of Oslo's delusions as exemplified by Beilin's statements, and Labor's blaming the Right for Oslo's failure, as a "Labor Party horror show of cowardice, aloofness and conceit."[44]

Another former Oslo supporter, *Maariv* commentator Amnon Dankner, now referred to Oslo as "The Big Scam." He decried those political leaders who developed and pushed the Oslo agreements as either not appreciating the dangers of what they were doing and therefore being "lousy politicians" or recognizing the potential dangers but choosing to hide them from the public and having, then, "intentionally and maliciously deceived" the nation. Dankner is no less critical of those who were now continuing to support Oslo "in a pathetic attempt to resurrect the peace process."[45]

Not surprisingly, the leaders of Labor's chief partner in pro-Oslo governments, the Meretz Party, likewise clung to the delusions of the "peace" process, distorted events surrounding Arafat's war, and chose to blame settlements and the Right for the absence of peace. Meretz chairman Yossi Sarid continued to argue that the terror was a natural response to Israel's presence in the territories and withdrawal would end the conflict.[46] Sarid, who has incessantly in his career attacked the Right for its supposedly demeaning perceptions of Arabs, characterized those Israelis living across the Green Line as "members of a different planet" and "wicked cancers . . . that should be eliminated."[47] In an Op-Ed in the *New York Times*, Sarid largely blamed Sharon for the violence and the absence of peace and equated him with Arafat, writing of the two of them "dancing their dance of bloodshed and despair." His main criticism of Arafat was that he "has foolishly played into Mr. Sharon's hands."[48]

While most Israelis felt Sharon was showing too much restraint in the face of the terror, another Meretz leader, deputy speaker of the Knesset Naomi Chazan, attacked the Israeli actions — killing of terrorist leaders, closures, roadblocks — as "excessive" and destructive of Israel's soul. Chazan alluded to reports of violations of proper behavior by some Israeli soldiers but invoked such reports not to insist on the need for troop discipline but rather to elaborate a blanket condemnation of the entire IDF response to terror. She acknowledged no legitimate Israeli interest in or claim on any part of the territories, regurgitated the old false alternative of Israel having to choose between controlling all the territories or fully withdrawing, cast the former as immoral and insisted that full withdrawal is the key to peace.[49] Despite Israeli concessions at Camp David and Taba and Arafat's rejection of them and resort to war, and despite all the PA's inveighing against Israel's very existence both before and after September, 2000, Chazan accorded the Palestinians' insistence that the terror was simply an effort to "end the occupation" equal legitimacy with Israeli complaints of an Arab war against the state's very survival.[50]

Chazan also faulted the government from another vantage, attacking Sharon for "humiliating and denigrating Arafat" in his criticisms of him.[51]

Yet another Meretz leader, Ran Cohen, in November, 2002, having suddenly discovered that the Palestinian Broadcasting Corporation, since its inception in 1994, had been putting out "subversive and racist" programming, much of it aimed at children, insisted something be done about it. Responding to a report that had documented PBC indoctrination of children to commit suicide attacks and seek to destroy Israel, Cohen urged the Israeli Minister of Communications to revoke the airwave licenses granted the PA. Nevertheless, Cohen at the same time joined with Peace Now in attacking the settlements as the obstacle to resolution of the conflict and still supported the delusional Peace Now perspective that full withdrawal would win Israel a full peace.[52]

The cognitive disconnect exhibited in Ran Cohen's on the one hand awakening to the murderous campaign against Israel's very existence orchestrated by the PA and yet his remaining true to the delusions that the conflict was essentially over borders and soluble by Israeli territorial concessions was not uncommon among those in the "peace camp" who were forced by Arafat's war to reassess their views. Some attempted to reconcile their inconsistent perspectives by maintaining that Arafat was the sole source of the terror war and the promotion of Israel's annihilation and that without Arafat the rest of the Palestinians, and the Arab world more broadly, would still be peace partners and so Oslo was still viable. But others among erstwhile Oslo supporters pointed to the absurdity of such a stance.

For example, Ehud Yaari, Israel's most prominent journalist on Arab affairs and, like Shavit, Asa-El, and Dankner, an early proponent of Oslo, wrote in June, 2001, of the "inherent contradiction" in recognizing that Arafat could not be won over to peace by Israeli concessions, seeing that the PA leadership and much of its constituency had not been reconciled by Oslo to the prospect of peaceful co-existence with the Jewish state, but believing that if Arafat were silenced Israel could safely make further Oslo-like concessions and the Palestinians, in response, would be miraculously transformed and peace would indeed be gained.[53] Yaari was also one of those mainstream journalists who now took up the issue of the government-promoted anti-Semitism and incitement to genocide being purveyed both by the PA and by Arab states.[54]

Yet another journalist long supportive of Oslo who now viewed things differently was Hirsh Goodman, founding editor of the *Jerusalem Report* and a prominent fixture of Israeli journalism. As an article discussing shifts in Israeli opinion noted in July, 2002, "Over many years [Goodman] knew, just knew, that the appropriate concessions, offered in the right way, would surely bring peace." The writer could have added that over these years Goodman was also vicious in his denunciations of those Israelis who would not endorse his rosy delusions. However, the author quotes Goodman as now saying, "I supported Oslo. I supported talking with Arafat. The greatest disappointment was to discover that despite everything I believed, everything I've promulgated, that asshole never gave up terror."[55]

Another major journalist, Israel's leading media commentator on military affairs, Ze'ev Schiff, likewise now acknowledged the PA's betrayal of its Oslo obligations, even though those betrayals had been occurring since 1993. Schiff now spoke of the error of trusting in any Palestinian cooperation in security matters.[56]

But among those journalists rethinking their early hopes for Oslo, some, such as Goodman and Schiff, like some Israeli politicians, at once acknowledged now the self-deluded thinking of Oslo's Israeli framers and implementers and yet still clung to visions of an agreement with the Palestinians along Oslo lines as the path to peace. For example, in an article published in April, 2002, Goodman stated that the terror is aimed at Israel's destruction and Israel is fighting for its survival. But he predicted that new leaders — he characteristically could not resist equating Arafat and Sharon as obstacles to his envisioned peace — will bring the conflict to its "logical end": Israel out of the territories and the Palestinians genuinely happy with a two-state solution.[57] Schiff similarly seemed to recognize finally the Palestinians' existential challenge to Israel. Yet he continued to suggest that Israeli settlement policy had been a key obstacle to peace and that the Palestinians would ultimately agree to a demilitarized state in the territories living in peace beside Israel; that Syria, too, would reconcile itself to peaceful coexistence; and that Israel would be able to withdraw safely from the Golan Heights and from "Palestinian" areas such as the Jordan Valley and largely return to its pre-1967 borders.[58]

There were also Israeli journalists who remained committed to indicting Israel despite Arafat's war and who did so by insisting that the war was somehow

Israel's fault and so Israeli reform was still the key to winning peace. Among such journalists were the three whom, as noted in Chapter Sixteen, *Yediot Acharonot's* Nahum Barnea had identified in November, 2000, as having failed the "lynch test": *Haaretz* reporters Gideon Levy, Amira Haas, and Akiva Eldar.[59]

Gideon Levy continued to embrace the view that Ehud Barak's offers to the Palestinians in 2000 had not been sufficiently generous and Israel bore as much responsibility as the Palestinians for the violence. Among Israel's sins, according to Levy, was its failure to agree in 1993 to withdraw to the pre-1967 borders in return for the Palestinians' "major historic concession at Oslo," their supposed reconciliation to Israel's existence.[60]

Levy also, bizarrely, decried the new Israeli unity in response to the terror as itself reprehensible, a danger to democracy, and indeed "a consensus that would shame no totalitarian regime." Moreover, Levy insisted that Israeli military measures in response to the terror were, in their inadvertent killing of innocent civilians, no less acts of terror than the bus and discotheque and restaurant bombings of the Palestinians. Perhaps most dishonestly, Levi totally ignored the genocidal message of Palestinian incitement. Rather, he declared, without evidence or explanation, that Palestinian media fare was "not much worse than the incitement on Israeli radio and television." He again ignored what the Palestinians themselves acknowledged to be their promotion of war in his suggesting that the terror can only be ascribed either to Israeli provocations or to Palestinian genes, and so must be attributed to the former.[61]

Amira Haas likewise continued her litany of contorted arguments and distortions of fact in the service of indicting Israel and legitimizing Palestinian attitudes and actions. In May, 2001, Haas was still insisting that it is Israel's presence in the territories that is the essential obstacle to peace and that "the vast majority in the Palestinian political organizations still support a solution of two states in the June 4, 1967 borders"; when, of course, the major Palestinian political organizations — the PA and its subsidiaries and the fundamentalist groups — were declaring to their constituents their dedication to Israel's ultimate destruction. Haas also advanced her Israel-bashing agenda by misrepresenting Israeli policies on such matters as water distribution and land leasing, falsely claiming for example, that Israeli settlements had ready access to water while Israel "sets quotas for Palestinian personal water consumption," and that Israel's "'national land' cannot be leased to non-Jews."[62]

Akiva Eldar, too, continued to argue that peace could be had if only Israel would leave the territories, and he persisted as well in invoking false claims to support his assertion. In an article in February, 2001, for example, Eldar wrote that "the Taba meeting clearly proved Israel does have a partner for the peace negotiations," even though, in fact, Arafat rejected Israel's Taba proposals without offering alternatives and the PA representatives still insisted Israel must accept the Palestinian "right of return," a stance observers overwhelmingly agree represents a mortal threat to Israel.[63] Israeli foreign minister at the time, Shlomo Ben-Ami, among the most eager enthusiasts of Oslo and Israel's chief negotiator at Taba, emerged from the talks newly convinced that Arafat would not agree to a deal because he "doesn't accept the legitimacy" of Israel.[64] Yet Eldar went on insisting to his readers that Arafat remained a partner and Israel was the problem.

In April, 2001, Eldar wrote that, "Even the most respected of the intelligence assessors in the IDF believe the war is over the settlements, not Tel Aviv, nor even the Jewish Quarter in the Old City of Jerusalem."[65] But, again, the truth was the opposite. For example, one of the most respected IDF intelligence assessors, General Eran Lerman, was quoted in late November, 2000, as stating, "Arafat stresses the temporary, conditional character of his peace agreement obligations and alludes to the stages theory for the liberation of Palestine."[66]

Journalist-commentator-author Amos Elon was another who persisted in seeing the conflict as not over the Palestinians' desire to expunge Israel but rather over borders. In an article in *The New York Review of Books* in December, 2002, Elon wrote in almost Beilin-like prose of how wonderful everything was becoming for Israel before the 1967 war and how that conflict really was a disaster for the nation, a "Pyrrhic victory," because Israel thereby acquired control of the territories, became addicted to perpetuating that control, and so set the stage for Palestinian terror. There is no reference to pre-1967 Palestinian terror. In Elon's fanciful history, the decade before 1967 was not only free of such terror but was also marked by "gradual detente between Israel and Egypt." Equally divorced from historical reality is his claim of Israel's having rejected numerous opportunities for peace. Those opportunities were squandered, Elon argues, because all post-1967 Israeli governments essentially insisted on maintaining control over the territories, with the differences among their plans being relatively insignificant. Details offered by Elon about the growth of the settlements and related Israeli policy in the territories are equally spurious. For example, he, like Amira Haas, makes assertions about water use in the territories — "[Palestinians'] water faucets go dry and . . . scarce water resources are taken over for the use of settlers" — that mimic Palestinian propaganda but are entirely false.

Not surprisingly, Elon also endorses the Palestinian version of Camp David and Taba, according to which Ehud Barak's offers were insufficiently forthcoming. Yes, Elon acknowledges, President Clinton did sweeten the proposal, and Israel agreed to Clinton's formula, and Arafat did not respond initially and then hedged his response; but, he insists, peace was still likely at hand if Israel had not elected Sharon.

Elon makes a point of acknowledging in the article, as though this were some sort of honest confession, that he does not "pretend to know what makes Arafat tick." But Elon's writings suggest rather that he did not want to know what made Arafat and those around him tick, because their stated intentions and actions flew in the face of all of Elon's formulas for peace through Israeli concessions. Elon tells us he was inclined to believe Arafat wanted a state living in peace beside Israel because, even though he had consistently articulated, in statements in Arabic, a more bellicose agenda, "he has often said he wants [that]."

Elon is less willing to take Ariel Sharon at his word. Sharon had said he was prepared to accept a democratic Palestinian state that has foresworn terror, but Elon still believes "Sharon is determined to prevent" such a denouement. Again, in Elon's formula, all would be well except for Israeli rejection of the proper path to peace. Of course, the settlements represent for Elon that rejection, whatever Barak offered, and uprooting the settlements and returning to the pre-1967 boundaries will, in Elon's view, gain for Israel the peace that was beckoning in the supposedly halcyon days that preceded the Six Day War.[67]

Among academic enthusiasts of the "peace process," too, some were disabused of their earlier delusions by Arafat's war while others continued to embrace visions of peace through Israeli self-indictment and self-reform.

Ron Pundak, one of the academics who represented Israel in the first Oslo negotiations, fell into the latter category. Pundak declared in September, 2002, two years into the war, that his one regret about Oslo was not that it was predicated on a false comprehension of Palestinian intentions and objectives or that it did not have an enforcement mechanism to address ongoing Palestinian incitement and terror. Rather, his regret was that Oslo did not prohibit growth in settlements.[68]

In a similar vein, David Newman, chairman of the Department of Politics and Government at Ben-Gurion University, wrote in April, 2002, that the reason the conflict continued was Israel's refusal to end its occupation of the West Bank and Gaza. Newman also insisted that the condemnations of Israel by Europe and by other elements of the international community were evidence of the rightness of his claim, and he dismissed disparagingly any suggestion that anti-Semitism played a role in European criticism of Israel. He presumably believed it was also not a factor in the widespread assaults on European Jews and Jewish institutions that accompanied the Palestinians' terror war.[69]

Prime Minister Sharon had expressed his support for a Palestinian state once the Palestinians were governed by a regime that accepted Israel's existence, and this stance converged with President Bush's vision of a future peace. But Newman insisted that, while Ehud Barak had called for ultimate establishment of a Palestinian state, Israel was now opposing that objective. Newman's argument gains logical consistency and coherence only if one assumes that "Palestinian state" means a state in all of the West Bank and Gaza, which, in fact, Israel did now oppose, for good strategic reasons and with the support of UN Security Council resolutions 242 and 338. Nor is the United States pushing

Israel to accept a Palestinian state so defined. Rather, such a state was Newman's agenda as the pathway to peace.[70]

Professor Moshe Zimmermann is a Hebrew University historian who, as noted in Chapter Fourteen, has insisted that Jews ought properly to see themselves in universalist rather than national terms and that the teaching of Zionist history in Israeli schools, in its diverging from a proper, universalist emphasis, is comparable to the education of Hitler Youth. After a terrorist bombing at a Hebrew University cafeteria killed nine in July, 2002, Zimmermann opined that such terror is natural because of the occupation. Despite the Palestinians' declaring quite openly an annihilationist agenda, at least in speeches in Arabic by PA leaders and in PA media and mosques, Professor Zimmermann still discerned in them a more pacific intent if only Israel would make the right reforms and concessions.[71]

As noted in Chapter Fourteen, Baruch Kimmerling, a sociologist at Hebrew University, had argued that Jews are not properly a people and must make amends for aspiring to peoplehood. In March, 2001, Kimmerling declared that Palestinians have a "moral right" to resist the occupation with any means at their disposal. This was his explanation, and justification, for Palestinian terror, even as he called it immoral. Kimmerling did not mention the Palestinians' agenda of supplanting Israel with a Palestinian state from the river to the sea, presumably because he was not fully certain of their "moral right" to that goal, or he at least was not prepared to endorse that "right" publicly.[72]

In arguing that all of the West Bank and Gaza properly belong to the Palestinians and that they have the right to do anything to achieve control over their territories, Kimmerling also ignores Israel's accommodation of Palestinian claims in those areas at Camp David and Taba, as well as UN Security Council acknowledgment of legitimate Israeli interests in the territories and of Israel's right to advance those interests in negotiations toward a settlement. Here again, Kimmerling prefers not to have such facts muddy his concept of "moral right" — a concept clearly defined for him by visions of a wished-for peace to be had by Israeli self-castigation and capitulation.

Ze'ev Sternhell is another Israeli academic who has refused to believe what the Palestinians have said are their goals and have done their best to translate into actions. Sternhell, a professor of political science at Hebrew University, had acknowledged that the Israeli version of nationalism, while regrettable, "was unusually moderate." But he had speculated that all would have been well in Arab-Israeli relations if only the Jews had been more self-effacing and less insistent in their desire for a nation.[73] In an article in June, 2001, Sternhell asserted that the Palestinians did not really mean it when they insisted on their "right of return" and that the Israelis were culpable for taking them at their word and thereby making peace more distant.[74]

While dismissing Palestinian interest in the "right of return," Sternhell — like many of his academic colleagues — was simply silent on the Palestinian demand for the ultimate dissolution of Israel. He would have others believe as he does that a state in the territories would satisfy Palestinian aspirations and end the conflict, and he apparently did not wish to confuse people by mentioning the Palestinians' stated intentions.

Also consistent with this wishful thinking, Sternhell declared elsewhere, "Settlement of the West Bank and Gaza Strip does not answer any real national need."[75] Of course, while some settlements were established for ideological, or historical-religious, reasons, others were founded in sparsely populated strategic areas to reinforce the legitimate Israeli security-based claim to those areas. But strategic considerations become meaningless for those who believe that full withdrawal will inexorably yield full and irreversible peace. Starting from this wishful premise, Sternhell's assertions that the settlements and the Israeli presence in the territories are the obstacle to peace — untrue by any measure of reality — become a tautology requiring no proof.

Not surprisingly, those academics, journalists, politicians, and others in Israel who still chose to construe the settlements as the chief obstacle to peace displayed very little sympathy for the settlers, even as the settlers were disproportionately the victims of the Palestinian terror war. Sternhell took this indifference one step further. In a May, 2001, article in *Haaretz*, he advised the Palestinians that it would be politically wise of them to focus their attacks more exclusively on the settlers.[76] For Sternhell, these people stood in the way of his fantasies of peace and so they were expendable.

Ari Shavit, writing in June, 2001, noted, and condemned, the indifference of much of the "peace" camp to the killing of settlers, including many women and children. "On almost a daily basis, Israeli citizens who live beyond the Green Line are being murdered by the historic allies of the Israeli peace movement, yet the movement is silent . . . Silence is also being observed by Israeli human rights groups. These human rights groups have taught Israelis for years that every drop of human blood is precious and that one must not distinguish between the blood of one group of human beings and another. Yet . . . the members of the Israeli human rights groups can find no place in their heart for any description of even one instance in which Jews have been killed on the highway by the special killing squads of the Palestinian dictatorship . . . Silence is also being observed by Israeli intellectuals and by the majority of columnists in the nation's newspapers . . . It is a blood-chilling silence and it raises the question whether . . . what has been presented here as the hallowed value of universalism was not in fact only an extremely particularist value that was intended to serve the specific needs of a specific cult of enlightened human beings."[77]

Shavit's piece did not elaborate on the political agenda of those whose attitude he condemns, nor did it cite Sternhell's going beyond silence to recommend to the Palestinians that they focus their attacks on settler targets. An editorial in the *Jerusalem Post* published in December, 2002, after many more murderous attacks, did both:

"Sternhell also spelled out the impeccable logic of throwing the settlers to the wolves: 'By adopting such an approach, the Palestinians would be sketching the profile of a solution that is the only inevitable one: The amended Green Line will be an international border and territory will be handed over to compensate the Palestinians for land that has already been or will be annexed to Israel.' In other words, settlements matter because the Arab-Israeli conflict is a border conflict. Settlements block a territorial compromise, so they are, in this thinking, a strategic obstacle to peace, perhaps more so than terrorism itself, which in theory can be stopped at any time . . .

"[But] what should not be debatable today is that the basic premise of Oslo . . . that the conflict was essentially a border conflict — has been disproved. In the summer and winter of 2000, the Palestinians first rejected a near total territorial capitulation by Israel, and followed with a war, in case the point has not been made clearly enough.

" . . . If there were no settlements, there would still have been a war . . . The stubborn focus on settlements, including by the Labor Party, is a distraction from confronting the real source of the conflict, which is the refusal to accept the legitimacy of Israel as a permanent Jewish state."[78]

The most notable of the new historians who changed his views in response to Arafat's war was Benny Morris, although Morris has suggested that his current perspectives are not new, that he had long held them but had simply not discussed them publicly. In any case, Morris now insisted that the Palestinians were obviously not interested in genuine peace; that their rejection of Clinton's proposals, which would have given them, according to Morris, 95 percent of the West Bank and all of Gaza, demonstrated this. Morris also noted that no figure in the Palestinian political establishment had ever been willing to renounce the "right of return," which he characterized as a formula for Israel's destruction. Moreover, Morris declared that he did not believe there was any realistic prospect, for generations at best, of the Palestinians giving up the "right of return" and the goal of Israel's destruction.

Morris also expressed opposition to Israel's accepting responsibility for the refugee problem even as *quid pro quo* for ostensible Palestinian renunciation of the "right of return." He insisted that to do so would be a lie, as the problem's essential cause was the war launched against Israel by the Palestinians and the Arab states. In addition, the Palestinians would inevitably disregard their renunciation and exploit Israel's acceptance of responsibility to press the "right of return."

Morris also faulted Ehud Barak for his willingness to cede the Temple Mount to Palestinian sovereignty. He asserted that if anyone should have exclusive control, it should be the Jews. In Morris's view, some shared authority could be acceptable, but there was no justice in acquiescing to exclusive Palestinian possession.[79]

Morris elaborated on these opinions in subsequent articles and interviews,[80] even as he still published tendentious history exhibiting many of the faults of his earlier works, such as his 2002 biography of Glubb Pasha.[81]

Unlike Morris, revisionist historian Avi Shlaim, generally less respectful of both historical and contemporary truth than even Morris, remained adamant in blaming Israel, and, more particularly now, Ariel Sharon, for the absence of peace. Shlaim supported his stance by ignoring many key recent events and mustering imaginative contortions of others. For example, in an article attacking Sharon in January, 2002, Shlaim noted Arafat's rejection of Barak's "offer of statehood encompassing Gaza and 95 percent of the West Bank," but he used this to demonstrate the culpability of Sharon. According to Shlaim's logic, Sharon, in now offering Arafat less, obviously knew Arafat would reject that, too; and so Sharon clearly was not interested in peace![82] In contrast, in an interview not long afterward, Shlaim asserted that Arafat "remains committed to a peaceful resolution of the conflict with Israel."[83]

In this interview, Shlaim also regurgitated many of the false claims about the 1948 war and its aftermath — such as that Israel had the military advantage in terms of manpower and equipment in 1948, and that there were opportunities for peace in the wake of the war that Israel had failed to pursue — that had been featured in his earlier publications.

Shlaim subsequently unleashed a venomous attack on Morris for his public criticism of the Palestinians and his recent perspectives regarding the prospects for genuine peace. Writing in the *Guardian* in February, 2002, Shlaim, essentially ignoring Palestinian terror, stated that the most salient event in recent months had been "the sound of Merkava tanks invading Palestinian cities on the West Bank and refugee camps in Gaza in the most flagrant violation of a long series of agreements that placed these areas under the control of the Palestinian Authority." Shlaim railed against an article by Morris that conveyed Morris's new views on the conflict and had appeared in the *Guardian* the previous day. Shlaim characterized the piece as "seething with contempt and hatred for the Arabs in general and the Palestinians in particular," and he insisted that "no evidence is available to sustain the argument of Arab intransigence." Shlaim again claimed that the chief culprit in the recent violence was Sharon — now attacked for his September, 2000, visit to the Temple Mount — even though PA officials had repeatedly acknowledged the violence was planned beforehand by Arafat. Shlaim also asserted that the Palestinians and "all the neighboring Arab states . . . recognize Israel's right to exist within its pre-1967 borders," and so all that was required for peace to reign was an Israeli withdrawal.[84]

Tom Segev is another revisionist historian who, despite the terror war, hewed to his stance that Israeli reform is the key to resolution of the conflict. The Palestinians were declaring in essence that their grievance is with the existence of a non-Arab, non-Moslem state in Palestine, and — perhaps more pertinently — Israeli media were now reporting on Palestinian declarations in this vein and Israeli political leaders were finally paying attention to them. But Segev persisted in his own comprehension of the conflict and dismissed any alternative understanding. As he phrased it in a column in the *New York Times* in November, 2001, "Many Israelis ignore the causes that lead Palestinians to wage a war of terror against them [i.e., according to Segev, Israeli actions], choosing instead to argue that they have been attacked not for anything they have done but for who they are." (It is noteworthy that in the same column Segev suggested that the United States had likewise been attacked on September 11 for what it had done to incite the Moslem world rather than, as many Americans would have it, simply for what America is.)[85]

Segev has been a longtime promoter of post-Zionism and has regarded its perspectives as tools for pushing Israelis toward the reforms and concessions that would ostensibly win peace. He now expressed regrets that Palestinian terror had triggered in Israel a rejection of such perspectives and a revitalization of Zionist ideals. In another *New York Times* Op-Ed, he lauded those Israelis still embracing post-Zionism and invoked in doing so the old sanctimonious assertion of many who have chosen to flee a besieged Jewish identity and have insisted their flight was for the sake of their "individuality." Segev said of their post-Zionist soul mates, "They do not live for nationalist ideals or the abstract ideology of Zionism. They live for life itself, as individuals." The notion that there are people who see their individual aspirations best capable of realization as citizens of a Jewish state, a nation created and sustained by Jewish self-determination, the same right of self-determination accorded other peoples around the globe, seemed still to be beyond Segev's comprehension.[86]

As an additional element of his denunciation of a resurgent Zionism, Segev invoked the ahistorical notion of a direction to history: "It is as if history had turned backward."[87] Indeed, Segev seemed to regard any bogus argument as preferable to rethinking his own delusional fantasies concerning the ongoing war against Israel and potential paths to peace.[88]

Within Israel's artistic and literary circles, as in other Israeli elites, some abandoned their former enthusiastic embrace of Oslo and of post-Zionism in the wake of the Palestinians' launching of their terror war. A notable example is the novelist Eyal Megged, son of Aharon Megged but formerly best known, and widely acclaimed, for two novels resonant with post-Zionist themes, with heroes alienated from their Jewish and Israeli identities and desperately seeking meaning elsewhere.

In the face of the terror that had wracked Israel even before September, 2000, and the PA's violation of its anti-incitement and anti-violence obligations under Oslo, Megged had already grown to doubt the pro-Oslo, post-Zionist verities of his literary and artistic friends. After September, 2000, he began criticizing the Oslo process and its Israeli initiators and supporters. He subsequently published a novel, *The Black Light*, whose Israeli protagonist is a Hebrew University professor estranged from his academic colleagues because he does not share their cult-like worship of Oslo. He leaves Israel, but, unlike Megged's earlier protagonists, he is driven to find meaning for his life within a Jewish and Zionist context and ultimately returns to Israel, having discovered for himself the meaning he was seeking.[89]

The Black Light was largely either ignored or panned by the doyens of the Israeli cultural elite, who apparently resented Megged's political conversion.[90] Indeed the more common reaction of that elite to Arafat's war has been perhaps to castigate the Palestinian leadership, to acknowledge its continued dedication to Israel's destruction and recognize in part the delusions of Oslo, but at the same time to cling to many of those delusions; or, alternatively, to remain unswerving enthusiasts of Oslo, their vision unaltered by Arafat's war.

A.B. Yehoshua represents an example of the former mentality. On the one hand he went a long way toward acknowledging that the Palestinians' objective is still Israel's annihilation; yet, he continued to insist that the solution to Israel's predicament lies in establishing borders between Israel and the Palestinians and, more particularly, in Israel's withdrawing from the territories. While to many Israelis, Arafat's war demonstrated — if further demonstration were needed — Israel's legitimate interest in at least parts of the territories, Yehoshua persisted in insisting that Israel has no such legitimate strategic interest and is, even in uninhabited areas, an alien interloper whose presence must end in order for peace to prevail and for Israelis to enjoy a "normal" national life. It remains unclear how, other than by wishful self-delusion, Yehoshua reconciles recognition of the Palestinians' annihilationist agenda with his conviction that they will allow Israelis to live a normal life if only the nation withdraws to the pre-1967 lines.[91]

Amos Oz is another who at least transiently acknowledged that the Palestinians' terror campaign was not initiated and pursued over the issue of borders. Oz wrote in early January, 2001, "Israel is offering the Palestinians a peace accord based on 1967 borders, with minor mutual amendments . . . The Palestinian nation is rejecting this agreement. Its leaders now demand a 'right of return' . . . In view of this Palestinian position, Israelis acting for peace must not pretend it is business as usual. Nor should we continue to argue, as we have for decades, that 'the sole obstacle to peace is Israel's occupation of the Palestinian territories.'"[92]

But despite this insight, for Oz it has indeed been, essentially, business as usual. The man who had said that Israel's doves must be the first to take up arms if the Palestinians violate their agreements with Israel and continue to pursue the nation's destruction has, in fact, advocated a much more pacific response to the terror war; and, even as a wide range of Israelis faulted Sharon's restraint in the face of the terror, Oz has excoriated Sharon for his military measures. Indeed, Oz has repeatedly equated Sharon with Arafat. He has written of "the Siamese twins, Mr. Sharon and Mr. Arafat — I now call them 'Mr. Sharafat,'"[93] has suggested that they are equally culpable for the carnage and has declared that, "The leadership of Mr. Sharon and Mr. Arafat . . . is a cowardly leadership."[94]

The basis for his vituperative attacks on Sharon is, apparently, Oz's continued faith that peace can be had if Israel would only withdraw to the pre-1967 lines and his outrage that Sharon is not acting on that faith and does not share it. In March, 2002, Oz proclaimed that "every Israeli" and "every Palestinian" knows the solution to the conflict is "peace between two states, established by the partition of the land . . . based on Israel's pre-1967 borders."[95] Oz has at various points urged a unilateral Israeli withdrawal and expressed the hope that the Palestinians would ultimately respond by granting Israel peace in return.

How does Oz reconcile this hope with his recognition that the war launched by Arafat after Camp David has been driven by Palestinian aspirations to Israel's extinction? Oz attempts to square this circle by insisting, strangely, that the Palestinians are really waging two wars against Israel, one for a state beside Israel and one for Israel's annihilation. He even declares that "any decent person ought to support" the former war while opposing the latter.[96] In explicating this bizarre theory, Oz repeatedly associates the war of extermination with the Islamists among the Palestinians, suggesting that the rest of the Palestinian community thinks in terms of more laudatory objectives.[97] But, of course, it was Arafat that rejected Barak and Clinton's proposals, and Arafat and his circle and virtually all their constituents insisted on the "right of return," which Oz acknowledges is a formula for Israel's destruction. As a concession to these inconvenient facts, Oz has also declared, despite the inconsistency, that "Yasser Arafat and his men are running both wars simultaneously, pretending they are one."[98]

But the pretending is all on Oz's part. Arafat and the Palestinian leadership, no less than the Islamist terror organizations, were stating very clearly their annihilationist objective, and their people have embraced that objective. Yet however loudly they proclaim it, Oz covers his ears and tries to outshout them with what he is convinced — what his delusions tell him — they truly want.

An example of a member of the nation's artistic elite who has apparently felt no obligation to rethink, even in passing, any of his intense Israel-indicting and Oslo-promoting views is David Grossman. According to Grossman, the terror war is the product of Israel not being forthcoming enough in its offers of withdrawal from the territories. He has also informed his readers that Israelis are dying in the terror war for the sake of the settlers. Grossman has assured his audiences that, if Israel would only do the right thing and essentially return to its pre-1967 boundaries, "from my conversations with Palestinian leaders . . . I am convinced there still is a chance for peace."[99]

Grossman argues that to blame the terror war on the Palestinians is to ignore the impact of thirty-three years of occupation that preceded the current hostilities. But, of course, the objectives articulated by the Palestinian leadership both before and after Oslo, and now, finally, being reported with some consistency in Israel's media, are the same objectives that the PLO articulated before the 1967 war.[100]

Mimicking *Haaretz's* Gideon Levy and resorting to the sort of intellectual dishonesty to which he has always appealed in buttressing his indictments of Israel, Grossman insists further that not to blame the terror on "Israeli provocation" is to endorse the racist view that the Palestinians are violent "by their nature." This ugly and nonsensical argument ignores entirely, of course, the reality of the path to violence being paved by indoctrination. (One could as logically assert that to insist that Nazi anti-Semitism was not provoked by the Jews is to suggest the Germans were anti-Semitic by nature and so is an unsavory racist claim.)[101]

Also, as in his earlier writings on the conflict, Grossman continues to maintain that Israel has no legitimate strategic interests in the territories. On the contrary, in the world according to Grossman, all strategic concerns would become essentially irrelevant in the peace that would prevail after adequate and appropriate Israeli accommodation of what he construes to be the Palestinians' territorial demands.[102]

As in the preceding years, there were also many lesser Israeli literary lights who continued, and even amplified, their attacks on Israel and the Zionist enterprise in the months following the start of the terror war. One who did so was Aharon Shabtai, in a collection of poems entitled *J'Accuse*. For example, in the poem "Passover 2002," referring to the Passover that opened with the terrorist murder of twenty-nine at a seder in Netanya, Shabtai's moral sensibilities lead him to cast the Palestinians as the Jews in slavery in Egypt and Sharon as the "cruel,/stupid Pharaoh."[103] Even the book's *New York Times* reviewer noted that "what is most striking about *'J'Accuse'* is Shabtai's insistence on a moral reckoning for Israel irrespective of the activities of the other side . . . Thus, there is no mention here of suicide bombers, the men who sent them and their predominantly Jewish victims."[104] But this is hardly surprising, for what passes for morality among so many in Israel's cultural elites is the perverse ascription of moral value to the acting out of fantasies of a world make right by Israeli self-castigation, self-reform, and, for some, even self-immolation.

In another example of post-Zionist and revisionist business as usual even in the face of Arafat's terror war, filmmaker Yeud Levanon directed *Islands on the Shore,* which takes the fraudulent claim by Teddy Katz of an Israeli massacre at Tantura during the War of Independence (discussed in Chapter Sixteen) and portrays it as fact. The film, set in the present, features a Palestinian heroine who uncovers the truth of the massacre in her PhD thesis and who promotes the Palestinian "right of return," and a villainous Israeli reserve general and politician who was responsible for the slaughter. Levanon's film was chosen to represent Israel at the 2003 Montreal International Film Festival.[105]

AMERICAN JEWS AND ARAFAT'S WAR

Among American Jews, many erstwhile supporters of Oslo responded to the Palestinians' terror war as did large numbers of Israelis who had nurtured pro-Oslo sentiments, with an awakening from the delusional verities of the Oslo accords. They now rethought their earlier belief that the Palestinian leadership around Arafat, and its constituents who had been indoctrinated to pursue Israel's extermination, could be Israel's "peace partners" and that sufficient Israeli concessions would resolve the conflict. They were supported in this reassessment even by President Clinton, who, according to the media, acknowledged that the breakdown of negotiations had not been over borders. Clinton was reported to have said that Camp David foundered not over territorial issues but over Palestinian demands that Israel accept the Palestinians' "right of return" — again, a formula for Israel's destruction.[106]

But some American Jews, including people in leadership positions of major Jewish organizations, refused to rethink their delusions. The executive vice president of the Reform movement's Central Conference of American Rabbis, Rabbi Paul Menitoff, in a letter to President Bush dated August 7, 2002, urged that the United States cut off all "diplomatic, military and financial support" for Israel if it did not accede to a peace accord based on the Taba discussions and Israel's return virtually to its pre-1967 boundaries.[107] Edgar Bronfman, President of the World Jewish Congress, similarly advocated pushing Israel toward such an agreement, suggested the settlements were the key obstacle to peace and echoed Professor Sternhell in advising the Palestinians that they would be wise to focus their terror attacks on the settlers. As Israel pursued construction of a security fence to render terrorist infiltration more difficult, Bronfman wrote to President Bush expressing concern that the fence, which was routed to include some settlements in strategically vital areas, might undermine Palestinian confidence in the possibility of peace. Bronfman encouraged President Bush to pressure Sharon on the issue of the fence.[108]

But American Jews who remained true believers in the Oslo process, or at least the most vocal among them, were particularly to be found among those affiliated with organizations whose *raison d'être* was the indictment of Israeli government policies and who were very often inclined now to blame Israel for Oslo's derailment and for Israeli-Palestinian tensions more broadly. The New Israel Fund, for example, continued to underwrite organizations dedicated to ignoring the terror war against Israel and to attacking Israeli reactions to Palestinian terror as though Israeli countermeasures were initiated without provocation and were prompted by Israel's supposed anti-Arab attitudes.[109]

Americans for Peace Now (APN) likewise proceeded along the same Israel-indicting path that had always been the organization's way. APN continued to campaign against the settlements as key obstacles to peace and indeed against any Israeli presence in the territories.

In November, 2001, APN sponsored a joint speaking tour of the United States by Yossi Beilin and PA Minister of Information and Culture Yasser Abed Rabbo. The pair had explicated the thrust of their joint message a few months earlier in a co-signed Op-Ed in the *New York Times*: Advocacy of the continuation of negotiations from the point of those concessions made by Israel at Taba, with the aim of establishing two states "based on the 1967 borders." The pair were evenhanded in declaring that, "Both sides have made mistakes over the past year," and in condemning "those on both sides who do not share our vision, and, tragically, who see violence as the route to an absolutist . . . end." The word *terror* never appeared in the article.[110]

Beilin and Rabbo were subsequently the choreographers of the Geneva Accord, an unofficial Israeli-Palestinian agreement for which they were hoping to win international support. In the accord, Beilin, the unelected representative of Israel then holding no public office and having no public mandate, granted on Israel's behalf concessions exceeding those offered at Taba, including greater territorial concessions, wider latitude to a Palestinian "right of return," and the ceding of elements of Israel's sovereignty and right of self-defense to international bodies. A ceremonial signing of the accord was held in Geneva on December 1, 2003, with a number of celebrities, such as Amos Oz and A.B. Yehoshua, in attendance. In the wake of the signing, APN sought to promote political support for the agreement in the United States.[111]

An APN fund-raising letter mailed shortly before the January, 2003, election in Israel urged its addressees to support APN's attacks on Israel's government. The letter, signed by Leonard Fein, complained of "an Israeli policy that is all about bellicosity." It criticized the Bush Administration for its sympathetic attitude toward Sharon and lamented that "the forces of good sense and decency in Israel are in disarray." Fein also expressed concern about the situation on American college campuses, where Israel is under incessant attack and Jewish students are too often ill-prepared to speak out in Israel's defense. But Fein's example of their poor preparation is that whatever pro-Israel education is given them is, in his view, "too often . . . less training than indoctrination. Our students are taught that Israel is right, the Palestinians wrong . . . ".

Earlier, in the wake of Arafat's launching of his terror war, Fein had briefly acknowledged that the peace camp had made mistakes. In an article published in March, 2001, he continued to cast the Israeli presence in the territories in all or nothing terms, to object to Israel's holding onto the territories as morally repugnant and corrupting and thereby to defend his insistence on full withdrawal. But he also stated that, "former Prime Minister Netanyahu . . . was, it turns out, quite correct to call for reciprocity." Fein still took swipes at Netanyahu but added, "the likelihood is that we of the left would, even [if Netanyahu had been more credible in the eyes of the peace camp], have chosen to turn a blind eye toward Palestinian violations, so desperately did we want to believe that peace was at hand."[112]

But that insight obviously did not prevent Fein from still insisting that a sufficiently forthcoming Israeli government could make dramatic headway on the path to peace and to fault Sharon for the persistence of the terror war.

Americans for Peace Now acknowledged that the differences in understanding of the Israeli-Palestinian conflict between most Israelis and the American Jewish supporters of organizations such as APN were widening. In fact, this growing gap was not simply a consequence of the Israelis being exposed to an accelerating campaign of Palestinian terror. It also reflected Israelis becoming better informed by their media of what PA leaders had been indicating all along were Palestinian objectives beyond Oslo. They were learning more about PA indoctrination and incitement, including the incitement to genocide by Palestinian media, mosques, and schools.

(Although key sources for this information on Palestinian indoctrination and objectives continued to be the "underground" Israeli monitoring groups such as MEMRI, PMW, and IMRA, and while the English-language *Jerusalem Post* tended to give greater attention to such stories than Israel's Hebrew press, the leading Hebrew press outlets were now picking up more stories from the monitoring groups and also generating more such stories on their own. Among subjects previously given short shrift and now more widely covered were vilification of Israelis and Jews and calls for their murder by PA-appointed mullahs, including in sermons broadcast on PA television[113]; denigration of Israelis and Jews, and incitement of children to pursue Israel's destruction, in PA schools[114]; PA incitement to anti-Israel violence in other venues, including the encouraging of children to pursue "martyrdom"[115]; PA delegitimization of Israel and declared dedication to its extinction[116]; state-sponsored anti-Semitism and delegitimization of Israel in Arab states, including Egypt[117]; PA denial of any Jewish historical connection to the Temple Mount and the Holy Land[118]; Christian victimization by the PA[119]; and PA corruption.[120])

This Palestinian indoctrination and incitement were not addressed by Americans for Peace Now in its lobbying, its public events, its advertising, or its fund-raising letters.

Nor did they receive much attention in American media.[121] America's "newspaper of record," the *New York Times*, which sets the tone for large segments of the nation's media, continued to report on the conflict with at best a studied evenhandedness but with more typically a clear policy agenda. The overall thrust of *Times* coverage entailed perfunctory condemnations of bombings and other attacks on Israeli civilians by Palestinian "militants" — the *Times* rarely used the word *terrorist* in this context — together with criticism of the Sharon government's policies and insistence that resolution of the conflict lay in the uprooting of settlements and Israel's return virtually to its pre-1967 lines.

The *Times* sought to bolster its vision of the path to peace by taking the lead in trumpeting the Palestinians' revisionist assessment of Camp David and Taba; that is, that Israel's offers were not really all that forthcoming; that Arafat was not actually that unreceptive; that Barak, Arafat, and Clinton had all made mistakes; that nevertheless the parties were very close to agreement before Sharon's election; and so the Camp David and Taba proposals remain appropriate and viable foundations for a definitive conflict-ending accord.[122] The *Times* also opened its Op-Ed pages disproportionately to Israelis who promoted a similar comprehension of the conflict, such as Yossi Beilin and his Knesset supporters, David Grossman, Amos Oz, and Tom Segev. And the *Times'* senior foreign affairs columnist, Tom Friedman, continued to hew in column after column to his decades-long, almost monomaniacal message that the settlements are the root of all problems and Israel's return to the pre-1967 lines is the key to peace.

(Friedman's delusional variation on Middle East reality predates his years as a journalist and commentator. As a student at Brandeis in the early 1970s, he took a leading role in a "Middle East Peace Group" that downplayed the significance of Palestinian terror and the strategic threats to Israel and cast American support for Israel as an obstacle to Middle East peace.[123] The basic tenets of Friedman's understanding of the Arab-Israeli conflict have evolved little over the intervening years. In the months since the Palestinians' launching of their terror war, he has soured somewhat on Arafat, toward whom he had typically been very indulgent. But Friedman continues to cling to visions of Israeli withdrawal to the pre-1967 lines leading to genuine peace, and he continues to urge — as he has for decades — that the United States pressure Israel to undertake the concessions that figure in his visions.)

Of course, to report on the Palestinians having promoted — in speeches by Arafat and his PA colleagues as well as in Palestinian media, mosques, and schools — demonization of Jews, delegitimization of any Jewish claim to any part of "Palestine," and the moral and religious necessity of Israel's destruction would run counter to that perspective on the conflict that the *Times* was advocating. This no doubt accounted in part for the newspaper's silence on the Palestinians' anti-Semitic and annihilationist indoctrination. Another factor, which also figured in shaping the paper's formulas regarding the nature of the conflict, was the *Times'* perennial reluctance to be perceived as taking "pro-Jewish" stances.

There was a notable irony in the *Times'* general silence regarding Palestinian, and indeed broader Arab, promotion of anti-Semitism, as during this same period the *Times* was also offering *meae culpae* for its chronic under-reporting of the Holocaust during World War II. A *Times* retrospective by Max Frankel on wartime coverage, published in November, 2001, bore the headline: "Turning Away From the Holocaust: Although editors knew of Hitler's extermination of Jews, they mostly hid the story on the inside pages." The full-page article chronicled in some detail the *Times'* underreporting of the genocide. In addition, although it offered several self-exculpatory explanations, the piece also acknowledged that "the reluctance to highlight the systematic slaughter of Jews was also undoubtedly influenced by the views of the publisher, Arthur Hays Sulzberger. He believed strongly and publicly that . . . Jews should be separate only in the way they worshiped. He thought they needed no state or political and social institutions of their own. He went to great lengths to avoid having the *Times* branded a 'Jewish newspaper.'"[124]

Frankel also states, "After the Nazis' slaughter of Jews was fully exposed at war's end, Iphigene Ochs Sulzberger, the influential daughter, wife, and mother of *Times* publishers, changed her mind about the need for a Jewish state and helped her husband, Arthur Hays Sulzberger, accept the idea of Israel and befriend its leaders. Later . . . the *Times* shed its sensitivity about its Jewish roots . . . and warmly supported Israel in many editorials." This last assertion no doubt came as a surprise to many *Times* readers, for whom what has been most notable is the newspaper's rarely more than lukewarm support for Israel even when that country has been under the most horrendous attack and, again, the *Times'* general silence on the nature of the Palestinian, and broader Arab, war against Israel.

In a radio interview broadcast the same day as publication of the article, Frankel was asked what had prompted the piece. He answered that the *Times* was "often berated" for its reporting on Israel and "the Palestinian issue" and "this terrible neglect in World War II. . . . The attitude of the *New York Times* came under minute examination by Jews, and they gave us a lot of grief. And I leapt at the chance to finally set the record straight."[125] But, of course, Frankel and the *Times* had done nothing, nor have they since then, to set the record straight on the newspaper's chronic critical omissions and distortions regarding Israel and the Arab-Israeli conflict.

The *Times* did depart from its usual pattern by publishing an article in a Sunday magazine in November, 2001, on "The Uncomfortable Question of Anti-Semitism." The piece discussed the resurgence of anti-Semitism in Europe since September, 2000, including in European media, and also the widespread Arab adoption of European anti-Semitic texts and anti-Semitic canards. It offered little about the PA's promotion of anti-Semitism but did contain some gratuitous slaps at Israel.[126]

The *Times* also published a piece by Susan Sachs in April, 2002, "Anti-Semitism Is Deepening Among Muslims," which provided some details of the promotion of anti-Semitism by Moslem governments and clerics and acknowledged that in many Moslem countries "the hatred of Jews as Jews . . . has been nurtured through popular culture for generations." The article, however, then evenhandedly cited Professor John L. Esposito, a longtime critic of Israel and apologist for Arab extremism who teaches at Georgetown, to the effect that both Jews and Moslems engage in hate-mongering; and George Washington University Professor of Islamic Studies Seyyid Hossein Nasr, who also stated that "it happens on both sides." There is, of course, nothing in Israeli government statements, Israeli government or mainstream nongovernment media, or Israeli school texts purveying views of Islam or Moslems or Arabs comparable to the demonizing attacks on Jews and Judaism that are epidemic in the Moslem world; yet Sachs never explicitly noted the difference. Indeed, she echoed Esposito and Nasr in blurring the difference. Sachs opined, "That Jews would be demonized by some Arabs, and Arabs demonized by some Jews may not be surprising after nearly a century of conflict over Palestine." In addition, she made no specific mention of Palestinian anti-Semitism or its promotion by the Palestinian Authority.[127]

The airbrushing out of the anti-Semitic and genocidal themes promoted by the Palestinian leadership and by other Arab, and Moslem, governments and religious leaders, and the concomitant misrepresentation of the nature of the Palestinian-Israeli conflict, are simply a staple of *Times* coverage. In a *Times* Sunday magazine story that was supposed to be considering how much anti-Semitism plays a role in the world's perspectives on Israel and on the Israeli-American relationship, the author, Ian Buruma, alludes to anti-Semitism in the Arab and broader Moslem world but the only specific statement he offers regarding it is, "*The Protocols of the Elders of Zion . . .* was widely read in prewar Japan and is enjoying a popular revival in the Middle East today." The Palestinian Islamist groups may openly acknowledge their goal is Israel's destruction, PA officials may insist that they have the same goal but will achieve it in stages according to Arafat's Plan of Phases, and Arab governments and media may likewise continue to assert that Israel is an illegitimate entity that must be expunged, but Buruma is critical of the "Manichaeism (which is, of course, what appeals to Christian fundamentalists too) that [the Arab war against Israel is] not only strategic but also existential." He comes back to the point, informing the reader that, "the politics of the Middle East may be murderous, but it is not helpful to see them as an existential battle . . . " Buruma then, in concluding, regurgitates *Times* evenhandedness: "Religious fanaticism is confounding the politics of Israel, as well as that of its enemies"; this even though no Israeli governmental or religious voice with any following attacks Islam and Moslems as Arabs and the wider Moslem world routinely attack Jews and Judaism.[128]

Perhaps most typical of the *Times'* attitude toward covering Arab, and more particularly Palestinian, anti-Semitism and genocidal incitement is an article by *Times* reporter William Orme that was published on October 24, 2000. On October 13, the day after the lynching of two Israeli reservists in Ramallah, the official Palestinian Authority television station broadcast a sermon by Sheik Ahmad Halabaya in which the sheik declared,

"Whether Likud or Labor, Jews are Jews . . . They are the terrorists. They are the ones who must be butchered and killed, as Allah the almighty said: Fight them; Allah will torture them at your hands, and will humiliate them . . . Have no mercy on the Jews, no matter where they are, in any country. Fight them, wherever you are. Wherever you meet them, kill them. Wherever you are, kill those Jews and those Americans who are like them . . . "[129]

Halabaya, in this official Palestinian Authority broadcast, also asserted that all of Israel properly belongs to the Arabs.

Orme, in his *Times* article published eleven days later, notes Israeli complaints of the PA's using its official media for incitement, and his tone is clearly dismissive of Israel's position. He writes at one point, "Israelis cite as one egregious example a televised sermon that defended the killing of the two soldiers. 'Whether Likud or Labor, Jews are Jews,' proclaimed Sheik Ahmad Abu Halabaya in a live broadcast from a Gaza City mosque the day after the killings." That is all Orme says of the sermon; nothing about Halabaya's exhortations to butcher Jews wherever one finds them, nothing about his assertions that all of Israel belongs to the Arabs, nothing about his invoking of Allah as calling for the torture and murder of the Jews.[130]

Orme's intent is clearly to make the Israeli complaints look unfounded and ridiculous. But beyond this, his omissions reflect the general *Times* policy of remaining silent on Palestinian and broader Arab anti-Semitism and its genocidal rhetoric.

On June 14, 2001, New York's two Senators, Charles Schumer and Hillary Clinton, sent a letter to President Bush lauding his efforts to achieve an Israeli-Palestinian cease-fire but noting that, "Unless the Palestinians take unequivocal steps to stop the rhetoric of hate emanating from official Palestinian Authority (PA) statements, media organizations and textbooks in Palestinian schools, any peace agreement will have little meaning . . . For nearly ten years, while Mr. Arafat and the Palestinian leadership were speaking the language of peace with Israel and the West, they were continuing their calls for the destruction of Israel to the Palestinian people and the Arab world."[131]

The Senators included in their letter illustrations of Palestinian incitement and hate-mongering, including a statement from a PA minister, made a few months before the outbreak of hostilities, that Oslo was merely a first step toward Israel's destruction; an article in an official PA newspaper calling for the killing of Jews wherever they are found; and citations from Palestinian school texts declaring that "there is no alternative to destroying Israel" and proposing that the Jews had been brought to "our land" in order to be annihilated.[132] But the *New York Times* could still not bring itself to cover the issue.

No doubt if the *Times* did more forthrightly report on the PA's anti-Jewish indoctrination and its incitement to the murder of Jews and the extermination of Israel, those elemental aspects of the conflict would be more widely reported in American media generally. In any case, *Times* attention to the subject would very likely inspire more informed public discussion of the essentials of the conflict. Coverage might even force organizations such as Americans for Peace Now to acknowledge and address the issue.

THE SECOND SHARON GOVERNMENT, THE WAR, AND THE ROAD MAP

Labor's withdrawal from the unity government in October, 2002, was prompted primarily by the struggle within Labor for leadership of the party. Defense Minister Ben-Eliezer had become party chairman after Ehud Barak's election loss to Sharon in January, 2001; but there were a number of potential challengers for the leadership post in an upcoming Labor Party primary scheduled for November 19. Ben-Eliezer, by withdrawing from the coalition over an issue of state funding of settlements, hoped to boost his standing among Labor rank and file. Leaving the government also freed him both to campaign to retain his party position and to do so in part by distancing himself still further from government policies.

However, Ben-Eliezer lost the Labor leadership in the November balloting to Amram Mitzna, a former mayor of Haifa who advocated such extensive Israeli concessions for "peace" that he was viewed as exceptionally "dovish" even by what had become over the preceding decade Labor Party standards. In the ensuing national campaign, Mitzna called for entering into unconditional negotiations with Arafat even without a cessation of terror and building a separation wall along the pre-1967 lines, which would presumably mark at some point the international border between Israel and a new Palestinian state. (At times

in the campaign, Mitzna was more vague and ambiguous about his preparedness to return to the pre-1967 lines; but full withdrawal had been the thrust of
his stance earlier, and his perspective appeared, despite new vagueness, to remain essentially unchanged.)

In the general election, Sharon and Likud won an overwhelming victory,
capturing thirty-eight Knesset seats (which grew to forty when a smaller party
holding two seats merged with Likud) to Labor's nineteen. Despite having various coalition configurations available to him, Sharon again sought to include
Labor in his government. However, sentiment in Labor, still shaped in large
part by those in the leadership who clung to visions of an Oslo-style path
to peace, was generally against such a course. A month after the election,
Sharon presented to the Knesset for ratification a sixty-eight-seat coalition
without Labor; and, in fact, he had less need of Labor involvement. Despite
the ongoing terror, he had won the trust of a very large part of the nation,
and he had also established himself on the international stage, particularly
in relations with the Bush Administration. In addition, a dramatically weakened Labor Party was in less of a position to undermine him either at home
or abroad.

(Not that Labor leaders have not tried to undermine him, and, in addition, to indict Israel for choosing him as prime minister, both domestically and
abroad. But their efforts have had relatively little impact. The perverse depths
to which such attacks have stooped is illustrated by an article by Avraham Burg
published in various newspapers, including the British paper the *Guardian*, during the summer of 2003. Burg had long been a fixture of the Labor leadership
and had served as Speaker of the Knesset from 1999 until early 2003. In the
piece, he casts Israel's predicament as having to choose either returning to the
pre-1967 lines, including ceding eastern Jerusalem, or retaining all the territories. Despite all of Israel's withdrawals in the context of Oslo and its Camp
David and Taba offers, Burg insists that the nation has essentially chosen to hold
onto all the territories and this has rendered it corrupt and unjust and is the
explanation for Palestinian terror. "They spill our blood . . . because they have
children and parents at home who are hungry and humiliated . . . The leaders
come from below — from the wells of hatred and anger, from the 'infrastructures' of [Israeli] injustice and moral corruption." It seems that in Burg's view
that corruption has been further entrenched by Israel's election of Sharon, which
apparently represents to him the nation's unwillingness to return to its pre-1967
boundaries and therefore its corrupt and immoral insistence on holding onto
all the territories; or, as he chooses to phrase it, Israel's choice of "Jewish racism
[over] democracy." "The nation today rests on a scaffolding of corruption, and
on foundations of oppression and injustice. As such, the end of the Zionist enterprise is already on our doorstep." But, again, while this sort of rhetoric from
some Labor leaders in opposition played well in Europe and elsewhere, even

among segments of the American Jewish population, it had little impact domestically.[133])

Various observers had explained Sharon's relatively restrained and limited military responses to the Palestinians' terror war over the life of the previous government as due to his desire to preserve the coalition with Labor. But Sharon did not substantially depart from that earlier pattern of action after formation of his new government. The terror continued, with an average of twenty-one people killed each month by Palestinian terrorists in the first six months of 2003. But Sharon — even while publicly addressing the role of Arafat and his PA lieutenants in inciting, supporting, and participating in the terror — still limited Israeli military responses to steps short of dismantling the PA and sweeping aside its leadership. He maintained this pattern despite calls by many within Likud and other voices in his coalition for more aggressive measures to stanch the persistent horrific loss of Israeli lives to Palestinian terror.

A major explanation for this appears to have been his reluctance to assume, particularly in Palestinian cities, the civil responsibilities that would have devolved upon Israel were the PA to be destroyed. On the contrary, Sharon repeatedly demonstrated through the course of his first government his willingness to withdraw from Palestinian cities and hand them over to the PA with the proviso that PA forces prevent a resurgence of terror emanating from those areas. But time after time such disengagement was followed in short order by new suicide bombings and other terror atrocities in Israel carried out by perpetrators from the evacuated towns. This was in keeping with Arafat's determination to persist in the terror war. Israel would then often reestablish in some form its presence in the previously transferred area.

The most significant development in the diplomatic sphere in the last months of the unity government and the ensuing period was the evolution of the so-called road map for ending the Israeli-Palestinian conflict.

The road map had disparate sources. The push for aggressive diplomatic intervention under the rubric of a "road map" came particularly from the European Union, as reflected in an EU initiative in late August, 2002.[134] The EU characterized its formulation as built upon President Bush's June 24 speech, in which the president had emphasized the need for the Palestinians to end their terror campaign, dismantle the terror infrastructure, and establish a Palestinian regime founded on democratic principles and untainted by terror, and he had cast these steps as essential preconditions to peace. But while invoking Bush's speech, the EU at the same time sought to promote a timetable for establishment of a Palestinian state, which suggested a process whose advancement would not be performance-based or predicated on Palestinian reform. In this respect, the EU proposals conformed less to Bush's vision than to PA desire for international intervention to establish a state essentially on the pre-1967 lines and to do so without significant reform and without precluding subsequent claims and actions against Israel aimed at its ultimate dissolution.

The Arab states, of course, also promoted international intervention to inhibit Israeli responses to the terror and advance the Palestinian agenda under an international umbrella.

Meanwhile, the United States, still eager to win support for its own war against terrorism and, increasingly, for a military confrontation with Saddam Hussein, remained very interested in placating Arab opinion and accommodating European pressures. President Bush, since October, 2001, had been explicitly expressing support for establishment of a Palestinian state following Palestinian reform and assurance of Israel's security. The American administration, in the wake of consultations at the United Nations in September, 2002, endorsed the concept of a road map that would proceed under the sponsorship of the "Quartet" of the EU, the UN, Russia, and the United States; the administration also emphasized the convergence of views among the four.

Over the next several months, even as the United States continued to speak of the Quartet's shared perspectives on the path to peace, there were indications of behind the scenes disagreement on the details of the road map's provisions, the mechanisms for its implementation, and the timing of its formal announcement. News reports spoke of various drafts. They also noted, for example, EU militating for rapid release of an agreed upon text and, seemingly, White House insistence on delay pending particular developments. Arab and European pressure continued and, in addition, British Prime Minister Tony Blair, who was encountering intense public opposition to his support for an American military campaign in Iraq, urged an American initiative on the Israeli-Palestinian front to demonstrate to his constituency that the Iraq campaign would be part of a larger effort to bring peace to the Middle East.[135]

Ultimately, the United States, still seeking to sideline Arafat, insisted on the establishment by the PA of an office of prime minister invested with genuine executive authority, and it made the appointment of a sufficiently empowered prime minister a precondition for formal release of the road map. The Bush Administration also enlisted European nations and some Arab states to press Arafat to acquiesce in creation of such a post.

Arafat, in the face of intense international pressure, gave ground and, in March, 2003, appointed as prime minister a veteran PLO colleague, Mahmoud Abbas, also known by the *nom de guerre* Abu Mazen. The Palestinian legislative council subsequently ratified the appointment and, on April 30, the State Department released the text of the road map.

The text incorporates conflicting emphases regarding the proper path forward. It is officially titled, "A Performance-Based Roadmap to a Permanent Two-State Solution to the Israeli-Palestinian Conflict," and the body of the document indicates that the ultimate criteria for moving forward with be performance criteria. But the road map also includes timelines and target dates, and there is clear tension between the determining factor for advancement of the process being the parties' fulfillment of their obligations and the determining factor being the calendar. The text also calls for resolution of the conflict on the basis of various relevant earlier initiatives, including agreements previously reached by the parties, UN Security Council Resolutions 242 and 338 and a recent "initiative" of Saudi Crown Prince Abdullah. But Abdullah spoke of possible Arab acceptance of Israel in return for Israeli withdrawal from all lands taken in 1967 that it still held — the West Bank, Gaza, and the Golan Heights — while UN Security Council Resolution 242 acknowledged that Israel has legitimate security reasons for not returning to the pre-1967 lines, supported Israel's not doing so, and called for negotiation of "secure and recognized boundaries."

The first phase of the road map required of the Palestinians the restructuring of their security forces, confiscating of illegal weapons and dismantling of the terrorist organizations. The Palestinians were also obliged to take steps toward establishing a transparent and democratic government. Israel was to withdraw to the positions it held in September, 2000, remove settlement outposts erected since March, 2001, and, "consistent with the Mitchell Report," freeze all settlement activity, including natural growth. This last went beyond Israel's obligations under Oslo, even beyond Rabin's informal unilateral undertakings, and is clearly biased against the Resolution 242 formula and toward an ultimate Israeli withdrawal to the pre-1967 lines.

The second phase of the road map was to entail movement toward establishment of an interim Palestinian state with attributes of sovereignty and provisional borders, with the end of 2003 a target date for completing this process.

Finally, in phase three, a full peace was to be achieved in 2005 "that ends the occupation that began in 1967" and "fulfills the vision of two states, Israel and sovereign, independent, democratic and viable Palestine, living side-by-side in peace and security."

For all the problematic inconsistencies and ambiguities of the text, looming still larger as potentially rendering the road map no more conducive to peace, nor even to a reduction of hostilities, than Oslo were what one could anticipate would likely be problems with its implementation. Would the Quartet truly insist upon PA dismantling of the terrorist infrastructure and ending of incitement? Even if the Quartet held fast to its demands in this vein, the task of persuading Palestinian authorities to execute their obligations regarding incitement and terrorism was daunting. Despite the trumpeting of Mahmoud Abbas's appointment as marking a revolution in Palestinian governance, control of Palestinian security forces, as of the Palestinian government generally, remained firmly in Arafat's hands and neither he nor his lieutenants were interested either in curbing their own terrorist cadres or reining in the Islamist groups.

But, in any case, there was no reason to believe that the members of the Quartet were prepared to press single-mindedly for dissolving the terrorist groups. On the contrary, two members of the Quartet, the United Nations and the European Union, had track records of supporting Palestinian terror in various ways and so could hardly be expected to exert themselves to defang its perpetrators.

As noted previously, the United Nations Human Rights Commission had, in April, 2002, declared anti-Israel terror a legitimate tool of Palestinian resistance. In April, 2003, the same month as publication of the road map, the Commission reaffirmed that stance. The United Nations Relief and Works Agency for Palestinian Refugees (UNRWA) has taught Palestinian children in UNRWA schools that it is their right and duty to pursue Israel's annihilation and has allowed UNRWA facilities to be used for terrorist recruitment and training; and UNRWA personnel have been involved in implementing terror attacks against Israel.[136] UN Secretary General Kofi Annan has consistently expended more energy attacking Israel for its responses to terror than criticizing the terror itself. At various points he has decried Israel's "draconian security measures" without even mentioning Palestinian terror. Terje Roed-Larsen, Annan's special envoy to the Middle East, has been perhaps less supportive of Palestinian terror than many others at the UN but has depicted it as no more reprehensible than Israeli settlement activity. (Hebrew University Professor Shlomo Avineri, a prominent veteran of the Israeli Left and unrepentant cheerleader for Oslo, wrote of Roed-Larsen: "So that there should be no mistake: I am against Jewish settlement in the territories; I strongly feel that setting them up was a major mistake . . . But anyone who compares settlement activities to suicide bombings targeting civilians is a moral cripple."[137])

Members of the EU have likewise chosen in various ways to lend their support to Palestinian terror. Beyond the six EU states that voted in the UN Human Rights Commission in April, 2002, to legitimize Palestinian terror (or, in UN terminology, "use of all available means" against "occupation"), another, Italy, abstained; only Germany and Britain voted against the resolution. But British foreign minister Jack Straw had earlier averred that he "understands" Palestinian terror.[138] In the April, 2003, Commission vote to endorse the Palestinians' use of terror, only Germany voted against; all the other EU members of the Commission abstained.[139] In addition, European governments and the EU have consistently vilified Israel for its military responses to terror, whatever the particular form of those responses, and soft-pedaled criticism of the PA. Moreover, there is strong evidence that EU money given to the Palestinians has been used to fund terror, as well as incitement in Palestinian media and

Palestinian schools, but EU foreign minister Chris Patten has dismissed the evidence and consistently sought to quash investigations of such funding.[140]

Some European political figures in EU states have also expressed support for the Arab goal of annihilating Israel. The Leader of the British House of Commons at the time of release of the road map, Peter Hain, had earlier declared that "the present Zionist state . . . will have to be dismantled."[141] (Arabs may insist that every inch of the Middle East properly belongs to them and may torment, abuse and even seek to exterminate those whom they perceive to be intruding on their exclusive right, as they have done to Kurds in Iraq and blacks in the Sudan and other ethnic, racial, and religious minorities living among them; but in Hain's view it is the Israelis who are guilty of "greedy oppression" and they must bow to Arab demands for the demise of their state.) In addition, there is wide endorsement in the EU of the Palestinians' claim to a "right of return," itself a formula for Israel's dissolution.

Given such UN and EU sentiment and predilections, Quartet insistence upon implementation of the basic tenet of the road map, an end to Palestinian terror and dismantling of the terrorist infrastructure, seemed highly unlikely.

Key figures in the Bush Administration nevertheless asserted in various venues the commitment of the United States to the road map's being performance-driven, with the *sine qua non* for progress remaining the Palestinians' stopping the terror and uprooting the terror groups. But there were early signs of likely softening of this commitment.

The person appointed by Arafat to the prime minister's post, Mahmoud Abbas, had indeed spoken out against Arafat's terror war as misguided and not serving Palestinian interests, but Abbas himself had a checkered history. He had earned a doctorate in Germany with a dissertation denying the Holocaust and had himself been involved in PLO terror operations in the past. Mohammed Dahlan, appointed by Abbas to be his security chief, also had differences with Arafat, and Arafat had tried to block his appointment; but Dahlan, like Abbas, had a history of involvement in terror, even in the context of the current terror war. For example, he was reliably reported to have been responsible for a bomb attack on an Israeli school bus that killed two teachers and seriously injured many children, including three siblings who all had parts of limbs blown off.[142] Dahlan was also identified as running a very lucrative racket selling protection, licenses, and border-crossing permits, which allegedly earned him about $250,000 a month.[143]

None of this prevented the American administration from enthusiastically embracing both men; and, of course, people do sometimes change and the two could not be entirely dismissed on the basis of their past records. But there were other troubling signs. While Prime Minister Sharon was openly voicing support for establishment of a Palestinian Arab state in the territories, as he did at the summit with Abbas and President Bush in Aqaba in June, 2003, Abbas refused to recognize the legitimacy of Israel as a Jewish state. On the contrary, he continued to insist on the Arab "right of return"; again, a formula for Israel's dissolution. In addition, both he and Dahlan declared repeatedly that they would not seek to disarm and dismantle the terror groups as to do so might trigger a Palestinian civil war.

The Bush Administration responded to this stance in a manner reminiscent of the first years of Oslo. At that time, the Rabin government, in the face of ongoing Palestinian terror and Arafat's failure to challenge the terror groups, embraced the suggestion by those around Arafat that he was too weak to do so. The government advanced the view that the proper Israeli step was to give Arafat more concessions, show the Palestinian people he can win gains for them, and thereby strengthen his public support and render him more capable of taking on the Islamist terror groups. Now, even as the Bush Administration continued to insist on the need to end the terror and destroy the terrorist infrastructure as a first priority in pushing forward the road map, it increasingly looked to Israel to make concessions in order ostensibly to strengthen Abbas by showing he can deliver benefits to the Palestinian people and thereby render him more able to challenge the terror groups. It pressed Israel to go ahead, despite Palestinian inaction on terror, with some of the steps that were ultimately part of its responsibilities under the road map, such as withdrawing forces from Palestinian cities, removing recently established settlement outposts, and decreasing the number of checkpoints. It also encouraged Israel to take other steps not part of the road map, such as allowing more Palestinians into Israel to work and releasing Palestinian prisoners. The focus thereby shifted from the Palestinians' need to take aggressive measures against the terror groups to the Israelis' need to accommodate the Palestinians.

A similar dynamic evolved around Abbas's brokering of an agreement with Hamas and Islamic Jihad under which the two groups would cease temporarily their attacks on Israel. Israel was against the cease-fire and refused to be a formal party to it both because it was an inadequate alternative to dismantling of the terror groups as called for in the road map and because it afforded the terrorists an opportunity to regroup and rearm. Yet the cease-fire was widely characterized as the most that could be expected of Abbas and as somehow a concession to Israel for which Israel ought to reciprocate by being more forthcoming with concessions of its own.

In addition to these difficulties with the initial unfolding of the road map, there loomed as well the fact that, again, for all the lauding of Abbas's appointment as inaugurating a new Palestinian leadership, real power, including power over Palestinian "security" forces, remained in the hands of Arafat, who showed no more interest than earlier in giving up his terror war.

The so-called cease-fire lasted from June to August, but during that time there were numerous attacks on Israelis. Israel in turn, responding to terrorist operations and also fearing a strengthening of terrorist capabilities, targeted some leaders of recent attacks as well as Palestinian arms-manufacturing and storage facilities. On August 19, 2003, a Palestinian suicide bombing of a bus in Jerusalem killed twenty-three passengers, including six children, and Hamas claimed responsibility. Israel then began more aggressively hunting down Hamas leaders. These events, and a resumption of more emphatic demands by the United States for dismantling of Hamas and other terror groups, led to a confrontation between Arafat and Abbas over control of the PA security apparatus and the PA's relations with Hamas. There followed threats in PA media against Abbas's life, and Abbas's resignation on September 6.

Arafat, in the face of American and European pressure to appoint another prime minister, subsequently selected his longtime associate Ahmed Qurei (*nom de guerre* Abu Ala). The appointment was greeted by the Quartet as a step toward resuscitating the road map, even though Arafat ceded no more real authority to Qurei than he had given to Abbas.

But beyond the specifics of recalcitrant Palestinian actions and counterproductive Quartet responses, which in themselves rendered the road map doomed as a formula for peace, lay the overarching problem that no one in the Arab camp was prepared to offer Israel genuine peace. Among the Palestinians, those with the power and the guns were still committed to pursuing Israel's ultimate destruction; and Palestinians in general, not least because of intense indoctrination under the PA in media, schools, and mosques to the effect that they were the rightful owners of all that was Israel, widely supported that goal and rejected co-existence with the Jewish state. (One representative poll during this period, for example, showed that even if Israel withdrew to its pre-1967 lines, giving up all of the West Bank, Gaza, and eastern Jerusalem, 59 percent of Palestinians would favor Hamas and Islamic Jihad continuing their war against Israel. Eighty percent would favor continued insistence on the "right of return."[144]) Consequently, any plan at this time that is predicated on the end point being genuine peace and that seeks to promote arrangements that are viable only in the context of genuine peace is, like Oslo, misconceived and doomed to failure.

The more realistic and appropriate goal of any diplomatic process at this time is not some delusional "peace" but rather arrangements that end current hostilities and decrease friction more generally; that is, an armistice that is potentially more effective than earlier arrangements. If I may, as a physician, invoke a medical model: There was much wrong with the Israeli-Arab status quo prior to Oslo, just as there is much wrong with the situation today; but in formulating potential diplomatic interventions, the key animating principle ought to be the first principle and obligation articulated in the Hippocratic Oath — "First do no harm." That is, in treating a sick patient, the first obligation is not to make the patient worse. Oslo took a "sick" situation and made it much sicker;

and any formula promoting arrangements predicated on delusions of peace, on the notion that genuine peace is attainable in the foreseeable future, will inevitably do the same.

What, then, would be a better course? For Israel, the goal remains what it has been, in the opinion of most Israelis, since 1967: to extricate the nation as much as possible from the lives of the Palestinian Arabs, facilitate as much as possible their pursuing their own, separate political course, while retaining control of strategic areas vital for the nation's defense, the most important of which are still, in general, sparsely populated by Palestinians. The strategic and demographic imperatives that inspired Yigal Allon's plan and rendered variations on the Allon Plan for twenty-five years central to Labor Party policy regarding disposition of the territories have not changed.[145] (Such an arrangement for the territories could likely be implemented while ceding to the Palestinians in the West Bank a contiguous area, or two areas separated by a narrow strip. But contiguity should in any case be weighed in the context of the principle aims of separation and security. Indeed, a major virtue of contiguity is that it allows more separation. Concerns about the economic viability of the Palestinian entity are also misplaced; separation and Israeli security are the essential conditions for a viable, stable armistice and for prosperity for both parties, and a Palestinian entity of any configuration can be rendered economically successful. A Palestinian government that wanted to nurture economic success would be able to do so either in cooperation with Israel or, if it preferred, without such cooperation, with aid and trade from the surrounding Arab nations and the world at large. Such trade might need to entail some minimal coordination with Israel for transport purposes, but — as long as potential military materials were not involved — Israel would have an interest in supporting this traffic and would undoubtedly do so.)

But if Israel's essential goals vis-à-vis the Palestinians and the territories can be relatively easily defined, there is no very easy or promising path for advancing toward those goals. Prior to Oslo, there were signs of emerging Palestinian leaders within the territories who had won local credibility through their role in the Intifada and might have served as interlocutors with whom Israel could negotiate viable political arrangements. Those leaders were intimidated to a considerable degree by the PLO leadership in Tunis and its representatives in the territories, but they had notable support and were accruing more. Whatever opportunity then existed ended with Oslo, with the PLO's entry in force into the territories, effective destruction of all moderate political challenge, and indoctrination of the population to more ambitious and eliminationist goals.

There are today signs of urban leaders in at least some West Bank cities desiring to get their areas back to normal functioning and working to extrude the terror cadres of both the Islamist groups and the PA, and if they were successful they might be interlocutors for Israel. But a number of these leaders have been intimidated by the PA and have withdrawn from public service and so the prospects here, too, at least in the short term, are not very promising.[146] Even if Israel were to prosecute its war against the terrorists more aggressively and wipe out the terrorist cadres and leadership and itself dismantle their infrastructure, it is not clear that the deeply indoctrinated population would tolerate a moderate leadership prepared to negotiate on the basis of less than maximal Palestinian demands.

In the absence of potential interlocutors, Israel could act unilaterally, and Prime Minister Sharon has proposed moving in this direction if the PA continues in its refusal to take steps necessary for a resumption of negotiations. In this vein, Israel could pursue more aggressively its military campaign against the terrorist groups and their leadership and then withdraw unilaterally to lines of its own choosing, proceeding, again, on the principles of seeking to retain as much as possible of key strategic terrain, such as the Jordan Valley, areas that border the nation's pre-1967 nine-mile waist or dominate its population centers, and positions vital for the defense of Jerusalem, while seeking also to separate itself as much as possible from the Palestinian population. In one respect, unilateral action would be easier today than before Oslo. Then, Israel had internationally recognized responsibility for civil administration of the territories and unilateral withdrawal would have entailed abandonment of that responsibility. Today, even if key figures involved in terrorism were removed, there would be an internationally recognized Palestinian administration in place upon which responsibility would devolve.

But, of course, there are many problems with unilateral withdrawal. Retaining key strategic areas would help provide Israel with protection from invasion from the East and would place much of the nation's population out of range of small arms, mortars, and short-range artillery and missiles. But, even if Israel had first diminished the capacities of the terror organizations and decimated their leadership, and even if it remained in control of borders between the territories and Jordan and Egypt and patrolled the Gaza coastline, the terror organizations would still have a presence in the territories and would be able to rebuild their forces and infrastructure. They would also still be capable of manufacturing some weapons, including rockets, and smuggling in others; so they would continue to present a threat to Israel and go on taking a toll of Israeli lives. Israel would then be obliged to undertake incursions into the territories and to do so in the face of predictable international censure for its "invasion" of what would have by then very likely been recognized as an independent Arab entity.

Indeed, the May, 2004, defeat, in a referendum polling Likud Party members, of Sharon's proposal for unilateral withdrawal from Gaza was spurred largely by voter concerns that the Palestinians would perceive Israel's withdrawal as a victory for their terror campaign, would be spurred to even more intensive efforts in the terror war, would have greater latitude in Gaza to do so, and would present even more severe security challenges to Israel and exact an even more horrific toll of Israeli victims. Other polls conducted around the same time showed that, while many Likud voters were against withdrawal under current conditions, most, like Israelis generally, favored withdrawal from Gaza in principle.[147]

Introduction of international forces after Israeli withdrawal could in theory obviate some of the difficulties of acting unilaterally. But, in the real world, the net result of such an intervention would almost certainly be negative for Israel. Indeed, the international community, not well disposed in any case toward Israel, would virtually inevitably follow Arab demands and balk at any involvement that reflected even tacit acceptance of Israel's unilaterally established borders. If they nevertheless agreed to enter the territories, they would likely do so with explicit declaration that Israel's borders were yet to be determined and were properly the pre-1967 lines. In addition, the intervening forces, whether acting under UN auspices or under some other flag, would likely not only fail to prevent Palestinian terror attacks against Israel but would provide some modicum of cover for such attacks and work to prevent Israel from responding militarily. It is impossible to comprehend any international parties seriously assigning their forces the task of controlling resurgent Palestinian terror groups.

Even an American presence, one that did seriously seek to eradicate terror and cultivate a moderate, democratized civil society, would be a problem for Israel, as any American casualties would be construed by at least some segments of the American public as casualties taken on Israel's behalf and would to some degree undercut American support for Israel. In addition, an American presence, too, would restrict Israel's capacity to respond to attacks.

A potentially more promising prospect, again in theory, would be the insertion of a moderate Arab police and civil force willing to combat violent elements and help build civil institutions. But even so-called moderate Arab governments, indeed even the two Arab states with which Israel has formal peace agreements, promote in their state-controlled media vicious anti-Semitic and anti-Israeli canards and have indoctrinated their populations to Israel's illegitimacy and so there are no obvious candidates for providing such a force. Indeed, it is more likely that if a moderate leadership emerged in the territories and were willing to negotiate with Israel on the basis of less than maximal Palestinian demands, that leadership would be vilified by the vast majority of Arab voices for having "betrayed" the Arab cause.

Jordan is the one Arab state that — despite the ugly hate-mongering in Jordanian media and the intense anti-Israel sentiments of its population — has cultivated substantive mutually beneficial connections with Israel. Jordan is also, of course, the Arab state with the strongest connections to the territories and could potentially intervene in the context of some mutually agreed upon affiliation with the Palestinian Arabs, such as a confederate arrangement. Moreover, the Jordanian government has its own reasons to fear the emergence of a revanchist Palestinian entity on its borders, would prefer to have Israel in control of the Jordan Valley, and has an interest in working to moderate Palestinian politics. But for Jordan to involve itself and defy popular Arab sentiment by cooperating with Israel would expose it to threats and potential retaliation from the larger Arab world, and indeed the Moslem world more broadly, even in the absence of Saddam Hussein. Moreover, the Hashemite court would have to worry about the Palestinians potentially joining with the Palestinian Arab population in Jordan to mount a threat to the regime. Clearly, Jordan continues to fear an independent Palestinian state; but it is less clear that that fear or other, related, concerns would suffice to render the regime willing to become deeply involved as a moderating force in areas that were unilaterally evacuated by Israel.

In sum, Israel can define its vital interests and seek to pursue them with circumspection, but there is little to suggest there is any way for it to do so and escape remaining subject to ongoing terror and armed conflict for the foreseeable future. Proceeding on the basis of open-eyed assessments of reality does not guarantee avoiding terror and war. But that is a point made at the beginning of this work: Israel in reality does not have the power to force the other side to grant it peace or to woo the other side to do so. Peace, if and when it comes, will do so at a time of the Arabs' choosing.

What Israel does have the capacity to do, and what has for half a century dramatically altered the conditions of Jewish life, is to defend itself. Indeed, for the forty-five years before Oslo it not only defended itself but brought in millions of Jewish refugees and gave them new lives and built a vibrant, modern, open, and democratic society comparable to the most admirable societies on the planet. Moreover, it is capable of continuing to nurture what it has built, and to defend it, even in the face of ongoing besiegement. Its most vulnerable point, its Achilles heel, is that psychological response to the Arab siege that twists people's sensibilities to a discounting and demeaning of all that is good in Israel and to an unconscionable romancing of the haters and would-be annihilators of Israel in the service of self-deluding fantasies that sufficient self-abnegation, self-abasement, and concessions will placate the besiegers and win "peace."

Epilogue

"An early build-up of a clear and positive feeling of belongingness to the Jewish group is one of the few effective things that Jewish parents can do for the later happiness of their children."
Kurt Lewin, German Jewish psychologist and refugee from Nazi Germany, in "Bringing Up the Jewish Child" (1940)[1]

To counteract fear and make the individual strong to face whatever the future holds, there is nothing so important as a clear and fully accepted belonging to a group whose fate has a positive meaning. A long-range view which includes the past and the future of Jewish life, and links the solution of the minority problem with the problem of the welfare of all human beings is one of these possible sources of strength . . . To build up such feeling of group belongingness . . . should be one of the outstanding policies in Jewish education.
Lewin, in "Self-Hatred Among Jews" (1941)[2]

The preceding chapters have traced the delusions of Oslo and the psychological and historical factors that led so many in Israel, and in Diaspora Jewish communities as well, to embrace those delusions.

That embrace has cost Israelis dearly. From Arafat's arrival in the territories in July, 1994, to his launching of his terror war in September, 2000, Palestinian attacks claimed 256 lives; they killed another 873 in the first three years of the terror war. Thousands of Israelis have been maimed and disabled. Nor is an end to the carnage in sight as Israel continues to confront a Palestinian leadership — much of it brought into the territories by Israel — dedicated to seeking its destruction, as well as a Palestinian population further radicalized over the past decade and indoctrinated to pursue the same objective. Beyond the Palestinians, Israel faces a broadly hostile Arab world steeped in the anti-Semitic invective and slander purveyed by its leaders, media, schools, and mosques and intensely supportive of the Palestinians' annihilationist agenda.

That Israel does not find itself in an even worse position is less of Israel's doing than the result of what was, despite all, a lucky turn of events. The nation was fortunate, in particular, in Arafat's rejecting the additional dramatic territorial concessions proffered by Barak at Camp David and thereafter at Taba. Arafat did so, it would seem, to avoid even the appearance of acquiescing to a final status agreement that left Israel intact. But his choice meant that he launched his terror war from a territorial base much less advantageous than the one with which the Barak government was prepared, even eager, to provide him. In this instance Israel reaped the benefit of Arafat's calculation. Clearly, however, the nation that determinedly pursues self-deluding, potentially suicidal, national policies and is dependent upon the missteps of its enemies to extricate it from its own folly will not survive very long.

What must Israel do to sustain itself in the face of ongoing besiegement to which there is no end in sight? The last several pages discussed the necessity of pragmatic policies that take full account of Israel's true predicament and set as their diplomatic goals the achievement of more secure armistice arrangements. Such arrangements must entail, in particular, the nation retaining those parts of the territories vital for its defense. Another aspect of those policies should be, of course, an alertness to changes in the Arab world that might signal the possibility of shifts away from its anti-Semitic demonizing of Israel and its exterminationist agenda toward the state. It is in Israel's interests to be responsive to developments that might offer opportunities for improved relations and even to engage in a continual testing for such developments.

It would obviously be helpful for the nation to have leaders that honestly confront Israel's strategic predicament, both its strengths and its challenges, and are predisposed neither to a pessimism that compromises judgment nor to utopian visions that discount genuine threats. Oslo agreements won at most a narrow approval in polls of Israeli opinion even though they were aggressively promoted by the government, suggesting the public at large was less vulnerable to the delusions of Oslo than the nation's Oslo-era leaders and that a more reality-oriented leadership could achieve much in inoculating the nation further against such delusions.

Ideologically driven politics are not necessarily delusion-prone, but those enamored of narrow ideology are predisposed to contort facts to fit the Procrustean bed of ideological tenets. Among the steps that would therefore be helpful in protecting the nation against the triumph of Oslo-like delusions would be whatever electoral reforms would serve to increase the likelihood of the election of pragmatic rather than ideology-driven leaders.

One useful change, often discussed but implemented only in the smallest incremental steps, would be to increase the threshold for party representation in the Knesset. This would make it more difficult for small, often ideologically rigid, parties to win seats. Perhaps more importantly, by increasing the representation of larger parties, such reform could potentially decrease the capacity of those small parties that do gain seats to wield power far beyond their relative strength by playing kingmakers in the complex coalition building now necessary to form governments.

An even more significant reform would be to have Knesset members, or at least a substantial portion of them, elected directly by local constituencies, as are American members of Congress, rather than through nationwide voting for party lists. The current system means that a politician's career is determined by his or her ability to win a high enough place on a party's list to gain a seat. This in turn enables party leaders, who determine list placements (or, in the wake of recent reforms in some parties, the party as a whole, which determines list placements through a poll of members), to enforce ideological discipline among Knesset members and candidates. Direct election would lead to politicians considering not only party orthodoxy but also the wishes of their constituents in shaping their positions on issues, and would likely translate into more pragmatism and less ideological rigidity.

In addition, both higher thresholds for party representation in the Knesset and direct election of Knesset members would likely move the parties that remain to become more pragmatic in that they would need to appeal to a broader constituency and so would have an interest in shaping platforms that are less narrowly rigid in ideological terms.

Screaming even more loudly for reform than election of Israel's legislature is the structure, mandate, and staffing of Israel's Supreme Court. There has long been debate in Israel over the issue of a constitution, but no area of national governance is more in need of introduction of constitutional controls than the judicial system. As discussed in Chapter Fourteen, the Supreme Court under Aharon Barak has appropriated to itself virtually dictatorial powers, including the right to pass judgment on any legislation or any executive procedure, with guidance solely — in the absence of a constitution — by imagined constitutional precepts that exist, in essence, only in Justice Barak's head. As noted, those precepts for Barak have been largely in the post-Zionist mold. But even if Barak and his Supreme Court colleagues were paragons of unimpeachable judicial restraint and sagacity, even if each were the embodiment of Plato's philosopher king, the institution of the Israeli Supreme Court as Barak has molded it would still be a threat to the nation's efforts to sustain a functioning democracy. That threat has been compounded by the Court's also appropriating to itself a dominant role in the selection of new justices, so that it is essentially self-perpetuating, without substantive input from the elected branches of government. Of course, this system not only assures ideological conformity among justices but also has a ripple effect throughout the judiciary, as anyone in the system aspiring to compete ultimately for a Supreme Court seat is under pressure to shape his or her career to fit that conformity.

A constitution would at least provide external, nationally endorsed principles that would serve as mandatory guidelines for Supreme Court actions. It would also introduce some of the checks and balances normal in democratic states, including the legislature's ability to advance constitutional amendments that would then likewise be obligatory guides for Supreme Court decisions and a substantive role for the executive and legislature in the nomination and approval of Supreme Court members.

In addition to government structures that facilitated to some degree Israeli adoption of delusional policies, the embrace of those policies was advanced as well by the circumstance that Israel's major media outlets were largely cheerleaders for the agenda of the Peace Movement. They also underreported, during the Oslo years, such essential stories as Palestinian incitement and PA support for and involvement in anti-Israel terror. This was true, for example, of all three major Hebrew newspapers.

The newspapers are privately owned, and the introduction of a news daily capable of competing with the established dailies and presenting a different perspective on the state of the nation and the challenges confronting it will likewise require the enterprise of private individuals. But the electronic media in Israel are state-controlled. Only relatively recently has there been some loosening of the government's monopoly on domestic electronic media and the dominant outlets are still state organs. During the Oslo years, those organs, too, shaped "news" to fit a pro-Oslo agenda. (It is noteworthy in this regard that, as indicated earlier, even in times of right-wing control of the government, the large state bureaucracy in Israel remained essentially in the hands of functionaries of the Left and this was true of state-owned media as well.) Steps toward further loosening the government's grip on electronic media and allowing a wider array of voices on the airwaves could also, by contributing to a better-informed public and facilitating more open debate of policy issues, help inoculate the public against embracing policies based on dangerous, self-defeating delusions.

But governmental reforms that promote fuller public discussion and understanding of vital issues and that increase chances for a more pragmatic national leadership less likely to enmesh the country in delusion-driven policies are, of course, only part, and the lesser part at that, of what is needed for Israel to pursue pragmatic policies in an ongoing, open-ended way. To do so requires, more importantly, that the nation's citizens be reconciled to living with a conflict that does cast its shadow over their lives and that they cannot by their own efforts resolve, a conflict whose peaceful resolution will come only at the pace and time chosen by the other side. Good leadership can help promote and sustain such a frame of mind. But, given the genuine distresses of living under these conditions, Israelis will be able to master their predicament only if they regard the virtues of life in Israel as outweighing the distresses.

Some clearly will not. Israel's population is highly educated and mobile, and some will look at life under siege and see life elsewhere as better. They will look at their children and the threats posed to them by terrorism, and will consider their children's military obligations, obligations that in Israel are not simply time away from getting on with the rest of one's life but entail significant likelihood of finding oneself in harm's way, and they will consider the real possibility that the conflict can at any time, as it has in the past, ignite into even more horrific scenarios, and they will conclude that their children would be safer and their own lives dramatically more at ease if they lived instead in the United States or western Europe or Australia or some other attractive and more tranquil place.

Other reactions to the stresses of living in an Israel under siege, such as fleeing into delusions that peace is attainable if only Israel assuages its foes by self-reform and sufficient concessions, can rightly be condemned for their violence to others, for their putting the lives of all Israelis at risk. In contrast, the decision by some to leave Israel and live elsewhere cannot in good conscience be censured by those of us who do not ourselves live in Israel and share the stresses of life there.

But what are the "virtues of being an Israeli" that might outweigh the allure of a more tranquil life elsewhere, or, more generally, might counter the corrosive effects of the siege, its potential for sowing doubt, alienation, loss of heart, and impulses to flight, whether psychological flight or physical or both?

While the quality of life in Israel is by many generic measures superior to that found in most of the world, the answer cannot lie there. Again, comparable amenities are available elsewhere. Some people will stay because of their social and family ties to others in Israel; but, for many, such ties will be insufficient counterweight to the allure of elsewhere. In addition, neither quality of life nor social ties can serve as counter to that other type of "flight," the flight to delusions of winning "normality" and a tranquil life through Israeli self-indictment, self-effacement, and concession.

Clearly the ultimate counterweight, the only one that renders living in Israel unique and makes all other places less attractive, is attaching value to the Jewish connectedness offered by Israel; that is, valuing one's Jewish identity and experiencing a fulfillment of that identity in Israel that so substantially outweighs the allures of elsewhere that the difficulties of life in Israel pale by comparison.

A concerted effort was made by academic and other supporters of the Peace Movement to undermine Israelis' sense of connectedness with the Jewish people, with Zionist aspirations, and with the state of Israel as fulfillment of those aspirations. The effort built on anti-Zionist strains long present within the universities, the arts, and elements of the kibbutz movement and the political Left in Israel. Prominent among the vehicles it utilized, in addition to the lectures and writings of university professors, were the mass media and the literary, plastic, and performing arts. Yoram Hazony sees the roots of the recent "post-Zionist" assault particularly in the history of Hebrew University, and he focuses on the need for institutions that will offer intellectual challenges to those waging this war of ideas. Hazony's own Shalem Center seeks to provide such an intellectual counterweight, and efforts of this sort are indeed important and should be expanded and supported.

But key to countering the post-Zionist assault is to preempt it. Key to nurturing connectedness with the Jewish people and with Israel as a fulfillment of Jewish aspirations is to educate the young in Jewish history, Jewish faith, Jewish ethics and comprehension of a moral life, Jewish culture; to educate them in the span of these elements of Jewish life over three millennia, in how they have molded the Jewish people and what they have contributed to the wider world. Educating the young in their intellectual and spiritual heritage can go far to inoculating them against the depredations of the "post-Zionist" institutions they encounter as adults. That preparatory education need not and should not be education comprehended in chauvinistic terms, nor education promoting a particular strain of Jewish religious practice, but education conceived in terms of conveying to children the spiritual and intellectual legacy of their forebears, the core of their own spiritual and intellectual inheritance.

Such education cannot, of course, assure strong emotional connection to the Zionist endeavor and to Israel, nor is it always necessary for establishing such connectedness. There are many people with little Jewish education who will feel the bond by virtue of temperament, or will be so put off by the blatant unfairness of the world's attacks on Israel, the cynical, kangaroo-court condemnations of the state on trumped-up charges or on the basis of supposed "standards" applied to no other state, the attempt to deprive Jews of that right of self-determination universally accorded all other peoples, that they will rally to the state, dedicate themselves to life there, out of sheer moral outrage and sense of justice and decency, even in the absence of much Jewish education. Some others, despite being well-educated, will be temperamentally unprepared to withstand the pressures of the siege, will seek to flee it either spiritually or physically or both, and will seek as well to cast their flight as some act of higher morality.

But for most people, education, and the institutions that provide it, will serve as the vital bulwark against the psychologically corrosive effects of the siege. They will provide the nurturing voice that teaches the child, and the adult he or she becomes, a truer valuing of himself and his society in the face of demeaning and abusive assaults. They will enable children, and the adults they grow to be, to derive their morality from something other than the indictments of accusers, to define themselves in terms other than those the haters would impose on them, and to comprehend steadfastly their place in the world equal to anyone else's, with a claim to the inalienable rights of all people, a claim morally superior to that of the world's haters and bigots.

The vital importance of education in this vein is indirectly attested to by those who have championed post-Zionist revisions in Israeli state institutions and an attenuation of Israelis' ties to the Jewish people and the Zionist endeavor. It is attested to by their devoting so much of their efforts to purging the Israeli school curricula of Jewish and Zionist content, to prying children's minds from any grasp of their intellectual, cultural, and spiritual heritage; their seeking to use ignorance as a tool to promote their deluded agenda of self-effacement for "peace." As Hillel Halkin observed, the educational reforms introduced in the 1990s were intended to advance the political goals of the post-Zionists by employing the education system to subject students to a "process of numbing and divorce" from their heritage.[3]

This use of Israel's schools by the post-Zionists is itself a reprise of a pattern seen in recent centuries in the Diaspora, where Jews eager to escape anti-Jewish pressures from surrounding societies and drawn by the allures of assimilation viewed with some negativity their Jewish heritage and educated their own children in less of it, conveying to them at most an attenuated comprehension of the faith, the culture and the history. Their children in turn, knowing less, had even less of a bond to hold them to their identity when confronted with anti-Jewish pressures and the allure of defection or at least of further self-effacement, and educated their own children in even less of their Jewish heritage in the light of their own predilections, in a downward spiral of ignorance and attenuated connectedness. Many caught up in this maelstrom chose to comprehend their course as a laudatory moving beyond parochialism to some higher identity, a self-delusion itself so parochial that it rendered the wholesale discounting of one's ethnic and cultural heritage a particularly Jewish idiosyncrasy; or, paraphrasing Cynthia Ozick, rendered universalism the parochialism of the Jews.

But the educational reforms of the post-Zionists in the 1990s that sought to cut Israelis off from their heritage were imposed on an education system that was already weak in its transmitting of Jewish history, Jewish religion, Jewish culture, Zionism, and Israeli history, so that many students exited the system ignorant of much that should have been offered them. Therefore, in arming students against the assault on their people, their faith and their nation mounted by their enemies and those wishing to appease their enemies, it is not sufficient to go back to the *status quo ante*; rather, new curricula are required that correct the inadequacies of the earlier schooling.

In the face of Arafat's terror war, there has been a coming together of Israelis and the reemergence of a broad consensus embracing Zionist principles and verities. This coming together was reflected in, for example, the formation in early 2001 of a Committee for National Responsibility consisting of prominent figures from across the Israeli political spectrum, and the Committee's approval, in October, 2001, of the Kineret Declaration. The Declaration consists of a list of principles regarding the nature of the state of Israel upon which the signatories agreed. Those principles conform in both spirit and specific content to the Zionist definition of the State of Israel as articulated in the nation's Declaration of Independence in 1948. Essential tenets are that Israel is a Jewish state, the National Home of the Jewish people, and that it is a democracy that respects and guarantees the rights of all its citizens.[4]

No doubt for some among the signatories, particularly among those whose own sentiments had drifted toward post-Zionist perspectives, as well as for many in the general public who had moved in a similar direction and now joined a reinvigorated Zionist mainstream, the turn in their views was essentially a reaction to their sudden comprehension of the murderous and uncompromising, indeed annihilationist, objectives of the other side. It was a reaction to the sudden dispelling of the delusional fantasy that a partial voluntary foregoing of those inalienable rights, the compromising of those rights in a manner not required of any other nation, and the conceiving of this self-abnegation as the expression of some higher morality, would suffice to win peace.

But Israelis had shared a similar broad consensus in the earlier decades of the nation's existence. Can they maintain the present one as the war goes on, as the acute attack becomes again chronic besiegement, whether in its current horrific form or some attenuated variation on Arafat's terror campaign?

The Kineret Declaration includes, as one of the corollaries to Israel's being a Jewish state, the nation's obligation to provide its Jewish citizens an education in Jewish history and the Jewish faith, and, indeed, to assist in providing Jewish education in Diaspora communities as well. But the capacity of the people of Israel to sustain a broad consensus regarding the essential rightness and value of the Jewish state in the face of chronic besiegement and vilification will in turn be largely a corollary of the provision to its people of Jewish education.

In this regard, the place of Jewish education converges with a role it has always played in the Diaspora, when education has been provided, as a vital buttress against the psychological assaults visited upon the Jews by surrounding societies. It has always served as a bulwark that neither was necessary for all who held to their Jewishness nor sufficient for some, who chose to flee in the face of abuses despite their Jewish learning. But it has been a key factor in the lives of many who valued their connections to the community too highly to surrender them for worldly advantage or relief from depredations.

The crucial role of Jewish education in Israel also converges with what must be its place in the Diaspora today. We see Jews today under assault even in America, as on university campuses — academia having always been a stronghold of bigoted ideologies whether of the Left or the Right, in Europe traditionally of both and in America more typically of the Left. Jews on campus are too often so abysmally ignorant of the history of their people, of Zionism, and of Israel that not only do some surrender to the assault but even those who know better and are not intimidated by the attacks and are inclined to fight back are too ill-informed to do so effectively. While Jews in the wider society in America are incessantly subjected to biased media coverage of Israel, even if the anti-Israel slant does not match the media defamation of Israel found in Europe, and are likewise, even when not inclined to be swayed by the bias or intimidated by it, too often ill-prepared to see clearly through the distortions and to respond effectively to them. It is the obligation of American Jews who have any interest in preserving their Jewish heritage and defending Israel to educate themselves and their children in both.

In recent centuries, the importance of educating Jews in Jewish faith and ethics, Jewish history, and Jewish culture as a defense against the psychological corrosiveness of anti-Jewish depredations, an importance which should have been obvious, has had to be restated, and in effect rediscovered, many times. In the dark days of the Nazi era, for example, as Jews were subjected to new levels of demonization in much of "civilized" Europe and were the objects of denigration elsewhere in the world as well, the psychologist Kurt Lewin, himself a refugee from Germany, felt it necessary to point out the importance of educating children to a positive Jewish group identity as a defense against the soul-withering depredations of anti-Jewish hatred. Lewin's essays "Bringing Up the Jewish Child" (1940) and "Self-Hatred Among Jews" (1941) offer truths that, again, should have been obvious.

Nor is education of this sort a uniquely Jewish, or Israeli, need, or a need only for chronically besieged or abused groups. In the United States, for example, it is widely recognized that to sustain people's intellectual and emotional investment in the social contract that is the American experiment requires, at the very least, education in civics, in the Constitution that defines the American experiment, and in the nation's history, the people and events that first shaped the Constitution and the polity and that have figured in their evolution over the last two centuries.

The American experiment, too, has had its bigoted indicters, those who have pointed to the recurrent gaps between national ideals and realities of national policy not to promote greater adherence to those ideals but rather to delegitimize the American endeavor. Such assaults cannot alter the truth that both the articulated premises and principles of the national contract and the curve of the nation's history, the struggle toward more perfect realization of that contract, have been and remain a uniquely promising and inspiring beacon to the wider world.

So, too, the Jewish *risorgimento,* the national rebirth of the Jewish people, its articulated aspirations and the history of its efforts to realize those aspirations, when honestly told, have been and continue to be an inspiration for much of mankind, including those who as members of victimized communities have yet to achieve their own communal self-determination or have taken the first steps in that direction but face daunting difficulties in the quest to transform their young polities into free, safe, and prosperous homelands for their people.

How ironic then that, in the face of the hatred directed against Israel, it is various Jews, in Israel and in the Diaspora, who most conspicuously embrace the calumnies of the haters and join the ranks of their supporters and fellow travelers. But it has been always thus. For those who are not broken by the siege, who are armed by nurturing education and upbringing against breaking, the task is to become themselves not only resistors but educators. The alternative, however disguised in claims of higher principle, is an ignoble capitulation to murderous bigotry and serves only to advance the world-diminishing campaign for hatred's victory and Israel's annihilation.

Endnotes

INTRODUCTION

1 Yigal Carmon, "The Story Behind the Handshake," *Commentary*, March, 1994, pp. 25–29.

2 Foreign Broadcast Information Service, "Near East and South Asia, Daily Report Supplement, Israel-PLO Agreement," Tuesday, September 14, 1993, pp. 4–5.

3 Efraim Karsh, *Arafat's War*, Grove Press, New York, 2003, p. 59.

4 Notable examples are the Middle East Media Research Institute and Palestinian Media Watch.

5 *Jerusalem Post International Edition*, June 1, 1996.

6 For example, in August, 1995, addressing the issue of recent terrorism and the challenge it presented to Israel, Rabin declared: "This is a war against the enemies of Israel and the enemies of peace. It is a war which we are waging today, to some extent, together with the Palestinian Authority, whose enemies they are also." (*Mideast Mirror*, July 22, 1995)

Similarly, in his last speech, Rabin stated: "There are enemies of peace who are trying to hurt us, in order to torpedo the peace process. I want to say bluntly, that we have found a partner for peace among the Palestinians as well: The PLO." (Federal News Service, November 4, 1995)

This rhetoric persisted throughout the term of the Rabin-Peres government. After the worst spate of terrorist violence, with fifty-nine Israelis killed in bombings in a nine-day period, an "anti-terrorism" conference was convened at Sharm al-Sheikh. Peres, in his comments at the opening ceremonies, again referred to the terrorists as "enemies of peace" while embracing Arafat as his peace partner. (Federal News Service, March 13, 1996) As Frank Gaffney noted in an Op-Ed in *The Washington Times* the previous day: "Mr. Arafat routinely tells his people in Arabic of his support for the 'martyrs' and 'heroes' that he condemns in English for Western consumption as 'terrorists' and 'enemies of peace.'" (*The Washington Times*, March 12, 1996)

7 For example, Environment Minister Yossi Sarid declared after a deadly terrorist attack: "The enemies of peace are making their best effort to stop the [peace] process. This is the main reason to accelerate the pace of peace." (United Press International, November 27, 1994)

8 BBC, March 28, 1995

9 Harold J. Kaplan, Benjamin J. Sadock, Jack A. Grebb, *Synopsis of Psychiatry*, seventh edition, Williams and Wilkins, Baltimore, 1994, p. 305.

10 See Rael Jean Isaac, "The Real Lessons of Camp David," *Commentary*, December, 1993, pp. 34–38.

11 Sander L. Gilman, *Jewish Self-Hatred*, Johns Hopkins University Press, Baltimore, 1986, p. 1.

12 Anna Freud, *The Ego and the Mechanisms of Defense*, International Universities Press, Madison, Conn, 1966, especially pp. 109–121. (First published in 1936.)

13 Anna Freud actually saw such projection, in developmental terms, as an early stage of identification with the aggressor, a stage at which the individual eschews taking to heart the indictment by redirecting it toward others, with embrace of the indictment

being a further developmental step. She also spoke of those who remained stuck in projecting the aggression and never moved to the next step. (Ibid., especially p. 119)

Interestingly, in autobiographical comments, Anna Freud described herself as having
been from childhood idiosyncratically predisposed to eschew projection and take all criticism
to heart. See Elisabeth Young-Bruehl, *Anna Freud*, Summit, New York, 1988, especially pp.
210–215.

[14] Kenneth Levin, *Unconscious Fantasy in Psychotherapy*, Jason Aronson, Northvale, New
Jersey, 1993.

[15] E.g., a three-part article published in the *Jerusalem Post*, February 2, February 28 and
March 7, 1993, the first under the title "Delusions of Peace"; also, "Nothing Doing," *The
New Republic*, May 24, 1993.

[16] E.g., "This Hubris Will Exact a Heavy Price," *Jerusalem Post*, September 10, 1993.

[17] Kenneth Levin, "Jews, Israelis, and the Psyche of the Abused," *Nativ*, fall, 1996 (in
Hebrew).

CHAPTER ONE

[1] In Aharon Megged, "One-Way Trip on the Highway of Self-Destruction," *The Jerusalem
Post*, June 17, 1994.

[2] From Max Nordau, speech to the First Zionist Congress, in *The Zionist Idea*, ed. Arthur
Hertzberg, Harper, New York, 1959, pp. 235–241. Citation is from p. 241.

[3] Moses Mendelssohn, cited in Gilman, *Jewish Self-Hatred*, p. 102.

[4] There was a school of economics in the eighteenth century, the physiocrats, that argued
that agriculture was the only genuinely productive endeavor. But indictments of the Jews for
their engagement in trade long antedated the physiocrats, were popular in areas largely un-
touched by physiocrat theories, and long outlived the demise of those theories.

[5] Cited in Lucy Dawidowicz, *What is the Use of Jewish History?*, Schocken, New York, 1992,
p. 252.

[6] Cited in Seymour Martin Lipset and Earl Raab, *Jews and the New American Scene*,
Harvard University, Cambridge, Mass., 1995, p. 13.

[7] Cited in Michael A. Meyer, *The Origins of the Modern Jew*, Wayne State University Press,
Detroit, 1967, p. 44. Meyer writes, "Psychologically there seems to be a trace of self-hate or
simple shame in Mendelssohn's strange reasonings" with regard to Yiddish.

[8] For attacks on the Jews' language, see Gilman, *Jewish Self-Hatred*. The subtitle of Gilman's
book is "Anti-Semitism and the Hidden Language of the Jews," and the book's focus is particularly anti-Semitic attacks on the language of the Jews and the embrace by Jews of elements of
those indictments.

[9] See Meyer, *The Origins of the Modern Jew*, p. 27.

[10] Isaiah Berlin, *Karl Marx: His Life and Environment*, Oxford University, Oxford, 4th edition, 1978, p. 73.

[11] Karl Marx, *Early Writings*, translated and edited by T.B. Bottomore, McGraw-Hill, New
York, 1964, p. 34.

[12] Ibid., p. 37.

[13] Ibid., p. 37.

[14] Frank E. Manuel, *A Requiem for Karl Marx*, Harvard University, Cambridge, Mass., 1995, p. 20.

[15] Harry Zohn, *Karl Kraus*, Twayne, New York, 1971. Also, Robert S. Wistrich, *The Jews of Vienna in the Age of Franz Joseph*, Littman Library, Oxford, 1989, especially pp. 497–519. Also, Gilman, *Jewish Self-Hatred*, especially pp. 233–243.

[16] The quotes are cited in Zohn, *Karl Kraus*, pp. 38 and 41.

[17] On Weininger, see Wistrich, *The Jews of Vienna*, especially pp. 516–536. Also, Gilman, *Jewish Self-Hatred*, especially pp. 244–248.

[18] Cited in Wistrich, *The Jews of Vienna*, p. 519.

[19] Otto Weininger, *Sex and Character*, Howard Fertig, New York, 2003.

[20] Ibid., p. 304.

[21] Some observers, including Wistrich, have suggested that Weininger's Jew-hatred was, like his misogyny, a product of his disturbed sexuality rather than a reflection of social and political stresses.

With regard to misogyny, Weininger himself attributed it generally, as he did most anti-Semitism, to projection: "Hatred of women is always only an unmastered hatred of one's own sexuality." (Cited in German in Wistrich, *The Jews of Vienna*, p. 524, note 108. Translation mine.) But even if Weininger's anti-Semitism is comprehended as founded on a self-loathing of psychosexual origin, the general point regarding the vulnerability of abused minorities to embrace the indictments of their abusers is the same. The social and political predicament confronted by members of an abused group, the predicament of Jews, for example, facing claims by the wider society that they are damaged and inferior, fosters not only straightforward absorption of the message of taint. It also inclines its victims to associate any sense of inadequacy and taint, of whatever origin, with their group identity.

CHAPTER TWO

[1] Shmuel Ettinger, "The Modern Period," in H.H. Ben-Sasson, ed., *A History of the Jewish People*, Harvard University, Cambridge, Mass., 1976, pp. 727–1096, p. 728.

[2] The earliest autobiographical account of voluntary conversion by a Jew to Christianity is that of one Judah ben David Halevi, who in the twelfth century became a monk in Germany and took the name Hermann. Hermann's "Letter on My Conversion" is in many respects typical of the genre and is discussed in Gilman, *Jewish Self-Hatred*, pp. 29–31. A still earlier apostate, a Spanish Jew who converted in 1106 and took the name Peter Alfonsi, wrote a *Dialogue* in which he has the convert Peter demonstrating the superiority of Christianity over Judaism to a Jew essentially representing Peter's earlier self. Both Peter Alfonsi's work and Hermann's autobiography are discussed by Jeremy Cohen, "The Mentality of the Medieval Jewish Apostate: Peter Alfonsi, Hermann of Cologne, and Pablo Christiani," in Todd D. Endelman, ed., *Jewish Apostasy in the Modern World*, Holmes and Meier, New York, 1987, pp. 20–47.

[3] Cited in H.H. Ben Sasson, "The Middle Ages," in Ben-Sasson, ed., *A History of the Jewish People*, pp. 385–723, p. 469.

[4] Ibid., p. 469.

[5] An early exponent of this view was the early German maskil, or promoter of the Jewish Enlightenment. David Friedlander. For Friedlander's views on Jewish reform see Michael A. Meyer, *The Origins of the Modern Jew*, pp. 57–84.

[6] For a succinct discussion of the size of Jewish populations over the course of Jewish history and of the difficulties involved in arriving at meaningful population data generally, and Jewish population data in particular, especially regarding ancient and medieval communities, see the *Encyclopedia Judaica* (Ketem Publishing, Jerusalem), Vol. 13, pp. 866–903.

[7] See, for example, Bat Ye'or, *The Dhimmi: Jews and Christians under Islam*, Fairleigh Dickinson University, Rutherford, N.J., 1985.

[8] Yosef Hayim Yerushalmi, *Zakhor: Jewish History and Jewish Memory*, University of Washington, Seattle, 1982.

[9] Cited in Ben-Sasson, *A History of the Jews*, p. 522.

[10] Cited in Yitzhak Baer, *A History of the Jews in Christian Spain*, Jewish Publication Society, Philadelphia, 1961–62, Vol. II, p. 145. It should be noted, however, that the writer of the letter, Joshua ha-Lorki, himself ultimately converted under pressure of the forced conversion campaign in Spain during that period. Later, as Jeronimo de Santa Fe, he represented the church in the disputation at Tortosa in 1413, in the midst of the second great wave of forced conversions in Spain.

[11] Cited in Ismar Schorsch, *From Text to Context: The Turn to History in Modern Judaism*, Brandeis University Press, Hanover, New Hampshire, 1994, pp. 384–385.

[12] Cited in Louis Finkelstein, ed., *The Jews: Their History, Culture and Religion*, 4th edition, 3 volumes, Schocken, New York, 1977, Vol. I, p. 321.

[13] Benzion Netanyahu, *The Origins of the Inquisition in Fifteenth Century Spain*, Random House, New York, 1995, p. 64.

[14] Ibid., p. 65.

[15] The historian who has most developed the view that the conversos, at this point second- and third-generation descendants of the forced converts of 1391 and 1412 and people whose Catholic education had been carefully supervised by Spanish authorities, were indeed overwhelmingly committed Catholics with very few "backsliders" among them, has been Benzion Netanyahu, most notably in his book *The Origins of the Inquisition in Fifteenth Century Spain*. Netanyahu argues that urban competition and resentment inspired false charges of converso heresy, and he marshals new and impressive evidence in support of his thesis.

Yitzhak Baer, in *A History of the Jews in Christian Spain*, maintains the position that substantial numbers of conversos were indeed secret Jews. Herman Salomon, in his introduction to the fourth edition of Cecil Roth's *A History of the Marranos* (Hermon Press, New York, 1974), notes that while in the introduction to the original, 1932, edition, Roth had spoken of the conversos' "unique devotion which could transmit the ancestral ideals unsullied, from generation to generation, despite the Inquisition...," he had amended this view in his forward to the third edition (1958). There Roth states: "Years have diminished, though it is to be hoped not entirely obliterated, the author's high romanticism of a quarter-century ago..." Salomon goes on to say: "In private communications with [me], Cecil Roth lamented that he had not sufficiently stressed the possibility that the New Christian problem was one of caste, rather than of religion; that people who were content to live as conforming, often as pious, Catholics, had been made to confess to the charges of 'judaizing' and 'believing in the Law of Moses,' and to denounce relatives and friends for having done so, in order to get out of the Inquisitorial labyrinth alive. Thus they had been made into 'Jews' by the very nature of the Inquisitorial procedure." (pp. viii–ix.)

Roth, in the earlier decades, was aware of the social and economic factors that figured in anti-converso sentiment, and of how those factors translated into anti-converso arguments that were in many respects more racist than religious, as reflected in the emphasis on "blood" distinctions between Old Christians and New Christians. The importance of the racist element is clearly stated in Roth's *The Spanish Inquisition*, first published in 1937, Robert Hale, London. But Roth nevertheless believed, at least then, that, whatever the true motives and beliefs of their enemies, conversos in large numbers were indeed secretly loyal to Judaism. A key point of Netanyahu is that such claims give too much credence to the confessions extracted by the Inquisition under torture. Netanyahu musters contemporary Jewish, converso, and Old Christian sources in support of his view that the conversos were overwhelmingly loyal to their Catholicism and that the accusations of Judaizing put forward by the conversos' enemies were essentially a cynical ruse.

CHAPTER THREE

[1] Cited in Hannah Arendt, *Rahel Varnhagen: The Life of a Jewish Woman*, revised edition, Harcourt, Brace, Jovanovich, New York, 1974, p. 120.

[2] Translated by Margaret Armour, in *The Poetry of Heinrich Heine*, selected and edited by Frederic Ewen, Citadel Press, New York, 1969, p. 285.

Heine wrote the poem shortly after his uncle, Salomon Heine, had provided an endowment to establish the hospital (1842), and Heine's relationship with his uncle, and his perspective on the relationship, cast some additional light on aspects of his anti-Jewish animus as reflected in the poem. Salomon was very wealthy, made extensive charitable contributions to the city of Hamburg and to Jewish institutions, and also supported much of his extended family, including Heine's father, after the failure of the latter's business, and Heine himself. He paid for Heine's education, financed his entrepreneurial endeavors, and provided stipends for him when Heine chose, to his uncle's incomprehension, to devote himself to writing. But Heine consistently felt that his uncle was not sufficiently generous in his support, given the level of Salomon's wealth. He also resented his dependence on his uncle, even as he was disinclined to forego the stipends, and chafed at his uncle's coolness to his life of art. Heine chose to see his uncle's attitude as an expression of that bourgeois Jewish sentiment that he repeatedly attacked. Heine also believed that his own Jewish origins blocked his being able to support himself as an artist — through, for example, an academic appointment — and so prevented him from "liberating" himself from dependence on his uncle; another manifestation of the Jewish "calamity transmitted from father to son."

For Heine's relationship with Salomon, see Jeffrey L. Sammons, *Heinrich Heine: A Modern Biography*, Princeton University, Princeton, 1979.

[3] Cited in Jacob Rader Marcus, *The Jew in the Medieval World*, Hebrew Union College, Cincinatti, 1990, p. 76.

[4] Comments by Voltaire attacking the Jews, beyond his indictments of their religion, include, "We find in them only an ignorant and barbarous people, who have long united the most sordid avarice with the most detestable superstition and the most invincible hatred for every people by whom they are tolerated and enriched. Still we ought not to burn them." The quote is from Voltaire's article "Juifs" in the *Dictionaire philosophique*. Cited in S. W. Baron, "The Modern Age," in Leo W. Schwarz, editor, *Great Ages and Ideas of the Jewish People*, Random House, New York, 1956, p. 324.

The thesis that Voltaire's anti-Jewish animus was secondary to his anti-Christian attitudes was rebutted by one observer who spent eight days as Voltaire's guest and afterwards concluded: "The only reason why M. de Voltaire gave vent to such outbursts against Jesus Christ is that He was born among a nation whom he detests." Cited in Bernard Lewis, *Semites and Anti-Semites*, W. W. Norton, New York, 1986, p. 87.

[5] See, for example, "Jewish Quarter," in *Encyclopedia Judaica*, Vol. 10, pp. 81–88.

[6] Dubnow expounded his views on the significance of Jewish autonomy in *History of the Jews in Russia and Poland from the Earliest Times Until the Present Day* (3 volumes, Ktav, New York, 1975) and *History of the Jews* (5 volumes, T. Yoseloff, South Brunswick, N.J., 1967–1973).

[7] For a succinct statement of this perspective, see Baron, "The Modern Age," in *Great Ages and Ideas of the Jewish People*, pp. 316–317. Baron also wrote a three-volume history of Jewish self-governance, *The Jewish Community: Its History and Structure to the American Revolution*, Jewish Publication Society, Philadelphia, 1942.

[8] Alexander Altmann, *Moses Mendelssohn: A Biographical Study*, University of Alabama, University, Alabama, 1973, p. 358.

[9] Cited in Hannah Arendt, *Rahel Varnhagen: The Life of a Jewish Woman*, p. 219.

[10] Ibid., p. 120.

[11] Gilman construes the statement as intentionally ironic, reflecting Heine's bitterness that despite his conversion he continued to be regarded widely as a Jew and to encounter the excoriation and rejection meted out to Jews. (*Jewish Self-Hatred*, p. 177.)

[12] Todd M. Endelman, "The Social and Political Context of Conversion in Germany and England, 1870–1914," in *Jewish Apostasy in the Modern World*, pp. 83–107, p. 89.

[13] See Todd M. Endelman, Introduction, *Jewish Apostasy in the Modern World*, p. 10 and note 6, pp. 18–19.

[14] Cited in Charles S. Liebman, *The Ambivalent American Jew*, Jewish Publication Society, Philadelphia, 1973, p. 67.

[15] On the demographic precariousness of German Jewry in the early decades of the twentieth century, due to small family size as well as defection, see Baron, "The Modern Age," in Schwarz, ed., *Great Ages and Ideas of the Jewish People*, p. 394.

[16] Cited in Michael A. Meyer, *The Origins of the Modern Jew*, p. 139.

[17] Ibid., p. 139.

[18] Cited in Ettinger, "The Modern Period," in Ben-Sasson, ed., *A History of the Jewish People*, p. 830.

[19] Cited in Barry Rubin, *Assimilation and Its Discontents*, Times Books, New York, 1995, p. 193.

[20] In recent years, the 1840 Damascus libel, represented as fact and as characteristic of Jewish depravity, has enjoyed new popularity in the Arab world. It is the subject of a book by Syrian Defense Minister Mustafa Tlas (*The Matzoh of Zion*) and articles in the state-run Egyptian press and Arab media elsewhere. It has even made it into the official proceedings of the United Nations through Syrian submissions to the United Nations Human Rights Commission in Geneva (Jewish Telegraph Agency, March 4, 1991).

[21] Cited by Ettinger, "The Modern Period," in Ben-Sasson, ed., *A History of the Jewish People*, p. 848.

[22] Cited in Rubin, *Assimilation and Its Discontents*, p. 19.

[23] "Gabriel Riesser," *Encyclopedia Judaica*, Vol. 14, pp. 166–169, p. 167.

[24] Many of the standard elements of modern anti-Semitic cant, even as purveyed by voices on the extreme Right, had their origins in anti-Jewish writings of European socialists and other left-wing radicals, and attacks on "the Jews" have remained a popular component of socialist and other leftist critiques of middle-class liberalism. See, for example, George Lichtheim, "Socialism and the Jews," *Dissent,* July–August, 1968, pp. 314–342. Also, papers by Robert S. Wistrich collected in *Between Redemption and Perdition* (Routledge, London, 1990); particularly, "Anti-Semitism as a Radical Ideology" (pp. 31–42) and "French Socialism and the Dreyfus Affair" (133–154).

[25] Robert S. Wistrich, *Revolutionary Jews from Marx to Trotsky,* Harper and Row, New York, 1976, pp. 7–8.

[26] Ferdinand Lassalle, *Une Page d'amour de Ferdinand Lassalle,* Brockhaus, Leipzig, 1878; cited in Gilman, *Jewish Self-Hatred,* p. 205.

[27] Cited in Wistrich, *Revolutionary Jews,* p. 46.

[28] Cited in Wistrich, *Revolutionary Jews,* p. 57. Wistrich suggests that Lassalle's anti-Jewish rhetoric in attacking middle-class liberals was a major source of the prominent place subsequently accorded anti-Semitic themes by Lassalle's successors in the leadership of German socialism and the German labor movement. However, anti-Semitic themes were already popular on the German Left.

[29] Cynthia Ozick, "Preamble: Universalism is the Ultimate Jewish Parochialism," in Edward Alexander, ed., *With Friends Like These: The Jewish Critics of Israel,* SPI, New York, 1993. On the issue of Jewish attraction to universalist perspectives, see also Charles S. Liebman, *The Ambivalent American Jew,* especially pp. 34–41.

[30] "Nietzsche Contra Wagner," in *The Portable Nietzsche,* edited and translated by Walter Kaufmann, Penguin, New York, 1959, pp. 675–676.

CHAPTER FOUR

[1] Cited in Gilman, *Jewish Self-Hatred,* pp. 222–223.

[2] Cited in Wistrich, *Between Redemption and Perdition,* p. 99.

[3] Theodor Herzl, *The Jewish State,* Dover, New York, 1988, p. 76.

[4] These statistics from Frankfurt, and the broader statistics in this section on Jewish populations in 1800 and 1880, are taken from Ettinger, "The Modern Period," in Ben-Sasson, ed., *A History of the Jewish People,* pp. 790–793.

[5] Ibid., p. 790.

[6] The standard resource on this subject is Peter G.J. Pulzer, *The Rise of Political Anti-Semitism in Germany and Austria,* John Wiley, New York, 1964.

[7] Early writing in this vein, noted by Gilman in *Jewish Self-Hatred,* includes that of the Vienna physician and Freud disciple Fritz Wittels, in his monograph *Die Taufjude* (Breitenstein, Vienna, 1904). Other examples are Hans Kohn, "Das kulturelle Problem des modernen Westjuden" (1921); Josef Prager, "Verdrangung und Durchbruch in der judischen Seele" (1923); and E.J. Lesser, "Karl Marx als Jude" (1924). Theodor Lessing's book, *Jewish Self-Hatred,* was particularly influential. See Gilman, especially pp. 293–308.

Development of the literature on Jewish self-hatred to some extent paralleled emergence and development of the new literature that was taking a more positive view of Eastern, Polish Jewry. The latter offered glosses on Eastern Jewry as in many respects more centered, more whole and more wholesome, its members often enjoying a psychological integrity that compared well to the fractured and conflicted sense of self that seemed to characterize the assimilating Jews of the West. This theme was most notably developed by Martin Buber. Not all those writing about Jewish self-hatred in the West shared this view of Eastern Jewry, but a number, including Kohn, Prager, and Lesser, did, and their papers listed above all appeared in Buber's journal, *The Jew*. On the history of this positive view of Eastern Jewry among some German Jews, see Steven E. Aschheim, *Brothers and Strangers: The East European Jew in German and German-Jewish Consciousness, 1800–1923,* University of Wisconsin, Madison, 1982, especially pp. 100–214.

[8] Cited in Gilman, *Jewish Self-Hatred,* pp. 222–223.

[9] Cited in Rubin, *Assimilation and Its Discontents,* p. 56.

[10] *Encyclopedia Judaica,* Vol. 12, p. 1570.

[11] *Allgemeine Israelitische Wochenschrift,* October 2, 1896; cited in Meir Ben-Horin, *Max Nordau, Philosopher of Human Solidarity,* Conference of Jewish Social Studies, New York, 1956, p. 180.

[12] Cited in Wistrich, *Between Redemption and Perdition,* p. 99.

[13] Cited in Rubin, *Assimilation and Its Discontents,* p. 59.

[14] Herzl, *The Jewish State,* p. 76.

[15] Rubin, *Assimilation and Its Discontents,* p. 189.

[16] Moses Hess, *Rome and Jerusalem,* Bloch, New York, 1945.

[17] Evolution of the musar movement is noted by Baron as an example of the influence of Hasidism on the Lithuanian yeshivot despite the latter's opposition to Hasidism. See Baron, "The Modern Age," in Schwarz, ed., *Great Ages and Ideas of the Jewish People,* pp. 374–375.

[18] Through the course of the nineteenth century, an estimated 84,500 Jews converted to Christianity in Russia, suggesting that conversion rates there did not differ dramatically from those elsewhere in Europe. But a sample study of one Russian Orthodox Church jurisdiction, which investigated what segments of the Jewish population chose the path of conversion, suggested a pattern very different from that in other places. In the sample, 72.5 percent of those who converted were destitute and desperate, victims of the czarist campaign to impoverish Russian Jewry, and turned to the church for succor. Another 5 percent were forcibly converted soldiers who had typically been inducted into the military as children under the "cantonist" laws. Still another 4 percent were convicts who, under Russian law, could have their sentences reduced or entirely canceled by conversion. It is also noteworthy that when, in 1905, Czar Nicholas II, as part of a series of concessions intended to stem political unrest, issued a "Law on Religious Tolerance" which permitted Jews who had converted to return to Judaism, the Ministry of Interior was inundated with petitions from Jews wishing to do so. (Michael Stanislawski, "Jewish Apostasy in Russia: A Tentative Typology," in Todd M. Endelman, *Jewish Apostasy in the Modern World,* pp. 189–203.)

[19] Seymour Martin Lipset, *"The Socialism of Fools": The Left, the Jews and Israel,* Anti-Defamation League of B'nai Brith, New York, 1969, p. 9.

[20] Cited in Ettinger "The Modern Period," in Ben-Sasson, ed., *A History of the Jewish People,* p. 911.

[21] Chaim Weizmann, "My Early Days," in Lucy Dawidowicz, ed., *The Golden Tradition,* Syracuse University, Syracuse, 1996, p. 381.

[22] Many historians argue that political oppression and abuse under the czars were major

factors, along with constantly worsening economic conditions, in spurring Jewish flight from Russia, and Ettinger offers statistics that show a correlation between the episodic worsening of pogroms in Russia and the numbers of Jews leaving the country (in Ben Sasson, ed., *A History of the Jewish People*, p. 861). Baron disputes this, claiming that the motivation to emigrate was overwhelmingly financial, to escape poverty and find work and a better life elsewhere, that there was no correlation between levels of persecution in Russia and numbers of emigrés, and that in fact decade by decade comparisons from 1870 onward show that the percentage of Jews among Russian emigrés to the United States consistently decreased even as abuse of the Jews worsened. Baron also asserts that during this period Galician Jews, who were not exposed to Czarist policies, emigrated to the United States in higher percentages than did Russian Jews. Baron does not offer statistics to support these assertions. Moreover, he ignores the fact that Poles were granted administrative autonomy in Galicia by the Austrian government in 1866 and subsequently instituted measures against the Jews, and the emigration from Galicia in the years that followed was likely driven by this orchestrated abuse as well as by economic conditions. (Baron, in Schwarz, ed., *Great Ages and Ideas of the Jewish People*, p. 398.)

[23] These distinguishing characteristics of the Jewish emigrés to America during the years being considered are taken from Ettinger, "The Modern Period," in Ben-Sasson, *A History of the Jewish People*, pp. 861–864.

[24] Ibid.

[25] Much of the populist anti-immigrant agitation during the last decades of the nineteenth century and into the early years of the twentieth targeted Jews and invoked anti-Jewish rhetoric. See, for example, discussion in Lipset, *"The Socialism of Fools": The Left, the Jews and Israel*, pp. 11–13.

[26] Myron Berman, *The Attitude of American Jewry Towards East European Jewish Immigration, 1881–1914*, Arno Press, New York, 1980, p. 27, note 30. According to Berman, there was a significant shift in the position of the American Jewish community toward Jewish immigration during these decades. In the 1880s and 1890s, the Jewish communal leadership sought to stem the arrival of indigent Jews as creating too much of a burden for the established community and even supported immigration restrictions. This attitude changed around the turn of the century; the organized community became more receptive to large-scale Jewish immigration and more prepared to aid the immigrants, and the leadership thereafter fought immigration restrictions. Berman does not explore the factors at work in bringing about this shift in policy.

[27] Cited in Finkelstein, *The Jews: Their History, Culture and Religion*, p. 500.

[28] Cited in Rubin, *Assimilation and Its Discontents*, p. 66.

[29] Ibid., p. 62.

[30] Ibid., p. 62.

[31] Cited ibid., p. 65.

[32] Cited ibid., p. 65.

[33] Cited in Ronald Steel, *Walter Lippmann and the American Century*, Little, Brown, Boston, 1980, p. 187.

[34] Cited in Rubin, p. 65.

[35] Cited ibid., p. 72.

[36] Cited ibid., p. 72.

[37] *Brandeis on Zionism: A Collection of Addresses and Statements by Louis D. Brandeis*, Zionist Organization of America, Washington, D.C., 1942, p. 11.

[38] Ibid., p. 23.

[39] Ibid., pp. 28–29.

[40] Ibid., p. 29.

[41] Ibid., p. 50.

[42] Citations from Gay Talese, *The Kingdom and the Power*, World, New York, 1966, p. 168.

CHAPTER FIVE

[1] Cited in Solomon Liptzin, *Germany's Stepchildren*, Meridian, Cleveland, 1961, pp. 180–181.

[2] Cited in Rubin, *Assimilation and Its Discontents*, p. 86.

[3] For a summary of discriminatory policies against the Jews pursued by the governments of eastern and central Europe in the decades between the wars, see Ettinger, "The Modern Period," in Ben-Sasson, ed., *A History of the Jewish People,* especially pp. 955–959.

[4] David Fromkin, *A Peace to End All Peace*, Avon, New York, 1989, p. 524.

[5] Ibid., p. 524.

[6] J.H. Patterson, *With the Judaeans in the Palestine Campaign*, Hutchinson, London, 1922, pp. 250–251.

[7] This pattern is discussed, for example, by Conor Cruise O'Brien in *The Siege* (Simon and Schuster, New York, 1986).

[8] Arthur D. Morse, *While Six Million Died*, Random House, New York, 1967, p. 105.

[9] A similar predilection to demonstrate even more forcefully one's national loyalty and to eschew more determinedly any Jewish "particularism" was, of course, a common response to heightened anti-Semitism during these years in other nations of the West as well. Rubin writes of the French Jewish political philosopher Raymond Aron: "He denied that his Jewish background set him apart from other Frenchmen but recalled how he felt inhibited from warning about Hitler in the 1930s lest his objectivity be questioned." (*Assimilation and Its Discontents*, p. 200.)

[10] Cited ibid, p. 58.

[11] Liptzin, *Germany's Stepchildren*, p. 223. The chapter on Zweig is on pp. 211–225.

[12] See ibid., pp. 152–169. Also, Gilman, *Jewish Self-Hatred*, especially pp. 300–302. Also Morse, *While Six Million Died*, pp. 159–160.

[13] Liptzin, *Germany's Stepchildren*, p. 165.

[14] Cited ibid., p. 168.

[15] See ibid., p. 200.

[16] The material on Toller is from Liptzin, *Germany's Stepchildren*, pp. 195–201. Liptzin also relates (pp. 173–183) the very similar course to disillusionment and despair of the German Jewish novelist Jakob Wassermann, whose autobiography, *My Life as a German and a Jew*, is cited in the opening of this chapter. While writing of the impossible position of Jews in Germany, Wassermann vehemently rejected any connection with Jews beyond the bounds of German Jewry, denigrated the wider Jewish world, and could never get past his despair and find his way to a sustaining bond with his Jewishness.

[17] See Gilman, *Jewish Self-Hatred*, on Erikson, especially pp. 8–11.

[18] The incident is related by Rubin, and the quote cited by him; *Assimilation and Its Discontents*, p. 214. Lessing also recalled "Once, in the street, my mother pointed to a man in a caftan and said 'There goes a Jew.' I then concluded that we were not really Jews." Cited in Aschheim, *Brothers and Strangers,* p. 47.

[19] See Ruth R. Wisse, *The Modern Jewish Canon*, Free Press, New York, 2000, especially pp. 66–87. Also, Gilman, especially pp. 281–285; also Rubin, especially pp. 42–45.

[20] On Kafka and Yiddish, see Wisse, pp. 71–75. Also, "An Introductory Talk on the Yiddish Language," in Kafka, *Dearest Father: Stories and Other Writings*, trans. Ernst Kaiser and Eithne Wilkins, Schocken, New York, 1954, pp. 381–386. Also, a fictional rendering of his discovery of Yiddish theatre, from Kafka's notebooks; *Dearest Father*, pp. 129–134.

[21] "A Report to the Academy," in *Selected Short Stories of Franz Kafka*, trans. Willa and Edwin Muir, Modern Library, New York, 1952, pp. 168–180.

[22] Ibid., pp. 202–255.

[23] Ibid., pp. 305–328.

[24] Cited in Rubin, *Assimilation and Its Discontents*, p. 44.

[25] Kafka, *Selected Short Stories*, pp. 181–187.

[26] Wisse, *The Modern Jewish Canon,* p. 76.

[27] See Wisse's exposition of *The Trial*, ibid., pp. 75–84.

[28] Cited in Gilman, *Jewish Self-Hatred,* p. 284.

[29] "Letter to His Father," *Dearest Father*, pp. 138–196. Quote is from p. 174.

[30] Ibid., p. 172.

[31] Ibid., pp. 171–174.

[32] Ibid., p. 174.

[33] For Henry Ford's activities in promoting anti-Semitism in America in the years between the wars, see especially Neil Baldwin, *Henry Ford and the Jews* (Public Affairs, New York, 2001).

[34] Cited by Rubin, *Assimilation and Its Discontents*, p. 64.

[35] Cited ibid., p. 86.

[36] Cited ibid., pp. 206–207.

[37] Ibid., p. 80.

[38] Cited ibid., p. 79. Rubin notes, "The leftist utopianism of some Jewish screenwriters and actors paralleled the rightist utopianism of the Jewish studio heads. The former romanticized a working class, multiethnic society, America as they wanted it to be; the moguls sought to be patrician, idealizing the upper crust and the small-town America they thought already existed." (p. 77) But both groups, in cultivating and communicating their vastly different utopias, widely shared an antipathy toward Jewish identity and assiduously eschewed any particularly Jewish content in their work.

[39] Cited in Ronald Steel, *Walter Lippmann and the American Century*, p. 189.

[40] Ibid., p. 189.

[41] Ibid., p. 192.

[42] Cited ibid., p. 194.

[43] Citations from Rubin, *Assimilation and Its Discontents*, p. 146.

[44] Arthur Miller, *Timebends: A Life,* Grove Press, New York, 1987, p. 24.

[45] Ibid., p. 37.

[46] Ibid., p. 71.

[47] Ibid., p. 70.

48 Ibid., pp. 214–215.
49 Ibid., p. 82.
50 Ibid., p. 167.
51 Ibid., p. 286.

CHAPTER SIX

1 Cited in David S. Wyman, *The Abandonment of the Jews*, Pantheon, New York, 1984, p. 105.

2 Cited in Rafael Medoff, *The Deafening Silence*, Shapolsky, New York, 1987, p. 110.

3 The American government's obstructionist policy toward the rescue of Jews, even when the Nazis' campaign of extermination was fully known and when many opportunities for the rescue of at least tens of thousands were clearly available, was first documented by Arthur D. Morse in *While Six Million Died*. About half of Morse's book is devoted to the nine years of Nazi rule in Germany before the West became aware of Hitler's Final Solution; Morse traces the ever worsening abuse of Germany's Jews, and then of the Jews of other nations that fell under the Nazis' control, and the consistent callousness of U.S. government policy toward Hitler's Jewish victims. He notes in particular that, except for a period of about one year, the Roosevelt Administration refused to allow immigration even to the extent permissible under the restrictive immigration quota system then in effect. Morse demonstrates the continuity be-tween U.S. policy over those nine years and policy during the years of the Holocaust. Morse also looks at some American Jewish efforts throughout the period to aid European Jewry and moderate U.S. government policies.

David S. Wyman, in *The Abandonment of the Jews*, focuses almost exclusively on American policy during the years when the Nazis' mass killing of Jews, and then the Nazis' intention to exterminate all of Europe's Jews, were known. (He had examined the Roosevelt Administration's obstructionist immigration policies from 1938 to 1941 in *Paper Walls: America and the Refugee Crisis, 1938–1941,* University of Massachusetts, Amherst, 1968.) Wyman generally looks in greater detail at American policy as formulated and executed by the White House and the State Department during these years as well as at U.S. interaction with the British Foreign Office and collusion with the British in obstructing plans for rescue. Wyman also considers the efforts of American Jews to promote rescue, the tremendous obsta-cles confronting them, and some factors at work within the community and its leadership that further compromised their efforts. He and Morse both look at the belated creation of the War Refugee Board and its successes in helping to save tens of thousands. Wyman gives greater at-tention to details of the politics surrounding the Board from its creation, the obstacles that continued to be placed in its path by other arms of the U.S. government, and the central role of the American Jewish community, particularly through the Jewish Joint Distribution Committee, in financing and otherwise advancing its work.

Wyman returns to the issue of conflicts within the Jewish community over promotion of rescue, the vital efforts of Peter Bergson, and Bergson's central role in the ultimate establish-ment of the War Refugee Board, in *A Race Against Death: Peter Bergson, America and the Holocaust,* co-authored with Rafael Medoff (New Press, New York, 2002).

4 Perhaps most prominent among those who have attacked criticism of American Jewish ef-

forts to help European Jewry during the Holocaust is the historian Lucy Dawidowicz. (See, for example, her article, "American Jews and the Holocaust," *New York Times Magazine*, April 18, 1982, pp. 47–48, 101–102, 106, 109–112, 114; also, "Indicting American Jews," *Commentary*, June, 1983 [reprinted in Dawidowicz, *What is the Use of Jewish History?*, pp. 179–202]; and "Could America Have Rescued Europe's Jews?" originally published in *This World*, fall, 1985, and reprinted in *What is the Use of Jewish History?*, pp. 157–178.) But there are difficulties with all of Dawidowicz's arguments. She at some points cast the issue of rescue in too stark terms, as though the question were whether or not the Holocaust could have been prevented. It is highly unlikely that any action, least of all any action by American Jews, could have averted the slaughter of millions of Jews by the Nazis. But tens of thousands were, in fact, saved by belated American efforts and there is overwhelming evidence to support the thesis that many more, perhaps numbering in the hundreds of thousands, could have been rescued. In one passage Dawidowicz writes that, while nothing would have diverted Hitler from his genocidal agenda, "No doubt that a more humane refugee policy on this country's part would have saved tens of thousands of lives." (*What is the Use of Jewish History?*, p. 176.) But that is the whole point.

Dawidowicz similarly cast the question of the role of American Jews, particularly the American Jewish leadership, in too stark terms, as whether they exerted themselves to help save European Jews or were essentially passive. Of course, there were efforts on the part of the American Jewish community to promote rescue. Those efforts had some belated and limited but nevertheless significant impact. It is perfectly reasonable to inquire then what within American Jewry prevented the community from mounting a more effective campaign for rescue. Again, Dawidowicz had an answer that was categorical: The obstacles confronting the community, the Nazi juggernaut and American governmental obstructionism, were impervious to any American Jewish effort. But this ignores both the many well-documented opportunities there, in fact, were for rescue (some of which Dawidowicz herself conceded) and the impact Jewish efforts did have in, again, the saving of tens of thousands of lives. The latter did not occur because European Jews were suddenly more accessible for saving, or because governmental resistance in the United States diminished. It occurred because of the increased effectiveness of the efforts of some Jews, making it all the more reasonable to look at what within the community contributed to its not mounting a more effective effort sooner.

For a response to Dawidowicz that addresses the weaknesses in her arguments, see the letter by David Wyman in answer to her *New York Times* article (*New York Times Magazine*, May 23, 1982, p. 94).

[5] Wyman, *The Abandonment of the Jews*, p. 21.

[6] Ibid., p. 24.

[7] Ibid., p. 51.

[8] Ibid., p. 47.

[9] Ibid., p. 76.

[10] On visa and immigration policy as applied to Jews trying to escape the Nazis before the war, see Morse, *While Six Million Died*, especially chapter 7, "Likely to Become a Public Charge," pp. 130–149. Also, Wyman, *Paper Walls*. Also, Henry L. Feingold, *The Politics of Rescue: The Roosevelt Administration and the Holocaust, 1939–1945* (Rutgers, New Brunswick, 1970), especially pp. 126–166. Feingold estimates that from 1938 until America's entry into the war, restrictive State Department procedures in issuing visas prevented the admission of between 67,000 and 75,000

refugees who could have been admitted to the United States under the immigration laws then in force (p. 166). For visa procedures as applied to Jews during the war, see Wyman, *The Abandonment of the Jews*, especially "Paper Walls: American Visa Policies," pp. 124–137.

[11] Wyman, *The Abandonment of the Jews*, p. 136.

[12] Hillel Levine, "The List of Mr. Sugihara," *New York Times*, September 18, 1994. Levine's book on Sugihara is *In Search of Sugihara*, Free Press, New York, 1996.

[13] Cited in Wyman, *The Abandonment of the Jews*, p. 182.

[14] Cited ibid., p. 105. The same sentiments were expressed in virtually identical words by the Colonial Secretary, Oliver Stanley, to his colleagues on the War Cabinet committee on refugees; Stanley, however, ties his concerns explicitly to Palestine. See Martin Gilbert, *Auschwitz and the Allies*, Holt, Rinehart and Winston, New York, 1981, p. 109.

British policy toward rescue, and the centrality of concerns regarding Palestine in the shaping of that policy, is discussed more fully in Gilbert, *Auschwitz and the Allies*, and in Bernard Wasserstein, *Britain and the Jews of Europe, 1939–1945*, Leicester University Press, London, 1979. See, for example, citations from Foreign Office records in Gilbert, including on pp. 224, 287, 291. See also quote from Foreign Office undersecretary Richard Law cited in Monty Noam Penkower, *The Jews Were Expendable* (University of Illinois, Urbana, 1983), p. 90. Foreign Secretary Anthony Eden characterized requests to open Palestine to Jews fleeing the Nazis as "extremist." (Penkower, p. 100.)

Gilbert writes in summary: "Many of the policymakers who opposed the appeals on behalf of refugees were particularly 'afraid' as they expressed it, of the 'danger' of 'flooding' Palestine, and indeed Britain, with Jews." (Gilbert, p. 339.)

British concerns about Palestine also figured in the omission of explicit reference to the plight of the Jews in all but a few statements by the Allies condemning the Nazis' crimes against civilian populations. A common argument is that the Allies were fearful mention of the Jews would serve Hitler's propaganda claims that the war was being waged by the Allies on the Jews' behalf and might stir up anti-Jewish and anti-war sentiment within Allied nations. Another argument put forward for the general Allied silence on the genocide of the Jews is that to distinguish the Jews from the other citizens of the occupied nations, to not simply include them among the Poles, Czechs, Russians and others being brutalized, would somehow be subscribing to the Nazis' distinction of Jews from other citizens of those nations. But a major reason in British calculations for excluding explicit mention of the Jews in Allied statements regarding Nazi crimes was that to refer to the Jews explicitly as a distinct persecuted group would elevate them to the status of a nationality, comparable to the other nations under occupation, and would lend support to demands that their distinctive nationhood be honored in postwar arrangements for those Jews who might survive. (See Gilbert, p. 74.)

Gilbert cites Churchill cautioning a Foreign Office official "against drifting into the usual anti-Zionist and anti-Semitic channel which it is customary for British officers to follow." (Ibid., p. 74.) See also Gilbert's references to Churchill's disagreements with Eden on Palestine policy and the White Paper, pp. 171–177.

[15] See Morse, *While Six Million Died*, pp. 299–300. Also, Wyman, *The Abandonment of the Jews*, p. 99. Also, Penkower, *The Jews Were Expendable*, p. 149.

[16] Wyman, *The Abandonment of the Jews*, pp. 77–78.

[17] Morse touches somewhat more on public and parliamentary calls for action in Britain than does Wyman. In his discussions of British and American reactions to Nazi persecution of

the Jews in the years before the war and the mass killings, Morse points to greater public responsiveness in Britain. On the *Kindertransport*, see Morse, *While Six Million Died*, p. 166. On the failed proposal to bring to the United States 20,000 children (not all of them were to be Jewish), see Wyman, *Paper Walls*, pp. 74–98; also Morse's chapter "Suffer the Children...," pp. 252–269. On the earlier, largely frustrated, attempts by the German Jewish Children's Aid group to bring Jewish children to the United States, see Morse, pp. 161–166.

Deborah Lipstadt, in *Beyond Belief* (Free Press, New York, 1986), in which she documents and discusses American media coverage of the Nazi assault on the Jews from 1933 through the years of the Holocaust, likewise notes greater public reaction in Britain to news of the mass murders, and more intense calls for rescue by religious, parliamentary and other leaders than by comparable echelons in the United States. Lipstadt also notes that leading British newspapers were much more candid and explicit in their coverage of news of the genocide, gave the story much greater prominence, and were more vocal in calls for rescue than were comparable media outlets in the United States. (See Lipstadt, pp. 189–191, 195.)

A Foreign Office note in February, 1943, refers to the "striking difference between the intense propaganda campaign regarding Hitler's Jewish victims carried on here and the apparently negligible publicity in the United States." (Cited by Lipstadt, p. 71 note)

But while the Foreign Office clearly felt the heat of public calls to action, and took steps to diminish this pressure, those steps never included modifying its policy of aggressively obstructing the rescue of Jews.

For fuller discussion of public calls for rescue in Britain as well as British government responses, see Wasserstein, and Gilbert.

[18] See Wyman, *The Abandonment of the Jews*, pp. 104–123. Also Morse, especially pp. 50–63; Feingold, *The Politics of Rescue*, especially pp. 197–207; Penkower, *The Jews Were Expendable*, pp. 98–121.

[19] Wyman, *The Abandonment of the Jews*, pp. 82–84. Also, Morse, pp. 72 ff, and Penkower, p. 148f. Morse and Penkower suggest that the original total number of Rumanian Jews transported to Transnistria was 185,000. Dawidowicz (*The War Against the Jews: 1933–1945*, Bantam, 1976 (hardcover, 1975)) states that "according to a conservative estimate, some 200,000 Rumanian Jews had been shipped to Transnistria", p. 521.

[20] Even at this late date, even with so much evidence to the contrary, there are still some who argue that in fact there was no possibility of rescuing any Jews from Europe and that therefore complaints of Administration callousness and obstruction are unfair. Particularly prominent among such voices are people who seem most concerned with countering any tarnishing of the image and legacy of President Roosevelt.

For example, a leading defender of Roosevelt in this vein, William J. vanden Heuvel, president of the Franklin and Eleanor Roosevelt Institute, offered such arguments in a *New York Times Magazine* article on December 22, 1996 ("The Holocaust Was No Secret," pp. 30–31). Problems with vanden Heuvel's assertions include his casting the issue as though it were one of whether or not the allies could have stopped the Holocaust. He states at one point, "There were no military options to liberate the prisoners of the extermination camps other than the direct assault and conquest by the Allied armies." Even this is not entirely true, as some people were saved even from the extermination camps by the efforts of the War Refugee Board (WRB) and others. But, of course, there were major opportunities for saving tens of thousands before they reached the death camps, or before they died in work camps or elsewhere, and, again, many tens of thousands were rescued. Elsewhere vanden Heuvel cites approvingly a claim by William D. Rubinstein, in his book *The Myth of Rescue*, that "not one plan or proposal, made anywhere in the democracies by either Jews or non-Jewish champions of the Jews after the Nazi conquest of Europe, could have rescued one single Jew who perished in the Holocaust." Once more, the evidence, including the tens of thousands who were rescued by such plans and proposals, make it difficult to comprehend how anyone could proffer such a statement and still claim to be a serious scholar.

A common refrain during the war from those involved in obstructing rescue efforts in the State Department and elsewhere in the administration, a refrain picked up by other governmental, and also media, voices opposed to rescue efforts, was that such projects would somehow detract from the war effort and that the surer way to end the mass killings was to focus exclusively on pursuing military victory; and vanden Heuvel obliquely echoes this argument. He states that so many Jews were being killed every day that any extension of the war due to diversion of resources to rescue would have consumed vastly more lives than those distracting efforts would have saved. But this too is a bogus argument. There is no evidence whatsoever that any of the efforts through which the WRB successfully rescued Jews extended the war by one minute and there is nothing to suggest that similar efforts made sooner or pursued with greater cooperation from other government agencies would have entailed prolonging the war. On the contrary, rescue would have inevitably advanced the war effort, as many of those saved would have had skills and knowledge, not least language skills and knowledge of local conditions, that could have been put to good use by military and intelligence services. Indeed this was the case for those who were saved. For example, some of the German Jews who were let into the United States provided important service in the armed forces and played key roles in the OSS. It is noteworthy in this regard that of the eight thousand German Jewish children admitted to Britain in the *Kindertransport*, over 1,000 subsequently served in the British military (Morse, *While Six Million Died*, p. 166).

Arthur Schlesinger, Jr., vanden Heuvel's colleague at the Roosevelt Institute, of which Schlesinger is chairman, has likewise written against those who suggest that Roosevelt should and could have done more to save Jews during the war. An example is his piece "Did FDR Betray the Jews? Or Did He Do More Than Anyone Else to Save Them?" in *Newsweek*, April 18, 1994. (Reproduced in *FDR and the Holocaust*, ed. Verne W. Newton, St. Martin's, New York, 1996, pp. 159–161). In the article, Schlesinger, like vanden Heuvel, casts the issue as whether or not FDR could have stopped the Holocaust. But, of course, Roosevelt's critics are not claiming he could have done so. They are arguing, rather, that he could have saved many more Jews who were lost to the Holocaust. Schlesinger also notes that Roosevelt ultimately led the fight against Nazism, which is also true but likewise does not address the concerns of his critics. Among Schlesinger's more specific assertions is that had the WRB been established earlier it would have accomplished little because conditions were not yet conducive to effective actions by the Board. But there were many well-documented opportunities prior to January, 1944, for effective intervention by an agency dedicated to rescue. The focus of Schlesinger's attack seems to be Wyman's arguments, but Schlesinger does not seriously address those arguments.

The most detailed effort to argue that there were simply no genuine opportunities to save European Jews, and that all claims of rescue opportunities lost are bogus, is the book cited by vanden Heuvel in his *New York Times Magazine* piece, William D. Rubinstein's *The Myth of*

Rescue (Routledge, London, 1997); and the book's dust jacket features laudatory blurbs from vanden Heuvel and Schlesinger. But as most reviewers of the book noted, there are major problems with Rubinstein's arguments.

Rubinstein, too, casts the issue at times as whether or not the Allies could have stopped the Nazi genocide, but again the argument of those who challenge American and British policy is not that alternative policies could have prevented the Holocaust but that many Jews could have been saved. On this latter issue, Rubinstein does indeed make the obviously absurd statement cited approvingly by vanden Heuvel to the effect that "no Jews who perished during the Nazi Holocaust could have been saved" (p. x) by any of the rescue efforts proposed at the time. But elsewhere he modifies this to suggest that only very small numbers of Jews could have been rescued and so critics who condemn the absence of greater rescue efforts are still vastly overblowing what could have been accomplished. In support of this thesis, Rubinstein asserts that the WRB in fact achieved much less than it is credited with having done, in his view having saved at most 20,000 lives, not the 150,000 to 200,000 widely mentioned, and he offers highly dubious grounds for this claim. But aside from these specifics, Rubinstein exhibits a very idiosyncratic perspective on what constitutes worthwhile rescue endeavors. For example, he offers, as analogous to advocacy of rescue during the war, the campaign to free Soviet Jews in the 1970s and 1980s, and he asserts that, while American Jews were able in the latter instance to win American government support, the campaign was a "total failure" because only 250,000 Soviet Jews were allowed to emigrate while another two million remained captive in the Soviet Union (p. 121).

Elsewhere, Rubinstein argues that the Western democracies including the United States, were very generous in their immigration policies vis-à-vis European Jews in the prewar years and that those who wanted to leave areas under Nazi control were able to do so. But there is, of course, impressive counterevidence to this claim, including the firsthand observations of American consular officials and journalists in Germany who wrote of Jews lined up at consulates desperate to get out but never able to do so and of many specific individuals who died because they were denied visas or because they had valid visa allotments but the State Department delayed their entry. Rubinstein also notes the widespread loathing of the Nazis in the West, but, as others have pointed out, this did not translate into support for admission of Jewish refugees, or, during the war, for rescue. Similarly, Rubinstein's arguments of how anti-Nazi Roosevelt was and how aggressively and effectively he pursued the war does not address those who criticize his actions vis-à-vis Jewish immigration and rescue.

Rubinstein's assertions that nothing the State Department or Foreign Office could have done differently during the war would have saved any Jews and so their behavior was unimpeachable ignore, among other data, what is known of the State Department and Foreign Office blocking the rescue of specific people who could easily have been saved but were lost. Those assertions also fly in the face of the many statements by Foreign Office officials expressing fears that rescue efforts might result in a flood of Jewish refugees. Rubinstein never cites any of those statements.

Regarding Foreign Office behavior and its motives, Rubinstein excoriates one writer on Allied inaction vis-à-vis rescue for calling Anthony Eden "a Jew hater" (William Perl, in *The Holocaust Conspiracy*, Shapolsky, New York, 1989). He offers in Eden's defense his impeccable anti-Nazi credentials. Not only is the latter point, once more, irrelevant, but Eden's personal secretary wrote of him in 1943: "Unfortunately, A.E. is immovable on the subject of Palestine. He loves Arabs and hates Jews." (Cited by Gilbert, *Auschwitz and the Allies,* p. 132.)

Rubinstein accuses Wyman of offering plans for rescue that were *post facto*, formulated after the events, and therefore ahistorical. But the rescue plans discussed by Wyman are in fact taken from proposals made at the time. Rubinstein claims that none of the proposed efforts would have worked, but, again, the WRB did utilize a number of them to good effect.

When Rubinstein deals with specific approaches to rescue, he likewise employs arguments that do not stand up under scrutiny. He dismisses, for example, suggestions at the time that neutral states be assured of financial support and postwar relocation for Jews they took in, claiming that this was not a genuine rescue plan because if Jews reached a neutral state they were already saved. But of course the intent was to make neutral states more amenable to taking in additional Jews, and it worked when the WRB finally acted on the proposal. To bolster this sort of argument, Rubinstein claims that no democracy turned back Jews who had escaped the Nazis, then in a note he acknowledges that Switzerland did turn away some Jews. In fact, Switzerland either refused to allow to enter into its borders or pushed back across the border at least 30,000 Jews; and Switzerland altered its policies after the WRB provided assurances of financial support for those taken in and of their later relocation. In a similar vein, Switzerland in January, 1944, offered to admit 5,000 Jewish children from France if Britain would assure them visas for Palestine. Britain refused and the children were not admitted. (See Penkower, *The Jews Were Expendable,* p. 140.)

Rubinstein is also silent on episodes involving neutrals such as that of the Struma, an essentially unseaworthy ship with nearly eight hundred Rumanian Jewish refugees aboard that limped into Istanbul harbor in December, 1941. The Turkish government offered to let the passengers disembark only if Britain agreed to admit them to Palestine. The British refused, the Turks had the ship towed out to sea, and it quickly sank, killing all but one of the refugees. Obviously, British assurances to neutral Turkey would have saved these people.

Equally weak arguments are offered by Rubinstein with regard, for example, to proposals that the Allies broadcast warnings to Jews of what transport to the East really meant. He argues that the Jews were forced into transports, they did not choose to go, and so warnings would have been meaningless. But, obviously, people, if forewarned, could have fled. Indeed of those who were told what awaited them in Poland, some ignored the information but others did flee and many among them were able to save themselves.

Another line of argument developed by Rubinstein is that assumptions about rescue plans not implemented are entirely hypothetical and therefore ahistorical. But of course his assumptions about the inevitable futility of such plans are equally hypothetical, yet that does not prevent him from asserting categorically that nothing could have worked.

The above offers but a few examples of the many flawed arguments in Rubinstein's book.

A very different line of argument against those who insist Roosevelt could have done more is Wasserstein's assertion that Churchill cared more than Roosevelt about the martyrdom of the Jews and yet Britain had a worse record than the United States, having, for example, never established an agency such as the WRB. Wasserstein is suggesting that one cannot infer indifference from lack of action. But Roosevelt had much more control over what the State Department and other Cabinet departments did than Churchill had over the Foreign Office and other arms of the British government. (Wasserstein's comments are reported in the "Transcript of the Summary of the Conference on 'Policies and Responses of the American

Government toward the Holocaust,' 11–12 November 1993," in Newton, ed., *FDR and the Holocaust*, p. 16.)

Dawidowicz ultimately concedes that the State Department obstructed efforts that could have saved many Jews, but she is defensive of Roosevelt. See her essay"Could America Have Rescued the Jews?," in *What Is the Use of Jewish History*, especially pp. 162–165.

Roosevelt and Hitler both rose to national power at virtually the same time, in early 1933. Morse, in looking at American responses to Nazi persecution of the Jews throughout the pre-war period as well as during the years of the mass killings, notes Roosevelt's callousness and general detachment and inaction during those earlier years as well.

[21] To cite but one example, at one point Roosevelt was angry with the *New York Times*, mainly over its criticism of the administration's plan to pack the Supreme Court, and the president hoped Arthur Sulzberger, then experiencing some financial difficulties, would lose control of the paper. When Sulzberger found a way to extricate himself from the financial crisis and retain control, Roosevelt reportedly complained that "It's a dirty Jewish trick" and apparently made other remarks in a similar vein. (See Susan E. Tifft and Alex S. Jones, *The Trust*, Little, Brown, Boston, 1999, p. 171.)

[22] Cited in Lipstadt, *Beyond Belief*, pp. 47–48.

[23] For American media coverage of the Holocaust during the years when the mass killings were known to be taking place, and when the Nazi policy of extermination was likewise known, see Part II of Lipstadt's book, pp. 135–278.

[24] Lipstadt cites the poll results (p. 240) as evidence of the high level of public disbelief, but Wyman's interpretation of the poll figures, as indicating the effectiveness of Jewish organizations in disseminating news of the mass killings, seems more appropriate.

[25] Wyman, *The Abandonment of the Jews*, pp. 77–78.

[26] Ibid., p. 86.

[27] Ibid., pp. 87–88.

[28] Ibid., pp. 88–89.

[29] Ibid., p. 88.

[30] Ibid., pp. 90–92.

[31] Ibid., pp. 96–97.

[32] Ibid., p. 97.

[33] Ibid., p. 120.

[34] Ibid., p. 143.

[35] Ibid., p. 143.

[36] Ibid., p. 147.

[37] Ibid., pp. 152–153.

[38] Ibid., p. 155.

[39] Ibid., p. 197 ff.

[40] Morse attributes Roosevelt's acquiescing to creation of the War Refugee Board mainly to this intervention of Treasury Department officials. But Wyman makes a very compelling case for the crucial impact as well of movement in Congress on the Rescue Resolution and fears in the administration that Congress would upstage the president and also expose the government's obstructionism. The Bergson group played an essential role in promoting Congressional action and Wyman therefore gives much credit to Bergson and his associates for bringing about the creation of the War Refugee Board. Penkower likewise emphasizes the im-

portance of the Bergson group and its work with Congress in spurring Roosevelt to establish the WRB.

In addition, Treasury officials, including Secretary of the Treasury Hans Morgenthau, acknowledged that it was the Congressional Resolution that made the president agree to set up the War Refugee Board. (See, for example, quotes from Morgenthau cited in Wyman and Medoff, *A Race Against Death*, p. 49, and in Medoff, *The Deafening Silence*, pp. 140–142.) Also, various newspapers at the time, including the *Christian Science Monitor* and the *Washington Post*, observed that the creation of the WRB was primarily due to the efforts of Bergson's Emergency Committee. (See Wyman and Medoff, p. 49.)

As noted, there was great resentment on the part of the mainstream Jewish leadership toward the Bergson group, and this resentment and hostility continued for decades after the war and expressed themselves in part in arguments to the effect that the impact of the group on the effort to promote rescue was nil or even negative. Dawidowicz is perhaps the most significant scholar to echo this sentiment, as she did in her *New York Times Magazine* piece and in "Indicting American Jews." But Dawidowicz offers no substantive, factual support for her attacks on Bergson and his circle, nothing that actually contradicts Wyman's assessment. Her main points of indictment appear to be Bergson's affiliation with the Irgun, which she reviles, and the fact that his work on the issue of rescue has been compared to that of the mainstream Jewish leadership and used to question the efforts of the latter. Dawidowicz is certainly on solid ground when she argues that there has been some unfair and overstated criticism of the efforts of the American Jewish leadership, criticism that underestimates the exertions it did make in support of rescue and underestimates as well the obstacles it faced. But none of her arguments addresses the issue of the contribution of the Bergson group to winning support, most importantly and effectively congressional support, for rescue, and none addresses Wyman's evaluation. The closest she comes to doing so is her suggesting, like Morse, that the actions of Treasury officials deserve exclusive credit for creation of the WRB. But, as noted, the available data, including statements by Treasury Secretary Morgenthau, contradict this view.

For responses to Dawidowicz's dismissal of the role of the Bergson group, see Wyman's letter in the *New York Times Magazine*, May 23, 1982; also, the letter of Paul O'Dwyer on the same page.

On the issue of how various factors weighed in finally prompting Roosevelt to create the WRB, the columnist Edgar Ansel Mowrer, long highly critical of the administration's inaction on rescue, attributed Roosevelt's sudden interest in rescue to the fact that "1944 is an election year and even Jews have votes"; but it is highly doubtful that the upcoming election alone would have swayed the president in the direction of efforts at rescue. (See Wyman, *The Abandonment of the Jews*, p. 204 note. Also, Lipstadt, *Beyond Belief*, p. 227.)

[41] Wyman, *The Abandonment of the Jews*, p. 156.

[42] Ibid., pp. 178–179.

[43] For Treasury's subsequent exposure to State Department obstructionism, and the course of events that led to Treasury Secretary Morgenthau's intervention with the president, see ibid., pp. 180–192, 203–204; also, Morse, *While Six Million Died*, especially pp. 78–99, and Penkower, *The Jews Were Expendable*, especially pp. 129–142.

[44] The full text of the Report is reprinted in Wyman and Medoff, *A Race Against Death*, pp. 187–201.

[45] For the work of the WRB, see Wyman, *The Abandonment of the Jews,* pp. 209–307; also, Morse, *While Six Million Died,* pp. 313–374. Britain never established any comparable rescue agency and the Foreign Office generally opposed the WRB and often fought against its efforts. Opinion within the Foreign Office is reflected in the statement by one official there that the efforts to rescue Jews by the WRB "is fundamentally all part of a Zionist drive and is liable to make much trouble for us in Palestine and with our relations with America over Palestine." (Cited in Penkower, *The Jews Were Expendable,* p. 143.)

[46] On the issue of bombing Auschwitz and/or the railheads, see Wyman, *The Abandonment of the Jews,* pp. 288–307; Morse, *While Six Million Died,* pp. 359–360; also, Gilbert, *Auschwitz and the Allies.* For other perspectives, including claims that bombing was not feasible, see, "The Holocaust, Auschwitz and World War II," in Newton, ed., *FDR and the Holocaust,* pp. 167–272.

[47] Cited in Wyman, *The Abandonment of the Jews,* p. 244.

[48] Ibid., p. 245.

[49] On Wallenberg, see ibid., pp. 240–243; also, Morse, *While Six Million Died,* pp. 362–374.

[50] Wyman, *The Abandonment of the Jews,* pp. 238–239.

[51] The historian who has perhaps looked most closely at this failure of American Jews to wield more effectively what political power they did have, Henry Feingold, has attributed it most to the twin factors of the secularization and acculturation of American Jewry. Both undermined communal solidarity and cohesion and also fostered the Balkanization of the American Jewish community and debilitating divisions in its leadership. Feingold also acknowledges the role of heightened anti-Semitism in America in the 1930s and early 1940s, both in accelerating the pace of secularization and acculturation and in more directly inhibiting Jewish political action on Jewish issues. He notes the intensity of that anti-Semitism but suggests that the Jewish community tended to perceive it as presenting an even greater threat than it actually did. See, for example, Henry L. Feingold, *Bearing Witness: How America and Its Jews Responded to the Holocaust,* Syracuse University, Syracuse, 1995.

[52] Cited in Rubin, *Assimilation and Its Discontents,* p. 84.

[53] Cited in Wyman, *The Abandonment of the Jews,* p. 94.

[54] For the response of major American Jewish organizations to immigration initiatives during this period, see in particular Medoff, *The Deafening Silence.* The issue is a major focus of the book.

[55] Wyman, *The Abandonment of the Jews,* p. 78. Feingold suggests more generally that the universalist predilections cultivated by many Jews, especially within the Jewish elite, undercut their ability to respond effectively to an exclusively Jewish catastrophe, and he argues that Wise's efforts were compromised by his "secularist, universalist outlook." See, for example, Feingold, *Bearing Witness,* p. 245.

[56] See Lipstadt, *Beyond Belief,* especially pp. 64–78.

[57] Rubin, *Assimilation and Its Discontents,* p. 84.

[58] Cited ibid., p. 84.

[59] Cited in Wyman and Medoff, *A Race Against Death,* p. 43.

[60] On the "free port" issue, see Medoff, *The Deafening Silence,* especially pp. 141–146.

[61] Wyman, *The Abandonment of the Jews,* p. 78. For a more detailed discussion of the black threat; the administration's efforts to dissuade the black leadership, particularly the chief orga-

nizer of the march, A. Philip Randolph; Randolph's refusal to bend; and the administration's finally capitulating, see Medoff, *The Deafening Silence*, pp. 165–167.

[62] Wyman, *The Abandonment of the Jews*, p. 316. For the stances of the Jews around Roosevelt, see also Feingold, *Bearing Witness*, e.g., pp. 232–235, 250.

[63] Wyman, *The Abandonment of the Jews*, p. 153.

[64] Ibid., p. 256.

[65] Ibid., p. 317. It should be noted that Medoff gives Dickstein more credit for seeking to use his position in Congress to promote rescue.

[66] Harrison E. Salisbury, *Without Fear or Favor*, Times Books, New York, 1980, p. 30.

[67] Gay Talese, *The Kingdom and the Power*, p. 168.

[68] See ibid., e.g., p. 93. Also, David Halberstam, *The Powers That Be*, Knopf, New York, 1979, p. 216. Also Harrison E. Salisbury, *Without Fear or Favor*, pp. 28–29. Tifft and Jones, in *The Trust*, concur that, from the time Adolph Ochs acquired the newspaper, the *Times* had a policy of eschewing promotion of Jewish causes. But they write that in 1914 Ochs was persuaded to defend Leo Frank, a Brooklyn Jew who was manager of a factory in Atlanta and was falsely convicted of sexually assaulting and murdering a young girl employed in the factory. Frank was subsequently killed by a lynch mob, the *Times* was attacked as the voice of interfering Jews and Ochs received anti-Semitic hate mail personally addressed to him. The result, according to Tifft and Jones, was that Ochs was reinforced in his determination that the paper would rigorously eschew identification with "Jewish" causes, and Ochs's stance has been adopted by his successors. See also the discussion of the *Times* and the Frank case in Talese, *The Kingdom and the Power*, pp. 169–170.

[69] Lipstadt, *Beyond Belief*, p. 155.

[70] Ibid., p. 220. Wyman makes the same point about the *Times*' influence on other papers (*The Abandonment of the Jews*, p. 323).

[71] Wyman, *The Abandonment of the Jews*, p. 321.

[72] Lipstadt, *Beyond Belief*, p. 278 note.

[73] Ibid., pp. 45–46.

[74] Ibid., pp. 109, 314.

[75] Wyman, *The Abandonment of the Jews*, p. 69. On Wise and Roosevelt, see also Penkower, *The Jews Were Expendable,* especially pp. 84–86.

[76] Cited in Medoff, *The Deafening Silence*, p. 113.

[77] Cited ibid., p. 122.

[78] Cited ibid., p. 178.

[79] Before the war, Hearst was an isolationist, and he was also inclined to believe that the Nazis and the Italian fascists were reformable and, more particularly, that the Nazis could be weaned from their anti-Jewish policies. He even opened his papers to columns by German and Italian officials. But during the war he and his syndicate stood virtually alone within the popular press in covering the plight of the Jews and editorializing for rescue. Lipstadt writes: "The Hearst chain became and remained active supporters of rescue activities, particularly those proposed by the Bergson group. On various occasions Hearst exhorted Americans to 'Remember... THIS IS NOT A JEWISH PROBLEM. It is a HUMAN PROBLEM'" (Lipstadt, *Beyond Belief*, p. 225). This was a perspective rarely advanced in America media. Similarly, Hearst's papers were among the few media outlets, and likely the only popular outlet, that emphasized that the Jews were Hitler's principle victims.

On the rescue issue, Wyman writes that in August, 1943, "Hearst ordered the thirty-four newspapers in his chain to publish the first of many major editorials supporting [Bergson's] Emergency Committee and appealing for nationwide backing of its proposals. The August editorial included a complete reprint of the Emergency Committee's recommendations. In September, the Hearst papers carried two more editorials advocating the Emergency Committee's rescue plans." (Wyman, *The Abandonment of the Jews*, p. 147.) Hearst's subsequent advocacy of rescue included editorializing vigorously in support of Congressional passage of the Rescue Resolution.

CHAPTER SEVEN

[1] Cited in Arthur Hertzberg, *The Jews in America*, Columbia University, New York, 1997, p. 341.

[2] Seymour Martin Lipset and Earl Raab, *Jews and the New American Scene*, p. 69.

[3] Hertzberg, *The Jews in America*, p. 311.

[4] See, for example, Hertzberg, ibid.

[5] See, for example, Charles S. Liebman, *The Ambivalent American Jew*, p. 131.

[6] Lipset and Raab, *Jews and the New American Scene*, p. 51.

[7] See, for example, ibid., pp. 49–54.

[8] Ibid., especially pp. 135–136.

[9] Margot Stern Strom and William S. Parsons, *Facing History and Ourselves: Holocaust and Human Behavior*, Intentional Educations, Watertown, Mass., 1982; also, second edition, Margot Stern Strom, Brookline, Mass., 1994.

[10] On the issue of government-sponsored promotion of Jew-hatred in the Arab and broader Moslem world and the promoters' often explicitly genocidal message, see in particular Bernard Lewis, *Semites and Anti-Semites* (Norton, New York, 1986), especially pp. 185–259; also, Robert Wistrich, *Muslim Anti-Semitism: A Clear and Present Danger*, American Jewish Committee, New York, 2002.

[11] *New York Times*, October 7, 1946.

[12] One writer who famously espoused this view was Arthur Koestler; see, for example, Koestler's *Thieves in the Night* (1946).

Barry Rubin, whose *Assimilation and Its Discontents* has been a valuable reference source for the present work, advances as a major theme of the book the thesis that the vulnerable position of Diaspora Jews in the modern period and the assaults to which they were subjected engendered in them both a unique self-consciousness and a powerful drive to demonstrate their worth and win themselves a place in the world. Rubin suggests that together these factors go far to account for the Jews' exceptional creativity. Rubin, however, does not view Diaspora Jews' creativity as an argument against a Jewish state.

[13] See, for example, Moshe Kohn, "Well-Kept Secret," *The Jerusalem Post*, April 3, 1998.

[14] Cited in *The Jerusalem Post*, November 2, 1991.

[15] Cited in Lipset and Raab, *Jews and the New American Scene*, p. 111.

[16] Cited in Hertzberg, *The Jews in America*, p. 341.

[17] Lipset and Raab, *Jews and the New American Scene*, p. 152.

[18] Ibid., p. 54.

[19] Jack Wertheimer, *A People Divided*, Basic Books, New York, 1993, p. 38.

[20] Lipset and Raab, *Jews and the New American Scene*, pp. 54 and 134.

[21] Hertzberg, *The Jews in America*, p. 354.

[22] On the UN General Assembly and Israel, see, for example, Allison Kaplan Sommer, "The UN's Outcast: Why is Israel Treated Differently Than All Other Nations?" Reform Judaism Online, winter, 2002.

[23] See, for example, Steven Edwards, "UN Backs Palestinian Violence: Arab, European Nations Pass Resolution Supporting Use of 'Armed Struggle'," *National Post* (Canada), April 16, 2002, p. A1.

[24] On UNRWA-administered Palestinian schools, see, for example, Matthew Kalman, "Canadian Funds Help Promote Hatred: Palestinian Schools Teach Glory of Martyrs, Deny Israel's Existence," *The Ottawa Citizen*, November 24, 2001; also, Charles A. Radin, "UN Role in Palestinian Camps in Dispute; Critics Say Extremism Appeased," *The Boston Globe*, July 8, 2002; also, Michael Wines, "Killing of UN Aide by Israel Bares Rift With Relief Agency," *New York Times*, January 4, 2003.

[25] Cited in "UNRWA Seeks to Calm Row over Palestinian Textbooks," *Jordan Times*, August 30, 2001.

[26] See, for example, Herb Keinon, "Shin Bet Documents Terrorists' Misuse of UNRWA Facilities," *The Jerusalem Post*, December 11, 2002.

[27] Lewis, *Semites and Anti-Semites*, p. 256.

[28] Wistrich, *Muslim Anti-Semitism: A Clear and Present Danger*.

[29] Hertzberg, *The Jews in America*, p. 357.

[30] Stanley Rothman and S. Robert Lichter, *Roots of Radicalism*, Transactions Publishers, New Brunswick, N.J., 1996. For their methodology, see especially pp. 205–212.

[31] Ibid., pp. 118–119.

[32] Cited by Rubin, *Assimilation and Its Discontents*, p. 148. For the Frankfurt Institute for Social Research, see also Paul Connerton, *The Tragedy of Enlightenment: An Essay on the Frankfurt School*, New York, 1980.

[33] Joseph Puder, "The New Israel Fund: Financing Palestinian Nationalism," in Edward Alexander, ed., *With Friends Like These*, pp. 225–261. The material on CONAME is on pp. 229–230. The article referred to as distributed by CONAME was by Paul Mayer.

[34] Rael Jean Isaac, "New Jewish Agenda: The Jewish Wing of the Anti-Israel Lobby," in Edward Alexander, ed., *With Friends Like These*, pp. 143–190.

[35] Ibid., p. 153.

[36] Ibid., especially pp. 179–181.

[37] Ibid., p. 169.

[38] Ibid., p. 170.

[39] Cited ibid., p. 162.

[40] Ibid, p. 149.

[41] Cited ibid., p. 155.

[42] See Puder, "The New Israel Fund."

[43] Cited in Rael Jean Isaac, "New Jewish Agenda," p. 183.

[44] Cited ibid., p. 187.

[45] Leonard Fein, *Where Are We? The Inner Life of America's Jews*, Harper and Row, New York, 1988; pp. 118–119. See also the chapter on Fein, "Too Mend the Universe," in Edward

Alexander, *The Jewish Wars: Reflections of One of the Belligerents,* South Illinois University, Carbondale, 1996, pp. 9–25.

[46] Ibid., p. 207.

[47] See, for example, Rael Jean Isaac, "New Jewish Agenda," p. 169. Also, Puder, "The New Israel Fund," p. 260.

[48] Cited in Rael Jean Isaac, "New Jewish Agenda," p. 174. See also Seymour Martin Lipset's explanation of the phenomenon of Jews so often leading the leftist attack on Israel; in Lipset, *The Socialism of Fools: The Left, the Jews and Israel,* p. 16.

[49] Rael Jean Isaac, "New Jewish Agenda," p. 175.

[50] Norman Podhoretz, "A Lamentation From the Future," *Commentary,* March, 1989, pp. 15–21.

CHAPTER EIGHT

[1] Theodor Herzl, *The Jewish State,* p. 154.

[2] Max Nordau, "Zionism," in Arthur Hertzberg, ed., *The Zionist Idea,* Harper, New York, 1966, pp. 242–245.

[3] Herzl himself saw the lie and distortion in this anti-Jewish indictment and also recognized the problem of many Jews taking it to heart. See, for example, Herzl, *The Jewish State,* p. 73.

[4] Cited in Barry Rubin, *Assimilation and Its Discontents,* p. 50.

[5] Cited in the biography of Herzl derived from Alex Bein, in Herzl, *The Jewish State,* pp. 53–54.

[6] For Ahad Ha-Am's perspective, see, for example, his, "The Jewish State and the Jewish Problem" (1897) and "The Negation of the Diaspora" (1909) in Arthur Hertzberg, ed., *The Zionist Idea,* pp. 262–269, 270–277.

[7] See, for example, Herzl, *The Jewish State,* p. 95.

[8] Cited in Yoram Hazony, *The Jewish State,* Basic Books, New York, 2000, p. 158.

[9] Herzl, *The Jewish State,* pp. 125–126.

[10] Ibid., p. 133.

[11] Cited in Hazony, *The Jewish State,* p. 139.

[12] Cited ibid., p. 138.

[13] Cited ibid., p. 139.

[14] Cited ibid., p. 141. See also Jehuda Reinharz, *Chaim Weizmann: The Making of a Zionist Leader,* Oxford, New York, 1985, pp. 123–125; also, Norman Rose, *Chaim Weizmann,* Viking, New York, 1986, p. 66.

[15] Cited in Hazony, *The Jewish State,* p. 182.

[16] Cited in Gilman, *Jewish Self-Hatred,* p. 273.

[17] Cited ibid., p. 274.

[18] Cited ibid., p. 274.

[19] Martin Buber, "Judaism and Mankind" (first published 1911), in Buber, *On Judaism,* ed. Nahum N. Glatzer, Schocken, New York, 1967, p. 32.

[20] Cited in Hazony, *The Jewish State,* p. 184.

[21] Cited ibid., p. 191. This was written in 1916. For Buber's later articulation of similar sentiments, see, for example, "The Jew in the World" (1934) and "Hebrew Humanism"

(1942) in Buber, *Israel and the World: Essays in a Time of Crisis*, Schocken, New York, 1963, pp. 167–172, 240–252.

22 The encounter is discussed in Hazony, *The Jewish State*, pp. 164–165. Also in Rose, *Chaim Weizmann*, pp. 145–146, and in Jehuda Reinharz, *Chaim Weizmann: The Making of a Statesman* (Oxford, New York, 1993), pp. 21–22. Reinharz offers more on Samuel's perspective at the time.

23 Cited in Hazony, *The Jewish State*, p. 164.

24 Ibid., p. 164.

25 Cited ibid., p. 164.

26 Interestingly, this discussion with Samuel is not mentioned at all in Weizmann's autobiography, *Trial and Error* (Harper, New York, 1949), although Weizmann does note other meetings around the same time with sympathetic British leaders, including Samuel, e.g., pp. 149–150.

27 Cited in Hazony, *The Jewish State*, p. 168.

28 Rose, *Chaim Weizmann*, p. 201.

29 Hazony, *The Jewish State*, p. 168.

30 Ibid., p. 168.

31 Rose, *Chaim Weizmann*, p. 265.

32 Cited ibid., p. 290.

33 Cited in Wyman and Medoff, *A Race Against Death*, p. 132.

34 Hazony, *The Jewish State*, p. 170.

35 Cited ibid., p. 170.

CHAPTER NINE

1 Cited in Shabtai Teveth, *Ben-Gurion: The Burning Ground*, Houghton Mifflin, Boston, 1987, pp. 611–612.

2 *Haaretz*, November 16, 1939; cited in Yoram Hazony, *The Jewish State*, p. 244.

3 As noted in Chapter Five, Churchill estimated that 90 percent of the British military in Palestine were opposed to Britain fulfilling its Mandate obligations to the Jews (David Fromkin, *A Peace to End All Peace*, p. 524). The civilian echelons of the administration were so hostile that Churchill circulated a memorandum to the Cabinet in 1921 suggesting "the removal of all anti-Zionist civil officials, however highly placed" (cited ibid., p. 524).

4 For the text of the Feisal-Weizmann agreement, see Walter Laqueur and Barry Rubin, eds., *The Israeli-Arab Reader*, sixth revised edition, Penguin, New York, 2001, pp. 17–18. See also, exchange of letters between Feisal and Felix Frankfurter, March 3–5, 1919, pp. 19–20.

5 Arguments that there were such British undertakings to the Arabs revolve around correspondence in 1915 and 1916 between Sir Henry McMahon and Feisal's father, Hussein ibn Ali, Sherif and Emir of Mecca. But there is debate as to whether McMahon's letters to Hussein constituted British pledges and, in any case, the letters do not entail commitments to Hussein regarding the territory later covered by the Mandate. See discussion of the McMahon-Hussein correspondence in David Fromkin, *A Peace to End All Peace*, especially pp. 182–185 and 504.

6 For a discussion of French and English jockeying in Syria and Feisal's role, see ibid., especially chapters 37 (pp. 332–347) and 48 (pp. 435–440).

7 It was an inquiry into Arab attacks in the spring of 1920 and revelation that the military

government had encouraged the assaults that led to London's quickly dissolving the military administration and establishing a civil administration in its place. But the ranks of both the British military contingent in Palestine and the civil service remained the same, continued to harbor the same attitudes and continued to work against London's fulfillment of British obligations to the Jews as subsequently formalized in the League of Nations Mandate. See ibid., pp. 447–448.

[8] See, for example, J. H. Patterson, *With the Judaeans in the Palestine Campaign.*

[9] Ibid., pp. 262–263.

[10] Ibid., pp. 250–251.

[11] See Teveth, *Ben-Gurion: The Burning Ground,* pp. 147–150.

[12] Cited ibid., p. 388.

[13] See especially Conor Cruise O'Brien, *The Siege,* on the tenures of the various British High Commissioners in Mandate Palestine and the relationship between their administrative styles and the intensity of Arab violence.

[14] See Hazony, *The Jewish State,* p. 201.

[15] Letter dated May, 1920, in *Dissenter in Zion: From the Writings of Judah L. Magnes,* ed. Arthur A. Goren, Harvard, Cambridge, Mass., 1982, p. 186.

[16] Martin Buber, "Toward the Decision" (March, 1919), in *A Land of Two Peoples: Martin Buber on Jews and Arabs,* ed. Paul R. Mendes-Flohr, Oxford, New York, 1983, pp. 39–41.

[17] See, for example, "At This Late Hour" (April, 1920), in *A Land of Two Peoples,* pp. 44–46.

[18] Buber, "Nationalism" (September, 1921), in *Israel and the World,* pp. 214–226.

[19] Magnes states in a journal entry for September 14, 1928, (document 62, *Dissenter in Zion,* p. 272), that because of this reservation he had not joined the Peace Association. But see Hazony, *The Jewish State,* p. 382, note 8.

[20] Hazony, *The Jewish State,* p. 206.

[21] Buber, "The National Home and National Policy in Palestine" and "The Wailing Wall," in *A Land of Two Peoples,* pp. 82–91, 93–95.

[22] See Magnes letter to Warburg of September 13, 1929, document 65, *Dissenter in Zion,* pp. 278–281.

[23] See Hazony, *The Jewish State,* p. 213.

[24] Magnes's interlocutor was Harry St. John Philby. See Magnes's article published in the *New York Times* on November 24, 1929; document 66, *Dissenter in Zion,* pp. 282–285.

[25] Ibid. Also, Hazony, *The Jewish State,* p. 215.

[26] Cited in Rubin, *Assimilation and Its Discontents,* p. 59.

[27] Buber, "And If Not Now, When?" (July, 1932), in *A Land of Two Peoples,* pp. 102–106.

[28] Cited in Teveth, *Burning Ground,* p. 399.

[29] Cited ibid., p. 400.

[30] Cited in Hazony, *The Jewish State,* p. 226.

[31] See the memorandum sent by Magnes on January 7, 1937, to Reginald Coupland, a member of the Peel Commission, and its summary of a potential agreement that Magnes reports emerged from contacts with Arab interlocutors in May and June, 1936; document 79, *Dissenter in Zion,* pp. 315–319.

[32] Cited in Teveth, *Burning Ground,* pp. 611–612.

[33] See, for example, "Twentieth Zionist Congress, August 3–17, 1937: A Weizmann Review," *New Judea*, August–September, 1937.

[34] Cited in Hazony, *The Jewish State*, p. 231.

[35] Cited in Teveth, *Burning Ground*, p. 619.

[36] *Haaretz*, November 16, 1939; cited in Hazony, *The Jewish State*, p. 244.

[37] Cited in Hazony, *The Jewish State*, p. 247.

[38] Buber, "Two Peoples," in *A Land of Two Peoples*, pp. 165–168.

[39] Buber, "Do Not Believe It!" in *A Land of Two Peoples*, pp. 153–154.

[40] Buber, "An Additional Clarification," in *A Land of Two Peoples*, pp. 158–160.

[41] See column under James Reston's byline, the *New York Times*, October 7, 1946.

[42] Cited in Gay Talese, *The Kingdom and the Power*, p. 92.

[43] Buber, "The Meaning of Zionism," in *A Land of Two Peoples*, pp. 180–184.

[44] Buber, "'Preface' to a Projected Volume on Arab-Jewish Rapprochement," in *A Land of Two Peoples*, pp. 259–261.

[45] Buber, "Instead of Polemics" (November, 1956), in *A Land of Two Peoples*, pp. 269–272.

[46] Buber, "Socialism and Peace," in *A Land of Two Peoples*, pp. 275–277.

[47] Cited in Hazony, *The Jewish State*, p. 256.

[48] Cited ibid., p. 259.

[49] See Goren, ed., *Dissenter in Zion*, pp. 461–520.

CHAPTER TEN

[1] Cited in Yoram Hazony, *The Jewish State*, p. 319.

[2] E.g., Martin Buber, "Zionism and 'Zionism'" (May, 1948), in *A Land of Two Peoples*, pp. 220–223.

[3] Hazony, *The Jewish State,* pp. 295–298.

[4] Various Christian authors recognized and praised elements of Buber's writing as evoking the Messianism of Christianity; for example, Oswald Spengler in his response to Buber's rendering of the Baal Shem. See Aschheim, *Brothers and Strangers,* especially p. 130.

[5] See, for example, Hazony, *The Jewish State,* pp. 299–302.

[6] Amnon Rubinstein, *From Herzl to Rabin: The Changing Image of Zionism*, Holmes and Meier, New York, 2000, p. 32.

[7] Cited in Tom Segev, *One Palestine Entire: Jews and Arabs Under the British Mandate*, Henry Holt, New York, 2000, p. 260.

[8] Ibid., p. 260.

[9] See, for example, Hillel Halkin's review of Hazony's book in *Commentary,* July 2000, pp. 63 ff. The anti-state tenets of elements of the Israeli socialist Left and the kibbutz movement are also discussed by Amnon Lord in his book *The Israeli Left: From Socialism to Nihilism*, The Ariel Institute, 2000 (Hebrew).

[10] Cited in Hazony, *The Jewish State*, p. 162.

[11] See, for example, Hillel Halkin's review of Hazony's *The Jewish State*.

[12] Hillel Halkin, while faulting Hazony for ignoring how much the animating ideas of Israel's Israel-indicting "post-Zionist" or "anti-Zionist" critics have been influenced by similar ideas in the United States and Europe (Halkin suggests that "in many ways, indeed, post-Zionism is the Americanization of Israeli life"), also suggests that the particular influence in Israel of the ideas

and concepts that Hazony is attacking is very much a consequence of the siege; that those ideas and concepts would have much less resonance and significance in "an economically prosperous Israel at peace with its neighbors and without a large and hostile Arab minority in its midst." (Ibid.)

13 Amos Oz, "Thoughts on the Kibbutz" in *Under This Blazing Light*, Cambridge University, Cambridge, 1995 (published in Hebrew in 1979), pp. 119–124; quote is on p. 124. See also, in the same volume, "How To Be a Socialist," pp. 133–138.

14 Oz, "The Kibbutz at the Present Time," in *Under This Blazing Light*, pp. 125–131, quote on p. 129.

15 See Hazony, p. 319. Also, remarks taken from Oz's 1976 memorial address on Lavon, in *Under This Blazing Light*, pp. 146–151. Also, Amos Oz, *Israel, Palestine, and Peace*, Harcourt Brace, San Diego, 1995, p. 15.

16 Cited by Hazony, *The Jewish State*, p. 319.

17 Amos Oz, *In the Land of Israel*, Harcourt Brace Jovanovich, San Diego, 1983, p. 131.

18 Ibid., p. 130. See also, Oz, *Israel, Palestine, and Peace*, p. 70.

19 Oz, *In the Land of Israel*, p. 130.

20 Oz, *Under This Blazing Light*, p. 82. See also Oz, *In the Land of Israel*, p. 148; also, *Israel, Palestine, and Peace*, p. 39.

21 For example, Lord Caradon, who served as Britain's ambassador to the United Nations at the time and who introduced Resolution 242 in the Security Council, told an interviewer some years later: "It would have been wrong to demand that Israel return to its positions of June 4, 1967, because those positions were undesirable and artificial. After all, they were just the places where the soldiers of each side happened to be on the day the fighting stopped in 1948. They were just armistice lines. That's why we didn't demand that the Israelis return to them, and I think we were right not to..." (*Beirut Daily Star*, June 12, 1974)

In 1969 the British Foreign Secretary stated in the House of Commons that the framers of the resolution did not envisage Israel withdrawing from "all the territories." Subsequently, George Brown, who had been Foreign Secretary at the time of the war and passage of the resolution, made the same point in his book, *Out of My Way*. (See Abba Eban, *Abba Eban: An Autobiography*, Random House, New York, 1977, p. 452.)

Also, Arthur Goldberg, ambassador of the United States to the United Nations at the time of the resolution, stated, "The notable omissions — which were not accidental — in regard to withdrawal are the words *the* or *all* and *the June 5, 1967 lines...* Rather, the resolution speaks of withdrawal from occupied territories without defining the extent of withdrawal. And the notable presence of the words 'secure and recognized boundaries,' by implication, contemplates that the parties could make territorial adjustments in their peace settlement encompassing less than a complete withdrawal of Israeli forces from occupied territories, inasmuch as Israel's prior frontiers had proved to be notably insecure." (Speech to American Israel Public Affairs Committee, May 8, 1973)

22 Cited in Dore Gold, "Defensible Borders for Israel," Jerusalem Center for Public Affairs, July 8, 2003.

23 Cited in Ephraim Karsh, "What Occupation?" *Commentary*, July–August, 2002, pp. 46–51, citation on p. 47.

24 Statistics cited ibid., p. 49.

25 Report of the Commissioner-General of the UNRWA for Palestine Refugees in the Near

East, July 1, 1978 – June 30, 1979; cited in *Judea-Samaria and the Gaza Strip: A 16-Year Study, 1967–1983*, Israel Ministry of Defense, November, 1983.

[26] Pearl Herman, *The United Nations Relief and Works Agency for Palestine Refugees in the Near East: A Report*, January, 2003, p. 11–12.

[27] Michael B. Oren, *Six Days of War: June 1967 and the Making of the Modern Middle East*, Oxford University, Oxford, 2002, p. 316.

[28] Rael Jean Isaac, *Israel Divided: Ideological Politics in the Jewish State*, Johns Hopkins, Baltimore, 1976, p. 86.

[29] Ibid., p. 96.

[30] See table of poll results ibid., p. 133.

[31] See *Hussein of Jordan: My "War" with Israel*, William Morrow, New York, 1969, especially pp. 60–67.

[32] For relevant opinion polls, see Daniel J. Elazar and Shmuel Sandler, *Israel's Odd Couple: The 1984 Knesset Elections and the National Unity Government*, Wayne State University, Detroit, 1990, p. 29.

[33] Rael Jean Isaac, *Israel Divided*, p. 155.

[34] Ibid., p. 152.

[35] Ibid., p. 156.

[36] Ibid., p. 150.

[37] See Rael Jean Isaac's observations on the *Haaretz* poll, ibid., p. 150.

CHAPTER ELEVEN

[1] Cited in Ze'ev Chafets, *Heroes and Hustlers, Hard Hats and Holy Men: Inside the New Israel*, William Morrow, New York, 1986, p. 63.

[2] Howard M. Sachar, *A History of Israel from the Rise of Zionism to Our Time*, 2nd ed., Alfred A. Knopf, New York, 2001, p. 833.

[3] See, for example, Arnold Blumberg, *The History of Israel*, Greenwood Press, Westport, Conn., 1998, p. 130.

[4] Cited in Ze'ev Chafets, *Heroes and Hustlers, Hard Hats and Holy Men: Inside the New Israel*, p. 63.

[5] Cited in Op-Ed by Moshe Kohn, *Jerusalem Post*, May 25, 1977.

[6] *Jerusalem Post*, May 18, 1977.

[7] Statistics cited in Tzvi Bar, "If We Want to Live," *Maariv*, October 13, 2000.

[8] See, for example, Amnon Rubinstein, "The Numbers Speak for Themselves," *Haaretz*, July 29, 2002.

[9] Amos Oz, *Israel, Palestine and Peace*, p. 12.

[10] Citations from Op-Ed by Moshe Kohn, *Jerusalem Post*, May 25, 1977.

[11] Cited ibid.

[12] Gloria H. Falk, "Israeli Public Opinion: Looking Toward a Palestinian Solution," *The Middle East Journal*, Volume 39, No.3, summer, 1985, pp. 247–269, p. 257.

[13] See Rael Jean Isaac, *Israel Divided*, p. 118.

[14] Cited in Mordechai Bar-On, *In Pursuit of Peace*, United States Institute of Peace Press, Washington, D.C., 1996, p. 106.

[15] On numbers of civilian casualties in the war versus press reports of casualty levels, see,

for example, Ze'ev Chafets, *Double Vision: How the Press Distorts America's View of the Middle East*, William Morrow, New York, 1985, pp. 300–302. Also, Frank Gervasi, "The War in Lebanon," in Stephen Karetzky and Norman Frankel, eds., *The Media's Coverage of the Arab-Israeli Conflict*, Shapolsky, New York, 1989, pp. 185–221, especially, pp. 187–191.

[16] E.g., Amos Oz, *The Slopes of Lebanon*, Harcourt Brace Jovanovich, San Diego, 1989, p. 30 (from *Yediot Acharonot*, (June 21, 1982), p. 33 (from *Davar*, June 22, 1982).

[17] Cited in Hazony, *The Jewish State*, p. 302.

[18] Amos Oz, *The Slopes of Lebanon*, p. 61.

[19] Amos Oz, *Israel, Palestine and Peace*, p. 46.

[20] The Israeli Left's indicting of the Right for supposedly suffering from a Holocaust syndrome continued over subsequent years. In a 1993 Op-Ed, *New York Times* columnist A.M. Rosenthal upbraided leftist Israeli academic Yaron Ezrahi for invoking the term to attack Israelis wary of Arab intentions. As Rosenthal notes in the article, "Yes, there is a mental malady that afflicts Israelis and other Jews but it is not the Holocaust syndrome. It is the tendency to confuse hope for the future with present reality."(*New York Times*, September 17, 1993)

[21] Amos Elon, *A Blood-Dimmed Tide: Dispatches from the Middle East*, Columbia University, New York, 1997, p. 235.

[22] See, for example, Efraim Karsh, *Arafat's War*, p. 50.

[23] Ze'ev Schiff and Ehud Yaari, *Intifada*, Simon and Schuster, New York, 1989.

[24] See Efraim Karsh, *Arafat's War*, p. 45.

CHAPTER TWELVE

[1] *Al-Ra'y*, Jordan, November 12, 1992; cited in Ze'ev Binyamin Begin, "Years of Hope," *Haaretz Magazine*, September 6, 2002.

[2] Mordechai Bar-On, *In Pursuit of Peace*, p. 217.

[3] Efraim Karsh, *Arafat's War*, p. 51.

[4] Ibid., p. 51.

[5] Bar-On, *In Pursuit of Peace*.

[6] Cited ibid., p. 262.

[7] *Al-Ra'y*, Jordan, November 12, 1992. (See note 1.)

[8] E.g., Husseini interview reported in *Al-Arabi*, Cairo, June 24, 2001; also a speech at the University of Jordan, July 22, 1995. Both are cited in Begin, "Years of Hope."

[9] Bar-On, *In Pursuit of Peace*, p. 165.

[10] Ibid., p. xviii.

[11] See, for example, ibid., p. 321.

[12] Ibid., p. 260.

[13] Ibid., p. 273

[14] Cited ibid., p. 273.

[15] Cited in *Jerusalem Post*, November 2, 1991.

[16] Cited in Mitchell E. Bard, *Myths and Facts: A Guide to the Arab-Israeli Conflict*, American-Israeli Cooperative Enterprise, Chevy Chase, Md., 2001, p. 26.

[17] Cited in Bar-On, *In Pursuit of Peace*, p. 273.

[18] Cited ibid., p. 282.

[19] Yossi Beilin, *Touching Peace*, Weidenfeld and Nicolson, London, 1999, p. 36.

[20] Cited in Bar-On, *In Pursuit of Peace*, p. 282.

[21] Ibid., p. 299.

[22] Cited in Hillel Halkin, "The Rabin Assassination: A Reckoning," in *The Mideast Peace Process: An Autopsy*, ed. Neal Kozodoy, Encounter, San Francisco, 2002, pp. 45–56, citation on p. 47. (Article originally published in *Commentary*, January, 1996.)

[23] Bar-On, *In Pursuit of Peace*, p. 321.

[24] Some critics of the New History perceive the warm reception almost invariably accorded criticism of Israel in Israeli and Western academia as having provided the major impetus to the revisionism of the new historians. See, for example, Efraim Karsh's preface to the second edition of his *Fabricating Israeli History: The "New Historians"* (Frank Cass, London, 2000), especially pp. xix ff.

[25] Bar-On, *In Pursuit of Peace*, p. 327.

[26] Benny Morris, *The Birth of the Palestinian Refugee Problem*, Cambridge University, Cambridge, 1987.

[27] Avi Shlaim, *Collusion Across the Jordan: King Abdullah, the Zionist Movement, and the Partition of Palestine*, Columbia University, New York, 1988.

[28] Ilan Pappe, *Britain and the Arab-Israeli Conflict, 1948–1951*, St. Martin's, New York, 1988.

[29] Efraim Karsh, *Fabricating Israeli History: The "New Historians,"* Frank Cass, London, 1997.

[30] E.g., ibid. Also, Shabtai Teveth, "Charging Israel With Original Sin," *Commentary*, September, 1989, pp. 24–33 (see also the correspondence in response to the Teveth article, *Commentary*, February, 1990, pp. 2–9); and Teveth, "The Palestinian Refugee Problem and Its Origins," *Middle Eastern Studies*, April, 1990, pp. 214–249.

[31] See, for example, Benny Morris, *1948 and After: Israel and the Palestinians*, Clarendon, Oxford, 1994, pp. 27, 47.

[32] See Karsh, *Fabricating Israeli History*, pp. 21–22.

[33] Morris, *The Birth of the Palestinian Refugee Problem*, p. 25.

[34] Karsh, *Fabricating Israeli History*, second revised edition, p. xvii.

[35] Morris, *The Birth of the Palestinian Refugee Problem*, p. 28.

[36] Karsh, *Fabricating Israeli History*, p. 64.

[37] Cited ibid., p. 66.

[38] Cited ibid., p. 67.

[39] E.g., Morris, *Birth of the Palestinian Refugee Problem*, pp. 52, 63, 131, 153, 164, 166, 198, 251, 261, 292.

[40] E.g., ibid., pp. 137, 162, 165.

[41] Ibid., p. 170.

[42] Bard, *Myths and Facts*, p. 56. Bard cites Moshe Aumann, "Land Ownership in Palestine, 1880–1948," in Michael Curtis, ed., *The Palestinians*, Transaction Books, 1975, p. 29.

[43] This work by Morris has also elicited many critiques in addition to those offered by Karsh. See, for example, Asher Susser, review of *1948 and After*, in *The Jerusalem Report*, April 18, 1991.

[44] For critiques of Shlaim and Pappe's theses regarding collusion between Israel and Transjordan in the 1947–1948 war and the involvement of Great Britain in that collusion, as well as Britain's alleged benevolence toward the nascent Jewish state, theses subscribed to as well

by Morris, see Karsh, *Fabricating Israeli History*, especially pp. 69–193; also, Avraham Sela, "Transjordan, Israel, and the 1948 War: Myth, Historiography, and Reality," *Middle Eastern Studies*, October, 1992, pp. 623–689; also Teveth, "Charging Israel With Original Sin."

Shlaim, Pappe, and Morris also argue that Arab leaders offered opportunities for peace in the wake of the 1947–1948 war and that these opportunities foundered mainly due to Israeli intransigence. Particularly noteworthy among the many rebuttals to such claims is Itamar Rabinovitch, *The Road Not Taken: Early Arab-Israeli Negotiations*, Oxford, New York, 1991.

[45] Tom Segev, *The Seventh Million: The Israelis and the Holocaust*, Hill and Wang, New York, 1993. (Originally published 1991 in Hebrew.)

[46] Ibid., p. 502.

[47] Ibid., p. 505.

[48] Ibid., p. 517.

[49] See, in particular, Shabtai Teveth, *Ben-Gurion and the Holocaust*, Harcourt Brace, New York, 1996.

[50] Amnon Rubinstein, *From Herzl to Rabin*, p. 219–220.

[51] Simha Flapan, *The Birth of Israel: Myths and Realities*, Pantheon, New York, 1987.

[52] Ibid., p. 4.

[53] Ibid., p. 10.

[54] Benny Morris, "The New Historiography: Israel Confronts Its Past," *Tikkun*, November–December, 1988, pp. 19–102, p. 21.

[55] E.g., Ilan Pappe, *The Making of the Arab-Israeli Conflict, 1947–1951*, I.B. Tauris, London, 1994, p. viii.

[56] E.g., Avi Shlaim, *The Iron Wall: Israel and the Arab World*, W. W. Norton, New York, 2000, p. xi.

[57] Morris, *1948 and After*, p. 27.

[58] Morris, "The New Historiography," p. 20.

[59] Ibid., p. 102.

[60] Avi Shlaim, *The Politics of Partition: King Abdullah, the Zionists and Palestine 1921–1951*, Columbia University, New York, 1990; see also the preface to the paperback edition, pp. vii–ix.

[61] Shlaim, *The Iron Wall*, p. 598.

[62] Morris, *1948 and After*, p. 47.

[63] Ilan Pappe, "A Report on the Refugee Problem," www.salon.org, April 4, 2000.

[64] See Yoram Hazony, *The Jewish State*, pp. 11–12.

[65] See ibid., p. 15.

[66] E.g., Amos Oz, *Under This Blazing Light*, p. 97.

[67] E.g., Amos Oz, *The Slopes of Lebanon*, pp. 64–65.

[68] E.g., ibid., p. 3.

[69] E.g., Amos Oz, *In the Land of Israel*, pp. 120–121.

[70] Ibid., pp. 121–122.

[71] E.g., ibid., p. 52.

[72] Oz, *Under This Blazing Light*, p. 91.

[73] Oz, *The Slopes of Lebanon*, p. 239.

[74] See also, for example, Amos Oz, *Israel, Palestine and Peace*, pp. xi, 36, 125.

[75] Oz, *Under This Blazing Light*, pp. 27–28.

[76] Amos Oz, *My Michael*, Bantam, New York, 1972. (Originally published in Hebrew in 1968.)

[77] A.B. Yehoshua, *Between Right and Right*, Doubleday, Garden City, New York, 1981 (originally published in Hebrew in 1980); see especially "The Golah: The Neurotic Solution," pp. 21–74.

[78] Ibid, p. 169.

[79] See, for example, ibid., p. 152.

[80] Cited in Hazony, *The Jewish State*, p. 25.

[81] David Grossman, *The Yellow Wind*, Farrar, Straus, and Giroux, New York, 1988. For Grossman's fictional dramatization of the effects of the Israeli presence in the territories, see, for example, the chapter "Swiss Mountain View — A Story," pp. 127–144.

[82] Ibid., p. 46.

[83] Ibid., p. 62.

[84] See also the discussion of Grossman's *The Yellow Wind*, in Edward Alexander, *The Jewish Wars*, pp. 1–8.

[85] David Grossman, *The Smile of the Lamb*, Farrar, Straus, and Giroux, New York, 1990. (Originally published in Hebrew in 1983.)

[86] See, for example, David Grossman, *See Under Love,* Farrar, Straus, and Giroux, New York, 1989 (originally published in Hebrew in 1986); and *The Book of Intimate Grammar*, Farrar, Straus, and Giroux, New York, 1994 (originally published in Hebrew in 1991).

[87] For a brief discussion of the prominence of rabidly anti-Zionist themes in Israeli poetry, film, theater, and the plastic arts during these years, see Hazony, *The Jewish State*, pp. 29–38. For the plastic arts, see also Avraham Levitt, "Israeli Art On Its Way to Somewhere Else," *Azure*, winter, 1998, pp. 120–145. For Israeli theater, see also Edward Alexander, "Anti-Semitism, Israeli-Style," in Alexander, ed., *With Friends Like These*, especially pp. 37–45; reprinted with slight modifications in Alexander, *The Jewish Wars*, pp. 36–43.

[88] Hazony, *The Jewish State*, p. 352.

[89] Amos Elon, *The Israelis: Founders and Sons*, Holt, Rinehart and Winston, New York, 1971, p. 268.

[90] Ibid., p. 275.

[91] Ibid., p. 279.

[92] Ibid., p. 265.

[93] Ibid., p. 267.

[94] Ibid., pp. 248–249.

[95] Ibid., p. 252 note.

[96] Ibid., p. 25.

[97] E.g., Amos Elon, *A Blood-Dimmed Tide*, p. 73.

[98] E.g., ibid., pp. 156–157.

[99] E.g., ibid., pp. 50, 62.

[100] E.g., ibid., p. 137.

[101] *Jerusalem Post*, July 6, 1982; cited in Alexander, *The Jewish Wars*, p. 34.

[102] Elon, *A Blood-Dimmed Tide*, p. 256.

[103] See statistics cited in Karsh, "What Occupation?" p. 49. The statistic for illiteracy in Jordan in 1998 is from S. Shawky, "Infant mortality in Arab countries: sociodemographic, perinatal and economic factors," posted on the World Health Organization Web site

(www.who.org). The statistic for life expectancy in Jordan in 2002 is from *The World Health Report, 2003;* likewise posted on the WHO Web site.

104 Elon, *A Blood-Dimmed Tide,* p. 268.

105 Elon, *Founders and Sons,* pp. 22–23. See also, *A Blood-Dimmed Tide,* p. 224.

106 Aharon Megged, "One-Way Trip on the Highway of Self-Destruction," *Jerusalem Post,* June 17, 1994.

107 Cited in Bar-On, *The Pursuit of Peace,* p. 307.

CHAPTER THIRTEEN

1 Mordechai Bar-On, *In Pursuit of Peace,* pp. 309–310.

2 *Yediot Acharonot,* August 30, 1993; cited by Yaacov Bar-Siman-Tov, "Peace-Making with the Palestinians: Change and Legitimacy," in Efraim Karsh, ed., *From Rabin to Netanyahu,* Cass, London, 1997, p. 177.

3 Yossi Beilin, *Israel: A Concise Political History,* St. Martin's, New York, 1993, p. 263.

4 Ibid., p. 265. In *Touching Peace,* Beilin suggests the 1967 victory turned out to be "the heaviest of curses," p. 9.

5 Beilin, *Israel: A Concise History,* pp. 119–120.

6 Ibid., p. 126.

7 Ethan Bronner, "Rewriting Zionism," *The Boston Globe Magazine,* November 27, 1994.

8 Beilin, *Israel: A Concise History,* p. 120.

9 E.g., Yossi Beilin, *Touching Peace,* p. 67.

10 Ibid., p. 145.

11 Ibid., p. 21.

12 Cited in Lally Weymouth, "Peres's Plan for Peace," *Washington Post,* November 28, 1995.

13 Hillel Halkin, "The Rabin Assassination: A Reckoning," p. 49.

14 *Haaretz* magazine, March 7, 1997.

15 Shimon Peres, *The New Middle East,* Henry Holt, New York, 1993.

16 Ibid., pp. 163–179.

17 Cited in Barry Rubin, *Assimilation and Its Discontents,* p. 142.

18 Cited in David Bar-Illan, "The New Middle East Version of the Protocols," *Jerusalem Post,* August 18, 1995.

CHAPTER FOURTEEN

1 Cited in Efraim Karsh, *Arafat's War,* p. 140.

2 Federal News Service, November 4, 1995.

3 Foreign Broadcast Information Service, "Near East and South Asia, Daily Report Supplement, Israel-PLO Agreement," Tuesday, September 14, 1993, pp. 4–5.

4 Karsh, *Arafat's War,* p. 59.

5 On May 10, 1994, for example, Arafat declared in a speech at a mosque in Johannesburg, "This agreement, I am not considering it more than the agreement which had been signed between our prophet Mohammed and [the] Quraysh... The same way Mohammed had accepted it, we are now accepting this peace effort." (*Haaretz,* May 23, 1994.)

6 In the same speech in Johannesburg cited in the previous note and delivered less than a week

after the signing of the Cairo Agreement, Arafat called for a Jihad to liberate Jerusalem. (*Haaretz,* May 23,1994.) Occasions of his subsequent calls for Jihad included, for example, a rally in Gaza in late 1994 (*Haaretz,* November 22, 1994) and a speech shortly thereafter before the Organization of the Islamic Conference (reported on Voice of Palestine Radio, December 15, 1994).

[7] Cited in *Maariv,* September 7, 1995.

[8] Voice of Palestine, November 11, 1995.

[9] *Haaretz,* July 27, 2002.

[10] Karsh, *Arafat's War,* p. 8.

[11] For example, Arafat referred to Sheikh Ahmed Yassin, the leader of Hamas, as "my brother Ahmed Yassin the warrior." (*New York Times,* July 2, 1994.)

[12] Cited in Ze'ev Binyamin Begin, "Years of Hope."

[13] E.g., PA police chief Nasser Yussef, quoted on Radio Monte Carlo, May 29, 1994.

[14] *An Nahar,* April 11, 1995, and *Al Quds,* April 14, 1995; cited in Morton A. Kline, *Three Years of PLO Violations,* Zionist Organization of America, New York, p. 6.

[15] Cited in *Jerusalem Post,* July 25, 1995.

[16] Cited in Douglas J. Feith, "Land for No Peace," *Commentary,* June, 1994, pp. 32–36.

[17] See, for example, Introduction, note 5.

[18] *Mideast Mirror,* August 22, 1995.

[19] See, for example, Introduction, note 6.

[20] Cited in Karsh, *Arafat's War,* pp. 4–5.

[21] Ibid., p. 58. The story of the speech, and the quoted remarks, first appeared in a Norwegian newspaper, *Dagen,* on February 16, 1996. Arafat subsequently denied the report, and some observers have questioned it as well; but others, including some Arab sources, attested to the veracity of the story, and Ehud Yaari, Israel's leading commentator on Arab affairs, asserted that the Israeli government had "full confirmation of [its] accuracy..." See Yaari, "Bend or Break!" *The Jerusalem Report,* April 4, 1996.

[22] Cited in Karsh, *Arafat's War,* p. 126.

[23] Cited ibid., p. 93.

[24] *The Jerusalem Post,* November 22, 1994.

[25] Cited in Ze'ev Begin, "Years of Hope."

[26] See, for example, articles by Yossi Melman in *Haaretz,* August 9 and August 16, 2002.

[27] Cited in Daniel Polisar, "The Myth of Arafat's Legitimacy," *Azure,* summer, 2002, pp. 29–87, citation on p. 35.

[28] Ibid., p. 31.

[29] Amotz Asa-El, "Industrial Parks Now," *Jerusalem Post,* October 4, 1996.

[30] Karsh, *Arafat's War,* p. 251.

[31] Leora Frankel-Schlosberg, "The Palestinian News Game: Walking on Eggs in the Arafat Era," *Columbia Journalism Review,* May/June, 1996, pp. 16–18.

[32] Polisar, "The Myth of Arafat's Legitimacy," pp. 58–66.

[33] On Al-Haq, see Polisar, "The Myth of Arafat's Legitimacy,"

[34] See discussion in Chapter Thirteen of the so-called Stockholm talks overseen by Beilin and Abu Mazen.

[35] The official's statements were made in a personal conversation with the author in Jerusalem in February, 1996. Adding to the curious nature of the conversation, there had been

a terrorist attack in Jerusalem just minutes earlier and the official repeatedly interrupted his assertions of his faith in the developing "peace" with the Palestinians, and in Israel's ability safely to make concessions previously viewed as entailing existential risks, with telephone calls to try and reach a family member whom he knew had been in the vicinity of the attack. The person was eventually located and fortunately was unhurt.

[36] On King Hussein's preference for Netanyahu over Peres in the May, 1996, election, see also Itamar Rabinovich, *Waging Peace*, Farrar, Straus, and Giroux, New York, 1999, p. 150.

[37] See, for example, the exchange between Rabin and BBC interviewer Yisrael Singer quoted in the Introduction and broadcast by the BBC March 28, 1995.

[38] Yaacov Bar-Siman-Tov, "Peace-Making with the Palestinians: Change and Legitimacy," in Efraim Karsh, ed., *From Rabin to Netanyahu*, p. 180.

[39] See editorial in *Jerusalem Post* critiquing Rabin's attacks on the settlers, "The Polarization Danger," December 9, 1993.

[40] See, for example, review of the activities of *agent provocateur* Avishai Raviv in Uri Dan and Dennis Eisenberg, "A Slanderous Tongue," *Jerusalem Post*, October 10, 1996.

[41] *Jerusalem Post International Edition*, June 1, 1996.

[42] Notable examples are the Middle East Media Research Institute and Palestinian Media Watch.

[43] Benny Morris, *Israel's Border Wars 1949–1956: Arab Infiltration, Israeli Retaliation, and the Countdown to the Suez War*, Clarendon, Oxford, 1993.

[44] Robert B. Satloff, review of *Israel's Border Wars, 1949–1956*, in *Middle Eastern Studies*, October, 1995, pp. 953–957; quote is from p. 953. Satloff's review also addresses Morris's casting Israel as the villain throughout the work and the spurious foundations of Morris's indictments.

[45] E.g., Benny Morris, "Objective History," *Haaretz Weekly Magazine*, June 10, 1994, p. 40; "A Second Look at the 'Missed Peace,' or Smoothing Out History: A Review Essay," *Journal of Palestine Studies*, autumn, 1994, p. 86; and "Falsifying the Record: A Fresh Look at Zionist Documentation of 1948," *Journal of Palestine Studies*, spring, 1995, pp. 57–58.

[46] E.g., Ilan Pappe, "A Lesson in New History," *Haaretz Weekly Magazine*, June 24, 1994, p. 54.

[47] E.g., Avi Shlaim, "The Debate About 1948," *International Journal of Middle East Studies*, August, 1995, p. 289.

[48] Cited in Yoram Hazony, *The Jewish State*, pp. 10–11.

[49] Ibid., p. 11.

[50] Amnon Rubinstein, in countering the arguments of the anti-Zionists and post-Zionists, makes the same point that Jews chose to come to Israel and that those who argue against Israel's right to exist as a Jewish state are seeking to deprive Jews of the self-determination accorded other peoples. See Rubinstein, *From Herzl to Rabin*, especially p. 212.

[51] *Yediot Acharonot*, May 1, 1995; cited in Hazony, *The Jewish State*, p. 45.

[52] Hazony, *The Jewish State*, p. 10.

[53] Ibid., pp. 11–12; also, p. 350, note 25.

[54] Joseph Agassi, *Liberal Nationalism for Israel: Towards An Israeli National Identity*, Gefen, Jerusalem, 1999, p. 18.

[55] Ze'ev Sternhell, *The Founding Myths of Israel*, Princeton University, Princeton, 1998, p. 15.

[56] Ibid., p. 4.

[57] *Jerusalem Post*, September 29, 1995; cited in Hazony, *The Jewish State,* p. 11.

[58] *Haaretz*, April 10, 1994; cited in Hazony, *The Jewish State,* p. 13.

[59] See, for example, Amos Oz, *The Slopes of Lebanon*, p. 224. Citations are from here.

[60] Amos Oz, *Israel, Palestine, and Peace*, p. 117.

[61] Oz, *The Slopes of Lebanon*, p. 112.

[62] Amos Elon, *A Blood-Dimmed Tide*, p. 253.

[63] Aharon Megged, "One-Way Trip on the Highway of Self-Destruction."

[64] Elon, *A Blood-Dimmed Tide*, p. 173.

[65] See, for example, discussion of Aloni in Edward Alexander, *The Jewish Wars*, especially pp. 115–116.

[66] Cited in the *Jewish Exponent*, October 16, 1992.

[67] Aloni had earlier criticized the Israeli education system because, in teaching children about the Holocaust, it conveyed that, "the Nazis did this to the Jews instead of the message that people did this to people." Cited in Alexander, *The Jewish Wars*, pp. 34, 115.

[68] *Jewish Exponent*, October 16, 1992.

[69] *Jerusalem Post*, March 8, 1993.

[70] *Yediot Acharonot*, April 13, 1995; cited in Hazony, *The Jewish State*, p. 41.

[71] Rubinstein, *From Herzl to Rabin*, p. 72.

[72] E.g., ibid., pp. 203–204.

[73] E.g., ibid., pp. 99–103.

[74] Ibid., p. 258.

[75] Hazony, *The Jewish State*, p. 42.

[76] Ibid., pp. 42–43.

[77] Daniel Polisar, "On the Quiet Revolution in Citizenship Education," *Azure*, summer, 2001, pp. 66–104, p. 76.

[78] Ibid., p. 79.

[79] Hazony, *The Jewish State*, pp. 43–44.

[80] Ibid., pp. 45–46.

[81] Ibid., p. 51.

[82] For an analysis and critique of Barak's interpretation of "Jewish and democratic," see Hillel Neuer, "Aharon Barak's Revolution," *Azure*, winter, 1998, pp. 13–49.

[83] See, for example, Mordechai Haller, "The Court that Packed Itself," *Azure*, autumn, 1999, pp. 65–91.

[84] Moshe Landau, interview with Ari Shavit, *Haaretz*, October 6, 2000. See also the critiques of the Court voiced by Ruth Gavison, Professor of Law at Hebrew University and founder of the Association for Civil Rights in Israel; e.g., her interview with Ari Shavit in *Haaretz Magazine*, November 12, 1999.

[85] Cited in Hazony, *The Jewish State*, pp. 51–52.

[86] For statements from other supreme court justices suggestive of the same agenda, see ibid., p. 52.

[87] Moshe Landau, interview in *Haaretz*, October 6, 2000.

[88] Hazony, *The Jewish State*, pp. 57 and 59.

[89] Ibid., pp. 59–61. The citations are from, respectively, pp. 59, 59, and 60.

[90] *Al Hamishmar*, April 17, 1992.

[91] Cited in Hazony, *The Jewish State*, p. 53.

[92] Ibid., pp. 54–55.

[93] Rubinstein, *From Herzl to Rabin*, p. 198.

[94] For a list of countries giving such preference, see Ruth Lapidoth, "The Right of Return in International Law, with Special Reference to the Palestinian Refugees," *Israel Yearbook on Human Rights*, #16, 1986, pp. 103–125, p. 121. The Law of Return is discussed on pp. 121–123.

[95] Rubinstein, *From Herzl to Rabin*, pp. 198–199. See also ibid., p. 122.

[96] Amnon Rubinstein, "Zionism's Compatriots," *Azure*, winter, 2004, pp. 111–122.

[97] Ibid. Citation is from p. 115.

[98] E.g., *Yediot Acharonot*, September 29, 1993; cited in Hazony, *The Jewish State*, pp. 59–60.

[99] Hazony, *The Jewish State*, p. 72.

[100] While many expressed concern that this seemed to be an implication of the agreement, others emphatically disputed that interpretation. Particularly notable among the latter was Amnon Rubinstein, in a letter to then Prime Minister Netanyahu dated January 8, 1997. The letter was posted on-line by Independent Media Review and Analysis on January 14, 1997 (imra@netvision.net.il).

[101] Arnold Blumberg, *The History of Israel*, p. 176.

[102] Hillel Halkin, "The Rabin Assassination: A Reckoning," p. 54.

[103] See, for example, Elon, *A Blood-Dimmed Tide*, p. 310. Also, Uri Savir, *The Process*, Random House, New York, 1998, p. 248.

[104] Halkin, "The Rabin Assassination: A Reckoning," p. 55.

[105] Arafat made these claims repeatedly. He was quoted to this effect by the German news agency DPA on February 28, 1996, and by the *Jerusalem Post* on March 22, 1996. Other PA officials echoed these claims; see, for example, the statement by PA Planning Minister Nabil Shaath in an interview with *Le Monde*, cited in *Haaretz*, March 6, 1996.

[106] See, for example, "Shaath Threatens Armed Conflict If Peace Fails," *Jerusalem Post*, March 15, 1996.

CHAPTER FIFTEEN

[1] Ari Shavit, "Why We Hate Him: The Real Reason," *Haaretz*, December 26, 1997.

[2] Yossi Beilin, *Touching Peace*, pp. 3–4.

[3] Ibid., pp. 270–271.

[4] Ibid., p. 3.

[5] E.g., ibid., pp. 83, 88, 164.

[6] Uri Savir, *The Process*, p. 254.

[7] Ibid., p. 311.

[8] Ehud Sprinzak, "Netanyahu's Safety Belt," *Foreign Affairs*, July/August 1998, pp. 18–28.

[9] Ibid., p. 18.

[10] Ibid., p. 22.

[11] Ehud Sprinzak, "How Israel Misjudges Hamas and Its Terrorism," *Washington Post*, October 19, 1997, p. C1.

[12] Efraim Karsh, "Peace Despite Everything," in Karsh, ed., *From Rabin to Netanyahu*, pp. 117–132, p. 118.

[13] *Israel Yearbook and Almanac*, 1997, Israel Business, Research, and Technical Translation/ Documentation, Jerusalem, 1997, p. 62.

[14] Ibid., p. 49.

[15] Ibid., p. 10.

[16] Ibid., p. 15.

[17] Cited in "Background-Note for the Record, Christopher Letter and JP Article," Aaron Lerner, Independent Media Review and Analysis (IMRA), December 7, 1997.

[18] On the issue of incitement, see also the Government of Israel Press Office policy paper of August, 1997, entitled "Palestinian Incitement to Violence Since Oslo: A Four-Year Compendium." The paper includes statements by PA officials asserting Palestinian claims to all of Israel, denigrating Jews and propounding anti-Semitic slanders.

[19] Shavit, "Why We Hate Him: The Real Reason."

[20] Ari Shavit, "Against the Tribe: Why We Hate Him, Part II," excerpted in the *Forward*, January 16, 1998.

[21] In August, 2001, the State Department informed Congress that it was planning, finally, to add American victims of Palestinian terror to the rewards program, this after members of both Houses of Congress had introduced legislation on the issue (Melissa Radler, "US Closer to Publicizing Rewards for Capture of Palestinian Terrorists," *Jerusalem Post*, August 10, 2001). But in an article published a year later ("Betrayed by the State Department," *Jerusalem Post*, August 11, 2002), Sherri Mandell, the mother of Koby Mandell, a thirteen-year-old who was killed by Palestinian terrorists in May, 2001, wrote that the State Department was still failing to advertise rewards for the capture of Palestinian murderers of Americans, in stark contrast to efforts made to publicize rewards for the apprehension of terrorist killers of Americans elsewhere.

[22] Barbara Demick, "Broadcasts' Warlike Tone Angers Israelis/ Listening to a PLO Network," *The Philadelphia Inquirer*, September 7, 1997.

CHAPTER SIXTEEN

[1] Cited in Efraim Karsh, *Arafat's War*, p. 198.

[2] See, for example, Charles Krauthammer, "The Peace of the Grave," *Jerusalem Post*, January 10, 2000, p. 8.

[3] Yossi Klein Halevi, "An Insane Gamble Turns Into a National Disgrace," *Los Angeles Times*, February 3, 2000.

[4] Ibid.

[5] For the text of Security Council Resolution 425, see Walter Laqueur and Barry Rubin, *The Israeli-Arab Reader*, pp. 221–222.

[6] Yossi Beilin, *Touching Peace*, p. 212.

[7] See, for example, the reference to Beilin's involvement in "secret" back-channel negotiations, in the *Jerusalem Post*, May 14, 2000.

[8] See, for example, Israel Harel, "Nobody Wants to Know," *Haaretz*, October 28, 1999.

[9] See Foreign Ministry Web site item, "Growing Concern in Israel at Rhetoric in Some Arab Countries," March 7, 2000.

¹⁰ See Pearl Herman, *The United Nations Relief and Works Agency for Palestine Refugees in the Near East: A Report*, 2003, p. 12.

¹¹ For example, in an Associated Press story of January 27, 2001, on the Taba talks, Palestinian negotiator Nabil Shaath was reported to have indicated that the sides were close to an agreement on borders, but he was quoted as saying that still unresolved was "the main issue of the right of return and its practical implementation."

¹² In March, 2001, Palestinian Authority Communications Minister Imad Al-Faluji stated in a speech in Lebanon: "Whoever thinks that the Intifada broke out because of the despised Sharon's visit to the Al-Aqsa Mosque [in September, 2000], is wrong... This Intifada was planned in advance, ever since President Arafat's return from the Camp David negotiations, where he turned the table upside down on President Clinton." (*Al-Safir* (Lebanon) March 3, 2001, translated by Middle East Media Research Institute. The statement by Faluji was also reported in translation by Middle East News Online, March 3, 2001.)

¹³ Itamar Marcus, "This Week in the Palestinian Media," Palestinian Media Watch, August 3, 2000.

¹⁴ See Karsh, *Arafat's War*, p. 178.

¹⁵ See note 11.

¹⁶ *Le Nouvel Observateur*, March 1, 2001. Arafat's initiation and orchestration of the violence was also described in an article consisting of excerpts from a book by Nofal and published in the Palestinian newspaper *Al-Ayyam* in September, 2001.

Earlier, as reported in the *New Yorker* in a January 29, 2001, article, Marwan Barghouti, head of Arafat's Tanzim militia, said of the descent into violence: "The explosion would have happened anyway [even if Sharon had not visited the Temple Mount.] It was necessary in order to protect Palestinian rights."

¹⁷ "White Paper Tiger Unleashed," *Haaretz*, November 24, 2000.

¹⁸ Ibid.

¹⁹ See, for example, Jacob Lefkovits Dallal, "Treasure Lost," *Jerusalem Post*, January 28, 2000.

²⁰ Ibid. Also, Tamar Hausman, "Wakf Dumping of Mount Material Angers Jerusalem Antiquities Officials," *Jerusalem Post*, December 20, 1999; also, Arieh O'Sullivan, "Fresh Artifacts From Temple Mount Ripe for Pillaging," *Jerusalem Post*, December 21, 1999.

²¹ "An Archaeological Atrocity," editorial, *Jerusalem Post*, December 24, 1999.

²² Cited in Dallal, "Treasures Lost."

²³ Etgar Lefkovits and Herb Keinon, "Concern at New Digging on Temple Mount," *Jerusalem Post*, January 22, 2001.

²⁴ Hausman, "Wakf Dumping of Mount Materials Angers Jerusalem Antiquities Officials."

²⁵ Lefkovits and Keinon, "Concern at New Digging on Temple Mount."

²⁶ Karsh, *Arafat's War*, p. 184.

²⁷ See, for example, Associated Press report of January 27, 2001, on statements by Nabil Shaath regarding the progress of the Taba negotiations.

²⁸ For example, in December, 2000, Peace Now renewed its call for the dismantling of settlements and cast Israel's policy on the settlements as blocking peace. See *Jerusalem Post*, December 5, 2000.

²⁹ Cited by Yoram Hazony, *The Jewish State*, p. 29.

³⁰ Ibid., p. 36.

[31] Benny Morris, *Righteous Victims: A History of the Zionist-Arab Conflict, 1881–1999*, Knopf, New York, 1999.

[32] Avi Shlaim, *The Iron Wall: Israel and the Arab World.*

[33] E.g., ibid., pp. 528–530.

[34] E.g., ibid., p. 556.

[35] Ibid., p. 605.

[36] Ibid., p. 600.

[37] Morris, *Righteous Victims*, p. 627.

[38] Ibid., pp. 667–668.

[39] Efraim Karsh, "New Historians, New Denial," *Times Literary Supplement*, May 5, 2000, pp. 27–28. For another incisive critique of the Morris and Shlaim books, see Anita Shapira, "The Past is Not a Foreign Country," *The New Republic*, November 29, 1999, pp. 26 ff.

[40] Tom Segev, *One Palestine Complete: Jews and Arabs Under the British Mandate*, p. 438. As noted earlier, the claims of a British pledge of Palestine to the Arabs have almost invariably centered on wartime correspondence between Sir Henry McMahon and Emir Hussein. David Fromkin, in *A Peace to End All Peace*, offers evidence that the McMahon-Hussein correspondence contained no such promise. See especially pp. 179, 182–183, 185, 528.

[41] See, for example, Fromkin, *A Peace to End All Peace*, p. 524.

[42] For example, in 1930, the League of Nations Permanent Mandates Commission protested the anti-Jewish content of the Shaw Commission report on the 1929 Arab attacks. The Passfield White Paper of 1930, which sought to restrict severely Jewish immigration and land acquisition, was based on the report and essentially ignored the Mandates Commission's objections. The Mandates Commission also objected to anti-Jewish steps proposed by Britain in 1936 and to the Peel Commission's proposal for a much reduced Jewish national enclave in 1937. With regard to Britain's repudiation of its obligations to the Jews in the 1939 White Paper, the Mandates Commission unanimously declared that "the policy set out in the White Paper is not in accordance with the interpretation which... the Commission had placed on the Palestine Mandate." See Shmuel Ettinger, "The Modern Period," in Ben-Sasson, *A History of the Jewish People*, pp. 1007, 1013. 1015; also, the discussion of League of Nations protests of British policy toward the Jews in Palestine in Howard M. Sachar, *A History of Israel*, second edition, especially pp. 199, 224.

[43] See references to this literature in Yehoshua Porath's review of Segev's book in *Azure*, spring, 2000.

[44] Tom Segev, *One Palestine Complete: Jews and Arabs under the British Mandate*, p. 497 note.

[45] Ibid., p. 140.

[46] Ibid., p. 430.

[47] Ibid., p. 461.

[48] See the discussion in Chapter Six of opportunities for escape to Palestine, particularly from Rumanian ports; and of Jews who died trying to reach Palestine but unable to get past the British blockade, such as the passengers aboard the *Struma*.

[49] The citations are from Robert S. Wistrich, *Muslim Anti-Semitism: A Clear and Present Danger*. Wistrich references for the quotes Moshe Pearlman, *Mufti of Jerusalem*, Gollancz, London, 1947.

[50] Tom Segev, *One Palestine Complete*, p. 508.

[51] Incisive reviews of the book include Anita Shapira, "Eyeless in Zion," *The New Republic*,

December 11, 2000, pp. 26–36; Yehoshua Porath,"Tom Segev's New Mandate," *Azure,* spring, 2000; Amos Perlmutter, "Bad Tidings to Zion," *National Review,* March 19, 2001, pp. 52–53.

52 *Haaretz,* December 22, 2000.

53 Ilan Pappe, *Journal of Palestine Studies,* spring, 2001.

54 Tom Segev, "A History Lesson," *Haaretz,* June 29, 2001.

55 Hazony, *The Jewish State,* p. 12.

56 Adi Ophir, Ariella Azoulay, and Debora Kohn, "100 Years of Zionism, 50 Years of a Jewish State; Israel at 50," *Tikkun,* #2, Volume 13, 1998, pp. 68–71.

57 Yaron Ezrahi, *Rubber Bullets,* Farrar, Straus, and Giroux, New York, 1997, p. 14.

58 Ibid., p. 223.

59 Ibid., p. 100.

60 Sidra Dekoven Ezrahi, "Brothers and Others," in Gail Twersky Reimer and Judith A. Kates, eds., *Beginning Anew: A Woman's Companion to the High Holy Days,* Simon and Schuster, New York, 1997, pp. 80–86.

61 Amos Elon, "Israel and the Evil of Zionism," *New York Review of Books,* December 19, 1996.

62 See Daniel Polisar, "On the Quiet Revolution in Citizenship Education," especially pp. 80–104.

63 Ibid., pp. 66–67.

64 Ibid.

65 Cited in Sarah Honig, "Crazier than Ben-Gurion," *Jerusalem Post,* September 10, 1999. See also Hillel Halkin's discussion of Naveh's book in "Was Zionism Unjust?" *Commentary,* November, 1999, pp. 29–35.

66 Yoram Hazony, Michael B. Oren, and Daniel Polisar, *The Quiet Revolution: A Comparative Study of Education Ministry Textbooks on the 20th Century,* The Shalem Center, Jerusalem, September, 2000.

67 Hillel Halkin, "Was Zionism Unjust?"

68 Mazal Mualem, "Labor Party Wants Women in Green Banned," *Haaretz,* January 8 2001.

69 Alan M. Dershowitz, *Haaretz,* August 31, 2000.

70 Cited in Daniel Doron, "What Open Debate?" *Jerusalem Post,* June 22, 2000, p. 8.

71 Gideon Levy, "Only Through Force," *Haaretz,* October 8, 2000.

72 Gideon Levy, "An Existential Exercise," *Haaretz,* October 16, 2000.

73 See, for example, *Jerusalem Post,* June 8, 2001.

74 Ari Shavit "Reeling under a Double-Barreled Curse," *Haaretz,* January 15, 2001.

75 Tanya Reinhart, "The Peace that Kills," www.tau.ac.il, December 6, 2000.

76 Ibid.

77 See Boris Shusteff, "We Are All Settlers," published on the Web site of the Freeman Center for Strategic Studies, November 22, 2000, www.freeman.org.

78 Interview in *Haaretz,* September 14, 2001; cited in Itamar Rabinovich, *Waging Peace: Israel and the Arabs 1948–2003,* Princeton University, Princeton, 2004, p. 162.

79 Associated Press interview with Shlomo Ben-Ami published in the *Jerusalem Post,* June 21, 2001.

CHAPTER SEVENTEEN

[1] Seth Gittell, "Ehrman Tape Makes Waves Among Brass," *Forward*, August 22, 1997, pp. 1,2.

[2] See, for example, "American Rabbis Want a 'Shared' Jerusalem," *Haaretz*, July 24, 2000.

[3] Cited in Marilyn Henry, "Smithsonian to Develop New Program to Mark Israel's 50th," *Jerusalem Post*, January 8, 1998. See also the editorial "The Smithsonian Does It Again," *The Washington Times*, December 29, 1997.

[4] Edward Alexander, "Introduction," in *With Friends Like These*, p. 8.

[5] Rael Jean Isaac, "A Trojan Horse Among Presidents," *Midstream*, May, 1993, pp. 2–7.

[6] Herbert Zweibon, letter in the *Jerusalem Post*, June 1, 1994.

[7] Ibid.

[8] Ibid.

[9] David Isaacs, "Information Packet Used to Tilt Opinion Toward Peace," *Jerusalem Post*, September 2, 1994, p. 4B.

[10] Ibid.

[11] The report was posted on the IPF Web site, www.peacepulse.org.

[12] Steve Feldman, "Israel Bash: At D.C. Conference, It Was No Holds Barred," *Jewish Exponent*, December 12, 1996, p. 1.

[13] Ibid.

[14] "Slim-Fast Tycoon Defends Syria's Assad: Predicts Peace Could Be Made 'In a Day or Two'," *Forward*, July 18, 1997, p. 4.

[15] "Blame Game Begins After Kiss," *Forward*, November 26, 1999, pp. 1, 5.

[16] Gittell, "Ehrman Tape Makes Waves Among Brass."

[17] Cited ibid., p. 2.

[18] "Blame Game Begins After Kiss."

[19] "Toasting a Tyrant," *Forward*, March 31, 2000, p. 8.

[20] Tom Rachman, "Yemeni President Leaves Conference," Associated Press, March 31, 2000; also, Marilyn Henry, "Yemeni President Dodges Questions on Israeli Visitors," *Jerusalem Post*, April 2, 2000.

[21] See Joseph Puder, "The New Israel Fund: Financing Palestinian Nationalism," in Edward Alexander, ed., *With Friends Like These*, pp. 225–261. The material on Neve Shalom is on pp. 252–256.

[22] Ibid., pp. 254–255.

[23] David Bar-Illan, "The Wrong Seeds," *Jerusalem Post*, January 28, 2000, p. 15B.

[24] Cited ibid.

[25] David Greenblatt, Letter to the Editor, *Jerusalem Post*, February 9, 2000, p. 8.

[26] See discussion in Chapter Seven of the priorities of Boston's Jewish Community Relations Council during the years 1997–1998.

[27] See Tom Rose, "NJCRAC's Mistake," *Forward*, July 12, 1996.

[28] "ADL Urges Arafat to Remove Anti-Semitism from Official PA Airwaves," U.S. Newswire, November 20, 1998.

[29] See, for example, "American Jewish Leaders Tour Arab States to Lobby for Syria Treaty," World Tribune.com, January 18, 2000.

[30] The text of the letter was posted on the Web site of Independent Media Review and Analysis (imra.org.il) September 25, 2000.

[31] See Rebecca Spence, "Arafat Eyed as Laureate For UJC's Isaiah Award, Stunning Jewish Leaders," *Forward*, October 15, 1999.

[32] Larry Cohler, "Once Lonesome Doves Challenge Hawks on Israel Policy," *Washington Post*, December 13, 1992.

[33] Gittell, "Ehrman Tape Makes Waves Among Brass."

[34] Natan Sharansky, "Oslo's Great Omission," *Haaretz*, January 24, 2001.

[35] See the piece on this issue by David Wurmser, in *Machor Rishon*, March 19, 2001.

CHAPTER EIGHTEEN

[1] Cited in Efraim Karsh, *Arafat's War*, pp. 213, 221; from MEMRI "Special Dispatch - PA" July 8, 2001.

[2] Yoram Hazony "Israel's Right and Left Converge," *New York Times*, April 26, 2002.

[3] Cited ibid.

[4] Cited in Robert Fulford, "You Can't Reason With Hatred: Israel's Best Minds Have Lost Faith in the Possibility of Peace," *National Post*, July 15, 2002.

[5] Ari Shavit, "Mister Nice Guy," *Haaretz Magazine*, June 14, 2001.

[6] Tom Gross, "Arafat Letter Hails Tel Aviv Bomber," *New York Daily News*, July 11, 2001.

[7] Chemi Shalev on "All Things Considered," National Public Radio, July 31, 2001.

[8] Cited in Karsh, *Arafat's War*, pp. 222–223.

[9] Janine Zacharia, "Arafat Misled Me, Bush Tells Mubarak," *Jerusalem Post*, January 29, 2002.

[10] Herb Keinon, "Cheney Sets Terms for Arafat Meeting," *Jerusalem Post*, March 20, 2002.

[11] See Gerald Steinberg, "Powell's Mission Still Alive — Barely," *Jerusalem Post*, April 15, 2002.

[12] Janine Zacharia, "Bush: Arafat Disappointed Me," *Jerusalem Post*, May 7, 2002.

[13] "Full Text of President Bush's Address," *Jerusalem Post*, June 25, 2002.

[14] See, for example, the President's November 6, 2003, speech before National Endowment for Democracy.

[15] Tom Carter, "UN Commission Backs Palestinian 'Armed Struggle,'" *Washington Times*, April 18, 2002; also, Herb Keinon, "Wiesenthal Raps EU Endorsement of Terror," *Jerusalem Post*, April 19, 2002. Of other EU states on the commission, Britain and Germany voted against the resolution and Italy abstained.

[16] Melissa Radler, "UN report clears Israel of alleged Jenin 'Massacre,'" *Jerusalem Post*, August 2, 2002.

[17] See, for example, Janine Zacharia, "State Department: No Conclusive Evidence Arafat Backed Terror," *Jerusalem Post*, July 21, 2002.

[18] Lamia Lahoud, "Poll: 80 percent of Palestinians Support Ongoing Terror," *Jerusalem Post*, September 29, 2002.

[19] Larry Derfner, "A Break in the Ranks," *Jerusalem Post*, February 8, 2002.

[20] Ibid.

[21] Robert S. Wistrich, *Muslim Anti-Semitism: A Clear and Present Danger.*

[22] Examples of Peres at least attempting to make Israel's case before hostile audiences in-

clude his rejection, at a meeting of the Socialist International in Lisbon, of Palestinian proposals for international observers in the territories (see Herb Keinon, et.al., "Peres and Arafat Meet," *Jerusalem Post*, July 1, 2001); his criticism of anti-Israel bias in European state policies (see, for example, Herb Keinon, "Peres Raps European Union's Bias," *Jerusalem Post*, April 20, 2001); and his defense, before foreign diplomats, of Israel's siege of Arafat's Ramallah headquarters (Gil Hoffman, et.al., "Envoys Slam Peres over Ramallah," *Jerusalem Post*, September 26, 2002).

[23] See Gil Hoffman, "National Unity Government Collapses," *Jerusalem Post*, October 31, 2002.

[24] See, for example, Barry Schweid, "Peres Calls Arafat a Peace Partner," AP Worldstream, May 1, 2001.

[25] E.g., ibid. Also, Saul Singer, "Making Excuses for Arafat," *Jerusalem Post*, March 22, 2002.

[26] For Peres on the continuing relevance of Oslo, see Gil Hoffman, "Ben-Eliezer Dealt Serious Blow in Stormy Labor Convention," *Jerusalem Post*, October 1, 2002. Regarding his belief in the ongoing viability of his vision of a New Middle East, see Melissa Radler, et.al., "Peres: 'New Middle East' Vision Remains Intact," *Jerusalem Post*, September 19, 2002.

[27] Gil Hoffman, "Palestinians Sincere, But Unable to Stop Terror — Ben-Eliezer," *Jerusalem Post*, August 23, 2002.

[28] See reference to Sneh's statement in Dafna Linzer, "Netanyahu Rebuffs Withdrawal Call," *Jerusalem Post*, April 11, 2002.

[29] See, for example, Clyde Haberman, "Dennis Ross's Exit Interview," *New York Times Magazine,* March 25, 2001; also Jack Katzenell, "Former US Peace Envoy Blames Arafat for Failure of Peace Process," AP Worldstream, April 13, 2001. Also, Eric Black, "Former Mideast Envoy Offers Insight into Last Year's Talks; Arafat 'Couldn't Do a Deal,' Ross Says," *Minneapolis Star Tribune*, May 6, 2001.

[30] See, for example, Yossi Beilin, "More War is not the Route to Israeli Security," *New York Times*, March 30, 2002.

[31] See, for example, Ari Shavit, "A Direct Threat to Democracy," *Haaretz*, November 14, 2001.

[32] E.g., Yossi Beilin, "More War is not the Route to Israeli Security."

[33] Ari Shavit, "Mister Nice Guy."

[34] Yossi Beilin, "The Urgency of Constructing Peace," *New York Times*, April 18, 2001.

[35] Yossi Beilin, "Back to a Coalition of Pragmatism," *Haaretz*, September 7, 2002.

[36] Shavit, "Mister Nice Guy."

[37] Ibid.

[38] See, for example, Herb Keinon, "Changing the Script," *Jerusalem Post*, May 11, 2001.

[39] Cited by Karsh, *Arafat's War*, p. 165.

[40] E.g., Gil Hoffman, "Peace Now Takes Aim at Settlements," *Jerusalem Post*, February 8, 2002.

[41] See, for example, Alexandra J. Wall, "Beilin Blasts Sharon," *Jewish Bulletin*, June 1, 2001. Also, Shavit, "Mister Nice Guy."

[42] "Sharon and Peres Mount Campaign Against Findings of Mitchell Report," *Haaretz*, May 10, 2001.

[43] Shavit, "A Direct Threat to Democracy."

[44] Amotz Asa-El, "Labor Knows Best," *Jerusalem Post*, December 7, 2001.

[45] Amnon Dankner, "The Big Scam," *Maariv*, July 13, 2001; translated by the Middle East Media Research Institute.

[46] E.g., Nina Gilbert, "Sarid: Terror War to Last as Long as Occupation," *Jerusalem Post*, March 2, 2002.

[47] Isi Liebler, "Yossi Sarid's Inciteful Remarks," *Jerusalem Post*, October 14, 2002.

[48] Yossi Sarid, "Sharon and Arafat in a Deadly Dance," *New York Times*, December 20, 2001.

[49] E.g., Naomi Chazan, "Preserving Israel's Soul," *Jerusalem Post*, February 22, 2002; also, Chazan, "Zero-Sum Game Has Only Losers," *Jerusalem Post*, May 16, 2002.

[50] Chazan, "Zero Sum Game."

[51] Ibid.

[52] David Bedein, "Israeli Peace Now MK Launches Attack Against Official Palestinian Media," Israel Resource News Agency, November 6, 2002.

[53] Ehud Yaari, "Oslo Revisited," *The Jerusalem Report*, July 2, 2001. The same point that it was not just Arafat that was the problem was made by, for example, Efraim Inbar. Inbar notes particularly the import of the Palestinian education system teaching that all of Israel properly belongs to the Arabs and the Palestinian population's essentially embracing that view. See Efraim Inbar, "Blaming Arafat is Too Easy," *Jerusalem Post*, August 13, 2001.

[54] Ehud Yaari, "Not Just Anti-Semitic Lies!" *The Jerusalem Report*, December 16, 2002.

[55] Robert Fulford, "You Can't Reason With Hatred: Israel's Best Minds Have Lost Faith in the Possibility of Peace."

[56] See, for example, Ze'ev Schiff, "Who Needs Security Cooperation? Israel Must Assume that the Palestinians Intend to Violate Security Agreements," *Haaretz*, April 13, 2001; also, "Arafat is Making Fools of Everyone — PA Released Two Who Admitted They Were Behind Disco Bombing," *Haaretz*, June 22, 2001.

[57] Hirsh Goodman, "The Real War of Independence," *The Jerusalem Report*, April 22, 2002.

[58] See, for example, Ze'ev Schiff, "Oslo May Be Dead, But Occupation is Not the Solution," *Haaretz*, November 24, 2000; also, "Q & A: Ze'ev Schiff on 'Strategic Dilemmas: Israel and the Mideast,'" *Haaretz*, September 25, 2003.

[59] See the reference in Chapter Sixteen to Barnea's article on the "lynch test," which appeared in the magazine *Seventh Eye*.

[60] Gideon Levy, "Just When We Were About to Give Them So Much," *Haaretz*, June 17, 2001.

[61] Gideon Levy, "Under the Volcano," *Haaretz*, June 10, 2001.

[62] Amira Haas, "All the Way from the Sea to the River," *Haaretz*, May 30, 2001.

[63] *Haaretz*, February 5, 2001.

[64] Cited by Associated Press, June 21, 2001.

[65] *Haaretz*, April 25, 2001.

[66] *Haaretz*, November 24, 2000.

[67] Amos Elon, "Israelis and Palestinians: What Went Wrong?" *The New York Review of Books*, December 19, 2002.

[68] Ron Pundak, "My regret about Oslo is it permitted settlement construction,"

Independent Media Review and Analysis, September 9, 2002, citing Israel Radio broadcast of the same day.

[69] David Newman, "A Time for Self-Criticism," *Jerusalem Post*, April 10, 2002.

[70] Ibid.

[71] Yisrael Harel, "The Fence of Hysteria and Illusion," *Haaretz*, August 9, 2002.

[72] Baruch Kimmerling, "The Right to Resist," *Haaretz*, March 27, 2001.

[73] Ze'ev Sternhell, *The Founding Myths of Israel*, p. 15. Sternhell is also discussed in Chapter Sixteen.

[74] Ze'ev Sternhell, "Hard Times on the Left," *Haaretz*, June 15, 2001.

[75] Ze'ev Sternhell, "Rejecting the Settlers' 'Holy War'," *Haaretz*, July 27, 2001.

[76] Ze'ev Sternhell, "Facing a Sleepwalking Government," *Haaretz*, May 11, 2001.

[77] Ari Shavit, "The Good People Are Silent," *Haaretz*, June 26, 2001.

[78] Editorial, *Jerusalem Post*, December 30, 2002.

[79] See interview with Morris by Miron Rappaport, *Yediot Acharonot*, November 23, 2001.

[80] See, for example, Benny Morris, "Peace? No Chance," *The Guardian*, February 21, 2002.

[81] Benny Morris, *The Road to Jerusalem — Glubb Pasha, Palestine and the Jews*, I.B. Tauris, London, 2002. On Morris's response to Arafat's war and his nevertheless having yet to distance himself from the false claims and tendentious arguments that have characterized his work, see also Efraim Karsh, "Revisiting Israel's 'Original Sin,'" *Commentary*, September, 2003, pp. 46–50.

[82] Avi Shlaim, "Sharon Needs to be Told to Stop Shooting and Start Talking," *International Herald Tribune*, January 10, 2002.

[83] Terry Gross, interview with Shlaim on "Fresh Air," National Public Radio, March 13, 2001.

[84] Avi Shlaim, "A Betrayal of History," *The Guardian*, February 22, 2002.

[85] Tom Segev, "Learning from Israel and Its Mistakes," *New York Times*, November 25, 2001.

[86] Tom Segev, "A Retreat to the Familiar Ground of Zionism," *New York Times*, August 12, 2001.

[87] Ibid.

[88] During this period, Segev published another book, *Elvis in Jerusalem: Post-Zionism and the Americanization of Israel* (Metropolitan Books, New York, 2002), which offered a compendium of his indictments of Zionism and a catalogue of what he perceives to be its failures. For a cogent critique of the book and of Segev's anti-Zionist arguments, see Hillel Halkin, "Not So Fast," *The New Republic*, July 1, 2002.

[89] Eyal Megged, *The Black Light* (Hebrew), Yediot Acharonot, Tel Aviv, 2002.

[90] See Carol Glick, "Blacklisting 'The Black Light'," *Jerusalem Post*, October 17, 2002.

[91] See, for example, A. B. Yehoshua, "For a Jewish Border," *Jerusalem Post*, July 19, 2002.

[92] Amos Oz, "Let Palestinians Govern Palestinians — Now," *New York Times*, January 6, 2001.

[93] Amos Oz, "Two Stubborn Men, and Many Dead," *New York Times*, March 12, 2002.

[94] Paul Kelbie, "Israeli Novelist Calls for a 'Semi-Detached Solution' to Decades of Bloodshed," *The Independent*, August 13, 2002.

[95] Oz, "Two Stubborn Men, and Many Dead."

[96] Amos Oz, "An End to Israel's Occupation Will Mean a Just War," *The Observer*, April 7, 2002.

[97] E.g., ibid. Also, "What We Israelis Must Do to Bring Peace to Our Land," *The Independent*, April 18, 2002.

[98] Oz, "An End to Israeli Occupation Will Mean a Just War."

[99] See, for example, David Grossman, "The Pain Israel Must Accept," *New York Times*, November 8, 2000; also, "Illusions of a Separate Peace," *New York Times*, July 12, 2002; also, "Fictions Embraced by an Israel at War," *New York Times*, October 1, 2002.

[100] E.g., Grossman, "Fictions Embraced by an Israel at War."

[101] Ibid.

[102] E.g., Grossman, "The Pain Israel Must Accept."

[103] Aharon Shabtai, *J'Accuse*, New Directions, New York, 2003.

[104] Jonathan Wilson, *New York Times Book Review*, July 6, 2003.

[105] Abigail Radoszkowicz, "Hagana Massacre Libel Resurfaces at Film Festival," *Jerusalem Post*, July 16, 2003.

[106] See, for example, Michael Hirsh, "Clinton to Arafat: It's All Your Fault," *Newsweek*, June 27, 2001.

[107] See, for example, Ami Eden, "Top Reform Executive Urges U.S. to Threaten Aid Cut-off to Israelis," *Forward*, September 6, 2002.

[108] See, for example, Itamar Levin, "Bronfman Calls on Bush to Press Sharon on Separation Fence Issue," Globes [online] (www.globes.co.il), August 5, 2003. Also, Joe Berkofsky, "Bronfman Letter on Fence Revives Debate on Jewish Criticism of Israel," Jewish Telegraphic Agency, August 13, 2003.

[109] See, for example, Evelyn Gordon, "Lies, Distortions, and Omissions," *Jerusalem Post*, November 5, 2002. Also, Gerald Steinberg, "How the New Israel Fund Supports the Propaganda War Against Israel," Independent Media Review and Analysis, May 15, 2003. For an update of recent New Israel Fund support of anti-Israel groups, see, "NIF — Some Improvements But Funding of Anti-Israel NGOs Continues," NGO Monitor Analysis, Vol. 2, # 12, August, 2004 (www.ngo.monitor.org).

[110] Yossi Beilin, and Yasir Abed Rabbo, "A Mideast Partnership Can Still Work," *New York Times*, August 1, 2001.

[111] For critiques of the Geneva Accord, see, Michael B. Oren and Yossi Klein Halevi, "Fantasy," *The New Republic*, December 15, 2002; Shlomo Avineri, "The Lies of Geneva," *Yediot Acharonot*, December 1, 2003; Ari Shavit, "The Dangers of the Geneva Accord," *Haaretz*, December 4, 2003.

[112] Leonard Fein, "Oslo is Dead, But the Search for Peace is Not," *Jewish Exponent*, March 15, 2001.

[113] On this issue, see, for example, "Islam's Mandatory War Against Jews and Israel in Palestinian Authority Religious Teaching," Palestinian Media Watch, special report #37, July 2, 2001; "Friday Sermon on PA TV: 'We Must Educate Our Children on the Love of Jihad,'" MEMRI, #240, July 11, 2001; "Sermon on PA TV: Blessings to Whoever Saved a Bullet to Stick in a Jew's Head," MEMRI, #252, August 7, 2001.

[114] See, for example, Limor Livnat, "A World of Falsehood," *Jerusalem Post*, March 9, 2001; Amos Harel, "Palestinian Schoolbooks Fan the Flames of Hatred," *Haaretz*, June 28, 2002; Itamar Marcus, "Planting the Seeds of the Next War: The Truth About the Palestinian

Schoolbooks," *Jerusalem Post*, June 29, 2003; Shira Schoenberg, "New PA Textbooks Full of Anti-Israel Propaganda," *Jerusalem Post*, July 22, 2003.

[115] E.g., Itamar Marcus, "PA Renews Efforts to Have Palestinian Children Die in Confrontations," *Palestinian Media Watch Bulletin*, October 1, 2002.

[116] For example, Aaron Lerner, "Interview: Faisal Husseini on Goal of State from the Jordan to the Sea," Independent Media Research and Analysis, April 15, 2001; Miriam Shaviv, "Intelligence Chief: Arafat Questions Our Right to the Land," *Jerusalem Post*, December 19, 2001; Efraim Karsh, "Euphemism for Annihilation," *Jerusalem Post*, August 21, 2003.

[117] See, for example, Herb Keinon, "Mubarak Invites Sharon to Sharm," *Jerusalem Post*, February 4, 2003.

[118] E.g., Efraim Inbar, "Fighting the Propaganda War," *Jerusalem Post*, June 11, 2001.

[119] See, for example, David Raab, "The Beleaguered Christians of the Palestinian-Controlled Areas," *Jerusalem Viewpoints*, January 1–15, 2003.

[120] See, for example, Khaled Abu Toameh, "PA Officials Stealing Aid, Own Documents Show," *Jerusalem Post*, January 2, 2003.

[121] There were a few American media outlets that were the exception and did report on these issues. Examples of relevant articles in those outlets are: Fiamma Nirenstein, "How Suicide Bombers Are Made," *Commentary*, September, 2001, pp. 53–55; Fiamma Nirenstein, "Jews and the Great Lie," WorldNetDaily, August 3, 2001; Joseph Farah, "The Jewish Temple," WorldNetDaily, August 14, 2003.

[122] See, for example, Deborah Sontag, "And Yet So Far: A Special Report: Quest for Mideast Peace: How and Why It Failed," *New York Times*, July 26, 2001. Also, Robert Malley, "Fictions About the Failure of Camp David," *New York Times*, July 8, 2001. Malley, a member of the National Security Council staff in charge of Arab-Israeli affairs at the time of Camp David, has been the chief purveyor of the revisionist thesis in the West. He articulated the revisionist view at length, with co-author Hussein Agha in "Camp David: The Tragedy of Errors," *New York Review of Books*, August 9, 2001. Dennis Ross rebutted Malley and Agha's slant on events in a letter to the *New York Review of Books*; "Camp David: An Exchange," September 20, 2001.

[123] For Friedman's student activities and writings on Israel in the years prior to Oslo, see Jerold S. Auerbach, "Thomas Friedman's Israel: The Myth of Unrequited Love," in Edward Alexander, ed., *With Friends Like These*, pp. 57–74.

[124] Max Frankel, "Turning Away From the Holocaust," *New York Times*, November 14, 2001.

[125] "Max Frankel Discusses the *New York Times*' 150th Anniversary," on *All Things Considered*, National Public Radio, November 14, 2001.

[126] Jonathan Rosen, "The Uncomfortable Question of Anti-Semitism," *New York Times*, November 4, 2001.

[127] Susan Sachs, "Anti-Semitism Is Deepening Among Muslims," *New York Times*, April 27, 2002.

[128] Ian Buruma, "How to Talk About Israel," *New York Times*, August 31, 2003.

[129] Translated by the Middle East Media and Research Institute, October 14, 2000.

[130] William A. Orme, Jr., "A Parallel Mideast Battle: Is It News or Incitement?" *New York Times*, October 24, 2000. See also, Andrea Levin, "*New York Times* Conceals Antisemitism," *Jerusalem Post*, November 17, 2000.

[131] The full text of the letter can be found at Senator Clinton's Web site: http://clinton.senate.gov

[132] Ibid.

[133] Avraham Burg, "The End of Zionism," *The Guardian*, September 15, 2003.

[134] See, for example, Gil Hoffman, et. al., "EU to Bring Peace 'Road Map' to Region," *Jerusalem Post*, August 30, 2002.

[135] See, for example, Douglas Davis and Herb Keinon, "Blair Pushing Bush for Progress on Palestinian Issue," *Jerusalem Post*, February 19, 2003.

[136] See, for example, Margot Dudkevitch, "Israeli Official: UN Personnel and Vehicles Used By Terrorists Throughout Mideast," *Jerusalem Post*, March 31, 2003.

[137] Shlomo Avineri, "The Moral Blindness of Terje Roed-Larsen," *Jerusalem Post*, August 23, 2002. For what could be expected of the UN in implementing the road map, see Anne Bayefsky, "Guess Who Drew the Road Map?" *Jerusalem Post*, June 12, 2003.

For additional anti-Israel actions by the UN just in the months during which the road map was taking form, in the fall of 2002, see Anne Bayefsky, "Elliot Abrams at a Fork in the Roadmap," *The New York Sun*, December 17, 2002.

[138] Douglas Davis, "Straw: I Understand Terrorism in 'Palestine,'" *Jerusalem Post*, September 25, 2001.

[139] Anne Bayevsky, "Guess Who Drew the Road Map?"

[140] See Douglas Davis, "Rogue States' Need Fans EU Greed," *Jerusalem Post*, July 9, 2002; also, "Slouching Toward Seriousness," *Jerusalem Post* editorial, February 9, 2003; also, Rachel Ehrenfeld, "Banking on Terror," *Jerusalem Post*, February 23, 2003; also, "Israeli Lawyer Accuses EU of Continuing to Fund Palestinian Terror — Calls for Chris Patten's Resignation," Independent Media Review and Analysis, March 2, 2003; also, Melissa Radler, "Defiant Defender of Israel," *Jerusalem Post*, March 21, 2003.

[141] Cited in Douglas Davis, "Biological Warfare," *The Spectator*, September 6, 2003.

[142] See, for example, Mathew Kalman, "Victims Suing Arafat: Claim Palestinian Leader Is Liable for Terror Attacks," *The Montreal Gazette*, November 27, 2001.

[143] See Karsh, *Arafat's War*, p. 249.

[144] See Janine Zacharia, "Palestinians Support Armed Struggle Even After Statehood — Poll," *Jerusalem Post*, October 22, 2003. (Report of poll conducted by Public Opinion Research of Israel and The Palestinian Center for Public Opinion.)

[145] There is evidence that Prime Minister Sharon is pursuing an Allon-like arrangement for the territories. On the subject of defensible borders, the current relevance of the Allon Plan, and Sharon's views, see Dore Gold, "Defensible Borders for Israel," *Jerusalem Letter/Viewpoints*, The Jerusalem Center for Public Affairs, June 15 – July 1, 2003; also, Yosef Goell, "What Are the Settlements Supposed to Achieve?" *Jerusalem Post*, December 9, 2002; also, Efraim Inbar, "The Allon Plan via the Road Map," *Jerusalem Post*, June 8, 2003.

[146] An example is Haider Irsheid, governor of Jenin, who resigned in July, 2003, after being abducted and beaten by members of the Al Aqsa Martyr's Brigades apparently acting with the support of Arafat. See, for example, Charles A. Radin, "Arafat is Said to Fund Truce Foes," *The Boston Globe*, July 23, 2003.

[147] For example, a *Yediot Acharonot* poll of May 4, two days after the referendum, that showed 53 percent of Likud voters supporting withdrawal. (Cited in Bret Stephens, "For Disengagement, Continued," *Jerusalem Post*, May 7, 2004.) Another *Yediot* poll, conducted on

the weekend ending May 16, showed 63 percent of Likud voters in favor of withdrawal. (Cited in Yosef Goell, "Withdrawal Syndrome, What Next?" *Jerusalem Post,* May 17, 2004.)

EPILOGUE

[1] In Kurt Lewin, *Resolving Social Conflicts,* Harper, New York, 1948, pp. 169–185; citation is from p. 183.

[2] Ibid., pp. 186–200; citation is from pp. 198–199.

[3] Hillel Halkin, "Was Zionism Unjust?"

[4] The text of the Kineret Declaration can be found in *Azure,* #13, summer, 2002, pp. 20–23.

BIBLIOGRAPHY

Agassi, Joseph. *Liberal Nationalism for Israel: Towards an Israeli National Identity.* Jerusalem: Gefen, 1999.

Alexander, Edward. *The Jewish Wars: Reflections of One of the Belligerents.* Carbondale: South Illinois University, 1996.

_____, ed. *With Friends Like These: The Jewish Critics of Israel.* New York: S.P.I. Books, 1993.

Altmann, Alexander. *Moses Mendelssohn: A Biographical Study.* University, Alabama: University of Alabama, 1973.

Arendt, Hannah. *Rahel Varnhagen: The Life of a Jewish Woman.* New York: Harcourt, Brace, Jovanovich, 1974.

Aschheim, Steven E. *Brothers and Strangers: The East European Jew in German and German-Jewish Consciousness, 1800–1923.* Madison: University of Wisconsin, 1982.

Baer, Yitzhak. *A History of the Jews in Christian Spain.* Philadelphia: Jewish Publication Society, 1961–62.

Baldwin, Neil. *Henry Ford and the Jews.* New York: Public Affairs, 2001.

Bard, Mitchell E. *Myths and Facts: A Guide to the Arab-Israeli Conflict.* Chevy Chase, Md.: American-Israeli Cooperative Enterprise, 2001.

Bar-On, Mordechai. *In Pursuit of Peace.* Washington, D.C.: United States Institute of Peace Press, 1996.

Baron, Salo W. *The Jewish Community: Its History and Structure to the American Revolution.* Philadelphia: Jewish Publication Society, 1942.

Bat Ye'or. *The Dhimmi: Jews and Christians under Islam.* Rutherford, N.J.: Fairleigh Dickinson University, 1985.

Begin, Ze'ev Binyamin. "Years of Hope," *Haaretz Magazine* (September 6, 2002).

Beilin, Yossi. *Israel: A Concise Political History.* New York: St. Martin's, 1993.

_____. *Touching Peace.* London: Weidenfeld and Nicolson, 1999.

Ben-Horin, Meir. *Max Nordau, Philosopher of Human Solidarity.* New York: Conference of Jewish Social Studies, 1956.

Ben-Sasson, H.H., ed. *A History of the Jewish People.* Cambridge, Mass.: Harvard University, 1976.

Berlin, Isaiah. *Karl Marx: His Life and Environment.* Oxford: Oxford University, 4th ed., 1978.

Berman, Myron. *The Attitude of American Jewry Towards Eastern European Jewish Immigration, 1881–1914.* New York: Arno Press, 1980.

Bibliography

Blumberg, Arnold. *The History of Israel.* Westport, Conn.: Greenwood Press, 1998.

Brandeis on Zionism: A Collection of Addresses and Statements by Louis D. Brandeis. Washington, D.C.: Zionist Organization of America, 1942.

Buber, Martin. *Israel and the World: Essays in a Time of Crisis.* New York: Schocken, 1963.

_____. *A Land of Two Peoples: Martin Buber on Jews and Arabs.* Paul R. Mendes-Flohr, ed. New York: Oxford, 1983.

_____. *On Judaism.* Nahum N. Glatzer, ed. New York: Schocken, 1967.

Carmon, Yigal. "The Story Behind the Handshake," *Commentary,* (March 1994): 25–29.

Chafets, Ze'ev. *Double Vision: How the Press Distorts America's View of the Middle East.* New York: William Morrow, 1985.

_____. *Heroes and Hustlers, Hard Hats and Holy Men: Inside the New Israel.* New York: William Morrow, 1986.

Dawidowicz, Lucy. *The War Against the Jews.* New York: Bantam, 1976.

_____. *What Is the Use of Jewish History?* New York: Schocken, 1992.

Dawidowicz, Lucy, ed. *The Golden Tradition.* Syracuse: Syracuse University, 1996.

Dubnow, Simon. *History of the Jews.* South Brunswick, N.J.: T. Yoseloff, 1967–73.

_____. *History of the Jews in Russia and Poland from the Earliest Times Until the Present Day.* New York: Ktav, 1975.

Eban, Abba. *An Autobiography.* New York: Random House, 1977.

Elazar, Daniel J. and Shmuel Sandler. *Israel's Odd Couple: The 1984 Knesset Elections and the National Unity Government.* Detroit: Wayne State University, 1990.

Elon, Amos. *A Blood-Dimmed Tide: Dispatches from the Middle East.* New York: Columbia University, 1997.

_____. *The Israelis: Founders and Sons.* New York: Holt, Rinehart and Winston, 1971.

Endelman, Todd D., ed. *Jewish Apostasy in the Modern World.* New York: Holmes and Meier, 1987.

Ewen, Frederic, ed. *The Poetry of Heinrich Heine.* New York: Citadel Press, 1969.

Ezrahi, Yaron. *Rubber Bullets.* New York: Farrar, Straus, and Giroux, 1997.

Fein, Leonard. *Where Are We? The Inner Life of America's Jews.* New York: Harper and Row, 1988.

Feingold, Henry L. *Bearing Witness: How America and Its Jews Responded to the Holocaust.* Syracuse: Syracuse University, 1995.

_____. *The Politics of Rescue: The Roosevelt Administration and the Holocaust, 1939–1945.* New Brunswick: Rutgers, 1970.

Finkelstein, Louis, ed. *The Jews: Their History, Culture and Religion.* New York: Schocken, 4th ed. 1977.

Flapan, Simha. *The Birth of Israel: Myths and Realities.* New York: Pantheon, 1987.

Freud, Anna. *The Ego and the Mechanisms of Defense.* Madison, Conn.: International Universities Press, 1966.

Fromkin, David. *A Peace to End All Peace.* New York: Avon, 1989.

Gilbert, Martin. *Auschwitz and the Allies.* New York: Holt, Rinehart and Winston, 1981.

Gilman, Sander L. *Jewish Self-Hatred.* Baltimore: Johns Hopkins, 1986.

Goren, Arthur A., ed. *Dissenter in Zion: From the Writings of Judah L. Magnes.* Cambridge, Mass.: Harvard University, 1982.

Grossman, David. *The Book of Intimate Grammar.* New York: Farrar, Straus, and Giroux, 1994.

_____. *See Under Love.* New York: Farrar, Straus, and Giroux, 1989.

_____. *The Smile of the Lamb.* New York: Farrar, Straus, and Giroux, 1990.

_____. *The Yellow Wind.* New York: Farrar, Straus, and Giroux, 1988.

Halberstam, David. *The Powers That Be.* New York: Knopf, 1979.

Halkin, Hillel. "The Rabin Assassination: A Reckoning," in Kozodoy, ed., *The Middle East Peace Process.* 45–56.

_____. "Was Zionism Unjust?" *Commentary,* (November 1999): 29–35.

Hazony, Yoram. *The Jewish State.* New York: Basic Books, 2000.

_____, Michael B. Oren, and Daniel Polisar. *The Quiet Revolution: A Comparative Study of Education Ministry Textbooks on the 20th Century.* Jerusalem: The Shalem Center, 2000.

Herzl, Theodor. *The Jewish State.* New York: Dover, 1988.

Hertzberg, Arthur. *The Jews in America.* New York: Columbia University, 1997.

_____, ed. *The Zionist Idea.* New York: Harper, 1959.

Hess, Moses. *Rome and Jerusalem.* New York: Bloch, 1945.

Isaac, Rael Jean. *Israel Divided: Ideological Politics in the Jewish State.* Baltimore: Johns Hopkins, 1976.

_____. "New Jewish Agenda," in Alexander, ed., *With Friends Like These:* 143–190.

_____. "The Real Lessons of Camp David," *Commentary,* (December 1993): 34–38.

Kafka, Franz. *Dearest Father: Stories and Other Writings.* New York: Schocken, 1954.

_____. *Selected Short Stories of Franz Kafka.* New York: Modern Library, 1952.

Karsh, Efraim. *Arafat's War.* New York: Grove Press, 2003.

_____. *Fabricating Israeli History: The "New Historians."* London: Frank Cass, 1997.

_____. *Fabricating Israeli History: The "New Historians."* London: Frank Cass, 2nd ed., 2000.

_____, ed. *From Rabin to Netanyahu.* London: Cass, 1997.

_____. "New Historians, New Denial," *Times Literary Supplement,* (May 5, 2000): 27–28.

_____. "Revisiting Israel's Original Sin," *Commentary,* (September 2003): 46–50.

_____. "What Occupation?" *Commentary,* (July–August, 2002): 46–51.

Kaufmann, Walter, ed. and trans. *The Portable Nietzsche.* New York: Penguin, 1959.

Bibliography

Kozodoy, Neal, ed. *The Mideast Peace Process: An Autopsy.* San Francisco: Encounter, 2002.

Lacquer, Walter and Barry Rubin. *The Israeli-Arab Reader.* New York: Penguin, 6th ed., 2001.

Levin, Kenneth. "Jews, Israelis, and the Psyche of the Abused," *Nativ,* (fall, 1996) (in Hebrew).

_____. "This Hubris Will Exact a Heavy Price," *Jerusalem Post,* (September 10, 1993).

_____. *Unconscious Fantasy in Psychotherapy.* Northvale, New Jersey: Jason Aronson, 1993.

Levine, Hillel. *In Search of Sugihara.* New York: Free Press, 1996.

_____. "The List of Mr. Sugihara," *New York Times,* (September 18, 1994).

Levitt, Avraham. "Israeli Art On Its Way to Somewhere Else," *Azure,* (winter 1998):120–145.

Lewin, Kurt. *Resolving Social Conflicts.* New York: Harper, 1948.

Lewis, Bernard. *Semites and Anti-Semites.* New York: W.W. Norton, 1986.

Lichtheim, George. "Socialism and the Jews," *Dissent,* (July–August 1968): 314–342.

Liebman, Charles S. *The Ambivalent American Jew.* Philadelphia: Jewish Publication Society, 1973.

Lipset, Seymour Martin. *"The Socialism of Fools": The Left, the Jews and Israel.* New York: Anti-Defamation League of B'nai Brith, 1969.

_____ and Earl Raab. *Jews and the New American Scene.* Cambridge, Mass.: Harvard University, 1995.

Lipstadt, Deborah. *Beyond Belief.* New York: Free Press, 1986.

Liptzin, Solomon. *Germany's Stepchildren.* Cleveland: Meridian, 1961.

Manuel, Frank E. *A Requiem for Karl Marx.* Cambridge, Mass.: Harvard University, 1995.

Marcus, Jacob Rader. *The Jew in the Medieval World.* Cincinnati: Hebrew Union College, 1990.

Marx, Karl. *Early Writings.* T. B. Bottomore, ed. New York: McGraw-Hill, 1964.

Medoff, Rafael. *The Deafening Silence.* New York: Shapolsky, 1987.

Megged, Aharon. "One-Way Trip on the Highway of Self-Destruction," *Jerusalem Post,* (June 17, 1994).

Meyer, Michael A. *The Origins of the Modern Jew.* Detroit: Wayne State University, 1967.

Miller, Arthur. *Timebends: A Life.* New York: Grove Press, 1987.

Morris, Benny. *The Birth of the Palestinian Refugee Problem.* Cambridge: Cambridge University, 1987.

_____. *Israel's Border Wars 1949–1956: Arab Infiltration, Israeli Retaliation, and the Countdown to the Suez War.* Oxford: Clarendon, 1993.

_____. "The New Historiography: Israel Confronts Its Past," *Tikkun,* (November–December, 1988).

_____. *1948 and After: Israel and the Palestinians.* Oxford: Clarendon, 1994.

_____. *Righteous Victims: A History of the Zionist-Arab Conflict, 1881–1999.* New York: Knopf, 1999.

_____. *The Road to Jerusalem — Glubb Pasha, Palestine and the Jews.* London: I.B. Tauris, 2002.

Morse, Arthur D. *While Six Million Died.* New York: Random House, 1967.

Netanyahu, Benzion. *The Origins of the Inquisition in Fifteenth Century Spain.* New York: Random House, 1995.

Newton, Verne W., ed. *FDR and the Holocaust.* New York: St. Martin's, 1996.

O'Brien, Conor Cruise. *The Siege.* New York: Simon and Schuster, 1986.

Oren, Michael B. *Six Days of War: June 1967 and the Making of the Modern Middle East.* Oxford: Oxford University, 2002.

Oz, Amos. *In the Land of Israel.* San Diego: Harcourt Brace Jovanovich, 1983.

_____. *Israel, Palestine, and Peace.* San Diego: Harcourt Brace, 1995.

_____. *The Slopes of Lebanon.* San Diego: Harcourt Brace Jovanovich, 1989.

_____. *Under This Blazing Light.* Cambridge: Cambridge University, 1995.

Pappe, Ilan. *Britain and the Arab-Israeli Conflict, 1948–1951.* New York: St. Martin's, 1988.

_____. *The Making of the Arab-Israeli Conflict, 1947–1951.* London: I.B. Tauris, 1994.

Patterson, J.H. *With the Judaeans in the Palestine Campaign.* London: Hutchinson, 1922.

Penkower, Monty Noam. *The Jews Were Expendable.* Urbana: University of Illinois, 1983.

Peres, Shimon. *The New Middle East.* New York: Henry Holt, 1993.

Perl, William. *The Holocaust Conspiracy.* New York: Shapolsky, 1989.

Podhoretz, Norman. "A Lamentation From the Future." *Commentary,* (March 1989): 15–21.

Polisar, Daniel. "The Myth of Arafat's Legitimacy," *Azure,* (summer 2002): 29–87.

_____. "On the Quiet Revolution in Citizenship Education," *Azure,* (summer 2001): 66–104.

Puder, Joseph. "The New Israel Fund," in Alexander, ed., *With Friends Like These:* 225–261.

Pulzer, Peter G.J. *The Rise of Political Anti-Semitism in Germany and Austria.* New York: John Wiley, 1964.

Rabinovitch, Itamar. *The Road Not Taken: Early Arab-Israeli Negotiations.* New York: Oxford, 1991.

_____. *Waging Peace.* New York: Farrar, Straus, and Giroux, 1999.

Reinharz, Jehuda. *Chaim Weizmann: The Making of a Statesman.* New York: Oxford, 1993.

_____. *Chaim Weizmann: The Making of a Zionist Leader.* New York: Oxford, 1985.

Rose, Norman. *Chaim Weizmann.* New York: Viking, 1986.

Rothman, Stanley and S. Robert Lichter. *Roots of Radicalism.* New Brunswick, N.J.: Transactions Publishers, 1996.

Rubin, Barry. *Assimilation and Its Discontents.* New York: Times Books, 1995.

Rubinstein, Amnon. *From Herzl to Rabin: The Changing Image of Zionism.* New York: Holmes and Meier, 2000.

_____. "The Numbers Speak for Themselves," *Haaretz,* (July 29, 2002).

_____. "Zionism's Compatriots," *Azure,* (winter 2004): 111–122.

Rubinstein, William D. *The Myth of Rescue.* London: Routledge, 1997.

Sachar, Howard M. *A History of Israel from the Rise of Zionism to Our Time.* New York: Alfred A. Knopf, 2nd ed., 2001.

Salisbury, Harrison E. *Without Fear or Favor.* New York: Times Books, 1980.

Sammons, Jeffrey L. *Heinrich Heine: A Modern Biography.* Princeton: Princeton University, 1979.

Savir, Uri. *The Process.* New York: Random House, 1998.

Shavit, Ari. "Why We Hate Him: The Real Reason," *Haaretz,* (December 26, 1997).

Schiff, Ze'ev and Ehud Yaari. *Intifada.* New York: Simon and Schuster, 1989.

Schorsch, Ismar. *From Text to Context: The Turn to History in Modern Judaism.* Hanover, N.H.: Brandeis University Press, 1994.

Schwarz, Leo W., ed. *Great Ages and Ideas of the Jewish People.* New York: Random House, 1956.

Segev, Tom. *One Palestine Entire: Jews and Arabs Under the British Mandate.* New York: Henry Holt, 2000.

_____. *The Seventh Million: The Israelis and the Holocaust.* New York: Hill and Wang, 1993.

Sela, Avraham. "Transjordan, Israel, and the 1948 War: Myth, Historiography, and Reality," *Middle Eastern Studies,* (October, 1992): 623–689.

Shapira, Anita. "The Past is Not a Foreign Country," *The New Republic,* (November 29, 1999).

Shlaim, Avi. *Collusion Across the Jordan: King Abdullah, the Zionist Movement, and the Partition of Palestine.* New York: Columbia University, 1988.

_____. *The Iron Wall: Israel and the Arab World.* New York: W.W. Norton, 2000.

_____. *The Politics of Partition: King Abdullah, the Zionists and Palestine 1921–1951.* New York: Columbia University, 1990.

Steel, Ronald. *Walter Lippmann and the American Century.* Boston: Little, Brown, 1980.

Sternhell, Ze'ev. *The Founding Myths of Israel.* Princeton: Princeton University, 1998.

Strom, Margot Stern. *Facing History and Ourselves: Holocaust and Human Behavior.* Brookline Mass.: Facing History and Ourselves National Foundation, 1994.

Bibliography

_____ and William S. Parsons. *Facing History and Ourselves: Holocaust and Human Behavior.* Watertown, Mass.: Intentional Educations, 1982.

Talese, Gay. *The Kingdom and the Power.* New York: World, 1966.

Teveth, Shabtai. *Ben-Gurion and the Holocaust.* New York: Harcourt Brace, 1996.

_____. *Ben-Gurion: The Burning Ground.* Boston: Houghton, Mifflin, 1987.

_____. "Charging Israel With Original Sin," *Commentary,* (February 1990): 2–9.

_____. "The Palestinian Refugee Problem and Its Origins," *Middle Eastern Studies,* (April 1990): 214–249.

Tifft, Susan E. and Alex S. Jones. *The Trust.* Boston: Little, Brown, 1999.

Wasserstein, Bernard. *Britain and the Jews of Europe, 1939–1945.* London: Leicester University Press, 1979.

Weininger, Otto. *Sex and Character.* New York: Howard Fertig, 2003.

Weizmann, Chaim. *Trial and Error.* New York: Harper, 1949.

_____. "The Twentieth Congress, August 3–17, 1937: A Weizmann Review," *New Judea* (August–September, 1937).

Wertheimer, Jack. *A People Divided.* New York: Basic Books, 1993.

Wisse, Ruth R. *The Modern Jewish Canon.* New York: Free Press, 2000.

Wistrich, Robert S. *Between Redemption and Perdition.* London: Routledge, 1990.

_____. *The Jews of Vienna in the Age of Franz Joseph.* Oxford: Littman Library, 1989.

_____. *Muslim Anti-Semitism: A Clear and Present Danger.* New York: American Jewish Committee, 2002.

_____. *Revolutionary Jews from Marx to Trotsky.* New York: Harper and Row, 1976.

Wyman, David S. *The Abandonment of the Jews.* New York: Pantheon, 1984.

_____. *Paper Walls: America and the Refugee Crisis 1938–1941.* Amherst: University of Massachusetts, 1968.

_____ and Rafael Medoff. *A Race Against Death: Peter Bergson, America and the Holocaust.* New York: New Press, 2002.

Yerushalmi, Yosef Hayim. *Zakhor: Jewish History and Jewish Memory.* Seattle: University of Washington, 1982.

Yeshoshua, A.B. *Between Right and Right.* Garden City, New York: Doubleday, 1981.

Zohn, Harry. *Karl Kraus.* New York: Twayne, 1971.

INDEX

Abbas, Mahmoud, 328, 503, 504, 506–7, 508
Abraham, S. Daniel, 453, 454, 455, 461
Addison, Joseph, 2–3
Advertising Council, 123
Agassi, Joseph, 304, 367
Ahad Ha-am (Asher Zvi Ginsberg), 187, 189, 190, 191, 192, 193, 209
Aharon, Itzhak Ben, 251–52
Al-Ahram (newspaper), 153
al-Assad, Hafez, 454
Albright, Madeline, 407, 452, 454, 462
Alexander II, Czar, 76, 196
Alexander III, Czar, 76, 186
Al-Faluji, Imad, 424
Al-Fajr (newspaper), 175
Algeria, 340
al-Husseini, Haj Amin Muhammad (Grand Mufti of Jerusalem), 99, 206, 217–18, 219, 434–35
Allgemeine Israelitische Wochenschrift, 51
Allon, Yigal, 239, 256, 257
Allon Plan, 239, 242, 243, 247, 253, 289, 305, 326, 509
All-Russia Social Democratic Party, 78
Almohades, 29
Aloni, Shulamit, 252
al-Shara, Farouk, 415
America-Israel Public Affairs Committee (AIPAC), 174, 457
American Air Corps, 132
American-Arab Anti-Discrimination Committee (ADC), 174
American Council for Judaism, 220
American Hebrew (journal), 86
American Jewish Committee, 86, 135, 221
American Jewish Congress, 126–27, 135, 177
American Jewry, 80–89: assimilation of, 86–87, 89, 110, 114; communal life of, 146–48; delusions among, 146, 165, 166, 448, 457, 493–94, 496; and German Jewish philanthropists, 208; immigrant

community of, 80–89, 531n26; and Jewish leadership (mainstream), 119, 123, 124, 126–27, 128, 129, 134, 135, 142, 143, 458–59, 460–61; and the Left, 113–14, 141, 143, 164–70; and relationship to Israel, 150, 154–56, 157–59, 160–61, 180–81; and response to anti-Semitism, 81–89, 109–10, 110–12, 113, 114, 116, 134, 164, 181; and response to Nazi campaign, 118, 126–31, 134, 534–35n4, 543n51; and the radical Left, 170–81; and remembrance of Holocaust by, 150–54, 180; and response to Oslo accords, xiii, 448–64, 493–94; and response to Yasser Arafat, 448–49, 459, 493; self-perception of, after WWII, 144–45; social liberalism and, 164, 165, 168; and Zionism, 87, 88, 154, 155, 156, 157, 159, 160
American League for a Free Palestine, 220
Americans for Peace Now (APN), 450, 451, 452, 454, 460, 461, 494, 495, 496, 500
Amir, Yigal, 388, 389
Anglo-American Committee of Inquiry, 162, 221
Annan, Kofi, 505
Anti-Defamation League, 166, 174, 409, 452, 459, 460
anti-Semitism, 153, 176, 529n24: in Arab states, 166, 167, 168–69, 317, 416, 417, 454, 498; in Austria, 8, 69–74, 169, 192, 416, 476, 481; and black Americans, 166; in central and western Europe, 3, 100, 484, 498; and the Communist Party, 79; in Czarist Russia, 74–76; delusions concerning, among Jews, 185, 208, 210, 212, 213, 214, 215, 261, 262–63, 381–82; in France, 71–72, 100, 168; and Friedrich Nietzsche, 62; in Germany, 64–69, 99–101, 192, 208, 210, 212, 213, 262–63, 492; among Jews, 185; in the New Left, 169–70, 174; in the *New York*

Index

Index

Index

Index

270, 276–77, 288, 290, 306, 338, 370, 395: Cairo Agreement and, 343, 344; corruption of, 270, 336, 337; Declaration of Principles and, 321, 322; Hamas and, 323, 351; and Israeli government, 271–72, 275, 319, 321, 322, 323, 332; Lebanon and, 264, 265, 266, 267; Peace Movement and, 275, 276, 278, 279, 280, 286, 289, 291, 320; as representative of Palestinian Arabs, 255, 279, 271, 275, 322; terrorism and, 238, 270–71, 287; and UN resolution 181, 276; U.S. government and, 272, 275, 286–87

Palestine Mandate. *See* League of Nations Mandate for Palestine

Palestine National Council (PNC), 272, 276, 306, 321, 322, 354, 403, 410

Palestinian Arabs, 162–63, 240, 269, 288: cultural elites' view of (Beilin, Elon, Grossman, Megged, Oz, Rubinstein, Savir), 305, 306, 308, 311, 316, 317, 319, 326–27, 328, 330, 368–69, 370, 372, 377, 395–96; Israelis' view of, 239–40, 272, 273, 308, 323; Israeli government's view of and negotiations with, 286, 287, 319, 323, 346, 349, 352, 356, 359; and Jordan, 270, 271, 336, 337–38, 341; leadership of, 162, 260, 267, 270, 331, 336, 341, 363; living conditions under Israelis, 160, 161, 240, 241–42, 255, 258, 269, 355; massacre of, 264; New Historian view of, 292–94, 295, 299, 302, 368; Oslo accords and, 333–34, 337, 353; Palestinian Authority and, 353, 422; Peace Movement and, 332, 345, 348–49; PLO and, 255, 270, 271, 275; and "right of return," 242, 303, 422, 485, 487, 493; terrorism of, 264, 325, 343–44, 349, 353, 356, 363, 502; Yasser Arafat and, 354, 399, 470. *See also* Intifada; Palestine Liberation Organization (PLO)

Palestinian Authority (PA), 322, 337, 343, 344, 348, 387, 359, 390, 398, 403, 404, 407, 409, 424, 472: anti-Semitism and, 166, 409, 417, 420, 476, 496–97; 498, 500; Declaration of Principles and, 322; education program of, x, 167–68, 331, 395, 420, 459–60, 495, 500; Islamic fundamentalists and, 347–48, 351–52, 353,

425, 508; Israeli perception of, 385, 427; media of, 355, 407, 417, 423, 460, 495, 499–500; monetary aid given to, 337, 354–55; Oslo accords and, 337, 344, 362, 369, 387, 388, 398, 403, 404, 429, 453; refugee camps and, 422; Temple Mount and, 399–400; terrorism and, 344, 348, 353, 369, 388, 390, 396, 402–3, 425; U.S. government and, 398, 407, 462, 468; Yasser Arafat and, 355–56, 426

Palestinian Broadcasting Corporation (PBC), 480

Palestinian Covenant, 321, 403, 410

Palestinian Interim Self-Government Authority, 322

Palestinian Media Watch, 420, 423

Palestinian National Charter, 387–88, 402

Pappe, Ilan, 294, 302–3

Paris Peace Conference, 91, 196, 288

Parthian Empire, 24

Passfield White Paper, 207

Patriarchate of Rabbi Judah the Prince, 24

Patterson, John, 203–4

Paulus, H.E.G., 58

Peace Association, 211, 212–13, 214, 215, 220

Peace Movement (Israeli), 244–45, 246, 247–48, 249, 254, 259, 260, 273, 275, 356, 357, 364: academic and cultural elites and, 310, 318–19, 429–30, 477, 518; Barak Administration and, 415, 420, 425, 426, 428, 429, 447, 477; delusions of , 277–78, 279–80, 292, 310, 316, 331, 361–62, 365, 392, 394, 428, 429, 436–37, 438, 440–41, 443–44, 480, 489; Labor Party and, 290–91, 292, 401, 476; Labor Zionism and, 292, 293; media and, 430, 517; Meretz party and, 331; Netanyahu Administration and, 404, 410–11; New Historians and, 292–93, 295, 302–3; Oslo accords and, 325, 358, 378, 405, 429, 444, 446; and perception of Palestinians, 345, 348–49; Rabin Administration and, 292, 319, 320, 324, 348; Shimon Peres and, 334; Yasser Arafat and, 332

Peace Now, 258–59, 275, 277, 286, 287, 289, 310, 320, 446, 475, 476, 478, 480

Peace of Mind (film), 456

KENNETH LEVIN earned an undergraduate degree in mathematics from the University of Pennsylvania, a B.A./M.A. in English language and literature from Oxford University, an M.D. degree from Penn and a Ph.D. in history from Princeton University. He is a clinical instructor in psychiatry at Harvard Medical School, has taught at various psychoanalytic training institutes in Boston and maintains a private practice in psychiatry. His previous books include *Freud's Early Psychology of the Neuroses: A Historical Perspective* and *Unconscious Fantasy in Psychotherapy*. Dr. Levin has written extensively on Israel and the Arab-Israeli conflict. His articles have appeared in *The New Republic, The Boston Globe, The Washington Times, The Jerusalem Post* and elsewhere and have also been distributed through the Knight-Ridder syndicate.